Unicoi County Tennessee

Death Record

Abstracts

1908-1936

Eddie M. Nikazy

HERITAGE BOOKS
2007

HERITAGE BOOKS
AN IMPRINT OF HERITAGE BOOKS, INC.

Books, CDs, and more—Worldwide

For our listing of thousands of titles see our website at
www.HeritageBooks.com

Published 2007 by
HERITAGE BOOKS, INC.
Publishing Division
65 East Main Street
Westminster, Maryland 21157-5026

Copyright © 1997 Eddie M. Nikazy

Other books by the author:
Abstracts of Death Records for Johnson County, Tennessee, 1908 to 1941
Carter County, Tennessee Deaths, 1926-1934
Carter County, Tennessee Record Abstracts, Death Records, 1908-1925
Carter County, Tennessee Record Abstracts, Marriages, 1871-1920
Forgotten Soldiers: History of the 2nd Tennessee Volunteer Infantry Regiment (USA), 1861-1865
Forgotten Soldiers: History of the 4th Tennessee Volunteer Infantry Regiment (USA), 1863-1865
Greene County, Tennessee Death Record Abstracts, 1908-1918
Sullivan County, Tennessee Death Records, 1908-1918, Volume 1
Sullivan County, Tennessee Death Records, 1919-1925, Volume 2
Washington County, Tennessee Death Record Abstracts, 1908-1916

All rights reserved. No part of this book may be reproduced or transmitted in any form or by any means, electronic or mechanical, including photocopying, recording or by any information storage and retrieval system without written permission from the author, except for the inclusion of brief quotations in a review.

International Standard Book Number: 978-0-7884-0747-3

Table of Contents

Preface:..v.

Death Record Abstracts:..1.

Name Index:..307.

PREFACE

Formed from Carter and Washington Counties in 1875, Unicoi County played an early role in the settlement of the frontier. Unicoi County was settled by many prominent families from North Carolina where most families came from nearby Mitchell, Yancey and Marshall Counties.

Many persons identified in this volume were direct descendants of early settlers of Tennessee. As the records also show, many people also moved to Unicoi County where it's county seat, Erwin, was a thriving railroad center and at one time was home of prosperous silk and pottery producing works.

This volume contains Tennessee death record abstracts for Unicoi County for the years 1908 through 1936. Death records were first filed for rural Tennessee counties beginning in 1908. Records, for the years 1908 through 1912 did not record the names of parents and in 1913 deaths were not recorded. Beginning in 1914, the State imposed more stringent recording requirements and the records included parents names, the name of the informant, and place of burial. The index contains 9,010 names. Records contained herein were compiled from microfilm of the original records.

Important facts about this volume:

1.) Name spelling variations have been preserved. The compiler made no effort to confirm or verify spelling.
2.) Record numbers shown in the compilation correspond with those on file in the Tennessee State Library and Archives.
3.) The place of birth is stated when the place of birth of the deceased, in parenthesis, or parents, in parenthesis, is recorded other than Unicoi County.
4.) An entry following the informant's name indicates the recorded place of residence.
5.) The cause of death is quoted as it appears in the official record.

1

SAMS, Robert; age: 1 year; death cause: "flucks"; died at Flag Pond, 6 Jul. 1911; record # 90781.

RILE, May; age: 11 years; death cause: "flucks"; died at Flag Pond, 15 Jul. 1911; record # 90782.

BOWING, Louis; age: 1 month and 25 days; death cause: "hives"; died at Flag Pond, 5 Jul. 1912; record # 90782.

RICE, Louis; age: 26 months; death cause: "croup"; died at Flag Pond, 1 Jun. 1912; record # 90783.

BOOTH, Ida; age: 18 years and 5 months; born: Washington County; married; death cause: not stated; died: 29 Jun. 1912; record # 90784.

TAYLOR, Neater May; age: 4 years; death cause: "whooping cough"; died in the 4th District, 1 Apr. 1912; record # 90786.

BARNETT, Nellie; age: 7 days; death cause: "unknown"; died in the 3rd District, 27 Jan. 1912; record # 90787.

GADDY, Eva; age: not stated; married; death cause: "consumption"; died in the 3rd District, 7 Dec. 1911; record # 90788.

LITTLE, Gracy Pearl; age: 3 days; death cause: "unknown"; died at Okalona, 17 Mar. 1912; record # 90789.

WHITRUN (?), Birtha; age: 2 days; death cause: "unknown"; died in the 4th District, 2 Dec. 1912; record # 90790.

SHELTON, Neley; age: 8 months; death cause: "flux"; died at Flag Pond, 4 Jul. 1912; record # 90791.

SHELTON, Arvile; age: 2 months; death cause: "croup"; died at Flag Pond, 20 Jun. 1912; record # 90792.

MCINTURFF, Edna Lee; age: 1 day; death cause: "unknown"; died in the 4th District, 24 Jun. 1912; record # 90793.

MCNABB, John Wilson; age: 1 day; death cause: "unknown"; died in the 4th District, 13 May 1912; record # 90794.

MCNABB, Eliza; age: 1 day; death cause: "unknown"; died in the 4th District, 13 May 1912; record # 90795.

BAKER, Nat; age: 4 days; death cause: "unknown"; died in the 4th District, 20 Jan. 1912; record # 90796.

TIPTON, Mack; age: 19 years; single; death cause: "killed by __ (illegible); died in the 4th District, 18 Aug. 1911; record # 90797.

PETERSON, J.D.; age: 36 years; married; merchant; death cause: "unknown"; died in the 4th District, 8 Oct. 1911; record # 90798.

WOODBY, Willie; age: 3 days; death cause: "unknown"; died: 27 Jun. 1912; record # 90799.

MCGLAUGHLIN, Malinda; age: 37 years; married; death cause: "consumption"; died in the 4th District, 22 Jul. 1911; record # 90800.

STREET, A.W.; age: 22 years; born: North Carolina; married; soldier; death cause: "consumption"; died: 2 Jun. 1912; record # 90801.

HOWELL, Emegene; age: 24 years; born: North Carolina; married; death cause: "consumption"; died: 16 Jul. 1911; record # 90802.

TAYLOR, Gracy; age: 11 years; death cause: "whooping cough"; died in the 4th District, 23 Feb. 1912; record # 90803.

TAYLOR, Leala Kate; age: 6 months; death cause: "whooping cough"; died in the 4th District, 24 Feb. 1912; record # 90804.

UNIDENTIFIED, Infant; male; death cause: "stillborn"; died in the 11th District, 20 Oct. 1010; record # 90805.

TAPP, Sarah; age: 69 years; single; death cause: "paralysis"; died in the 11th District, 19 Feb. 1911; record # 90806.

LINVILLE, Perna; age: 13 months; death cause: "cholera"; died in the 1st District, 2 Jun. 1911; record # 90807.

UNIDENTIFIED, Female; Name: Bertha; age: 6 months; death cause: "pneumonia"; died in the 5th District, __ Feb. 1911; record # 90808.

LAWING, John; age: 48 years; married; death cause: "drowned"; died in the 5th District, 6 May 1909; record # 90810.

RYBERN, Antom; age: 3 months; death cause: "stomach trouble"; died in the 5th District, 11 Aug. 1910; record # 90811.

UNIDENTIFIED, female; age: 4 days; death cause: "strangulation"; died in the 5th District, date not stated; record # 90812.

UNIDENTIFIED, male; age: 3 days; death cause: "ruptured blood vessels"; died: 28 Dec. 1910; record # 90813.

HENSLEY, James Thomas; age: 21 years; born: North Carolina; single; death cause: "spinal trouble"; died in the 5th District, 30 Apr. 1911; record # 90814.

DOUGLAS, Archie; age: 5 months; death cause: "brain trouble"; died in the 5th District, __ May 1911; record # 90815.

CLOUD, Daisy Lee; age: 6 weeks; born: Kingsport; death cause: "spinal trouble"; died in the 5th District, 1 Oct. 1910; record # 90816.

3

VANCE, Mack; age: 33 years; born: North Carolina; married; death cause: "accident"; died in the 5th District, 10 Dec. 1910; record # 90817.

DUNCAN, Pearl; age: 27 years; married; death cause: "unknown"; died in the 5th District, 21 Feb. 1911; record # 90818.

TONEY, W.C.; age: 52 years; married; mail carrier; death cause: "pneumonia"; died in the 5th District, 19 Apr. 1911; record # 90819.

BURGEN (?), Ellen; age: 85 years; born: North Carolina; married; death cause: "paralysis"; died in the 5th District, 6 Jun. 1911; record # 908120.

PIERCE, James H.; age: 2 months; death cause: "hives"; died in the 5th District, 25 Feb. 1911; record # 90821.

KEPLINGER, Vestie; age: 5 weeks; death cause: "unknown"; died in the 5th District, __ Jan. 1911; record # 90822.

ANDERSON, Mary; age: 33 years; married; death cause: "fever"; died in the 5th District, 20 Jun. 1911; record $ 90823.

HARRIS, Dora; age: 33 years; married; death cause: "childbirth"; died in the 5th District, 25 Apr. 1911; record # 90824.

UNIDENTIFIED, Infant; male; age: 1 month; death cause: "bowel trouble"; died in the 5th District, 23 May 1911; record # 90825.

UNIDENTIFIED, Infant; female; age: 1 month; death cause: "bowel trouble"; died in the 5th District, 23 May 1911; record # 90826.

SMITH, Ella; age: 2 years; death cause: "croup"; died in the 4th District, 18 Jun. 1911; record # 90827.

HOPSON, Etta; age: 7 weeks; death cause: "fever"; died in the 4th District, 27 Jun. 1911; record # 90828.

WHITSON, John; age: 74 years; born: Tennessee; married; death cause: "heart trouble"; died in the 4th District, 22 Apr. 1911; record # 90829.

HOWELL, Harmon; age: 6 weeks; death cause: "hives"; died in the 4th District, 8 Nov. 1911; record # 90830.

MCLAUGHLIN, Alvin; age: 26 years; single; death cause: "consumption"; died in the 4th District, 23 Jul. 1910; record # 90831.

MCCURY, Loyd; age: 8 months; death cause: "hives"; died in the 4th District, 28 Jun. 1911; record # 90832.

MCLAUGHLIN, Wik; age: 83 years; born: Unicoi County; married; death cause: "old age"; died in the 4th District, 23 Jun. 1911; record # 90833.

WHITE, Cordie; age: 1 year and 10 months; death cause: "croup"; died in the 4th District, 9 Apr. 1911; record # 90834.

DAVIS, Jackson; age: 61 years; born: North Carolina; married; death cause: "consumption"; died in the 3rd District, 5 Jun. 1911; record # 90835.

HARRIS, Minnie; age: 30 years; born: Carter County; married; death cause: "pneuralgia of stomach"; died in the 3rd District, 2 Jun. 1911; record # 90836.

CARROLL, Rosy; age: 20 years; single; death cause: "dropsy"; died in the 3rd District, 20 Apr. 1911; record # 90837.

FRY, Lucy; age: 16 years; born: North Carolina; death cause: "dropsy"; died in the 3rd District, 2 Aug. 1910; record # 90838.

TONEY, Lucinda; age: 72 years; born: Carter County; married; death cause: "dropsy"; died in the 3rd District, 4 Feb. 1911; record # 90839.

CARROLL, Mattison; age: 53 years, born: Carter County; married; death cause: "consumption"; died in the 3rd District, 20 Dec. 1910; record # 90840.

ROWE, Guy; age: 8 months; death cause: "brain fever"; died in the 3rd District, 13 May 1911; record # 90841.

WOODLEY, Teddy; age: 9 months; born: North Carolina; death cause: "diarrhea"; died in the 3rd District, 26 May 1911; record # 90842.

AUSBON, Ida; age: 2 years; death cause: "croup"; died in the 4th District, 7 Apr. 1911; record # 90843.

WRIGHT, Thomas J.; age: 90 years; born: Alton, Illinois; married; minister; death cause: "old age"; died in the 2nd District, 6 Sep. 1910; record # 90844.

SHELL, Samuel; age: 30 years; married; death cause: "typhoid fever"; died in the 2nd District, 25 Aug. 1910; record $ 90845.

FRY, Matilda; age: 62 years; born: Spruce Pine, NC.; married; death cause: "lagrippe"; died in the 2nd District, 8 Jun. 1911; record # 90846.

MILLER, Neal; age: 62 years; born: Mitchell County, NC.; married; death cause: "stomach trouble"; died in the 2nd District, 22 Apr. 1911; record # 90847.

5

DAVIS, Ollie; female; age: 16 years; born: Carter County; married; death cause: "consumption"; died in the 2nd District, 25 May 1911; record # 90848.

UNIDENTIFIED, Infant; female; age: 1 day; death cause: not stated; died in the 2nd District, 16 May 1911; record # 90849.

MILLER, J.B.; age: 85 years; born: Crabtree, Carter County; married; death cause: "brights disease"; died in the 2nd District, 10 May 1911; record # 90850.

SNEYD, Jewel; age: 8 months; death cause: "cholera"; died in the 2nd District, 10 Aug. 1911; record # 90851.

SNEYD, Isaac; age: 5 months; death cause: not stated; died in the 2nd District, 30 Oct. 1911; record # 90852.

GRINDSTAFF, Mary; age: 78 years; born: Radford County, NC.; married; death cause: "brights disease"; died in the 2nd District, 14 Oct. 1910; record # 90853.

GRINDSTAFF, __ (illegible); female; age: 22 years; married; death cause: "typhoid fever"; died in the 2nd District, 31 Oct. 1910; record # 90854.

GRINDSTAFF, Anna May; age: 1 year; death cause: "typhoid fever"; died in the 2nd District, 29 Jan. 1911; record # 90855.

BIRCHFIELD, Samuel; age: 50 years; single; death cause: "typhoid fever"; died in the 2nd District, 20 Jun. 1911; record # 90856.

BIRCHFIELD, Sarah; age: 74 years; born: Limestone Cove; married; death cause: "typhoid fever"; died in the 2nd District, 14 Jan. 1911; record # 90857.

BIRCHFIELD, Julia; age: 38 years; single; death cause: "pneumonia fever"; died in the 2nd District, 10 May 1911; record # 90858.

BIRCHFIELD, Infant: sex: not stated; age: 2 days; death cause: "deformed"; died in the 2nd District, 14 May 1911; record # 90859.

WOODBY, Infant; male; death cause: "stillborn"; died in the 2nd District, 2 May 1911; record # 98060.

HENSLEY, Lewsindy; age: 2 years; death cause: "croup"; died in the 1st District, 15 Feb. 1912; record # 90861.

HENSLEY, April; age: 1 month; death cause: "croup"; died in the 1st District, 17 Feb. 1912; record # 90862.

RAY, Newman; age: 2 days; death cause: not stated; died in the 1st District, 4 Jun. 1912; record # 90863.

SHELTON, Purel; age: 19 years; born: Madison County, NC.; single; death cause: "burnt"; died in the 1st District, 7 Feb. 1912; record # 90864.

RAMSEY, Liney; age: 52 years; born: Washington County; married; death cause: "female trouble"; died in the 1st District, 4 Mar. 1912; record # 90865.

SNEYD, Alven; age: 9 months; death cause: "measles"; died in the 1st District, 14 Jun. 1912; record # 90866.

GOUGE, Cheerfully; age: 9 years; born: Mitchell County, NC.; death cause: "accident"; died in the 1st District, 25 Sep. 1911; record # 90867.

CAMPBELL, Annie; age: 3 weeks; death cause: "convulsions"; died in the 1st District, __ 1911; record # 90866.

FRANCIS, Dr. Joseph; age: 75 years; born: Washington County; single; dentist; death cause: "dropsy"; died in the 1st District, 13 May 1912; record # 90869.

GOUGE, Bonnie; age: 3 years; death cause: "convulsions"; died in the 1st District, 14 Sep. 1911; record # 90870.

WYATT, Penley; age: 30 years; born: Yancey County, NC.; married; death cause: "paralysis"; died in the 1st District, __ Aug. 1911; record # 90871.

BAKER, David; age: 73 years; born: Limestone Cove; married; death cause: "heart failure"; died in the 1st District, 26 Sep. 1911; record # 90872.

GARLAND, Delia; age: 20; single; death cause: "typhoid fever"; died in the 1st District, 20 Mar. 1911; record # 90873.

DAVIS, Margaret; age: 23 years; born: Carter County; married; death cause: "consumption"; died in the 1st District, 12 Feb. 1912; record # 90874.

WOODBY, Docia; age: 75 years; married; death cause: "paralysis"; died: 16 Jun. 1912; record # 90876.

ABNER, English; age: 3 years; death cause: "burned"; died: 26 Dec. 1912; record # 90876.

HAUN, Ethel; age: 16 years; death cause: "typhoid fever"; died: Scott County, Huntsville, TN. on __ 29, 1911; record # 90877.

ANDERSON, Mary; age: 35 years; married; death cause: "typhoid fever"; died: 9 Jul. 1911; record # 90878.
WHITE, Salie; age: 24 years; married; death cause: "typhoid fever"; died: 11 Aug. 1911; record # 90879.
AYERS, Tilde; age: 5 years; death cause: "croup"; died at Rock Creek on 28 Jun. 1912; record # 90880.
ANDERSON, James; age: 3 months; death cause: not stated; died at Rock Creek on 23 Jul. 1911; record # 90881.
NELSON, Isaac; age: 4 months; death cause: "bealing in head"; died at Erwin on 5 Dec. 1911; record # 90882.
NELSON, Silvin; age: 4 months; death cause: "bold hives"; died at Erwin on 5 Dec. 1911; record # 90883.
NELSON, Martha Ann; age: 5 months; death cause: "measles"; died at Rock Creek on 6 Feb. 1912; record # 90884.
UNIDENTIFIED, Infant; male; age: 3 months; death cause: not stated; died at Erwin on 26 Feb. 1912; record # 90885.
UNIDENTIFIED, Infant; male; lived 1 day; death cause: not stated; died at Erwin on 26 Dec. 1911; record # 90886.
PHILLIPS, Bessie; age: 8 years; born: Jonesborough; death cause: "pellagra"; died at Johnson City on 5 Dec. 1911; record # 90887.
HORTON, Lewis; lived 1 day; death cause: "premature"; died at Erwin on 20 Aug. 1911; record # 90888.
WOHLFORD, Charlott; age: 3 months; death cause: "indigestion"; died at Erwin on 19 Jun. 1912; record # 90889.
LOVE, John R.; age: 68 years; married; death cause: "paralysis"; died at Erwin on 26 Mar. 1912; record # 90890.
TONEY, Ruby; age: 4 years; death cause: "whooping cough"; died at Erwin on 29 Feb. 1912; record # 90891.
DEHAVEN, Mary R.; age: 5 months; death cause: "spinal meningitis"; died at Erwin on 18 Nov. 1911; record # 90892.
BORDON, Virginia; age: 9 years; born: Bluefield, West Virginia; death cause: "membranous croup"; died at Erwin on 14 Oct. 1911; record # 90893.
MORELAND, Orville; age: 19 years; born: Johnson City; single; death cause: "accident"; died in Chicago, Illinois, on 2 Jul. 1912; record # 90894.

DAVIS, W.D.; age: 48 years; born: Greeneville; married; death cause: "pellagra"; died at Erwin on 9 Oct. 1911; record # 90895.
BROWN, W.S.; age: 51 years; married; death cause: "heart trouble"; died in the 11th District on 21 Jan. 1912; record # 90896.
MCINTURFF, David; age: 78 years; born: Carter County; married; death cause: "uremia"; died in the 11th District, 15 Oct. 1911; record # 90897.
ANDERSON, Taylor; age: 12 years; death cause: "germ in bowels"; died in the 11th District on 24 Mar. 1912; record # 90898.
WILSON, Lela; age: 5 years; death cause: "croup"; died in 9th District on 13 Jan. 1912; record # 90899.
UNIDENTIFIED, Infant; female; age: 15 months; first name: Irene; death cause: "flux or dysentery"; died: 9th District, 3 Jan. 1912; # 90900.
SHEVLEY, M.; age: 6 years; death cause: "croup"; died at Chucky, TN. on 25 Nov. 1911; record # 90901.
STILLMAN, Lede Elizabeth; age: 4 months; death cause: "unknown"; died in the 4th District on 6 Mar. 1912; record # 90902.
FOSTER, Ethel; age: 12 months; death cause: "fever"; died: 8 Mar. 1912; record # 90903.
HENSLEY, Clayton; age: 24 days; death cause: "croup"; died in the 8th District on 27 Jun. 1912; record # 90904.
SHEHAN, Jack; age: 30 years; married; death cause: "knife wound"; died in the 8th District on 11 Jan. 1912; record # 90905.
LEWIS, Lida; age: 2 years; death cause: "burned"; died in the 8th District on 27 Jun. 1912; record # 90906.
HENSLEY, Golman; age: 1 year; death cause: "flux"; died in the 8th District on 24 Jul. 1911; record # 90907.
CHANDLER, Vestel; age: 15 months; death cause: "flux"; died in the 8th District on 26 Jul. 1911; record # 90908.
GENTRY, Guy; age: 1 year; death cause: "croup"; died in the 8th District on 20 Dec. 1911; record # 90909.
TIPTON, Mary, Mrs.; age: 71 years; born: Washington County; single; death cause: "pneumonia fever"; died in the 8th District on 14 Nov. 1911; record # 90910.
TILSON, Catherine; age: 80 years; born: Yancey County, NC.; married; death cause: "heart failure"; died in the 8th District on 22 Sep. 1911; record # 90911.

WATTS, Arthur; age: 6 years; death cause: "flux"; died in the 8th District on 22 Aug. 1911; record # 90912.

FOSTER, Cecil; age: 9 months; death cause: "flux"; died in the 8th District on 13 Jul. 1911; record # 90913.

LEDFORD, Blanch; age: 3 days; death cause: "croup"; died in the 8th District on __ Feb. 1911; record # 90914.

RIDDLE, Leroy; age: 20 years; single; death cause: "consumption"; died in the 8th District on 5 May 1912; record # 90915.

EDWARDS, Eliza; age: 4 years; death cause: "fever"; died in the 8th District on 16 Nov. 1912; record # 90916.

HOWELL, Rufus; age: 8 months; death cause: "croup"; died in the 8th District on 10 Mar. 1912; record # 90917.

MCNABB, Isaac; age: 62 years; married; death cause: "suicide by hanging"; died in the Jonesboro Jail on 31 Mar. 1912; record # 90918.

FOWLER, John; age: 32 years; married; death cause: "cars wrecked"; died at Dunlee, Virginia on 7 Oct. 1911; record # 90919.

RAY, A__; female; age: 7 months; death cause: not stated; died in the 7th District on 16 Apr. 191_; record # 90920.

ILLEGIBLE, Everet; age: 35 months; death cause: "pneumonia fever"; died in the 7th District on 15 Feb. 1912; record # 90921.

CARL (?), Sarah; age: 78 years; single; death cause: "heart trouble"; died in the 7th District on 11 Apr. 1912; record # 90922.

NORRIS, D.B.; age: 58; single; death cause: "unknown"; died in the 11th District on 21 Mar. 1912; record # 90923.

JONES, Julia A.; age: 76 years; born: Carter County; married; death cause: "general breakdown"; died in the 11th District on 11 Nov. 1911; record # 90924.

BOWMAN, Joseph; age: 87 years; born: Carter County; married; death cause: "general breakdown"; died in the 11th District on 11 Nov. 1911; record # 90925.

GLENARD, Infant; age: 1 year and 20 days; death cause: "membranous croup"; died in the 9th District on 25 Sep 1911; record # 90926.

UNIDENTIFIED, female; age: 24 years; named: Ola; death cause: "throat trouble"; died in the 12th district on 1 Nov. 1911; record # 90927.

EDWARD, Bertha Lee; age: 4 months; death cause: "fever"; died in the 12th District on 15 Sep. 1911; record # 90928.

UNIDENTIFIED, female; age: 4 years; named: Shirley; death cause: "croup"; died in the 12th District on 10 Nov. 1912; record # 90929.

HOYL, L. Zira; age: 73 years; born: Relford, North Carolina; married; death cause: "spinal and heart"; died: 29 Apr. 1912; record # 90930.

HOYL, H.S.; age: 74 years; born: South Carolina; death cause: "paralysis"; died in the 12th District on 9 Apr. 1912; record # 90931.

CRAIN, Vaughn; age: 23 days; death cause: "hives"; died at Flag Pond on 23 Mar. 1912; record # 90932.

SELLERS, Infant; female; age: 2 months; death cause: "measles"; died at Flag Pond on 15 Feb. 1912; record # 90933.

RAMSEY, Linnie; age: not stated; born: Greene County; married; death cause: "epilepsy"; died: 9th District, 3 Mar. 1912; record # 90934.

PARKER, Vegan May; age: 2 years; death cause: "croup"; died in the 12th District on __ Oct. 1912; record # 90935.

PARKER, Dollie; age: 8 days; death cause: "yellow jaundice"; died in the 12th District on 1 Jul. 1912; record # 90936.

TITTLE, Mary C.; age: 60 years; married; death cause: "blood poison"; died in the 12th District on 7 Mar. 1912; record # 90937.

STOCTON, Minty; age: 4 years; death cause: "croup"; died at Flag Pond on 8 Sep. 1911; record # 90938.

BLANKENSHIP, Infant; male; lived 1 day; death cause: "hives"; died at Flag Pond on 19 Sep. 1911; record # 90939.

BLANKENSHIP, Infant; male; lived 1 day; death cause: "hives"; died at Flag Pond on 19 Sep. 1911; record # 90940.

MCFARLINGTON, Infant; female; age: 13 days; death cause: "fever"; died at Flag Pond on 21 Feb. 1912; record # 90941.

WILLIS, May; age: 3 months; death cause: "hives"; died at Flag Pond on 12 Jul. 1911; record # 90942.

RAY, Infant; male; lived 1 day; death cause: "fever"; died at Flag Pond on 18 Mar. 1912; record # 90943.

MOORE, Samuel; age: 84 years; born: Flag Pond; married; death cause: "rheumatism"; died at Flag Pond on 27 Jun. 1912; record # 90944.

RICE, Cora; age: 18 months; death cause: "croup"; died at Flag Pond on 10 Oct. 1912; record # 90945.

HENSLEY, J.A.; age: 85 years; born: Yancey County, NC.; married; death cause: "paralysis"; died: Flag Pond, 19 Dec. 1911; record 90946.

EDWARDS, R.G.; age: 44 years; born: Yancey County, NC.; married; death cause: "consumption"; died: Flag Pond, 5 May 1912; # 90947.

STOCTON, Infant; male; lived 1 day; death cause: not stated; died at Flag Pond on 25 Feb. 1912; record # 90948.

CRAIN, Mamie; age: 28 years; born: Madison County, NC.; married; death cause: "case of midwifery"; died at Flag Pond, 22 Dec. 1911; record # 90949.

GUINN, Infant; sex: not stated; age: 3 weeks; death cause: "unknown"; died in the 9th District, 3 Mar. 1909; record # 90950.

GILLIS, Emiline; age: 71 years; born: Washington County; married; death cause: "general breakdown"; died in the 9th District, 26 may 1909; record # 90951.

WATTS, Nelson; age: 1 month; death cause: "croup"; died in the 8th District on 10 Apr. 1909; record # 90952.

RANDOLPH, Martha; age: 8 years; born: Yancey County, NC.; death cause: "unknown"; died in the 8th District on 15 Feb. 1909; # 90953.

RANDOLPH, Walcie; male; age: 9 months; born: Yancey County, NC.; death cause: "unknown"; died: 8th District, 31 Mar. 1909;# 90954.

RANDOLPH, Elizabeth; age: 70 years; married; death cause: "heart failure"; died in the 8th District on 3 Mar. 1909; record # 90955.

RANDOLPH, V.L.; age: 3 weeks; death cause: "unknown"; died in the 8th District on 10 Jul. 1908; record # 90956.

HOLCOMB, Elizabeth; age: 72 years; born: Madison County, NC.; married; death cause: "unknown"; died 25 Oct. 1908; record # 90957.

TIPTON, M.J.; female; age: 41 years; married; death cause: "consumption"; died 26 Mar. 1909; record # 90958.

HIGGINS, J.H.; age: 35 years; married; death cause: "consumption"; died: 14 Jun. 1909; record # 90959.

LEDFORD, Kitty L.; lived 2 days; death cause: "unknown"; died: 28 Jun. 1909; record # 90960.

CHANDLER, Dora; age: 3 months; death cause: "unknown"; died: 21 Jun. 1909; record # 90961.

CHANDLER, Dessie; age: 2 months; death cause: "unknown"; died: 20 Jun. 1908; record # 90962.

WHITE, E.T.; age: 25 years; married; death cause: "railroad accident"; died: 24 Nov. 1909; record # 90963.

JONES, Lizzie; age: 27 years; married; death cause: "consumption"; died: 10 Nov. 1909; record # 90965.

MCEWEN, Leroy; age: not stated; single; death cause: "unknown"; died: 10 May 1910; record # 90964.

MCINTURFF, Samuel; age: 70 years, 4 months, 7 days; born: Carter County; married; death cause: illegible; died: 11 Mar. 1910; # 90966.

ILLEGIBLE, William Arthur; age: 4 months; death cause: illegible; died: 16 Aug. 1909; record # 90967.

MILLER, Ollie; age: 10 months; death cause: "whooping cough"; died: __ Nov. 1909; record # 90968.

BARNES, Parker; age: 24 years; single; death cause: "consumption"; died 14 Nov. 1909; record # 90969.

BENNET, Josephine; age: 2 years; death cause: "unknown"; died: 8 Mar. 1910; record # 90970.

JOHNSON, James; age: 4 months; death cause: "pneumonia"; died: 15 Feb. 1910; record # 90971.

WEEMS, Oscar; age: 3 years; born: Knoxville; death cause: "burn"; died: 7 Jun. 1910; record # 90972.

BOGART, Elizabeth; age: 39 years; married; death cause: "fever"; died: 14 Jan. 1910; record # 90973.

HENSLEY, Robert W.; age: 16 years; death cause: "accidentally shot"; died: 19 Nov. 1910; record # 90974.

HENSLEY, Vernon; age: 1 year and 4 months; death cause: "croup"; died: 23 Oct. 1910; record # 90975.

HENSLEY, Elvira; age: 83 years; born: Madison County, NC.; death cause: "cancer"; died: 27 Aug. 1910; record # 90976.

CHANDLER, Clyde; age: 11 months; death cause: "croup"; died: 15 Oct. 1910; record # 90977.

TILSON, Brownlow; age: 3 years; death cause: "pneumonia"; died: 24 Jan. 1911; record # 90978.

HIGGINS, J.H. Sr.; age: 60 years; married; death cause: "dropsy"; died: 25 Dec. 1910; record # 90979.

EDWARDS, Harve; age: 1 year; death cause: "flux"; died: 24 Jun. 1911; record # 90980.

WATTS, Mary Elizabeth; age: 3 months; death cause: "unknown"; died: 16 Jun. 1910; record # 90981.

TIPTON, William Monroe; age: 3 months; death cause: "croup"; died: 2 Jan. 1911; record # 90982.

WATTS, John; age: 45 years; born: Yancey County, NC.; married; death cause: "consumption"; died: 13 Jan. 1911; record # 90983.

STEPHENS, Isaac; age: 20 years; born: Yancey County, NC.; single; death cause: "killed by a log"; died 4 Jun. 1911; record # 90984.

STEPHENS, Ora; age: 1 month and 9 days; death cause: "croup"; died: 14 May 1911; record # 90985.

FRITTS, Willie; age: 23 months; death cause: "croup"; died: 21 Oct. 1910; record # 90986.

FRITTS, Rally; age: 24 days; death cause: illegible; died: 16 Sep. 1910; record # 90987.

PRESNELL, Ernest; age: "about 2 years'; death cause: "fever"; died: 25 Nov. 1910; record # 90988.

UNIDENTIFIED, Infant; female; age: 27 days; death cause: "croup"; died: 7 Feb. 1911; record # 90989.

SHELTON, Norman; age: 21 days; death cause: "unknown"; died: 1 Mar. 1911; record # 90990.

NOLAND, Valda; age: 14 years; born: Haywood, North Carolina; death cause: "diphtheria"; died: 11 Dec. 1910; record # 90991.

UNIDENTIFIED, Infant; sex: not stated; lived 3 hours; death cause: not stated; died: 30 Aug. 1910; record # 90992.

GOUGE, Howard; age: 13 months; death cause: "spinal"; died at Bakersfield, North Carolina on 23 May 1911; record # 90993.

BROOKS, Ader; age: 8 months and 12 days; born: Yancey County, NC.; death cause: "diarrhea"; died: 3 Aug. 1910; record # 90994.

FOSTER, Charlie; age: 3 years, 4 months and 28 days; death cause: "spasms"; died: 18 Oct. 1910; record # 90995.

MCINTURFF, E.M.; age: 87 years; born: Carter County; married; death cause: "a fall"; died: 22 Jan. 1910; record # 90996.

RIGGS, Gladys; age: 5 months; death cause: "bowel trouble"; died: 3 Jul. 1909; record # 90997.

WHITSON, Arnold Lee; age: 16 months; born: Lee Springs, TN.; death cause: "dysentery"; died: 17 Aug. 1909; record # 90998.

WHITSON, Ruth; age: 11 months and 3 weeks; death cause: "croup"; died: 30 Oct. 1909; record # 90999.

BRITT, James; age: 17 years; single; death cause: "pneumonia"; died: 4 Jan. 1910; record # 91000.

SUTPLIN (?), Alice; age: 29 years; born: Virginia; married; death cause: "consumption"; died: 18 Jan. 1910; record # 91001.

LEDFORD, Susan; age: 78 years; born: Snow Creek, NC.; married; death cause: "general debility"; died: 7 Feb. 1910; record # 91002.

BENSON, Wyeth; age: 11 months; death cause: "excema; died: 3 May 1910; record # 91003.

PATE, J.E.; age: 87 years; born: Yancey County, NC.; married; death cause: "general debility"; died: 21 Dec. 1909; record # 91004.

HUGHS, Cliford L.; age: 1 year and 2 months; death cause: not stated; died: 5 Jul. 1910; record # 91005.

WALKER, Carrie; age: 3 years; death cause: not stated; died at Unaka Springs on 5 Mar. 1910; record # 91006.

TREDWAY, Berthe; age: 23 years; born: Washington County; married; death cause: illegible; died at Bumpus Cove on 20 May 1910; # 91007.

BRYANT, Sam; age: 45 years; born: North Carolina; married; death cause: "consumption"; died: 5 Feb. 1910; record # 91008.

HENSLEY, Evert; age: 15 days; death cause: "hives"; died at Flag Pond on 27 Feb. 1911; record # 91009.

LEWIS, Henry; age: 3 years; death cause: "typhoid fever"; died at Flag Pond on 4 Jan. 1911; record # 91010.

HIGGINS, Vance; age: 15 days; death cause: "hives"; died at Flag Pond on 5 Dec. 1910; record # 91011.

EDWARDS, Clyed; age: 2 months; born: Madison County, NC.; death cause: "hives"; died at Madison County, NC. on 5 Oct. 1910; # 91012.

BLANKENSHIP, Mattie; age: 26 days; death cause: "hives"; died at Flag Pond on 11 Sep. 1910; record # 91013.

DUNKEN, Anzo; female; age: 24 years; born: Yancey County, NC.; married; death cause: "pneumonia"; died at Flag Pond on 19 Apr. 1911; record # 91014.

DUNKEN, Walter; lived 1 day; death cause: "hives"; died 9 Apr. 1911; record # 91015.

DUNKEN, Fred; lived 1 day; death cause: "hives"; died 9 Apr. 1911; record # 91016.

15

SHELTON, David; age: 79 years; born: Madison County, NC.; married; death cause: "brain hemorrhage"; died at Flag Pond on 18 May 1911; record # 91017.

SHELTON, Eliphus; age: 65 years; born: Madison County, NC.; married; death cause: "heart dropsy"; died at Flag Pond on 5 Dec. 1910; # 91018.

BLANKENSHIP, Fred; age: 7 years; death cause: "flux"; died at Flag Pond on 24 Jun. 1911; record # 91019.

MASHBURN, Bessie; age: 21 years; married; death cause: "consumption"; died at Flag Pond on 3 May 1911; record # 91020.

RICE, Lizzie; lived 8 days; death cause: "hives"; died at Flag Pond on 20 Aug. 1910; record # 91021.

LEWIS, Mary; age: 2 years; death cause: "flux"; died at Flag Pond on 20 Jun. 1911; record # 91022.

MCINTOSH, I.N.; age: 48 years; born: Yancey County, NC.; married; death cause: "shot"; died at Flag Pond on 3 Jun. 1910; record # 91023.

RICE, Mary; age: 4 weeks; death cause: "hives"; died at Flag Pond on 4 Mar. 1910; record # 91024.

RICE, Floyd; age: 1 year; death cause: "flux"; died at Flag Pond on 21 Jun. 1911; record # 91025.

MUREY, Yety; age: 9 years; death cause: "flux"; died at Flag Pond on 23 Jun. 1911; record # 91026.

BOWMAN, Hattie; age: 4 years; death cause: "flux"; died at Flag Pond on 14 Jun. 1911; record # 91027.

EFFLER, Clerie Bell; age: 1 year; death cause: "flux"; died at Flag Pond on 6 Jul. 1911; record # 91028.

RAMSEY, Johny; age: 1 year and 4 months; death cause: "flux"; died at Flag Pond on 14 Jul. 1911; record # 91029.

HORN, Idy; age: 49 years; married; death cause: "paralysis"; died at Flag Pond on 14 Feb. 1911; record # 91030.

GENTRY, Elizabeth; age: 64 years; born: Madison County, NC.; single; death cause: "fever"; died at Flag Pond on 29 Jan. 1911; record 91031.

LOID, Dary; male; age: 45 years; married; death cause: "heart failure"; died at Flag Pond on 23 Apr. 1911; record # 91032.

HENSLEY, Tomes; age: 51 years; born: Madison County, NC.; married; death cause: "flux"; died at Flag Pond on 15 Jul. 1911; record 91033.

CARTER, Ethel; age: 14 years, 1 month and 10 days; born: Madison County, NC.; death cause: "flux"; died at Flag Pond on 11 Jul. 1911; record # 91034.

HENSLEY, Barbarey; age: 86 years; born: Washington County; married; death cause: "old age"; died at Flag Pond on 5 Jan. 1911; record 91035.

GUIN, Vale; age: 1 year; death cause "flux"; died at Flag Pond on 7 Jul. 1911; record # 91036.

HARE, Grave; age: 3 years; death cause: "fever"; died at Flag Pond on 15 Mar. 1911; record # 91037.

RIGGS, Gladys; age: 5 months; death cause: "diarrhea and flux"; died in the 4th District on 15 Jul. 1909; record # 91038.

JONES, Pheoba; age: 55 years; born: Sullivan County; single; death cause: "heart failure"; died: 4th District, 16 Feb. 1909; record # 91039.

MCCURRY, Wash; age: 54 years; born: Mitchell County, NC.; married; death cause: "heart trouble"; died in the 4th District on 21 Dec. 1908; record # 91040.

BOWMAN, Emeline; age: "about 60 years"; married; death cause: "paralysis"; died in the 4th District, 23 Feb. 1909; record # 91044.

CARROLL, Arther; age: 17 years and 7 months; death cause: "stomach trouble"; died in the 3rd District on 14 Feb. 1909; record # 91045.

BOWMAN, Loyd; age: 5 months; born: Carter County; death cause: "bold hives"; died in the 3rd District on 30 May 1909; record 91043.

JONES, Birdie; age: 21 years; married; death cause: "pneumonia fever"; died in the 3rd District on 12 Apr. 1909; record # 91044.

HAYNES, Lesley; lived 1 day; death cause: not stated; died in the 3rd District on 6 Feb. 1909; record # 91045.

ANDERSON, William Loyd; age: 1 year, 3 months and 15 days; death cause: "drowned by falling in spring"; died in the 3rd District on 7 May 1909; record # 91046.

MCINTURFF, Willy (?); age: 72 years; married; death cause: "lagrippe"; died in the 3rd District on 19 Apr. 1909; record # 91047.

BIRCHFIELD, Vistie; age: 2 months; death cause: "fever"; died in the 2nd District on 21 Dec. 1908; record # 91048.

BIRCHFIELD, William; age: 72 years; married; death cause: "fever"; died in the 2nd District on 8 Dec. 1908; record # 91049.

GOUGE, John; age: 73 years; born: Mitchell County, NC.; married; death cause: "paralysis"; died: 2nd District on 6 Jan. 1909; record 91050.

WOODLY, Sarah; age: 22 years; married; death cause: "child bed fever"; died in the 2nd District on 9 Mar. 1909; record # 91051.

RICE, Joshua Taylor; age: 23 years, 1 month and 1 day; single; death cause: "typhoid fever"; died in Kansas City, MO. on 28 Jul. 1908; record # 91052.

HENSLEY, Joseph; age: 62 years; married; death cause: "dropsy"; died at Flag Pond on 30 Oct. 1908; record # 91053.

BANKS, James; age: 1 year and 10 months; born: Carmon, NC.; death cause: "diarrhea"; died at Flag Pond on 22 Jun. 1909; record # 91054.

MURRAY, Thomas; age: 1 year and 2 months; death cause: "spinal"; died: 20 Aug. 1908; record # 91055.

MURRAY, Finettie; lived 1 day; death cause: "smothered by __ (illegible)"; died at Flag Pond on 31 Jan. 1909; record # 91056.

MASHBURN, Martha May; age: 7 months; death cause: "bold hives"; died at Flag Pond on 6 Apr. 1909; record # 91057.

BLANKENSHIP, Estell; female; lived 1 day; death cause: not stated; died at Flag Pond on 26 Nov. 1908; record # 91058.

STOCTON, Ollia May; age: 1 year and 5 months; death cause: "vomiting"; died at Flag Pond on 1 Aug. 1908; record # 91059.

MCINTOSH, Betsy; age: 77 years; born: Madison County, NC.; single; death cause: not stated; died: Flag Pond, 9 Apr. 1909; record # 91060.

CLARK, Nancy; age: 81 years; married; death cause: not stated; died at Flag Pond on 8 Dec. 1908; record # 91061.

RAMSEY, J.W.; age: 51 years; born: Madison County, NC.; married; death cause: "brain hemorrhage"; died at Flag Pond on 11 Feb. 1909; record # 91062.

RAY, Infant; male; age: not stated; death cause: not stated; died: 23 Feb. 1909; record # 91063.

SHELTON, Marion W.; age: 1 year and 1 month; death cause: "poison"; died at Flag Pond on 8 Jun. 1909; record # 91064.

SAMS, Joshah; age: 80 years, 6 months and 16 days; born: Buncombe County, NC.; single; death cause: "uremic poison"; died at Flag Pond on 13 Aug. 1908; record # 91065.

WALDROP, Milla; age: 1 year, 4 months and 10 days; death cause: illegible; died in the 7th District, 25 Jun. 1909; record # 91066.

WALDROP, Jordan Fields; age: 3 years and 6 months; death cause: illegible; died in the 7th District on 27 Jun. 1909; record # 91067.

BOWMAN, Joseph Arlee; age: 1 year and 6 months; death cause: illegible; died in the 7th District on 4 Aug. 1908; record # 91068.

MASTERS, Ada May; age: 3 months and 25 days; death cause: "bold hives"; died in the 7th District on 15 Aug. 1909; record # 91069.

ERWIN, Mary; age: 93 years; midwife; widow; death cause: "old age"; died in the 7th District on 13 Jun. 1909; record # 91070.

FOSTER, Maud; lived 3 days; death cause: "bold hives"; died in the 12th District on 30 Apr. 1909; record # 91071.

SHELTON, Jesse; female; age: "7 on August 17th"; death cause: "burned by fire"; died in the 12th District on __ Mar. 1909; record # 91072.

SHELTON, Mary; age: 2 years; death cause: "summer disease"; died in the 12th District on 29 Jun. 1909; record # 91073.

FOSTER, Thomas; age: not stated; married; death cause: not stated; died in the 12th District on 16 Nov. 1908; record # 91074.

MARRIS, Mary; age: 75 years; single; death cause: "old age"; died in the 12th District on 23 Oct. 1908; record # 91075.

CALLAHAN, William; age: 78 years; born: Madison County, NC.; married; death cause: "enlargement of stomach"; died in the 7th District on 30 Nov. 1908; record # 91076.

KUSECKER, Infant; female; lived 2 days; death cause: "bowel hemorrhage"; died in the 11th District on 15 Jan. 1909; record # 91077.

WHITE, Tommy; age: 1 month; death cause: "stomach and bowels"; died in the 11th District on 3 Jul. 1909; record # 91078.

NORRIS, R.N.; age: 25 years; single; death cause: "lung trouble"; died in the 11th District on 28 May 1908; record # 91079.

BARNES, Lizzie; age: 30 years; married; death cause: "lung trouble"; died in the 11th District on 2 Nov. 1908; record # 91080.

SCOTT, L.D.; age: 78 years; born: "Botetot" County, VA.; married; death cause: "rheumatism"; died in the 5th District on 4 Mar. 1909; record # 91084.

MILLER, Ollie; age: 10 months; death cause: "whooping cough"; died at Rock Creek on __ Jan. 1909; record # 91085.

19

JACKSON, C.B.; age: 29 years; married; death cause: "malaria"; died in the 5th District on 14 Jun. 1909; record # 91083.

WHITEHORN, Lottie; age: 23 years; born: Washington County; single; death cause: "fever"; died at Erwin on 14 Nov. 1909; record 91084.

ROSEMAN, Martha; black; age: 63 years; born: Yancey County, NC.; widow; death cause: "heart failure"; died at Yancey County, NC.; on 20 Dec. 1908; record # 91085.

HARRISON, Robert Taylor; age: 8 months; death cause: "dysentery"; died at Erwin on 15 Jun. 1909; record # 91086.

BENNET, Josephine; age: 1 year; death cause: not stated; died at Erwin on 27 Apr. 1909; record # 91087.

CRAIN, Retha; age: 64 years; married; death cause: "tumor on inside"; died at Flag Pond on 19 Jan. 1910; record # 91088.

HIGGINS, Infant; sex: not stated; age: not stated; death cause: not stated; died at Flag Pond on 24 Apr. 1910; record # 91089.

RAY, Julia; age: 40 years; born: Madison County, NC.; single; death cause: not recorded; died at Flag Pond on 20 Jun. 1910; record 91090.

HARRIS, Infant; sex: not stated; death cause: "dead when born"; died at Flag Pond on 3 Jun. 1910; record # 91091.

BLANKENSHIP, Jasper; lived 1 day; death cause: not stated; died at Flag Pond on 18 Aug. 1909; record # 91092.

MATHIS, Phenhica (?); age: 8 years; death cause: "pneumonia fever"; died at Flag Pond on 30 Mar 1910; record # 91093.

BALEY, Minnie L.; age: 22 years; single; death cause: "appendicitis"; died at Flag Pond on 10 Sep. 1909; record # 91094.

GUINN, Malinda; age: 64 years; born: Madison County, NC.; married; death cause: "cancer of stomach"; died at Flag Pond on 19 Nov. 1909; record # 91095.

GILLIS, Nancy; age: "about 45 years"; born: Madison County, NC.; married; death cause: "female trouble"; died at Flag Pond on 1 Aug. 1909; record # 91096.

MCINTOSH, Isaac; age: 61 years; born: Yancey County, NC.; married; death cause: "killed"; died at Flag Pond on 3 Jun. 1910; record 91097.

TIPTON, Martha; age: 28 years; born: Yancey County, NC.; married; death cause: "consumption"; died at Flag Pond on 18 Mar. 1910; record # 91098.

20

HIGGINS, Elizabeth; age: 86 years; born: Washington County; single; death cause: "old age"; died at Flag Pond on 15 Sep. 1909; record # 91099.

BOWMAN, Gravir (?); male; age: 12 months; death cause: "hives"; died at Flag Pond on __ Oct. 1909; record # 91100.

MORE, Mamey; age: 21 days; death cause: "croup"; died at Flag Pond on 15 Mar. 1910; record # 19101.

TILSON, William Harrison; born: 10 Dec. 1888; single; parents: John TILSON and Mary Ann GUINN, death cause: "revolver wound to head - murder"; informant: father (Kittyton); died: 1 Jan. 1914; buried; Clouse Cemetery; record (1914) # 7.

HAMMER, Mary Ella; born: 3 Jan. 1914; parents: Daniel W. HAMMER (Washington County) and Elizabeth NAVE (Carter County); death cause: "acute indigestion"; informant: father (Erwin); died: 29 Jan. 1914; buried: Johnson City; record (1914) # 6.

DUNCAN, John Samuel; born: 19 Dec. 1913; parents: Samuel T. DUNCAN (McDowell County, NC.) and Lula B. MARTIN (Franklin County, Illinois); death cause: "convulsions"; informant: father (Erwin); died: 30 Jan. 1914; record (1914) # 5.

EDWARDS, Gertie; born: 18 Jun. 1913; parents: Willard EDWARDS (Bee Loy, NC.) and Louttie LEDFORD (Bee Loy, NC.); death cause: "whooping cough"; informant: J.W. LEDFORD (Kittyton); died: 13 Jan. 1914; buried: Edwards Cemetery; record (1914) # 4.

HOPSON, Bert; born: 18 Oct. 1913; parents: J.A. HOPSON (Mitchell County, NC.) and Hassie PETERSON (Yancey County, NC.); death cause: "influenza and pneumonia"; informant: W.A. SAMS (Unicoi); died: 4 Jan. 1913; buried: Peterson Cemetery; record (1914) # 3.

DUNCAN, Ida; born: 23 Jul. 1879 in Mitchell County, NC.; married; parents: John WHITSON (Mitchell County, NC.) and Alzie SLAGLE (Mitchell County, NC.) death cause: "dropsy"; informant: R.V. BYRD (Unicoi); died: 11 Jan. 1914; buried: Peterson Cemetery; record # 2.

DAVIS, John; born: 26 Aug. 1851; widower; parents: Acey DAVIS and Susan WHITEHEAD (Carter County); death cause: "cerebral hemorrhage"; informant: J.L. WOODBY (Unicoi); died: 24 Jan. 1914; record (1914) # 1.

ERWIN, Pearl; born: 25 May 1888; single; parents: Phillip ERWIN and Caldona RAY (North Carolina); death cause: "larynx and heart disease"; informant: Albert CALLAHAN (Fontville); died: 13 Feb. 1914; buried: Erwin Cemetery; record (1914) # 15.

WOODBY, Samuel; born: 11 Sep. 1913; parents: Joe B. WOODBY (Yancey County, NC.) and Jane HEAD (Carter County); death cause: "influenza and gastritis"; informant: father (Unicoi); died: 26 Feb. 1914; buried: Peterson Cemetery; record (1914) # 14.

COOPER, Landon Nathaniel; born: 4 Jan. 1867; single; parents: James T. COOPER (Carter County) and Margaret K. MCNABB (Carter County); death cause: "pulmonary tuberculosis"; informant: Emma COOPER (Unicoi); died: 22 Feb. 1914; buried: family cemetery; record (1914) # 13.

BIRCHFIELD, Robert; born: 3 Mar. 1832 in North Carolina; widower; parents: H. BIRCHFIELD (North Carolina) and Polly BAKER; death cause: "diabetes"; informant: M.E. BIRCHFIELD (Erwin); died: 4 Feb. 1914; buried: 12th District; record (1914) # 12.

WHITE, Fay Banner; born: 2 Jan. 1914; parents: J.C. WHITE and Virginia TINKER; death cause: "indigestion"; informant: father (Erwin); died: 12 Feb. 1914; record (1914) # 11.

MCINTURFF, Earnest Ray; born: 19 Jul. 1912; parents: Jessie MCINTURFF and Julia CLICK (North Carolina); death cause: "meningitis"; informant: father (Erwin); died: 4 Mar. 1914; buried: Jobe Cemetery; record (1914) # 10.

HUSKINS, John; born: 15 Mar. 1837 in McDowell County, NC.; married; parents: Robert HUSKINS (North Carolina) and Catherine PLOTT (North Carolina); death cause: "asthma"; informant: Lizzie HUSKINS (Erwin); died: 4 Mar. 1914; buried: Martin Creek, 12th District; record (1914) # 9.

SHELTON, Nathan Garfield; born: 15 Jan. 1881; married; parents: Levi SHELTON (North Carolina) and Amanda SHELTON (North Carolina); death cause: "tuberculosis of lungs"; died: 6 Mar. 1914; buried: Flag Pond; record (1914) # 8.

WORSHAM, Rebecca; born: 2 May 1834 in Washington County, VA.; widow; parents: Joseph MEADOWS (Virginia) and mother's name illegible; death cause: "pneumonia"; informant: James WORSHAM (Erwin); died: 11 Mar. 1914; buried: Bristol, TN.; record (1914) # 21.

BENNETT, Frank; age: "about 25 years"; born: North Carolina; single; parents: Amos BENNETT (North Carolina) and __ MCCURRY; death cause: "brain tumor"; informant: A.S. HAMPTON (Erwin); died: 30 Mar. 1914; buried: 12th District; record (1914) # 20.

HOLCOMB, Earl; born: 12 Jan. 1910; parents: W.P. HOLCOMB and Belle GILLIS; death cause: "whooping cough"; informant: father (Kittyton); died: 19 Mar. 1914; buried: Holcomb Cemetery; record (1914) # 19.

HOLCOMB, William M.; age: 68 years; born: North Carolina; widower; parents: Abner HOLCOMB (North Carolina) and Mary ROBERTS (North Carolina); death cause: "pneumonia"; died: 2 Mar. 1914; buried: Holcomb Cemetery, 8th District; record (1914) # 18.

FRITZ, Infant; female; parents: Andy H. FRITZ (Johnson City) and Lula Duncan FRITZ; death cause: "stillborn"; died in the 12th District, 1 Apr. 1914; record (1914) # 17.

TIPTON, Ruba Mae; born: 13 Aug. 1912; parents: father not stated and Sarah TIPTON; death cause: "whooping cough"; informant: J.W. CHANDLER (Kittyton); died: 31 Mar. 1914; buried: Clear Branch; record (1914) # 16.

BAILEY, Theodore; born: 22 Apr. 1914; parents: Milton O. BAILEY (Yancey County, NC.) and Mary L. PETERSON (Green Mountain, NC.) death cause: "born at the 7th month"; informant: father (Erwin); died in the 12th District on 22 Apr. 1914; record (1914) # 29.

HOWELL, Infant; female; parents: Frank HOWELL (Yancey County, NC.) and Mae MCINTURFF; death cause: "stillborn"; informant: J.M. JONES (Unicoi); died: 19 Apr. 1914; buried: Jones Cemetery; record (1914) # 28.

WATTIS, Infant; male; parents: Bert WATTIS and Atha LEWIS (North Carolina); death cause: "still born"; died: 10 Apr. 1914; record # 27.

PRICE, Infant; male; born: 25 Feb. 1914; parents: (illegible) PRICE and Sara TILSON; death cause: illegible; died: 22 Apr. 1914; buried: Gillis Cemetery; record (1914) # 26.

23

BECK, Infant; female; parents: Julian J. BECK (Virginia) and Myrtle (illegible) (Henry County, VA.); death cause: "stillborn"; informant: Mrs. J.J. BECK (Erwin); died: 15 Apr. 1914; record (1914) # 25.

WALDRUP, Martha; age: 64 years; born: Madison County, NC.; single; parents: Joe WALDRUP (Madison County, NC.) and Nancy RICE (Madison County, NC.); death cause: "intestinal nephritis"; informant: Will SPARKS (Flag Pond); died: 14 Apr. 1914; buried: Sweetwater, TN.; record (1914) # 24.

RICE, Infant; unnamed; male; born: 17 Dec. 1913; parents: J.W. RICE and Lue BRIGGS; death cause: "died suddenly"; informant: E.J. RICE (Flag Pond); died: 25 Apr. 1914; buried: Rice Creek; record # 23.

ROBERTS, Chester; born: 24 Feb. 1914; parents: T.Z. ROBERTS (Grayson County, VA.) and mother's name illegible (Mitchell County, NC.); death cause: illegible; died: 15 Apr. 1914; record (1914) # 22.

PRICE, Nora; born: 19 Mar. 1908; parents: W.P. PRICE (Yancey County, NC.) and Callie BRADFORD (Yancey County, NC.); death cause: illegible; informant: father (7th District); died: 22 May 1914; record (1914) # 35.

LUCAS, Julia Katherine Creech; born: 9 Feb. 1860 in North Carolina; married; parents: Parrott CREECH (North Carolina) and Sarah CANADY (North Carolina); death cause: "uraemic poison"; informant: J.W. LUCAS (Unicoi); died: 17 May 1914; buried: Swingle Cemetery; record (1914) # 31.

GOUGE, Bruce; born: 4 Nov. 1912; parents: Walter GOUGE (Mitchell County, NC.) and Hattie RATCLIFFE (Kentucky); death cause: "lobar pneumonia"; died in the 4th District on 10 May 1914; buried: Gouge Cemetery; record (1914) # 33.

MCINTURFF, William R.; born: 6 Aug. 1889; married; parents: D.J. MCINTURFF and Lucenda BORDERS; death cause: "tubercular peritonitis"; informant: N.K. MCINTURFF (Unicoi); died: 29 May 1914; record (1914) # 32.

GOUGE, Infant; male; parents: B.L. GOUGE (North Carolina) and Effie HOWELL (North Carolina); death cause: "stillborn"; informant: father (Erwin); died: 3 May 1914; buried: Jobe Cemetery; record (1914) # 31.

MILLER, Soloman; born: 2 May 1841 in North Carolina; married; parents: Andy MILLER (North Carolina) and Nancy PETERSON

(North Carolina); death cause: "old age"; informant: W.E. EDWARDS (Erwin); died: 19 May 1914; buried: Jobe Cemetery; record (1914) # 30.

TILSON, Rebecca; born: 20 Nov. 1827 in Washington County; widow; parents: Jessie BALIS and Nancy SHANAN (?)(Washington County); death cause: "stomach disorder and old age"; informant: E.B. SAMS (Kittyton); died: 25 Jun. 1914; buried: Tilson Cemetery; record # 46.

TALLEY, William Albert; born: 17 Aug. 1913; parents: E.K. TALLEY (Carter County) and mother not stated; death cause: "malnutrition"; informant: Robert WILLIS (Roan Mountain); died: 23 Jun. 1914; record (1914) # 24.

CAMPBELL, Lois Reed; born: 6 Dec. 1887 in Ohio; widow; parents: A.M. REED (Ohio) and Estella MCMILLEN (Ohio); death cause: "shock following operation"; informant: father (Belfountain, Ohio); died: 9 Jun. 1914; buried: Belfountain, Ohio; record (1914) # 44.

TOPP, Infant; male; parents: Jim TOPP and Ethel MILLER; death cause: "stillborn"; informant: father (Erwin); died: 17 Jun. 1914; buried: 11th District; record (1914) # 43.

HAMPTON, Infant; male; parents: George HAMPTON and Celie WILLIAMS (North Carolina); death cause: "stillborn"; informant: H. WILLIAMS (Erwin); died: 18 Jun. 1914; buried: Martins Creek; record (1914) # 42.

LOGAN, Mahaley Erwin; black; born: 18 Mar. __; age: 23 years, 9 months and 6 days; single; born: McDowell County, NC.; parents: Larkin LOGAN (North Carolina) and Eather BRIDGES (North Carolina); death cause: "pellagra"; informant: H.H. HILL (Erwin); died: 24 Jun. 1914; buried: Martins Creek; record (1914) # 41.

MILLER, Edna; born: 27 Dec. 1873; married; parents: Vinson TOPP and Caroline AMBERUST; death cause: "anemia"; informant: Fuller MILLER; died: 19 Jun. 1914; buried: 11th District; record (1914) # 40.

PEAKE, Julia; born: 1 Aug. 1880 in North Carolina; married; parents: W.H. HENSLEY (North Carolina) and Mary J. LETTERMAN (North Carolina); death cause: "pellagra"; informant: J.W. PEAKE (Erwin); died: 20 Jun. 1914; buried: Martins Creek; record (1914) # 39.

INGLE, Estel; born: 5 Jun. 1914; parents: A. INGLE (North Carolina) and Vista RAY (North Carolina); death cause: "thrush"; informant: father (Erwin); died: 22 Jun. 1914; buried: Martins Creek; record # 38.

HONEYCUTT, William M.; born: __ Aug. 1859 in Georgia; married; parents: William HONEYCUTT (North Carolina) and Claricy STANLEY (North Carolina); death cause: "gunshot wound - shock from anesthesia for amputation of knee"; informant: Hick HONEYCUTT (Unicoi); died: 4 Jun. 1914; buried: Mosley Creek, 2nd District; record (1914) # 37.

BLANKENSHIP, Infant; female; parents: W.B. BLANKENSHIP and Elen TILSON; death cause: "stillborn"; died at Flag Pond on 7 Jun. 1914; record (1914) # 36.

MITCHELL, Elizabeth Lee; born: 23 Apr. 1914; parents: J.H. MITCHELL (Virginia) and Rosa MITCHELL (Virginia); death cause: "acute indigestion"; informant: father (Erwin); died: 2 Jul. 1914; buried: Martins Creek; record (1914) # 58.

BURLISON, Isaac; born: 17 Aug. 1856 in North Carolina; married; parents: D.W. BURLISON (North Carolina) and Nancy WILSON (North Carolina); death cause: "pellagra"; informant: Margaret E. BURLISON (Erwin); died: 25 Jul. 1914; buried: Jobe Cemetery; record (1914) # 57.

FOSTER, William David; born: 18 Jul. 1863 at Clear Branch, TN.; married; parents: David FOSTER and Jane CHANDLER (North Carolina); death cause: "cholera"; informant: David DUNCAN (Chestod (?), TN.); died: 21 Jul. 1914; buried: Unaka Springs; record # 56.

BOOSHE, Charles; born: 28 Feb. 1867; married; parents: not stated; death cause: "railroad accident, scalds of entire body"; died: 20 Jul. 1914; buried: Peterson Cemetery; record (1914) # 55.

CHANDLEY, Anorman (?); female; born: 15 Apr. 1893; parents: Lair CRAIN (Buncombe County, NC.) and Rachel ALLEN (Yancey County, NC.); death cause: "appendicitis"; informant: D.F. WILLIS (Flag Pond); died: 6 Aug. 1914; buried: Flag Pond; record (1914) # 54.

LEWIS, Luther; born: 24 Dec. 1913; parents: M. Daniel LEWIS (Yancey County, NC.) and Lilly LEWIS (Yancey County, NC.); death cause: "spinal meningitis"; informant: Leroy LEWIS (Flag Pond); died: 13 Jul. 1914; record (1914) # 53.

JOHNSON, Moses; born: 9 Jul. 1870 in Mitchell County, NC.; married; parents: E. JOHNSON (Mitchell County) and Polly HONEYCUTT (Mitchell County); death cause: "typhoid fever"; informant: W.H.

JONES (Unicoi); died: 2 Sep. 1914; buried: Gouge Cemetery; record (1914) # 63.

JEWELL, George Raymond; born: 13 Jun. 1914; parents: father "unknown" and Eliza JEWELL; death cause: "acute indigestion"; informant: Jane BAILEY (Erwin); died: 20 Aug. 1914; buried: Martin Creek; record (1914) # 62.

BOGART, Infant; female; parents: Charles BOGART and Gertrude CASH; death cause: "stillborn"; informant: father (Erwin); died: 16 Aug. 1914; buried: Martin Creek; record (1914) # 61.

DANIEL, Infant; age: illegible; sex: illegible; parents: W. DANIEL (Virginia) and Nannie PARISH (North Carolina); death cause: "premature"; died: 15 Aug. 1914; buried: Jobe Cemetery; record # 60.

FAGAN, Robert T.; born: 11 Sep. 1878; married; parents: James M. FAGAN and Alice ELLIS; death cause: illegible; informant: Mrs. L.L. MINTON (Johnson City); died: 24 Aug. 1914; buried: Fagan Cemetery; record (1914) # 59.

LAWING, Leonard; born: 26 Nov. 1911; parents: Daniel LAWING and Alise RICE; death cause: "accident, log rolled and crushed skull"; informant: father (Flag Pond); died: 12 Sep. 1914; buried: Lawing Cemetery; record (1914) # 73.

SHELTON, Champ; born: 27 Aug. 1914; parents: Fate SHELTON (North Carolina) and Girtha CUTSHALL (North Carolina); death cause: "whooping cough"; informant: I.M. RICE (Flag Pond); died: 24 Sep. 1914; buried: Rays Cemetery; record (1914) # 72.

MCINTURFF, Julia Neal; born: 4 Jul. 1878; married; parents: William BAKER (Roanoke, VA.) and Edna LYLE (Carter County); death cause: "eclampsia"; informant: Mrs. Edna Lyle BAKER (Unicoi); died: 26 Sep. 1914; buried: Swingle Cemetery; record (1914) # 71.

JONES, Pauline; born: 26 Sep 1914; parents: Doctor Lewis JONES (Yancey County, NC.) and Mary Adams WHITSON (Mitchell County, NC.); death cause: "cyanosis"; died: 5 Oct. 1914; buried: Peterson Cemetery; record (1914) # 70.

RAMSEY, Infants (twins); females; parents: M.B. RAMSEY (North Carolina) and Clara MORRIS (North Carolina); death cause: "premature"; informant: father (Erwin); died: 22 Aug. 1914; buried: Jobe Cemetery; record (1914) # 69.

27

BROOKS, Vernie Elizabeth; born: 25 Apr. 1914 in Washington County; parents: Robert BROOKS (Washington County) and Nora DANIELS; death cause: "acute indigestion"; informant: father (Erwin); died: 1 Sep. 1914; buried: Martin Creek; record (1914) # 68.

MILLER, Willard; born: 13 Sep. 1914; parents: N.T. MILLER and Mary M. HONEYCUTT; death cause: "infant"; informant: father (Erwin); died: 13 Sep. 1914; record (1914) # 67.

CHITWOOD, Harvey; born: 31 May 1875; married; parents: "unknown"; death cause: "fell between rail cars and car severed head from body"; died: 14 Sep. 1914; buried: Jobe Cemetery; record (1914) # 66.

WOODLY, Cany L.; born: 31 Aug. 1914; parents: John WOODLY and Lydia DAVIS; death cause: "acute indigestion"; informant: Frank L. DAVIS (Unicoi); died: 6 Oct. 1914; record (1914) # 65.

HENSLEY, Julia Ann; born: 10 Dec. 1848 in North Carolina; widow; parents: William K. HENSLEY (North Carolina) and Elmira CHANDLER (North Carolina); death cause: "old age"; informant: J.E. HUSKINS (Kittyton); died: 30 Sep. 1914; buried: Hensley Cemetery; record (1914) # 64.

JONES, Paul; born: 27 Sep. 1914; parents: Doctor Lewis JONES (Yancey County, NC.) and Mary Adams WHITSON (Mitchell County, NC.); death cause: "unknown, found dead in bed"; informant: C.N. WILCOX, MD.; died: 12 Oct. 1914; buried: Peterson Cemetery; record not numbered.

HOYL, Dora; born: 13 Oct. 1912; parents: J.M. HOYL (Greene County) and S. ROBERTS (Virginia); death cause: "diphtheria"; informant: Father (Erwin); died: 6 Oct. 1914; died in the 12th District; record not numbered.

JEWELL, Eliza; born: __ Jun. 1840; single; parents: George JEWELL (North Carolina) and Hannah PETERSON (North Carolina); death cause: "abscess of stomach"; informant: Jane BAILEY (Erwin); died: 10 Oct. 1914; buried: Martin Creek; record not numbered.

BANNER, Julia E.; born: 6 Aug. 1883; married; parents: M.L. TOPP and Emma JOHNSON; death cause: "stomach trouble"; informant: father (Erwin); died: 21 Oct. 1914; buried: Martin Creek; record not numbered.

JULIAN, Polly Eveline; born: 10 Mar. 1879 in Mitchell County, NC.; married; parents: Wilson EDWARDS (Mitchell County) and Martha GOUGE (North Carolina); death cause: "tuberculosis"; informant: G.L. JULIAN (Roan Mountain); died: 30 Oct. 1914; buried: Martin Creek; record not numbered.

ROGERS, Corbet; born: 24 May 1895; single; parents: Will ROGERS and Cassie BAKER; building trade; death cause: "fell from top of Unicoi Courthouse"; died: 20 Oct. 1914; buried: Tucker Cemetery; record not numbered.

BURGESS, Roy; born: 24 Aug. 1899 in North Carolina; parents: E.D. BURGESS (North Carolina) and Mamie ENGLAND (North Carolina); death cause: "diabetes"; informant: father (Erwin); died: 22 Oct. 1914; buried: Martin Creek; record not numbered.

ANDERS, Essie May; born: 16 Sep. 1914; parents: Wordin ANDERS and SARA P__ (illegible); death cause: "hives"; informant: father (Erwin); died: 28 Oct. 1914; buried: Martin Creek; record not numbered.

CAPPS, Ruth; born: 4 Dec. 1912; parents: M.R. CAPPS (North Carolina) and Annie May LAWS; death cause: "measles and pneumonia"; informant; father (Erwin); died: 28 Oct. 1914; buried: Jobe Cemetery; record not numbered.

PETERS, Hugh; born: 23 Feb. 1919 in West Virginia; parents: T.H. PETERS (North Carolina) and Belle BRINKLEY (Virginia); death cause: "typhoid"; informant: mother (Erwin); died: 30 Oct. 1914; buried: Jobe Cemetery; record not numbered.

HERRELL, Samuel; born: 23 Oct. 1882 in Magnetic City, NC.; married; parents: William HERRELL (Mitchell County, NC.) and Celia GARLAND (Mitchell County, NC.) death cause: "aneurysm of carotid artery, died instantly"; informant: Celia HERRILL (Magnetic City, NC.); died: 11 Nov. 1914; buried: Rowe Cemetery; record not numbered.

EDWARDS, Nancy; "aged lady, age unknown"; parents: illegible; death cause: not stated; informant: M.W. WILSON (Kittyton); died: 14 Mar. 1914; record not numbered.

TILSON, Infant; born: 10 Nov. 1914; parents; E__ (illegible) TILSON and Nora TILSON; death cause: not stated; died: 12 Nov. 1914; buried: Clear Spring; record not numbered.

BIRCHFIELD, Martha; age: 76 years; widow; parents: father's name illegible and Sarah OBRIEN; death cause: "paralysis"; died: 30 Nov. 1914; record not numbered.

MASTERS, Worley; age: 59 years; widower; parents: W.N. BALES and Dicie MASTERS; death cause: "sudden death, cause not stated"; informant: Doctor L.S. TILSON (Erwin); died: 2 Nov. 1914; buried: Martin Creek; record not numbered.

WILLIAMS, Jessie; born: 10 Oct. 1911 in North Carolina; parents: Vannis WILLIAMS (North Carolina) and Bessie HAMPTON; death cause: "tonsillitis"; informant: father (Erwin); died: 26 Nov. 1914; buried: Martin Creek; record not numbered.

DAVIS, Hazel Elton; born: 16 Sep. 1914; parents: R.H. DAVIS and Lola RICE (North Carolina); death cause: "pneumonia"; informant: Mrs. Mary VANCE (Erwin); died: 3 Nov. 1914; buried: Jobe Cemetery; record not numbered.

GOUGE, William; born: 16 Nov. 1869 in North Carolina; married; parents: Nat GOUGE and Dicey HONEYCUTT; death cause: "traumatism"; died: 16 Nov. 1914; buried: North Carolina; record not numbered.

CAMPBELL, Infant; female; parents: W.A. CAMPBELL (Virginia) and Josephine ANDERSON; death cause: "stillborn"; informant: father (Erwin); died: 20 Nov. 1914; buried: Jobe Cemetery; record not numbered.

WESTALL, Herman; born: 13 Aug. 1909 in North Carolina; parents: T.B. WESTALL (North Carolina) and Mary BUTNER (North Carolina); death cause: "pneumonia"; informant: mother (Erwin); died: 24 Nov. 1914; buried: Martin Creek; record not numbered.

LEWIS, Cora L.; age: 6 years, 2 months and 4 days; parents: W.S. LEWIS (Virginia) and Phebe E. BANNER; death cause: "pneumonia"; informant: father (Erwin); died: 26 Nov. 1914; buried: Martin Creek; record not numbered.

HENSLEY, Infant; female; parents: Henry HENSLEY and Dora HENSLEY (Yancey County, NC.) death cause: "unknown"; informant:

Mary BAILEY (Flag Pond); died: 25 Nov. 1914; buried: Rice Creek; record not numbered.

EDWARDS, Theidry (?); born: 22 Nov. 1914; parents: G. EDWARDS (Bee Loy, NC.) and Rosie BRIGGS; death cause: "bold hives"; informant: Walter BLANKENSHIP (Flag Pond); died: 24 Dec. 1914; buried: above Higgins Chapel; record not numbered.

MOORE, Thomas Henry; born: 17 Dec. 1889; single; parents: William N. MOORE (North Carolina) and Rebecca __ (illegible)(North Carolina); death cause: "tuberculosis of hips"; informant: Ralph MOORE (Flag Pond); died: 22 Dec. 1914; buried: Flag Pond; record not numbered.

BRIGGS, William H.; born: 2 Jun. 1880; parents: P. BRIGGS and mother's name illegible; death cause: "lung trouble"; died in the 10th District on 18 Dec. 1914; buried: Flag Pond; record not numbered.

STREET, Infant; female; parents: Monroe STREET (Mitchell County, NC.) and Bertie ERWIN (Washington County); death cause: "stillborn"; informant: Mrs. J.L. ERWIN (Unicoi); died: 24 Dec. 1914; buried: Rowe Cemetery; record not numbered.

WARREN, Infant; female; parents: J.M. WARREN (Buncombe County, NC.) and Rosa __ (illegible)(Haywood County, NC.) death cause: "miscarriage at 5th month"; died: 15 Dec. 1914; buried: Peterson Cemetery; record not numbered.

SNEYD, Infant; female; parents: Will SNEYD (Washington County) and Ollie WOODLY; death cause: "stillborn"; informant: F.W. WOODLY (Unicoi); died: 30 Dec. 1914; buried: Birchfield Cemetery; record not numbered.

TILSON, Elizabeth; born: 4 Dec. 1830 in Washington County; widow; parents: John BEALS and Elizabeth NELSON; death cause: not stated; informant: George TILSON (Kittyton); died: 30 Dec. 1914; buried: Tilson Cemetery; record not numbered.

PETERS, J.S.; born: __ Apr. 1872; married; parents: G.W. PETERS and Martha LONG; death cause: "burnt"; informant: father (Piney Flats, TN.) died: 19 Dec. 1914; buried: Piney Flats; record not numbered.

THOMAS, John R.; born: 18 Dec. 1877; married; parents: Paul THOMAS and Hannah HALL; death cause: "tuberculosis"; informant:

31

L.D. THOMAS (North Carolina); died: 18 Dec. 1914; buried: North Carolina; record not numbered.

MCNABB, Ralph; born: 29 Oct. 1913; parents: G.S. MCNABB and Bell ERWIN; death cause: "broncho pneumonia"; informant: father (Erwin); died: 20 Dec. 1914; buried: Jobe Cemetery; record not numbered.

HENSLEY, Elsie; born: 21 Mar. 1899; parents: Dr. T.C. HENSLEY and Mary BRIGGS; death cause: "pneumonia"; died: 23 Dec. 1914; buried: Flag Pond; record not numbered.

LEWIS, Ora; age: 3 years, 10 months and 29 days; parents: N.S. LEWIS and mother's name illegible; death cause: "typhoid fever"; died: 11 Dec. 1914; buried: Martin Creek; record not numbered.

HARRIS (?), Will; born: 4 Mar. 1875 in North Carolina; married; parents: Gather HARRIS and Callie BRIGGS; death cause: "pulmonary tuberculosis"; informant: Horace HARRIS (?); died: 31 Dec. 1914; record not numbered.

JONES, Illegible; born: 12 Dec. 1912; parents: illegible; death cause: "scarlet fever"; informant: George NEAS (Erwin); died in the 12th District on 16 Dec. 1914; record not numbered.

MCCURRY, Luther; born: 12 Nov. 1914; parents: M.C. MCCURRY (North Carolina) and Laura MCINTURFF; death cause: "pneumonia and meningitis"; informant: father (Erwin); died: 12 Jan. 1915; record (1915) # 451.

KING, Harry H.; born: 14 Dec. 1878 in Virginia; married; parents: W.L. KING (Virginia) and Sarah WILLIAMS (Virginia); death cause: "pulmonary tuberculosis"; informant: N.E. MILLER (Jonesboro); died: 17 Jan. 1915; buried: Limestone, TN.; record (1915) # 452.

LOGAN, Mollie; parents: George LOGAN (Simpson County, KY.) and Cinthia CROUSE (Allegheny County, NC.); death cause: "stillborn - delivered at 6th month"; died: 27 Jan. 1915; buried: Peterson Cemetery; record (1915) # 453.

HORN, Frank; born: 5 Jan. 1855 in Cleveland County, NC.; married; parents: "unknown"; death cause: "dropsy"; informant: Lee HORN (Flag Pond); died: 14 Jan. 1915; buried: Hensley Cemetery; record # 454.

SHELTON, John B.; born: 18 Jan. 1915; parents: Billie SHELTON (Madison County, NC.) and Usby WATTS; death cause: "croup";

informant: C.E. HENSLEY (Kittyton); died: 18 Feb. 1915; buried: Watts Cemetery; record (1915) # 455.

WOODBY, Infant; male; parents: Henry WOODBY and Sammie LACY (Carter County); death cause: "stillborn"; informant: R.L. WOODBY (Unicoi); died: 26 Feb. 1915; buried: Banks Cemetery; record # 456.

BAILEY, Infant; female; parents: Morgan BAILEY and Ada HARRIS; death cause: "stillborn"; died: 16 Feb. 1915; buried: Martins Creek; record (1915) # 457.

NEAL, Marion Albert; born: 9 May 1914; parents: R.A. NEAL and Anna SMITH; death cause: "erysipelas"; informant: George M. NEAS (Erwin); died: 19 Feb. 1915; buried: Martin Creek; record (1915) # 458.

WOMACK, Elizabeth; born: 2 Feb. 1911; parents: E.L. WOMACK and Leta JENNINGS; death cause: "scarlet fever"; informant: Lela WOMACK; died: 21 Feb. 1915; buried: Jobe Cemetery; record # 459.

LINVILLE, Howard Ray; born: 19 Jun. 1914; parents: William A. LINVILLE (Mitchell County, NC.) and Nancy Elizabeth NELSON (Washington County); death cause: "entero colitis, pneumonia"; informant: Mrs. N. NELSON (Unicoi); died: 28 Feb. 1915; buried: Jones Cemetery; record (1915) # 460.

CRAIN, R__ (illegible); born: 29 Jan. 1915; parents: Mack CRAIN and Texie HIGGINS (North Carolina); death cause: "diphtheria"; informant: L.E. BLANKENSHIP (Flag Pond); died: 28 Feb. 1915; buried: Higgins Chapel; record (1915) # 461.

TIPTON, Dianna; born: 3 Dec. 1897; parents: John D. TIPTON (Virginia) and Jane HIGGINS; death cause: "pulmonary tuberculosis"; informant: T.N. MASHBURN (Flag Pond); died: 21 Feb. 1915; buried: Higgins Cemetery; record (1915) # 462.

HOLCOMB, Enid; born: 8 Mar. 1907; parents: U.S. HOLCOMB and Florence RIDDLE (North Carolina); death cause: "lobar pneumonia"; informant: Robert WILLIS (Earnestville); died: 1 Feb. 1915; buried: Holcomb Cemetery; record (1915) # 463.

RICE, Denlie; born: 28 Apr. 1913; parents: T.G. RICE and Altha BRIGGS; death cause: "burnt"; informant: father (Erwin); died: 28 Mar 1915; buried: Flag Pond; record (1915) #464.

33

HARRIS, Dwight; born: 23 Feb. 1915; parents: Fletch HARRIS and Diana PHILLIPS; death cause: "bold hives"; informant: J.M. HARRIS (Flag Pond); died: 26 Mar. 1915; buried: Flag Pond; record # 465.

TIPTON, Infant; male; parents: Charles TIPTON and Cleo CORM (?); death cause: "stillborn"; informant: father (Erwin); died: 15 Mar. 1915; buried: Jobe Cemetery; record (1915) # 466.

SHELTON, Infant; female; parents: Rod SHELTON and Debie Jane BLANKENSHIP; death cause: "born before full term"; born/died: 17 Mar 1915; informant: Father (Flag Pond); buried: Shelton Cemetery; record (1915) # 467.

SHELTON, Infant; female; parents: Rod SHELTON and Debie Jane BLANKENSHIP; death cause: "born before full term"; born/died: 17 Mar 1915; informant: Father (Flag Pond); buried: Shelton Cemetery; record (1915) # 468 (twin of above).

WILLIS, Robert C.; born: 18 Jan. 1915; parents: W.J. WILLIS and H__ (illegible) JONES; death cause: not stated; died in the 8th District on 10 Mar. 1915; record (1915) # 469.

LEWIS, David; born: 10 Jun. 1863 in North Carolina; parents: Bill LEWIS (North Carolina) and A. HARRELL; death cause: "unknown"; informant: Deborah LEWIS (Kittyton); died: 5 Mar. 1915; buried: Lewis Cemetery; record (1915) # 470.

WOODBY, Gladys Sally; born: 28 Feb. 1915; parents: Frank L. DAVIS (Mitchell County, NC.) and Marry WOODBY; death cause: "broncho pneumonia"; informant: Charley DAVIS (Unicoi); died: 6 Mar. 1915; buried: Woodby Cemetery; record (1915) # 471.

WOODBY, George (?); age: 18 years; parents: E.P. WOODBY and Caroline CAMPBELL (North Carolina); death cause: "pneumonia fever"; informant: father (Unicoi); died: 4 Mar. 1915; buried: Woodby Cemetery; record (1915) # 472.

WRIGHT, Infant; male; parents: Ollie WRIGHT and Bessie DENTON (Sullivan County); death cause: "unknown"; born/died: 6 Mar. 1915; buried: Wright Cemetery; record (1915) # 473.

HARRIS, Tom; born: 23 Feb. 1915; parents: Fletch HARRIS and Diana PHILLIPS; death cause: "bold hives"; informant: J.F. HARRIS (Flag Pond); died: 15 Mar. 1915; record (1915) # 474.

HENSLEY, Starling S.; born: 20 Oct. 1833 in Madison County, NC.; parents: Berry HENSLEY (North Carolina) and __ KEITH (North Carolina); death cause: "pellagra"; informant: T.C. HENSLEY (Erwin); died: 28 Mar. 1915; buried: Flag Pond; record (1915) # 475.

STREET, Infant; female; parents: Landon STREET (Mitchell County, NC.) and Mary COCHRAN (Carter County); death cause: "stillborn"; died: 2 Apr. 1915; buried: Unicoi; record (1915) # 476.

CRAIN, Berry; born: 27 Apr. 1915; parents: Bradie CRAIN and R__ (illegible) COATS; death cause: "unknown"; informant: Thomas HOYLE; died: 28 Apr. 1915; buried: Higgins Chapel; record # 477.

CARPENTER, John W.; born: 26 Nov. 1873 in West Virginia; married; parents: Frank CARPENTER (West Virginia) and Sarah E. SIMONS (West Virginia); death cause: "brights disease"; died 4 Apr. 1915; buried: Martin Creek; record (1915) # 478.

RUNNION, Infant; female; parents: Thomas C. RUNNION and Sue E. GUINN; death cause: "stillborn"; informant: father (Erwin); died: 22 Apr. 1915; buried: Martin Creek; record (1915) # 479.

TAPP, Sada; age: 67 years; born: Washington County; widow; parents: father unknown and Margaret WHITE (Washington County); death cause: "pneumonia"; informant: D.J. WHITE (Erwin); died: 20 Apr. 1915; buried: Fishery, 11th District; record (1915) # 480.

TILSON, William E.; born: 29 Apr. 1827 in Washington County; parents: P__ (illegible) TILSON (Washington County, Virginia) and Nancy ALLEN (Washington County, Virginia); death cause: "nephritis and uremia"; informant: L.S. TILSON (Erwin); buried: Tilson Cemetery; record (1915) # 481.

WOODBY, Infant; female; parents: D.F. WOODBY (North Carolina) and M.L. RIDDLE; death cause: "stillborn"; informant: G.F. GUINN (Kittyton); died: 17 Apr. 1915; buried: Mt. Pleasant; record # 482.

HEAD, Thurman; born: 27 Apr. 1915; parents: William HEAD and Myrtle MCCURRY (Yancey County, NC.); death cause: "miscarriage - 6 months"; informant: Mrs. W.M. MCCURRY (Unicoi); died: 28 Apr. 1915; record (1915) # 483.

BARRY, Everett J.; born: 27 Mar. 1915; parents: Charles A BAKER and Cenia JONES (Yancey County, NC.); death cause: "premature birth";

informant: W.A. SAMS (Unicoi); died: 11 Apr. 1915; buried: Swingle Cemetery; record (1915) # 484.

WHITSON, Jennie; born: 23 Jul. 1883; married; parents: M. Ephram MCLAUGHLIN and Mary Ann COLE (Johnson County); death cause: "tuberculosis"; informant: E.B. MCLAUGHLIN (Unicoi); died: 4 Apr. 1915; buried: Jones Cemetery; record (1915) # 485.

HAMMETT, John; born: 19 Sep 1829; married; parents: Newton HAMMETT (Carter County) and Millie HEADRICK (Carter County); death cause: not stated; died: 3 Apr. 1915; buried: Anderson Cemetery; record (1915) # 486.

GOUGE, Ezekiah; born: 25 Apr. 1892; married; parents: Robert GOUGE and Ollie WOODY (North Carolina); death cause: not stated; informant: D. GOUGE (Unicoi); died: 3 May 1915; buried: Gouge Cemetery; record (1915) # 487.

TEAGUE, Bell; born: 16 Mar. 1912 in Avery County, NC.; parents: Waits TOWNSEND (Coldwell County, NC.) and Nola TEAGUE (Hampton, TN.); death cause: "bowel perforation"; informant: father (Unicoi); died: 14 May 1915; buried: Baker Cemetery; record # 488.

JARRETT, Infant; male; parents: George JARRETT (North Carolina) and Sallie SHEPPARD (Carter County); death cause: "premature birth"; born/died: 3 May 1915; buried: Mableton; record (1915) # 489.

COOPER, Infant; female; parents: Guy COOPER (Johnson City) and D. BROKUS; death cause: "stillborn"; informant: father (Erwin); died: 26 May 1915; buried: Jobe Cemetery; record (1915) # 490.

BLEVINS, William M.; age: "about 70 years"; born: Carter County; widower; parents: Charles BLEVINS (Carter County) and mother not stated; death cause: "organic heart disease"; died in the 11th District on 6 May 1915; record (1915) # 491.

BAILEY, Infant; male; parents: Milton A. BAILEY (Green Mountain, NC.) and Mary L. PETERSON (Green Mountain, NC.); death cause: "stillborn"; born/died: 15 May 1915; buried: Martin Cemetery; record (1915) # 492.

SHELTON, Esau; age: "unknown"; widower; parents: "unknown"; death cause: "paralysis"; informant: Edd RAY (Flag Pond); died: 12 Jun. 1915; buried: Shelton Cemetery; record (1915) # 493. .

COOPER, Milburn; age: 50 years; born: Carter County; married; parents: James COOPER (Washington County) and Margaret MCNABB (Washington County); death cause: "heart trouble"; informant: Orville COOPER (Unicoi); died: 4 Jun. 1915; record (1915) # 494.

PRICE, Infant; male; parents: Will PRICE and Rettie LAWS (Washington County); death cause: "stillborn"; died: 9 Jun. 1915; buried: Jobe Cemetery; record (1915) # 495.

HENDRICK, E.D.; black; age: 30 years; born: Blair, South Carolina; parents: "unknown"; death cause: "hit by train"; died: 17 Jun. 1915; buried: South Carolina; record (1915) # 496.

WALKER, Infant; female; born: 15 Apr. 1915; parents: Wash WALKER (North Carolina) and Essie BENNETT (North Carolina); death cause: "spina bifida"; informant: father (Erwin); died: 21 Jun. 1915; record (1915) # 497.

HONEYCUTT, Jack; born: 8 Jul. 1913; parents: Dillard HONEYCUTT and Bell GIBBS (Mitchell County, NC.); death cause: "cholera infantum"; informant: George D. FOWLER (Erwin); died: 23 Jun. 1915; buried: Rock Creek; record (1915) # 498.

HIGGINS, G.W.; born: 13 Oct. 1867; married; parents: John H. HIGGINS and Catherine WHITE (North Carolina); death cause: "typhoid fever"; died in the 8th District, 28 Jun. 1915; buried: Tipton Cemetery; record (1915) # 499.

TAYLOR, Rebecca; born: 15 Dec. 1849; married; parents: John H. HIGGINS and Leveasy ARWOOD (North Carolina); death cause: "paralysis"; informant: J.W. TAYLOR (Kittyton); died: 18 Jun. 1915; buried: Tipton Cemetery; record (1915) # 500.

DICKERSON, Mrs. O.E.; born: 29 May 1893; married; parents: J.W. BROWN and Elizabeth DEADRICK; death cause: "heart disease"; informant: L.S. TILSON (Erwin); died: 24 Jun. 1915; buried: Johnson City; record (1915) # 501.

DUNCAN, Franklin Madison; born: 10 Dec. 1830 in Tennessee; married; parents: Abner DUNCAN (Tennessee) and Catherine DUGGER (Tennessee); death cause: "paralysis"; informant: J.L. DUNCAN; died: 16 Jul. 1915; buried: Cheston, Tennessee; record (1915) # 502.

SHELTON, Infant; female; parents: __ (illegible) Milton SHELTON (North Carolina) and Carlotta HENSLEY; death cause: "born at 7 months"; informant: O.H. GRINDSTAFF (Kittyton); died: 30 Jul. 1915; buried: Shelton Cemetery; record (1915) # 503.

ANDERSON, Shep M.; born: 27 Nov. 1825 in Carter County; widower; parents: Isaac ANDERSON (Carter County) and Elizabeth MCINTURFF (Illinois); death cause: not stated; informant: I.H. ANDERSON (Johnson City); died: 28 Jul. 1915; buried: Anderson Cemetery; record (1915) # 504.

HUSKINS, Louzretia; born: 10 Jul. 1847; married; parents: __ TAPP and mother not stated; death cause: "typhoid fever"; informant: J.W. HUSKINS (Erwin); died at Rock Creek on 10 Jul. 1915; record # 505.

SHIPLEY, Geneve; born: 25 Apr. 1913; parents: Roy SHIPLEY and Mary HENSLEY (North Carolina); death cause: "cholera infantum"; informant: Mrs. May SHIPLEY (Erwin); died: 25 Jul. 1915; record (1915) # 506.

CLOUSE, Mary J.; born: 17 Sep. 1865; married; parents: Thomas FOSTER and Naoma CHANDLER (North Carolina); death cause: "pulmonary tuberculosis"; informant: W.J. CLOUSE (Kittyton); died: 2 Jul. 1915; buried: Foster Cemetery; record (1915) # 507.

HENSLEY, Harrie; born: 2 Apr. 1915; parents: Rosco HENSLEY and Celia HIGGINS (North Carolina); death cause: "cholera infantum"; died in the 8th District, 18 Jul. 1915; buried: Edwards Cemetery; record (1915) # 508.

HIGGINS, Thugie (?); born: 27 Jul. 1837 in North Carolina; widow; parents: Van JONES (North Carolina) and Bell BRIGGS (North Carolina); death cause: "cancer of cervix and eye"; informant: R.P. JONES (Kittyton); died: 27 Jul. 1915; buried: Tipton Cemetery; record (1915) # 509.

STOCTON, James H.; born: 23 Jun. 1877; married; parents: J.W. STOCTON (Cleveland County, NC.) and Rebecca BRIGGS (Georgia); death cause: "tuberculosis"; informant: T.J. STOCTON (Flag Pond); died: 11 Jul. 1915; buried: Flag Pond; record (1915) # 509.

GILLIS, Leonard Ezekiel; born: 13 Jun. 1914; parents: Lattie GILLIS and Vivian BARNES; death cause: "ate washing powder"; informant: J.B. LAWING (Flag Pond); died: 1 Aug. 1915; buried: Lawing Cemetery; record (1915) # 510.

FOSTER, Jean; born: 7 Feb. 1915; parents: John MATHIS and Josie HUSKINS; death cause: illegible; informant: J.E. HUSKINS (Kittyton); died: 3 Aug. 1915; buried: Mt. Pleasant; record (1915) # 511.

WHITE, Charles, Jr.; born: 20 May 1915; parents: Charles WHITE and Jennie Myrtle __ (illegible); death cause: "malnutrition"; informant: father (Erwin); died: 15 Sep. 1915; record (1915) # 512.

HUGHES, Infant; female; parents: Walter HUGHES (Gate City, VA.) and May A. ALLEN (North Carolina); death cause: "stillborn"; informant: father (Erwin); died: 29 Sep. 1915; buried: Jobe Cemetery; record (1915) # 513.

MASHBURN, Andy Clifford; born: 20 Aug. 1915; parents: Melvin MASHBURN and Estell CHANDLER (Clear Branch, TN.) death cause: "unknown"; informant: T.M. MASHBURN (Flag Pond); died: 20 Sep. 1915; buried: Higgins Chapel; record (1915) # 514.

TIPTON, Sarah Elizabeth; born: 22 Oct. 1853 in Washington County; married; parents: Cale HAIR (Washington County) and Eliza FOSTER (Jonesboro); death cause: not stated; informant: Mrs. Amanda WHITTAMORE (Johnson City); died: 3 Sep. 1915; buried: Mableton, TN.; record (1915) # 515.

GRINDSTAFF, Jessie; born: 23 Sep. 1915; parents: Elbert GRINDSTAFF and Charlotte CARVER (Carter County); death cause: "tumor of head"; informant: father (Unicoi); died: 27 Oct. 1915; buried: Grindstaff Cemetery; record (1915) # 516.

BIRCHFIELD, Charley; born: 2 Sep. 1915; parents: Nathan BIRCHFIELD and Hattie COCHRAN (North Carolina); death cause: "acute indigestion"; informant: father (Unicoi); died: 7 Oct. 1915; buried: Birchfield Cemetery; record (1915) # 517.

WOODBY, Susan; born: 14 Aug. 1875 in Carter County; married; parents: William CARVER (Carter County) and Rachel SWANER (Carter County); death cause: "tuberculosis"; informant: George CARVER (Unicoi); died: 27 Oct. 1915; buried: Carter County; record (1915) # 518.

WILLIAMS, El__ (illegible); born: __ Jul. 1914; parents: Frank WILLIAMS (North Carolina) and Nancy ANDERS; death cause: "bronchial pneumonia"; informant: E.G. ANDERS (Erwin); died: 31 Oct. 1915; buried: Martin Creek; record (1915) # 519.

39

MCNABB, Hannah; born: 2 Jul. 1841 at Buffalo, Carter County; parents; W.M. PHILLIPS (North Carolina) and Vina PHILLIPS (North Carolina); death cause: "pellagra and uremic coma"; informant: R.G. MCNABB (Erwin); died: 13 Oct. 1915; record (1915) # 520.

BLANKENSHIP, Dwight; born: 12 Oct. 1915; parents: Oscar BLANKENSHIP and Bertha PHILLIPS; death cause: not stated; informant: Fletch HARRIS (Flag Pond); died: 14 Oct. 1915; buried: Sams Creek; record (1915) # 521.

HARRIS, Lydia; born: 19 Sep. 1915; parents: Walter HARRIS and Radie CRAIN; death cause: "unknown"; informant: Horace BLANKENSHIP (Flag Pond); died: 12 Oct. 1915; buried: above Higgins Chapel; record (1915) # 522.

HARRIS, Lydia; duplicate of record 522, record (1915) # 523.

BLANKENSHIP, Dwight; duplicate of record 521, record (1915) # 524.

JONES, Leonard; born: 12 Oct. 1915; parents: father not stated and Mary E. GILBERT; death cause: "unknown"; died: 14 Oct. 1915; buried: Foster Cemetery; record (1915) # 525.

MCCURRY, Jay M.; born: 27 Jan. 1911; parents: W.M. MCCURRY (Yancey County, NC.) and Ina PETERSON (Yancey County, NC.); death cause: "appendicitis, peritonitis"; informant: father (Unicoi); died: 21 Oct. 1915; buried: family cemetery; record (1915) # 526.

FOSTER, Gladys; born: 24 Sep. 1915; parents: Emory FOSTER and Allice JONES; death cause: "eczema"; informant: father (Erwin); died: 10 Oct. 1915; buried: Martin Creek; record (1915) # 527.

EDWARDS, Lydia; born: 25 Sep. 1866; married; parents: Phillip ERWIN and Martha TOMPKIN; death cause: "dropsy"; informant: A. EDWARDS (Kittyton); died: 9 Nov. 1915; buried: Clouse Cemetery; record (1915) # 528.

ALEXANDER, Mary Catherine; born: 6 Jun. 1843 in Washington County; married; parents: Frank KEEBLER and Elizabeth WRIGHT; death cause: "weak heart"; informant: F. ALEXANDER (Indian Springs, TN.); died: 29 Nov. 1915; buried: Marion, Virginia; record (1915) # 529.

BLANTON, John; age: 25 years; single; parents: "unknown"; death cause: "train ran over legs"; died: 8 Nov. 1915; buried: Knoxville, Tennessee; record (1915) # 530.

SAMS, Leonard; born: 17 Oct. 1915; parents: M.S. SAMS and Mary LEDFORD (North Carolina); death cause: "unknown"; informant: J.W. LEDFORD (Kittyton); died: 6 Nov. 1915; buried: Edwards Cemetery; record (1915) # 531.

WHITTAMORE, Samuel; born: 29 Sep. 1883; married; parents: Tom WHITTAMORE and Mary ROBISON; death cause: "tuberculosis of stomach and intestines and excessive cigarette smoking"; informant: Deck WHITTAMORE (Johnson City); died: 18 Nov. 1915; buried: Anderson Cemetery; record (1915) # 532.

MILLER, John Preston; born: 24 Dec. 1849 in Washington County; married; parents: Shepperd MILLER and Annie CARY; death cause: "valvulor heart disease"; informant: Mrs. Susan Caroline MILLER (Unicoi); died: 10 Nov. 1915; buried: Swingle Cemetery; record # 533.

STREET, David; born: 4 Dec. 1869 in North Carolina; widower; parents: Clingman STREET (Mitchell County, NC.) and Eveline TROUTMAN (Mitchell County, NC.); death cause: "tuberculosis"; informant: James STREET (Unicoi); died: 5 Dec. 1915; buried: Street Cemetery; record (1915) # 534.

GARLAND, Minnie; born: 16 Mar. 1911; parents: father not stated and Jane GARLAND (Mitchell County, NC.); death cause: "double pneumonia"; informant: mother (Unicoi); died: 11 Dec. 1915; buried: McInturff Cemetery; record (1915) # 535.

WALLACE, Luther; born: 24 Mar. 1911 in Yancey County, NC.; parents: S.W. WALLACE (Yancey County) and Mary WALLACE (North Carolina); death cause: "croup"; informant: father (Erwin); died: 23 Dec. 1915; buried: Jobe Cemetery; record (1915) # 536.

WEAVER, William S.; born: 19 Jan. 1913; parents: A.C. WEAVER and Minnie DRAPER; death cause: "pneumonia"; informant: father (Erwin); died: 4 Dec. 1915; buried: Knoxville, Tennessee; record (1915) # 537.

GREER, Helen; born: 25 Nov. 1915; parents: Ed GREER and Annie L. TAYLOR; death cause: "unknown"; informant: E.G. ANDERS (Erwin); died: 9 Dec. 1915; buried: Jobe Cemetery; record (1915) # 538.

WILLIAMS, Leona; age: 3 years; parents: Frank WILLIAMS (North Carolina) and Nancy ANDERS; death cause: "bronchial pneumonia"; informant: E.G. ANDERS (Erwin); died: 20 Dec. 1915; buried: Martin Creek; record (1915) # 539.

GILBERT, Mary; born: 18 Nov. 1828 in Carter County; widow; parents: John BARRY (Ireland) and Jamima POLAND (Johnson County); death cause: illegible; informant: Jane HUSKINS (Erwin); died: 31 Dec. 1915; buried: Martin Creek; record (1915) # 540.

FOSTER, Infant; female; parents: J.H. FOSTER and Amelda SAMS (?); death cause: "stillborn"; informant: father (Kittyton); died: 30 Dec. 1915; buried: Foster Cemetery; record (1915) # 541.

BIRCHFIELD, Mattie C.; born: 17 Aug. 1879; married; parents: E.J. RIGGS and Darthula J. BETTIS; death cause: "scarlet fever"; informant: Mrs. Lula M. TUTTLE (Charlotte, NC.); died: 20 Dec. 1915; buried: Birchfield Cemetery; record (1915) # 542.

CRAIN, Infant; male; parents: Braddie CRAIN and Rentha COATS; death cause: "unknown"; informant: John COATS (Flag Pond); born/died: 18 Dec. 1915; buried: above Higgins Chapel; record # 543.

ERWIN, Jack Stuart; born: 3 Jul. 1915 in South Carolina; parents: R.H. ERWIN and Verna GARLAND (North Carolina); death cause: "bile duct obstruction"; informant: mother (Fordville, Tennessee); died: 19 Dec. 1915; buried: Erwin Cemetery; record (1915) # 544.

HUSKINS, Samuel; born: 23 Dec. 1915; parents: father "unknown" and Anna Lee HUSKINS; death cause: "found dead in bed"; informant: B.M. ALLRED (Erwin); died: 5 Jan. 1916; record (1916) # 435.

BAXTER, Infant; male; parents: L.D. BAXTER and Elizabeth HUGHES; death cause: "catarrh jaundice"; informant: father (Erwin); died: 24 Jan. 1916; buried: Martins Creek; record (1916) # 436.

BAKER, Will; born: 24 Apr. 1892; railroad fireman; parents: J.W. BAKER and Margaret KUNER; death cause: "injury from train wreck in North Carolina"; informant: D.W. BAKER (Erwin); died: 28 Jan. 1916; buried: Jobe Cemetery; record (1916) # 437.

MOORE, William N.; age: 59 years; married; parents: not stated; death cause: "lobar pneumonia"; informant: C.P. GENTRY (Kittyton); died: 24 Jan. 1916; buried: "above Flag Pond"; record (1916) # 438.

HENSLEY, Lofton; born: 26 Nov. 1897; single; parents: C.E. HENSLEY and Rebecca J. HENSLEY; death cause: "lagrippe"; informant: father (Kittyton); died: 25 Jan. 1916; buried: Hensley Cemetery; record # 439.

INGLE, Willie Viola; born: 13 Feb. 1913; parents: __ (illegible) Claimon INGLE (Marshall, North Carolina) and Maggie HUGHES (Yancey County, NC.); death cause: "burn"; died: 13 Feb. 1916; buried: Bailey Cemetery; record (1916) # 440.

BRIGGS, Infant; male; parents: Rosco BRIGGS and Tilda Mae RICE; death cause: "stillborn"; informant: Mrs. J.O. BLANKENSHIP (Flag Pond); died: 4 Feb. 1916; buried: Rice Creek; record (1916) # 441.

HENSLEY, Leon; born: 20 Oct. 1915; parents: James HENSLEY and Annettie METCALF; death cause: "pneumonia fever"; informant: A.S. BAILEY (Flag Pond); died: 20 Feb. 1916; buried; Sams Creek; record (1916) # 442.

COLEMAN, Minnie; born: 30 Aug. 1879 in Carter County; married; parents: Don STREET (Mitchell County, NC.) and Eva STEVENS (Carter County); death cause: "double pneumonia"; informant: John COLEMAN (Unicoi); died: 18 Feb. 1916; buried: Brumett Cemetery; record (1916) # 443.

WILLIS, Juda; born: 6 Mar 1811 in North Carolina (age 104 years, 11 months and 18 days); married; parents: Francis TOLLEY (North Carolina) and Darkey TOLLEY (North Carolina); death cause: "breast cancer and old age"; informant: Sam VANCE (Unicoi); died: 24 Feb. 1916; buried: Cochran Cemetery; record (1916) # 444.

CLARK, Luther, Jr.; parents: Luther CLARK and Lockie WOODBY; death cause: "stillborn"; informant: E. HOWELL (Unicoi); died: 15 Feb. 1916; buried: Woodby Cemetery; record (1916) # 445.

DAVIS, James C.; born: 14 Feb. 1861 in Washington County; married; parents: Thomas D. DAVIS and Catherine L__ (illegible); death cause: not recorded; informant: Mrs. J.C. DAVIS (Erwin); died: 17 Feb. 1916; buried: Jobe Cemetery; record (1916) # 446.

TITTLE, Mollie; born: 20 Nov. 1889 in Carter County; married; parents: James DAUGHERTY and Sarahan GRINDSTAFF (North Carolina); death cause: "hookworm disease"; informant: Thomas DAUGHERTY (Unicoi); died: 17 Feb. 1916; buried: Garland Cemetery; record # 447.

HORVILLE, William; age: 77 years; born: North Carolina; widower; parents: John HORVILLE (North Carolina) and Sallie OLLIS (North Carolina); death cause: "lobar pneumonia"; died: 23 Feb. 1916; buried: Garland Cemetery; record (1916) # 448.

43

MCEWEN, Calvin; born: 22 Aug. 1838 in Shelby County, TN.; retired school teacher; married; parents: Will MCEWEN (Shelby County) and Tabitha MCKINNEY (Glade Springs, TN.); death cause: "cerebral hemorrhage"; informant: Mrs. Calvin MCEWEN (Unicoi); died: 12 Feb. 1916; record (1916) # 449.

LINVILLE, Dana Landon; born: 23 Feb. 1916; parents: James LINVILLE and Nannie HUMPHREYS (Carter County); death cause: "premature birth"; informant: W.A. SAMS (Unicoi); died: 25 Feb. 1916; buried: Tipton Cemetery; record (1916) # 450.

MARKLAND, Emory Alfred; born: 2 Feb. 1916; parents: Blain MARKLAND and Edna PARSLEY (Kentucky); death cause: "unknown"; informant: father (Erwin); died: 3 Feb. 1916; record # 451.

RICHARDSON, William; born: 29 Oct. 1915; parents: J.S. RICHARDSON (Carter County) and Fine BLEVINS; death cause: "unknown, found dead in bed"; informant: John S. RICHARDSON (Embreeville); died: 14 Feb. 1916; buried: Cove Cemetery; record (1916) # 452.

PENLAND, Louise Poteet; born: 21 Dec. 1840 at Milligan, Carter County; married; parents: Pinkney WILLIAMS (Buffalo, Carter County) and Rose HAUN (Dry Creek, Carter County); death cause: "lobar pneumonia"; informant: R.L. PENLAND (Unicoi); buried: Swingle Cemetery; record (1916) # 453.

BROWN, Floyd Ray; born: 25 Jan. 1916; parents: father not stated and Blanch BROWN; death cause: "bold hives"; informant: Louise BROWN (Erwin); died: 4 Mar 1916; buried: Fishery Cemetery; record # 454.

HENSLEY, Infant; male; parents: J.B. HENSLEY and Martha HENSLEY; death cause: "stillborn"; informant: J.E. HENSLEY (Kittyton); born/died: 29 Mar. 1916; buried: Hensley Cemetery; record (1916) # 455.

BLEVINS, Martha; age: 70 years; widow; parents: Quillen WHITE and Mary HAMPTON; death cause: "pneumonia"; informant: Bill BLEVINS (Embreeville); died: 15 Mar. 1916; buried: Cove Cemetery; record (1916) # 456.

COLDWELL, M_ (illegible); male; born: 6 Mar. 1916; parents: Thomas J. COLDWELL (Virginia) and Lona E. VAUGHN (Virginia); death cause: "infancy"; informant: father (Erwin); died: 16 Mar. 1916; buried: Jobe Cemetery; record (1916) # 457.

LETTERMAN, Noah; age: 39 years; born: Yancey County, NC.; married; parents: Milton LETTERMAN (Yancey County) and Carolina BUCHANAN (Yancey County); death cause: "influenza and heart disease"; informant: Hannah LETTERMAN (Erwin); died: 11 Mar. 1916; record (1916) # 458.

HOWELL, Infant; male; parents: Dudley J. HOWELL (Yancey County, NC.) and Rachel DAVIS; death cause: "premature birth"; informant: W.A. SAMS (Unicoi); born/died: 29 Mar. 1916; buried: Peterson Cemetery; record (1916) # 459.

MCNABB, Myrtle Marie; parents: Taylor MCNABB and Rebecca HENSON (Washington County); death cause: "stillborn"; died in the 4th District, 29 Mar. 1916; record (1916) # 460.

BRUMETT, James; age: 74 years; born: Unicoi County; married; parents: William BRUMETT (Carter County) and Melinda BRITT (Carter County); death cause: "pneumonia"; informant: Thomas BRUMITT (Unicoi); died: 20 Mar 1916; record (1916) # 461.

DUNCAN, Mary Catherine; born: 23 Jan. 1839 in Johnson County; parents: Jacob DUGGER (Johnson County) and Mary BROWN (Johnson County); death cause: "organic heart disease"; informant: W.F. DUNCAN (Chestra); died: 17 Mar. 1916; buried: Shallow Ford; record (1916) # 462.

MOSLEY, Edward; born: 10 May 1882 in North Carolina; married; parents: William MOSLEY (North Carolina) and Sallie BUCHANAN (North Carolina); death cause: "epileptic convulsions, pneumonia"; informant: David GOUGE (Unicoi); died: 31 Mar. 1916; buried: Gouge Cemetery; record (1916) # 463.

HUSKINS, Mary Ann; born: 12 Apr. 1853 in Washington County; widow; parents: William TAPP (Washington County) and Elizabeth MATON (Carter County); death cause: "apoplexy"; informant: Matt TAPP (Erwin); died: 25 Apr. 1916; buried: Fishery Cemetery; record (1916) # 464.

HENSLEY, Infant; male; parents: Joe HENSLEY and Mary SHELTON; death cause: "stillborn, fall by mother"; informant: W.K. HENSLEY (Kittyton); died: 26 Apr. 1916; buried: Hensley Cemetery; record # 465.

HENSLEY, Infant; male; parents: Joe HENSLEY and Mary SHELTON; death cause: "stillborn, fall by mother"; informant: W.K. HENSLEY (Kittyton); died: 26 Apr. 1916; buried: Hensley Cemetery; record # 466.

TILSON, G. Tilman; born: 14 Apr. 1884; married; parents: Henry TILSON and Elizabeth SAMS; death cause: not stated; informant: father (Kittyton); died: 28 Apr. 1916; buried: Sams Cemetery; record (1916) # 467.

BROWN, Infant; male; parents: Sam BROWN and Emma TIPTON; death cause: "stillborn"; informant: father (Kittyton); died: 28 Apr. 1916; buried: Clear Branch Cemetery; record (1916) # 468.

GOUGE, Bulow; born: 12 Mar. 1871 in Mitchell County, NC.; married; parents: Leonard GOUGE (Mitchell County) and Phebe BURLESON (Mitchell County); death cause: "gastritis and stomach ulcer"; informant: Phebe GOUGE (Erwin); died: 19 Apr. 1916; buried: North Carolina; record (1916) # 469.

TAYLOR, Infant; male; parents: Frank TAYLOR and Paddie BENNETT (North Carolina); death cause: illegible; informant: father (Erwin); born/died: 28 Apr. 1916; buried: Jobe Cemetery; record (1916) # 470.

RUNYON, Julia; born: 28 Apr. 1894; married; parents: James SIMMONS and Emmaline MASHBURN; death cause: "infection following child birth"; informant: Will SIMMONS (Erwin); died: 27 Apr. 1916; record (1916) # 471.

ERWIN, Annie Thelma; born: 30 Apr. 1915; parents: G.C. ERWIN (McDowell County, NC.) and Ellen EDWARDS (McDowell County, NC.); death cause: "pneumonia fever"; informant: father (Erwin); died: 27 Apr. 1916; record (1916) # 472.

GARDNER, Infant; female; parents: Dock GARDNER (North Carolina) and Sarah FORBES (North Carolina); death cause: not stated; informant: Cinda CAMPBELL (Unicoi); died: 1 Apr. 1916; record (1916) # 473.

MCLAUGHLIN, Mary Ann; age: "about 59 years"; born: Johnson County; married; parents: Jesse COLE (Johnson County) and Margaret BERRY (Johnson County); death cause: "valvulor heart insufficiency"; informant: C.N. WILCOX (Unicoi); died: 9 Apr. 1916; record # 474.

GILLIS, Infant; male; parents: D.C.S. GILLIS and Annis SAMS; death cause: "miscarriage at the 5th month"; informant: W.A. SAMS (Unicoi); died: 21 Apr. 1916; buried: Swingle Cemetery; record (1916) # 475.
HAIRE, Georgia Pearl; born: 31 Jul. 1915; parents: George HAIRE (Buncombe County, NC.) and Maggie HARVEL (Mitchell County, NC.) death cause: "acute indigestion"; informant: father (Unicoi); died: 1 Apr. 1916; buried: Peterson Cemetery; record (1916) # 476.
PATRICK, George William; born: 17 Aug. 1815; parents: George PATRICK (Virginia) and Cora BENETT (Mitchell County, NC.); death cause: "bronchial pneumonia"; informant: father (Unicoi); died: 27 Apr. 1916; buried: Peterson Cemetery; record (1916) # 477.
COOPER, James Taylor; born: 22 Dec. 1832 in Carter County; widower; parents: Andy COOPER (Carter County) and Elizabeth TAYLOR (Carter County); death cause: "paralysis"; informant: Emma COOPER (Unicoi); died: 29 Apr. 1916; buried: family cemetery; record # 478.
MATHES, Lizzie; parents: Loda MATHES (Washington County) and Lula FOSTER; death cause: "suffocation, premature birth"; informant: C.B. FOSTER (Embreeville); born/died: 3 Apr. 1916; buried: Liberty Cemetery; record (1916) # 479.
CRAIN, Ralph Elroy; born: 13 Mar. 1916; parents: Hezekiah CRAIN (North Carolina) and Hattie BLANKENSHIP (North Carolina); death cause: "pneumonia fever"; informant: Harrison HALL (Flag Pond); died: 25 May 1916; buried: Laurel, North Carolina; record (1916) # 480.
GARLAND, Elisha; born: 28 Oct. 1848 in North Carolina; married; parents: Christianbury GARLAND (North Carolina) and Jane BURLESON (North Carolina); death cause: "intestinal nephritis"; informant: P.T. GARLAND (McDowell, Illinois); died: 15 May 1916; buried: Bell Cemetery; record (1916) # 481.
JOHNSON, Leurla; parents: G.B. JOHNSON (North Carolina) and Jane DAVIS; death cause: "stillborn"; informant: father (Unicoi); born/died: 23 May 1916; buried: Davis Cemetery; record (1916) # 482.
BROWN, Joseph A.; born: 19 Nov. 1828 in Washington County; married; parents: Jesse BROWN (Richmond, Virginia) and Elizabeth WAKEFIELD (Burke County, NC.); death cause: "cerebral hemorrhage"; informant: Mrs. Sarah HULING (Erwin); died: 17 May 1916; buried: Brown Cemetery; record (1916) # 483.

47

TILSON, Margaret; born: 24 Jun. 1849; married; parents: William BROWN and Rachel CLOUSE; death cause: "stomach and heart failure"; informant: W.A. TILSON (Kittyton); died: 7 May 1916; buried: Clear Branch Cemetery; record (1916) # 484.

ELLIS, Charles D.; age: "about 20 years"; single; parents: Landon ELLIS and Carie SLAGLE; death cause: "accident, struck on head by ore bucket"; informant: A.E. MCCORKLE (Johnson City); died: 20 May 1916; buried: Elizabethton; record (1916) # 485.

BARNETT, Marial Alderson Snead; born: 30 Sep. 1852 in Russell County, VA.; married; parents: Ralph SNEAD and Mary Jane SNEAD; death cause: "brights disease"; died: 9 May 1916; buried: Erwin; record (1916) # 486.

HARMON, Harold Francis; born: 27 Mar, 1915 in Washington County; parents: Arthur L. HARMON and Mary A. SWATZEL; death cause: "pneumonia"; informant: father (Erwin); died: 13 May 1916; buried: Greeneville; record (1916) # 487.

RUNION, David; born: 22 Apr. 1916; parents: Cornelius RUNION and Julia SUMMONDS (North Carolina); death cause: "illio colitis"; died: 25 May 1916; buried: Jobe Cemetery; record (1916) # 488.

JONES, Naomi; black; born: 22 Jan. 1916; parents: Ransom JONES (North Carolina) and Ellie ALLISON; death cause: "illio colitis"; informant: father (Erwin); died: 25 May 1916; buried: Martins Creek; record (1916) # 489.

LYLE, Floyd Alvey; born: 18 Dec. 1915; parents: Frank LYLE and Martha TAPP; death cause: "whooping cough"; informant: father (Erwin); died: 11 Jun. 1916; buried: Fishery Cemetery; record # 490.

TOMPKINS, Martha; born: 27 Mar. 1830 in Washington County; widow; parents: Thomas TILSON (Virginia) and Gennet TILSON (Virginia); death cause: "old age"; informant: G.W. TOMPKINS (Kittyton); died: 5 Jun. 1916; buried: Clear Branch; record # 491.

MCCURRY, Infant; female; parents: William MCCURRY (Yancey County, NC.) and Ina PETERSON (Yancey County, NC.); death cause: "cyanosis"; informant: father (Unicoi); born/died: 14 Jun. 1916; record (1916) # 492.

ALBERTSON, Infant; male; parents: Jack ALBERTSON (Cranberry, NC.) and Ethel FORD (West Virginia); death cause: "stillborn";

informant: father (Erwin); died: 26 Jun. 1916; buried: Jobe Cemetery; record (1916) # 493.

MILLER, Minnie; born: 14 Apr. 1884 in Elk Park, NC.; married; parents: John CASH (North Carolina) and Delia JONES (North Carolina); death cause: "pellagra"; informant: Henry MILLER (Erwin); died: 29 Jun. 1916; buried: Martins Creek; record (1916) # 494.

EFFLER, Dathia Evelyn; born: 30 Aug. 1915; parents: father not stated and Jane EFFLER; death cause: "unknown"; informant: Everette EFFLER (Kittyton); died: 24 Jun. 1916; buried: Effler Cemetery; record (1916) # 495.

LEWIS, Willard Ray; born: 27 Jan. 1916; parents: William LEWIS (Virginia) and Febe BANNER; death cause: "acute indigestion"; informant: W.S. LEWIS (Erwin); died: 9 Jul. 1916; buried: Martins Creek; record (1916) # 496.

BARLOW, Chafon; age: "about 31 years"; married; parents: not stated; death cause: not stated; informant: Mrs. Robert FAGAN (Johnson City); died: 8 Jul. 1916; buried: Carter County; record (1916) # 497.

TAYLOR, Louttia; born: 20 Aug. 1889 in North Carolina; married; parents: Mat BENETT (North Carolina) and Cordi BENNET (North Carolina); death cause: "sarcoma"; informant: Frank TAYLOR (Erwin); died: 15 Jul. 1916; buried: Martins Creek; record (1916) # 498.

GILBERT, S.C.; born: 17 Jan. 1855; married; parents: Henry GILBERT (South Carolina) and Berzillia DEWITT (South Carolina); death cause: "stomach and liver disease"; informant: Mrs. Mary GILBERT (Ernestville); died: 29 Jul. 1916; buried; Clear Branch Cemetery; record (1916) # 499.

MCNABB, Emma; age: "about 53 years"; born: Carter County; married; parents: Boyd SMITH (Carter County) and Elizabeth CROW (Carter County); death cause: "tuberculosis of stomach"; informant: Mrs. Jane BROWN (Unicoi); died: 10 Jul. 1916; buried: Fishery Cemetery; record (1916) # 500.

MATHES, Ninah; born: 15 Jan. 1915; parents: father not stated and Lenrie MATHES; death cause: "poisoned by eating pills"; informant: Sanis MATHES (Embreeville); died: 3 Jul. 1916; buried: Liberty Cemetery; record (1916) # 501.

BUCHANAN, Vertie Flora; born: 6 Mar. 1916; parents: Dot BUCHANAN (North Carolina) and Hattie GREENE (North Carolina); death cause: "__ (illegible) of brain"; informant: father (Embreeville); died: 22 Jul. 1916; record (1916) # 502.

BROYLES, John Sumerfield; born: 27 Apr. 1840 in Washington County; married; parents: Jacob BROYLES (Washington County) and Lucinda BROYLES (Washington County); death cause: "paralysis"; informant; Frank E. BROYLES (Erwin); died: 23 Jul. 1916; record (1916) # 503.

LAWSON, Deffina D.; born: 3 Jan. 1826 in Greene County; school teacher; widow; parents: John W, BARTTIG (Greene County) and Martha BUSTER (Greene County); death cause: "influenza and paralysis"; informant: Thomas LAWSON (Erwin); died: 28 Jul. 1916; buried: Hot Springs, North Carolina; record (1916) # 504.

JONES, Perl; born: 15 May 1915; parents: Danal JONES and Martha JONES, death cause: not stated; informant: mother (Kittyton); died: 15 Jul. 1916; buried: Foster Cemetery; record (1916) # 505.

LOVE, Martha C.; born: 8 Jul. 1849; widow; parents: Louis BANNER (Kentucky) and Viana WHITSON (North Carolina); death cause: "heart failure"; informant: D. LOVE (Erwin); died: 3 Aug. 1916; record # 506.

WAUGH, Julia Ann; black; born: 26 Dec. 1883 in Ashe County, NC.; married; parents: John WAUGH (North Carolina) and Alice COOK (North Carolina); death cause: "mitral stenosis, aneurysm and syphilis"; informant: John WAUGH; died: 5 Aug. 1916; record (1916) # 507.

TIPTON, Birtha; age: 1 month and 16 days; parents: Joseph TIPTON and Nancy BARNETT (North Carolina); death cause: "indigestion and anemia"; informant: Charles S. BARNETT (Unicoi); died: 30 Aug. 1916; buried: Tipton Cemetery; record (1916) # 508.

MCLEMORE; Venie; born: 14 Jul. 1911; parents: Henry MCLEMORE (North Carolina) and Julia MOSLEY; death cause: "bronchial pneumonia"; informant: N.L. MCLEMORE (Unicoi); died: 19 Aug. 1916; buried: Mosley Cemetery; record (1916) # 509.

BIRCHFIELD, Infant; female; parents: S.L. BIRCHFIELD and Martha YOUNG (Mitchell County, NC.); death cause: "stillborn"; informant: father (Unicoi); died: 27 Aug. 1916; buried: Birchfield Cemetery; record (1916) # 510.

PETERSON, Peter; born: 1 Apr. 1843 (age: 76 years, 6 months and 27 days); born: Mitchell County, NC.; married; parents: Peter PETERSON (North Carolina) and Dicey STOUT (Yancey County, NC.) death cause: "nephritis"; informant: Mrs. Peter PETERSON (Unicoi); died: 27 Sep, 1916; buried: Peterson Cemetery; record (1916) # 511.

GUINN, Clide; born: 27 Jul. 1916; parents: A.B. GUINN and Zora TILSON; death cause: "croup"; informant: G.F. GUINN (Kittyton); died: 6 Sep. 1916; buried: Clear Branch; record (1916) # 512.

RIDDLE, George; born: 28 Sep. 1884; single; parents: John RIDDLE (North Carolina) and Sarah M. HIGGIN; death cause: "tuberculosis"; informant: J.M. BLANKENSHIP (Kittyton); died: 4 Sep. 1916; buried: Sams Cemetery; record (1916) # 513.

LEWIS, Haret; born: 26 Jul. 1896 in North Carolina; single; parents: David LEWIS (North Carolina) and Sarah LEWIS (North Carolina); death cause: "measles"; died in the 8th District on 11 Sep. 1916; buried: Lewis Cemetery; record (1916) # 514.

WILLIS, Hester; born: 10 Nov. 1881; married; parents: Elbert JONES and Margaret EDWARDS; death cause: "heart failure"; informant: J.C. WILLIS (Kittyton); died: 24 Sep. 1916; buried: Edwards Cemetery; record (1916) # 515.

MCINTURFF, A__ (illegible); female; born: __ Feb. 1862; married; parents: Samuel TINKER and Magie EFFLER; death cause: illegible; informant: W.A. MCINTURFF (Erwin); died: 15 Sep. 1916; buried: Fishery Cemetery; record (1916) # 516.

CRAIN, Carl; born: 19 Aug. 1915; parents: Joe CRAIN and Dora HIGGINS; death cause: "cholera infantum"; informant: father (Erwin); died: 6 Sep. 1916; buried: Martins Creek; record (1916) # 517.

PARR (?), George Washington; born: 21 Nov. 1913; parents: R.C. PARR (Virginia) and Mary Jane ROBERTS; death cause: "pneumonia"; informant: father (Erwin); died: 5 Oct. 1916; buried: Martins Creek; record (1916) # 518.

RAY, James Harrison; age: not stated; married; parents: Riley RAY (North Carolina) and Julia Ann SHELTON (North Carolina); death cause: "typhoid fever"; informant: Riley RAY (Flag Pond); died: 29 Oct. 1916; buried: Ray Cemetery; record (1916) # 519.

JACKSON, W.C.; born: 19 Sep 1842 in North Carolina; widower; parents: Austin JACKSON (North Carolina) and Mary RAILY; death cause: "heart lesion"; informant: Mrs. W.C. JACKSON (Erwin); died: 25 Oct. 1916; buried: Jobe Cemetery; record (1916) # 520.

TIPTON, Julia Ann; age: 80 years; widow; parents: William JONES (North Carolina) and Bell BRIGGS (North Carolina); death cause: "brights disease"; informant: Mrs. S.W. COLE (Erwin); died: 20 Oct. 1916; record (1916) # 521.

BOGART, Infant; male; parents: C.G. BOGART and Gertrude C__ (illegible); death cause: "premature birth"; informant: father (Erwin); died: 1 Oct. 1916; record (1916) # 522.

PENLAND, Milton F.; born: 4 Aug. 1840 in Yancey County, NC.; widower; physician; parents: Milton PENLAND (Buncombe County, NC.) and Elvira HORTON (Yancey County, NC.); death cause: "nephritis and pneumonia"; informant: Mrs. Joseph STREET (Unicoi); died: 9 Oct. 1916; buried: Swingle Cemetery; record (1916) # 523.

BIRCHFIELD, Ezekiel; born: 15 Jun. 1826 in Unicoi County; widower; parents: Nathaniel BIRCHFIELD (Tennessee) and Lila GARLAND (North Carolina); death cause: "mitral regurgitation"; informant: N. BIRCHFIELD (Unicoi); died: 25 Oct. 1916; buried: Birchfield Cemetery; record (1916) # 524.

BLEVINS, Infant; female; parents: Frank BLEVINS and Lenis WHITE; death cause: "stillborn"; informant: father (Embreeville); died: 31 Oct. 1916; buried: Tucker Cemetery; record (1916) # 525.

RUNIONS, Carie L.; born: 22 Feb. 1895; married; parents: Nelson TINKER and Jane CALLAHAN; death cause: "heart disease"; died in the 7th District on 17 Nov. 1916; buried: Tinker Cemetery; record (1916) # 526.

INGLE, Clifford; born: 11 Sep. 1916; parents: Isaac INGLE (North Carolina) and Lockie BRIGGS; death cause: not stated; informant: father (Flag Pond); died: 9 Nov. 1916; buried: Flag Pond; record # 527.

NELSON, Blanie; female; born: 17 Jun. 1894; parents: Will NELSON and Annie MASTERS; death cause: "tuberculosis"; informant: J.W. MASTERS (Embreeville); died: 7 Nov. 1916; buried: Mt. Wesley Cemetery; record (1916) # 528.

STANTON, Clint; born: 14 Jul. 1901; parents: Billie STANTON and Jane BROYLES; death cause: "typhoid fever"; informant: father (Embreeville); died: 8 Nov. 1916; buried: Liberty Cemetery; record (1916) # 529.

WHITSON, Alzina; born: 28 Aug. 1842 in North Carolina; widow; parents: David SLAGLE and Judie WATKINS; death cause: "arterial sclerosis"; informant: R.A. WHITSON (Unicoi); died: 29 Nov. 1916; buried; Peterson Cemetery; record (1916) # 530.

HALE, Mary C.; born: 7 Nov. 1852 in Washington County; widow; parents: Jesse B. ERWIN (Washington County) and Elizabeth MCMAHAN (Madison County, NC.); death cause: "ulcer of stomach and hemorrhage"; informant: L.S. TILSON (Erwin); died: 5 Nov. 1916; record (1916) # 531.

HICKS, Sarah; born: 3 Mar. 1862 in Johnson County; married; parents: Henry CAMPBELL (Johnson County) and Mary GRINDSTAFF (Johnson County); death cause: "typhoid fever"; informant: H.H. HICKS (Unicoi); died: 30 Nov. 1916; buried: Hicks Cemetery; record (1916) # 532.

HILMAN, Mattie; born: 6 Nov. 1884 in Mitchell County, NC.; married; parents: William URST (?) and Nancy HARRELL (North Carolina); death cause: "pulmonary tuberculosis"; informant: Rouben MCLEMORE (Unicoi); died: 21 Nov. 1916; buried: Mosley Cemetery; record (1916) # 533.

HENSLEY, B.L.; born: 28 Jun. 1832 in North Carolina; widower; parents: William HENSLEY (North Carolina) and Polly HOWELL (North Carolina); death cause: "diarrhea"; informant: H.C. HENSLEY (Kittyton); died: 29 Nov. 1916; buried: Falls Branch Cemetery; record (1916) # 534.

ADAMS, Anee Lee; born: 20 Dec. 1916; parents: James ADAMS (North Carolina) and Eliza WESLEY; death cause: "infant only 4 hours old"; informant: father (Chestra); died: 20 Dec. 1916; record (1916) # 535.

MATHES, Emeline; born: 6 Sep. 1844 in Yancey County, NC.; widow; parents: David ANGEL and Peggy KING (Virginia); death cause: "old age"; informant: Joseph MATHES (Flag Pond); died: 11 Dec. 1916; buried: Sams Creek; record (1916) # 536.

COLE, S.W.; born: 25 Dec. 1854 in Arkansas; married; parents: "unknown"; death cause: "typhoid fever"; informant: S.W. COLE (Erwin); died: 3 Dec. 1916; buried: Jobe Cemetery; record (1916) # 537.

BRUMMETT, Dorothy Mae; born: 3 Mar. 1911 in Ohio; parents: James BRUMMETT and Lissie BRUMMETT; death cause: "bowel perforation"; informant: Joe BRUMMETT (Unicoi); died: 15 Dec. 1916; record (1916) # 538.

DAY, William Lenard; born; 18 Nov. 1914; parents: William DAY and Myrtle HAMPTON; death cause: "fire burning"; informant: father (Erwin); died: 30 Dec. 1916; buried: Rock Creek; record (1916) # 539.

FOSTER, Infant; male; parents: Andy FOSTER and Litty CHANDLER; death cause: "unknown"; informant: I.T. CHANDLER (Kittyton); born/died: 23 Jan. 1917; buried: Foster Cemetery; record (1917) # 429.

SAMS, Jack Gleason; born: 17 Dec. 1916; parents: Rufus SAMS and Lizzie PHILLIPS; death cause: "diphtheria"; informant: Hobart METCALF; died: 28 Jan. 1917; buried: Sams Creek; record # 430.

PRICE, Nolie Mae; born: 25 Dec. 1916; parents: father not stated and Minnie PRICE; death cause: "croup"; informant: J.H. CHANDLER (Kittyton); died: 26 Jan. 1917; buried: Hensley Cemetery; record # 431.

YELTON, Effie Isabell Bailey; born: 12 May 1894 in North Carolina; parents: E.L. BAILEY (North Carolina) and Vista STREET (North Carolina); death cause: "pulmonary tuberculosis"; informant: E.L. BAILEY (Erwin); died: 22 Jan. 1917; buried: Martins Creek; record (1917) # 432.

KILBY, James Albert; born: __ Nov. 1916 in Johnson City; parents: J.H. KILBY (Johnson City) and Mary WILSON (Johnson City); death cause: "malnutrition"; informant: father (Erwin); died: 30 Jan. 1917; buried: Jobe Cemetery; record (1917) # 433.

WALKER, W.A.; born: 3 Feb. 1854 in North Carolina; widower; parents: J.M. WALKER (North Carolina) and Sallie __ (North Carolina); death cause: "heart failure"; informant: Frank WALKER (Embreeville); died: 24 Jan. 1917; buried: Flag Pond; record # 434.

YOUNG, Wilma; born: 23 Aug. 1916; parents: F.W. YOUNG (North Carolina) and Missouri GREEN (North Carolina); death cause: "pneumonia"; informant: father (Embreeville); died: 18 Jan. 1917; record (1917) # 435.

GUINN, William Franklin; born: 12 Apr. 1848; widower; parents: Isaac GUINN and Elizabeth LAWING; death cause: "brights disease"; informant: Carl SAMS (Flag Pond); died: 11 Jan. 1917; record # 436.

DOVE, Catherine; born: 4 Sep. 1844; widow; parents: John NELSON and Nancy WHITSON; death cause: "dropsy"; informant: Newton NELSON (Unicoi); died: 1 Jan. 1917; buried: Jones Cemetery; record (1917) # 437.

MATHES, Velma; born: 10 Feb. 1910; parents: father not stated and Altha MATHES (Yancey County, NC.); death cause: "diphtheria"; informant: Sam METCALF (Flag Pond); died: 10 Feb. 1917; buried: Sams Creek; record (1917) # 439.

PHIBBS, William David; born: 16 Mar. 1878; married; parents: W.W. PHIBBS and Cinthy SAMMONS; death cause: "accidental crushing under engine"; informant: father (Knoxville); died: 13 Feb. 1917; buried: Knoxville; record (1917) # 438.

LUNDY, Terry Jr.; born: 30 Jan. 1917; parents: T.H. LUNDY (Virginia) and Virginia HAYMON (Virginia); death cause: "rickets"; informant: father (Erwin); died: 17 Feb. 1917; buried: Jobe Cemetery; record (1917) # 440.

BLANKENSHIP, Thiery; female; parents: Cling BLANKENSHIP and Minnie BLANKENSHIP; death cause: "unknown"; informant: Earl BLANKENSHIP (Flag Pond); born/died: 15 Feb. 1917; buried: Coffee Ridge; record (1917) # 441.

SMITH, Harrison; born: 3 Jul. 1893; married; parents: Henry SMITH and Nancy HUSKINS; death cause: "pneumonia and heart failure"; informant: Nancy SMITH (Unicoi); died: 16 Feb. 1917; buried: Fishery Cemetery; record (1917) # 442.

HENSLEY, Lula; born: 4 Feb. 1917; parents: Noah HENSLEY and Ushy WATTS; death cause: "croup"; informant: J.E. HUSKINS (Kittyton); died: 19 Feb. 1917; buried: Hensley Cemetery; record (1917) # 443.

HENSLEY, Mary; age: not stated; married; parents: not stated; death cause: "double pneumonia"; died: 20 Feb. 1917; buried: Fishery Cemetery; record (1917) # 444.

CRAIN, Lewis E.; born: 29 Jan. 1819 in North Carolina; married; parents: Billie CRAIN (North Carolina) and Polly GUTHRIE (North

Carolina); death cause: "old age"; informant: Carl SAMS (Flag Pond); died: 23 Feb. 1917; buried: Flag Pond; record (1917) # 445.

TITTLE, John; age: 38 years; single; parents: John R. TITTLE and Rebecca TAPP; death cause: "__ (illegible) of brain"; informant: T.M. TAPP (Erwin); died: 25 Feb. 1917; buried: Fishery Cemetery; record (1917) # 446.

HENSLEY, Anas; age: "about 40 years"; born: North Carolina; married; parents: Larance HENSLEY (North Carolina) and Rachel LEDFORD (North Carolina); death cause: "pneumonia"; died in the 5th District, 27 Feb. 1917; buried: Fishery Cemetery; record (1917) # 447.

RAY, Infant; female; parents: Shelt RAY (North Carolina) and Aga RAY (North Carolina); death cause: "stillborn"; informant: Arch RAY (Flag Pond); born/died: 24 Feb. 1917; buried: Sams Creek; record # 448.

PASE (?), Infant; female; parents: T.V. PASE (Pennsylvania) and Esther MORLEY (Ohio); death cause: "stillborn"; informant: father (Erwin); born/died: 14 Feb. 1917; record (1917) # 449.

PRICHARD, Charles; born: 8 Aug. 1899; single; parents: N.D. PRICHARD and Mary VANCE (North Carolina); death cause: "measles and pneumonia"; informant: father (Embreeville); died: 8 Mar. 1917; buried: Cove Cemetery; record (1917) # 450.

BLANKENSHIP, Etter Isabell; born: 31 Jul. 1913; parents: George W. BLANKENSHIP and Mary Jane FOSTER; death cause: "measles and croup"; informant: father (Embreeville); died: 19 Mar. 1917; buried: Cove Cemetery; record (1917) # 451.

GREGG, Hester Beale; age: 50 years; born: Johnson County; married; parents: John BEALE (North Carolina) and Mary LYONS (Sullivan County); death cause: "cancer of throat and stomach"; informant: John HODGE (Johnson City); died: 19 Mar. 1917; buried: Carter County; record (1917) # 452.

TINKER, Maree R.; born: 26 Dec. 1913; parents: S.W. TINKER and Cora MASHBURN; death cause: "measles"; informant: father (Embreeville); died: 21 Mar 1917; buried: Cove Cemetery; record (1917) # 453.

LOYD, Flow Ellen; born: 18 Feb. 1912; parents: I.A. LOYD and Jennie PAYNE; death cause: "measles"; informant: father (Embreeville); died: 21 Mar. 1917; buried: Cove Cemetery; record (1917) # 454.

WOODBY, Ephafes (?); age: 42 years; married; parents: Alford WOODBY and Elvira GILBERT; death cause: "pulmonary tuberculosis"; informant: W.H. JONES (Unicoi); died: 28 Mar. 1917; buried: Woodby Cemetery; record (1917) # 455.

TILSON, Elsie Mae; born: 8 May 1914; parents: Walter TILSON and Nancy Ann HARRIS; death cause: illegible; informant: father (Kittyton); died: 24 Mar. 1917; buried: Guinn Cemetery; record # 457.

TINKER, Lizzie; born: 21 Apr. 1911; parents: W.S. TINKER and Cora MASHBURN; death cause: "measles"; informant: Bob MASHBURN (Embreeville); died: 24 Mar. 1917; buried: Cove Cemetery; record (1917) # 456.

WHITE, Christopher; born: 24 Mar. 1882; married; parents: C.C. WHITE and Mary WHITE; death cause: "heart disease"; died: 24 Mar. 1917; buried: Fishery Cemetery; record (1917) # 458.

CLARK, Lockey; born: 8 Jul. 1899; married; parents: Ephafes WOODBY and Caroline CAMPBELL (North Carolina); death cause: "pulmonary tuberculosis"; informant: W.H. JONES (Unicoi); died: 25 Mar. 1917; buried: Woodby Cemetery; record (1917) # 459.

CASEY, Ernest; born: 27 Jun. 1909; parents: Joe CASEY and Millie RODGERS; death cause: "pneumonia"; informant: father (Embreeville); died: 28 Mar. 1917; buried: Cove Cemetery; record (1917) # 460.

FORNOR (?), Jacob; born: 8 Nov. 1873 in Greene County; single; parents: J.S. FORNER (Greene County) and Rebecca HARDIN (Greene County); death cause: "heart failure"; informant: father (Kittyton); died: 29 Mar. 1917; buried: Clear Branch; record (1917) # 461.

BRUMMETT, Infant; female; parents: Sam BRUMMETT and Ethel WHITE; death cause: "malformation"; informant: father (Unicoi); born/died: 10 Mar. 1917; buried: Brummett Cemetery; record # 462.

TINKER, Phillip Edmon; born: 31 Oct. 1916; parents: S.W. TINKER and Cora MASHBURN; death cause: "measles and malaria"; informant: father (Embreeville); died: 1 Apr. 1917; buried: Cove Cemetery; record (1917) # 463.

BLANKENSHIP, Mildred; born: 27 Dec. 1916; parents: John BLANKENSHIP and Ida ROBARDS; death cause: "measles"; died: 1 Apr. 1917; buried: Cove Cemetery; record (1917) # 464.

BAXTER, Bird D.; born: 10 Feb. 1844 in Greene County; married; parents: Green BAXTER (Greene County) and Letticia BAXTER (Greene County); death cause: "lagrippe"; died in the 9th District, 10 Apr. 1917; buried: Clear Branch; record (1917) # 465.

PAINTER, George Ernest; lived 1 day; parents: James PAINTER and Bessie ESTEP; death cause: "cerebral hemorrhage"; informant: A.J. WILLIS, MD.; died: 11 Apr. 1917; buried: Cove Cemetery; record (1917) # 466.

VANCE, Polly; age: 56 years; married; parents: William CAMPBELL (Johnson County) and Mary FRY; death cause: not stated; informant: Sam VANCE (Unicoi); died: 11 Jan. 1917; buried: Campbell Cemetery; record (1917) # 467.

TOLLEY, Ida Susand; born: 11 Jan. 1917; parents: E.K. TOLLEY (Carter County) and Nancy Jane TOLLEY; death cause: "entero colitis"; informant: Lace TOLLEY (Roan Mountain, TN.); died: 20 Apr. 1917; buried: Tolley Cemetery; record (1917) # 468.

BISHOP, Andrew J.; age: 60 years; born: Pike County, KY.; married; parents: "unknown"; death cause: "myocarditic"; died: 1 May 1917; buried: Jobe Cemetery; record (1917) # 469.

LYLE, Martha J.; born: 6 Mar. 1844; widow; parents: Henry AMBROSE and Rhoda TILSON; death cause: "liver inflammation"; informant: John LYLE (Erwin); died: 3 May 1917; buried: Jobe Cemetery; record # 470.

RANDOLPH, Lizzie; age: 55 years; married; parents: A.S. JONES and Birtha RANDOLPH; death cause: "drowning"; died: 5 May 1917; buried: Hensley Cemetery; record (1917) # 471.

ALLEN, Sarah; born: 11 Jun. 1833; widow; parents: Gabriel MCINTURFF and Axie NELSON; death cause: "heart disease"; informant: I.G. ALLEN (Erwin); died: 10 May 1917; buried: Martins Creek; record (1917) # 472.

WATSON, Edith C.; born: 21 Apr. 1917; parents: William WATSON (Washington County) and Rebecca MASHBURN; death cause: "hives"; informant: W.M. MASHBURN (Kittyton); died: 12 May 1917; buried: Clear Branch; record (1917) # 473.

HONEYCUTT, Infant: female; parents: Hobart TROUTMAN (North Carolina) and Sadie HONEYCUTT; death cause: "drowned, thrown in the creek following birth"; informant: Sadie HONEYCUTT (Erwin Jail); born/died: 23 May 1917; buried: Garland Cemetery; record # 474.

LEDFORD, Troy E.; born: 8 Jul. 1900; parents: Alford LEDFORD (Yancey County, NC.) and Mary Jane TIPTON; death cause: "nephritis"; informant: father (Erwin); died: 24 May 1917; buried: Martins Creek; record (1917) # 475.

HUSKINS, William; born: 27 Mar. 1890; married; parents: Elbert HUSKINS and Annie PRICE; death cause: "tuberculosis of stomach"; informant: Frank H. BRITT (Erwin); died: 25 May 1917; record # 476.

TIPTON, Isaac; born: 16 Oct. 1834 (?); age: 33 (?) years; married; parents: A.B. TIPTON and Hester JOHNSON; death cause: "tuberculosis"; informant: W.F. KIPPLIN (Johnson City); died: 26 May 1917; buried: Unicoi; record (1917) # 477.

HAYNES, John; born: 6 Jul. 1832 in Scott County, VA.; widower; parents: William HAYNES (Virginia) and Katherine WINNIGER (Virginia); death cause: "uremic coma, brights disease"; informant: Samuel HAYNES (Gate City, VA.); died: 14 Jun. 1917; buried: Camron, TN.; record (1917) # 478.

MONK, Edward L.; born: 22 Jun. 1914; parents: J.C. MONK (Tazewell County, VA.) and Fanny B. TONEY; death cause: "meningitis"; informant: father (Erwin); died: 20 Jun. 1917; buried: Jobe Cemetery; record (1917) # 479.

GUINN, Nettie Geneva; born: 25 May 1917; parents: A.B. GUINN and Zora TILSON; death cause: "flucks"; informant: G.F. GUINN (Kittyton); died: 21 Jun. 1917; buried: Clear Branch; record # 480.

M_ (illegible), Infant; female; parents: Luther M_ (illegible) and Sylvia P_ (illegible); death cause: "stillborn"; died: 29 Jun. 1917; buried: Morrell Cemetery; record (1917) # 481.

WOODBY, Maud Ailene; born: 17 Apr. 1915; parents: D.F. WOODBY (North Carolina) and M.L. RIDDLE; death cause: "cholera infantum"; died: 30 Jun. 1917; buried: Clear Branch; record (1917) # 482.

BAKER, Jane; born: 12 Apr. 1840; married; parents: John GARLAND (North Carolina) and Susand WHITEHEAD (Johnson County); death cause: "pellagra"; informant: C.H. BAKER (Unicoi); died: 30 Jun. 1917; buried: Bell Cemetery; record (1917) #483.

CLAWSON, Ben; age: "about 60 years"; married; parents: not stated; death cause: "dropped dead, suppose heart disease"; died: 2 Jul. 1917; buried: Johnson City; record (1917) # 484.

GENTRY, Mary Louise; born: 1 Apr. 1917; parents: Newton GENTRY and Laura GUINN; death cause: "acute indigestion"; informant: Jennie MOORE (Flag Pond); died: 2 Jul. 1917; buried: Gentry Cemetery; record (1917) # 485.

RAMSEY, Glenn Fowler; born: 9 Aug. 1917; parents: John RAMSEY and Virgie CUTSHALL (North Carolina); death cause: "chronic indigestion"; informant: Jennie MOORE (Flag Pond); died: 3 Jul. 1917; buried: Ramsey Cemetery; record (1917) # 486.

CARVER, Stacy; female; born: 25 Apr. 1874 in North Carolina; married; parents: John HUGHES (North Carolina) and Rebecca COOPER (North Carolina); death cause: "typhoid fever"; informant: P.P. CARVER (Unicoi); died: 4 Jul. 1917; buried: Carter County; record (1917) # 487.

BURGESS, Edward; born: 8 May 1860 in North Carolina; married; parents: Mitchell BURGESS (North Carolina) and Ellen MCINTOSH (North Carolina); death cause: "__ (illegible) hernia"; informant: Mrs. Edward BURGESS (Erwin); died: 5 Jul. 1917; buried: Martins Creek; record (1917) # 488.

WILLIAMS, Harley; born: 31 Jul. 1916; parents: C.R. WILLIAMS (North Carolina) and Eliza HENSLEY; death cause: "hives"; informant: J.E. HUSKINS (Kittyton); died: 5 Jul. 1917; buried: Hensley Cemetery; record (1917) # 489.

BLACKBURN, Silas; born: 26 Jun. 1857 in North Carolina; married; parents: Andrew Jackson BLACKBURN (North Carolina) and mother "unknown"; death cause: "cancer of bladder"; informant: Mrs. Silas BLACKBURN (Erwin); died: 8 Jul. 1917; record (1917) # 490.

EDWARDS, Infant; female; parents: J.F. EDWARDS (North Carolina) and Ola FREEMAN (North Carolina); death cause: "premature birth"; informant: J.F. EDWARDS (Erwin); born/died: 11 Jul. 1917; record (1917) # 491.

GUINN, Lilly B.; age: 30 years; born: South Carolina; married; parents: "unknown"; death cause: "puerperal eclampsia"; informant: C.F.

GUINN (Erwin); died: 12 Jul. 1917; buried: Clear Branch; record (1917) # 492.

HARRIS, Jude; born: 16 Jul. 1917; parents: Frank HARRIS and Jennie WHALEY (Washington County); death cause: "unknown"; died: 19 Jul. 1917; buried: Martins Creek; record (1917) # 493.

JONES, Lora (Mrs. Charles); age: 25 years; born: Sullivan County; married; parents: James __ (illegible) and Sis FERGUSON (Sullivan County); death cause: "unknown"; informant: C.B. JONES (Unicoi); died: 19 Jul. 1917; buried: Fordtown, TN.; record (1917) # 494.

FURCHES, Elsie May; born: 13 Nov. 1916; parents: M.Z. FURCHES (North Carolina) and Vergie ROGERS; death cause: "diarrhea"; informant: father (Embreeville); died: 21 Jul. 1917; buried: Cove Cemetery; record (1917) # 495.

FOWLER, __ (illegible); male; born: 26 Jul. 1944; born: St. John Newfoundland; married; minister; parents: John FOWLER (Canada) and Sara __ (Canada); death cause: "brights disease"; informant: George D. FOWLER (Erwin); died: 28 Jul. 1917; buried: Georgia; record (1917) # 496.

BOGART, E.P.; born: 6 Mar. 1853 in Washington County; single; parents: S.W. BOGART and Mary ERWIN; death cause: "unknown"; informant: E.G. BOGART (Erwin); died: 29 Jul. 1917; buried: Garland Cemetery; record (1917) # 497.

THOMAS, Goldie; born: 29 Jul. 1917; parents: William THOMAS (North Carolina) and Pearl LAWING; death cause: "unknown"; informant: father (Erwin); died: 29 Jul. 1917; buried: Martins Creek; record (1917) # 498.

THOMAS, Pearl; born: 14 Jan. 1900; married; parents: Elbert LAWING and Fanny PATE; death cause: "childbirth"; informant: father (Erwin); died: 30 Jul. 1917; buried: Martins Creek; record (1917) # 499.

MCLEMORE, Velma; born: 5 Apr. 1916; parents: Nathan MCLEMORE and Minnie HONEYCUTT; death cause: "acute indigestion"; died: 31 Jul. 1917; buried: Mosley Cemetery; record (1917) # 500.

DURBIN, Infant: female; parents: Charles Thomas DURBIN (Ohio) and Rachel SMITH; death cause: "stillborn"; informant: father (Erwin); died: 27 Aug. 1917; buried: Martins Creek; record (1917) # 501.

TURNER, Milus Edward; born: 20 Oct. 1916; parents: Abraham TURNER and Allie BUTCHER; death cause: "spinal meningitis"; informant: J.A. TURNER; buried: Oakland Cemetery; record # 502.

FURCHES, Virgie; born: 10 Jan. 1877; married; parents: Elihue ROGERS and Jane HUSKINS; death cause: "pulmonary tuberculosis"; informant: M.Z. FURCHES (Embreeville); died: 2 Aug. 1917; buried: Cove Cemetery; record (1917) # 503.

CHANDLER, Silas L.; born: 7 Mar 1832 in Madison County, NC.; married; parents: Lark CHANDLER (North Carolina) and Sallie MCALF (North Carolina); death cause: "cancer"; informant: G.B. CHANDLER (Kittyton); died: 7 Aug. 1917; buried: Mt. Pleasant; record (1917) # 504.

JENNINGS, Charles E.; born: 23 Sep. 1843 in Virginia; widower; parents: father unknown and Catherine JEWEL (Virginia); death cause: "dysentery"; informant: E.L. WOMACK (Erwin); died: 10 Aug. 1917; buried: Roanoke, Virginia; record (1917) # 505.

NELSON, Barbara Ellen; born: 12 Feb. 1838 in Sullivan County; widow; parents: Henry JONES and Elizabeth FEATHERS; death cause: "aortic regurgitation"; informant: Lizzie MCINTURFF (Unicoi); died: 16 Aug. 1917; buried: Jones Cemetery; record (1917) # 506.

HARRIS, Joseph; born: 20 Oct. 1840; married; parents: Jocinth HARRIS and Nancy HARRIS; death cause: "heart failure"; informant: A. HARRIS (Flag Pond); died: 20 Aug. 1917; buried: Higgins Chapel; record (1917) # 507.

RAY, Albert; born: 31 Jul. 1917; parents: Nelson RAY and Ida FRANKLIN (Madison County, NC.); death cause: "unknown, found dead"; informant: Edd RAY (Flag Pond); died: 31 Aug. 1917; record (1917) # 508.

CASTEEL, Infant; female; parents: Jack CASTEEL (Scott County, VA.) and Amanda CASTEEL (Scott County, VA.); death cause: "stillborn"; died: 20 Aug. 1917; buried: Anderson Cemetery; record (1917) # 509.

TIPTON, Infant; male; parents: Mack TIPTON (Mitchell County, NC.) and Citta GARLAND (Mitchell County, NC.); death cause: "stillborn"; informant: father (Unicoi); died: 6 Aug. 1917; buried: Marbleton; record (1917) # 510.

HARRIS, Ruthanna; age: "unknown"; widow; parents: William HENSLEY (North Carolina) and Polie HOWARD (North Carolina); death cause: "old age"; informant: J.M. CLOUSE (Kittyton); died: 6 Sep 1917; buried: Hensley Cemetery; record (1917) # 511.

MCCALL, Louvinia; born: 1 Apr. 1892 in North Carolina; married; parents: Howard HILL (North Carolina) and M_ RAY (North Carolina); death cause: "uremia and blood poison from abscessed tooth"; informant: Louise HILL (Erwin); died: 9 Sep. 1917; buried: Martins Creek; record (1917) # 512.

HONEYCUTT, Infant; male; parents: Matt HONEYCUTT (North Carolina) and Hattie MILLER (North Carolina); death cause: "unknown, premature birth"; born/died: 29 Sep. 1917; buried: Martins Creek; record (1917) # 514.

WILSON, D.M.; born: 19 May 1862 in North Carolina; married; parents: John M. WILSON and Sarah CHAPEEL (Alabama); death cause: "jaundice and fever"; informant: W.A. WILSON (Ashville, NC.); died: 27 Sep. 1917; buried: Martins Creek; record (1917) # 513.

DAUGHERTY, Infant; male; parents: Thomas DAUGHERTY (Carter County) and Sabra CAMPBELL; death cause: "stillborn"; informant: father (Unicoi); died: 16 Sep. 1917; buried: Campbell Cemetery; record (1917) # 515.

SHELTON, Sylvia; born: 31 Jul. 1917; parents: Creed SHELTON and Bessie WALLIN; death cause: "croup"; informant: Edd RAY (Flag Pond); died: 4 Oct. 1917; record (1917) # 516.

BRUMETT, Thomas J.; born: 2 Jul. 1856 in Carter County; married; parents: William P. BRUMETT and Malinda BRITT (Carter County); informant: J. BRUMETT (Unicoi); died: 6 Oct. 1917; buried: Brumett Cemetery; record (1917) # 517.

POORE, William; born: 20 Dec. 1916; parents: Burnie POORE and Liza MASHBURN; death cause: "diphtheria"; informant: W.M. MASHBURN (Kittyton); died: 9 Oct. 1917; buried: Clear Branch; record (1917) # 518.

BENETT, James; born: 6 Aug. 1881 in Mitchell County, NC.; single; parents: Matt BENETT (Yancey County, NC.) and Cordelia WOODBY; death cause: "pulmonary tuberculosis from service in

Panama"; informant: Thomas E. SANGER (Unicoi); died: 10 Oct. 1917; buried; Garland Cemetery; record (1917) # 519.

PRESNELL, Soloman; born: 14 Oct. 1844 in North Carolina; married; parents: Westley PRESNELL (North Carolina) and Caroline MITCHELL; death cause: "syphilis"; informant: Gilbert PRESNELL (Embreeville); died: 15 Oct. 1917; buried: Cove Cemetery; record (1917) # 520.

LEDFORD, Mary; born: 18 Sep. 1888 in North Carolina; married; parents: H.L. RIDDLE (North Carolina) and Mary MCINTOSH (North Carolina); death cause: "typhoid fever"; died: 7 Nov. 1917; buried: Edwards Cemetery; record (1917) # 521.

STREET, Dosser (?); born: 14 Jan. 1877 in Mitchell County, NC.; married; parents: Doak STREET (Mitchell County, NC.) and Jane CROWDER (Yancey County, NC.); death cause: "gall stones"; informant; Milton STREET (Elizabethton); died: 13 Nov. 1917; buried: Carter County; record (1917) # 522.

WILSON, Infant; female; parents: John B. WILSON (North Carolina) and Lenore BIRCHFIELD (North Carolina); death cause: "premature birth"; informant: father (Erwin); born/died: 19 Nov. 1917; record (1917) # 523.

MILLER, Sam Ray; born: 18 Mar 1916 in Mitchell County, NC.; parents: Elkanan MILLER (Mitchell County, NC.) and Lizzy WHALEY; death cause: "gastritis and internal irritation"; informant: Walker BARNETT (Johnson City); died: 23 Nov. 1917; buried: Washington County; record (1917) # 524.

MARKIN, Infant; male; parents: Garfield MARKIN and Haley OVERBEY; death cause: "difficult labor and large infant"; born/died: 1 Nov. 1917; buried: Cove Cemetery; record (1917) # 525.

RUNNIAN, Vestal Ray; born: 23 May 1916; parents: W.J. RUNNIAN (Marshall County, NC.) and Maggie COBBIL; death cause: "burned to death, clothing caught fire"; informant: father (Chestra); died: 8 Dec. 1917; buried: Tinker Cemetery; record (1917) # 526.

TIPTON, Mary; born: __ Apr. 1827 in North Carolina; widow; parents: George EDWARDS (North Carolina) and Nancy BENNET (North Carolina); death cause: "old age"; informant: H.G. TIPTON (Kittyton); died: 1 Dec. 1917; buried: Tipton Cemetery; record (1917) # 527.

COTHRAN, James Whitlock; born: 19 May 1845; widower; parents: Robert COCHRAN and Mary MAHATHEY; death cause: "artero sclerosis"; informant: James COCHRAN (Unicoi); died: 9 Dec. 1917; buried: Carter County; record (1917) # 528.

TILSON, George W.; born: 1 Jan. 1880; single; parents: A.B. TILSON and Eliza J. GILLIS; death cause: "tuberculosis"; informant: father (Kittyton); died: 10 Dec. 1917; buried: Tilson Cemetery; record # 529.

MILLER, Julia; born: 11 Jul. 1882; married; parents: Kendrick MCLAUGHLIN (Washington County) and Susan KEENER (Carter County); death cause: "pthisis pulmonalis"; informant: W.J. CONSTABLE (Unicoi); died: 10 Dec. 1917; buried: Swingle Cemetery; record (1917) # 530.

ROBERTS, George; born: 28 Dec. 1915; parents: J.E. ROBERTS (Virginia) and Cenia BURNET (North Carolina); death cause: "laryngitis"; informant: William MILLER (Erwin); died: 10 Dec. 1917; buried: Martins Creek; record (1917) # 531.

PATE, Infant; male; born: 7 Aug. 1917; parents: Tom PATE (North Carolina) and Eller TIPTON; death cause: "croup"; informant: G.F. TILSON (Ernestville); died: 11 Dec. 1917; buried: Coffee Ridge; record (1917) # 532.

HIGGINS, William L.; born: 12 Aug. 1917; parents: Edgar HIGGINS and Pearl MURRAY; death cause: "hives or croup"; informant: W.E. HIGGINS (Flag Pond); died: 11 Dec. 1917; buried: Higgins Chapel; record (1917) # 533.

HOYLE, Sara Cordelia; born: 15 Jan. 186_; age: 49 years, 11 months and 4 days; married; parents: William HIGGINS and Amanda E. SMITH; death cause: "pneumonia"; informant: Diana HOYLE (Flag Pond); died: 19 Dec. 1917; buried: Higgins Chapel; record # 534.

TIPTON, Rucker; born: 26 Sep. 1914 in Mitchell County, NC.; parents: Moses TIPTON (Mitchell County) and Celia BUCHANAN (Mitchell County); death cause: "liver disease"; informant: father (Chestra); died: 19 Dec. 1917; buried: Martins Creek; record (1917) # 535.

JEWELL, George; born: __ Apr. 1833; widower; parents: John JEWELL and mother unknown; death cause: "dropsy"; informant: J.W. HOWELL (Erwin); died: 21 Dec. 1917; buried: Martins Creek; record # 536.

STOCKTON, Dewey; born: 21 Apr. 1915; parents: Luther STOCKTON and Dora MASHBURN; death cause: "hives"; informant: Diana HOYLE (Flag Pond); died: 22 Dec. 1917; buried: Higgins Chapel; record (1917) # 537.

HEAD, Mary; born: 19 Jan. 1902; parents; John HEAD (Carter County) and Manda COCHRAN (Carter County); death cause: "tuberculosis"; informant: Eller HEAD, brother (Unicoi); died: 22 Dec. 1917; buried: home cemetery; record (1917) # 538.

CLOUSE, Georgia; born: 15 Mar. 1828 in Tennessee; widow; parents: Jacob CLOUSE and Sallie TILSON; death cause: "old age"; informant: W.A. TILSON (Kittyton); died: 25 Dec. 1917; buried: Clouse Cemetery; record (1917) # 539.

DICKSON, Nola; born: 16 May 1885 in Washington County; married; parents: Riley B. DANIELS (Carter County) and Belle COWELL (Washington County); death cause: "nephritis"; informant: James DICKSON (Erwin); died: 25 Dec. 1917; buried: Jobe Cemetery; record (1917) # 540.

MORE, Eliza; born: 23 Jan. 1884; married; parents: Amos DAVIS and Harriett MOSLEY; death cause: "pulmonary tuberculosis"; informant: Miller MORE (Unicoi); died: 28 Dec. 1917; buried; Gouge Cemetery; record (1917) # 541.

RAMSEY, Rachel; age: "supposed 100 years"; born: North Carolina; widow; parents: Daniel PAYNE (North Carolina) and mother "unknown"; death cause: "suppose pellagra"; informant: B.S. WALKER (Flag Pond); died: 2 Jan. 1918; buried: Ramsey Cemetery; record #522.

WHITSON, Ancrinus; male; born: __ May 1900 in North Carolina; parents: John F. WHITSON (North Carolina) and Huldy HUNTER (North Carolina); death cause: "killed by train"; informant: William Matt WHITSON (Ramseytown, NC.); died: 9 Jan. 1918; buried: Ramseytown, North Carolina; record (1918) # 523.

BLANKENSHIP, Ray; born: 20 Jun. 1917; parents: William E. BLANKENSHIP and Betsy Jane STOCKTON; death cause: "unknown"; informant: Cullus MCINTOSH (Flag Pond); died: 12 Jan. 1918; buried: Rice Creek; record (1918) # 524.

FORBES, Minnie Lucille; born: 1 Jan. 1812; parents: Milburn FORBES (Mitchell County, NC.) and Bessie FRAZIER (Mitchell County, NC.);

death cause: "open fireplace, clothing caught fire"; informant: father (Danle, Virginia); died: 15 Jan. 1918; buried: Marbleton; record # 525.

KINARD, John Andrew; born: 29 Jul. 1866 in Newberry County, South Carolina; married; parents: Martin Luther KINARD (Newberry County) and Sofia HARTMAN (Newberry County); death cause: "cerebral hemorrhage"; informant: Mrs. J.A. KINARD (Erwin); died: 13 Jan. 1918; buried: South Carolina; record (1918) # 526.

FORBES, Masey; female; born: 20 Mar 1903 in Mitchell County, NC., parents: father not stated and Bessie FRAZIER; death cause: "homicide, gunshot wound in shoulder"; informant: Andy FRAZIER (Unicoi); died: 17 Jan. 1918; buried: Marbleton; record (1918) # 527.

PATE, Linda; born: 18 Jan. 1839; married; parents: John HIGGINS and Sinda ARWOOD; death cause: "old age"; informant: A.L. BAILEY (Flag Pond); died: 18 Jan. 1918; buried: Sam Creek; record # 528.

MCINTURFF, Elizabeth J.; born: 24 Sep. 1866; married; parents: Charles NELSON and Barbara Ellen JONES (Sullivan County); death cause: "carcinoma of stomach"; informant: W.H. MCINTURFF (Unicoi); died: 3 Feb. 1918; buried: Jones Cemetery; record # 529.

BAKER, Maggie; born: 17 Sep. 1917; parents: Fonzo STREET (Mitchell County, NC.) and Love Lee BAKER (Washington County); death cause: "bronchitis"; died: 3 Feb. 1918; buried: Cole Cemetery; record (1918) # 530.

ALLISON, Sarah Elizabeth; born: 25 Sep. 1844 in Irdell County, NC.; married; parents: John REED (North Carolina) and Mary HENLINE (North Carolina); death cause: "bronchial pneumonia"; informant: N.H. ALLISON (Erwin); died: 5 Feb. 1918; buried: North Carolina; record (1918) # 531.

GARLAND, __ (illegible), Buller; male; age: 67 years, 5 months and 10 days; born: Mitchell County, NC.; married; parents: Julias GARLAND (Mitchell County) and Susan SLAGLE (Mitchell County); death cause: "rheumatism and heart disease"; informant: A.G. GARLAND; died: 7 Feb. 1918; record (1918) # 532.

JOHNSON, Eva May; born: 4 Feb. 1915; parents: Simpson JOHNSON (North Carolina) and Tina GOUGE; death cause: "lobar pneumonia"; informant: father (Unicoi); died: 9 Feb. 1918; buried: Gouge Cemetery; record (1918) # 533.

67

SCOTT, Gladys; black; born: 26 Jun. 1905 in Spartinburg, SC.; parents: Jim CALDWELL (Spartainburg) and Emma __ (illegible)(South Carolina); death cause: "accidental gunshot"; informant: Emma SCOTT (Erwin); died: 12 Feb. 1918; buried: Spartainburg, SC.; record # 534.

TILSON, Margaret; born: 4 Nov. 1853; single; parents: John A. TILSON (Washington County) and Rebecca BALIS (Washington County); death cause: "unknown"; died: 19 Feb. 1918; buried: Tilson Cemetery; record (1918) # 535.

SIMMONS, Fred; born: 26 Dec. 1916; parents: G. William SIMMONS and Martha J. CL_ (illegible); death cause: "bronco penumonia"; informant: George W. SIMMONS (Erwin); died: 19 Feb. 1918; buried: Jobe Cemetery; record (1918) # 536.

CHANDLER, Annie E.; born: 9 Dec. 1884 in Campbell County, Georgia; married; parents: Richard PARKER and Margaret MOSS; death cause: "cancer of uterus"; informant: J.P. CHANDLER (Erwin); died: 19 Feb. 1918; buried: Palmetta, Georgia; record (1918) # 537.

PAYNE, Vivian Margaret; born: 5 Feb. 1918; parents: A.J. PAYNE (Carter County) and Ida BOWMAN; death cause: "bronco pneumonia"; died: 24 Feb. 1918; buried: Unicoi County; record # 538.

SCRUGGS, Louie Davis, Jr.; born: 21 Jan. 1918; parents: L.D. SCRUGGS (North Carolina) and Ida J. WHITE; death cause: illegible; informant: father (Erwin); died: 26 Feb. 1918; buried: Jobe Cemetery; record (1918) # 539.

LAWING, Elbert; age: 49 years; married; parents: William LAWING and Lucinda HARRIS; death cause: __ (illegible) and peritonitis"; informant: W.M. LAWING (Erwin); died: 28 Feb. 1918; buried: Martins Creek; record (1918) # 540.

GOOD, Margaret Louise; parents: A.C. GOOD and Kate PROPST; death cause: "stillborn"; informant: father (Erwin); died: 23 Feb. 1918; buried: Martins Creek; record (1918) # 541.

LOVE, Roy; born: 28 Sep. 1910; parents: Dillard LOVE and Gertrude STEWARD (?)(North Carolina); death cause: "burned to death in burning building"; informant: father (Erwin); died: 3 Mar. 1918; buried: Martins Creek; record (1918) # 542.

LOVE, Paul; born: 19 Mar. 1908; parents: Dillard LOVE and Gertrude STEWARD (?)(North Carolina); death cause: "burned to death in burning building"; informant: father (Erwin); died: 3 Mar. 1918; buried: Martins Creek; record (1918) # 543.

LOVE, Grant; born: 28 Jul. 1906; parents: Dillard LOVE and Gertrude STEWARD (?)(North Carolina); death cause: "burned to death in burning building"; informant: father (Erwin); died: 3 Mar. 1918; buried: Martins Creek; record (1918) # 544.

HIGGINS, Pansy; born: 7 Mar. 1918; parents: Arthur HIGGINS (North Carolina) and Bertha EDWARDS; death cause: "unknown"; informant: J.M. BLANKENSHIP (Kittyton); died: 7 Mar. 1918; buried: Higgins Cemetery; record (1918) # 545.

LEDFORD, M_; male; born: 19 Jun. 1916; parents: O.M. LEDFORD (North Carolina) and M.J. JONES; death cause: "pneumonia fever"; died: 9 Mar. 1918; buried: Edwards Cemetery; record (1918) # 546.

CALLOWAY, Saunders; born: 18 Jul. 1916; parents: Daniel CALLOWAY (South Carolina) and Elizabeth SMITH (North Carolina); death cause: "laryngitis"; informant: Dan CALLOWAY (Erwin); died: 11 Mar. 1918; buried: Jobe Cemetery; record # 547.

EDWARDS, Wilson; born: 6 Jun. 1847 in Mitchell County, NC.; married; parents: O.B. EDWARDS (North Carolina) and L_ MASTERS (North Carolina); death cause: "cancer of bowels"; informant: D. EDWARDS (Erwin); died: 12 Mar. 1918; buried: Martins Creek; record # 548.

ABELL, Thomas B.; born: 27 Oct. 1917; parents: Thomas F. ABELL (Abingdon, VA.) and mother's name illegible; death cause: "meningitis"; informant: T.F. ABELL (Erwin); died: 17 Mar 1918; buried: Jobe Cemetery; record (1918) # 549.

CARROLL, Delila; born: 16 Jun. 1827 in Greene County; widow; parents: Greenberry CARROLL (Greene County) and Betsy MCGEE; death cause: "unknown"; informant: Florence WHITTAMORE (Johnson City); died: 14 Mar. 1918; record (1918) # 550.

EDWARDS, Infant; female; parents: W.B. EDWARDS and Lula HARRIS; death cause: "unknown"; informant: Edd EDWARDS (Kittyton); born/died: 21 Mar. 1918; buried: Hensley Cemetery; record (1918) # 551.

69

FOSTER, Infant; female; parents: Silas FOSTER and April COOPER (Poplar, North Carolina); death cause: "unknown"; born/died: 31 Mar. 1918; buried: Foster Cemetery; record (1918) # 552.

FOSTER, Infant; duplicate record of above; record # 553.

BAYER, Francis Louise; parents: A.L. BAYER (Montreal, Canada) and mother's name illegible (born: Virginia); death cause: "stillborn"; informant: father (Erwin); born/died: 22 Mar. 1918; buried: Jobe Cemetery; record (1918) # 554.

EVANS, Sadie Jane; born: 6 Jun. 1875; married; parents: Bob TAYLOR (Carter County) and Sarah B. FOSTER; death cause: "kidney and heart disease"; informant: G.C. EVANS; died: 25 Mar. 1918; record # 555.

TREDWAY, Infant; male; parents: Carver TREDWAY and June RAY; death cause: "unknown"; informant: Arch RAY (Flag Pond); born/died: 16 Apr. 1918; buried: Sams Creek; record (1918) # 556.

BARTLEY, Miss F.P.; born: 23 Apr. 1838 in Greene County; single; parents: J.W. BARTLEY and Martha BUSTER; death cause: "heart and kidney disease"; informant: Thomas LAWSON (Erwin); died: 10 Apr. 1918; buried: Hot Springs, North Carolina; record (1918) # 557.

GARLAND, Will; born: 12 Oct. 1884 in North Carolina; married; parents: Charles GARLAND (North Carolina) and Manerva PARKER (North Carolina); death cause: "pneumonia"; informant: Harley GARLAND (Erwin); died: 17 Apr. 1918; buried: North Carolina; record (1918) # 558.

FRITTS, Lula Pearl; born 2 May 1884; married; parents: J.L. DUNCAN and Mary Ellen RAY; death cause: "lung disease"; informant: W.F. DUNCAN; died, 7th District, 22 Apr. 1918; buried: Bailey Cemetery; record (1918) # 551.

DEVALUT, Georgia Sprinkle; born: 6 Mar 1878 in Marion, Virginia; married; parents: Thurman B. MEREDITH (Pulaski, Virginia) and Ella RAIDER (Smyth, Virginia); death cause: "Adison disease"; informant: Mrs. Ella GIBBS (Pulaski, Virginia); died: 27 Apr. 1918; buried: Jobe Cemetery; record (1918) # 560.

GARLAND, Susan; born: 26 Sep 1812 (age 105) in Johnson County; widow; parents: John WHITEHEAD (Johnson County) and Hannah RAINBOLT (Johnson County); death cause: "age and diarrhea"; informant: N. PATE (Unicoi); buried: Swingle Cemetery; record # 561.

KIRK, Jim; age: 27 years; married; parents: Daniel KIRK and Rebecca HAMILTON; death cause: "hepatitis"; informant: Robert KIRK (Erwin); died: 1 May 1918; record (1918) # 562.

HILL, Howard; age: 74 years; born: Marion County, Virginia; married; parents: "unknown"; death cause: "heart disease and pneumonia"; informant: Bert HILL (Erwin); died: 4 May 1918; buried: Martins Creek; record (1918) # 563.

STARNES, Oscar Caney; parents: Oscar STARNES (Ashe County, NC.) and Mary REECE (Augusta County, VA.); death cause: "premature birth, lived 8 hours"; informant: father (Erwin); born/died: 6 May 1918; buried: Jobe Cemetery; record (1918) # 564.

BRYANT, Franky Jean; born: 5 Sep. 1882 in Yancey County, NC.; married; parents: David TIPTON (Yancey County) and Eliza TIPTON (Yancey County); death cause: "_-_ (illegible) of heart valves"; informant: Thomas RIDDLE (Unicoi); died: 12 May 1918; buried: Peterson Cemetery; record (1918) # 565.

BAILEY, Cordia; born: 1903; parents: John BAILEY and Ellen HAMPTON; death cause: "typhoid and whooping cough"; informant: J.W. HOWELL (Erwin); died: 15 May 1918; buried: Martins Creek; record (1918) # 566.

DEVERT, Tom; black; age: "about 35 years"; born: North Carolina; parents: "unknown"; death cause: "killed by unknown persons in attempt to rape Georgia Lee COLLINS"; died: 19 May 1918; body was burned; record (1918) # 567.

COLLINS, Georgia Lee; born: 8 May 1903 in Washington County; worked in silk mill; parents: G.V. COLLINS (Washington County) and Fannie WEBB (Sullivan County); death cause: "strangled and assaulted by a Negro, then thrown into river"; informant: father (Erwin); died: 19 May 1918; buried: Martins Creek; record (1918) # 568.

COCHRAN, Hannah; born: 27 Oct. __; age: 24 years, 6 months and 27 days; married; parents: John COCHRAN (Carter County) and Amanda COCHRAN (Carter County); death cause: "thisis pulmonalis"; informant: father (Unicoi); died: 24 May 1918; buried: father's homeplace; record (1918) # 569.

MCINTURFF, David; born: 22 Mar. 1856; married; parents: Wesley MCINTURFF (Carter County) and Rachel PRICE (Carter County);

death cause: "tumor (?) in head"; informant: Mrs. Matt WHITTIMORE (Unicoi); died: 30 May 1918; record (1918) # 570.

PETERSON, Infant; female; parents: Robert PETERSON (North Carolina) and Esther PETERSON (North Carolina); death cause: "stillborn"; informant: father (Erwin); buried: Martins Creek; record (1918) # 571.

RANDOLPH, Haden; born: 4 Sep. 1915 in North Carolina; parents: W.M. RANDOLPH (Ramsey, North Carolina) and Nelly SPARKS (North Carolina); death cause: "diabetes"; informant: father (Erwin); died: 5 Jun. 1918; buried: Huntdale; record (1918) # 572.

CAMPBELL, William; age: 79 years; born: Johnson County; widower; parents: John CAMPBELL (Johnson County) and Dashia HEATON (Johnson County); death cause: "paralysis"; informant: David CAMPBELL (Unicoi); died: 7 Jun. 1918; buried: Campbell Cemetery; record (1918) # 573.

WHITE, Sarah A.; born: 7 Apr. 1854; widow; parents: David KEENER (Carter County) and Cynthia WALTERS (Washington County); death cause: "operation for abdominal tumor"; informant: Emma WHITE (Unicoi); died: 8 Jun. 1918; buried: Jobe Cemetery; record # 574.

WHITE, Sarah A.; duplicate record of above; record # 575.

LINVILLE, Emily; born: 24 Mar. 1848 in Carter County; widow; parents: Golf HYDER (Carter County) and __ FLETCHER (Washington County); death cause: "dysentery and arthritis"; informant: W.A. LINVILLE (Unicoi); died: 17 Jun. 1918; buried: Anderson Cemetery; record (1918) # 576.

MCINTURFF, Scott Howard; born: 17 Jun. 1918; parents: Walter MCINTURFF and Ella BOWMAN; death cause: "croup"; informant: father (Unicoi); died: 17 Jun. 1918; buried: McInturff Cemetery; record (1918) # 577.

TINKER, J.C.; born: 13 Jun. 1918; parents: Wesley TINKER and Cora MASHBURN; death cause: "cranial hemorrhage"; informant: father (Embreeville); died: 18 Jun. 1918; buried: Cove Cemetery; record (1918) # 578.

FAGAN, Bessie M.; born: 24 May 1881 in Bluff City, Tennessee; widow; parents: L.H. GEISLER (Bluff City) and Mary MAUK (Bluff City);

death cause: "typhoid fever"; informant: Mavine GEISLER (Bluff City); died: 23 Jun. 1918; record (1918) # 579.

ELLIS, Jack Keith; born: 13 Aug. 1914; parents: Dan M. ELLIS and Carry HICKS; death cause: "appendicitis"; informant: O.L. MCLAIN (Johnson City); died: 25 Jun. 1918; buried: Oak Hill Cemetery, Johnson City; record (1918) # 580.

PACE, Infant; male; parents: Benjamin Franklin PACE (North Carolina) and F_ (illegible)(North Carolina); death cause: "bronchial tube obstruction"; informant: father (Erwin); born/died: 25 Jun. 1918; buried: Jobe Cemetery; record (1918) # 581.

PARKER, Manuel Love; born: 6 Mar. 1918; parents: Handy PARKER (North Carolina) and Essie SMITH (North Carolina); death cause: "pertussis"; informant: W.S. PARKER (Erwin); died: 27 Jun. 1918; buried: Martin Creek; record (1918) 582.

RENFRO, Eistella; born: 20 Jan. 1916; parents: Thomas RENFRO (North Carolina) and Millie HAMPTON (North Carolina); death cause: "cholera infantum"; informant: father (Erwin); died: 30 Jun. 1918; buried: Martins Creek; record (1918) # 583.

HERRELL, George; born: 23 Jan. 1918; parents: Spencer HERRELL (Mitchell County, NC.) and Martha MOSLEY (Mitchell County, NC.); death cause: "strophulus confertus"; died: 30 Jun. 1918; buried: Rowe Cemetery; record (1918) # 584.

ROBBINS, Nora; born: 15 Jul. 1861 in Virginia; married; parents: James CARVIN (Virginia) and Elizabeth MOYER (Virginia); death cause: "brights disease"; informant: Ruth JESSE (Erwin); died: 12 Jul. 1918; buried: Jobe Cemetery; record (1918) # 585.

MCCURRY, Oliver; born: 30 Mar. 1843 in Yancey County, NC.; widower; parents: Malcolm MCCURRY (Yancey County) and Betsy DEATON (Yancey County); death cause: "inflammation of airways"; died: 13 Jul. 1918; buried: Coles Cemetery; record (1918) # 586.

MILLER, Samuel K.; born: 11 Mar. 1882 in Washington County; single; parents: John Preston MILLER (Washington County) and Susan SWEENEY (Washington County); death cause: "measles, thesis pulmonitis"; informant: Joda MILLER (Bristol); died: 18 Jul. 1918; buried: Swingle Cemetery; record (1918) # 587.

MILLER, Ralph; born: 21 Jul. 1819; parents: Oscar MILLER and mother's name illegible; death cause: "unknown"; informant: W.E. MILLER (Erwin); died: 28 Jul. 1918; record (1918) # 588.

BAILY, John Lester; born: 24 Jan. 1915 in North Carolina; parents: W.F. BAILY (North Carolina) and Nancy PRESNELL (North Carolina); death cause: "dysentery"; informant: father (Chestra); died: 29 Jul. 1918; buried: Tinker Cemetery; record (1918) # 589.

WATTS, Usley; female; age: 60 years; divorced; parents: William WATTS (North Carolina) and Lula HENSLEY; death cause: "flux"; informant: J.M. WATTS (Kittyton); died: 2 Aug. 1918; buried: Watts Cemetery; record (1918) #590.

RICE, Jessie; age: 60 years; married; parents: William J. RICE and Matilda RICE; death cause: "old age"; informant: W.A. RICE (Flag Pond); died: 2 Aug. 1918; buried; Rice Creek Cemetery; record # 591.

BAILEY, Ellen; born: 25 Dec. 1878; married; parents: Back TITTLE and Sarah HAMPTON; death cause: "tuberculosis"; informant: John BAILEY (Erwin); died: 2 Aug. 1918; buried: Martins Creek; record (1918) # 592.

WATTS, Texie P.; born: 15 Oct. _; age: 2 years, 9 months and 24 days; parents: Bert WATTS and A_ LEWIS (North Carolina); death cause: "clothing caught fire"; informant: father (Clear Branch); died: 9 Aug. 1918; buried: Clear Branch; record (1918) # 593.

WEST, John; born: __ Aug. 1877 in Carter County; married; parents: Thomas J. WEST (Washington County) and Martha STREET (Mitchell County, NC.); death cause: "killed on railroad track"; informant: Mrs. Julia JENKINS (Unicoi); died: 10 Aug. 1918; record (1918) # 594.

HAMPTON, William Woodward; born: 10 Apr. 1917; parents: Sherman HAMPTON and Senia E. MASTERS; death cause: dysentery; informant: father (Erwin); died: 15 Aug. 1918; buried: Martins Creek; record (1918) # 595.

CAMPBELL, Elenor Kirkwood; born: 26 Sep. 1914; parents: John Wiley CAMPBELL (Campbell County, Virginia) and Agnes METTOL; death cause: "diphtheria"; informant: J.W. CAMPBELL; died: 19 Aug. 1918; buried: Jobe Cemetery; record (1918) # 596.

WATTS, Clay; born: 19 Aug. 1918; parents: Anderson WATTS (North Carolina) and Tillie ATKINS (North Carolina); death cause:

"suffocation"; informant: father (Embreeville); died: 20 Aug. 1918; buried: Cove Cemetery; record (1918) # 597.

WHITE, Criss; born: 22 Oct. 1848 in Georgia; married; parents: William WHITE and Sarah MCINTURFF; death cause: "cerebral hemorrhage, high blood pressure"; died: 22 Aug. 1918; buried: Rock Creek; record (1918) # 598.

TITTLE, Hazel Mae; born: 18 Nov. 1916; parents: Walter TITTLE and Lucy MATHES; death cause: "cholera infantum"; informant: father (Embreeville); died: 22 Aug. 1918; buried: Liberty Cemetery; record (1918) # 599.

HOWELL, Christine; born: 31 Jul. 1918; parents: Geter HOWELL (Yancey County, NC.) and Cora BENNETT (Yancey County, NC.); death cause: "bronchitis"; informant: father (Unicoi); died: 19 Aug. 1918; buried: Peterson Cemetery; record (1918) # 600.

RICE, William Jackson; born: 29 Apr. 1894; married; parents: John Calvin RICE and Malinda SHELTON (North Carolina); death cause: "homicide, gunshot wound in head and chest"; informant: J.C. RICE (Erwin); died: 31 Aug. 1918; buried: Flag Pond; record (1918) # 601.

FORTUNE, Infant; sex: not stated; parents: J.E. FORTUNE (Virginia) and Mary FLACK (North Carolina); death cause: "stillborn"; died: 15 Aug. 1918; record (1918) # 602.

BROWN, Infant; male; parents: Sam BROWN and Eula TIPTON; death cause: "stillborn"; informant: father (Kittyton); died: 19 Aug. 1918; buried: Clear Branch; record (1918) # 603.

BANNER, Phoeba Ann; born: 20 Oct. 1850; widow; parents: not stated; death cause: "liver disease"; informant: J.G. TONEY (Erwin); died: 2 Sep. 1918; buried: Martins Creek; record (1918) # 604.

BRITT, Alice; age: 41 years; born: Carter County; married; parents: Reuben PATE (Yancey County, NC.) and Mary WOODBY (Carter County); death cause: "anemia"; informant: David BRITT (Unicoi); died: 7 Sep. 1918; buried: Britt Cemetery; record (1918) # 505.

SMITH, Kelly Lena; female; born: 25 Jul. 1918; parents: Sam SMITH and Annie AMBROSE; death cause: "broncho pneumonia"; informant: father (Erwin); died: 9 Sep. 1918; buried: Unicoi; record (1918) # 606.

WOODBY, Mary Elizabeth; born: 10 Aug. 1902; parents: William P. WOODBY and Margaret GILBERT; death cause: "diarrhea";

informant: William H. JONES (Unicoi); died: 11 Sep. 1918; buried: Woodby Cemetery; record (1918) # 607.

BRAKINS, Dora; born: 17 Jul. 1882; married; parents: Thomas FOSTER and Naoma CHANDLER (North Carolina); death cause: "tuberculosis of lungs"; informant: J.H. FOSTER (Kittyton); died: 20 Sep. 1918; buried: Foster Cemetery; record (1918) # 608.

CROW, William Edward; born: 18 Feb. 1917; parents: A.C. CROW (North Carolina) and Pansy RENFRO (North Carolina); death cause: "dysentery"; informant: father (Erwin); died: 22 Sep. 1918; buried: Jobe Cemetery; record (1918) # 609.

LOYD, Velma; born: 19 Jun. 1918 in Illinois; parents: Ben LOYD and Blanche PAYNE; death cause: "bronchial pneumonia"; informant: father (Erwin); died: 29 Sep. 1918; buried: Martins Creek; record # 610.

TUCKER, Joe L., Jr.; born: 17 Oct. 1915; parents: Joe L. TUCKER and Mamie TONEY; death cause: "diphtheria"; informant: J.L. TUCKER (Erwin); died: 5 Oct. 1918; buried: Jobe Cemetery; record (1918) # 611.

GRIFFITH, Ethel; born: 29 Aug. 1891 in Illinois; married; parents: William JOHNSON (Ohio) and Anna GAMBOL; death cause: "influenza"; informant: J.T. GRIFFITH (Ellenwood, Illinois); died: 5 Oct. 1918; buried: Ellenwood, Illinois; record (1918) # 612.

DOYLE, A.P.; born: 18 Jun. 1890 in Montgomery County, VA.; married; parents: George P. DOYLE (Montgomery County, VA.) and mother's name unknown; death cause: "pneumonia, influenza"; informant: Mrs. A.P. DOYLE (Erwin); died: 8 Sep 1918; record (1918) # 613.

HARRISON, W.B.; age: "about 35 years"; parents: "unknown"; death cause: "lobar pneumonia"; died: 9 Oct. 1918; buried: Martins Creek; record (1918) # 614.

WHITEHEAD, Anna Thackes; age: 47 years; married; parents: George W. THACKES (Nelson County, VA.) and Rebecca HUMPHREYS (Albermaryle County, VA.) death cause: "influenza"; informant: Dr. Cloyd WHITEHEAD; died: 12 Oct. 1918; buried: Arlington, Virginia; record (1918) # 615.

GREENWELL, Infant; male; born: 12 Oct. 1918; parents: Ed GREENWELL and Annie TAYLOR; death cause: "premature birth"; informant: Noah CODY (Erwin); died: 12 Oct. 1918; buried: Jobe Cemetery; record (1918) # 616.

DUNCAN, Dovie; born: 18 Sep. 1908 in Asheville, North Carolina; parents: David DUNCAN (Yancey County, NC.) and Jessie Ida WHITSON (Mitchell County, NC.) death cause: "typhoid fever"; died: 13 Oct. 1918; buried: Peterson Cemetery; record (1918) # 617.

COUSINS, Isaac S.; born: 7 Feb. 1888; married; parents: W.M. COUSINS (North Carolina) and Sarah WILLIS (North Carolina); death cause: "influenza"; informant: Mrs. Isaac COUSINS (Erwin); died: 14 Oct. 1918; buried; Johnson City; record (1918) # 618.

ROBBINS, Thomas Arson; born: 17 May 1884 in Kentucky; married; parents: A.D. ROBBINS (Virginia) and Mary KRIDER (Kentucky); death cause: "pneumonia"; informant: Mrs. Laura ROBBINS (Elihue, Kentucky); died: 14 Oct. 1918; buried; Somerset, Kentucky; record (1918) # 619.

WILSON, Mattie Molloy; born: 11 Sep. 1918; parents: Mattie WILSON (Mitchell County, NC.) and May DEYTON (Washington County); death cause: "__ (illegible) hernia"; died: 14 Oct. 1918; buried: Peterson Cemetery; record (1918) # 620.

SPARKS, Infant; male; born: 13 Oct. 1918; parents: J.B. SPARKS (North Carolina) and Bell WEST (North Carolina); death cause: "Spanish influenza"; informant: David HYLMAN (Unicoi); died; 15 Oct. 1918; buried: Mosley Cemetery; record (1918) # 621.

ERWIN, William Ryburn; born: 11 Nov. 1914; parents: William M. ERWIN and Allie RYBURN; death cause: "accidentally burned to death in barn"; informant: father (Erwin); died: 17 Oct. 1918; buried; Jobe Cemetery; record (1918) # 622.

RYBURN, Walter, Jr.; born: 17 Jun. 1912; parents: Walter RYBURN and Antonette WINTZER (?)(Pennsylvania); died: 17 Oct. 1918; buried: Jobe Cemetery; record (1918) # 623.

COPESTICK, Daniel Bellyse; born: 5 Oct. 1886 in New Jersey; married; parents: William COPESTICK (England) and __ BELLYSE (England); death cause: "influenza"; informant: Mrs. D.B. COPESTICK (Erwin); died: 17 Oct. 1918; buried: East Liverpool, Ohio; record (1918) # 624.

TINKER, Sam; born; 8 Aug. 1901; single; parents: John TINKER and Darkey SAMS; death cause: "influenza"; informant: father (Embreeville); died: 20 Oct. 1918; buried: Clear Branch; record # 625.

GRINDSTAFF, Jane; born: 29 Jan. 1908; parents: Isaac GRINDSTAFF and Julia GRINDSTAFF; death cause: "Spanish influenza"; informant: father (Unicoi); died: 22 Oct. 1918; buried: Grindstaff Cemetery; record (1918) # 626.
SHELTON, C.L. born: 14 Jan. 1918; parents: Melvin SHELTON (North Carolina) and Pearl GUINN; death cause: "influenza"; informant: father (Flag Pond); died: 23 Oct. 1918; buried: Flag Pond; record # 627.
GRINDSTAFF, Mollie; born: 18 Jun. 1911; parents: Isaac GRINDSTAFF and Julia GRINDSTAFF; death cause: "Spanish influenza"; informant: father (Unicoi); died: 23 Oct. 1918; buried: Grindstaff Cemetery; record (1918) # 628.
MCINTURFF, Basel Cole; born: 12 Sep. 1917; parents: D.J. MCINTURFF and Martha NELSON; death cause: "Spanish influenza"; informant: father (Erwin); died: 24 Oct. 1918; record (1918) # 629.
HAREN, Elizzie Pearl; born: 4 May 1917; parents: Z.G. HEREN (Greene County) and Lizzie PETERSON (Yancey County, NC.); death cause: "influenza"; informant: father (Erwin); died: 24 Oct. 1918; buried: Martins Creek; record (1918) # 630.
TINKER, Willard Oliver; born: 6 Apr. 1917; parents: Palmer TINKER and Savannah INGLE; death cause: "influenza"; informant: father (Erwin); died: 25 Oct. 1918; buried: Martins Creek; record # 631.
CODY, Charlie; born: 5 Apr. 1918; parents: Harrie CODY and Julie GRINDSTAFF (North Carolina); death cause: "influenza and pertussis"; informant: W.C. CODY (Embreeville); died: 20 Oct. 1918; buried: Cove Cemetery; record (1918) # 632.
SHELTON, Nella; born: 30 May 1894; married; parents: George RICE and Liza NORTON (Madison County, NC.); death cause: "influenza"; informant: father (Flag Pond); died: 28 Oct. 1918; buried: Rice Creek; record (1918) # 633.
DUNCAN, John; age: 31 years; born: North Carolina; married; parents: Isaac DUNCAN (North Carolina) and Sallie PATE (North Carolina); death cause: "influenza and pneumonia"; informant: Mrs. John DUNCAN (Erwin); died: 28 Oct. 1918; record (1918) # 634.
RICE, Flossie; born: 13 Jul. 1906; parents: George RICE and Liza NORTON (Madison County, NC.); death cause: "influenza"; informant:

father (Flag Pond); died: 29 Oct. 1918; buried: Rice Creek; record (1918) # 635.

CODY, Harrie; born: 26 Feb. 1895; married; parents: W.C. CODY and Sarah MURRY, death cause: "influenza, pneumonia and meningitis"; informant: W.C. CODY (Embreeville); died: 30 Oct. 1918; buried: Cove Cemetery; record (1918) # 636.

BOONE, Infant; female; parents: Troy Sherman BOONE (North Carolina) and Ollie __ (illegible); death cause: "stillborn"; informant: Troy BOONE (Erwin); died: 8 Oct. 1918; buried: Martins Creek; record (1918) # 637.

DEVAULT, Infant; female; parents: James T. DEVAULT and Mabel EVANS (Virginia); death cause: "stillborn"; informant: J.J. DEVAULT (Erwin); died: 14 Oct. 1918; buried: Jobe Cemetery; record # 638.

RICE, Matilda; born: 1 Nov. 1900; single; parents: W.S. RICE and Nancy RICE; death cause: "influenza"; informant: father (Flag Pond); died: 1 Nov. 1918; buried: Rice Creek; record (1918) # 639.

RICE, Quillian; born: 22 May 1893; single; parents: George RICE and Liza NORTON (Madison County, NC.); death cause: "influenza"; informant: father (Flag Pond); died: 1 Nov. 1918; buried: Rice Creek; record (1918) # 640.

CASTEEL, John; born: 5 Feb. 1915; parents: Millard CASTEEL (Scott County, VA.) and Rosea HILL (Mitchell County, NC.); death cause: "influenza"; informant: Mrs. Millard CASTEEL (Johnson City); died: 2 Nov. 1918; buried: Anderson Cemetery; record (1918) # 641.

TOLLY, E.K.; age: 34 years; born: Carter County; married; parents: Avery TOLLY (Carter County) and Susan WHITEHEAD (Carter County); death cause: "Spanish influenza and tuberculosis"; informant: Green SPARIES (Unicoi); died: 2 Nov. 1918; buried: Tolly Cemetery; record (1918) # 642.

PETERSON, Ada; age: 21 years and 3 months; born: North Carolina; married; parents: A.N. BENNETT (North Carolina) and Rena HENSLEY (North Carolina); death cause: "influenza and pneumonia"; died: 3 Oct. 1918; buried: Huntdale, North Carolina; record # 643.

BENNETT, William Glen Street; born: 30 Sep. 1917; parents: Glenn STREET (Mitchell County, NC.) and Derkie BENNETT (Yancey

County, NC.); death cause: "influenza and pneumonia"; died: 3 Nov. 1918; buried: Peterson Cemetery; record (1918) # 644.

PETERSON, Bindett; born: 5 Jun. 1912; parents: Charles PETERSON (Yancey County, NC.) and Hannah LAUGHREN (Yancey County, NC.); death cause: "influenza and pneumonia"; informant: Robert PETERSON (Unicoi); died: 3 Nov. 1918; buried: Peterson Cemetery; record (1918) # 645.

MASTERS, Alexander; born: 1 Nov. 1828 in North Carolina; widower; parents: father unknown and __ RAY (North Carolina); death cause: "general debility and old age"; informant: William MILLER (Erwin); died: 4 Nov. 1918; buried: Martins Creek; record (1918) # 646.

RICE, Infant; male; born: 5 Nov. 1918; parents: E.J. RICE and Bertha BRIGGS; death cause: "influenza"; informant: father (Flag Pond); died: 6 Nov. 1918; buried: Rice Creek; record (1918) # 647.

BENNETT, William; born: __ May 1897; single; parents: Harrison BENNETT (Yancey County, NC.) and Nancy Jane MCCURRY (Yancey County, NC.); death cause: "influenza, phtisis pulmonitis"; informant: father (Unicoi); died: 9 Nov. 1918; buried: Peterson Cemetery; record (1918) # 648.

WILLIS, Bert; born: __ Aug. 1908; parents: Bob WILLIS (North Carolina) and Nancy Ann TOLLY (Carter County); death cause: "Spanish influenza"; informant: J.B. SPARKS (Unicoi); died: 13 Nov. 1918; buried: Clark Cemetery; record (1918) # 649.

PROFFITT, Lockie; born: 28 Dec. 1887; married; parents: John S. TILSON and Margaret BROWN; death cause: "influenza, pneumonia and child birth"; informant: Wesley PROFFITT (Flag Pond); died: 13 Nov. 1918; record (1918) # 650.

GARLAND, Dutrey (?); female; born: 17 Aug. 1896 in North Carolina; married; parents: Clayton FRY (North Carolina) and Jane BROWN (North Carolina); death cause: "influenza and pneumonia"; informant: Lacy GARLAND (Unicoi); died: 14 Nov. 1918; buried: McInturff Cemetery; record (1918) # 651.

JONES, Walter; born: 13 Aug. 1906; parents: Albert JONES and Delia HOPSON (Mitchell County, NC.); death cause: "influenza"; died: 15 Nov. 1918; buried: Swingle Cemetery; record (1918) # 652.

NELSON, Mary E.; born: 16 Sep. 1918; parents: Ralph NELSON and Ethel BRADFORD; death cause: "bold hives"; informant: Joe NELSON (Erwin); died: 16 Nov. 1918; buried: Jobe Cemetery; record # 653.

HAMBRICK, Samuel W.; born: 18 Nov. 1918; parents: Samuel HAMBRICK and Mary DAVIS; death cause: "unknown, lived 3 hours"; informant: father (Erwin); died: 18 Nov. 1918; buried: Jobe Cemetery; record (1918) # 654.

BRIGGS, James Holt; born: 25 May 1918; parents: Walter BRIGGS and Effie HENSLEY; death cause: "spinal meningitis"; died: 25 Nov. 1918; buried: Flag Pond; record (1918) # 655.

HARRINGTON, W.B.; born: 18 Oct. 1844 in North Carolina; parents: unknown; death cause: "paralysis"; informant: Fred HARRINGTON (Erwin); died: 26 Nov. 1918; buried: Jobe Cemetery; record # 656.

PETERSON, Infant; sex: not stated; parents: Dave PETERSON and Ada BENNETT (North Carolina); death cause: "stillborn"; informant: father (Erwin); died: 2 Nov. 1918; buried: Huntdale, North Carolina; record (1918) # 657.

FORD, Mart; born: 13 Jun. 1836; widower; blacksmith; parents: "unknown"; death cause: "old age"; informant: Josh FORD (Chestra); died: 3 Dec. 1918; buried: Piney Flats, Tennessee; record (1918) # 658.

LAMBERT, Helen May; born: 25 Sep. 1918; parents: W.G. LAMBERT (Ohio) and P_ (illegible) May BLAKELY (West Virginia); death cause: "colitis"; informant: father (Erwin); died: 3 Dec. 1918; record # 659.

HOPSON, Phoeba; born: 4 Nov. 1856 in Mitchell County, NC.; widow; parents: Jacob MASTERS (Mitchell County) and Celia HUGHES (Mitchell County); death cause: "unknown, complained of hurting around heart"; informant: Rob BYRD (Unicoi); died: 4 Dec. 1918; buried: Swingle Cemetery; record (1918) # 660.

JONES, Virgie; born: 2 Dec. 1910; parents: J.E. JONES and __ (illegible) SHELTON; death cause: "influenza and pneumonia"; informant: J.E. HUGHES (Kittyton); died: 6 Dec. 1918; buried: Foster Cemetery; record (1918) # 661.

BALEY, Mary; born: 10 May 1858 in Mitchell County, NC.; married; parents: John BRINKLEY (Mitchell County) and Sallie BRINKLEY (Mitchell County); death cause: "influenza"; informant: John BALEY (Flag Pond); died: 7 Dec. 1918; buried: Rice Creek; record # 662.

JONES, David Silas; born: 15 Oct. 1908; parents: James E. JONES and Elvira SHELTON; death cause: "influenza and pneumonia"; informant: mother (Kittyton); died: 8 Dec. 1918; buried: Foster Cemetery; record (1918) # 663.

TIPTON, Su Ema; born: 2 Aug. 1892; married; parents: Ell EDWARDS and Nevoy HIGGINS; death cause: "influenza and pneumonia"; informant: S.H. BROWN (Kittyton); died: 10 Dec. 1918; buried: Tipton Cemetery; record (1918) # 664.

PAYNE, Reba Maudann; born: 25 Jul. 1913 in Carter County; parents: Alex J. PAYNE (Carter County) and Ida Pearl BOWMAN; death cause: "influenza and asthma"; informant: father (Erwin); died: 15 Dec. 1918; record (1918) # 665.

PAYNE, Selmon Jesse; born: 4 Aug. 1915; parents: Alex J. PAYNE (Carter County) and Ida Pearl BOWMAN; death cause: "influenza and asthma"; informant: father (Erwin); died: 15 Dec. 1918; record # 666.

COIN, Harvey Lee; born: 28 Jun. 1898; single; parents: S.A. COIN and Emmie TOMPKINS; death cause: "influenza and pneumonia"; informant: father (Erwin); died: 18 Dec. 1918; buried: Jobe Cemetery; record (1918) # 667.

TOLLEY, Edna May; born: 25 Dec. 1917; parents: Clarenc TOLLEY (North Carolina) and Salda MILLER (North Carolina); death cause: "broncho pneumonia"; informant: father (Erwin); died: 25 Dec. 1918; buried: Swingle Cemetery; record (1918) # 668.

HUTTON, Ralph; born: 1 Dec. 1918; parents: Arthur D. HUTTON (Washington County, Virginia) and Lula BALES; death cause: "stillborn"; informant: father (Erwin); died: 1 Dec. 1918; record # 669.

BLAKE, Infant; male; parents: Howard BLAKE and Dora WHITE (Kentucky); death cause: "stillborn"; informant: father (Erwin); died: 24 Dec. 1918; record (1918) # 670.

STREET, Mary; born: 1 Mar. 1879 in Carter County; married; parents: John COR__ (illegible)(Carter County) and Sarah SIMERLY (Carter County); death cause: "influenza and pneumonia"; informant: Hubert COOPER (Unicoi); died: 3 Jan. 1919; record (1919) # 405.

MCINTURFF, Elith; age: 6 days; parents: James MCINTURFF and Mollie HENSON; death cause: "bold hives"; informant: John

MCINTURFF (Unicoi); died: 4 Jan. 1919; buried: McInturff Cemetery; record (1919) # 406.

ILLEGIBLE, Bessie; born: 8 Oct. 1894; married; parents: Steve GILBERT and Mary TAYLOR (North Carolina); death cause: "influenza"; informant: G.F. GUINN (Kittyton); died: 5 Jan. 1919; buried: Clear Branch; record (1919) # 407.

MCLAUGHLIN, Robert; born: 24 Oct. 1918; parents: Robert MCNABB and Lola MCLAUGHLIN; death cause: "unknown, found dead in bed"; died: 6 Jan. 1919; record (1919) # 408.

ALLEN, James Virgil; born: 7 Apr. 1912; parents: Isaac ALLEN and Cassie WHALEY; death cause: "influenza and pneumonia"; informant: father (Erwin); died: 15 Jan. 1919; buried: Martins Creek; record # 409.

WILLIAMS, Bradie; born: 17 Jan. 1919; parents: C.R. WILLIAMS (North Carolina) and Elzie HENSLEY; death cause: not stated; informant: R.J. HENSLEY (Kittyton); died: 17 Jan. 1919; buried: Hensley Cemetery; record (1919) # 410.

WOLF, Phill; born: 5 Jun. 1915; parents: Henry WOLF and Lizie EDWARDS; death cause: "pneumonia fever"; informant: G.F. GUINN (Kittyton); died: 12 Jan. 1919; buried: Clear Branch; record # 411.

WATTS, Arthur; born: 7 Sep. 1917; parents: Bert WATTS and Altha LEWIS (?); death cause: "influenza and pneumonia"; informant: father (Kittyton); died: 21 Jan. 1919; buried: Tilson Cemetery; record # 412.

METCALF, Woodrow Edward; born: 19 Jan. 1919; parents: George METCALF (North Carolina) and Lilly SMITH (West Virginia); death cause: not stated; informant: father (Erwin); died; 21 Jan. 1919; buried: Jobe Cemetery; record (1919) # 413.

CARVER, Hattie Ettie; born: 31 Jan. 1917; parents: Doc CARVER (Mitchell County, NC.) and Bertie L. HILL (Mitchell County, NC.); death cause: "bronchitis and convulsions"; died: 23 Jan. 1919; buried: Peterson Cemetery; record (1919) # 414.

WARD, William Reese, Jr.; born: 31 Aug. 1897 in Kentucky; single; parents: William Reese WARD (Kentucky) and Grace STANLEY (Kentucky); death cause: "ensyphilitis"; informant: father (Hazard, Kentucky) died: 24 Jan. 1919; buried: Richmond, Kentucky; record (1919) # 415.

GARLAND, Howard Allen; born: 23 Mar. 1918; parents: John GARLAND (Poplar, NC.) and Credy HONEYCUTT; death cause: "influenza and pneumonia"; informant: father (Erwin); died: 24 Jan. 1919; buried: Martins Creek; record (1919) # 416.

ARNETT, Edwin; parents: John ARNETT (Carter County) and Allie MILLER (Carter County); death cause: "stillborn"; died: 29 Jan. 1919; buried: Jobe Cemetery; record (1919) # 417.

SPARKS, Joseph William; born: 5 Jul. 1864 in North Carolina; married; parents: Sidney SPARKS (North Carolina) and Sindy __ (illegible) (North Carolina); death cause: "gunshot wound"; informant: D.C. SPARKS (Flag Pond); died: 2 Feb. 1919; record (1919) # 418.

EDWARDS, Morton; born: 10 Jul. 1904; parents: G.W. EDWARDS and Celia JONES; death cause: "accidentally shot with shotgun while hunting"; informant: H.G. TILSON (Kittyton); died: 3 Feb. 1919; buried: Sams Cemetery; record (1919) # 419.

FURCHES, Rena Jane; born: 19 Apr. 1870; married; parents: father not stated and Vina HUSKINS; death cause: "rheumatism and inflammation; informant: W.J. FURCHES (Erwin); died: 6 Feb. 1919; record (1919) # 420.

HAMPTON, Sarah; age: 74 years; born: Washington County; parents: William HAMPTON (Washington County) and Malina HAMPTON (Washington County); death cause: "influenza and pneumonia"; informant: J.W. HOWELL (Erwin); died: 7 Feb. 1919; buried: Martins Creek; record (1919) # 421.

WHITE, Edith Louise; born: 18 Oct. 1918; parents: Jesse WHITE and Hester EDWARDS (North Carolina); death cause: "pneumonia"; informant: father (Chestra); died: 9 Feb. 1919; buried: Martins Creek; record (1919) # 423.

LINVILLE, Loyd; born: 28 Mar 1912; parents: James LINVILLE and Nannie HUMPHREY (Carter County); death cause: "influenza"; informant: Mrs. Mary HUMPHREY (Unicoi); died: 8 Feb. 1919; buried: Humphrey Cemetery; record (1919) # 422.

JONES, Oran Hutsel; born: 25 Oct. 1918; parents: Rufus JONES and Roxy BRITT; death cause: "croup"; informant: father (Erwin); died: 9 Feb. 1919; record (1919) # 424.

GARLAND, Callie; born: 22 Jun. 1867 in North Carolina; married; parents: Clingman ATKINS (North Carolina) and Polly STANLEY (North Carolina); death cause: "brights disease"; informant: W.A. GARLAND (Erwin); died: 13 Feb. 1919; buried: Martins Creek; record (1918) 425.

FOSTER, Elmer; age: not stated; married; parents: William Arthur FOSTER and Cordie JOHNSON (Relief, North Carolina); death cause: "meningitis"; died: 18 Feb. 1919; buried; Martins Creek; record # 426.

ROWE, W. Harrison; born: 8 Mar. 1840 in Carter County; married; parents: Dill ROWE and Rebecca __; death cause: "dropsy and organic heart trouble"; informant: Bessie ROWE (Unicoi); died: 2 Mar. 1919; record (1919) # 427.

HIGGINS, William T.; born: 16 Dec. 1844; married; parents: Ellis HIGGINS (Yancey County, NC.) and Ruth TILSON (Washington County); death cause: "old age and dropsy"; informant: Mrs. Amanda E. HIGGINS (Flag Pond); died: 10 Mar. 1919; buried: Higgins Cemetery; record (1919) # 428.

DUNCAN, Pauline; born: 9 Feb. 1916; parents: Frank DUNCAN and Gertrude STEVENS; death cause: "killed by being run over by wagon"; informant: father (Erwin); died: 13 Mar. 1919; buried: Jobe Cemetery; record (1919) # 429.

GARLAND, Bonnie; born: 28 Sep. 1916; parents: John GARLAND (North Carolina) and Liza DILLINGER; death cause: "brain abscess"; informant: mother (Unicoi); died: 19 Mar. 1919; record (1919) # 430.

PETERS, Nealey Belle; age: 32 years; widow; parents: Davis SMITH and Nancy WHALEY (Washington County); death cause; "pthisis pulmonalis"; informant: James COLEMAN (Unicoi); died: 27 Mar. 1919; buried: Jones Cemetery; record (1919) # 431.

SPARKS, Sindy; age: 80 years; born: North Carolina; widow; parents: father not stated and Nancy RICE (North Carolina); death cause: "senility"; informant: Zeb WALDROP (Flag Pond); died: 27 Mar. 1919; buried: Hensley Cemetery; record (1919) # 432.

NORRIS, Richard Herman; born: 6 Mar. 1919; parents: Charles NORRIS and Adie JOHNSON (North Carolina); death cause: "jaundice"; informant: father (Erwin); died: 29 Mar. 1919; buried: Martins Creek; record (1919) # 433.

WOODBY, William; age: 35 years and 6 months; married; parents: Alfred WOOBY and Fannie E. GILBERT (North Carolina); death cause: "pulmonary tuberculosis"; informant: Maryan SNEYD (Unicoi); died: 30 Mar. 1919; buried: Woodby Cemetery; record (1919) # 434.

CAMPBELL, James; age: 77 years; married; parents: John C. CAMPBELL and Dasha HELTON; death cause: not stated; informant: David CAMPBELL (Unicoi); died: 30 Mar. 1919; buried: Campbell Cemetery; record (1919) # 435.

PATE, Infant; male; parents: Dewey PATE and Litha DAVIS; death cause: "stillborn"; informant: Emaline HYDER (Hampton, Tennessee); died: 16 Mar. 1919; buried: Gouge Cemetery; record (1919) # 436.

HEAD, Infant; female; parents: Hunler HEAD and Martha BRITT; death cause: "stillborn"; died: 27 Mar. 1919; buried: Head Cemetery; record unnumbered.

MCINTURFF, Infant; male; parents: Walter MCINTURFF and Ellia BOWMAN; death cause: "stillborn, mother had the flu"; died: 27 Mar 1919; buried: McInturff Cemetery; record (1919) # 437.

HEAD, Julia; age: "about 47 years"; married; parents: John HAMMET and Maggie ROBERSON (Carter County); death cause: "tuberculosis of lungs"; informant: Mrs. Maggie HAMMET (Johnson City); died: 2 Apr. 1919; buried: Anderson Cemetery; record (1919) # 438.

GILLIS, William J.; born: 15 Feb. 1859 in Washington County; married; parents: Alfred GILLIS (Washington County) and Emeline GUINN (Washington County); death cause: "carcinoma of prostate"; died: 5 Apr. 1919; buried; Clear Branch; record (1919) # 440.

ELLIOTT, Razor; born: 14 Jan. 1917; parents: Jessie ELLIOTT and Rebecca (?) ELLIS; death cause: "influenza"; informant: Jess ELLIOTT (Embreeville); died: 4 Apr. 1919; buried: Elizabethton, Tennessee; record (1919) # 439.

LLOYD, Gleason; born: 6 Jun. __; age: 1 year, 10 months and 4 days; parents: Lattie LLOYD and Kitty MORROW; death cause: "lobar pneumonia"; informant: father (Kittyton); died: 8 Apr. 1919; buried: Lloyd Cemetery; record (1919) # 441.

MILLER, Smith; age: 26 years; born: North Carolina; single; soldier; parents: Daniel MILLER (North Carolina) and Sinda BARNETT

(North Carolina); death cause: "killed in train crash"; died: 8 Apr. 1919; buried: Relief, North Carolina; record (1919) # 442.

CAMPBELL, Mary; born: 10 Apr. 1842 in Johnson County; widow; parents: A.J. GRINDSTAFF (Johnson County) and Malinda PRITCHARD (Mitchell County, NC.); death cause: not stated; informant: Sarah A. GRINDSTAFF (Unicoi); died: 9 Apr. 1919; buried: Limestone Cove; record (1919) # 443.

HENSLEY, Irene; born: 27 Mar 1919; parents: Walter HENSLEY (North Carolina) and Mary MCANICH (Scotland); death cause: not stated; informant: Mary HENSLEY (Erwin); died: 10 Apr. 1919; buried: Martins Creek; record (1919) # 444.

JOY, Henry G.; age: "about 32 years; married; parents: "unknown"; death cause: "bronchial pneumonia"; died: 10 Apr. 1919; buried: Lenoir, North Carolina; record (1919) # 445.

TAYLOR, Sam; age: 38 years; married; parents: not stated; death cause: "typhoid fever"; informant: wife; died: 10 Apr. 1919; buried: Elizabethton, Tennessee; record (1919) # 446.

WATTS, Rosa Belle; born: 11 Dec. 1918; parents: Monroe WATTS (Yancey County, NC.) and Rachel WILLIAMS (Yancey County, NC.); death cause: "unknown"; informant: father (Erwin); died: 20 Apr. 1919; buried: Jobe Cemetery; record (1919) # 447.

SAMS, Ezekel G.; born: 12 Dec. 1849 in North Carolina; married; parents: John SAMS (North Carolina) and Winnie __ (illegible) (North Carolina); death cause: illegible; informant: W.R. GENTRY (Flag Pond); died: 26 Apr. 1919; buried: Sams Cemetery; record # 448.

METCAFF, Estell; born: 3 Feb. 1918; parents: Willie METCALF (Madison County, NC.) and Lora CLICK (Yancey County, NC.); death cause: "nose bleed"; informant: A.L. BALEY (Flag Pond); died: 27 Apr. 1919; buried: Sams Creek; record (1919) # 449.

O'BRIEN, Benjamin Fletcher; born: 2 Feb. 1847; widower; parents: William D. O'BRIEN (Pennsylvania) and Vina GARLAND; death cause: "apoplexy, strokes"; informant: Lola LOVE (Erwin); died: 29 Apr. 1919; buried: Jobe Cemetery; record (1919) # 450.

HIGGINS, Pansey; parents: W.E. HIGGINS and Iva An TIPTON; death cause: "stillborn"; informant: D.C. HIGGINS (Kittyton); died: 18 Apr. 1919; buried: Higgins Cemetery; record (1919) # 451.

HAYNES, Anna Lee; born: 4 May 1919; parents: A.W. HAYNES (North Carolina) and Jane HAYNES; death cause: "unknown"; informant: father (Flag Pond); died: 4 May 1919; buried: Clear Branch; record (1919) # 452.

PHILLIPS, Kate; born: 24 Feb. 1859; single; parents: Samuel MOORE (North Carolina) and Charity MOORE; death cause: "heart disease"; informant: Edd STOCKTON (Flag Pond); died: 5 May 1919; buried: Flag Pond; record (1919) # 453.

WILLIS, Rossie Elen; born: 9 Jun. 1918; parents: Robert WILLIS (North Carolina) and Nancy An TOLLY (Carter County); death cause: "acute indigestion"; informant: father (Unicoi); died: 14 May 1919; buried: Clark Cemetery; record (1919) # 454.

STOCKTON, Nellie; born: 10 Dec. 1918; parents: Luther STOCKTON and Dora MASHBURN; death cause: "unknown"; informant: father (Unicoi); died: 26 May 1919; buried: Higgins Cemetery; record # 455.

ESTEP, Infant; male; parents: father not stated and Bessi ESTEP; death cause: "unknown"; informant: Bessie WILLIAMS (Kittyton); born/died: 30 May 1919; buried: Foster Cemetery; record (1919) # 456.

PARKER, Miley; parents: Elisah PARKER (North Carolina) and Daicy JONES (North Carolina); death cause: "stillborn"; died: 9 May 1919; record (1919) # 457.

BARNETT, Infant; female; parents: Smith BARNETT (North Carolina) and Mary CARVER (North Carolina); death cause: "stillborn"; informant: father (Unicoi); died: 9 May 1919; buried: Grindstaff Cemetery; record (1919) # 458.

DAVIDSON, Horace; born; __ Jan. 1877; single; parents: James DAVIDSON and Sallie SMITH; death cause: "tubercular pha__ (illegible)"; informant: W.F. KIPPLING (Johnson City); died: 2 Jun. 1919; buried: Roan Mountain, Tennessee; record (1919) # 459.

JONES, Joe A.; born: 24 Dec. 1873 in Washington County; married; parents: John JONES (Sullivan County) and Lizzie WHALEY (Washington County); death cause: "tuberculosis of bowels"; informant: father (Erwin); died: 5 Jun. 1919; buried: Jobe Cemetery; record # 460.

DAVIS, Thomas; age: 45 years; married; parents: James DAVID (North Carolina) and Tilha BUTLER (North Carolina); death cause:

"tuberculosis"; informant: John DAVIS (Unicoi); died: 7 Jun. 1919; buried: Gouge Cemetery; record (1919) # 461.

WHITE, Mary Lucinda; age: 67 years; widow; parents: Leander SIMMONS (North Carolina) and Mary R. TIMMERSON (North Carolina); death cause: "dysentery"; died in the 5th District 8 Jun. 1919; record (1919) # 462.

NELSON, David Samuel; born: 20 Jun. 1919; parents: Phillip NELSON and Millie MILLER; death cause: "bold hives"; informant: father (Unicoi); buried: Rock Creek Cemetery; record (1919) # 463.

FOX, Charlie B.; born: 2 Feb. 1908 in Johnson City; parents: Charles Burnie FOX and Bessie SMITH; death cause: "nephritis"; informant: C.B. FOX (Erwin); died: 1 Jul. 1919; buried: Martins Creek; record (1919) # 464.

KITE, Hazel C.; born: 20 Oct. 1917; parents: Luther KITE and Chevis DAVIS; death cause: "spinal meningitis"; died: 3 Jul. 1919; buried: Milligan, Tennessee; record (1919) # 465.

HENSLEY, Maggie; born: 29 Jun. 1884; married; parents: D.C. FOSTER and L.E. HENSLEY; death cause: "peritonitis and appendicitis"; informant: W.B. FOSTER (Kittyton); died: 5 Jul. 1919; buried: Hensley Cemetery; record (1919) # 466.

CAMPBELL, Edith; born: 5 Aug. 1918; parents: Jackson CAMPBELL and Jane LEDFORD; death cause: "gastro enteritis"; informant: father (Unicoi); died: 5 Jul. 1919; buried: Garland Cemetery; record # 466 (duplicate record).

PRESNELL, Harrison; born: __ 1847 in Wilkes County, NC.:, age: 71 years, 11 months and 20 days; married; parents: Peter PRESNELL (Wilkes County, NC.) and Susie __ (Wilkes County, NC.); death cause: "typhoid fever"; informant: David A. PRESNELL (Chestra); died: 5 Jul. 1919; record (1919) # 467.

HAYNES, Buena Vista; born: __ Nov. 1873 in Scott County, VA.; married; parents: Wiley B. HARRELL (Hawkins County) and Mary A. DARTER (Hawkins County); death cause: "diarrhea"; informant: J.K. HAYNES (Erwin); died: 11 Jul. 1919; buried: Yuma, Virginia; record (1919) # 468.

JONES, Orra Clive; male; born: 29 Jan. 1903 in Ohio; parents: W.H. JONES and Anna BAKER; death cause: "well caved in, crushed skull"; informant: father (Erwin); died: 11 Jul. 1919; record (1919) # 469.

BENNETT, Binder; born: 9 May 1913 in North Carolina; parents: Rice BENNETT (North Carolina) and Oma HUGHES (North Carolina); death cause: "dysentery"; informant: father (Erwin); died: 13 Jul. 1919; buried: Poplar, North Carolina; record (1919) # 470.

SHOUN, Infant; female; parents: Roy SHOUN (Mountain City) and Willie NORRIS; death cause: "premature birth"; born/died: 17 Jul. 1919; buried: Jobe Cemetery; record (1919) # 471.

SHULTZ, Daniel; age: 75 years; married; blacksmith; parents: "unknown"; death cause: "gall stones"; informant: Jack SHULTZ (Unicoi); died: 20 Jul. 1919; buried: Gouge Cemetery; record # 472.

HENSLEY, Noah; born: 23 May 1881; married; parents: J.C. HENSLEY and Tilda FOSTER; death cause: "colic"; informant: Lizie WATTS (Kittyton); died: 28 Jul. 1919; buried; Hensley Cemetery; record # 473.

FOSTER, Maud; born: 31 Jul. 1918; parents: J.H. FOSTER and Elizie TILSON; death cause: not stated; informant: father (Kittyton); died: 31 Jul. 1919; buried: Mt. Pleasant; record (1919) # 474.

PADGETT, Infant; male; born: 15 Aug. 1919; parents: Mack PADGETT and Sada TINKER; death cause: "premature birth"; informant: father (Embreeville); died: 15 Aug. 1919; buried: Cove Cemetery; record (1919) # 475.

FANNING, Ruby; born: 3 Feb. 1918; parents: Frank FANNING and Geneva BARNES; death cause: "cholera infantum"; informant: father (Erwin); died: 15 Aug. 1919; buried: Martins Creek; record # 476.

PADGETT, Sadie; born: 19 Mar. 1899; married; parents: John TINKER and Darkey SAMS; death cause: "peritonitis, premature labor, edema of lungs"; informant: John TINKER (Embreeville); died: 23 Aug. 1919; buried: Liberty Cemetery; record (1919) # 477.

GENTRY, Sarah; born: 14 Nov. 1854; married; parents: Samuel MOORE (North Carolina) and Charity BROWN (North Carolina); death cause: "stomach trouble"; informant: E.B. SAMS (Kittyton); died: 31 Aug. 1919; buried: Rice Creek; record (1919) # 478.

WILLIAMS, Infant; female; parents: R.L. WILLIAMS (Virginia) and Mynter ADKINS (Virginia); death cause: "stillborn"; informant: father (Erwin); died: 14 Aug. 1919; buried: Jobe Cemetery; record # 479.

PATE, Ella Tipton; age: 27 years; married; parents: John D. TIPTON and Jane HIGGINS; death cause: "consumption"; informant: Mrs. J.D. TIPTON (Kittyton); died: 3 Sep. 1919; buried: Tipton Cemetery; record (1919) # 480.

MCINTOSH, Elsie Mae; born: 8 May 1918; parents: Clifford MCINTOSH and Annie HENSLEY; death cause: "intestinal nephritis"; informant: father (Flag Pond); died: 3 Sep. 1919; buried: Rice Creek; record (1919) # 481.

WORSHAM, Thelma; born: 22 Jul. 1902 in Virginia; parents: W.J. WORSHAM (Virginia) and __ BIRDWELL; death cause: "typhoid fever"; informant: father (Erwin); died: 4 Sep. 1919; buried: Martins Creek; record (1919) # 482.

LEDFORD, Texie; born: 5 Sep. 1917; parents: W.C. LEDFORD (North Carolina) and Marier FENDER (North Carolina); death cause: "croup"; informant: father (Kittyton); died: 5 Sep. 1919; buried: Ledford Cemetery; record (1919) # 483.

HENSLEY, Mary; born: 17 Sep. 1919; parents: John HENSLEY and Elizith RICE; death cause: "unknown"; informant: father (Flag Pond); died: 17 Sep. 1919; buried: Rice Creek; record (1919) # 485.

EDWARDS, Amanda; born: 21 Jun. 1867; married; parents: Andrew HENSLEY and Rheuhana HARRIS; death cause: "tuberculosis of lungs"; informant: Andy EDWARDS (Kittyton); died: 2 Oct. 1919; buried: Hensley Cemetery; record (1919) # 486.

TOLLEY, Rex; age: 15 years, 4 months and 4 days; parents: J.R. TOLLEY (Yancey County, NC.) and Hattie DUFFY (Germany); death cause: "gunshot wound, homicide"; informant: J.W. HOWELL (Erwin); died: 2 Oct. 1919; buried: Rock Creek; record (1919) # 487.

GARLAND, Infant; female; born: 2 Oct. 1919; parents: David GARLAND (North Carolina) and Joanna SLAGLE; death cause: father (Unicoi); died: 4 Oct. 1919; buried: Marbleton; record (1919) # 488.

WOODBY, Alford; age: 78 years; born: North Carolina; married; parents: E.P. WOODBY and Melvira GILBERT; death cause: "lobar pneumonia"; informant: John WOODBY (Unicoi); died: 11 Oct. 1919; buried: Woodby Cemetery; record (1919) # 489.

NELSON, Jasper; born: 16 Jan. 1846; married; parents: John NELSON and Nancy NELSON (North Carolina); death cause: "atrophy of liver"; informant: W.A. LINVILLE (Unicoi); died: 11 Oct. 1919; buried; Jones Cemetery; record (1919) # 490.

HARISON, William; age: "about 83 years"; born: North Carolina; widower; parents: James HARISON (North Carolina) and Nancy HARES (North Carolina); death cause: "paralysis"; informant: Henry SMITH (Unicoi); died: 16 Oct. 1919; buried: Fishery Cemetery; record (1919) # 491.

JONES, Urah Haskell; born: 17 May 1899 in Pactolus; single; parents: Charles JONES (Knoxville) and Mary GALLOWAY (Knoxville); death cause: "locked bowels"; informant: Ethel JONES (Chestra); died: 28 Oct. 1919; buried: Pactolus, Tennessee; record (1919) # 492.

BOONE, Zeb; born: 27 Oct. 1919; parents: Sam BOONE (North Carolina) and Irene WALTERS (Pennsylvania); death cause: "unknown"; died: 30 Oct. 1919; buried: Jobe Cemetery; record # 493.

JONES, Julia B.; born: 10 Dec. 1886; married; parents; Robert L. TAPP and Mollie JOHNSON; death cause: "pulmonary tuberculosis"; informant: J.C. HENSLEY (Erwin); died: 31 Oct. 1919; buried: Fishery Cemetery; record (1919) # 494.

STOCTON, Infant; female; parents: Wesley STOCTON and Jane HIGGINS (North Carolina); death cause: "stillborn"; informant: father (Unicoi); died: 29 Oct. 1919; buried: Fishery Cemetery; record # 495.

GARRISON, W.T.; born: 10 May 1856 in Carter County; married; parents: James GARRISON and Hannah CULBERT; death cause: "cerebral hemorrhage"; informant: W.R. MEREDITH (Erwin); died: 8 Nov. 1919; buried: Valley Forge, Tennessee; record (1919) # 496.

POTTER, Clyde; born: 18 Aug. 1997; single; electrician; parents: Wesley J. POTTER and Idie HUSKINS; death cause: "contacted 13,000 volt electrical wire"; informant: Oscar POTTER (Embreeville); died: 11 Nov. 1919; buried; Johnson City; record (1919) # 497.

BARRY, David M.; age: 67 years; born: Carter County; married; parents: John BARRY (North Carolina) and Peggy MCKINNEY (Johnson

County); death cause: "heart trouble"; died: 24 Nov. 1919; buried: Washington County; record (1919) # 498.

BRUMMETT, Celia; born: 20 Jun. 1918; parents: William BRUMMETT and M_ (illegible) COLEMAN (Carter County); death cause: "cholera infantum"; died: 20 Nov. 1919; record (1919) # 499.

PETERS, Francis Love; parents: T.H. PETERS (North Carolina) and M.B. BRINKLEY (Virginia); death cause: "stillborn"; informant: father (Erwin); died: 20 Nov. 1919; buried: Jobe Cemetery; record # 500.

HOWELL, Tinetta (?); age: 55 years; born: Yancey County, NC.; married; parents: Willis BAILEY (North Carolina) and Polly LEDFORD (North Carolina); death cause: "pellagra"; informant: J.W. HOWELL (Erwin); died: 2 Dec. 1919; buried: Martins Creek; record (1919) # 501.

PEOPLES, William J.; age: 89 years; married; parents: W.J. PEOPLES and Elizabeth S__ (illegible); death cause: "kidney trouble, uremic poisoning"; died: 3 Dec. 1919; buried: Milligan College, Tennessee; record (1919) # 502.

GREGG, Julius D.; age: 70 years; married; parents: Harrison GREGG (North Carolina) and Margaret DUGGER; death cause: "cerebral hemorrhage"; informant: John GREGG (Johnson City); died: 4 Dec. 1919; record (1919) # 503.

NELSON, John; born: 18 Apr. 1883; married; parents: Ike NELSON and Rebecca PHILLIPS; death cause: "gunshot wound by a boy named BLACKBURN"; informant: father (Erwin); died: 9 Dec. 1919; buried: Jones Cemetery; record (1919) # 504.

JONES, John; age: "about 67 years"; born: Sullivan County; married; parents: Henry JONES and Elizabeth FEATHERS; death cause: "cerebral hemorrhage"; informant: J.M. JONES (Unicoi); died: 11 Dec. 1919; buried: Fishery Cemetery; record (1919) # 505.

RIGGS, Ellis J.; born: 5 Jan. 1844; married; parents: Jessie RIGGS and Celia M. SHELTON; death cause: "lobar pneumonia"; informant: Emma RIGGS (Unicoi); died: 12 Dec. 1919; buried; Birchfield Cemetery; record (1919) # 506.

TITLE, Infant; female; born: 11 Dec. 1919; parents: Alex TITTLE (Washington County) and __ HUSKINS (Washington County); death cause: "broncho pneumonia"; informant: father (Erwin); died: 17 Dec. 1919; buried: Jobe Cemetery; record (1919) # 507.

BRUMMETT, Susan; age: 63 years; born: North Carolina; married; parents: Sidney BRANCH (North Carolina) and Emely BENFIELD (North Carolina); death cause: "leakage of heart"; died: 20 Dec. 1919; buried: Brummett Cemetery; record (1919) # 508.

DAY, William Done; born: 4 Mar. 1876; widower; parents: Alexander DAY and Mary MILLER; death cause: "carcinoma of throat"; informant: C.W. DAY (Erwin); died: 24 Dec. 1919; buried: home cemetery; record (1919) # 509.

PADGETT, Fay; born: 31 May 1919; parents: Algire PADGETT (Washington County) and May HENSLEY; death cause: "unknown, found dead in bed"; informant: father (Erwin); died: 27 Dec. 1919; buried: Embreeville; record (1919) # 510.

RUNIONS, Brask; born: 14 Nov. 1919; parents: Dolphus RUNIONS and Mary HIGGINS; death cause: "bold hives"; informant: J.L. HIGGINS (Flag Pond); died: 1 Jan. 1920; record (1920) # 374.

BYRD, Ira Kenneth; born: 21 Dec. 1919; parents: Jacob B. BYRD (Illinois) and Ollie GARLAND (North Carolina); death cause: "pneumonia"; informant: J.B. BYRD (Unicoi); died: 17 Jan. 1920; buried: Martins Creek; record (1920) # 375.

CROW, Edward Marshall; age: "about 30 years"; married; parents: Ed CROW and __ (illegible) TIPTON (North Carolina); death cause: "pulmonary tuberculosis"; informant: M.E. BIRCHFIELD (Erwin); died: 28 Jan. 1920; buried: Jobe Cemetery; record (1920) # 376.

CHANDLER, Infant; male; parents: Arthur CHANDLER (North Carolina) and Annie CRAIN; death cause: "stillborn"; informant: J. CRAIN (Erwin); died: 30 Jan. 1920; buried: Martins Creek; record (1920) # 377.

LEWIS, Charles Edgar; born: 4 Mar. 1875 in Sullivan County; railroad engineer; married; parents: __ (illegible) LEWIS (Virginia) and Callie MORRELL (Virginia); death cause: "influenza and pneumonia"; informant: Mrs. C.E. LEWIS (Erwin); died: 7 Feb. 1920; buried: Jobe Cemetery; record (1920) # 378.

NELSON, Harold M.; born: 21 Nov. 1919; parents: Ralph M. NELSON and Ethel BRADFORD; death cause: "bold hives"; informant: father

(Erwin); died: 12 Feb. 1920; buried: Rock Creek Cemetery; record (1920) # 379.

MCCURRY, Retha; born: 7 Jan. 1920 in Yancey County, NC.; parents: Sid MCCURRY (Yancey County) and Lillie HOWELL (Yancey County); death cause: "unknown, found dead in bed"; informant: father (Erwin); died: 14 Feb. 1920; buried: Huntsdale, North Carolina; record (1920) # 380.

HEDRICK, Lina; born: 17 May 1872 (?) in Mitchell County, NC.; age given as 47 years, 6 months and 28 days; married; parents: Peter PETERSON (Mitchell County) and Sarah __ (illegible); death cause: "cancer of uterus, shock from operation"; informant: M.A. HEDRICK; died: 15 Feb. 1920; buried: Peterson Cemetery; record (192) # 381.

LINDSAY, Mary A.; born: 20 Aug. 1832 in Virginia; widow; parents: John WILSON (Bedford County, VA.) and Mary A. WILSON (Bedford County, VA.); death cause: "lobar pneumonia"; informant: Mary L. RULE (Erwin); died: 17 Feb. 1920; buried: Roanoke, Virginia; record (1920) # 382.

MCCURY, Sarah; born: 8 Dec. 1893 in Yancey County, NC.; married; parents: Lawson PETERSON (North Carolina) and Camelia TIPTON; death cause: "influenza and abortion"; informant: L.M. MCCURRY; died: 8 Feb. 1920; buried: Peterson Cemetery; record (1920) # 383.

LOVE, Virginia A.; born: 21 Mar. 1919; parents: William LOVE (Virginia) and N. PETERSON (North Carolina); death cause: "whooping cough"; informant: Anne LOVE (Erwin); died: 22 Feb. 1920; buried: Rock Creek Cemetery; record (1920) # 384.

DEATON, Infant; female; born: 11 Dec. 1919 in Yancey County, NC.; parents: F.H. DEATON (Yancey County) and C_ (illegible) DEATON (Yancey County); death cause: "broncho pneumonia"; informant: father (Erwin); died; 22 Feb. 1920; record (1920) # 385.

MCLAIN, Wade H.; born: 24 Apr. 1892 in Van Hill, Tennessee; railroad fireman; married; parents: C.L. MCLAIN (Van Hill) and mother's name illegible; death cause: "cancer of liver"; informant: wife (Van Hill); died: 23 Feb. 1920; buried: Jobe Cemetery; record (1920) # 386.

ANDERSON, Lucinda; born: 21 Jan. 1848 in Carter County; married; parents: Christopher BOWMAN (Carter County) and Sarafina JOHNSON (Carter County); death cause: "pneumonia"; informant: E.L.

95

ANDERSON (Johnson City); died: 23 Feb. 1920; buried; Anderson Chapel; record (1920) # 387.

WHITE, Jane; age: 44 years; married; parents: D.J. WHITE and Martha GARLAND; death cause: "influenza and pneumonia"; informant: Will WHITE (Erwin); died: 25 Feb. 1920; buried; Fishery Cemetery; record (1920) # 388.

BARRY, Manetia; born: 23 Feb. 1920; parents: David BARRY (North Carolina) and mother's name illegible; death cause: "unknown"; informant: father (Erwin); died: 25 Feb. 1920; buried; Jobe Cemetery; record (1920) # 389.

MOORE, Charity; born: 10 Sep. 1835 in North Carolina; widow; parents: not stated; death cause: "senility"; informant: W.R. GENTRY (Flag Pond); died: 16 Feb. 1920; buried; Blankenship Cemetery; record # 390.

CALLAHAN, Emily; born: 22 Apr. 1829 in Madison County, NC.; single; parents: John TATEMAN (Buncombe County, NC.) and Cordelia SPRINKLES (Madison County, NC.); death cause: "lobar pneumonia"; informant: Lydia BLANKENSHIP (Flag Pond); died: 29 Feb. 1920; buried; Higgins Chapel; record (1920) # 391.

MCNABB, Infant; male; parents: G.S. MCNABB and Belle ERWIN; death cause: "stillborn"; informant: L.S. TILSON (Erwin); died: 4 Feb. 1920; buried: Jobe Cemetery; record (1920) # 392.

EDWARDS, Infant; female; parents: Edd EDWARDS and Jane PRICE (North Carolina); death cause: "stillborn"; informant: Dolly EDWARDS (Kittyton); died: 15 Feb. 1920; record (1920) # 393.

GRAY, Infant; female; parents: A.M. GRAY and Hester RAMSEY; death cause: "cord around neck"; born/died: 24 Feb. 1920; buried; Cove Cemetery; record (192) # 394.

RAY, Infant; male; parents: father not stated and Sirelda RAY; death cause: "stillborn"; died: 8 Feb. 1920; buried: Ray Cemetery; record (1920) # 395.

DICKSON, Monica Brown; born: 9 Mar. 1919; parents: M.C. DICKSON (Sullivan County) and Mattie CAUDELL (Virginia); death cause: "whooping cough and pneumonia"; informant: James DICKSON (Erwin); died: 2 Mar. 1920; buried: Jobe Cemetery; record # 396.

BLEVINS, Lockie; born: 17 Jul. 1906; parents: D.B. BLEVINS and Lizzie SMITH; death cause: "peritonitis, appendicitis"; informant: father (Unicoi); died: 6 Mar 1920; record (1920) # 397.

TIPTON, G_ (illegible); born: 28 Sep. 1853; married; parents: Strom TIPTON (North Carolina) and Elizabeth TIPTON (North Carolina); death cause: "influenza and pneumonia"; informant: W.S. HAMPTON (Erwin); died: 6 Mar. 1920; buried: Martins Creek; record # 398.

BOYD, Clyde Eldrige; born: 16 Jun. 1919; parents: William BOYD (North Carolina) and Edna SWAFORD (North Carolina); death cause: "broncho pneumonia"; informant: T.W. MCKINNEY (Erwin); died: 8 Mar. 1920; buried: Mt. Mitchell, North Carolina; record (192) # 399.

HENSLEY, Elizabeth; born: 13 Dec. 1846; single; parents: Sam TILSON (Washington County) and Annie CRAIN (Madison County, NC.); death cause: "senility"; informant: Leroy HIGGINS (Flag Pond); died: 16 Mar. 1920; buried: Higgins Chapel; record (1920) # 400.

MILLER, Cecil M.; born: 29 Dec. 1900; married; parents: George MILLER and Hester AMBROSE; death cause: "post partum hemorrhage"; informant: Hyder MILLER (Erwin); died: 12 Mar. 1920; buried: Martins Creek; record (1920) # 401.

LAMON, Irene; born: 24 Jun. 1919 in Atlanta, Georgia; parents: Ira LAMON (Virginia) and Edith R_ (illegible) (New York); death cause: "malnutrition"; informant: father (Erwin); died: 16 Mar. 1920; buried: Martins Creek; record (1920) # 402.

CLOCESE, Infant; male; born: 15 Mar. 1920; parents: Grover CLOCESE and Orpah WILLIS; death cause: "unknown"; died: 16 Mar. 1920; buried: Edwards Cemetery; record (1920) # 403.

MOOSHA, Essie McCurry; born: 14 Feb. 1899 in Yancey County, NC.; parents: V.S. MCCURRY (Yancey County) and Melissa TIPTON (Yancey County); death cause: "ruptured uterus, childbirth"; informant: William E. MOOSHA (Erwin); died: 26 Mar. 1920; buried: North Carolina; record (1920) # 404.

METCALF, Lovada; born: 28 Feb. 1877 in Madison County, NC.; married; parents: Marion HENSLEY (Madison County) and Margaret HENSLEY (Madison County); death cause: "pulmonary tuberculosis"; informant: George METCALF (Flag Pond); died: 27 Mar. 1920; buried: Sams Creek Cemetery; record (1920) # 405.

WOODBY, Hezekiah; born: __ May __ in Tennessee; age: 86 years, parents: Eppy WOODBY (Tennessee) and Polly DOUGLAS (Tennessee); death cause: "unknown"; informant: James WOODBY (Unicoi); died: 28 Mar. 1920; buried; Woodby Cemetery; record # 406.

CASEY, Clyde Garnett; born: 7 Mar. 1902; parents: George B. CASEY (Virginia) and Virginia B. S__ (illegible) (Virginia); death cause: "caught between engine and tank"; informant: father (Erwin); died: 30 Mar. 1920; buried: Virginia; record (1920) # 407.

FOSTER, Infant; male; parents: father not stated and Emma FOSTER; death cause: "unknown"; informant: E. HUSKINS (Kittyton); born/died: 6 Mar. 1920; buried: Foster Cemetery; record (1920) # 408.

NELSON, Infant; male; parents: Joe NELSON and Germa MCCURY (North Carolina); death cause: "stillborn"; informant: father (Erwin); died: 18 Mar 1920; buried: Jobe Cemetery; record (1920) # 409.

MOOSHA, Infant; male; parents: William C. MOOSHA and Essie MCCURRY (North Carolina); death cause: "stillborn"; informant: father (Erwin); died: 26 Mar. 1920; buried: Green Mountain, North Carolina; record (1920) # 410.

BAILEY, Lonn; born: 22 Apr. 1902; parents: John BAILEY and Ellen HAMPTON; death cause: "tuberculosis of lungs"; informant: Pitman WILLIAMS (Erwin); died: 5 Apr. 1920; buried: Martins Creek; record (1920) # 411.

RICE, Betsie; born: 21 May 1832 in Wilkes County, NC.; single; parents: Ellis WATTS (Wilkes County) and Betsie WATTS (Madison County, NC.); death cause: "dropsy"; informant: L.J. HIGGINS (Flag Pond); died: 9 Apr. 1920; buried; Higgins Chapel; record (1920) # 412.

BOOTHE, M.F.; age: 77 years; born: Washington County; married; parents: John BOOTHE (Washington County) and Mary PARKS (Washington County); death cause: "heart disease"; informant: Mrs. Mollie DAVIS (Erwin); died: 18 Apr. 1920; buried: Boothe Cemetery; record (1920) # 413.

WILLIAMS, Anna; age: 2 years; born: North Carolina; parents: Sam WILLIAMS (North Carolina) and Hanah HIGGINS (North Carolina); died: 14 Apr. 1920; buried: Martins Creek; record (1920) # 414.

STANIFORTH, Infant; male; parents: Edward P. STANIFORTH (Saltville, Virginia) and Glenna PETERSON (Bluefield, West Virginia);

death cause: "stillborn"; informant: father (Erwin); died: 15 Apr. 1920; buried: Jobe Cemetery; record (1920) # 415.

PATE, Nathan; born: 5 Apr. 1846 in Mitchell County, NC.; married; parents: Eson PATE (Yancey County, NC.) and Hannah HONEYCUTT (Yancey County, NC.); death cause: "catarrh, gastro enteritis": died in the 4th District, 15 Apr. 1920; buried; Swingle Cemetery; record # 416.

FOSTER, Sallie; age: 62 years, 3 months and 20 days; born: North Carolina; married; parents: M_ Bailey (North Carolina) and Beckie TIPTON (North Carolina); death cause: "influenza and endo carditis"; informant: Cordelia BAILEY (Erwin); died: 18 Apr. 1920; buried: Martins Creek; record (1920) # 417.

KELEY, May; born: 22 Apr. 1920; parents: R.M. KELEY (Virginia) and S_ BANNER; death cause: "unknown"; informant: J.M. KELEY (Erwin); died: 24 Apr. 1920; buried: Martins Creek; record # 418.

EFFLER, Infant; male; parents: George EFFLER and Emma MORROW; death cause: "stillborn"; died: 22 Apr. 1920; buried; Effler Farm; record (1920) # 419.

HENSLEY, Harrison; born: 20 Oct. 1919; parents: __ (illegible) HENSLEY (Yancey County, NC.) and Della HENSLEY (Madison County, NC.); death cause: "scarlet fever"; informant: John HENSLEY (Flag Pond); died: 10 May 1920; buried; Rice Cemetery; record # 420.

TILSON, Andy; born: 9 Jul. 1886; single; parents: John TILSON (Washington County) and Annie GUINN; death cause: "appendicitis, post operation"; informant: L.S. TILSON (Erwin); died: 18 May 1920; record (1920) # 421.

TAYLOR, Jacob; age: 73 years; married; parents: Mike TAYLOR and Sarah LEWIS; death cause: "paralysis, 3rd stroke"; informant: Jeff TAYLOR (Embreeville); died: 15 May 1920; buried: Ritchie Cemetery; record (1920) # 422.

STORY, Anna; born: 30 Aug. 1880 in Washington County; married; parents: Joseph M. BEALS (Washington County) and Nancy D. HUSKINS (Lincoln County, NC.); death cause: "heart disease"; informant: T.A. BEALS (Erwin); died: 15 May 1920; buried: Embreeville; record (1920) # 423.

BARNETT, Willie Denton; female; age: 31 years, 9 months and 29 days; married; parents: H.M. DENTON and Sallie JONES; death cause:

"pulmonary tuberculosis"; informant: J.M. BARNETT (Erwin); died: 16 May 1920; record (1920) # 424.

MCLAUGHLIN, Amanda Jane; born: 15 Jul. 1849 in Cherokee, Tennessee; widow; parents: W.D. HARVEY (Cherokee, TN.) and Amanda HARVY (Cherokee, TN.); death cause: "pulmonary hemorrhage"; informant: J.H. MCLAUGHLIN (Erwin); died: 17 May 1920; buried: Jobe Cemetery; record (1920) # 425.

HENSLEY, Josephine; born: 28 Apr. 1920; parents: Oscar HENSLEY and Texie HENSLEY (Yancey County, NC.); death cause: "influenza and pneumonia"; informant: father (Flag Pond); buried: Rice Creek; record (1920) # 426.

MERCEY, Ruby; born: 10 Jun. 1919; parents: William S. MERCEY (Virginia); parents: Hilda SMITH (Ohio); death cause: "scalded by hot water"; informant: father (Congo, West Virginia); died: 27 May 1920; buried: Welsville, Ohio; record (1920) # 427.

TINKER, Rosie; born: 12 Apr. 1902; married; parents: S.C. TIPTON and Amanda SMITH; death cause: "childbirth"; informant: Amanda TIPTON (Kittyton); died: 28 May 1920; buried: Tilson Cemetery; record (1920) # 428.

HAMPTON, Robert A.; born: 4 Jun. 1856; married; parents: Daniel HAMPTON and Katie MASTERS; death cause: "pneumonia"; informant: W.S. HAMPTON (Erwin); died: 28 May 1920; buried: Martins Creek; record (1920) # 429.

BAILEY, Naron; age: 70 years; born: North Carolina; married; parents: Morgan BAILEY (North Carolina) and mother "unknown"; death cause: "intestinal nephritis"; informant: Morgan BAILEY (Erwin); died: 28 May 1920; buried: Martins Creek; record (1920) # 430.

YOUNG, Infant; female; parents: Ralph YOUNG (North Carolina) and Catherine ALBERTSON (North Carolina); death cause: "stillborn"; informant: father (Erwin); died: 22 May 1920; buried: Jobe Cemetery; record (1920) # 431.

TINKER, Infant; male; parents: Charley TINKER and Rousa TIPTON; death cause: "stillborn"; informant: Amanda TIPTON (Kittyton); died: 28 May 1920; buried: Tilson Cemetery; record (1920) # 432.

DUNKLEBURGER, Mabel Leone; born: 1 Dec. 1919; parents: A.C. DUNKLEBURGER (Indiana) and Addie B. FOREMAN (Kansas);

death cause: "cholera infantum"; informant: father (Erwin); died: 1 Jun. 1920; buried; Jobe Cemetery; record (1920) # 433.

PIERCY, Hattie; born: 13 Apr. 1876 in Yancey County, NC.; married; parents: Jeff BAILEY (Yancey County) and Emaline EDWARDS (Washington County); death cause: "childbirth, hemorrhage"; informant: Hubert PIERCY (Unicoi); died: 3 Jun. 1920; buried: Peterson Cemetery; record (1920) # 434.

WHITE, Emma Erwin; born: 9 Dec. 1859 in Washington County; widow; parents: Jessie B. ERWIN (Washington County) and Elizabeth MCMAHAN (North Carolina); death cause: "apoplexy"; informant: L.D. SCRUGGS (Erwin); died: 8 Jun. 1920; buried: Jobe Cemetery; record (1920) # 435.

BUCHANAN, Elvira A.; born: 17 Jun. 1849 in McDowell County, NC.; divorced; parents: Charles M. LOWRY (North Carolina) and Elizabeth WHITBURN; death cause: "killed by a locomotive at Unicoi crossing"; died: 9 Jun. 1920; buried: Swingle Cemetery; record (192) # 436.

SNEYD, Blain; parents: Ed STEVENS and Samantha SNEYD; death cause: "stillborn"; died: 27 Jun. 1920; buried: Sneyd Cemetery; record (1920) # 437.

GOUGE, Georgia; born: 25 Dec. 1897; married; parents: Jasper CROWELL and Dora PEW; death cause: "influenza and pulmonary tuberculosis"; informant: Hoy GOUGE (Unicoi); died: 10 Jul. 1920; buried: family cemetery, Unicoi; record (1920) # 438.

WILLIAMS, Ernest; born: 4 Oct. 1919; parents: Hiram WILLIAMS (North Carolina) and Nita LOVELACE; death cause: "unknown"; informant: father (Erwin); died: 27 Jul. 1920; buried: Martins Creek; record (192) # 439.

EDWARDS, Fred; born: 4 Jul. 1920; parents: Fred EDWARDS and Sara (?) SNEYD; death cause: "stillborn"; informant: Emeline HYDER (Hampton, Tennessee); died: 11 Jul. 1920; buried: Birchfield Cemetery; record (1920) # 440.

WOODBY, Bertie; parents: John WOODBY and Lydia DAVIS; death cause: "stillborn"; informant: father (Unicoi); died: 1 Jul. 1920; buried: Woodby Cemetery; record (1920) # 441.

CASEY, Clifton; born: 8 Mar. 1913; parents: Joe CASEY and Mollie ROGERS; death cause: "indigestion"; informant: father (Embreeville); died: 1 Aug. 1920; buried: Cove Cemetery; record (1920) # 442.

HUGHES, Rebecca; age: 63 years; born: Relief, North Carolina; marital status; not stated; parents: David HUGHES (North Carolina) and Eliza BRYANT (North Carolina); death cause: "pleurisy"; informant: Charles GRIFFITH (Erwin); died: 3 Aug. 1920; buried: Relief, North Carolina; record (1920) # 443.

TITTLE, Addie; born: 3 Jun. 1919; parents: Walter TITTLE and Lucy MATHES; death cause; "cholera infantum"; informant: father (Unicoi); died: 8 Aug. 1920; buried: Martins Creek; record (1920) # 444.

O'BRIEN, Emma; born: 1 May 1893 in West Virginia; married; parents: Eben __ (illegible) (West Virginia) and Jane LUTS (West Virginia); death cause: "appendicitis, peritonitis"; informant: Charles O'Brien; died: 10 Aug. 1920; buried: East Liverpool, Ohio; record (1920) # 445.

TUCKER, Paul Lewis; born: 19 Oct. 1903; parents: J.L. TUCKER and Mamey TONEY; death cause: "sarcoma"; informant: father (Erwin); died: 11 Aug. 1920; record (1920) # 446.

HARRIS, Siddie Pearl; born: 14 Aug. 1919; parents: J.L. HARRIS and Francis SMITH; death cause: "dysentery"; informant: father (Erwin); died: 20 Aug. 1920; buried: Martins Creek; record (1920) # 447.

RAY, Claude; born: 23 Aug. 1918; parents: father not stated and Sirelda RAY; death cause: "fits"; informant: Faye SHELTON (Flag Pond); died: 22 Aug. 1920; buried: Ray Cemetery; record (1920) # 448.

PATE, Margaret; born: 20 Mar. 1894; divorced; parents: James RAMSEY (North Carolina) and Hassaltine BOYD (North Carolina); death cause: "pulmonary tuberculosis"; informant: Elizabeth RAMSEY (Flag Pond); died: 24 Aug. 1920; buried: Ramsey Cemetery; record (1920) # 449.

BAILY, Rosy; parents: Ed BAILY (North Carolina) and Pollie DAVIS; death cause: "stillborn"; informant: J.A. HARDIN (Unicoi); died: 21 Aug. 1920; buried: Davis Cemetery; record (1920) # 450.

MCLAUGHLIN, Wilder; parents: William MCLAUGHLIN and Pearl SMITH (Mitchell County, NC.); death cause: "stillborn"; informant: father (Unicoi); died: 24 Aug. 1920; buried; Peterson Cemetery; record (1920) # 451.

OXENDINE, Rosa Eveline; born: 13 May 1919; parents: Luther OXENDINE and Rosetta KITTS; death cause: "meningitis and dysentery"; informant: L.D. KITTS (Maynardsville); died: 5 Sep. 1920; buried: Cove cemetery; record (1920) # 452.

BLEVINS, Alfred, Sr.; age: 67 years; married; parents: Walter BLEVINS and Mary HENSLEY; death cause: "dropsy"; informant: Muncy PHILLIPS (Embreeville); died: 5 Sep. 1920; buried: Cove Cemetery; record (1920) # 453.

LAWING, Stanley; born: 22 Apr. 1900; married; parents: J.B. LAWING and Julina GUINN; death cause: "infection following a bruise"; informant: father (Erwin); died: 6 Sep. 1920; buried; Martins Creek; record (1920) # 454.

WILSON, Garfield; born: 4 Mar. 1919; parents: Mart WILSON and Elmira MCINTOSH; death cause: "spinal trouble"; informant: S.J. MCINTOSH (Kittyton); died: 8 Sep 1920; buried: Mount. Pleasant; record (1920) # 455.

BROYLES, Mrs. John; born: 6 May 1854; age: 66 years, 4 months and 2 days; born: Georgia; widow; parents: Jacob ELDRIDGE (Georgia) and mother not stated; death cause: "brights disease"; informant: Frank E. BROYLES (Erwin); died: 8 Sep. 1920; record (1920) # 456.

TIPTON, Charles Sherman; age: illegible; single; parents: J.H. TIPTON and Nancy BARNET (Carter County); death cause: "gastro catarrh"; informant: Paul S. KINNING (Johnson City); died: 12 Sep. 1920; record (1920) # 457.

EDWARDS, Joseph B.; born: 17 May 1860; married; parents: Howell EDWARDS (North Carolina) and Jane HENSLEY (North Carolina); death cause: "flux and dysentery"; informant: Lula EDWARDS (Kittyton); died: 15 Sep. 1920; buried: Hensley Cemetery; record # 458.

EDWARDS, Ester; age: 67 years; widow; parents: Isaac POORE and mother not stated; death cause: "heart disease"; informant: William EDWARDS (Erwin); died: 15 Sep. 1920; record (1920) # 459.

BOONE, Grace; born: 4 Feb. 1892 in North Carolina; married; parents: Thomas GIBBS (North Carolina) and Molly WILSON (North Carolina); death cause: "childbirth"; informant: Paul BOONE (Erwin); died: 23 Sep. 1920; record (1920) # 460.

103

STAFFORD, Harry Jack; born: 1 Apr. 1916; parents: B.H. STAFFORD (Virginia) and Anna Clyde G_ (illegible); death cause: "accidental gunshot wound in stomach"; informant: father (Erwin); died: 26 Sep. 1920; record (1920) # 461.

BUCHANAN, Clarence; born: 2 Dec. 1913 in Mitchell County, NC.; parents: A. BUCHANAN (Mitchell County) and Mollie EDWARDS (Mitchell County); death cause: "obstruction of bowels"; informant: Are BUCHANAN (Erwin); died; 27 Sep. 1920; buried: Jobe cemetery; record (1920) # 462.

SHUTLER, Infant; male; parents: Dan N. SHUTLER and Maggie BLEVINS; death cause: "stillborn"; informant: father (Erwin); died: 6 Sep. 1920; buried: Martins Creek; record (1920) # 463.

WOODWARD, Infant; male; parents: father not stated and Mary Jane WOODWARD; death cause: "miscarriage"; informant: J.B. WOODWARD (Flag Pond); died: 17 Sep. 1920; buried: Tilson Cemetery; record (1920) # 464.

BOONE, Infant: female; parents: Paul BOONE (North Carolina) and Grace GIBBS (North Carolina); death cause: "stillborn"; informant: father (Erwin); died: 22 Sep. 1920; buried: Jobe Cemetery; record (1920) # 465.

HOPSON, Paul; born: 3 Feb. 1917 in North Carolina; parents: M. HOPSON (North Carolina) and Stella WOMACK (North Carolina); death cause: "dysentery"; informant: father (Erwin); died: 4 Oct. 1920; record (1920) # 466.

MILLER, Arther; born: 15 Aug. 1920; parents: Sam MILLER (North Carolina) and Lizzie BOWMAN; death cause: "hives"; informant: father (Erwin); died: 9 Oct. 1920; buried: Jobe Cemetery; record (1920) # 467.

FORD, Robert Joseph; born: 12 May 1920 in West Virginia; parents: George FORD (Pennsylvania) and Ermer RILEY (West Virginia); death cause: "unknown, found dead in bed"; informant: father (Erwin); died: 20 Oct. 1920; record (1920) # 468.

SHULL, Francis Ellen; born: 4 Feb. 1841 in Virginia; widow; parents: Hewy DEAN (Virginia) and Ellen WALL (Virginia); death cause: "old age"; informant: G.F. SHULL (Erwin); died: 21 Oct. 1920; buried: Winchester. Virginia; record (1920) # 469.

GILLIS, Orville; born: 12 Jan. 1920; parents: William L. GILLIS and Vivian BARNES; death cause: "diphtheria"; died: 24 Oct. 1920; record (1920) # 470.

FURCHES, Nancy; born: 2 May 1882 in North Carolina; married; parents: Garth ENGLE and mother not stated; death cause: "blood poison following operation for appendicitis"; informant: W.F. FURCHES (Erwin); died: 28 Oct. 1920; buried: Martins Creek; record (1920) # 471.

BOONE, Infant; male; parents: Sam BOONE (North Carolina) and Irene WALTERS (Pennsylvania); death cause: "stillborn"; informant: father (Erwin); died: 14 Oct. 1920; buried: Jobe Cemetery; record # 472.

PHILIPS, Carson; born: 18 Jan. 1872 in Madison County, NC.; married; parents: Jack PHILIPS (North Carolina) and Matilda PHILIPS (North Carolina); death cause: "typhoid fever"; informant: Thomas PETERSON (English, NC.); died: 7 Nov.1920; buried; English, North Carolina; record (1920) # 473.

HENSLEY, Barnet; born: _ May 1848; age: 72 years; married; parents: Armstrong HENSLEY (North Carolina) and mother not stated; death cause: "accidental by falling tree"; informant: R.C. HENSLEY (Kittyton); died: 8 Nov. 1920; buried; Edwards Cemetery; record # 474.

BOWMAN, Lillian Virginia; born: 29 Nov. 1919 in Bakerfield, North Carolina; parents: James CAROL (Monroe, Canada) and Cleda BOWMAN (Johnson City); death cause: "stomach trouble and teething"; informant: Lee BOWMAN (Erwin); died: 9 Nov. 1920; buried: Okalona Cemetery; record (1920) # 475.

HENLEY, Rose; age: 28 years; single; parents: Charlie HENLEY (Washington County) and Mary POORE (Washington County); death cause: "appendicitis and gangrene"; informant: Paul K. KEPLINGER (Jonesboro); died: 10 Nov. 1920; buried; Jonesboro; record # 476.

BRITTON, Cauthus; female; born: 26 Sep. 1860; married; parents: Thomas ROBINSON and Mary Ann MOSER; death cause: "diabetes"; informant: M.M. ROBINSON (Jackson, Tennessee); died: 11 Nov. 1920; buried: Johnson City; record (1920) # 477.

GARLAND, Infant; male; parents: David GARLAND and Lurla PATTON; death cause: "7 month infant"; informant: father (Unicoi); born/died: 12 Nov. 1920; buried: Woodby Cemetery; record # 478.

HARRIS, Richard Pinkson; born: 16 Apr. 1855 in Washington County; married; parents: Hugh HARRIS and Elizabeth HENSLEY; death cause: "heart disease"; informant: Jason HARRIS (Erwin); died: 13 Nov. 1920; record (1920) # 479.

GARRETT, Infant; female; parents: James GARRETT and Susan PELINGS (?); death cause: "malnutrition"; died: 20 Nov. 1920; buried: Anderson Cemetery; record (1920) # 480.

BRUMMETT, Samuel; parents: Samuel BRUMMETT and Ethel WHITE; death cause: "premature birth"; born/died: 24 Nov. 1920; buried: Soistra; record (1920) # 481.

BRUMMETT, Ethel; parents: Samuel BRUMMETT and Ethel WHITE; death cause: "premature birth"; born/died: 24 Nov. 1920; buried: Soistra; record (1920) # 482.

HARRIS, John; age: 49 years; married; parents: Harrison HARRIS and Jude BANNER; death cause: "dysentery"; informant: J.W. HOWELL (Erwin); died: 2 Dec. 1920; buried: Martins Creek; record (1920) # 483.

SHULLAND, Hobert; age: 11 months; parents: Melvin SHULLAND and mother's name illegible; death cause: "whooping cough"; died: 12 Dec. 1920; record (1920) # 484.

KENEDY, Linnie; born: 21 Sep. 1838 in North Carolina; widow; parents: William SELF (North Carolina); and mother not stated; death cause: "old age and kidney trouble"; informant: C.A. KENEDY (Embreeville); died: 19 Dec. 1920; buried: Morganton, North Carolina; record # 485.

JEWELL, Robert; born: 19 Dec. 1920; parents: Charley JEWELL and Lola May ANDERS; death cause: "premature birth"; informant: father (Erwin); died: 22 Dec. 1920; buried: Martins Creek; record # 486.

EDWARDS, Dessie; born: 6 Mar. 1918; parents: George EDWARDS and Celia JONES; death cause: not stated; informant: Estell BLANKENSHIP (Kittyton); died: 22 Dec. 1920; buried: Sams Creek; record (1920) # 487.

CARTER, John Henry; born: 6 Aug. _; age: 61 years, 4 months and 22 days; divorced; parents: William CARTER and Jane BRIGGS; death cause: "homicide, shot"; informant: Minta CARTER (Flag Pond); died: 23 Dec. 1920; buried: Carter Farm; record (1920) # 488.

PHILLIP, Bertha May; born: 15 May 1901 in North Carolina; single; parents: W.W. PHILLIP (North Carolina) and Mary FOSTER (?)

(North Carolina); death cause: illegible; informant: father (Erwin); died: 24 Dec. 1920; buried: Red Hill, North Carolina; record (1920) # 489.

HESTER, Roy; born: 8 Dec. 1920; parents: George HESTER (Wilkes County, NC.) and Emeline CAMPBELL; death cause: not stated; informant: father (Unicoi); died: 26 Dec. 1920; buried: Baker Cemetery; record (1920) # 490.

HARRIS, Jane; age: 79 years; born: North Carolina; widow; parents: Ezekiel HONEYCUTT (North Carolina) and Mary BAILEY (North Carolina); death cause: "dropped dead"; died in the 5th District, 29 Dec. 1920; record (1920) # 491.

CARVER, Polly; age: 72 years; born: North Carolina; widow; parents: Obediah BUTLER and mother not stated; death cause: "anemia and neuralgia"; informant: Joe CARVER (Unicoi); died: 5 Jan. 1921; buried: Peterson Cemetery; record (1921) # 301.

SHELTON, Elvira; born: 5 Jul. 1833 in Yancey County, NC.; widow; parents: Joe HUGHES (North Carolina ?) and Emiline BENNETT (North Carolina); death cause: "old age"; informant: Lizzie WATTS (Kittyton); died: 6 Jan. 1921; buried: Hensley Cemetery; record # 302.

RUNION, Ruth G.; born: 16 Nov. 1920; parents: David RUNION (West Virginia) and Francis __ (illegible) (Virginia); death cause: "bold hives"; informant: father (Erwin); died: 6 Jan. 1921; buried: Jobe Cemetery; record (1921) # 303.

MASHBURN, Malinda; born: 10 Jan. 1851 in Washington County; married; parents: Samuel HIGGINS (Washington County) and Lizzie HIGGINS (Washington County); death cause: "dropsy"; informant: John MASHBURN (Flag Pond); died: 10 Jan. 1921; buried: Higgins Chapel; record (1921) # 304.

HARRIS, Allice; born: 30 Jul. 1920; parents: __ (illegible) HARRIS and Flossie LAWING; death cause: "pertusis and pneumonia"; died at Flag Pond, 12 Jan. 1921; record (1921) # 305.

NORRIS, Nannie A.; born: 12 Sep. 1845 in Carter County; single; parents: Richard HARRIS (Washington County) and Sindy MCINTURFF (Carter County); death cause: "pneumonia"; informant: W.A. MCINTURFF (Erwin); died in the 11th District, 15 Jan. 1921; record (1921) # 306.

EDWARDS, Elizabeth: born: 16 Apr. 1881; married; parents: John JONES and Elizabeth WHALEY; death cause: "brights disease"; informant: Frank EDWARDS (Erwin); died: 23 Jan. 1921; buried: Fishery Cemetery; record (1921) # 307.

LANE, Marie; born: 12 Jul. 1920; parents: J.A. LANE and Lula B. CASEY (Virginia); death cause: "unknown, found dead in bed"; informant: G.B. CASEY (Erwin); died: 28 Jan. 1921; buried: Piney Flats, Tennessee; record (1921) # 308.

MCINTURFF, Infant: male; parents: James MCINTURFF and Mattie HENSON; death cause: "stillborn, mother fell"; informant: father (Unicoi); died: 1 Jan. 1921; buried: home cemetery; record # 309.

BOGART, Infant; male; parents: Charles BOGART and Gertrude CASH (Georgia); death cause: "stillborn"; informant: father (Erwin); died: 14 Jan. 1921; buried: Martins Creek; record (1921) # 310.

RAMSEY, Infant; male; born: 1 Feb. 1921; parents; Will RAMSEY and Beca PRICE; death cause: not stated; informant: Jim PRICE (Kittyton); died: 2 Feb. 1921; buried: Ramsey Cemetery; record (1921) # 311.

COOPER, Neuona (?); female; born: 26 Jun. 1877 in Mitchell County, NC.; married; parents: John TIPTON (Virginia) and C_ (illegible) PETERSON (Yancey County, NC.); death cause: "septicemia, tonsillitis"; informant: Sam COOPER (Erwin); died: 8 Feb. 1921; buried: Martins Creek; record (1921) # 312/

RICE, Lu Case; female; born: 18 Dec. 1920; parents: Marion RICE and Cordelia CODA; death cause: "whooping cough"; informant: father (Flag Pond); died: 9 Feb. 1921; record (1921) # 313.

PATE, Eddie Burton; born: 28 Jun. 1920; parents: Milton PATE (North Carolina) and Brigette MATHUS; death cause: "pertusis and pneumonia"; informant: D.S. GILLIS (Flag Pond); died: 10 Feb. 1921; buried: Pate Farm; record (1921) # 314.

BIDDIX, Cordie; born: 20 Jan. 1921; parents: Arthur BIDDIX (North Carolina) and Mabel MCBEE (North Carolina); death cause: "unknown, found dead in bed"; informant: father (Erwin); died: 12 Feb. 1921; record (1921) # 315.

CLAYTON, Edna; born: 5 Dec. 1912; parents: Odis P. CLAYTON (Caldwell County, NC.) and Eriasey FRAZIER (Mitchell County, NC.);

death cause: "blood poison"; died: 16 Feb. 1921; buried: Martins Creek; record (1921) # 316.

SIMMONS, William Harry; born: 31 May 1918; parents: Will SIMMONS and Martha CLAUSE; death cause: "pneumonia"; informant: father (Erwin); died: 20 Feb. 1921; buried: Jobe Cemetery; record (1921) # 317.

MCKAY, Josie; born: 10 Mar. 1848; single; parents: James MCKAY and Mary NICKLAS; death cause: "lesion of heart"; informant: C.L. HARRISON (Erwin); died: 22 Feb. 1921; buried: Jobe Cemetery; record (1921) # 318.

HAMPTON, Laurie; born: 15 Feb. 1919; parents: W.S. HAMPTON and Gertie TIPTON; death cause: "lobar pneumonia"; informant: father (Erwin); died: 26 Feb. 1921; buried: Martins Creek; record # 319.

GILBERT, Edward Floyd; born: 17 Apr. 1919; parents: Carl R. GILBERT and Melda TINKER; death cause: "lobar pneumonia"; informant: father (Erwin); died: 27 Feb. 1921; buried: Martins Creek; record (1921) # 320.

RAY, Thomas; born: 1 Mar. 1845; age: 76 years; born: North Carolina; widower; Civil War veteran; parents: Stephen RAY (North Carolina) and Nancy REESE (North Carolina); death cause: not stated; informant: R.A. RAY (Flag Pond); died: 2 Mar. 1921; buried: Ray Cemetery; record (1921) # 321.

WHITE, Will W.; born: 18 Jan. 1897; married; parents: Daniel WHITE and Elizabeth WHITE; death cause: "diabetes"; informant: C.C. WHITE (Erwin); died: 2 Mar. 1921; buried: Johnson City; record (1921) # 322.

BUTLER, Mary Jane; born: 18 __ 1851 (month not stated); age: 71 years; widow; parents: Ashley MORGAN and Betsy WHITEHEAD (Carter County); death cause: not stated; informant: W.J. SLAGEL (Unicoi); died: 8 Mar 1921; buried: Magnetic, North Carolina; record (1921) # 323.

TILSON, Eva May; born: 16 Feb. 1921; parents: William TILSON and Barbey TAYLOR (North Carolina); death cause: not stated; informant: Frank GUINN (Kittyton); died: 12 Mar. 1921; buried: Clear Branch; record (1921) # 324.

CAPPS, William Manual; born: 16 Mar 1842; age: 78 years, 11 months and 22 days; born: North Carolina; married; parents: John CAPPS and mother unknown; death cause: "heart disease"; informant: M.R. CAPPS (Erwin); died: 12 Mar. 1921; record (1921) # 325.

MEEK (?), Elizabeth Jane; age: 81 years and 6 months; widow; parents: J.H. WALKER (Virginia) and Louisa CLARKSON; death cause: "paralysis"; died: 15 Mar. 1921; buried: Knoxville, Tennessee; record (1921) # 326.

DIXON, William Henry; age: 73 years, 2 months and 21 days; married; parents: father unknown (born East Tennessee) and R_ (illegible) DIXON; death cause: "cancer of stomach"; informant: J.C. DIXON (Bluefield, West Virginia); died: 18 Mar. 1921; buried: Milligan, Tennessee; record (1921) # 327.

GALLOWAY, Maude; born: 10 Jun. 1895 in Pike County, Kentucky; married; parents: R.N. MCINTURFF (Carter County) and Ida L. TIMBERLAKE (Fayette County, Tennessee); death cause: "brights disease"; informant: father (Erwin); died: 21 Mar. 1921; record # 328.

CARVER, John William; born: 2 Oct. 1920; parents: Doc CARVER (Mitchell County, NC.) and Berthie HILL (Mitchell County, NC.); death cause: "bronchitis"; died: 26 Mar. 1921; buried: Peterson Cemetery; record (1921) # 329.

BOONE, Zeb Vance; born: 25 Apr. 1878 in Burnsville, North Carolina; married; blacksmith; parents: J.S. BOONE (Burnsville) and Emely RAY (Burnsville); death cause: "erysipelas of head"; informant: H.P. BOONE (Johnson City); died: 27 Mar. 1921; buried: Jobe Cemetery; record (1921) # 330.

BAILEY, Texie; born: 22 Jul. 1908 in North Carolina; parents: Don BAILEY (North Carolina) and Lida CONLEY (North Carolina); death cause: "abscessed appendix"; died: 31 Mar. 1921; buried: North Carolina; record (1921) # 331.

GALLOWAY, Edna Leah; parents: Joseph H. GALLOWAY (Washington County) and Mande MCINTURFF (Pike County, Kentucky); death cause: "stillborn"; informant: father (Erwin); died: 7 Mar. 1921; buried: Jobe Cemetery; record (1921) # 332.

GUINN, infant; female; parents: Orville GUINN and Maud FOSTER; death cause: "stillborn"; died; 8 Mar. 1921; buried: Clear Branch; record (1920) # 333.

JOHNSON, Enylu (?); female; born: 10 Sep. 1920; parents: Jake JOHNSON (North Carolina) and Carry TAYLOR (North Carolina); death cause: "double pneumonia"; died in the 5th District, 7 Apr. 1921; record (1921) # 334.

MCINTURFF, Walter; born: 5 Jan. 1896; married; parents: D.J. MCINTURFF and Mary TONEY; death cause: "testiary syphilis"; informant: Maggie WHITTAMORE (Johnson City); died: 15 Apr. 1921; buried: Unicoi; record (1921) # 335.

BARNETT, Marie; born: 17 May 1917 in North Carolina; parents: Marion BARNETT (North Carolina) and Ellen MILLER (North Carolina); death cause: "dysentery"; informant: S.E. BARNETT (Erwin); died: 19 Apr. 1921; record (1921) # 336.

HARRIS, Patty; age: 70 years; born: North Carolina; married; parents: Jason HARRIS and Nancy HENSLEY; death cause: "pellagra"; informant: Jim HARRIS (Erwin); died: 22 Apr. 1921; buried; Fishery Cemetery; record (1921) # 337.

COOPER, M_ (illegible; born: 17 Dec. 1893 in North Carolina; marital status: not stated; parents: Sam COOPER (North Carolina) and Jane _ (illegible); death cause: "shot in bowels, hemorrhage"; informant: father (Erwin); died: 25 Apr. 1921; buried: Martins Creek; record # 338.

CAMPBELL, Allice; born: 16 May 1877; married; parents: James STOUT and Ellen CAMPBELL; death cause: "dropsy"; informant: James CAMPBELL (Unicoi); died: 28 Apr. 1921; buried: Campbell Cemetery; record (1921) # 339.

HARVEY, Mary Francis; born: 8 Aug. 1920; parents: Bob HARVEY and Lillian ANDERSON; death cause: "pneumonia and whooping cough"; informant: father (Erwin); died: 29 Apr. 1921; record # 340.

HENSLEY, Infant; male; parents: Walter HENSLEY and Stella SHELTON (North Carolina); death cause: "stillborn"; informant: Elizer HENSLEY (Flag Pond); died: 1 Apr. 1921; buried: Hensley Cemetery; record (1921) # 341.

PICKERING, Infant; female; parents: Robert PICKERING and Betty A. LANE; death cause: "stillborn"; informant: father (Erwin); died: 10 Apr. 1921; buried: Jobe Cemetery; record (1921) # 342.

CLOUSE, Infant; sex: not stated; parents: Groar CLOUSE and Orpha WILLIS; death cause: "stillborn"; died: 29 Apr. 1921; record # 343.

MILLER, Infant; male; parents: Nat MILLER (North Carolina) and Lizzie SNEYD; death cause: "stillborn"; informant: Robert HYDER (Hampton, Tennessee); died: 21 Apr. 1921; buried: Hyder Cemetery; record (1921) # 344.

MASTERS, Nancy A.; born: 11 Mar. 1836 in Virginia; widow; parents: father not stated and Polly EALEM (Virginia); death cause: "brights disease"; informant: Maggie E. MASTERS (Erwin); died: 1 May 1921; buried: Martins Creek; record (1921) # 345.

LOWE, Sinda Tipton; born: 16 Feb. 1891; married; parents: A.B. TIPTON (North Carolina) and Hester JOHNSON (Carter County); death cause: "pulmonary tuberculosis"; informant: M.C. TIPTON (Unicoi); died: 8 May 1921; buried: Tipton Cemetery; record # 346.

BARNETT, Henry; born: 5 Apr. 1880 in North Carolina; widower; parents: Isaac BARNETT (North Carolina) and Susan WILLIAMS (North Carolina); death cause: "homicide, gunshot wound"; informant: father (Unicoi); died: 9 May 1921; buried: Buchanan Cemetery; record (1921) # 347.

CHURCH, Katherin; age: 78 years; born: North Carolina; married; parents: __ GREENFIELD and Kate GREENFIELD (North Carolina); death cause: "heart disease"; informant: Larkin CHURCH (Unicoi); died: 12 May 1921; buried: Peoples Cemetery; record (1921) # 348.

BOONE, Mary; age: 54 years; born: North Carolina; married; parents: Robert MCINTOSH (North Carolina) and Emma ANGLER (North Carolina); death cause: "cancer of stomach"; informant: Sam BOONE (Erwin); died: 13 May 1921; buried: Burnsville, North Carolina; record (1921) # 349.

HARRIS, Maud; age: 27 years; married; parents: Elbert LAWING and Fannie PATE (Virginia); death cause: "post partum hemorrhage"; died in the 5th District, 20 May 1921; record (1921) # 350.

PEAK, Helen Boone; born: 20 Mar. 1921; parents: Rube PEAK (Yancey County, NC.) and Mollie HENSLEY (Yancey County, NC.); death cause: "acute indigestion"; informant: G.B. HENSLEY (Erwin); died: 21 May 1921; buried: Martins Creek; record (1921) # 351.

HARRIS, Archlene; born: 14 May 1921; parents: Jake HARRIS and Maud LAWING; death cause: "unknown"; informant: father (Erwin); died: 24 May 1921; buried: Martins Creek; record (1921) # 352.

WATTS, Silas; age: 50 years; born: North Carolina; married; parents: Anderson WATTS (North Carolina) and Vira HENSLEY (North Carolina); death cause: "just fell dead"; died: 26 May 1921; buried: North Carolina; record (1921) # 353.

BARNETT, Martha; born: 12 May 1921; parents: James BARNETT (North Carolina) and Rosetta MILLER; death cause: "unknown"; informant: father (Erwin); died: 27 May 1921; buried: Jobe Cemetery; record (1921) # 354.

CROW, Charlie Lee; born: 16 May 1919; parents: Marshall CROW and Maude KEENER; death cause: "tubercular meningitis"; informant: W.C. BIRCHFIELD (Erwin); died: 28 May 1921; buried: Jobe Cemetery; record (1921) # 355.

COLEMAN, Roy; parents: Will COLEMAN and Elizabeth BRUMMETT; death cause: "premature birth, lived 4 hours"; born/died: 29 May 1921; buried: Brummett Cemetery; record (1921) # 356.

PARSLEY, Victoria; born: 2 Aug. 1992 in Moher, West Virginia; married; parents: James MAYNARD and Susan DAVIS; death cause: "puerperal eclampsia"; informant: Thomas J. PARSLEY (Erwin); died: 29 May 1921; buried: McInturff Cemetery; record (1921) # 357.

MCVEY, Sarah Jane; born: 17 Sep. 1919; parents: Silas MCVEY (Mitchell County, NC.) and Dela JOHNAS (Mitchell County, NC.); death cause: "dysentery"; informant: mother (Erwin); died: 30 May 1921; buried: Martins Creek; record (1921) # 358.

FORD, Sara Rosa; born: 26 Dec. 1869; married; parents: Isaac HORTON (Virginia) and Margaret DAVIS; death cause: "exopthalmic goiter"; informant: R.E.L. FORD (Erwin); died: 30 May 1921; buried: Jobe Cemetery; record (1921) # 359.

DAVIS, Elizabeth; born: 7 Aug. 1820; age: 101 years, 9 months and 29 days; born: Tennessee; widow; parents: Michel FRY (Germany) and Susey BURNS (Germany); death cause: not stated; informant: David

113

CAMPBELL (Unicoi); died: 31 May 1921; buried; Fry Cemetery; record (1921) # 360.

PARSLEY, Vivian Pearl; parents: T.J. PARSLEY (Kentucky) and Victoria MAYNARD (Moher, West Virginia); death cause: "stillborn"; informant: Thomas J. PARSLEY (Erwin); died: 29 May 1921; buried: McInturff Cemetery; record (1921) # 361.

TIPTON, James Oscar; born: 14 Feb. 1913; parents: John D. TIPTON and Maggie RUNION; death cause: "dengue"; informant: father (Erwin); died: 6 Jun. 1921; buried: Jobe Cemetery; record (1921) # 362.

BARR, Florence Virginia; born: 22 Jan. 1910 (?) in Georgia; parents: W.E. CAMPBELL (Georgia) and Mandy MASSEY (Georgia); death cause: "heart disease"; informant: W.M. BARR (Erwin); died: 6 Jun. 1921; buried: Martins Creek; record (1921) # 363.

PAGGET, Charlie; born: 28 May 1921; parents: Geter BARNETT (North Carolina) and Dasie PAGGET (Washington County); death cause: "premature birth"; died: 9 Jun. 1921; buried: Embreeville; record (1921) # 364.

TIPTON, Harrison; born: 12 Jun. 1921; parents: M.C. TIPTON (North Carolina) and Elizabeth G_ (illegible) (North Carolina); death cause: not stated; informant: father (Unicoi); died: 13 Jun. 1921; record # 365.

CAMPBELL, Dorris; born: 23 Jan. 1921; parents: William CAMPBELL (Virginia) and Sara LITTERFORD; death cause: "dysentery"; informant: father (Erwin); died: 15 Jun. 1921; record (1921) # 366.

RUNNION, Louise; adopted child; age: 2 months; parents: David RUNNION (West Virginia) and Florence _ (illegible) (Virginia); death cause: "unknown"; informant: father (Erwin); died: 15 Jun. 1921; buried: Jobe Cemetery; record (1921) # 367.

COGGINS, Charlie; born: 4 May 1902; single; parents: Will COGGINS (North Carolina) and Minnie MILLER (North Carolina); death cause: "accidentally drowned"; informant: father (Erwin); died: 26 Jun. 1921; buried: Martins Creek; record (1921) # 368.

BEAN (?), Kate; born: 2 Dec. 1835 in Tennessee; widow; parents: Samuel ERWIN and Mary PARKS (?); death cause: "nephritis"; died in the 7th District, 28 Jun. 1921; record (1921) # 369.

MORGAN, Elna Woods; parents: C. MORGAN (North Carolina) and Bessie WOODS; death cause: "stillborn"; informant: John C. MORGAN (Erwin); died: 16 Jun. 1921; record (1921) # 370.

HENSLEY, Banner; age: 24 years; born: North Carolina; married; parents: Reuben HENSLEY (North Carolina) and Eliza SHELTON (North Carolina); death cause: "2 gunshot wounds, homicide"; informant: Ike SHELTON (Flag Pond); died: 2 Jul. 1921; buried: Shelton Cemetery; record (1921) # 371.

SHEHAN, Albert; born: 18 Aug. 1891; age: 30 years, 10 months and 14 days; born: North Carolina; parents: father not stated and Bessie E. SHEHAN (North Carolina); death cause: "tuberculosis"; informant: Ethel SHEHAN (Erwin); died: 2 Jul. 1921; buried: Martins Creek; record (1921) # 372.

ILLEGIBLE, female; born: 9 Nov. 1832; born: Washington County; widow; parents: Jesse BROWN (Virginia) and Elizabeth WAKEFIELD (North Carolina); death cause: "liver disease"; died: in the 5th District, 4 Jul. 1921; record (1921) # 373.

HAUN, R.L.; born: 11 Mar. 1846; married; parents: George HAUN and Elizabeth HONEYCUTT (North Carolina); death cause: "nephritis"; informant: Julia HAUN (Erwin); died: 8 Jul. 1921; buried: family cemetery; record (1921) # 374.

LEWIS, Audie; born: 20 Oct. 1917; parents: Mallie LEWIS (North Carolina) and Mary HENSLEY; death cause: "flux"; died: 7 Jul. 1921; buried: Hensley Cemetery; record (1921) # 375.

HUFFINE, Franklin Taylor; born: 10 Aug. 1917; parents: John HUFFINE and Lee BAYLESS; death cause: "dysentery"; informant: Frank HENSLEY (Jonesboro); died: 7 Jul. 1921; record (1921) # 376.

ROBERTS, Velma; born: 14 Aug. 1920 in North Carolina; parents: John ROBERTS and Dora BUCHANAN; death cause: "colitis"; died: 9 Jul. 1921; buried: Buchanan Cemetery; record (1921) # 377.

HILBERT (?), Mae; born: 30 Sep. 1897 in Franklin County, Illinois; widow; parents: Sherman MARTIN (Franklin County, IL.) and Catherine HICKS (Franklin County, IL.); death cause: "typhoid fever"; informant: S. DUNCAN (Erwin); died: 10 Jul. 1921; record # 378.

WHITE, Jesse; born: 3 Mar. 1864; married; parents: Lee WHITE (North Carolina) and Mary WOLFE (North Carolina); death cause: "railroad accident, head crushed"; informant: Hester WHITE (Erwin); died: 15 Jul. 1921; record (1921) # 379.

ROWMAN, Martha Carroll; age: 20 years; born: 7 Aug. _; married; parents: Edmon CARROLL and Emma WHITSON; death cause: "typhoid fever"; informant: William CARROLL (Unicoi); died: 18 Jul. 1921; buried: Carroll Cemetery; record (1921) # 380.

BRUMMETT, Roscoe; born: 3 Jan. 1896; single; parents: Thomas BRUMMETT (Carter County) and Anne BUCK (Carter County); death cause: "tuberculosis"; died: 25 Jul. 1921; buried: Brummett Cemetery; record (1921) # 381.

SMYER, Earl; born: 23 Apr. 1915 in Johnson City; parents: L.T. SMYER (Conover, North Carolina) and Addie V. SCOTT (Johnson City); death cause: "typhoid fever"; died: 28 Jul. 1921; buried: Jobe Cemetery; record (1921) # 382.

HENSLEY, Harry; parents: Wylie HENSLEY (Yancey County, NC.) and Vinetta WILSON (Madison County, NC.); death cause: "stillborn"; informant: mother (Kittyton); died: 15 Jul. 1921; record (1921) # 383.

SHELTON, Infant; female; parents: Ike SHELTON (North Carolina) and Dora C_ (illegible); informant: father (Flag Pond); died: 27 Jul. 1921; buried: Ray Cemetery; record (1921) # 384.

BARNETT, Jack; born: 31 Mar. 1921; parents: R.C. BARNETT (North Carolina) and Sarah LAWS (North Carolina); death cause: cholera infantum"; informant: R.L. LAWS (Erwin); died: 8 Aug. 1921; record (1921) # 385.

MCNABB, Annie Elizabeth; age: 10 years, 3 months and 1 day; parents: Grover S. MCNABB and Ella B. ERWIN; death cause: "accidental drowning"; informant: father (Erwin); died: 8 Aug. 1921; buried: Jobe Cemetery; record (1921) # 386.

OLLIS, Arther; born: 8 May 1914; parents: Tilman OLLIS (North Carolina) and Emma STALLING (North Carolina); death cause: "dysentery"; informant: father (Erwin); died: 11 Aug. 1921; buried: Martins Creek; record (1921) # 387.

HUGHES, Willie; born: 20 Nov. 1919; parents: Toma HUGHES and Dora HUGHES; death cause: "cholera infantum"; informant: father (Erwin); died: 13 Aug. 1921; buried: Martins Creek; record # 388.

WILLIAMS, Rex Frank; age: 34 years; parents: not stated; death cause: "killed in automobile wreck"; died: 16 Aug. 1921; buried: Morganton, North Carolina; record (1921) # 389.

LINVILLE, Minnie Ray; born: 1 Jul. 1921; parents: James LINVILLE and Nanie HUMPHREY (Carter County); death cause: not stated; informant: Henry HUMPHREY (Unicoi); died: 17 Aug. 1921; buried: Humphrey Cemetery; record (1921) # 390.

KIRK, Becky; age: 74 years; born: Washington County; widow; parents: _ (illegible) HAMPTON (North Carolina) and Katherine HAMPTON (North Carolina); death cause: "infection following an injury"; died in the 5th District, 21 Aug. 1921; buried: Rock Creek; record # 391.

TITTLE, Sam; born: 12 Jul. 1848; married; parents: John TITTLE and Nancy TITTLE; death cause: "intestinal nephritis"; informant: Charlie TITTLE (Erwin); died: 22 Aug. 1921; buried: Fishery Cemetery; record (1921) # 392.

AUSBIN, Hobert Lee; born: 14 Aug. 1921; parents: Hobert AUSBIN (Washington County, VA.) and Amanda TUGGLE (Russell County, VA.); death cause: illegible; died: 23 Aug. 1921; buried: McInturff Cemetery; record (1921) # 393.

JONES, Hoy; born: 17 Apr. 1910; parents: father not stated and Martha Ann JONES; death cause: "infection from accidental gunshot wound in abdomen"; died: 15 Aug. 1921; buried: Earnestville; record # 394.

WILLIAMS, Mable; born: 30 Apr. 1903 in North Carolina; single; parents: Millard WILLIAMS (North Carolina) and Ella HICKS (North Carolina); death cause: "pulmonary tuberculosis"; informant: father (Erwin); died: 28 Aug. 1921; buried: Jobe Cemetery; record # 395.

ELLIOTT, Walter Logue; born: 4 Nov. 1888 in North Carolina; married; locomotive engineer; parents: James O. ELLIOTT (North Carolina) and Jennie MORRISON (North Carolina); death cause: "typhoid fever"; informant: C.B. ELLIOTT (Union Mills, North Carolina); died: 2 Sep. 1921; buried: Statesville, North Carolina; record (1921) # 396.

LEONARD, Ralph; born: 11 Jul. 1921; parents: John LEONARD and Bashie BAILEY; death cause: "unknown, found dead in bed"; informant: father (Erwin); died: 4 Sep. 1921; buried: Jonesboro; record # 397.

GARLAND, Mynete; born: 21 Apr. 1903 in North Carolina; single; parents: A.G. GARLAND (North Carolina) and Adinie GRIFFITH

(North Carolina); death cause: "typhoid fever"; informant: father (Earnestville); died: 6 Sep. 1921; buried: Martins Creek; record # 398.

ROBINSON, Ethel Mae; born: 9 Apr. 1894; married; parents: J.B. LAWING and Jalinee GUINN; death cause: "__ (illegible) of ovaries"; informant: E.B. ROBINSON (Erwin); died: 7 Sep. 1921; buried: Martins Creek; record (1921) # 399.

FAGAN, Eliza; born: 16 Feb. 1836; parents: Sam MCCORKLE (Sullivan County) and Lucina COLBAUGH (Sullivan County); death cause: "ptomaine poison"; died: 9 Sep. 1921; buried: Fagan Cemetery; record (1921) # 400.

LIPE, William Feamster; born: 26 Feb. 1860 in Iredell County, North Carolina; married; parents: Abraham LIPE (Iredell County) and Sarah DEATON (Iredell County); death cause: "struck by motor car"; informant: Mrs. W.F. LIPE (Erwin); died: 10 Sep. 1921; buried: Jobe Cemetery; record (1921) # 401.

WHITE, Carrie Adlin; born: 11 Aug. 1921; parents: James W. WHITE and Phoebe HAMPTON; death cause: illegible; informant: father (Erwin); died: 12 Sep. 1921; buried: Martins Creek; record # 402.

BRITT, Isaac; age: "about 72 years"; born: Carter County; widower; parents: James BRITT (North Carolina) and Nancy UNDERWOOD (North Carolina); death cause: "obstruction of bowels"; died: 23 Sep. 1921; buried: Britt Cemetery; record (1921) # 403.

PATTERSON, Jack; born: 28 Jun. 1919; parents: J.C. PATTERSON (North Carolina) and Lula MCVAY (North Carolina); death cause: "diphtheria"; informant: father (Erwin); died: 28 Sep. 1921; buried: Martins Creek; record (1921) # 404.

GARLAND, Paulin; born: 8 Apr. 1914; parents: Stakes GARLAND (North Carolina) and Latten BROWN; death cause: "diphtheria"; died: 30 Sep. 1921; record (1921) # 405.

MCINTURFF, Infant; female; parents: Enos MCINTURFF and Julia TEAGUE; death cause: "stillborn"; informant: John TEAGUE (Unicoi); died: 30 Sep. 1921; buried: Garland Cemetery; record (1921) # 406.

BOONE, Infant; male; parents: Charles BOONE (North Carolina) and Lyda TUCKER (North Carolina); death cause: "stillborn"; informant: father (Erwin); died: 26 Sep. 1921; buried: Jobe Cemetery; record (1921) # 407.

HUSKINS, Ellie; age: 42 years; married; parents: L.H. GRIFFITH (North Carolina) and Mary BAILEY; death cause: "infection following childbirth"; informant: J. HUSKINS (Erwin); died: 1 Oct. 1921; buried: Martins Creek; record (1921) # 408.

WEST, William; age: 60 years; born: North Carolina; married; parents: James WEST (North Carolina) and Sarah ARRWOOD; death cause: "pulmonary tuberculosis"; informant: Burna WEST (Unicoi); died: 6 Oct. 1921; buried: Mosley Cemetery; record (1921) # 409.

BAKER, Mildred; born: 6 Oct. 1914; parents: Floyd BAKER (North Carolina) and Edgle BAILEY (North Carolina); death cause: "typhoid fever"; informant: father (Erwin); died: 8 Oct. 1921; buried: Jobe Cemetery; record (1921) # 410.

BARNETT, Elizabeth; age: 78 years; born: North Carolina; widow; parents: "unknown"; death cause: not stated; informant: R.D. JONES (Johnson City); died: 21 Oct. 1921; buried: Peoples Cemetery; record (1921) # 411.

HARRIS, William Harrison; born: 4 Aug. 1844 in Marion, North Carolina; married; parents: father unknown and Kissie HARRIS (Marion, North Carolina); death cause: "old age"; informant: J.F. HARRIS (Erwin); died in the 12th District, 6 Nov. 1921; record # 412.

HUNNICUTT, Martha C.; born; 10 Nov. _; age: 70 years, 11 months and 29 days; born: Yancey County, NC.; married; parents: Thomas BRYANT (Yancey County) and Elvira MCCURRY (Yancey County); death cause: "heart lesion"; informant: F.B. HUNNICUTT (Erwin); died: 8 Nov. 1921; buried: Jobe Cemetery; record (1921) # 413.

STRONG, John; age: 54 years; born: Virginia; married; parents: George STRONG and mother "unknown"; death cause: "asthma and lung hemorrhage"; informant: Ollie STRONG (Erwin); died: 12 Nov. 1921; record (1921) # 414.

WILLIAMS, Nellie Clo; born: 28 Mar. 1921; parents: W.T. WILLIAMS (Yancey County, NC.) and __ MCCURRY (Yancey County, NC.); death cause: "broncho pneumonia"; informant: father (Erwin); died: 13 Nov. 1921; buried: Martins Creek; record (1921) # 415.

DRYMAN, Olga; parents: C.F. DRYMAN (North Carolina) and Maggie SULLINS (North Carolina); death cause: "premature birth"; informant:

119

father (Erwin); born/died: 17 Nov. 1921; buried: Jobe Cemetery; record (1921) # 416.

THOMAS, Billie; age: 23 years; born: North Carolina; married; parents: Dempsy THOMAS (North Carolina) and Ester COOK (North Carolina); death cause: "tuberculosis"; informant: Maggie THOMAS (Erwin); died: 17 Nov. 1921; record (1921) # 417.

WARRICK, Mary Imogene; born: 21 May 1921; parents: Fredlen WARRICK (North Carolina) and Susie POTEAT (North Carolina); death cause: "hemorrhage from bowels"; informant: father (Erwin); died: 24 Nov. 1921; buried: Jobe Cemetery; record (1921) # 418.

WOHLFORD, Stacy Roetta; born: 6 Mar. 1878; age: 45 years; married; parents: S.W. RYBURN (Virginia) and Stacy CRUMLEY; death cause: "breast cancer"; informant: C.R. WOHLFORD (Erwin); died: 25 Nov. 1921; buried: Jobe Cemetery; record (1921) # 419.

RUNION, Margaret; born: 8 Sep. 1920; parents: W.F. RUNION (North Carolina) and Maggie COFFEE; death cause: "pneumonia"; informant: W.T. RUNION (Erwin); died: 2 Dec. 1921; buried: Martins Creek; record (1921) # 420.

BAILEY, Jane; born: 25 Aug. __ in North Carolina; age: 52 years; married; parents: W.M. EDWARDS (North Carolina) and Martha GOUGE; death cause: "unknown"; informant: S.G. BAILEY (Erwin); died: 7 Dec. 1921; buried: Martins Creek; record (1921) # 421.

JONES, Cora Belle; born: 7 May 1896; married; parents: David SMITH and Julia ORTON; death cause: "tuberculosis of lungs"; informant: E.L. JONES (Erwin); died: 8 Dec. 1921; buried: Fishery Cemetery; record (1921) # 422.

LOYD, Edward; born: 13 Dec. 1921; parents: Ben LOYD and Blanche PAYNE; death cause: "died suddenly after birth"; died: 13 Dec. 1921; buried: Martins Creek; record (1921) # 423.

PETERS, J.F.; born: 19 Apr. 1852 in North Carolina; widower; parents: Hugh PETERS (England) and mother not stated; death cause: "bronchial pneumonia"; died in the 5th District, 15 Dec. 1921; buried: Lexington, North Carolina; record (1921) # 424.

WHITE, Fred; born: 17 Dec. 1921; parents: __ (illegible) WHITE and Edney May __ (illegible); death cause: "premature"; informant: Flecher WHITE (Erwin); died: 17 Dec. 1921; record (1921) # 425.

COLE, Mildred; born: 16 Dec. 1921; parents: E.L. COLE (Virginia) and Ana May HENSLEY (North Carolina); death cause: "convulsions"; died: 17 Dec. 1921; buried: Martins Creek; record (1921) # 426.

SAYLOR, Sarah; born: 25 Oct. 1884; married; parents: Jessie BAKER and Lizzie NICHOLS; death cause: "peritonitis from pregnancy"; informant: C.A. TAYLOR (Erwin); died: 17 Dec. 1921; buried: Bluff City, Tennessee; record (1921) # 427.

BRICE, Hezekiah; born: 12 Mar. 1854 in South Carolina; married; parents: William BRICE (South Carolina) and mother unknown; death cause: "paralysis"; died in the 10th District, 21 Dec. 1921; record # 428.

BRUMMETT, Dewitt; age: 5 years; parents: J.R BRUMMETT and Nancy CARROLL; death cause: "fell from horse, brain injury"; died: 22 Dec. 1921; buried: Carroll Cemetery; record (1921) # 429.

MILLER, William Elbert; born: 15 Dec. 1921; parents: J.O. MILLER and Bunia TROUTMAN; death cause: "pneumonia"; informant: father (Erwin); died: 9 Jan. 1922; buried: Unicoi; record (1922) # 262.

ENGLISH, Anderson; born: 15 Jun. 1904 in Marion, North Carolina; parents: W.G. ENGLISH (Madison County, NC.) and Ollie MCKINNEY (Marion, NC.); death cause: "lobar pneumonia"; informant: Duie ENGLISH (Flag Pond); died: 12 Jan. 1921; buried: Madison County, North Carolina; record (1922) # 263.

PHILLIPS, Fidell; born: 3 May 1846 in Madison County, North Carolina; married; parents: Robin PHILLIPS (Madison County) and Veney PHILLIPS (Madison County); death cause: "diabetes"; informant: R.M. SAMS (Flag Pond); died; 13 Jan. 1922; buried; Sams Cemetery; record (1922) # 264.

PHILLIPS, W.W.; age: 53 years; born: Toecane, North Carolina; married; parents: C.W. PHILLIPS (North Carolina) and Sarah GOUGE (North Carolina); death cause: "tuberculosis of lungs"; informant: W.C. PHILLIPS (Erwin); died: 21 Jan. 1922; buried: Red Hill, North Carolina; record (1922) # 265.

BLANKENSHIP, Grace; born: 16 Feb. 1921; parents: Fate BLANKENSHIP (Madison County, NC.) and Jennie CRAIN (Madison County, NC.); death cause: "lobar pneumonia"; informant: Lydia BLANKENSHIP (Flag Pond); died: 23 Jan. 1922; buried: Higgins Chapel; record (1922) # 266.

TREADWAY, Jane; born: 30 Jul. 1890; married; parents: N.W. RAY (Madison County, NC.) and Agie RAY (Madison County, NC.); death cause: "post partum hemorrhage"; informant: Arch RAY (Flag Pond); died: 25 Jan. 1922; buried: Willis Cemetery; record (1922) # 267.

HENSLEY, Clingman; born: 10 Apr. 1845 in Yancey County, NC.; married; parents: Jessie HENSLEY (Yancey County) and Matly HENSLEY (Yancey County); death cause: "lobar pneumonia"; informant: A.L. BAILEY (Flag Pond); died: 27 Jan. 1922; buried: Sams Creek; record (1922) # 268.

MCNABB, Mandie; born: 25 Dec. 1915; parents: Joe MCNABB and Lura BLEVINS; death cause: "gastritis"; informant: William BLEVINS (Flag Pond); died: 28 Jan. 1922; buried: Tucker Cemetery; record # 269.

SNEYD, Dasha Susana; born: 8 Jul. 1919; parents: Seth SNEYD and Zela STOUT (Johnson County); death cause: not stated; informant: Joseph SNEYD (Unicoi); died: 30 Jan. 1922; buried: Sneyd Cemetery; record (1922) # 270.

MOORE, Frank; born: 15 Jan. 1887; married; parents: William N. MOORE and Rebecca RUNION; death cause: "homicide, gunshot"; informant: John B. SAMS (Flag Pond); died: 31 Jan. 1922; buried: Flag Pond Cemetery; record (1922) # 271.

METCALF, Victor; born: 31 May 1903 in Madison County, NC.; parents: W.E. METCALF (Madison County) and Laura METCALF; death cause: "homicide, revolver wound"; informant: Hobert METCALF (Flag Pond); died: 31 Jan. 1922; buried; Metcalf Cemetery; record (1922) # 272.

WALDROP, Infant; female; parents: father not stated and Carrie WALDROP; death cause: "stillborn"; informant: Zeb WALDROP (Flag Pond); died: 4 Jan. 1922; buried: Hensley Cemetery; record # 273.

CRAIN, Infant; male; parents: Lattie CRAIN and Martha CRAIN (Madison County, NC.); death cause: "stillborn"; informant: father (Flag Pond); died: 15 Jan. 1922; buried: Higgins Cemetery; record # 274.

TREADWAY, Infant; male; parents: Carver TREADWAY and Jane TREADWAY; death cause: "stillborn"; informant: Arch RAY (Flag Pond); died: 25 Jan. 1922; buried: Willis Cemetery; record # 275.

HAUN, G.W.; born: 28 Mar. 1868; married; parents: Daniel HARRIS and Margaret PERRY (?); death cause: "brights disease"; informant: Retta HAUN (Erwin); died: 1 Feb. 1922; record (1922) # 276.

RICE, Marion; born: 30 May 18__; age: 66 years, 10 months and 21 days; married; parents: Billie RICE and Rachel TINKER; death cause: "influenza and pneumonia"; informant: Henry RICE (Flag Pond); died: 7 Feb. 1922; buried: Flag Pond Cemetery; record (1922) # 277.

TAYLOR, Bula Grace; born: 15 Oct. 1919; parents: Jeff TAYLOR and Nancy GARLAND; death cause: "gastro interitis"; died: 8 Feb. 1922; buried: Tucker Cemetery; record (1922) # 278.

BRUMMETT, Nancy Evangeline; born: 24 Jan. 1894; married; parents: Edward CARROLL (Carter County) and Emma WHITSON (Carter County); death cause: "heart disease and pneumonia"; died: 11 Feb. 1922; buried: Carroll Cemetery; record (1922) # 279.

MOORE, Infant; male; born: 11 Feb. 1922; parents: R.L. MOORE (Australia) and Mary Ann WILLIS (Australia); death cause: "convulsions"; informant: father (Erwin); died: 14 Feb. 1922; buried: Martins Creek; record (1922) # 280.

HUGHES, Julia; age: 40 years; married; parents: Daniel HAUN and Margaret PERRY; death cause: "tuberculosis of lungs"; informant: Retta HAUN (Erwin); died: 20 Feb. 1922; record (1922) # 281.

EDWARDS, Vinna; born: 9 Feb. 1847 in North Carolina; widow; parents: Daniel TIPTON (North Carolina) and Sallie ROBINSON (North Carolina); death cause: "bronchitis"; informant: George EDWARDS (Erwin); died: 26 Feb. 1922; buried: North Carolina; record (1922) # 282.

MILLER, Samuel Washington; age: 54 years; born: 1 May __ in North Carolina; married; blacksmith; parents: T. MILLER (North Carolina) and Sallie BENNETT (North Carolina); death cause: "heart failure"; died in the 5th District, 26 Feb. 1922; record (1922) # 283.

HENSON, Hubert; born: 11 Feb. 1922; parents: father not stated and Bell HENSON; death cause: "stillborn"; informant: J.A. HARDIN (Unicoi); died: 11 Feb. 1922; buried: Barnett Cemetery; record (1922) # 284.

WILSON, Infant; male; parents: Walts WILSON (Yancey County, NC.) and Betie WILLIAMS; death cause: "stillborn"; informant: Mollie

BANNER (Erwin); died: 13 Feb. 1922; buried; Martins Creek; record (1922) # 285.

HOWELL, James Ray; born: 19 Mar 1899; single; parents: W.T. HOWELL and Martha Jane HOPKINS; death cause: "burned to death in building"; informant: father (Erwin); died: 2 Mar. 1922; record # 286.

EDWARDS, Ira; born: 4 Feb. 1922; parents: John EDWARDS and Alis WHITE; death cause: "unknown, found dead in bed"; informant: father (Erwin); died: 4 Mar. 1922; buried: Martins Creek; record # 287.

PHIPPS, Larkin; born: 26 Dec. 1858 in Virginia; married; parents: Jackson PHIPPS (Virginia) and Polly OSBORNE (Virginia); death cause: "acute __ (illegible) following operation"; informant: J.E. BARE (Erwin); died: 13 Mar. 1922; buried: Jobe Cemetery; record # 288.

SHEPPEARD, Fred; born: 22 Jun. 1921; parents: Arthur SHEPPEARD (Mitchell County, NC.) and Annie HORTON (Yancey County, NC.); death cause: "bronchitis"; informant: Taylor HORTON (Unicoi); died: 13 Mar. 1922; buried: Peoples Cemetery; record (1922) # 289.

MCINTOSH, Rausa; born: 20 Sep. 1847 in Washington County; married; parents: Andy MOORE and Polly BRIGGS (North Carolina); death cause: "dropsy"; informant: W.J. MCINTOSH (Kittyton); died: 14 Mar. 1922; buried: Mt. Pleasant; record (1922) # 290.

MCKINNEY, John W.; born: 27 Jun. 1913; parents: John W. MCKINNEY (North Carolina) and Mary_ BURNS (North Carolina; death cause: "heart disease"; informant: father (Erwin); died: 18 Mar. 1822; record (1922) # 291.

STRAFFINSTEAD, Elizabeth; born: 5 Jun. 1835 in Madison County, NC.; widow; parents: Bod DOBSON (Madison County) and Rebecca PENERAL (Madison County); death cause: "cancer of lips"; died: 21 Mar. 1922; buried: Rice Creek; record (1922) # 292.

GREENWAY, Laura Jane; born: 17 Jul. 1855 in Virginia; widow; parents: J Adison HUFFMAN (Virginia) and mother's name illegible; death cause: "nephritis and dropsy"; informant: Mrs. J.W. GARRISON (Erwin); died: 24 Apr. 1922; buried: Afton, Tennessee; record # 293.

COLEMAN, Bettie; born: 1 Nov. 1890 in Carter County; married; parents: J.A. TOLLEY (North Carolina) and Susan WHITEHEAD (Carter County); death cause: "tuberculosis"; informant: J.C.

COLEMAN (Unicoi); died: 25 Apr. 1922; buried: Tolley Cemetery; record (1922) # 294.

YOUNG, Hellen; born: 24 Feb. __; age: 14 years; parents: Anderson YOUNG (North Carolina) and Bashie FREEMAN (North Carolina); death cause: "tuberculosis"; informant: Dewey FRY (Unicoi); died: 25 Apr. 1922; buried: Banks Cemetery; record (1922) # 295.

BOOTH, Augusta P.; born: 6 May 1840; widow; parents: William HATCHER and Mary BOOTH; death cause: "nephritis, uremia"; informant: A.V. BOOTH (Erwin); died: 30 Apr. 1922; buried: home cemetery; record (1922) # 296.

PECK, Infant; male; parents: H.S. PECK (North Carolina) and Sarah FOSTER; death cause: "stillborn"; informant: M.C. FOSTER (Kittyton); died: 13 Apr. 1922; buried: Foster Cemetery; record # 297.

HARRIS, Infant; male; parents: Quillin HARRIS and Flossie LAWING death cause: "stillborn"; died at Flag Pond, 17 Apr. 1922; record # 298.

POORE, Estell; born: 24 Feb. 1922; parents: Burnie POORE and Liza MASHBURN; death cause: "unknown"; informant: James MASHBURN (Flag Pond); died: 1 May 1922; buried: Sams Creek; record (1922) # 299.

LOVE, Gladie; born: 23 Jul. 1903 in Illinois; parents: Dillard LOVE and Gertrude STEWART (North Carolina); death cause: "influenza and tuberculosis"; informant: Cordie CRAIN (Erwin); died: 3 May 1922; buried: Martins Creek; record (1922) # 300.

DAVIS, Walter; born: 31 May 1905; parents: William DAVIS and Nora __ (illegible); death cause: "blood poison"; informant: father (Hampton, Tennessee); died: 4 May 1922; buried: Livingston Cemetery; record (1922) # 301.

KERNS, J.D.; born: 10 May 1895 in West Virginia; married; parents: William KERNS (West Virginia) and Myrtle ROGINS (West Virginia); death cause: "electrocution"; informant: Mrs. Annie KERNS (Erwin); died: 19 May 1922; record (1922) # 302.

BRIGGS, Fairy; parents: Homer BRIGGS (Yancey County, NC.) and Flora PROFFITT (Yancey County, NC.); death cause: "unknown"; informant: father (Flag Pond); born/died: 21 May 1922; buried: Rice Creek; record (1922) # 303.

125

SIMMONS, Sana; age: 35 years; married; parents: Tom NELSON and Molly DAY; death cause: "septicemia"; informant: Henry SIMMONS (Erwin); died: 23 May 1922; record (1922) # 304.

CHANDLEY, Cullen; age: 29 years, 9 months and 27 days; born: Madison County, NC.; parents: Howard CHANDLEY (Madison County) and Angeline HENSLEY (Madison County); death cause: "homicide, pistol wound"; informant: Banner CHANDLEY (North Carolina); died: 4 Jun. 1922; buried: North Carolina; record # 305.

YELTON, Carroll Reese; born: 19 Apr. 1922; parents: H.L. YELTON (North Carolina) and Georgia __ (illegible); death cause: "gastro intestinal inflammation"; informant: father (Erwin); died: 7 Jun. 1922; record (1922) # 306.

HUGHES, Rachel; born: 5 Jan. 1860 in Carter County; married; parents: Pres NORRIS (Carter County) and Vina BAKER (Carter County); death cause: "heart disease"; informant: Will HUGHES (Erwin); died: 8 Jun. 1922; record (1922) # 307.

KEENE, William Mathis; born: 5 Aug. 1837 in Carter County; widower; parents: Enoch KEENE (Virginia) and Ora __ (Virginia); death cause: "__ (illegible) of lungs"; informant: G.F. KEENE (Unicoi); died: 9 Jun. 1922; buried: Bowman Cemetery; record (1922) # 308.

HURD, Virginia Caroline; born: 5 Nov. 1921; parents: Luther C. HURD (Virginia) and Flossie __ (illegible); death cause: "cholera infantum"; informant: father (Erwin); died: 10 Jun. 1922; record (1922) # 309.

LAWS, Netta; age: 25 years; born: North Carolina; married; parents: Sam INGRAM (North Carolina) and R. TAYLOR (North Carolina); death cause: "childbirth, infection"; informant: J.W. LAWS (Erwin); died: 19 Jun. 1922; buried: Spruce Pine, North Carolina; record # 310.

GRINDSTAFF, Lovada; born: 29 May 1920; parents: Sherman GRINDSTAFF and Bertie BLEVINS (Carter County); death cause: "burned, children playing with matches"; informant: J. MARTIN (Unicoi); died: 20 Jun. 1922; record (1922) # 311.

LEACH, Will H.; born: 13 Jul. 1870 in Garber, Tennessee; married; parents: E.W. LEACH (Cherokee, TN.) and Sarah E. OSBORNE (Cherokee, TN.); death cause: "heart disease"; informant: O.C. HALE (Erwin); died: 21 Jun. 1922; buried: Johnson City; record (1922) # 312.

HOWELL, Luvada; age: 74 years; born: North Carolina; married; parents: Rickels ADKINS (North Carolina) and mother unknown; death cause: not stated; informant: H.A. TOLLEY (Erwin); died: 23 Jun. 1922; record (1922) # 313.

MILLER, John; born: 23 Jul. 1846 in North Carolina; married; parents: not stated; death cause: "paralysis"; informant: J.C. ROBERTS (Erwin); died: 24 Jun. 1922; buried: Indian Creek; record (1922) # 314.

SMITH, Clay; age: 27 years; single; parents: John SMITH and mother not stated; death cause: "sudden, unknown cause"; died in the 13th District, 18 Jun. 1922; record (1922) # 315.

LAWS, Infant; female; parents: John LAWS (North Carolina) and Hattie INGRAM (North Carolina); death cause: "stillborn"; informant: father (Erwin); died: 1 Jun. 1922; record (1922) # 316.

MILLER, Infant; male; parents: Johny S. MILLER and Kate BOGART; death cause: "stillborn"; informant: father (Erwin); died: 19 Jun. 1922; record (1922) # 317.

BARNETT, J.D.; age: 1 year and 11 months; parents: Aron BARNETT (North Carolina) and Magra (?) SIZEMORE (North Carolina); death cause: "cholera"; informant: father (Unicoi); died: 3 Jul. 1922; record (1922) # 318.

VANDEGRIFF, John W.; born: 15 Jun. 1859 in Roanoke, Virginia; married; parents: Thomas VANDEGRIFF (Virginia) and Mary Elizabeth LITTLE (Virginia); death cause: "prostate cancer"; died: 8 Jul. 1922; buried: Salem, Virginia; record (1922) # 319.

METCALF, John; born: 24 Oct. 1838 in Madison County, NC.; married; parents: Ham METCALF (Madison County) and Jennie METCALF (Madison County); death cause: "pneumonia"; informant: A.B. BAILEY (Flag Pond); died: 11 Jul. 1922; buried: Sams Creek; record # 320.

CASTEEL, John David; age: 4 months; parents: Jack CASTEEL (Scott County, VA.) and Amanda CASTEEL (Scott County, VA.); death cause: "colitis"; informant: father (Johnson City); died: 22 Jul. 1922; buried: Anderson Chapel; record (1922) # 321.

JONES, Gaither B.; born: 4 Sep. 1892; married; parents: W.H. JONES and Mary HENSLEY; death cause: "fargugitis"; informant: H.E. HUSKINS (Kittyton); died: 24 Jul. 1922; buried: Hurley Cemetery; record (1922) # 322.

EDENS, Infant; male; parents: Ernest EDENS and Rhoda MASTERS; death cause: "stillborn"; informant: father (Erwin); died: 5 Jul. 1922; record (1922) # 232.

PAINTER, Infant; male; parents: George K. PAINTER and __ (illegible) GREEN; death cause: "stillborn"; informant: father (Erwin); died: 11 Jul. 1922; record (1922) # 324.

PADGETT, Emily; age: "about 56 years"; widow; parents: Edwin STANTON and mother "unknown"; death cause: "pellagra"; informant: Daisy PADGETT (Erwin); died: 1 Aug. 1922; buried: Liberty Cemetery; record (1922) # 325.

WHITE, Mary E.; born: 20 Jan. 1876; widow; parents: N.K. MCINTURFF and Barbara Ann COBBLE; death cause: "pellagra"; informant: Evert WHITE (Unicoi); died: 6 Aug. 1922; buried: Jones Cemetery; record (1922) # 327.

WHALEY, C_ (illegible); born: 11 Apr. 1847; widow; parents: Sam TIPTON (North Carolina) and mother not stated; death cause: "dysentery"; informant: James WHALEY (Erwin); died: 4 Aug. 1922; buried: Garland Cemetery; record (1922) # 326.

NORRIS, Rena; born: 7 Aug. 1922; parents: Ben NORRIS and Delia COCHRAN and mother not stated; informant: father (Unicoi); died: 7 Aug. 1922; buried: Peoples Cemetery; record (1922) # 328.

BRIGGS, Cinda; born: 13 Oct. 1855 in Madison County, NC.; married; parents: Tom TIPTON (Madison County) and Sally BAILEY (Madison County); death cause: "heart disease"; informant: John SAMS (Flag Pond); died: 24 Aug. 1922; buried: Rice Creek Cemetery; record # 329.

WILLIAMS, Dora; born: 2 Apr. 1896; married; parents: George HAMPTON and Lizzie HAMPTON; death cause: "typhoid fever"; informant: M. HAMPTON (Erwin); died: __(illegible) Aug. 1922; record (1922) # 330.

HIGGINS, Lydia May; born: 29 Jul. 1922; parents: L.D. HIGGINS (White Rock, NC.) and Rhue Nanie RUNIONS; death cause: "bold hives"; informant: father (Flag Pond); died: 25 Aug. 1922; buried: Higgins Cemetery; record (1922) # 331.

LUTTRELL, Infant; male; parents: Albert LUTTRELL and Gladys HENSLEY; death cause: "stillborn"; informant: father (Erwin); died: _ Aug. 1922; record (1922) # 332.

RAMSEY, Infant; female; parents: Will RAMSEY and Beca PRICE; death cause: "stillborn"; informant: father (Kittyton); died: 16 Aug. 1922; buried: Ramsey Cemetery; record (1922) # 333.

GENTRY, John B.; born: 7 Oct. 1854 in North Carolina; married; parents: John GENTRY (North Carolina) and Jane EDWARDS (North Carolina); death cause: not stated; informant: A.R. GENTRY (Kittyton); died: 2 Sep. 1922; buried: Rice Creek Cemetery; record (1922) # 334.

LEWIS, Elizabeth; age: 85 years; born: North Carolina; widow; parents: Joseph TIPTON (England) and mother "unknown"; death cause: "colitis, apoplexy"; died in the 5th District, 2 Sep. 1922; record (1922) # 335.

OLLIS, Margaret; born: 30 May 1997; married; parents: Tom MILLER and Beckie VANCE; death cause: "eclampsia"; informant: James OLLIS (Erwin); died: 10 Sep. 1922; record (1922) # 336.

SNEYD, Infant; male; parents: James SNEYD and Addie CAMPBELL; death cause: not stated; informant: father (Unicoi); born/died: 12 Sep. 1922; buried: Birchfield Cemetery; record (1922) # 337.

MCNABB, William Clifton; born: 6 Jul. 1904; single; parents: Grover MCNABB and Ella B. ERWIN; death cause: "heart lesion"; informant: father (Erwin); died: 13 Sep. 1922; buried: Jobe Cemetery; record (1922) # 338.

GADDY, Sara A. Bowman; born: 26 Sep. 1892; married; parents: Scott BOWMAN (Carter County) and Alice BRITT (Carter County); death cause: "typhoid fever"; informant: father (Unicoi); died: 23 Sep. 1922; buried: McInturff Cemetery; record (1922) # 339.

NORTON, Stella Iris; born: 20 Jan. 1922; parents: Alfred NORTON and Mary Ellen GILLIS; death cause: "fever"; informant: mother (Flag Pond); buried: President Madison Cemetery; record (1922) # 340.

JONES, Thomas J.; born: 5 Aug. 1851; married; parents: Henry JONES and mother not stated; death cause: "aortic insufficiency"; informant: W.H. JONES (Erwin); died: 28 Sep. 1922; buried: Unicoi County; record (1922) # 341.

BROWN, Margaret Elizabeth; born: 20 Oct. 1921; parents: W.H. BROWN and Hester CARTER; death cause: "colitis"; informant: father (Erwin); died: 28 Sep. 1922; record (1922) # 342.

129

BOWERS, Infant; female; parents: H.V. BOWERS (North Carolina) and May PROFFIT (North Carolina); death cause: "stillborn"; informant: father (Erwin); died: 6 Sep. 1922; record (1922) # 344.

BOWERS, Infant; female; parents: V.B. BOWERS, Jr. (North Carolina) and Lois ISAACS (North Carolina); death cause: "stillborn"; informant: mother (Erwin); died: 7 Sep 1922; buried: Elk Park, North Carolina; record (1922) # 343.

OLLIS, Infant; male; parents: James OLLIS (North Carolina) and Margaret MILLER; death cause: "stillborn"; informant: father (Erwin); record (1922) # 345.

SMITH, Infant; male; parents: Press SMITH and mother's name illegible; death cause: "stillborn"; informant: father (Erwin); died: 15 Sep. 1922; record (1922) # 346.

HIGGINBOTHOM, Lora Tilson; born: 14 Nov. 1884; married; parents: L.S. TILSON (MD) (Washington County) and Eliza J. PARKS (Washington County); death cause: "endo carditis"; informant: father (Erwin); died: 1 Oct. 1922; buried: Jobe Cemetery; record (1922) # 347.

WITCHER, Infant; male; born: 28 Sep. 1922; parents: Ruben WITCHER and Lela WILLIS; death cause: "hemorrhage"; informant: father (Erwin); died: 1 Oct. 1922; record (1922) # 348.

PADGETT, Ed; age: 26 years; born: North Carolina; married; parents: S. PADGETT (North Carolina) and Carrie WALL (North Carolina); death cause: "suicide, shot through heart"; informant: H.J. PADGETT (South Carolina); died: 3 Oct. 1922; buried: North Carolina; record # 349.

RICE, Mary; born: 8 Aug. 1905 in Yancey County, NC.; married; parents: John SWINEY (Yancey County) and Delie BAILEY (Yancey County); death cause: "suicide, poison ate wild parsnip"; informant: Dana RICE (Flag Pond); died: 4 Oct. 1922; buried: Rice Creek; record (1922) # 350.

JONES, George C. Jr.; parents: Chester JONES and Anna Belle SMITH; death cause: "8 month baby"; born/died: 4 Oct. 1922; buried: Jones Cemetery; record (1922) # 351/

LUTTRELL, Isaac Washington; age: 70 years; born: Washington County; married; parents: father not stated and Linda LUTTRELL (Washington County); death cause: "paralysis"; informant: Grady

HUTCHINS (Erwin); died: 5 Oct. 1922; buried: Jobe Cemetery; record (1922) # 352.

HIGGINS, Leroy; born: 11 Oct. 1882; single; parents: Stewart HIGGINS and Elizabeth TILSON; death cause: "appendicitis"; died: 14 Oct. 1922 in the 10th District; record (1922) # 353.

JACKSON, Jarrett; born: 20 Aug. 1922; parents: G.C. JACKSON (Virginia) and __ (illegible) BROOKS (Virginia); death cause: "diphtheria"; died: 30 Oct. 1922; record (1922) # 354.

MARTIN, Helen Lea; born: 15 Feb. 1918; parents: Samuel MARTIN and Josie GRINDSTAFF; death cause: "diphtheria"; died: 20 Oct. 1922; buried: Peterson Cemetery; record (1922) # 355.

RICE, V.; male; born: 11 Aug. 1919; parents: N.B. RICE and Leota BLANKENSAY; death cause: "clothing caught fire"; informant: father (Flag Pond); died: 27 Oct. 1922; buried: Rice Creek Cemetery; record (1922) # 356.

OSBORNE, John; born: 30 Apr. 1883 in Ohio; married; potter; parents: Joseph OSBORNE (England) and mother "unknown"; death cause: "tuberculosis of lungs"; informant: Mrs. John OSBORNE (Ohio); died: 31 Oct. 1922; buried: East Liverpool, Ohio; record (1922) # 357.

CARTER, Infant; male; parents: W.B. CARTER and Minny SHELTON (North Carolina); death cause: "stillborn"; informant: father (Flag Pond); died: 21 Oct. 1922; buried; Carter Farm; record (1922) # 358.

MCCANDLESS, Della; born: 1 Jul. 1869 in Marshall, North Carolina; widow; parents: R.K. DEAVER (North Carolina) and Myra Jane PHILLIPS (North Carolina); death cause: "heart lesion"; informant: Clarence A. MCCANDLESS (Erwin); died: 5 Nov. 1922; buried: Jobe Cemetery; record (1922) # 359.

O'BRIEN, Carry; born: 31 Aug. 1901; single; parents: Joseph O'BRIEN and Etter MOORE; death cause: "endo carditis"; informant: father (Erwin); died: 6 Nov. 1922; record (1922) # 360.

FOSTER, Elbert; age: 74 years; married; parents: Dan FOSTER and Elizabeth TITTLE; death cause: "apoplexy"; informant: John FOSTER (Erwin); died; 12 Nov. 1922; buried: Mt. Pleasant; record (1922) # 361.

WILLIAMS, Silas; age: 76 years; married; parents: P_ (illegible) WILLIAMS and mother not stated; death cause: "paralysis"; informant:

Joe A. WILLIAMS (Kittyton); died: 18 Nov. 1922; buried: Hensley Cemetery; record (1922) # 362.

WEBB, Will; age: 14 years; parents: father "unknown" and Texie WEBB (North Carolina); death cause: "unknown, found dead in bed"; informant: Ulys WEBB (Erwin); died: 20 Nov. 1922; buried: Poplar, North Carolina; record (1922) # 363.

ATKINS, Jason; age: 87 years; born: North Carolina; widower; parents: B_ (illegible) ADKINS (North Carolina) and E_ (illegible) WHITSON (North Carolina); death cause: "old age"; informant: Jim ADKINS (Erwin); died: 20 Nov. 1922; buried: Unicoi County; record # 364.

LEWIS, John M.; born: 1 Apr. 1920; parents: L.J. LEWIS and Ada BRIGGS; death cause: "meningitis"; informant: father (Erwin); died: 29 Nov. 1922; record (1922) # 365.

SNEYD, Seth; born: 23 Nov. 1882; married; parents: Joseph SNEYD and Susan CAMPBELL; death cause: "mitral regurgitation"; informant: Joseph SNEYD (Unicoi); died: 23 Nov. 1922; buried: Sneyd Cemetery; record (1922) # 366.

CAPPS, Sana; age: 78 years; born: North Carolina; widow; parents: Alfred LEDFORD (North Carolina) and Autie _ (illegible); death cause: "nephritis"; informant: Autie CLARK (Erwin); died: 26 Nov. 1922; record (1922) # 367.

HOPSON, Nick; born: 6 Oct. 1851 in North Carolina; widower; parents: George HOPSON (North Carolina) and Delia STANLEY (North Carolina); death cause: "cancer of face"; informant: Jake HOPSON (Unicoi); died: 26 Nov. 1922; record (1922) # 368.

STREET, Ulyses C.; born: 4 Feb. 1893 in Buladeen, North Carolina; married; parents: Stephen G. STREET (North Carolina) and Martishy J. DAY (North Carolina); death cause: "typhoid fever"; informant: James C. STREET; died: 5 Dec. 1922; buried: Swingle Cemetery; record (1922) # 369.

PATE, John; born: 19 Apr. 1872 in North Carolina; married; parents: M.S. PATE (North Carolina) and Jane HIGGINS (Washington County); death cause: "paralysis"; informant: Walter MATHIS (Flag Pond) died: 6 Dec. 1922; buried: Sams Creek; record (1922) # 370.

BUTNER, Selma; born: 29 Nov. 1922; parents: Sam BUTNER (North Carolina) and Dolly BREWER; death cause: "premature birth";

informant: mother (Erwin); died: 17 Dec. 1922; buried: Martins Creek; record (1922) # 371.

WHITE, Harrel; born: 24 Oct. 1922; parents: J.C. WHITE and Virginia TINKER; death cause: illegible; informant: father (Erwin); died: 26 Dec. 1922; buried: Jobe Cemetery; record (1922) # 372.

LAWS, Infant; male; born: 24 Dec. 1922; parents: D.M. LAWS and Anna WORSHAM; death cause: "bronchial pneumonia"; informant: father (Erwin); died: 28 Dec. 1922; buried: Jobe Cemetery; record (1922) # 373.

WEBB, Mary; born: 26 Apr. 1861 in Virginia; widow; parents: L.D. COLLIER (Virginia) and Sarah COX (Virginia); death cause: "cancer of womb"; died: 31 Dec. 1922; buried: Jobe Cemetery; record # 374.

MOORE, Infant; male; parents: J.L. MOORE (Australia) and Mary WILLIS (Australia); death cause: "stillborn"; informant: father (Erwin); died: 24 Dec. 1922; buried: Martins Creek; record (1922) # 375.

SHELTON, Eli; born: 10 Aug. 1905 in Madison County, NC.; parents: Jasper SHELTON (Madison County) and Dosha BLANKENSHIP; death cause: "homicide, revolver wound in back"; informant: mother (Flag Pond); died: 1 Jan. 1923; buried: Madison County, North Carolina; record (1923) # 294.

RICE, Malinda Jane; born: 24 Mar. 1858; divorced; parents: Rev. H.W. GILBER (North Carolina) and mother "unknown"; death cause: "heart disease"; informant: James C. RICE (Erwin); died: 4 Jan. 1923; buried: Clear Branch; record (1923) # 295.

SMITH, Glenna; born: 25 Jan. 1922; parents: Sam SMITH and Annie AMBROSE; death cause: "flu"; informant: father (Erwin); died: 5 Jan. 1923; buried: Fishery Cemetery; record (1923) # 296.

WILLIAMSON, Infant; female; parents: George WILLIAMSON and Dora CALLAHAN; death cause: "premature birth"; informant: J.W. CALLAHAN (Erwin); born/died: 6 Jan. 1923; buried: Tinker Cemetery; record (1923) # 297.

WILLIAMSON, Dora Bell Callahan; age: 25 years; married; parents: J.W. CALLAHAN (Madison County, NC.) and Margaret JERVIS (Washington County); death cause: "childbirth, pneumonia"; informant: father (Fordville, Tennessee); died: 10 Jan. 1923; buried: Tinker Cemetery; record (1923) # 298.

133

ROBERSON, Margaret; age: 1 year; born: Johnson City; parents: W.E. ROBERSON (Cocke County) and Estella CLOUSE; death cause: "pneumonia"; informant: J.A. CALLAHAN (Erwin); died: 12 Jan. 1923; buried: Tinker Cemetery; record (1923) # 299.

HOPSON, W.C.; age: 78 years; born: Mitchell County, NC.; widower; parents: George HOPSON (North Carolina) and Delila HOPSON (North Carolina); death cause: "unknown"; informant: David A. HUGHES (Erwin); died: 12 Jan. 1923; buried: Martins Creek; record (1923) # 300.

RUNION, Infant; male; born: 5 Jan. 1923; parents: James RUNION and __ (illegible) METCALF; death cause: "broncho pneumonia"; informant: W.K. RUNION (Erwin); died: 15 Jan. 1923; buried: Tinker Cemetery; record (1923) # 301.

BLEVINS, Callie; age: 66 years; widow; parents: William HENSLEY and Kattie SUTS; death cause: "heart trouble"; informant: G.M. YATES (Embreeville); died: 18 Jan. 1923; buried: Bunker Cove; record (1923) # 302.

SHELTON, Millard; age: 27 years; married; parents: John SHELTON (North Carolina) and Sarah WATTS; death cause: "pellagra"; informant: father (Erwin); died: 18 Jan. 1923; buried: Martins Creek; record (1923) # 303.

HIGGINS, Ralph Gay; born: 19 Dec. 1919; parents: Woodward HIGGINS and Vergie HASTON; death cause: "pneumonia"; informant: father (Unicoi); died: 20 Jan. 1923; buried: Fishery Cemetery; record (1923) # 304.

SHIPLEY, Fred; born: 17 Jan. 1923; parents: Roy SHIPLEY and Maggie HENSLEY (North Carolina); death cause: "unknown"; informant: father (Erwin); died: 20 Jan. 1923; buried: Jobe Cemetery; record # 305.

KEENER, Stella; born: 6 Oct. 1903; single; parents: Will KEENER and Ida __ (illegible); death cause: "childbirth, flu and pneumonia"; informant: C.C. KEENER (Erwin); died: 23 Jan. 1923; buried: Fishery Cemetery; record (1923) # 306.

STARNES (?), William; born: 25 Dec. 1843; widower; parents: "unknown"; death cause: "influenza and pneumonia"; informant: William SALTZ (Erwin); died: 23 Jan. 1923; record (1923) # 307.

RIDDLE, Molly; born: 11 Nov. 1890 in North Carolina; married; parents: Ruben GOUGE (North Carolina) and Martha PARKER (North Carolina); death cause: "influenza"; informant: W.L. RIDDLE (Erwin); died: 24 Jan. 1923; buried: Martins Creek; record (1923) # 308.

BOOTHE, Elizabeth; born: 1 May 1850; married; parents: Dr. William REED and Martha MILLER; death cause: "influenza and pneumonia"; informant: Lora BOOTHE (Erwin); died: 26 Jan. 1923; buried: family cemetery; record (1923) # 309.

LOVE, Phoeba; born: 10 Apr. 1834 in Washington County; parents: __ STOUT (Washington County) and mother "unknown"; death cause: "cancer of __ (illegible); informant: O.C. HALE (Erwin); died: 26 Jan. 1923; buried: Martins Creek; record (1923) # 310.

WOODLEY, Elizabeth; born: 6 May 1842; married; parents: William BRUMMETT and Sinda BRITT; death cause: "tuberculosis"; informant: Charles WOODLEY (Unicoi); died: 27 Jan. 1923; buried: Woodley Cemetery; record (1923) # 311.

GILLIS, David Lewis; born: 7 Oct. 1922; parents: Lattie GILLIS and Vivian BARNES; death cause: not stated; informant: W. Lattie GILLIS (Flag Pond); died: 28 Jan. 1923; buried; President Madison Cemetery; record (1923) # 312.

GARLAND, Verna Erwin; born: 23 Sep. 1894 in Bakersville, North Carolina; married; invalid; parents: Guss GARLAND (Bakersville, NC.) and Adina M. GRIFFITH (Red Hill, NC.); death cause: illegible; informant: father (Erwin); died: 28 Jan. 1923; buried: Martins Creek; record (1923) # 313.

HIGGINS, Sam; age: "about 72 years"; widower; parents: Ellis HIGGINS and Barbara TILSON; death cause: "pulmonary hemorrhage"; informant: Margaret HENSLEY (Erwin); died: 29 Jan. 1923; buried: Higgins Chapel; record (1923) # 314.

MASHBURN, Infant; female; parents: T.M. MASHBURN and Estell CHANDLER; death cause: "stillborn, caused by flu"; informant: father (Flag Pond); died: 5 Jan. 1923; buried: Higgins Chapel; record # 315.

TIPTON, Ora; born: 26 Apr. 1918; parents: Fred TIPTON and Nora TAYLOR (Yancey County, NC.); death cause: "meningitis"; informant: father (Erwin); died: 2 Feb. 1923; buried: Clear Branch; record # 316.

135

ILLEGIBLE, Mary L.; born: 10 Aug. 1857; widow; parents: John TINKER and Marien LILLBURN; death cause: "unknown"; died in the 12th District, 2 Feb. 1923; record (1923) # 317.

MCCURRY, Cleophus; age: 28 years; born: North Carolina; single; soldier; parents: J.H. MCCURRY (North Carolina) and Anna GREEN (North Carolina); death cause: "paralysis"; informant: father (Unicoi); died: 8 Feb. 1923; buried: Garland Cemetery; record (1923) # 318.

JACKSON, Edward; age: "about 34 years"; married; parents: Calvin JACKSON and Anne ODEN (North Carolina); death cause: "influenza"; informant: Bertha JACKSON (Erwin); died: 12 Feb. 1923; buried: Jobe Cemetery; record (1923) # 319.

BOWMAN, Daniel; born: 4 Apr. 1851 in Carter County; single; parents: Joseph BOWMAN (North Carolina) and Catherine CLINE (North Carolina); death cause: "gall stones"; informant: Mary E. SMITH (Unicoi); died: 13 Feb. 1923; buried: Jones Cemetery; record # 320.

HELTON, Infant; female; born: 13 Feb. 1923; parents: Oscar HELTON and Dora LUTTRELL (North Carolina); death cause: "premature"; informant: father (Erwin); died: 14 Feb. 1923; record (1923) # 321.

KEENER, Nellie; born: 8 Jan. 1923; parents: Claud KEENER and Myrtle BENNETT (North Carolina); death cause: "flu"; informant: father (Erwin); died: 16 Feb. 1923; record (1923) # 322.

INGRAM, Nathaniel; age: 73 years; born: Carter County; married; shoe cobbler; parents: William INGRAM and mother not stated; death cause: "age and arthritis"; informant: W.H. INGRAM (Unicoi); died: 25 Feb. 1923; buried: Swingle Cemetery; record (1923) # 323.

WILLIAMS, Kid Turley; born: 6 Feb. 1921; parents: David WILLIAMS (North Carolina) and Martha BENNETT (North Carolina); death cause: "influenza and pneumonia"; informant: father (Erwin); died: 28 Feb. 1923; buried: Martins Creek; record (1923) # 324.

HAYNES, Frank; parents: Arthor HAYNES (Yancey County, NC.) and Jane CHANDLER; death cause: "stillborn"; informant: father (Flag Pond); died: 4 Feb. 1923; buried: Kittyton; record (1923) # 325.

HUTCHINS, Rosa; born: 31 Jan. 1923; parents: Jess HUTCHINS (North Carolina) and Celia WILCOX (North Carolina); death cause: "hives"; informant: John STREET (Unicoi); died: 8 Mar. 1923; buried: Rowe Cemetery; record (1923) # 326.

BROWN, Barbara Elizabeth; born: 5 Jan. 1837 in Wytheville, Virginia; widow; parents: Phillip BARNETT (Lexington, Virginia) and Mary CRIGGER (Wytheville); death cause: "bronchial pneumonia"; informant: R.W. BROWN (Son); died: 8 Mar. 1923; buried: Graham, West Virginia; record (1923) # 327.

HONEYCUTT, Dawson; born: 16 May 1900 in Greeneville, South Carolina; single; locomotive fireman; parents: W.R. HONEYCUTT (South Carolina) and Nonie ESKEW (South Carolina); death cause: "fell between railroad cars"; informant: father (Erwin); died: 8 Mar. 1923; buried: Greeneville, South Carolina; record (1923) # 328.

SHEHAN, George; age: "about 53 years"; born: North Carolina; married; parents: E_ (illegible) SHEHAN (North Carolina) and Josie HUSKINS (North Carolina); death cause: "intestinal nephritis"; informant: Martha SHEHAN (Erwin); died: 9 Mar. 1923; buried: Mt. Pleasant; record (1923) # 320.

ERWIN, Eliza; age: 70 years and 5 months; born: Washington County; widow; parents: William E. TILSON (Washington County) and Katherine SAMS (Madison County, NC.); death cause: "acute indigestion and heart trouble"; informant: L.S. TILSON (Erwin); died: 9 Mar. 1923 ("she died within 50 feet of birthplace"); record # 330.

NORRIS, William P.; born: 25 Nov. 1855 in Carter County; married; parents: C.C. NORRIS (Carter County) and Rachel MCINTURFF (Carter County); death cause: not stated; informant: A.C. NORRIS (Johnson City); died: 14 Mar. 1923; buried: Peoples Cemetery; record (1923) # 331.

HENSLEY, Zeb D. Vance; age: "about 53 years"; born: North Carolina; parents: John HENSLEY (North Carolina) and Delia BAILEY (North Carolina); death cause: "gunshot wound received in Erwin fight"; informant: Mary HENSLEY (Erwin); died: 26 Mar. 1923; buried: Martins Creek; record (1923) # 332.

LAWING, Infant; male; parents: W.A. LAWING and Parlee ALFRED; death cause: "stillborn"; informant: father (Erwin); died: 20 Mar. 1923; record (1923) # 333.

PETERSON, Infant; male; parents: Robert PETERSON (North Carolina) and Ester MILLER (North Carolina); death cause: "stillborn";

informant: father (Erwin); died: 28 Mar. 1923; buried: Martins Creek; record (1923) # 334.

ANDREWS, Elsie; born: 22 Mar. 1906; single; parents: E.B. ANDREWS and Martha JACKSON; death cause: "spinal meningitis"; informant: father (Erwin); died: 6 Apr. 1923; buried: Martins Creek; record (1923) # 335.

TITTLE, Wayne; born: __ Jan. 1923 in Kentucky; parents: Ike TITTLE and Blanch LOYD; death cause: "unknown"; informant: father (Erwin); died: 10 Apr. 1923; buried: Martins Creek; record (1923) # 336.

HENSLEY, Vance; born: 11 Apr. 1923; parents: __ (illegible) HENSLEY and Lizzie HENSLEY; death cause: "bold hives"; informant: Estell HARRIS (Flag Pond); died: 14 Apr. 1923; record (1923) # 337.

CAMPBELL, Harmon; born: 2 Apr. 1923; parents: Arthur CAMPBELL and Emma SNEYD; death cause: not stated; informant: George HESTER (Unicoi); died: 14 Apr. 1923; buried: Baker Cemetery; record (1923) # 338.

ROWE, Cirifina (?); born: 12 Aug. 1849; widow; parents: Wilson BAKER and Biddie GARLAND; death cause: "intestinal nephritis"; informant: Charles MCINTURFF (Erwin); died: 17 Apr. 1923; buried: Unicoi; record (1923) # 339.

MORRELL, A_ (illegible) Andrew; born: 21 Aug. 1921; parents: H.F. MORRELL and _ HUFF (West Virginia); death cause: "cerebral hemorrhage"; informant: father (Erwin); died: 18 Apr. 1923; record (1923) # 340.

STREET, Hassie Mae Garland; age: 32 years, 3 months and 22 days; born: Mitchell County, NC.; married; parents: Gutch GARLAND (Mitchell County) and Isabell GARLAND (Mitchell County); death cause: "influenza and pneumonia"; informant: Charles STREET (Unicoi); died: 22 Apr. 1923; buried: Marbleton; record (1923) # 341.

SHELTON, Nicy; born: 1 Mar. 1836 in Madison County, NC.; widow; parents: David SHELTON (Madison County) and Nancy SHELTON (Madison County); death cause: "dropsy"; informant: G.W. SHELTON; died: 23 Apr. 1923; buried: Flag Pond; record (1923) # 342.

LOYD, Infant; male; born: 2 Apr. 1923; parents: Ben LOYD and Blanch PAYNE; death cause: "unknown"; informant: father (Erwin); died: 23 Apr. 1923; record (1923) # 343.

ROBERTS, Cora; age: "about 45 years"; married; parents: Worly MASTERS and Dice MASTERS; death cause: "pellagra"; informant: Jim ROBERTS (Erwin); died: 26 Apr. 1923; record (1923) # 344.

HARRIS, Adeline; age: "about 57 years"; married; parents: Joseph MURRAY and Nancy HENSLEY; death cause: "intestinal nephritis"; informant: Charlie HARRIS (Erwin); died: 2 May 1923; buried: Flag Pond; record (1923) # 345.

WILLIAMS, Joe; age: "about 35 years"; born: North Carolina; parents: James WILLIAMS (North Carolina) and Rachel WILLIAMS (North Carolina); death cause: "gunshot wound, killed in drunken fight"; died: 10 May 1923; buried: Martins Creek; record (1923) # 346.

PARSONS, Richard C.; born: 3 Dec. 1890 in Athens, Tennessee; married; assistant train master; parents: R.D. PARSONS and _ SAMPSON; death cause: "tubercular laryngitis"; informant: R.W. LAWSON (Erwin); died: 13 May 1923; buried: Jobe Cemetery; record (1923) # 347.

INGRAM, William; born: 12 Feb. 1911; parents: F.H. INGRAM (Virginia) and Flossie KELLY; death cause: "mitral regurgitation"; informant: father (Erwin); died: 14 May 1923; record (1923) # 348.

GREGG, John M.; born: 17 Oct. 1859 in Johnson County; married; parents: Harrison GREGG (North Carolina) and Hannah WHITEHEAD (Carter County); death cause: "heart disease"; informant: J.H. GREGG; died: 15 May 1923; record (1923) # 349.

PHILLIPS, Dorthy Ryden; born: 9 Oct. 1921; parents: Homer PHILLIPS (North Carolina) and __ (illegible) RYDEN; death cause: "meningitis"; informant: father (Erwin); died: 23 May 1923; buried: Bluff City, Tennessee; record (1923) # 350.

BAUMGARDNER, Ruth Ann; born: 20 Sep. 1922 in Virginia; parents: T.C. BAUMGARDNER (North Carolina) and Fisher HORD (North Carolina); death cause: "colitis"; informant: Mrs. Tom ROBERTS (Erwin); died: 28 May 1923; record (1923) # 351.

PAUL, Infant; male; parents: A.E. PAUL and Eva ALLEN; death cause: "stillborn"; informant: Eva ALLEN (Erwin); died: 10 May 1923; record (1923) # 352.

OLIVER, William; born: 30 Jul. 1921; parents: John OLIVER and Effie BAILY; death cause: "dysentery"; informant: father (Erwin); died: 1 Jul. 1923; record (1923) # 353.

ROGERS, Joe; born: 29 Jan. 1923; parents: Will ROGERS and Fine BAKER; death cause: "colitis"; informant: father (Erwin); died: 3 Jun. 1923; record (1923) # 354.

WILSON, Harry; born: 31 May 1923; parents: R.C. WILSON (North Carolina) and Julia TITTLE; death cause: "unknown"; informant: father (Erwin); died: 6 Jun. 1923; record (1923) # 355.

FOX, Gladys; age: "about 3 years"; parents: M.A. FOX and Cora _ (illegible); death cause: "double pneumonia"; informant: father (Erwin); record (1923) # 356.

HIGGINS, Amanda E.; born: 16 Dec. 1847; widow; parents: Thomas SMITH and Sarah HOLCOMB; death cause: "dropsy"; died in the 10th District, 14 Jun. 1923; buried: Higgins Cemetery; record (1923) # 357.

MCCAMEY, Nancy; remainder of record illegible; record (1923) # 358.

TIPTON, Kathern; born: 2 Sep. 1922; parents: Charles TIPTON and Cleo COIN; death cause: "cholera infantum"; informant: father (Erwin); died: 22 Jun. 1923; record (1923) # 359.

DUNBAR, Loade Jr.; born: 5 May 1922; parents: Loade DUNBAR (Greene County) and Ellen SPAIRS (Greene County); death cause: "cholera infantum"; informant: father (Erwin); record (1923) # 360.

BANNER, Alvin Lee; born: 17 Oct. 1919; parents: Martin Lee BANNER and Linda HENSLEY; death cause: "diphtheria"; informant: father (Erwin); died: 27 Jun. 1923; record (1923) # 362.

FULLER, Frank; age: 55 years; born: Front Royal, Virginia; single; president of Erwin __ (illegible) Corporation; parents: "unknown"; death cause: "heart trouble"; died: 24 Jun. 1923; record (1923) # 361.

JONES, Infant; male; parents: Chester JONES and Anna SMITH; death cause: "premature birth"; informant: father (Erwin); died: 13 Jun. 1923; buried: Jones Cemetery; record (1923) # 363.

CASTEEL, Jane; age: 65 years; married; parents: John HICKS (Virginia) and Nancy CORRELL (Virginia); death cause: "colitis"; informant: Sid

CORRELL (Johnson City); died: 3 Jul. 1923; buried: Anderson Cemetery; record (1923) # 364.

CASTEEL, Millard; age: 37 years; born: Virginia; married; parents: John CASTEEL and Jane HICKS; death cause: "dysentery"; informant: Sid CORRELL (Johnson City); died: 8 Jul. 1923; buried: Anderson Chapel; record (1923) # 365.

HARTSOCK, Winnie Elizabeth; born: 8 Aug. 1851 in Scott County, VA.; widow; parents: John MEAD (Scott County) and __ MEAD (Russell County, VA.); death cause: "nephritis"; informant: Addie G. BUNDY (Erwin); died: 10 Jul. 1923; record (1923) # 366.

PRATER, Salina Geer; born: 10 Apr. 1841; married; parents: Ransom GEER (North Carolina) and Mary HARVICK (South Carolina); death cause: "apoplexy"; informant: Mrs. C.W. ADAMS (Erwin); died: 19 Jul. 1923; buried: Jobe Cemetery; record (1923) # 367.

MURRY, Miney; born: 1 Oct. 1921; parents: Geter MURRY and Tilda WALDROP (North Carolina); death cause: "cholera infantum"; informant: father (Erwin); record (1923) # 368.

BARRON, Infant; female; born: 26 Jul. 1923; parents: Roy L. BARRON and Mary VANCE; death cause: "premature birth"; informant: father (Erwin); died: 27 Jul. 1923; record (1923) # 369.

BENNETT, Mae; born: 9 May 1908 in North Carolina; single; parents: Mat BENNETT (North Carolina) and Cinda WEBB (North Carolina); death cause: "peritonitis"; informant: father (Erwin); died: 29 Jul. 1923; record (1923) # 370.

PETERSON, __ (illegible); born: 4 Jan. 1840 in North Carolina; married; parents: Massy PETERSON (North Carolina) and Poly MCKINNEY (North Carolina); death cause: "dysentery"; died in the 4th District, 29 Jul. 1923; record (1923) # 371.

ILLEGIBLE: records 372 - 374.

HENSLEY, Infant; male (twins); born: 2 Aug. 1923; parents: Hobart HENSLEY and Cordie KEENER; death cause: "premature birth"; informant: father (Erwin); died: 2 Aug. 1923; records # 374 and 375.

TINKER, Infant; male; born: 15 Jun. 1923; parents: S.W. TINKER and Cory MASHBURN; death cause: illegible; died: 14 Aug. 1923; record (1923) # 376.

BOYD, Infant; male; parents: D.A. BOYD (Virginia) and Elizabeth BRADSHAW (North Carolina); death cause: "blue baby"; informant: father (Erwin); born/died: 9 Aug. 1923; buried: Jobe Cemetery; record (1923) # 377.

TINKER, Hazeline; born: 12 Jun. 1923; parents: L_ (illegible) EDWARDS and Ina TINKER; death cause: "bold hives"; informant: mother (Unicoi); died: 19 Aug. 1923; buried: Jones Cemetery; record (1923) # 378.

TILSON, Dellar Mae; born: 27 Jun. 1916; parents: J.F. TINKER and Mamie HIGGINS; death cause: "spinal meningitis"; informant: father (Erwin); died: 20 Aug. 1923; buried: Martins Creek; record # 379.

HENSLEY, Joseph H.; born: 1 May 1922; parents: Hobart HENSLEY and Florence Cordie KEENER; death cause: "colitis"; informant: father (Erwin); died: 20 Aug. 1923; record (1923) # 380.

MILLER, Nancy Isabel; born: 25 Nov. 1846 in Iredell County, NC.; widow; parents: John MILLER (North Carolina) and Nancy Isabell MARLOW (North Carolina); death cause: "carcinoma of mammary gland"; informant: J.F. MILLER (Unicoi); died: 22 Aug. 1923; buried: Jones Cemetery; record (1923) # 381.

TITTLE, Cora Lee; born: 26 Dec. 1883; married; parents: John AMBROSE (North Carolina) and Nancy MILLER; death cause: "tuberculosis of throat"; informant: Fannie AMBROSE (Erwin); died: 24 Aug. 1923; buried: Jobe Cemetery; record (1923) # 382.

CAROTHEN, Pauline; born: 12 Oct. 1922; parents: Jim CAROTHEN and Myrtle HONEYCUTT; death cause: "measles and pneumonia"; informant: Jim CAWTHEN (Erwin); died: 2 Sep. 1923; record # 383.

TIPTON, Biddie; born: __ Aug. 1861; age: 62 years and 1 month; born: North Carolina; widow; parents: Joel COOPER (North Carolina) and Rebecca RAMSEY (North Carolina); death cause: "dysentery"; informant: Joel TIPTON (Erwin); died: 11 Sep. 1923; buried: Poplar, North Carolina; record (1923) # 384.

TIPTON, Rosa Belle; born: 6 Nov. 1891 in North Carolina; married; parents: Sam BRYANT (North Carolina) and Dora LEWIS (North Carolina); death cause: "tuberculosis of lungs"; informant: Steve TIPTON (Erwin); died: 13 Aug. 1923; record (1923) # 385.

POPE, John Richard; born: 27 Jan. 1844 in "Chatim" County, North Carolina; married; parents: John Richard POPE (North Carolina) and mother unknown; death cause: "paralysis"; informant: Henry C. POPE (North Carolina); died: 13 Sep. 1923; record (1923) # 386.

HAUN, Effie; age: "about 30 years"; married; parents: John MCINTURFF and Sara CLARK; death cause: "tuberculosis of lungs"; informant: Jesse MCINTURFF (Erwin); died: 14 Sep. 1923; record (1923) # 387.

GOUGE, James Denman; born: 8 Sep. 1923; parents: L.T. GOUGE (Carter County) and Ethel BLEVINS (Carter County); death cause: "ictorus"; died: 17 Sep. 1923; buried: Carter County; record # 388.

WIGGAND, Virginia; born: 1 Sep. 1923; parents: Raymond WIGGAND (Virginia) and Pansy PETERSON (North Carolina); death cause: "premature birth"; died: 19 Sep. 1923; record (1923) # 389.

HONEYCUTT, Lemuel; age: 37 years; born: North Carolina; parents: Elisha HONEYCUTT (North Carolina) and Bettie BARNETT (North Carolina); died: 20 Sep. 1923; buried: North Carolina; record # 390.

MCINTURFF, Mattie; age: 18 years; single; parents: John MCINTURFF and Sarah CLARK; death cause: "typhoid fever"; informant: Jesse MCINTURFF (Erwin); died: 21 Sep. 1923; record (1923) # 391.

GREGG, Nettie; born: __ May 1921; parents: Orville GREGG and Rhoda SHEPARD (North Carolina); death cause: illegible; informant: Frank SHEPARD (Unicoi); died: 25 Sep. 1923; buried: Unicoi Cemetery; record (1923) # 392.

SHULTZ, __ (illegible); female; born: 24 Sep __, age: 74 years; born: Henry County, Virginia; widow; parents: J.T. PHILPOT (Virginia) and mother's name illegible; death cause: "cancer of stomach"; informant: A.W. SHULTZ (Erwin); died: 24 Sep. 1923; buried; Henry, Virginia; record (1923) # 393.

WHITE, Elizabeth; born: 27 Sep __ ; age: 71 years; born: Washington County; widow; parents: father not stated (North Carolina) and Rose Elizabeth __ (not stated)(North Carolina); death cause: "mitral lesion"; informant: C.C. WHITE (Erwin); died: 28 Sep. 1923; buried: Johnson City; record (1923) # 394.

TAPP, William Henry; born: 25 Sep. 1890; single; parents: Matt L. TAPP (Washington County) and Clarcia Emme JOHNSON (Carter

County); death cause: "acute indigestion"; informant: Lottie TAPP (Erwin); died: 29 Sep. 1923; buried: Fishery Cemetery; record # 395.

EDWARDS, Lula; born: 5 Aug. 1921; parents: William EDWARDS and Mae NELSON; death cause: "cholera infantum"; informant: father (Erwin); died: 30 Sep. 1923; buried: Garland Cemetery; record # 396.

DUNCAN, Infant; male; parents: J.N. DUNCAN and Ollie SCARBOURH; death cause: "stillborn"; informant: father (Erwin); died: 7 Sep. 1923; record (1923) # 397.

STOCKTON, Gladys Hazel; born: 20 Jan. 1923; parents: R.W. STOCKTON and Jane HIGGINS (North Carolina); death cause: "broncho pneumonia"; informant: father (Erwin); died: 7 Oct. 1923; buried: Fishery Cemetery; record (1923) # 398.

JOHNSON, Rachel R.; born: 11 Apr. 1838; born: Burke County, North Carolina; widow; parents: Alfred WARLICK (North Carolina) and Elizabeth FISHER (North Carolina); death cause: "apoplexy"; informant: G.W. JOHNSON (Erwin); died: 10 Oct. 1923; buried: Morganton, North Carolina; record (1923) # 399.

RUNIONS, Wilma; born: 8 Jul. 1920; parents: James S. RUNION and Velma METCALF; death cause: "broncho pneumonia"; informant: W.H. JONES (Erwin); died: 14 Oct. 1923; record (1923) # 400.

HAMPTON, Hannah; age: "about 60 years"; single; parents: Daniel HAMPTON and Kate MASTERS; death cause: "general breakdown"; died in the 12th District, 17 Oct. 1923; record (1923) # 401.

BYRD, __ (illegible); male; born: 15 Sep 1923; parents: Arthur BYRD (North Carolina) and Mollie TIPTON (North Carolina); death cause: "whooping cough"; informant: father (Unicoi); died: 21 Oct. 1923; buried: Peterson Cemetery; record (1923) # 402.

FOSTER, Johnathan; age: "about 70 years"; widower; parents: David FOSTER and mother unknown; death cause: "tuberculosis of lungs"; informant: G.W. FOSTER (Erwin); died: 23 Oct. 1923; record # 403.

STALLINGS, Maggie E.; born: 29 Aug. 1860; married; parents: George CROSSWHITE and Jennie ALLEN; death cause: "gastric hemorrhage"; informant: G.E. STALLINGS (Erwin); died: 25 Oct. 1923; buried: Martins Creek; record (1923) # 404.

PETERSON, Chester; born: 4 Aug. 1922; parents: Doss PETERSON (North Carolina) and Darliskey BRYANT (North Carolina); death cause: "lobar pneumonia"; informant: father (Erwin); died: 26 Oct. 1923; buried: Green Mountain, North Carolina; record (1923) # 405.

ILLEGIBLE - Record # 406.

MCINTURFF, Bruce K.; born: 17 Jul. 1922; parents: N.J. MCINTURFF and Myrtle NELSON; death cause: "measles"; informant: father (Erwin); died: 1 Nov. 1923; record (1923) # 407.

MILLER, Lillie; born: 8 Aug. 1859 in Virginia; married; parents: J.S. YODER (Virginia) and mother unknown; death cause: "asthma and heart failure"; informant: Walter LOVE (Erwin); died; 8 Nov. 1923; buried: Jobe Cemetery; record (1923) # 408.

LETTERMAN, Sara Jane; age: "about 52 years"; born: North Carolina; married; parents: Nathan DEATON (North Carolina) and Louise BYRD (North Carolina); death cause: "suicide, hanged herself"; informant: Ed LETTERMAN (Erwin); died: 9 Nov. 1923; buried: Green Mountain, North Carolina; record (1923) # 409.

GARLAND, Hobart; age: "about 2 years"; parents: Tom GARLAND (North Carolina) and Mattie HOWELL (North Carolina); death cause: "measles"; informant: father (Erwin); died: 10 Nov. 1923; record # 410.

HUGHES, Caroline; age: "about 2 years"; parents: P_ (illegible) HUGHES and Minnie WILLIAMS; death cause: "measles"; informant: Tom GARLAND (Erwin); died: 10 Nov. 1923; record (1923) # 411.

GOUGE, Phebe; age: 76 years; born: Mitchell County, NC.; widow; parents: father's name illegible and Nancy GARLAND; death cause: "pneumonia"; informant: A.M. GOUGE (Erwin); died: 19 Nov. 1923; buried; North Carolina; record (1923) # 412.

AMBROSE, James H.; age: "about 34 years"; widower; parents: John AMBROSE and Nan MILLER; death cause: "tuberculosis of lungs"; informant: Nan MILLER (Erwin); died: 22 Nov. 1923; buried: Jobe Cemetery; record (1923) # 413.

MCNABB, Gertrude; born: 23 Jul. 1909; parents: Taylor MCNABB and Rebecca HINSON; death cause: not stated; informant: father (Unicoi); died; 30 Nov. 1923; buried: family cemetery; record (1923) # 414.

HONEYCUTT, Dave; born: 3 Jul. 1923; parents: Sidney HONEYCUTT (Mitchell County, NC.) and Sarah HONEYCUTT (Relief, Mitchell County, NC.); death cause: "spinal meningitis"; informant: father (Erwin); died: 6 Dec. 1923; record (1923) # 415.

SHEHAN, Ned; age: "about 65 years"; born: North Carolina; married; parents: Aaron SHEHAN (North Carolina) and Sally HENSLEY (North Carolina); death cause: "heart disease"; informant: Elizabeth SHEHAN (Erwin); died: 16 Dec. 1923; record (1923) # 416.

THOMAS, Infant; male; born: 16 Dec. 1923; parents: Pat THOMAS (North Carolina) and Ella GRINDSTAFF (North Carolina); death cause: "unknown"; informant: father (Erwin); died; 17 Dec. 1923; buried: Roses Branch Cemetery; record (1923) # 417.

FOX, Ula; age: 21 months; parents: John FOX and Lizzie LAWS; death cause: "measles"; informant: father (Erwin); died: 18 Dec. 1923; buried; Green Mountain, North Carolina; record (1923) # 418.

LAWING, Clara Bell; born: 5 Dec. 1922; parents: William LAWING and Bessie THOMAS (North Carolina); death cause: "unknown"; informant: father (Erwin); died: 22 Dec. 1923; buried: Martins Creek; record (1923) # 419.

MCINTOSH, Ray; age: "about 3 years"; parents: Mark MCINTOSH and Rhoda JONES; death cause: "measles"; informant: Martha JONES (Erwin); died: 25 Dec. 1923; record (1923) # 420.

HENSLEY, J.B.; born: 17 Dec. 1923; parents: McKinley HENSLEY (Yancey County, NC.) and B_ (illegible) MCKINNEY (McDowell County, NC.); death cause: "unknown"; informant: father (Erwin); died: 25 Dec. 1923; record (1923) # 421.

MCCURRY, Infant; male; parents: J.C. MCCURRY (North Carolina) and Bertha PHILLIPS (North Carolina); death cause: "stillborn"; informant: father (Erwin); died: 12 Dec. 1923; record (1923) # 422.

CLEVELAND, Infant; female; parents: M.C. CLEVELAND (North Carolina) and Uma MATHIS (North Carolina); death cause: "stillborn"; informant: father (Erwin); died: 14 Dec. 1923; record (1923) # 423.

DUPLICATE - Record # 424 in a duplicate of record # 423.

DAVIS, Infant: female; parents: Netron DAVIS and mother's name illegible; death cause: "stillborn"; informant: father (Unicoi); died: 22 Dec. 1923; buried: Gouge Cemetery; record (1923) # 425.

BAILEY, Mary Lee; age: "about 2 years"; parents: Morgan BAILEY and Ada HARRIS; death cause: "unknown"; informant: father (Erwin); died: 8 Jan. 1924; record (1924) # 208.

FOSTER, Hobart; age: "about 9 months"; parents: Arthor FOSTER and Corda JOHNSON (North Carolina); death cause: "measles relapse"; informant: father (Erwin); died: 8 Jan. 1924; record (1924) # 209.

TONEY, Harry; born: 30 Dec. 1923; parents: W.C. TONEY and Christine SCOTT (Johnson City); death cause: "hemorrhage"; informant: father (Erwin); died: 12 Jan. 1924; record (1924) # 210.

NORRIS, Mary Elizabeth; born: 2 Dec. 1843 in Tennessee; single; parents: Richard M. NORRIS and Lucinda MCINTURFF; death cause: "influenza"; informant: H.F. NORRIS (Unicoi); died: 17 Jan. 1924; buried: Peoples Cemetery; record (1924) # 211.

WILSON, Sara; age: 15 years; born: North Carolina; parents: Jeb WILSON (North Carolina) and Luvina BRYANT (North Carolina); death cause: "endo carditis"; informant: father (Erwin); died: 20 Jan. 1924; buried: Huntdale, North Carolina; record (1924) # 212.

CRAIN, Junior; born: 5 Jan. 1923; parents: Sam CRAIN and Ella HENSLEY; death cause: "whooping cough"; informant: Joe CRAIN (Erwin); died: 22 Jan. 1924; record (1924) # 213.

ODOM, Nancy; born: __ May 1841; age: 82 years; born: North Carolina; widow; parents: Fred LEDFORD (North Carolina) and __ WHITSON (North Carolina); death cause: "influenza"; informant: John K. MILLER (Erwin); record (1924) # 214.

EDWARDS, Infant; female; parents: Clifton EDWARDS and Creola CHANDLER; death cause: "stillborn"; informant: father (Erwin); died: 5 Jan. 1924; buried: Clear Branch; record (1924) # 215.

TIPTON, Infant; male; parents: Walter TIPTON and Bessie BENNETT; death cause: "stillborn"; informant: father (Erwin); died: 11 Jan. 1924; record (1924) # 216.

BRITT, Infant; female; born: 7 Nov. 1923; parents: W.H. BRITT and Maude SUTPHIN; death cause: "bronchial pneumonia"; informant: father (Unicoi); died: 3 Feb. 1924; record (1924) # 217.

JONES, Dartha; born: 17 Aug. 1923; parents: Bud JONES and Eliza FOSTER; death cause: "whooping cough"; informant: father (Erwin); died: 17 Feb. 1924; record (1924) # 218.

BLEVINS, Oscar Silas; born: 14 Dec. __; age: 24 years, 2 months and 7 days; born: North Carolina; parents: Charlie BLEVINS (North Carolina) and Ida GREEN (North Carolina); death cause: "killed by train"; informant: Dora BLEVINS (Jonesboro); died: 21 Feb. 1924; buried: Forbes, North Carolina; record (1924) # 219.

CHASE, Daniel; age: "about 57 years"; married; parents: "unknown"; death cause: "paralysis"; informant: Mrs. Hubert CHASE (Erwin); died: 24 Feb. 1924; record (1924) # 220.

INGLE, Elizabeth J.; born: 1 May 1852 in North Carolina; married; parents: Robert CHAPMAN (North Carolina) and Betsy SWATHARD; death cause: "influenza and pneumonia"; informant: W.G. INGLE (Unicoi); died: 26 Feb. 1924; buried: Erwin Cemetery; record # 221.

WINDELL, Jane; age: "about 68 years"; widow; parents: John PHILLIPS and mother unknown; death cause: "unknown"; informant: Mrs. John LYLE (Erwin); died: 26 Feb. 1924; buried: Fishery Cemetery; record (1924) # 222.

HARRIS, Lula May; born: 28 Jul. 1923; parents: Clay HARRIS and Jennie PHILLIPS; death cause: "heart disease"; informant: John F. ANDERSON (Flag Pond); died: 28 Feb. 1924; buried: Flag Pond Cemetery; record (1924) # 223.

CAMPBELL, Infant; male; parents: William E. CAMPBELL and Adda GOUGE; death cause: "stillborn"; informant: father (Unicoi); died: 2 Feb. 1924; buried; Campbell Cemetery; record (1924) # 224.

STOCKTON, Infant; female; parents: Luther STOCKTON and Dora MASHBURN; death cause: "stillborn"; informant: Diana HOYLE (Flag Pond); died: 22 Feb. 1924; buried: Flag Pond Cemetery; record # 225.

NELSON, Joe; age: 57 years; married; parents: John NELSON and mother unknown; death cause: "cancer of stomach"; informant: L.S. TILSON (Erwin); died: 11 Mar. 1924; record (1924) # 226.

GREEN, Thomas Duncan; born: 26 Mar. 1921 in Kentucky; parents: William GREEN (Kentucky) and Flossie WILLOUGHBY (Alabama); death cause: "erysipelas"; informant: father (Erwin); died: 15 Mar 1924; record (1924) # 227.

HUTCHINS, Dora; born: 2 Mar. 1924; parents: Jess HUTCHINS (North Carolina) and Celia GILLIS (North Carolina); death cause: "unknown, found dead in bed"; informant: John STREET (Unicoi); died: 17 Mar. 1924; buried: Rowe Cemetery; record (1924) # 228.

BEAM, Mary; age: 40 years; born: North Carolina; single; parents: Daniel BEAM (North Carolina) and Manda BENNETT (North

Carolina); death cause: "lobar pneumonia"; informant: A.M. PITMAN; died: 20 Mar. 1924; record (1924) # 229.

HIGGINS, J.D.; born: 3 Oct. 1923; parents: Ernest HIGGINS and Eller LOYD; death cause: "whooping cough"; informant: father (Erwin); died: 21 Mar. 1924; buried: Martins Creek; record (1924) # 230.

EDWARDS, Infant; male; born: 17 Feb. 1924; parents: Jason EDWARDS (North Carolina) and Bessie BENNETT (North Carolina); death cause: "premature birth"; informant: father (Erwin); died: 23 Mar. 1924; record (1924) # 231.

SHIPLEY, Vivian; age: 2 years; parents: Roy SHIPLEY and Maggie HENSLEY; death cause: "influenza and pneumonia"; informant: Mrs. J.A. SHIPLEY (Erwin); died: 27 Mar. 1924; record (1924) # 232.

SNEYD, Walter; born: 23 Mar. 1924; parents: James SNEYD and Addie CAMPBELL; death cause: "deformed child"; informant: mother (Unicoi); died: 27 Mar. 1924; buried: Birchfield Cemetery; record (1924) # 233.

BOONE, Infants (twins); females; parents: Mort BOONE (North Carolina) and Estelle MCMAHAN (North Carolina); death cause: "premature birth"; informant: father (Erwin); died: 27 Mar 1924; record (1924) # 234.

SMITH, Infant; male; parents: father not stated and Rever SMITH; death cause: "stillborn"; informant: Sam SMITH (Erwin); died: 22 Mar. 1924; record (1924) # 235.

FORTUNE, Infant; male; parents: Hubert FORTUNE (Virginia) and Gertrude NORTH (North Carolina); death cause: "stillborn"; informant: father (Erwin); died: 27 Mar. 1924; record (1924) # 236.

BOONE, Infants (twins); females; parents: Mont BOONE (North Carolina) and Estelle MCMAHAN (North Carolina); death cause: "stillborn"; informant: father (Erwin); died: 27 Mar 1924; record # 237.

ALLEN, William; age: 62 years; widower; parents: Harvey ALLEN and Martha MCCALL (Virginia); death cause: "asthma and dropsy"; died: 3 Apr. 1924; record (1924) # 238.

LAUGHREN, Dosser M.; born: 12 Mar. 1924; parents: Arcinus LAUGHREN (North Carolina) and Allie EDWARDS (North Carolina); death cause: "unknown"; died: 6 Apr. 1924; record (1924) # 239.

SHELTON, Allis; female; born: 24 Feb. 1924; parents: William SHELTON and M_ (illegible) BLANKENSHIP; death cause: "unknown"; informant: father (Erwin); died: 14 Apr. 1924; record (1924) # 240.

LEWIS, Fred F.; born: 8 Sep. 1903 in Virginia; parents: Jessie L. LEWIS (Virginia) and Sarah Z. J_ (illegible) (Virginia); death cause: "pulmonary hemorrhage"; informant: Elbert PATE (Johnson City); died: 19 Apr. 1924; record (1924) # 241.

TITTLE, Charlie Bean; born: 8 Jun. 1874; married; parents: Russell TITTLE and Rebecca TAPP; death cause: "suicide, hanged himself"; informant: James F. TITTLE (Erwin); died: 20 Apr. 1924; record (1924) # 242.

PHILLIPS, Thomas Warren; born: __ Aug. 1881; age: 42 years; married; parents: Henderson P. PHILLIPS (Mitchell County, NC.) and Rachel E. BRITT (Carter County); death cause: "cerebral hemorrhage"; informant: W.L. PHILLIPS (Unicoi); died: 23 Apr. 1924; buried: Jobe Cemetery; record (1924) # 243.

PATE, Infant; male; born: 5 Apr. 1924; parents: Zeb PATE (Yancey County, NC.) and Carrie TIPTON; death cause: "bold hives"; informant: Richard METCALF (Flag Pond); died: 26 Apr. 1924; record (1924) # 244.

CRAIN, Infant; male; born: 14 Apr. 1924; parents: Joe CRAIN and Dora HIGGINS; death cause: "unknown"; informant: father (Erwin); died: 27 Apr. 1924; record (1924) # 245.

GREEN, Kathrn; born: 27 Apr. 1924; parents: Percy GREEN and Lena GREEN; death cause: "unknown"; informant: father (Erwin); died: 28 Apr. 1924; buried: Jobe Cemetery; record (1924) # 246.

COLLINS, Minnie; born: 2 Mar. 1882; married; parents: I.R. LOVE and Sarah HAMPTON; death cause: "general breakdown"; informant: L.C. COLLINS (Erwin); died: 30 Apr. 1924; record (1924) # 247.

NORRIS, Infant; female; parents: Bob NORRIS and Jena BAILEY (North Carolina); death cause: "stillborn"; informant: father (Erwin); died: 1 Apr. 1924; buried: Martins Creek; record (1924) # 248.

MILLER, Elbert C.; born: 12 Jun. 1847; widower; parents: "unknown"; death cause: "aortic regurgitation"; informant: William MILLER

(Erwin); died: 1 May 1924; buried: Poplar, North Carolina; record (1924) # 249.

HAYNES, George G.; born: 11 Apr. 1867; married; state legislator; parents: Nathaniel T. HAYNES and Vene BOWMAN; death cause: "nephritis"; informant: Madison P. HAYNES (Philadelphia, PA.); died: 3 May 1924; buried: Marbleton; record (1924) # 250.

HENSLEY, Willard L.; born: 12 Oct. 1920; parents: Charles HENSLEY (North Carolina) and Ellen INGLE; death cause: not stated; informant: T.C. INGLE (Erwin); died: 13 May 1924; record (1924) # 251.

GRINDSTAFF, Earl; born: 28 Apr. 1924; parents: Elbert GRINDSTAFF and Charlotte CARVER (Carter County); death cause: "hives"; informant: father (Erwin); died: 15 May 1924; record (1924) # 252.

WYNNE, Lamar Andrew Jr.; born: 7 Aug. 1922; parents: Lamar Andrew WYNNE (South Carolina) and Dora DUNCAN (South Carolina); death cause: "pneumonia"; informant: father (Erwin); died: 15 May 1924; buried: Westminister, South Carolina; record (1924) # 253.

MCCURRY, Rosie; age: 84 years; born: North Carolina; widow; parents: Tom SILVERS (North Carolina) and Nellie SILVERS (North Carolina); death cause: "heart failure"; died: 17 May 1924; buried: Martins Creek; record (1924) # 254.

HORTON, David M.; born: 18 Oct. 1844 in North Carolina; married; parents: Zephine (?) HORTON (North Carolina) and Vostie (?) PIERCY (North Carolina); death cause: "pneumonia"; died in the 5th District, 18 May 1924; buried: Erwin; record (1924) # 255.

GANT, L. James; born: 22 Oct. 1848 in Kingsport, widower; parents: Elcany GANT (Virginia) and Nancy LILBURNE (Virginia); death cause: "aortic dilatation of heart"; informant: F.W. BAKER (Erwin); died: 29 May 1924; buried: Jonesboro; record (1924) # 256.

DUNCAN, Infant; female; parents: W.G. DUNCAN (North Carolina) and Ida KING (North Carolina); death cause: "stillborn"; informant: father (Erwin); died: 18 May 1924; buried: Erwin; record (1924) # 257.

THOMAS, Infant; male; parents: W.C. THOMAS (North Carolina) and Sarah EDWARDS; death cause: "stillborn"; informant: father (Erwin); died: 21 May 1924; buried: Erwin; record (1924) # 258.

ELLIS, Infant; male; born: 29 May 1924; parents: R.J. ELLIS and Kate SHELL; death cause: "unknown"; informant: W.P. LOVE (Erwin); died: 2 Jun. 1924; buried: Erwin; record (1924) # 259.

BUCHANAN, Mollie; born; 17 Mar. 1887 in North Carolina; married; parents: R.A. EDWARDS (North Carolina) and Susan WILLIAMS (North Carolina); death cause: "flu, abortion"; informant: Ave BUCHANAN (Erwin); died: 6 Jun. 1924; buried; Erwin; record # 260.

TIPTON, May; born: 30 Jan. 1916 in North Carolina; parents: Steve TIPTON (North Carolina) and Rosa BRYANT (North Carolina); death cause: "synacitis"; informant: father (Erwin); died: 8 Jun. 1924; buried: Erwin; record (1924) # 261.

KEEVER, D.N.; born: 22 Jan. 1834 in North Carolina; married; parents: Jacob KEEVER (North Carolina) and mother unknown; death cause: "intestinal nephritis"; informant: Drew KEEVER (Erwin); died: 11 Jan. 1924; buried: Erwin; record (1924) # 262.

HAMPTON, Fred; born: 12 Jun. 1904; single; parents: George HAMPTON and Celia WILLIAMS (Yancey County, NC.); death cause: "phisis pulmonalis"; informant: Paul HUGHES (Unicoi); died: 12 Jun. 1924; buried: Peterson Cemetery; record (1924) # 263.

PHILLIPS, Zeb; born: 24 Apr. 1873; married; parents: Fidel PHILLIPS and Mary L. SAMS; death cause: "carcinoma of stomach"; informant: Dwight PHILLIPS (Unicoi); died: 13 Jun. 1924; buried: Unicoi; record (1924) # 264.

BOWMAN, Ruth Geneva; born: 31 May 1924; parents: Edd BOWMAN and Rosa JONES; death cause: "bold hives"; informant: J. BOWMAN (Unicoi); died: 23 Jun. 1924; buried: Unicoi; record (1924) # 265.

CHANDLER, Nervie Jane; born: 20 Mar. 1839 in North Carolina; married; parents: Birt BANKS (North Carolina) and Sallie BLANKENSHIP (North Carolina); death cause: "general breakdown"; died at Clear Branch on 29 Jun. 1924; buried: Mt. Pleasant; record (1924) # 266.

BRITT, Jacob; born: __ Apr. 1856 in Unicoi, former Carter County; parents: James BRITT and Nancy UNDERWOOD; death cause: "general anasarca"; died: 30 Jun. 1924; buried: Rowe Cemetery; record (1924) # 267.

BUCHANAN, Infant; male; parents: Ave BUCHANAN (North Carolina) and Millie EDWARDS (North Carolina); death cause: "stillborn";

informant: father (Erwin); died: 2 Jun. 1924; buried: Erwin; record (1924) # 268.

SPARKS, Infant; male; parents: V.R. SPARKS (North Carolina) and Ruth STEWART (North Carolina); death cause: "stillborn"; informant: father (Erwin); died: 14 Jun. 1924; buried: Erwin; record (1924) # 269.

FOSTER, Infant; male; parents: father not stated and Leona FOSTER; death cause: "stillborn"; informant: Axie FOSTER (Clear Branch); died: 16 Jun. 1924; buried: Foster Cemetery; record (1924) # 270.

CALLAHAN, William Elbert Jr.; parents: William Elbert CALLAHAN and Bessie FINCHER; death cause: "stillborn"; informant: father (Erwin); died: 23 Jun. 1924; buried: Erwin; record (1924) # 271.

COFFEE, Judy; age: 38 years; married; parents: Dave SMITH and Nan WHALEY; death cause: "pellagra"; informant: J.W. COFFEE (Erwin); died: 2 Jul. 1924; buried: Erwin; record (1924) # 272.

TOLLEY, Mary L.; age: 6 months; parents: Clarence TOLLEY (North Carolina) and Goldie MILLER (North Carolina); death cause: "cholera infantum"; informant: father (Erwin); died: 5 Jul. 1924; buried: Unicoi; record (1924) # 273.

RIDDLE, Viola; born: 16 Jan. 1923 in North Carolina; parents: Richard RIDDLE (North Carolina) and Effie __ (North Carolina); death cause: "unknown"; informant: father (Erwin); died: 10 Jul. 1924; buried: Martins Creek; record (1924) # 274.

HENSLEY, Louisa; born: 20 may 1865; married; parents: John HONEYCUTT and Litha HONEYCUTT (North Carolina); death cause: "heart trouble"; informant: J.N. HENSLEY (Clear Branch); died: 11 Jul. 1924; buried: Foster Cemetery; record (1924) # 275.

LAWING, Julina; born: 8 Nov. 1874; married; parents: D.T. GUINN and Lindy RUNION; death cause: "carcinoma of liver"; informant: J.B. LAWING (Erwin); died: 18 Jul. 1924; buried: Erwin; record # 276.

HOWELL, Dave; born: 24 Feb. 1881 in North Carolina; married; parents: Zeb HOWELL (North Carolina) and Meniva BRYANT (North Carolina); death cause: "typhoid fever"; informant: Ruth HOWELL (Erwin); died: 18 Jul. 1924; buried: Fishery Cemetery; record # 277.

TIPTON, Mose; age: 66 years; born: North Carolina; married; parents: John D. TIPTON (North Carolina) and Caroline PETERSON (North Carolina); death cause: "knife wound in a fight with drunk man";

informant: Dock TIPTON (North Carolina); died: 24 Jul. 1924; buried: Erwin; record (1924) # 278.

BIRCHFIELD, Rosa Leah; born: 9 Jun. 1923; parents: Isaac BIRCHFIELD (Mitchell, NC.) and Mary MCVAY (Mitchell, NC.); death cause: "cholera infantum"; died: 25 Jul. 1924; buried: Peterson Cemetery; record (1924) # 279.

PRESNELL, Pheba; born: 9 Apr. 1924; parents: Charley PRESNELL (Burnsville, NC.) and Dufey BISHOP (Marshall, NC.); death cause: "unknown"; informant: father (Erwin); died: 29 Jul. 1924; buried: Erwin; record (1924) # 280.

HENSLEY, Rome; born: 5 Jul. 1906; single; parents: Albert HENSLEY (North Carolina) and Sarah CHANDLER; death cause: "gall stone"; informant: Bak MARTIN (Clear Branch); died at Appalachian Hospital, Johnson City, 30 Jul. 1924; buried: Mt. Pleasant; record (1924) # 281.

PRESNELL, Joseph; born: 9 Apr. 1924; parents: Charley PRESNELL (Burnsville, NC.) and Duffy BISHOP (Marshall, NC.); death cause: "unknown"; informant: father (Erwin); died: 2 Jul. 1924; buried: Erwin; record (1924) # 282.

HUGHES, David; parents: Paul HUGHES (Mitchell County, NC.) and Celia WILLIAMS (Yancey County, NC.); death cause: "born dead"; died: 8 Jul. 1924; buried: Peterson Cemetery; record (1924) # 283.

MCINTURFF, Infant; female; parents: Noah MCINTURFF and Myrtle NELSON; death cause: "stillborn"; informant: father (Erwin); died: 18 Jul. 1924; buried: Erwin; record (1924) # 284.

TINKER, Infant; male; parents: Edward TINKER and Verna EXXLER; death cause: "stillborn"; informant: Anna Mae DOUGALL (Flag Pond); died: 29 Jul. 1924; buried: Mt. Pleasant; record (1924) # 285.

MILLER, Susie; born: 1 Aug. 1838 in Tennessee; widow; parents: Adam SWINIE and Vicy SWINIE; death cause: "old age"; informant: Mollie MILLER (Unicoi); died: 2 Aug. 1924; buried: Unicoi; record # 286.

DAVIS, Charley; age: 82 years; born: Tennessee; married; parents: William DAVIS and Mary WOODBY; death cause: "heart failure"; died in the 2nd District, 3 Aug. 1924; buried: Gouge Cemetery; record # 287.

FOX, Guindolyn; born: 13 Jul. 1912; parents: C.B. FOX and Mary E. SMITH; death cause: "drowned"; informant: father (Erwin); died: 4 Aug. 1924; buried: Erwin; record (1924) # 288.

DUNCAN, John Columbus; age: 64 years; born: Marion, North Carolina; married; parents: Samuel DUNCAN (North Carolina) and Malisa DUNCAN; death cause: "cancer"; informant: S.T. DUNCAN (Erwin); died: 17 Aug. 1924; buried: Erwin; record (1924) # 289.

SHEHAN, Celia; age: 26 years; widow; parents: Robert JONES and Catherine EDWARDS; death cause: "pellagra"; informant: T.F. WILLIS (Erwin); died: 19 Aug. 1924; buried: Erwin; record # 290.

SHEHAN, Shely; age: 25 years; widow; parents: Robert JONES and Catherine EDWARDS; death cause: "pellagra"; informant: Katherine JONES (Erwin); died: 23 Aug. 1924; buried: Erwin; record # 291.

WILLIS, David; born: 30 Jun. 1837 in North Carolina; married; parents: not stated; death cause: not stated; died in the 8th District, 25 Aug. 1924; buried: Smith Cemetery; record (1924) # 292.

TITTLE, Infant; male; born: 29 Aug. 1924; parents: James TITTLE and Reana ROGERS; death cause: "infant"; informant: father (Erwin); died: 30 Aug. 1924; buried: Erwin; record (1924) # 293.

BRIGGS, Infant; female; parents: Homer BRIGGS and Flora May BRIGGS; death cause: "stillborn"; died: 20 Aug. 1924; buried: Blankenship Cemetery; record (1924) # 294.

NORRIS, W. Otto; born: 30 Jan. 1883 in Ohio; married; parents: Jim NORRIS (Ohio) and Georgia KEMPFIELD (Ohio); death cause: "cerebral hemorrhage"; informant: Mrs. Otto NORRIS (Erwin); died: 1 Sep. 1924; buried: Erwin; record (1924) # 285.

MARTIN, Warren G.; born: 28 Dec. 1923; parents: Samuel MARTIN and Jossie GRINDSTAFF; death cause: "diphtheria"; informant: father (Unicoi); died: 1 Sep. 1924; buried: Unicoi; record (1924) # 296.

ROBERTS, Benni; born: 21 Sep. 1905; single; parents: T.B. ROBERTS (Virginia) and Lidia MASTERS; death cause: "shot, killed in a drunken fight"; informant: father (Erwin); died: 21 Sep. 1924; buried: Erwin; record (1924) # 297.

PAISLEY, Margaret Marion; born: 26 Sep. 1922; parents: G.W. PAISLEY (Kentucky) and Elizabeth PRESNELL (Boonford, North Carolina); death cause: "unknown"; informant: father (Erwin); died: 23 Sep. 1924; buried: Rock Creek; record (1924) # 298.

SAMS, John Dan; age: 43 years; married; parents: L.S. SAMS (Washington County) and mother's name illegible; death cause:

155

"murdered with gun"; died: 28 Sep. 1924; buried: Sams Cemetery; record (1924) # 299.

SAMS, Conway; age: 30 years; parents: T.C. SAMS and Sarah Beck FOSTER; death cause: "killed instantly in a drunken fight"; informant: L.S. TILSON (Erwin); died: 29 Sep. 1924; buried: Higgins Creek; record (1924) # 300.

SAMS, John Dan; age: 41 years; parents: L.S. SAMS and Margaret WHITSON; death cause: "killed in drunken fight"; died: 29 Sep. 1924; buried: Coffee Ridge, Sams Cemetery; record (1924) # 301.

RICE, Infant; male; parents: Newberry RICE and Leota BLANKENSHIP; death cause: "stillborn"; informant: Anna MACDOUGALL (Flag Pond); died: 1 Sep. 1924; buried: Blankenship Cemetery; record # 302.

RICE, Infant; male; parents: Newberry RICE and Leota BLANKENSHIP; death cause: "stillborn caused by flu"; informant: NB. RICE (Flag Pond); died: 1 Sep. 1924; buried: Flag Pond; record # 303.

MATHIS, Clarence David; born: 26 Dec. 1923; parents: Ben MATHIS and Trissie MCCAN (Arkansas); death cause: "unknown"; informant: father (Erwin); died: 2 Oct. 1924; record (1924) # 305.

MARSH, Gracy Louise; born: 5 May 1923; parents: George MARSH (North Carolina) and Edith CAPPS; death cause: "diphtheria"; informant: father (Erwin); died: 8 Oct. 1924; buried: Erwin; record (1924) # 306.

NORRIS, Josephine; born: 11 Dec. 1859; marriage status: illegible; parents: William MCINTURFF and Sallie BIRCHFIELD; death cause: "apoplexy"; informant: Shelor NORRIS (Unicoi); died: 10 Oct. 1924; buried: Peoples Cemetery; record (1924) # 307.

BATES, Robert; born: 24 Sep. 1843; widower; parents: Hoogis BATES and Ruth COX; death cause: "asthma and pneumonia"; informant: James C. BATES (Unicoi); died: 16 Oct. 1924; buried: Bluff City; record (1924) # 308.

BECKET, Infant; male; born: 19 Oct. 1924; parents: Floyd BECKET and Josie KEPLINGER; death cause: "hemorrhage"; informant: father (Erwin); died: 21 Oct. 1924; buried: Keplinger Cemetery; record # 309.

REEDY, Rebecca; born: __ Nov. 1862; age: 62 years, 11 months and 14 days; widow; parents: Dave LOUDY and mother "unknown"; death cause: "apoplexy"; informant: Mrs. J.W. BARNETT (Erwin); died: 25 Oct. 1924; buried: Erwin; record (1924) # 310.

SAMS, Clinton; born: 9 Sep. 1924; parents: Conway SAMS and Menerva INGLE; death cause: "unknown"; informant: Walter GILLIS (Erwin); died: 26 Oct. 1924; buried: Higgins Creek Cemetery; record (1924) # 311.

BENFIELD, Mary; born: __ Apr. 1852; age: 72 years and 6 months; born: Carter County; widow; parents: William BRUMMETT (Carter County) and Melinda BRITT (Carter County); death cause: "gastro enteritis"; informant: David BRUMMITT (Unicoi); died: 27 Oct. 1924; buried: Lyons Cemetery; record (1924) # 312.

LAWSON, James Wesley; born: 14 Jul. 1923; parents: R.W. LAWSON (North Carolina) and Lettie BROWN (Virginia); death cause: "unknown"; informant: father (Erwin); died: 31 Oct. 1924; buried: Erwin; record (1924) # 313.

TIPTON, Hobart; born: 28 Mar. 1917 in North Carolina; parents: Sam TIPTON (North Carolina) and Sarah BEAM (North Carolina); death cause: "tetanus"; informant: mother (7th District); died: 2 Nov. 1924; buried: Erwin; record (1924) # 314.

FREEMAN, Ann Eliza; born: 3 May 1877; married; parents: Dope (?) SOUTHERLAND and __ (illegible) SHELTON (North Carolina); death cause: "inflammation following appendicitis operation"; informant: G.A. FREEMAN (Unicoi); died: 6 Nov. 1924; buried: Bethesda Cemetery, Washington County; record (1924) # 315.

FOX, Henry Grady Jr.; born: 30 Oct. 1924; parents: H.G. FOX (North Carolina) and Fannie WHITE; death cause: "premature birth"; informant: father (Erwin); died: 8 Nov. 1924; buried: Jobe Cemetery; record (1924) # 316.

MARTIN, Clifton; born: 28 Oct. 1921; parents: L.G. MARTIN (North Carolina) and Lora FOSTER; death cause: "croup"; informant: father (Clear Branch); died: 10 Nov. 1924; buried: Tumbling Hill Cemetery; record (1924) # 317.

MCCURRY, Ethel; born: 16 Jul. 1903 in North Carolina; married; parents: Andrew EDWARDS (North Carolina) and Margaret MCINTURFF (North Carolina); death cause: "round cell sarcoma";

informant: Ernest MCCURRY (Erwin); died: 12 Nov. 1924; buried: Erwin; record (1924) # 318.

ALTMAIER, Peter; age: 55 years; single; potter; born: Germany; death cause: "pulmonary tuberculosis"; died: 17 Nov. 1924; buried: Erwin; record (1924) # 319.

FRYE, H.M.; born: 13 Feb. 1922; parents: H.M. FRYE (North Carolina) and Della YOUNG (North Carolina); death cause: "tubercular meningitis"; informant: father (Erwin); died: 15 Nov. 1924; buried: Limestone Cove; record (1924) # 320.

BURTON, Mrs. M.J.; born: 10 Jan. 1853 in North Carolina; widow; parents: "unknown"; death cause: "lobar pneumonia": died: 16 Nov. 1924; buried: Green Mountain, North Carolina; record (1924) # 321.

BENNETT, Matthew; born: 9 Dec. 1849 in Yancey County, NC.; married; parents: William BENNETT (North Carolina) and Elizabeth BENNETT (North Carolina); death cause: "paralysis"; died in the 4th District, 17 Nov. 1924; buried: Erwin; record (1924) # 322.

YARNELL, James S.; born: 22 Apr. 1838; widower; parents: Martin YARNELL and Harriett BELL; death cause: "nephritis"; informant: Mrs. Lela Yarnell WYATT (Etowah, Tennessee); died: 19 Nov. 1924; buried: Knoxville; record (1924) #323.

MCCURRY, Ruby; born: 12 Mar. 1924; parents: Ernest MCCURRY (North Carolina) and Ethel MCCURRY (North Carolina); death cause: "broncho pneumonia"; informant: father (Erwin); died: 26 Nov. 1924; buried: Erwin; record (1924) # 324.

FOSTER, Fred; born: 15 Dec. 1900; single; parents: Jonathan FOSTER and Geneva HUSKINS; death cause: "automobile accident, neck broken"; informant: Andy FOSTER (Erwin); died: 27 Nov. 1924; buried: Clear Branch; record (1924) # 325.

HOYLE, Andrew; age: 59 years, born: 1865; widower; parents: Hiram HOYLE and Zisa BLANKENSHIP; death cause: "heart disease"; died: 27 Nov. 1924; buried: Flag Pond; record (1924) # 326.

JONES, Roda; age: 28 years; single; parents: Robert JONES and Catherine JONES; death cause: "pellagra"; informant: George HIGGINS (Erwin); died: 28 Nov. 1924; buried: Erwin; record # 327.

LAND, Infant; male; parents: F.E. LAND (North Carolina) and Matta ROSS (North Carolina); death cause: "premature, stillborn"; informant: father (Erwin); died: 5 Nov. 1924; buried: Erwin; record (1924) # 329.

BANNER, Mary; born: 5 Jul. 1897; married; parents: Pinkston HARRIS and Critty HENSLEY; death cause: "heart disease"; informant: Monroe BANNER (Erwin); died: 28 Nov. 1924; buried: Erwin; record # 328.

HENSLEY, May; parents: Walter HENSLEY and Estella SHELTON (Madison County, NC.); death cause: "stillborn"; died at Flag Pond, 12 Nov. 1924; record (1924) # 330.

WALKER, Infant; male; parents: Fayette WALKER and Dina HONEYCUTT (North Carolina); death cause: "stillborn"; informant: father (Erwin); died: 12 Nov. 1924; buried: Earnestville; record # 331.

NORRIS, Alex; born: 20 Aug. 1849; widower; parents: Richard NORRIS and mother "unknown"; death cause: "diarrhea"; informant: Mrs. S.B. PARDUE (Erwin); died: 6 Dec. 1924; buried: Unicoi; record # 332.

HARRIS, Armstrong; born: 6 Apr. 1843; married; parents: Jason HARRIS and Nancy HENSLEY; death cause: "tuberculosis"; informant: Estel HARRIS (Erwin); died: 13 Dec. 1924; buried: Flag Pond; record (1924) # 333.

ILLEGIBLE, Martha; born: 22 Sep. 1878; married; parents: J.W. GOUGE (North Carolina) and Rachel FORBES (North Carolina); death cause: "dropsy"; informant: James GOUGE (Unicoi); died: 24 Dec. 1924; buried: Gouge Cemetery; record (1924) # 334.

TURBYFIELD, Homer; born: 22 Dec. 1912; born: Green Mountain, North Carolina; parents: George TURBYFIELD (North Carolina) and Molly BYRD (North Carolina); death cause: "accidental gunshot wound"; informant: father (Green Mountain, NC.); died: 25 Dec. 1924; buried: Green Mountain, NC.; record (1924) # 335.

BURGNER, Wilma; parents: father not stated and Birdie L. BURGNER; death cause: "premature birth"; informant: mother (Erwin); born/died: 4 Dec. 1924; buried: Erwin; record (1924) # 336.

HEAD, Lucy; parents: Elbert HEAD and Louise GRINDSTAFF; death cause: "stillborn"; informant: father (Unicoi); died: 6 Dec. 1924; record (1924) # 337.

RIDDLE, Infant; male; parents; Cornelius RIDDLE (North Carolina) and Clara HARR; death cause: "stillborn"; informant: father (Erwin); died: 20 Dec. 1924; buried: Erwin; record (1924) # 338.

TITTLE, Anna; born: 17 Feb. __; age: 77 years; widow; parents: Henry AMBROSE and Rody TILSON; death cause: "brights disease"; informant: Rody LEWIS (Erwin); died: 1 Jan. 1925; buried: Fishery Cemetery; record (1925) # 253.

JONES, Leonard Hester; born: 25 Dec. 1924; parents: Chester JONES and Anna Bell SMITH; death cause: "broncho pneumonia"; informant: Sam JONES (Unicoi); died: 5 Jan. 1925; buried: Jones Cemetery; record (1925) # 254.

HIGGINS, Mildred; born: 1 May 1922; parents: M.B. HIGGINS (North Carolina) and Annie RANDLOPH (North Carolina); death cause: "meningitis"; informant: father (Erwin); died: 7 Jan. 1925; buried: Fishery Cemetery; record (1925) # 255.

JACKSON, Infant; male; parents: Everett JACKSON (Virginia) and Alta FLETCHER (Virginia); death cause: "unknown"; informant: father (Erwin); born/died: 13 Jan. 1925; buried: Erwin; record (1925) # 256.

HOWELL, Luke; age: 22 years; born: North Carolina; single; parents: Sid HOWELL (North Carolina) and Minnie HOWELL (North Carolina); death cause: "pulmonary tuberculosis"; informant: father (Erwin); died: 15 Jan. 1925; buried: Erwin; record (1925) # 257.

CHANDLER, Mary; born: 25 Dec. 1842; widow; parents: Thomas FOSTER and Sallie FOSTER; death cause: "lobar pneumonia"; informant: J.H. CHANDLER (Clear Branch); died: 25 Jan. 1925; buried: Chandler Cemetery; record (1925) # 258.

BANKS, John; age: 76 years; married; parents: Moses BANKS (Carter County) and Ruthie DAVIS; death cause: "brights disease"; informant: Nancie BANKS (Unicoi); died: 25 Jan. 1925; buried: Banks Cemetery; record (1925) # 259.

STORY, Hattie; age: 37 years; married; parents: Jim BOONE (?) or POORE (?) and Delia EDWARDS; death cause: "nephritis"; informant: Ed STORY (Erwin); died: 27 Jan. 1925; buried: Erwin; record # 260.

PAGETT, Claude; born: 11 Jan. 1925; parents: Mack PAGETT and Bell FRANCIS (North Carolina); death cause: "unknown, found dead in bed"; informant: mother (Erwin); died: 30 Jan. 1925; buried: Liberty Cemetery; record (1925) #261.

PETERSON, Sarah A.; born: 10 Apr. 1862 in North Carolina; married; parents: Sam HONEYCUTT (North Carolina) and Melinda FORBES (North Carolina); death cause: "heart failure"; informant: M.C. PATTERSON (Erwin); died: 2 Feb. 1925; buried: Erwin; record # 262.

TAPP, Jake; age: 84 years; married; parents: John TAPP and Polly CLOUSE; death cause: "influenza"; informant: Mrs. Jake TAPP (Erwin); died: 4 Feb. 1925; buried: Erwin; record (1925) # 263.

SNEED, Jessie L.; born: 30 Jan. 1925; parents: Alford SNEED and Betty PATE; death cause: "bold hives"; informant: father (Unicoi); died: 5 Feb. 1925; buried: Sneed Cemetery; record (1925) # 264.

BARRY, L.C.; born: 9 Feb. 1858; widower; parents: John W. BARRY and mother "unknown"; death cause: "aortic insufficiency"; informant: John BARRY (Huntdale, NC.); died: 12 Feb. 1925; buried: Huntdale, North Carolina; record (1925) # 265.

COOPER, Ethel; born: 29 Mar. 1905; married; parents: J.T. HIGGINS (North Carolina); and Caldonie STOCKTON; death cause: "endo carditis"; informant: father (Erwin); died: 16 Feb. 1925; buried; Fishery Cemetery; record (1925) # 266.

NORTON, Singleton; age: "about 75 years"; born: North Carolina; married; parents: "unknown"; death cause: "old age and brights disease"; died in the 5th District, 17 Feb. 1925; buried: Erwin; record # 267.

WARLISK, Jane; born: 24 Oct. 1858 in Madison County, NC.; widow; parents: S.J. MOORE (North Carolina) and M_ (illegible) MELTON (North Carolina); death cause: "heart degeneration"; informant: Orville COOPER; died: 3rd District, 18 Feb. 1925; buried: Barnett Cemetery; record (1925) # 268.

BARNETT, Sarah; born: 1 Apr. 1896 in North Carolina; married; parents: John PETERSON (North Carolina) and Becky LAWS (North Carolina); death cause: "miscarriage, pneumonia"; informant: Robert LAWS (Erwin); died: 22 Feb. 1925; buried: Erwin; record (1925) #269.

HONEYCUTT, M.R.; born: 31 Aug. 1863 in South Carolina; married; parents: M.R. HONEYCUTT (South Carolina) and mother "unknown"; death cause: "dropsy"; died in the 5th District, 27 Feb. 1925; buried: Greeneville, South Carolina; record (1925) # 270.

161

BARNETT, Infant; male; parents: __ (illegible) BARNETT (North Carolina) and Sarah LAWS (North Carolina); death cause: "stillborn"; informant: Bob LAWS (Erwin); died: 15 Feb. 1925; buried: Martins Creek; record (1925) # 271.

BOONE, Charley; age: 5 months; parents: Charles P. BOONE (North Carolina) and Lydia TUCKER; death cause: "broncho pneumonia"; informant: father (Erwin); died: 7 Mar. 1925; buried: Erwin; record (1925) # 272.

HENSLEY, Sallie; born: 16 Apr. 1840 in North Carolina; widow; parents: Jack BURNS (North Carolina) and Nancy ENGLAND (North Carolina); death cause: "dropsy, pneumonia and brights disease"; informant: Hannah LETTERMAN (North Carolina); died: 9 Mar. 1925; buried: Erwin; record (1925) # 273.

WOODBY, Junior; born: 1 Nov. 1923; parents: Charley WOODBY and Lizzie JOHNSON; death cause: "lobar pneumonia"; informant: Henry FRY (Unicoi); died: 15 Mar. 1925; buried: Woodby Cemetery; record (1925) # 274.

MURAY, Jessie; age: 62 years; married; parents: "unknown"; death cause: "acute indigestion"; informant: W.S. ERWIN (Erwin); died: 18 Mar. 1925; buried: Erwin; record (1925) # 275.

WOODWARD, Lucinda; born: 17 Jan. 1834 in North Carolina; widow; parents: James SAMS (North Carolina) and Mary __ (Illegible); death cause: "senility"; informant: Lockie WOODWARD (Erwin); died: 18 Mar. 1925; buried: Erwin; record (1925) # 276.

BLANKENSHIP, Lenore Lillian; born: 28 May 1907; single; parents: Lewis J. BLANKENSHIP and Laura E. LAWING; death cause: "pulmonary tuberculosis"; informant: father (Erwin); died: 19 Mar. 1925; buried: Erwin; record (1925) # 277.

JONES, Gilbert; born: 6 Sep. 1924; parents: J.E. JONES and Allas PHILLIPS (Yancey County, NC.); death cause: "abscess of coroted glands"; informant: father (Clear Branch); died: 20 Mar. 1925; buried: Willis Cemetery; record (1925) # 278.

SAMS, Sarah; born: 26 Apr. 1845 in Madison County, NC.; widow; parents: John GILLIS (Greene County) and Ruth TILSON (Greene County); death cause: "accidental burns, fell in fire"; informant: E.B.

162

SAMS (Clear Branch); died: 31 Mar. 1925; buried: Gillis Cemetery; record (1925) # 279.

BAILEY, Infant; male; parents: John BAILEY (North Carolina) and Leona HUGHES (North Carolina); death cause: "stillborn"; informant: father (Erwin); died: 20 Mar. 1925; buried: Erwin; record # 280.

BAILEY, David; age: 73 years; born: North Carolina; parents: John BAILEY (North Carolina) and Marrie BRYANT (North Carolina); death cause: "flu"; informant: Edd BAILEY (Unicoi); died: 2 Apr. 1925; record (1925) # 281.

MORRIS, Mary Lois; born: 26 Jul. 1924; parents: Dudly H. MORRIS and Rosa WISE (North Carolina); death cause: "broncho pneumonia"; informant: father (Erwin); died: 7 Apr. 1925; buried: Johnson City; record (1925) # 283.

MCINTURFF, Sarah Ellen; born: 2 Jun. 1897; single; parents: W.H. MCINTURFF and Lizzie NELSON; death cause: "anemia"; informant: father (Erwin); died: 19 Apr. 1925; buried: Unicoi; record # 284.

RICHARDSON, Lovada; born: 27 Apr. 1904; married; parents: L.A. DUNBAR and Mary E. S_ (illegible); death cause: "nephritis"; informant: father (Erwin); died: 29 Apr. 1925; buried: Martins Creek; record (1925) # 285.

EXXLER, Infant; female; parents: George EXXLER and Annie MORROW; death cause: "stillborn"; died: 20 Apr. 1925; buried: Exxler Cemetery; record (1925) # 286.

TITTLE, Infant; female; parents: Ike TITTLE and Blanch CLOYD (Washington County); death cause: "stillborn"; informant: father (Erwin); died: 25 Apr. 1925; buried: Erwin; record (1925) # 287.

EDENS, Etta T.; born: 7 Oct. 1867; married; parents: Marshal JOHNSON (Virginia) and Hattie BORING; death cause: "carcinoma of __ (illegible)"; informant: H.K. EDENS (Erwin); died: 15 May 1925; buried: Erwin; record (1925) # 288.

FOSTER, James Luther; born: 15 Sep. 1924; parents: J.C. FOSTER and Lena MATHIS; death cause: "broncho pneumonia"; informant: M.C. FOSTER (Erwin); died: 15 may 1925; buried: Erwin; record # 289.

ROGERS, Infant; male; parents: W.M. ROGERS and Fina BAKER; death cause: "premature birth"; informant: father (Erwin); born/died: 16 May 1925; buried: Erwin; record (1925) # 291.

CAMPBELL, John; born: 20 Oct. 1850 in Mitchell County, NC.; married; minister; parents: Bady CAMPBELL and Julia HERRELL (Mitchell County, NC.); death cause: "gastro enteritis"; informant: Cinda CAMPBELL (Unicoi); died: 22 May 1925; buried: Buffalo; record (1925) # 292.

CASTEEL, Jack; age: 55 years; born: Virginia; married; parents: Bill CASTEEL (Virginia) and Polly BLEVINS (Virginia); death cause: "gall stone operation and infection"; informant: Mrs. Jack CASTEEL (Johnson City); died: 22 May 1925; buried: Anderson Cemetery; record (1925) # 293.

FURCHES, Earl; born: 20 Aug. 1923; parents: Marvin FURCHES and Dollie BROYLES; death cause: "bronchial pneumonia"; informant: father (Erwin); died: 22 May 1925; buried: Washington County; record (1925) # 294.

WILSON, John; age: "about 65 years"; born: North Carolina; married; parents: "unknown"; death cause: "unknown"; died in the 5th District, 23 May 1925; buried: Erwin; record (1925) # 295.

EATON, Frank L.; born: 15 Mar. 1881 in Virginia; married; parents: William F. EATON (Virginia) and Fannie LINKENS (Virginia); death cause: "myo carditis"; informant: Mrs. F.L. EATON (Erwin); died: 26 May 1925; buried: Pearisburg, Virginia; record (1925) # 296.

EDWARDS, Infant; male; parents: J.S. EDWARDS (North Carolina) and May PETERSON (North Carolina); death cause: "stillborn"; informant: father (Erwin); died: 21 May 1925; buried: Green Mountain, North Carolina; record (1925) # 297.

O'BRIAN, Infant; female; parents: Clifton O'BRIAN and Nancy PETERSON; death cause: "stillborn"; informant: father (Erwin); died: 31 May 1925; buried: Jobe Cemetery; record (1925) # 298.

GOUGE, James; born: 11 Jun. 1853 in Carter County; married; parents: Thomas GOUGE (Bakersville, NC.) and Sarah BLEVINS (North Carolina); death cause: "high blood pressure and lung congestion"; informant: Dalton GOUGE (Unicoi); died: 3 Jun. 1925; buried: Limestone Cove; record (1925) # 299.

SLAGLE, Claude Elizabeth; born: 24 Jun. 1923; parents: Bill SLAGLE (North Carolina) and Hettie GOUGE (North Carolina); death cause:

"meningitis"; informant: father (Erwin); died: 14 Jun. 1924; buried: North Carolina; record (1925) # 300.

BANNER, David S.; born: 18 Sep. 1924; parents: D.S. BANNER and Alha PRESNELL (North Carolina); death cause: "colitis"; informant: father (Erwin); died: 18 Jun. 1925; buried; Erwin; record (1925) # 301.

DAVIS, Rebecca; born: 12 Aug. 1893; married; parents: James BRUMMETT and Amanda __ (illegible); death cause: "pulmonary tuberculosis"; died: 24 Jun. 1925; buried: Douglas; record (1925) # 302.

DAVIS, Gladys; born: 25 Feb. 1925; parents: John M. DAVIS (North Carolina) and Sarah TREADWAY; death cause: "mitral insufficiency"; informant: father (Erwin); died: 24 Jun. 1925; buried: Bethesda, Washington County; record (1925) # 303.

CASH, John; age: "about 70 years"; married; parents: "unknown"; died in the 12th District, 27 Jun. 1925; buried: Martins Creek; record # 304.

SIZEMORE, Joseph H.; born: 23 May 1922; parents: Jay SIZEMORE and Carry B. HARRISON; death cause: "illio colitis"; informant: father (Erwin); died: 3 Jul. 1925; buried: Erwin; record (1925) # 305.

FOX, H_ (illegible); born: 1 Mar. 1857 in North Carolina; widow; parents: "unknown"; death cause: "colitis"; informant: Hershel FOX (Erwin); died: 3 Jul. 1925; buried: "Jubiler", North Carolina; record (1925) # 306.

WILLIAMS, Child (name not stated); born: 14 Jun. 1921; parents: Hiram WILLIAMS and Heta LOVELACE; death cause: "unknown"; informant: father (Erwin); died: 4 Jul. 1925; record (1925) # 307.

SHEHAN, John; born: 12 Jan. __; age: 70 years; widower; parents: Aaron SHEHAN and Sarah HENSLEY; death cause: "heart failure"; died in the 12th District, 8 Jul. 1925; record (1925) # 308.

F_, Alvin; born: 3 May 1925; parents: Francis FARMER (?) and Ida CHANDLER; death cause: "unknown"; informant: father (Erwin); died: 11 Jul. 1925; buried: Erwin; record (1925) # 309.

WEST, Martha; born: 3 May 1853 in Mitchell County, NC.; widow; parents: John A. STREET and Mattie CAMPBELL; death cause: "carcinoma of uterus"; died in the 4th District, 12 Jul. 1925; buried: Swingle Cemetery; record (1925) # 310.

TIPTON, Aaron Burl; age: 74 years; born: North Carolina; married; parents: Joseph TIPTON (North Carolina) and Julia HONEYCUTT

(North Carolina); death cause: illegible; informant: Alvin TIPTON (Erwin); died: 17 Jul. 1925; buried: Buffalo; record (1925) # 312.

FRANKLIN, Emma; born: 13 Sep. 1876 in Maryland; married; parents: Lewis WELD and Emily WILSON (Maryland); death cause: illegible; died in the 5th District, 24 Jul. 1925; buried: Erwin; record # 313.

VINES, Lafayett; born: 3 May 1842; married; parents: William VINES and Rosa DUNCAN; death cause; "paralysis"; informant: D.A. VINES (Johnson City); died: 24 Jul. 1925; buried: Jonesboro; record # 314.

CAMPBELL, Brownlow; born: 3 Jul. 1907 in North Carolina; parents: J.L. CAMPBELL (North Carolina) and Mary HUGHES (North Carolina); death cause: "accidentally killed by train"; informant: Cad CAMPBELL (Erwin); died: 27 Jul. 1925; buried: Forbes, North Carolina; record (1925) # 315.

STOCKTON, Eliza; born: 2 Oct. 1858; married; parents: Bill CARTER and Jane HARDIN; death cause: "influenza"; informant: Anna MACDOUGALL (Flag Pond); died: 28 Jul. 1925; buried; Stockton Cemetery; record (1925) # 316.

CARTER, Francis Marion; born: 29 Jul. 1925; parents: Frank CARTER (Virginia) and Bessie HOLLAND (North Carolina); death cause: "premature birth"; informant: father (Erwin); died: 30 Jul. 1925; buried: Erwin; record (1925) # 317.

EDWARDS, Infant; female; parents: John EDWARDS and Allie WHITE; death cause: "stillborn"; informant: father (Erwin); died: 1 Jul. 1925; buried: Erwin; record (1925) # 318.

SPARKS, Infant; female; parents: Lewis SPARKS and Clara PHILLIPS; death cause: "stillborn"; informant: Anna MACDOUGALL (Flag Pond); died: 9 Jul. 1925; buried: Moore Cemetery; record (1925) # 319.

LOVETT, Infant; male; parents: Stuart LOVETT (North Carolina) and Bertha GARLAND (North Carolina); death cause: "stillborn"; informant: father (Erwin); died: 18 Jul. 1925; buried: Erwin; record (1925) # 320.

MCINTURFF, Mary; age: 66 years; widow; parents: Preston NORRIS and Cindy TONEY; death cause: "cerebral hemorrhage"; informant: J.A. MCINTURFF (Unicoi); died: 10 Aug. 1925; buried: Unicoi; record (1925) # 321.

PETERSON, Lee; born: 15 Aug. 1923; parents: Tice PETERSON (North Carolina) and Zora DEATON (North Carolina); death cause: "unknown"; died in the 5th District, 21 Aug. 1925; buried: Erwin; record (1925) # 322.

MYERS, Margaret; born: 25 Aug. 1852; widow; parents: Daniel PETTET and Marie LOURY; death cause: "uremia"; informant: W.T. WILSON (Erwin); died: 21 Aug. 1925; buried: Elizabethon, Tennessee; record (1925) # 323.

MATHES, Willard; born: 7 May 1925; parents: Ben MATHES and Tressie MCCANN (Missouri); death cause: "bold hives"; informant: father (Erwin); died: 24 Aug. 1925; buried: Martins Creek; record (1925) # 324.

HARDIN, Carl; born: 12 Mar 1914; parents: W.H. HARDIN and Dessie HARDIN; death cause: "blood poison from splinter in foot"; informant: father (Flag Pond); died: 27 Aug. 1925; buried: Rice Creek; record (1925) # 325.

CHANDLER, Wiley; born: 20 Sep. 1924; parents: Wolford CHANDLER and Betsy LEWIS; death cause: not stated; informant: J.H. CHANDLER (Clear Branch); died: 31 Aug. 1925; buried; Chandler Cemetery; record (1925) # 326.

MORRIS, W.H.; born: 8 Jan. __; age: 55 years; born: North Carolina; married; parents: William MORRIS (North Carolina) and Lucy BALLARD; death cause: "unknown, dropped dead"; informant: Mrs. W.H. MORRIS (Erwin); died: 7 Sep. 1925; buried: New Victory Cemetery; record (1925) # 327.

BRUMMETT, Casey; born: 11 Sep. 1925; parents: Samuel BRUMMETT and Ethel WHITE; death cause: "bronchitis"; informant: father (Unicoi); died: 14 Sep. 1925; buried: Soista Cemetery; record (1925) # 328.

EDWARDS, Infant; male; parents: Clifton EDWARDS and Carrie RIDDLE; death cause: not stated; informant: Lula RIDDLE (Clear Branch; born/died: 16 Sep. 1925; record (1925) # 329.

ARROWOOD, Madeline; parents: John W. ARROWOOD (North Carolina) and Pearle COLE (Virginia); death cause: "premature birth"; informant: father (Erwin); born/died: 17 Sep. 1925; buried: Chunker, Washington County; record (1925) # 330.

LEWIS, Evert; born: 12 Aug. 1925; parents: W.S. LEWIS (North Carolina) and C.J. HENSLEY; death cause: not stated; informant: father (Clear Branch); died: 20 Sep. 1925; buried: Hensley Cemetery; record (1925) # 331.

EDWARDS, (Unknown); female; age: "about 35 years"; married; parents: "unknown"; death cause: "tuberculosis of bowels"; died: 21 Sep. 1925; county burial at Erwin; record (1925) # 332.

EDWARDS, Infant; parents: Clifton EDWARDS and Carrie Martha RIDDLE; death cause: "edema of lungs, lived 6 hours; died: 21 Sep. 1925; buried: Clear Branch; record (1925) # 333.

GRIFFITH, Infant; male; parents: G. GRIFFITH (North Carolina) and Mary MCKINNEY (North Carolina); death cause: "stillborn"; informant: father (Erwin); died: 6 Sep. 1925; buried: Erwin; record (1925) # 334.

LUNCEFORD, Brownlow: born: 25 May 1909; parents: M.P. LUNCEFORD and Delia WILSON; death cause: "unknown, abscess of left leg"; informant: father (Marbleton); died: 5 Oct. 1925; buried: Harvey Cemetery; record (1925) # 335.

THURMAN, Robert; age: 76 years; widower; parents: "unknown"; death cause: "angina pectoris"; informant: Jim HARVEY (Erwin); died: 7 Oct. 1925; buried: Roanoke, Virginia; record (1925) # 336.

YOUNG, Ileen; born: 17 Mar. 1922; parents: Sam H. YOUNG and Rosa DUGGER; death cause: "diphtheria"; informant: S.H. YOUNG (Erwin); died: 19 Oct. 1925; buried: near Milligan; record (1925) # 337.

SHEHAN, Harry; born: 17 Jan. 1924; parents: Wiley FORBES (North Carolina) and Viola SHEHAN; death cause: "diarrhea"; informant: Wiley FORBES (Erwin); died: 20 Oct. 1925; record (1925) # 338.

BRIGGS, Margaret M.; born: 20 Nov. 1853; widow; parents: Samuel MOORE and Charity BROWN; death cause: "heart disease"; informant: Deckey SMITH (Flag Pond); died: 22 Oct. 1925; buried: Rice Creek; record (1925) # 339.

BENNETT, Walter Lee; born: 12 Apr. 1923; parents: Jonnie BENNETT and Annie DUNBAR; death cause: "lobar pneumonia"; informant: father (Erwin); died: 22 Oct. 1925; buried: Martins Creek; record # 340.

LUCAS, Infant; female; parents: Troy LUCAS (Scott County, VA.) and Laky GIBSON (Scott County, VA.); death cause: "stillborn"; informant: father (Erwin); died: 12 Oct. 1925; buried: Erwin; record (1925) # 341.

MILLER, Infant; female; parents: Allie MILLER and Lucy RIDDLE; death cause: "slow labor"; informant: father (Embreeville); born/died: 30 Oct. 1925; buried: Embreeville; record (1925) # 342.

TAYLOR, R.L.; born: 4 Oct. 1844 in North Carolina; widower; parents: Wesley TAYLOR (North Carolina) and Callie PHILLIPS (North Carolina); death cause: "heart disease"; informant: W.J. TAYLOR (Erwin); died: 4 Nov. 1925; buried: Coffee Ridge; record (1925) # 343.

AMBROSE, Alfred M.; born: 16 Jun. 1924; parents: Charles AMBROSE and Ethel KISSICKER (West Virginia); death cause: "double pneumonia"; informant: father (Erwin); died: 6 Nov. 1925; buried: Fishery Cemetery; record (1925) # 344.

FRYE, Della; born: 20 Jun. 1895 in North Carolina; married; parents: Anderson YOUNG (North Carolina); and Bash FREEMAN (North Carolina); death cause: "tuberculosis"; informant: H.M. FRYE (Unicoi); died: 14 Nov. 1925; buried: Buchanan Cemetery; record (1925) # 345.

PETERSON, Samuel; age: 85 years; born: North Carolina; parents: John PETERSON (North Carolina) and Sisey BRYANT (North Carolina); death cause: "aortic insufficiency"; informant: James PETERSON (Erwin); died: 21 Nov. 1925; buried: Green Mountain, North Carolina; record (1925) # 346.

HONEYCUTT, Arvill Lee; born: 25 Oct. 1925; parents: C.C. HONEYCUTT (Yancey County, NC.) and Lilly ADKINS (Yancey County, NC.); death cause: "unknown, found dead in bed"; informant: father (Erwin); died: 23 Nov. 1925; buried: Erwin; record (1925) # 347.

GARLAND, Carcil M.; male; born: 6 Feb. 1910; parents: Bill GARLAND and Mary Lee SHULTZ; death cause: "sugar diabetes"; informant: father (Unicoi); died: 24 Nov. 1925; buried: Garland Cemetery; record (1925) # 348.

SHELTON, Infant; female; parents: Coatney SHELTON (Madison County, NC.); death cause: "stillborn"; informant: father (Erwin); died: 6 Nov. 1925; buried: Erwin; record (1925) # 349.

WILLIAMS, Infant; male; parents: Steve WILLIAMS (Virginia) and Ollie BULLOCK (Kentucky); death cause: "stillborn"; informant: father (Erwin); died: 10 Nov. 1925; buried: Erwin; record (1925) # 350.

BLANKENSHIP, Tom; age: "about 60 years"; married; parents: Jasper BLANKENSHIP and Polly RUNION; death cause: "pellagra"; informant: L.S. TILSON (Erwin); died: 21 Dec. 1925; buried: Flag Pond; record (1925) # 351.

WHITE, Catherine; born: 7 Dec. 1925; parents: James W. WHITE and Phebia E. HAMPTON; death cause: "bronchial pneumonia"; informant: mother (Erwin); died: 22 Dec. 1925; buried: Martins Creek; record (1925) # 352.

TRAYLOR, Hazel Katherine; born: 18 Oct. 1925; parents: Bill TRAYLOR (North Carolina) and Dessie LETTERMAN (North Carolina); death cause: "unknown, found dead in bed"; informant: B.L. LETTERMAN (Erwin); died: 23 Dec. 1925; buried: Martins Creek; record (1925) # 353.

WHITEHEAD, A.L.; age: 56 years; born: Virginia; married; parents: Kincaid WHITEHEAD (Virginia) and mother "unknown"; death cause: "brights disease, high blood pressure"; died: 26 Dec. 1925; buried: Erwin; record (1925) # 354.

BUCKNER, Eugenie Kate; age: 40 years, 7 months and 7 days; born: North Carolina; married; parents: John CHANDLER (North Carolina) and Lucindy BRIGGS (North Carolina); death cause: "pellagra"; informant: George W. BUCKNER (Erwin); died: 30 Dec. 1925; buried: Erwin; record (1925) # 355.

BARTLEY, Martha E.; parents: W.E. BARTLEY (Virginia) and Carrow JACOBS (Virginia); death cause: "stillborn"; informant: father (Erwin); died: 30 Dec. 1925; buried: Wise County, Virginia; record # 356.

LINDSLEY, Caroline; born: 20 Jan. 1901; single; bank clerk; parents: Frank LINDSLEY (New York) and Rowina RYBURN (Virginia); death cause: "fractured skull from fall"; informant: Mrs. William ERWIN; died: 1 Jan. 1926; buried: Erwin; record (1926) # 2170.

MCCURRY, Lillie Howell; age: 23 years; born: North Carolina; married; parents: Will HOWELL (North Carolina) and Ida LEWIS (North Carolina); death cause: "gangrenous appendix"; informant: Sidney MCCURRY (Erwin); died: 14 Jan. 1926; buried: Erwin; record # 2171.

HARRIS, Lindy; born: 23 Sep. 1920; parents: William HARRIS and Jossie HARRIS; death cause: "diphtheria"; informant: father (Erwin); died: 23 Jan. 1926; buried; Erwin; record (1926) # 2172.

GILBERT, Sarah E.; born: 3 Jan. 1856; married; parents: Lewis BANNER and Viana WHITSON; death cause: "brights disease and heart disease"; informant: R.W.H. GILBERT (Erwin); died: 11 Jan. 1926; buried: Erwin; record (1926) # 2173.

LOVE, W.C.; age: 74 years; married; parents: William LOVE (North Carolina) and Nancy A. HARTSEL; death cause: "apoplexy"; informant: Bob ROBERTS (Erwin); died: 29 Jan. 1926; buried: Erwin; record (1926) # 2174.

BOWMAN, Earnest Taylor; born: 7 Jun. 1923; parents: John BOWMAN (Mitchell County, NC.) and Nettie BIRCHFIELD (Mitchell County, NC); death cause: "gastritis"; informant: Mrs. Sallie INGRAM (Unicoi); died: 23 Jan. 1926; buried: Horton Cemetery; record (1926) # 2175.

BROWN, Catherine; born: 9 May 1847; age: 78 years, 8 months and 2 days; divorced; parents: William BROWN and Rachel C_ (illegible); death cause: "cancer of throat"; informant: M.J. BROWN (Clear Branch); died: 11 Jan. 1926; buried: Clear Branch; record # 2176.

TIPTON, Neoma; born: 10 Feb. 1926; parents: Joseph TIPTON and Nancy BARNETT (Mitchell County, NC.); death cause: not stated; informant: Frank TIPTON (Unicoi); died: 10 Feb. 1926; buried: Tipton Cemetery; record (1926) # 4848.

MILLER, Francis; age: 36 years; married; parents: John HAMMITT and Maggie ROBINSON; death cause: "pulmonary tuberculosis"; informant: Hugh OWENS (Johnson City); died: 5 Jan. 1926; buried: Anderson Chapel; record (1926) # 4849.

WHITE, Masy; age: "unknown"; born: Greene County; divorced; parents: H. DICKERSON and D. CARRELL; death cause: "influenza"; informant: Walter BLEVINS (Johnson City); died: 17 Jan. 1926; buried: Anderson Chapel; record (1926) # 4850.

BARNETT, Barnett; born: 7 Feb. 1845 in Ohio; widower; parents: J.W. BARNETT (Ohio) and H.C. SNEAD (Ohio); death cause: "brights and general wear out"; informant: William BARNETT (Erwin); died: 3 Feb. 1926; buried: Erwin; record (1926) 4851.

SAMS, Galden; born: 11 Dec. 1925; parents: Robert SAMS and Mabel KENLY; death cause: "influenza"; informant: mother (Erwin); died: 16 Feb. 1926; buried: Higgins Creek; record (1925) # 4852.

SMITH, Pauline; born: 26 Jun. 1925; parents: Sam SMITH and Annie AMBROS; death cause: "pneumonia"; informant: father (Erwin); died: 20 Feb. 1926; buried: Fishery Cemetery; .record (1926) # 4853.

PETERSON, Boyd; born: 9 Feb. 1926; parents: David PATERSON (North Carolina) and Andie GARLAND (North Carolina); death cause: "unknown"; informant: Ben PETERSON (Erwin); died: 20 Feb. 1926; buried: 21 Feb. 1926 at Green Mountain, NC; record (1926) # 4854.

PETERSON, Loyd; born: 9 Feb. 1926; parents: David PATERSON (North Carolina) and Ander GARLAND (North Carolina); death cause: "unknown"; informant: S.G. PATERSON (Erwin); died: 21 Feb. 1926; buried: 23 Feb. 1926 at Green Mountain, NC; record (1926) # 4855.

TILSON, Leroy S.; born: 13 Feb. 1854; married; physician; parents: William E. TILSON and Katherine SAMS; death cause: "pellagra"; informant: W.E. TILSON (Erwin); died: 26 Feb. 1926; buried: Jobe Cemetery; record (1926) # 4856.

DAVIS, Thurla; age: 23 years; single; parents: John DAVIS (North Carolina) and Guda GOUGE; death cause: "goiter"; informant: Ernest DAVIS (Unicoi); died: 20 Mar. 1926; buried: Gouge Cemetery; record (1926) # 8063.

BAKER, Ezkill; born: 9 Jul. 1840; married; parents: Wilson BAKER and Biddie GARLAND; death cause: "paralysis"; informant: Martha C. BAKER (Unicoi); died: 17 Mar. 1926; buried: Cole Cemetery; record (1926) # 8064.

GRINDSTAFF, Eliza; born: _ Sep. 1854; married; parents: James BRITT and Nancy BRITT; death cause: "organic heart disease"; died in the 4th District, 5 Mar. 1926; buried: Britt Cemetery; record # 8065.

BAKER, Ezekiel; born: 9 Jul. 1840 in Carter County; married; parents: Wilson BAKER (Carter County) and Biddy GARLAND (Carter County); death cause: "apoplexy"; died in 2nd District, 17 Mar. 1926; buried: Cole Cemetery; record (1926) # 8066.

SOUGER, Thomas Early; born: 8 Feb. 1869 in Virginia; married; parents: Christian SOUGER (Virginia) and Virginia EARLY (Virginia);

death cause: "tuberculosis"; informant: Mrs. T.E. SOUGER (Unicoi); died: 7 Mar. 1926; buried: Swingle Cemetery; record (1926) # 8067.

TIPTON, Neoma; born: 10 Feb. 1926; parents: Joseph TIPTON and Nancy BARNETT (Mitchell County, NC.); death cause: not stated; informant: Mrs. Frank TIPTON (Unicoi); died: 10 Feb. 1926; buried: Tipton Cemetery; record (1926) # 4868.

PRITCHARD, Lena J.; born: 20 Nov. 1881; married; parents: J.O. AKERS (Virginia) and Liza T_ (illegible); death cause: "apoplexy"; informant: L.N. PRITCHARD (Erwin); died: 18 Mar 1926; buried: Erwin; record (1926) # 8069.

RUNYON, Minnie Lee; age: 28 years; born: 14 Jul. __; married; parents: James HURDT (North Carolina) and Elizabeth SLIGER; death cause: illegible; died: 30 Mar. 1926; buried: Erwin; record (1926) # 8070.

FARMER, Martha E.; born: 14 Jan. 1846 in Virginia; widow; parents: Abraham FULWILDER (Virginia) and Martha Ann CONELY (Virginia); death cause: "pneumonia and bronchitis"; died in the 5th District, 2 Feb. 1926; record (1926) # 8071.

GARLAND, Valdine; born: 23 Nov. 1919; parents: Earl GARLAND and Cleo WEEKS; death cause: "gangrenous appendix"; informant: father (Erwin); died: 8 Feb. 1926; buried: Carter County; record # 8072.

TILSON, Sarah; born: 9 Feb. 1856; parents: illegible; death cause: "unknown"; informant: E.D. TILSON (Clear Branch); died: 19 Mar. 1926; buried: Clear Branch; record (1926) # 8073.

WILLIS, Ardella; born: 25 Sep. 1886; parents: Charles FOSTER and M.E. HENSLEY; death cause: "heart failure"; informant: Pery WILLIS (Clear Branch); died: 18 Mar 1926; buried: Foster Cemetery; record (1926) # 8074.

MARTIN, Marvin; born: 21 Jan. 1924; parents: L.G. MARTIN (North Carolina) and Lora FOSTER; death cause: "hernia"; informant: father (Clear Branch); died: 20 Feb. 1926; buried: Foster Cemetery; record (1926) # 8075.

BRIGGS, Peter; born: 2 Feb. 1854 in Georgia; married; parents: Therman BRIGGS (Georgia) and Oma STROND (Georgia); death cause: "broncho pneumonia"; died at Flag Pond, 5 Mar. 1926; buried: Rice Creek; record (1926) # 8076.

BRIGGS, Julia Finnettie; born: 12 Apr. 1926; parents: Homer BRIGGS and Flora May PROFFITT; death cause: "unknown"; died: 12 Apr. 1926; buried: Blankenship Cemetery; record (1926) # 10830.

MACKINTOSH, Cora Lee; born: 16 May 1901 in Madison County, NC.; married; parents: M.O. PACK (Poke County, NC.) and Mary Jane LEWIS (Madison County, NC.); death cause: "tuberculosis"; informant: Anna MACDOUGALL (Flag Pond); died: 4 Apr. 1926; buried: Rice Creek; record (1926) # 10831.

BANKS, Helen Marie; born: 10 May 1925; parents: Walter BANKS and Mae MCKINNEY (Carter County); death cause: "spinal affliction"; informant: Robert BANKS (Unicoi); died: 3 Apr. 1926; buried: Banks Cemetery; record (1926) # 10832.

SUTPHIN, Glenna May; born: 31 May 1926; parents: Elbert HICKS (Mitchell County, NC.) and Maud SUTPHIN (Washington County); death cause: "strangulation on milk"; informant: U.S. BOWMAN, JP; died: 5 Apr. 1926; buried: Swingle Cemetery; record (1926) # 10833.

MCLAUGHLIN, Willetta Manson; born: 25 Sep. 1920; parents: William K..MCLAUGHLIN and Francie E. WILCOX; death cause: "struck by an automobile crossing pike"; informant: father (Unicoi); died: 4 Apr. 1926; buried: Jones Cemetery; record (1926) # 10834.

GRIFFIN, Pat (male); age: "about 65 years"; born: New York; single; parents: "unknown"; death cause: "heart disease"; died: 15 Apr. 1916; buried: Erwin; record (1926) # 10835.

HARVEY, Alfred; age: 23 years; married; parents: Thomas HARVEY and Mariah HARVEY; death cause: "pulmonary tuberculosis"; informant: Sam HARVEY (Erwin); died: 21 Apr. 1926; buried: Erwin; record (1926) # 10836.

MORGAN, Laura C.; born: 17 Apr. __; age: 69 years; widow; parents: John PATTON and mother "unknown"; death cause: "carcinoma of uterus"; informant: Clarence MORGAN (Erwin); died: 23 Apr. 1926; buried: Erwin; record (1926) # 10838.

B_ (illegible), Cordelia; born: 3 Aug. 1923 in Washington County; parents: Eugen B_ (illegible)(Carter County) and Mirra PRICE (Washington County); death cause: "flu, pneumonia"; died: 3 Apr. 1926; buried: Tucker Cemetery; record (1926) # 10839.

THOMAS, Ruby; born: 11 Jun. 1923; parents: Grady THOMAS (North Carolina) and Mary OLLIS (North Carolina); death cause: "accidental burn"; informant: father (Erwin); died: 15 Apr. 1926; buried: Martins Creek; record (1926) # 10840.

STOCKTON, Alta Madge; age: 8 months; parents: L.H. STOCKTON and Dora MASHBURN; death cause: "pneumonia"; informant: father (Erwin); died: 17 Apr. 1926; buried: Flag Pond; record (1926) # 10841.

BAILEY, Delcina; born: 25 Oct. 1861 in North Carolina; married; parents: Charles BYRD (North Carolina) and Eliza GRIFFITH (North Carolina); death cause: "intestinal nephritis"; informant: Hiram BAILEY (North Carolina); died: 23 Feb. 1926; buried: Erwin; record # 10842.

CAMPBELL, Eray; born: 28 Nov. 1925; parents: Jack CAMPBELL and Dora GOUGE; death cause: "diarrhea"; informant: Sarah CAMPBELL (Unicoi); died: 24 May 1926; buried: Campbell Cemetery; record (1926) # 13262.

DAUGHERTY, James; age: 61 years; single; parents: Joseph DAUGHERTY and Rachel SWANNER; death cause: "heart dropsy"; informant: Thomas DAUGHERTY (Unicoi); died: 21 Apr. 1926; record (1926) # 13263.

WOODFIN, David Oscar; age: 72 years, 6 months and 5 days; born: North Carolina; widower; parents: John WOODFIN (North Carolina) and Lula LEWIS (North Carolina); death cause: "hemaplegia"; informant: Mrs. John RENFRO (Asheville, North Carolina); died: 1 May 1926; record (1926) # 13264.

CHANDLER, Fannie; born: 20 Oct. 1906; married; parents: father "unknown" and Cora TITTLE; death cause: "pulmonary tuberculosis"; informant: J.F. CHANDLER (Erwin); died: 2 May 1926; buried: Erwin; record (1926) # 13265.

HARVEY, Thomas V.; born: 22 Sep. 1878; widower; parents: Dewey HARVEY and Harriett E. SWANN; death cause: "anemia"; informant: Sam HARVEY (Erwin); died: 10 May 1926; record (1926) # 13266.

RICE, Malinda; born: 8 Sep. 1858 in North Carolina; married; parents: John SHELTON (North Carolina) and Malinda METCALF (North Carolina); death cause: "angina pectoris"; informant: John C. RICE (Erwin); died: 31 May 1926; buried: Rice Creek; record # 13267.

BLACK, Ralph; born: 4 Jul. 1924 in Alabama; parents: G.B. BLACK (Alabama) and Julia WHITEHEAD (Alabama); death cause: "bronchial pneumonia"; informant: G.S. BLACK (Erwin); died: 25 May 1926; buried: Dothan, Alabama; record (1926) # 13268.

HEAD, Carl; born: 3 May 1926; parents: W.J. HEAD and Dora BYRD (Carter County); death cause: "lobar pneumonia"; informant: Blake HEAD (Unicoi); died: 21 Jun. 1926; buried: O'Brien Cemetery; record (1926) # 15636.

CARRELL, Andy; born: 3 Mar. 1876 in Lee County, Virginia; married; parents: George CARRELL (Washington County) and Jane DENTON (Washington County); death cause: "accidentally fell from tree dislocating neck"; informant: J.R. ANDERSON (Johnson City); died: 21 Jun. 1926; buried: Anderson Cemetery; record (1926) # 15637.

MCNABB, Sarah Ellen; born: 1 May 1903; married; parents: David CAMPBELL (North Carolina) and Sarah HONEYCUTT (North Carolina); death cause: "influenza and pneumonia"; informant: Julia JENKINS (Unicoi); died: 30 Jun. 1926; buried: Limestone Cove; record (1926) # 15638.

MILLER, Ora Ellen; born: 16 Dec. 1894 in Ohio; married; parents: H.R. FELTY (Ohio) and Allice DAVIS (Ohio); death cause: "pulmonary tuberculosis"; informant: C.N. MILLER (Erwin); died: 24 Jun. 1926; buried: East Liverpool, Ohio; record (1926) # 15539.

REAVES, Kittie; born: 24 Oct. 1854; widow; parents: Ozy WILLIAMSON and Elizabeth SEATON; death cause: "carcinoma of cervix, hysterectomy"; informant: R.B. REAVES (Greeneville); died: 15 May 1926; buried: Greeneville; record (1926) # 15640.

TILSON, Axie; born: 28 Mar 1854; single; parents: George TILSON and Katie BAILS; death cause: not stated; informant: John TILSON (Clear Branch); died: 19 Jun. 1926; buried: Tilson Cemetery; record (1926)

MCINTOSH, Infant; female; parents: Lincoln MCINTOSH and Opal CARROLL (Straight Fork, TN.); death cause: "premature birth"; informant: father (Clear Branch); born/died: 26 Jun. 1926; buried: Mt. Pleasant; record (1926) # 15642.

DAVIS, Elizabeth; born: 17 Oct. 1865; widow; parents: Ivens CAMPBELL and Betsy CAMPBELL; death cause: "goiter"; informant:

John DAVIS (Erwin); died: 14 Jul. 1926; buried: Davis Cemetery; record (1926) # 18394.

BIRCHFIELD, Cordelia; born: 20 Nov. 1873 in Washington County; married; parents: Bob YOUNG (North Carolina) and Jane DANIELS; death cause: "paralysis"; informant: David BIRCHFIELD (Unicoi); died: 22 Jul. 1926; buried: Buchanan Cemetery; record (1926) # 18395.

BRITT, Minnie E.; born: 28 Mar. 1892 in North Carolina; married; parents: Charles SHERILL (North Carolina) and Hattie CASWELL (North Carolina); death cause: "pulmonary tuberculosis"; died: 29 Jul. 1926; buried: Douglas Cemetery; record (1926) # 18396.

GRIFFITH, Bertha; born: 16 May 1918 in North Carolina; parents: W.M. GRIFFITH (North Carolina) and Nellie HOLLOWAY (North Carolina); death cause: "mitral insufficiency"; informant: father (Erwin); died: 12 Jul. 1926; buried: Huntdale, North Carolina; record # 18397.

SIMMONS, Evelin; born: 17 Feb. 1926; parents: Noah SIMMONS and Annie RENFRO (North Carolina); death cause: "unknown"; informant: father (Erwin); died: 19 Jul. 1926; buried: Rock Creek; record # 18398.

PETERSON, Birdie; born: 18 Nov. 1894 in North Carolina; married; parents: John DUNCAN (North Carolina) and Loretta HONEYCUTT (North Carolina); death cause: "liver inflammation"; informant: Charles C. PETERSON (Erwin); died: 23 Jul. 1926; buried: Green Mountain, North Carolina; record (1926) # 18399.

HARRIS, Charles; born: 12 Aug. 1910; parents: William HARRIS and Oma GLOVER; death cause: "myocarditis"; informant: Carl HARRIS (Erwin); died: 23 Jun. 1926; buried: Fishery Cemetery; record # 18400.

FRANKLIN, Infant; female; parents: Harry FRANKLIN and Annabeth TABB (Georgia); death cause: "premature birth"; informant: father (Erwin); born/died: 4 Jun. 1926; buried: Erwin; record (1926) # 18401.

WOODBY, Infant; male; parents: Jim WOODBY and Julie BARRY; death cause: "premature birth"; informant: father (Erwin); born/died: 3 Apr. 1926; buried: Limestone Cove; record (1926) # 18402.

PEAK, Rachel; age: 25 years; born: North Carolina; married; parents: M.G. EDWARDS (North Carolina) and Caroline FINDER (North Carolina); death cause: "pellagra"; informant: Garrett EDWARDS (Erwin); died: 9 Jul. 1926; buried: Madison County, North Carolina; record (1926) # 18403.

WILLIAMS, Infant; male; born: 30 Jun. 1926; parents: William WILLIAMS and Nellie COLLINS; death cause: "not stated, found dead in bed"; informant: father (Luttrell, TN.); buried: Luttrell Cemetery; record (1926) # 18404.

CAMPBELL, C_ (illegible); born: 17 Mar. 1852; widow; parents: Wesley METCALF and Rachel PRICE; death cause: "cerebral hemorrhage"; informant: Ada METCALF (Unicoi); died: 10 Aug. 1926; buried: McInturff Cemetery; record (1926) # 20815.

FURCHES, Sheridan; born: 4 May 1926; parents: W.T. EDWARDS (North Carolina) and Edna REEVES; death cause: "pneumonia"; informant: father (Erwin); died: 14 Aug. 1926; buried: Martins Creek; record (1926) # 20816.

ILLEGIBLE, Josephus; born: 17 Apr. __; age: 17 years; parents: Robert _ (illegible) and Prescilla TAYLOR; death cause: illegible; died: 21 Aug. 1926; buried: Earnestville; record (1926) # 20817.

RANDOLPH, M.Z.; age: 68 years; born: North Carolina; widower; parents: William RANDOLPH and Visa PHILIPS (North Carolina); death cause: "cerebral hemorrhage"; died: 2 Jul. 1926; buried: Martins Creek; record (1926) # 20818.

HARRIS, Luther; age: 19 years; single; parents: W.M. HARRIS and Oma GLOVER; death cause: "unknown"; informant: Carl HARRIS (Erwin); died: 7 Jun. 1926; buried: Fishery Cemetery; record # 20819.

RIDDLE, Pearl; age: 10 months; parents: W.L. RIDDLE and Rettie BRADFORD (North Carolina); death cause: "bold hives"; informant: Tom RIDDLE (Erwin); died: 4 Aug. 1926; buried: Martins Creek; record (1926) # 20820.

MCKINNEY, T.W.; born: 27 Jul. 1866 in North Carolina; married; parents: Henry MCKINNEY (North Carolina) and Sarah WISEMAN (North Carolina); death cause: "pernicious anemia"; informant: Mrs. T.W. MCKINNEY (Erwin); died: 21 Aug. 1926; buried; Erwin; record (1926) # 20821.

HASTINGS, Nancy Jane; born: 6 Jun. 1855 in North Carolina; married; parents: Samuel STOCKTON (North Carolina) and Elizabeth H_ (illegible); death cause: "cerebral hemorrhage"; informant: J.C. HASTINGS (Erwin); died: 11 Aug. 1926; buried: Flag Pond; record (1926) # 20822.

LOYD, Fred; born: 4 Mar. 1913; parents: Laddie LOYD and Kittie MORROW; death cause: "unknown"; died: 15 Sep. 1926; buried: Loyd Cemetery, Flag Pond; record (1926) # 23172.

MCNABB, A.W.; born: 23 Jun. 1859; married; parents: Davie MCNABB and Vinie LOOPER; death cause: "carcinoma of prostate"; informant: Charles MCNABB (Unicoi); died: 11 Sep. 1926; buried: McNabb Cemetery; record (1926) # 23173.

FRANKLIN, Hester; born: 3 Jun. 1861 in North Carolina; married; parents: Joe WOLDRUP (North Carolina) and Millie RAY (North Carolina); death cause: "colesystitis"; informant: Fred FRANKLIN (Erwin); died: 10 Sep. 1926; buried: Martins Creek; record # 23175.

MILLER, Wayne; born: 24 Nov. 1922; parents: C.O. MILLER (Virginia) and May BAXTER; death cause: "diphtheria"; informant: Mrs. Ed GARLAND (Erwin); died: 16 Sep. 1926; buried: Erwin; record (1926) # 23176.

MCCURRY, Maxine; age: 5 months; parents: Harrison MCCURRY (North Carolina) and Marie SPARKS (North Carolina); death cause: "double pneumonia"; informant: Tim SPARKS (Erwin); died: 28 Sep. 1926; record (1926) # 23177.

TIPTON, Infant; sex: not stated; born: 20 Sep. 1926; parents: Sam TIPTON (North Carolina) and Bell BARNETT; death cause: "unknown"; informant: father (Erwin); died: 30 Sep. 1926; buried: Erwin; record (1926) # 23178.

GRINDSTAFF, Russell; age: 69 years; married; parents: Zack GRINDSTAFF and Annie DAVIS; death cause: "aortic insufficiency"; informant: Mrs. Russell GRINDSTAFF (Unicoi); died: 12 Oct. 1926; buried: Garland Cemetery; record (1926) # 25631.

HONEYCUTT, Lucy; born: 25 Oct. 1918; parents: C.H. HONEYCUTT (North Carolina) and Allie PETERSON (North Carolina); death cause: "typhoid fever"; informant: father (Unicoi); died: 8 Oct. 1926; buried: Peterson Cemetery; record (1926) # 25632.

HOPSON, Neoma; born: 30 May 1917; parents: Bob HOPSON (North Carolina) and Uncella LUCAS; death cause: "pneumonitis"; informant: J.A. HOPSON (Unicoi); died: 10 Oct. 1926; buried: Unicoi; record (1926) # 25633.

CARROLL, Sarah A. Brummett; age: 39 years; married; parents: Thomas BRUMMETT and Annie BUCK; death cause: "preama"; informant: Sam BRUMETT (Unicoi); died: 24 Oct. 1926; record (1926) # 25634.

MCCALL, Julia; born: 20 Sep. 1877 in North Carolina; married; parents: Jim HOWE (North Carolina) and Laura PRICE (North Carolina); death cause: "angina pectoris"; informant: Mary RAY (Erwin); died: 18 Oct. 1926; buried: Erwin; record (1926) # 25635.

BALL, Lula; born: 4 Mar. 1893; single; parents: George BALL and Mary E. BROWN; death cause: "bowel obstruction, appendix operation"; informant: Mrs. Sallie BAYLESS (Jonesboro); died: 26 Oct. 1926; buried: Mt. Wesley Cemetery; record (1926) # 25636.

BENNETT, Bayless; age: 75 years; married; parents: Amos BENNETT and mother "unknown"; death cause: "apoplexy"; informant: Lee BENNETT (Erwin); died: 18 Oct. 1926; buried: Kingsport; record (1926) # 25637.

MILLER, Helen; born: 22 Oct. 1926; parents: Ernest MILLER (North Carolina) and Mamie RIDDLE; death cause: "unknown"; informant: father (Erwin); died: 29 Oct. 1926; buried: Martins Creek; record (1926) # 25638.

HENSLEY, Joel; age: 73 years; married; parents: W.R. HENSLEY and Elvina CHANDLER; death cause: "pellagra"; died: 5 Oct. 1926; buried: Hensley Cemetery; record (1926) # 25639.

CHANDLER, C_ (illegible); born: 19 Sep. 1900; parents: Isaac CHANDLER and mother's name illegible; death cause: "pellagra"; informant: father (Clear Branch); died: 22 Oct. 1926; record # 25640.

GENTRY, John; born: 11 Nov. 1926; parents: Kabe GENTRY and Bonnie HIGGINS; death cause: "unknown"; informant: Anna MCDOUGALL (Flag Pond); died: 13 Nov. 1926; buried: Lawing Cemetery; record (1926) # 28125.

SNEYD, Daisey Lee; born: 24 Jan. 1924; parents: A.T. SNEYD and Bettie PATE; death cause: "typhoid fever"; informant: father (Unicoi); died: 10 Nov. 1926; buried: Sneyd Cemetery; record (1926) # 28126.

STREET, Helen Maria; born: 18 Mar. 1925; parents: Glenn STREET and Destie Lee BENNETT (North Carolina); death cause: "whooping cough"; informant: Teter HOWELL (Unicoi); died: 20 Nov. 1926; buried: Peterson Cemetery; record (1926) # 28127.

PRICE, Infant; male; parents: Paris PRICE and Iva BUCKLES; death cause: "convulsions"; informant: father (Erwin); born/died: 17 Nov. 1926; buried: Greene County; record (1926) # 28128.

MOORE, Julius; age: 61 years; born: North Carolina; married; parents: Jackson MOORE (North Carolina) and Polly BRYANT (North Carolina); death cause: "homicide, gunshot wound in abdomen"; informant: Mrs. Julius MOORE (Flag Pond); died: 14 Nov. 1926; buried: Rocky Fork, Tennessee; record (1926) # 28129.

COOK, Betsy; age: 90 years; born: North Carolina; widow; parents: "unknown"; death cause: "old age"; informant: W.M. LAWING (Erwin); died: 11 Nov. 1926; buried: Erwin; record (1926) # 28130.

HIGGINS, Infant; male; parents: Arthur HIGGINS (North Carolina) and _ EDWARDS; death cause: not stated; informant: father (Clear Branch); died: 25 Nov. 1926; record (1926) # 27131

WILSON, Lillian E. Dalton; born: 23 Jun. 1896; married; post mistress; parents: Lewis DALTON and Matilda HAYNES; death cause: "apoplexy"; informant: L.C. DALTON (Knoxville); died: 8 Nov. 1926; buried: Greenwood Cemetery; record (1926) # 28132.

STACK, Elizabeth; born: 3 Oct. 1859 in North Carolina; married; parents: John NEWMAN (Germany) and Sarah BEESON (North Carolina); death cause: "pellagra"; informant: C.E. STACK (Erwin); died: 4 Dec. 1926; buried: Kearnsville, NC.; record (1926) # 30783.

WILLIAMS, Ruth; born: 6 Nov. 1902; single parents: Dr. __ (illegible) WILLIAMS and Francis HENSLEY (North Carolina); death cause: "cancer of thyroid"; informant: mother (Erwin); died: 5 Dec. 1926; buried: Erwin; record (1926) # 30784.

LOY, Artie Louise; born: 17 Jul. 1892; married; parents: John BRADLEY and Cynthia LEDERWOOD; death cause: "self inflicted gunshot wound"; informant: S.W. LOY (Erwin); died: 20 Dec. 1926; buried: Knoxville; record (1926) # 30785.

TINKER, Robert C.; age: 57 years; married; parents: father unknown and Margaret TINKER; death cause: "nephritis"; died in the 7th District, 22 Mar. 1926; buried: Earnestville; record (1926) # 30786.

181

SAMS, Catherine; born: 21 Dec. 1926; parents: Will SAMS and Cora SHELTON; death cause: "unknown"; informant: father (Erwin); died: 23 Dec. 1926; buried: Erwin; record (1926) # 30787.

BAILEY, Catherine; born: 25 Sep. 1924; parents: Sam BAILEY (North Carolina) and Clara FANNING; death cause: "malnutrition"; informant: father (Erwin); died: 30 Dec. 1926; record (1926) # 30788.

JEWEL, Infant; female; born: 10 Mar. 1926; parents: father not stated and Lola JEWEL; death cause: "unknown"; informant: J.W. HOWELL (Erwin); died: 12 Apr. 1926; record (1926) # 30789.

JEWEL, Infant; female; age: 3 months; parents: father not stated and Ellen JEWEL; death cause: "measles and pneumonia"; informant: J.W. HOWELL (Erwin); died: 6 Mar. 1926; record (1926) # 30790.

BAILEY, June; age: "about 76 years"; born: North Carolina; widow; parents: __ MORRIS and mother not stated; death cause: "old age"; died: 6 Jan. 1926; record (1926) # 30791.

EDWARDS, Stella M.; born: 16 Jun. 1926; parents: father not stated and Mary EDWARDS; death cause: not stated; informant: Bonnie EDWARDS (Clear Branch); died: 3 Dec. 1926; buried; Lewis Cemetery; record (1926) # 30792.

WATTS, William; born: 15 Mar. 1878; parents: Dempsy WATTS and Adline FOSTER; death cause: not stated; informant: N.J. WATTS (Clear Branch); died: 22 Dec. 1926; buried: Foster Cemetery; record (1926) # 30793.

HENSLEY, Sarah; born: 11 Dec. 1861; married; parents: Samuel HIGGINS and Elizabeth HIGGINS; death cause: "old age"; informant: W.E. HIGGINS (Flag Pond); died: 11 Dec. 1926; buried: Higgins Chapel; record (1926) # 30794.

HARDING, Ford; born: 1 Oct. 1926; parents: Sam HARDING and Sarah RAY; death cause: "bold hives"; died: 31 Dec. 1926; buried: Blankenship Cemetery; record (1926) # 30795.

SPARKS, Ralph; born: 11 Dec. 1926; parents: Green SPARKS (Yancey County, NC.) and Belle WEST; death cause: illegible; informant: G.B. SPARKS (Unicoi); died: 15 Dec. 1926; buried: Swingle Cemetery; record (1926) # 30796.

WHITE, Irene; born: 24 Aug. 1925 in Virginia; parents: Landon WHITE and Josie HUGHES; death cause: "diphtheria"; informant: father (Erwin); died: 14 Oct. 1926; buried: Rock Creek; record # 30797.

EDENS, Manda; born: 27 Apr. 1884; married; parents: Stuart HIGGINS and mother "unknown"; death cause: "unknown"; informant: M.F. EDENS (Elizabethton); died: 2 Jan. 1927; buried: Flag Pond; record (1927) # 2093.

HUGHES, Garth; born: 6 May 1920 in North Carolina; parents: Holden HUGHES (North Carolina) and Mollie PETERSON (North Carolina); death cause: "measles and pneumonia"; informant: father (Erwin); died: 6 Jan. 1927; buried: Poplar, North Carolina; record (1927) # 2094.

MONTGOMERY, Clarence; born: 23 Dec. 1876 in Georgia; married; undertaker; parents: Hugh MONTGOMERY (Georgia) and Jennie JONES (Georgia); death cause: "gastric indigestion"; informant: Jones MONTGOMERY (Rome, Georgia); died: 8 Jan. 1927; buried: Jellico, Tennessee; record (1927) # 2095.

DEYTON, Dolly; born: __ May 1891 in North Carolina; married; parents: John RENFRO (North Carolina) and Sallie WELCH (North Carolina); death cause: "brights and eclampsia"; informant: Joe DEATON (Erwin); died: 10 Jan. 1927; buried: Green Mountain, North Carolina; record (1927) # 2096.

MEREDITH, Anna Virginia; born: 18 Mar. 1845 in Virginia; widow; parents: J.H. WILLIAMS (Giles County, VA.) and mother "unknown"; death cause: "dropsy"; informant: J.F. MEREDITH (Erwin); died: 19 Jan. 1927; buried: Pembroke, Virginia; record (1927) # 2097.

PETERSON, Infant; male (twins); parents: Doss PETERSON (North Carolina) and __ (illegible) BRYANT; death cause: "premature births"; died: 21 Jan. 1927; buried: Green Mountain, North Carolina; record (1927) # 2098 and 2099.

NEWEL, Edwin Tollison; born: 27 Jun. 1918 in South Carolina; parents: Sam H. NEWEL (North Carolina) and Evelyn TOLLISON (South Carolina); death cause: "accidental gunshot wound"; died: 22 Jan. 1927; buried: South Carolina; record (1927) # 2100.

ERWIN, C.H.; born: 15 May 1881; married; circuit court clerk; parents: D.J.N. ERWIN and Susan C. YOUNG (Washington County); death

183

cause: "double pneumonia"; informant: W.S. ERWIN (Erwin); died: 25 Jan. 1927; buried: Erwin; record (1927) # 2101.

LAWSON, Walter Herbert; born: 23 Jan. 1927; parents: R.W. LAWSON (North Carolina) and Lettie BROWN (North Carolina); death cause: "__ (illegible) hemorrhage"; informant: father (Erwin); died: 28 Jan. 1927; record (1927) # 2102.

MILLER, Infant; male; born: 10 Jan. 1927; parents: Frank MILLER and Aroura POORE; death cause: "7 month baby"; informant: father (Embreeville); died: 13 Jan. 1927; record (1927) # 2103.

RIDDLE, Sara; age: 48 years; born: North Carolina; married; parents: William A. EDWARDS (North Carolina) and mother "unknown"; death cause: "heart failure"; informant: Frank WHALEY (Erwin); died: 1 Jan. 1927; buried: Erwin; record (1927) # 2104.

CLOUSE, James M.; born: 5 Sep. 1867; married; parents: John CLOUSE and Elizabeth TINKER; death cause: "pernicious anemia"; informant: Frank W. BAKER (Erwin); died: 4 Jan. 1927; buried: Erwin; record (1927) # 2105.

LEDFORD, Infant; female; born: 4 Dec. 1926; parents: O.M. LEDFORD (North Carolina) and M.J. JONES; death cause: not stated; informant: J.E. JONES (Clear Branch); died: 7 Jan. 1927; record (1927) # 2106.

BRUMMETT, Sarah Louise; born: 2 Aug. 1840; single; parents: William BRUMMETT and Melinda BRITT; death cause: "hemiplegia"; informant: Sam BRUMMETT; died: 2 Feb. 1927; buried: farm home; record (1927) # 4283.

BAILEY, Marie; born: 25 Nov. 1923; parents: Sam BAILEY (Yancey County, NC.) and Clara FANNING; death cause: "measles"; informant: father (Erwin); died: 5 Feb. 1927; buried: Erwin; record (1927) # 4194.

O'BRIEN, Jack; born: 8 Feb. 1927; parents: Clifton O'BRIEN and Nancy PETERSON (North Carolina); death cause: "premature birth"; informant: father (Erwin); died: 11 Feb. 1927; buried: Jobe Cemetery; record (1927) # 4295.

TOWNSEND, Mary Lou; born: 9 Jul. 1921; parents: W.J. TOWNSEND (South Carolina) and Lillian DUNCAN (South Carolina); death cause: "pneumonia, whooping cough"; informant: father (Erwin); died: 23 Feb. 1927; buried: Anderson, South Carolina; record (1927) # 4296.

RAY, Gathen C.; born: 8 Jul. 1874; married; parents: Elbert RAY (North Carolina) and Harriett BRIGGS (North Carolina); death cause: "carcinoma of stomach"; informant: Mrs. J.H. MCLAUGHLIN (Erwin); died: 28 Feb. 1927; buried: Martins Creek; record (1927) # 4297.

ERWIN, Phillip; born: 9 Apr. 1841; married; parents: Sam ERWIN and Polly PARKS; death cause: "intestinal nephritis"; informant: W.M. ERWIN (Erwin); died: 3 Feb. 1927; record (1927) # 4298.

GILBERT, Guy F.; born: 17 Jan. 1927; parents: Darsie GILBERT and Birdie SIMMONS; death cause: "influenza"; informant: Mary E. GILBERT (Erwin); died: 6 Feb. 1927; buried; Clear Branch; record (1927) # 4299.

SAMS, Margaret Lee; born: 3 Apr. 1863; married; parents: "unknown"; death cause: "paralysis"; died in the 1st District, 3 Mar. 1927; buried: Sams Cemetery; record (1927) # 6781.

DUNBAR, Joseph; age: "about 42 years"; married; parents: "unknown"; death cause: "unknown"; died: 9 Mar. 1927; buried: Peoples Cemetery; record (1927) # 6782.

LUTTRELL, Infant (twins); male; parents: William LUTTRELL and Effie NELSON; death cause: "premature, twins"; informant: father (Erwin); died: 10 Feb. 1927; record (1927) # 6782 and 6783.

MCKINNEY, Robert T.; age: 59 years; born: North Carolina; married; parents: Reuben MCKINNEY (South Carolina) and Minerva BAKER (South Carolina); death cause: "influenza and pneumonia"; informant: Rex MCKINNEY (Erwin); died: 5 Mar. 1927; buried: North Carolina; record (1927) 6785.

TILSON, A.B.; born: 1 Jan. 1850; widower; parents: G. TILSON and Katy BALES (North Carolina); death cause: illegible; informant: Tildy TILSON (Clear Branch); died: 24 Mar. 1927; buried; Tilson Cemetery; record (1927) # 6786.

HENSLEY, John; born: 19 Mar. 1840 in North Carolina; parents: W.A. HENSLEY (North Carolina) and Cinda HIGGINS (North Carolina); death cause: not stated; informant: R.B. HENSLEY (Clear Branch); died: 28 Mar. 1927; record (1927) # 6787.

TILSON, William H.; born: 21 Mar. 1877; married; parents: A.B. TILSON and E.J. GILLIS; death cause: not stated; informant: Sarah

PRICE (Clear Branch); died: 18 Feb. 1927; buried: Gillis Cemetery; record (1927) # 6788,
MOORE, Caroline; age: "about 54 years"; widow; parents: father not stated and Elizabeth METCALF; death cause: "pneumonia, paralysis"; died: 15 Apr. 1927; buried: Guinn Cemetery; record (1927) # 9180.
MCLAUGHLIN, Dozine; age: "about 47 years"; born: Mitchell County, NC.; married; parents: Oliver MCCURRY (Mitchell County) and mother "unknown"; death cause: "not stated, died in the Appalachian Hospital at Johnson City"; died: 2 Apr. 1927; informant: Oscar MCLAUGHLIN (Unicoi); record (1927) # 9181.
GRAY, R.M.; age: 46 years; born: Virginia; married; parents: R.M. GRAY (Virginia) and May MCCURRY; death cause: "car wreck, neck broken"; informant: R.L. BYERS (Abingdon, VA.); died: 11 Apr. 1927; buried: Abingdon, Virginia; record (1927) # 9182.
MOORE, Rebecca Jane; born: 26 Jul. 1857; widow; parents: B. RYNON and Elizabeth BUCKNER (North Carolina); death cause: "apoplexy"; informant: Kittie SALTS (Erwin); died: 30 Apr. 1927; buried: Flag Pond; record (1927) # 9183.
BANNER, Paul; born; __ Oct. 1923; parents: Martin BANNER and Lindy HENSLEY; death cause: "lobar pneumonia"; informant: father (Erwin); died: 9 Mar 1927; buried: Martins Creek Cemetery; record (1927) # 9184.
TINKER, Kathleen; age: 1 year and 1 month; parents: George TINKER and Leona MULLINS; death cause: "small pox, measles"; informant: father (Erwin); died: 15 Apr. 1927; buried: Jones Cemetery; record (1927_ # 9185.
KEESECKER, Wilbur; born: 5 Apr. 1918; parents: W.A. KEESECKER (West Virginia) and Ida Ray TAPP; death cause: "pertussis and pneumonia"; informant: W.O. KEESECKER (Erwin); died: 27 Apr. 1927; buried: Fishery Cemetery; record (1927) # 9186.
WILLIAMS, Sanders; born: 1 Mar 1904; born: North Carolina; married; parents: W.T. WILLIAMS (North Carolina) and Rena MCCURRY (North Carolina); death cause: "pulmonary tuberculosis"; informant: father (12th District); died: 18 Apr. 1927; buried: Martins Creek; record (1927) # 9187.

WATTS, Blake; born: 2 Jul. 1909; parents: William WATTS and Nancy JONES; death cause: "pulmonary tuberculosis"; informant: Bessie WATTS (Erwin); died: 24 Apr. 1927; record (1927) # 9188.

WILLIAMS, Edith Mae; born: 24 Dec. 1925; parents: W.T. WILLIAMS (North Carolina) and Rena MCCURRY (North Carolina); death cause: "influenza and pulmonary tuberculosis"; informant: father (Erwin); died: 28 Apr. 1927; buried: Martins Creek; record (1927) # 9189.

TIPTON, Richard; born: 11 Nov. 1923; parents: J.H. TIPTON and Elizie MASHBURN; death cause: not stated; informant: mother (Clear Branch); died: 17 Apr. 1927; buried: Tipton Cemetery; record # 9190.

GREENE, R.L.; born: 15 Jul. 1873 in Green Acre, North Carolina; married; parents: W.M. GREENE (North Carolina) and Biddie BLEVINS (North Carolina); death cause: "cancer of neck"; informant: Roscoe GREENE (Unicoi); died: 15 May 1927; buried: Buchanan Cemetery; record (1927) # 11654.

WHITE, Margaret Adelia; born: 13 Jan. 1849 in Yancey County, NC.; married; parents: Leander SIMMONS (McDowell County, NC.) and Mary JIMISON (McDowell County, NC.); death cause: "heart disease"; died: 20 May 1927; buried: Jones Cemetery; record (1927) # 11655.

RANGE, George E.; born: 25 Jul. 1888; married; parents: John RANGE and Ruth RANGE; death cause: "automobile accident"; informant: Mrs. George RANGE (Erwin); died: 4 May 1927; buried: Gray Station; record (1927) # 11656.

CROW, Joe; born: 1 Aug. 1876; married; parents: William CROW and Enidien HIGGINS; death cause: "heart disease and rheumatism"; informant: wife (Erwin); died: 8 May 1927; buried; Martins Creek; record 91927) # 11657.

TITTLE, Elmer; age: 13 years; parents: Frank TITLE and Rosa TITTLE; death cause: "accidental drowning"; died: 9 May 1927; buried: Martins Creek; record 91927) # 11658.

MARKLAND, D.W.; born: 23 Sep. 1858 in Carter County; married; parents: Nelson MARKLAND (Carter County) and Lukinizie WILSON (Carter County); death cause: "angina pectoris"; informant: wife (Erwin); died: 9 May 1927; buried; Stoney Creek; Carter County; record (1927) # 11659.

CAPP, Willie; born: 29 May 1918 in Washington County; parents: Luda L. CAPP (Washington County) and Eda FOSTER; death cause: "peritonitis"; died: 15 May 1927; buried: Liberty, Washington County: record (1927) # 11660.

FURCHES, Nancy Ruth; born: 3 Jul. 1920; parents: W.T. FURCHES (North Carolina) and Nancy ENGLE; death cause: "typhoid fever"; informant: father (Erwin); died: 17 May 1927; buried: Martins Creek; record (1927) # 11661.

HUSKINS, W_ (illegible); age: 68 years; married; parents: John HUSKINS and Jane GRINDSTAFF; death cause: "aortic insufficiency"; informant: J.H. HUSKINS (Erwin); died: 19 May 1927; buried: Martins Creek; record (1927) # 11662.

MITCHELL, Rosa Florence; born: 26 Sep. 1874 in Virginia; married; parents: John MITCHELL (Virginia) and __ (illegible) TURNER (Virginia); death cause: "carcinoma of liver"; informant: J.H. MITCHELL (Erwin); record (1927) # 11663.

MATHES, Amanda; age: 38 years; married; parents: William COOPER and Tildy FOISTER; death cause: "cancer of uterus"; died: 26 May 1927; buried: Martins Creek; record (1927) # 11664.

ALLRED, B.M.; born: 26 Jun. 1876 in North Carolina; married; parents: Joseph ALLRED (North Carolina) and mother's name illegible; death cause: "apoplexy"; informant: Mrs. B.M. ALLRED (Erwin); died: 6 May 1927; buried: Evergreen Cemetery; record (1927) # 11665.

TITTLE, Sarah Alice; age: 63 years; widow; parents: Tom FOSTER and Oma CHANDLER; death cause: "heart disease"; informant: Walter TITTLE (Erwin); died: 3 May 1927; record (1927) # 11666.

WIGGAND, P.P.; age: 59 years; born: Virginia; married; parents: "unknown"; death cause: "unknown"; died: 7 May 1927; buried: Evergreen Cemetery; record (1927) # 11667.

EPPERSON, Ernest; born: 28 Oct. 1926; parents: J.B. EPPERSON and Minnie DAUGHETY; death cause: "whooping cough"; died: 12 May 1927; buried: Elizabethton; record (1927) # 11668.

HARRIS, Willard Brady; born: 28 Mar. 1927; parents: Sam HARRIS and Bessie GILLIS; death cause: "unknown, found dead in bed"; informant: father (Erwin); died: 17 May 1927; buried: Martins Creek; record (1927) # 11669.

WILLIAMS, Ethel; age: 43 years; married; parents: Sam WATTS (North Carolina) and Lizzie BALES; death cause: "nephritis, uremia poison"; informant: Retman WILLIAMS (Erwin); died: 23 May 1927; buried: Martins Creek; record (1927) # 11670.

FINDER, Bonnie; age: 46 years; married; parents: John BLANKENSHIP and Emeline GHANDLER (North Carolina); death cause: "cerebral hemorrhage"; died in the 11th District, 9 May 1927; record # 11671.

LANDERS, Maggie Hensley; age: 24 years and 20 days; married; parents: James HENSLEY (North Carolina) and Dortherly HENSLEY (North Carolina); death cause: "ruptured uterus"; died: 3 Jun. 1927; record (1927) # 14149.

ROBINSON, Jack Owen; parents: James A. ROBINSON (Farmington, TN.) and Ula Louise MCINTURFF; death cause: "premature birth"; born/died: 25 Jun. 1927; buried: Martins Creek; record (1927) # 14150.

RAYBURN, Margaret Sarah; born: 28 Oct. 1852 in North Carolina; widow; parents: Richard TURNER (North Carolina) and mother "unknown"; death cause: "intestinal nephritis"; died: 1 Jun. 1927; buried: Glenwood, North Carolina; record (1927) # 14151.

WHITE, Edna May; born: 2 May __ in Kentucky; married; parents: Mose PARKLEY (Kentucky) and Charlotte JAMES (Kentucky); death cause: "miscarriage, peritonitis"; informant: F.B. WHITE (Erwin); died: 19 Jun. 1927; buried; McInturff Cemetery; record (1927) # 14152.

BROCKINS, John; age: 66 years; married; parents: father "unknown" and Betsy BROCKINS; death cause: "carcinoma of urinary bladder"; informant: M.R. BROCKINS (Erwin); died: 23 Jun. 1927; buried: Tinker Cemetery; record (1927) # 14153.

HARRIS, Judy; age: 77 years; widow; parents: Joe MURRY and Lizzie BONNER; death cause: "nephritis"; informant: Henry HARRIS (Erwin); died: 9 Jun. 1927; buried: Martins Creek Cemetery; record (1927) # 14154.

ALDRIDGE, William A.; born: 1 Mar. 1842 in Virginia; widower; disabled veteran; parents: not stated; death cause: "aortic insufficiency"; died: 22 Jun. 1927; buried: Martins Creek; record (1927) # 14155.

GILLIS, Minnie Belle; age: 3 years; parents: Walter GILLIS and Polly INGLE; death cause: "broncho pneumonia"; informant: father (Erwin); died: 9 May 1927; buried: Martins Creek; record (1927) # 14156.

189

MYNATT, William C.; born: __ May 1854; married; parents: Sawyers MYNATT and Alizy ZACHARY; death cause: "paralysis"; informant: H.C. MYNATT (Knoxville); died: 12 Jun. 1927; buried: Mynatt Cemetery; record (1927) # 14157.

BAILEY, Reece; born: 25 Apr. 1927; parents: E.D. BAILEY (Yancey County, NC.) and Polly DAVIS; death cause: "diarrhea"; informant: Earl BAILEY (Unicoi); died: 10 Jul. 1927; buried: Woodby Cemetery; record (1927) # 16741.

HEAD, Jessie; born: 3 Nov. 1904; single; parents: S.J. HEAD (Carter County) and Dora BYRD (Carter County); death cause: "typhoid fever"; informant: Blake HEAD (Erwin); died: 28 Jul. 1927; buried: O'Brien Cemetery; record (1927) # 16742.

TEAGUE, Sad Allen; born: 10 Jun. 1927; parents: John TEAGUE and Etta GRINDSTAFF; death cause: "bold hives"; informant: John TEAGUE (Unicoi); died: 11 Jun. 1927; buried: Bell Cemetery; record (1927) # 16743.

BAILEY, Reece; duplicate of record 16741; record (1927) # 16744.

HEAD, Jessie; duplicate of record 16742; record (1927) # 16745.

BROWN, Lucinda Jane McInturff; born: 16 Dec 1835 in Carter County; widow; parents: John C. MCINTURFF and Rachel SCOTT; death cause: "acute indigestion"; informant: W.L. PHILLIPS (Unicoi); died: 13 Jul. 1927; buried: Fishery Cemetery; record (1927) # 16746.

MASHBURN, Helen; born: 16 Mar. 1927; parents: Jake MASHBURN and Mary SAMS; death cause: "spinal meningitis"; died: 7 Jul. 1927; buried: Martins Creek; record (1927) # 16747.

JOHNSON, Patrick H.; born: 23 Sep. 1843; widower; parents: James JOHNSON (North Carolina) and mother not stated; death cause: "intestinal nephritis"; informant: D.A. JOHNSON (Jonesboro); died: 16 Jul. 1927; buried: Washington County; record (1927) # 16748.

MAUK, T.M.; born: 8 Jul. 1875; married; parents: Abe MAUK and Florence CLARK; death cause: "dropsy"; informant: wife (Erwin); died: 17 Jul. 1927; buried: Knoxville; record (1927) # 16749.

TITTLE, Loretta; age: 54 years; married; parents: father's name illegible and Noma ANGLE; death cause: "typhoid fever"; informant: Otis HIGGINS (Erwin); died: 20 Jul. 1927; buried: Fishery Cemetery; record (1927) # 16750.

ROBERTS, Annie; born: 17 Jun. 1872; married; parents: Harrison HARRIS and __ BANNER; death cause: "pulmonary tuberculosis"; informant: Bob ROBERTS (Erwin); died: 30 Jul. 1927; buried: Erwin; record (1927) # 16751.

BRADFORD, Bessie Marie; born: 25 May 1927; parents: J.E. BRADFORD and Bethel HIGGINS; death cause: "colitis"; informant: father (Erwin); died: 3 Jul. 1927; buried: Bailey Cemetery; record (1927) # 16752.

LONG, Dana Jr.; born: 19 Sep. 1926; parents: Dana LONG and Etta SHELTON (North Carolina); death cause: "pneumonia and whooping cough"; informant: John LONG (Erwin); died: 11 Jul. 1927; buried: Martins Creek; record (1927) # 16753.

BROOKINS, Serley; age: 86 years, 4 months and 23 days; widow; parents: __ LEDFORD and mother "unknown"; death cause: "gastric __ (illegible)"; informant: E. LEDFORD (Erwin); died; 14 Jul. 1927; buried: Martins Creek; record (1927) # 16754.

FOSTER, Dortha E.; born: 18 Jun. 1927; parents: father not stated and Leora FOSTER; death cause: not stated; informant: J.H. FOSTER (Clear Branch); died: 23 Jul. 1927; buried: Foster Cemetery; record (1927) # 16755.

EDWARDS, Sallie; born: 3 Jan. 1857; widow; parents: Haskie C_ (illegible) (North Carolina) and Ellen TINKER; death cause: not stated; informant: S.A CONN (Erwin); died: 4 Jul. 1927; buried: Tinker Cemetery; record (1927) # 16756.

SIMMONS, Annie; age: 87 years; married; parents: Earl MCINTOSH and __ BANNER; death cause: "pellagra"; died: 1 Aug. 1927; buried: Martins Creek; record (1927) # 19090.

SIMMONS, George W.; age: 77 years; born: North Carolina; single; parents: Leander SAMMONS (North Carolina) and mother "unknown"; death cause: not stated; informant: Jake ANDERSON (Erwin); died: 11 Aug. 1927; buried: Jobe Cemetery; record (1927) # 19091.

FREOY, Forest; born: 3 May 1907 in North Carolina; parents: I.G. FREOY (North Carolina) and Ollie PARKER (North Carolina); death cause: "typhoid fever"; informant: A.E. POTEET (Unicoi); died: 20 Aug. 1927; buried: Martins Creek; record (1927) # 19092.

JOHNSON, Mrs. J.A.; born: 10 Feb. 1889; married; parents: Will FURCHESS and Rena HUSKINS; death cause: "ruptured gall bladder"; informant: J.A. JOHNSON (Erwin); died: 31 Aug. 1927; buried: Martins Creek; record (1927) # 19093.
BLASY, Hellen Lola; born: 2 Jul. 1917 in Ohio; parents: John BLASY (Ohio) and mother's name illegible; death cause: "colitis"; died: 19 Aug. 1927; buried: Cincinnati, Ohio; record (1927) # 19094.
HARRIS, James; age: 41 years; married; parents: Andy KING and Patty HARRIS; death cause: "killed by lightening"; informant: wife (Erwin); died: 28 Aug. 1927; buried: Fishery Cemetery; record (1927) # 19095.
LAWING, Mrs. D.T.; born: 2 Apr. 1897 in North Carolina; married; parents: W.M. MILLER (North Carolina) and T_ (illegible) BENNETT (North Carolina); death cause: "influenza and pneumonia"; informant: D.T. LAWING (Erwin); died: 14 Aug. 1927; buried: Martins Creek; record (1927) # 19096.
COCHRAN, George; born: 21 Oct. 1901; single; parents: J.T. COCHRAN and Sudie GARLAND; death cause: "pellagra"; informant: father (Unicoi); died: 2 Sep. 1927; buried: Buchanan Cemetery; record (1927) # 21274.
RALDOLPH, Vissie; born: 16 Jun. 1838 in North Carolina; widow; parents: George PHILLIPS (North Carolina) and __ BIRD (North Carolina); death cause: "old age"; died: 21 Sep. 1927; buried: Ramsey Cemetery; record (1927) # 21275.
CARROLL, George; born: 10 Sep. 1861; married; parents: David CARROLL and mother "unknown"; death cause: "pneumonia"; informant: wife (Erwin); died: 28 Sep. 1927; record (1927) # 21276.
WHITSON, Mollie; age: 42 years; born: North Carolina; married; parents: J.W. WHITSON (North Carolina) and Polly PETERSON (North Carolina); death cause: "influenza, pulmonary tuberculosis"; informant: wife (Erwin); died: 30 Sep. 1927; buried: Huntdale, North Carolina; record (1927) # 21277.
KERNS, Myrtle Jane; born: 16 Mar. 1875 in West Virginia; married; parents: David ROGERS (West Virginia) and Rachel TRICKETT (West Virginia); death cause: "operation for locked bowels"; died: 30 Sep. 1927; buried: Erwin; record (1927) # 21278.

SMITH, David; born: 3 Jan. 1859 in Carter County; married; parents: Alexander SMITH (Carter County) and Jane TIPTON (Carter County); death cause: "myocarditis"; informant: Fred SMITH (Unicoi); died: 6 Sep. 1927; record (1927) # 21279.

HUSKINS, Mary; born: 15 Sep. 18__; age: 54 years; married; parents: A.L. SMITH and Jane TIPTON; death cause: "dysentery"; died: 15 Sep. 1927; buried: Fishery Cemetery; record (1927) # 21280.

CRAIN, Vira Eulalia; age: 4 months; parents: Arthur CRAIN and Esteller CHANDLER; death cause: not stated; informant: G.B. CHANDLER (Clear Branch); died: 22 Sep. 1927; buried: Mount Pleasant Cemetery; record (1927) # 21281.

COLEMAN, Dorchis Marie; born: 21 Feb. 1927; parents: J.C. COLEMAN and Clercia TOLLEY; death cause: "croup"; informant: father (Unicoi); died: 16 Oct. 1927; buried: Brummett Cemetery; record (1927) # 23442.

HEAD, Amanda Cochran; age: 65 years; widow; parents: Robert COCHRAN (Virginia) and Mary MAHAFFEY (Virginia); death cause: "atrophy of liver"; died: 24 Oct. 1927; buried: Head Cemetery, Unicoi; record (1927) # 23443.

CARROLL, Norma Edna; born: 24 Oct. 1926; parents: William CARROLL and Sarah Ann BRUMMETT; death cause: "spinal meningitis"; died: 26 Oct. 1927; buried: Brummett Cemetery; record (1927) # 23444.

MCCURRY, Pauline; born: 18 May 1927; parents: Pink MCCURRY (North Carolina) and Cora PETERSON (North Carolina); death cause: not stated; died: 20 Sep. 1927; buried: Peterson Cemetery; record (1927) # 23445.

HAMMIT, Infant; male; parents: J.S. HAMMIT and Vada WHITLOCK (Kentucky); death cause: "instrumental delivery"; informant: father (Erwin); born/died: 5 Aug. 1927; buried: Boones Creek, Tennessee; record (1927) # 23446.

RICHARDSON, Irene; born: 10 May 1927; parents: Alern RICHARDSON and Ida LOCKNER; death cause: illegible; informant: Fred LOCKNER (Embreeville, Tennessee); died: 20 Oct. 1927; record (1927) # 23447.

DEADERICK, Mary A.; age: 87 years; married; parents: James H. WALKER and Louise CLARKSON; death cause: "brights disease and cerebral hemorrhage"; informant: Paul DEADERICK (Unaka Springs); died: 5 Oct. 1927; buried: Johnson City; record (1927) # 23448.

KAGLEY, Harold Westley; age: 14 years, 4 months and 22 days; born: Illinois; parents: J.H. KAGLEY (Virginia) and Ada ALLEN; death cause: "lobar pneumonia"; informant: father (Erwin); died: 22 Nov. 1927; buried: Martins Creek; record (1927) # 23449.

MCCURRY, Cora; born: 22 Feb. 1871 in North Carolina; married; parents: Lawson PETERSON (North Carolina) and Cora TIPTON (North Carolina); death cause: "heart disease"; informant: Ike MCCURRY (Unicoi); died: 18 Nov. 1927; record (1927) # 25606.

MCNABB, Jessie; female; born: 2 May 1927; parents: Clinton MCNABB and Rosha BUCK (Carter County); death cause: "hepatitis"; informant: Frank RICH (Unicoi); died: 21 Nov. 1927; buried: Taylor McNabb Cemetery; record (1927) # 25607.

PETERSON, Cemillie; age: 81 years; widow; parents: __ TIPTON (North Carolina) and mother not stated; death cause: "dysentery"; informant: Noah PETERSON (Unicoi); died: 22 Nov. 1927; buried: Unicoi; record (1927) # 25608.

TINKER, J.W.; born: 4 Nov. 1869 in Virginia; married; parents: Robert TINKER and Uisie CLAIBORNE (Virginia); death cause: "influenza and pneumonia"; informant: wife (Erwin); died: 1 Nov. 1927; record (1927) # 25609.

BROWN, Lizzie Lucille; lived 2 days; parents: E.A. BROWN (Virginia) and Blanche HOBGOOD; death cause: "premature infant"; informant: father (Erwin); died: 14 Nov. 1927; buried: Evergreen Cemetery; record (1927) # 25610.

BARNETT, S.B.; age: 77 years; widower; parents: David BARNETT (Mitchell County, NC.) and mother not stated; death cause: "colitis"; died: 23 Nov. 1927; buried: Tiger Creek; record (1927) # 25611.

WATSON, Annie; born: 11 Apr. 1881 in North Carolina; married; parents: B.F. F_ (illegible) and Annie BIETZ (North Carolina); death cause: "carcinoma of liver"; died: 24 Nov. 1927; buried: Erwin; record (1927) # 25612.

WHITE, Mrs. M.C.; born: 6 Feb. 1844; widow; parents: Alec SMITH and Celia GOODWIN; death cause: "heart disease"; informant: C.T. NORRIS (Erwin); died: 29 Nov. 1927; buried: Erwin, Tennessee; record (1927) # 25613.

BOLMAN, Mrs. Everet; born: 24 Apr. 1893; married; parents: J.S. SAYLOR (Nebraska) and Bessie HOGAN (North Carolina); death cause: "cancer of uterus"; informant: father (Erwin); died: 29 Nov. 1927; buried: Erwin; record (1927) # 25614.

DAY, Mrs. Walter; born: 30 Apr. 1896; married; parents: Grant HAMPTON and Sarah Ann LOVE; death cause: "pellagra"; informant: Walter DAY (Erwin); died: 30 Nov. 1927; buried: Erwin, Tennessee; record (1927) # 25615.

BENNETT, C.I.; age: 55 years; born: North Carolina; married; parents: Arch BENNETT (North Carolina) and Jane HENSLEY; death cause: "probably froze to death"; informant: Mrs. Ike BENNETT (Erwin); died: 21 Nov. 1927; buried: Erwin; record (1927) # 25616.

HAMPTON, Lizzie; age: 65 years; widow; parents: Bill TREADWAY and Sarah HAMPTON; death cause: "pellagra"; informant: Matt HAMPTON (Erwin); died: 10 Nov. 1927; buried: Martins Creek; record (1927) # 25617.

BANNER, Mollie E.; age: 69 years; married; parents: "unknown"; death cause: "myocarditis following foot infection"; died in the 12th District, 18 Nov. 1927; record (1927) # 25618.

SAMS, Leroy S.; age: "about 65 years; widower; parents: not stated; death cause: "murdered, skull fractured, body burned"; died: 23 Dec. 1927; buried: Sams Cemetery; record (1927) # 28459.

CAMPBELL, Elisha; age: 50 years; married; parents: William CAMPBELL and Mary FRY; death cause: "heart failure"; informant: Geter BARNETT (Unicoi); died: 13 Dec. 1927; buried: Campbell Cemetery; record (1927) # 28460.

GRINDSTAFF, Alf; born: 18 Dec. 1844; married; parents: Jackson GRINDSTAFF and Louise GRINDSTAFF; death cause: "heart disease"; informant: Jim GRINDSTAFF (Unicoi); died: 22 Dec. 1927; buried: Britt Cemetery; record (1927) # 28461.

FULTON, B.F.; born: 1 Jun. 1850 in Nebraska; widower; parents: "unknown"; death cause: "brights disease, high blood pressure"; died: 8 Dec. 1927; buried: Jobe Cemetery; record (1927) # 28462.

JONES, Louis David; age: 19 years; married; parents: Henry JONES and Julia TAPP; death cause: "murdered, gunshot in abdomen"; informant: father (Erwin); died: 12 Dec. 1927; buried: Fishery Cemetery; record (1927) # 28463.

DEATON, J.W.; born: 5 Jun. 1927; parents: F.R. DEATON (North Carolina) and Mile EDWARDS (North Carolina); death cause: "broncho pneumonia"; died: 13 Dec. 1927; buried: Green Mountain, North Carolina; record (1927) # 28464.

HENSLEY, W.H.; born: 15 Oct. 1860 in North Carolina; married; parents: Howard HENSLEY (North Carolina) and Rose SILVERS (North Carolina); death cause: "cancer of stomach"; informant: wife (Erwin); died: 28 Dec. 1927; record (1927) # 28465.

HONEYCUTT, Connie; age: 68 years; born: North Carolina; parents: Joe TIPTON (North Carolina) and mother "unknown"; death cause: "flu and broncho pneumonia"; died in the 5th District, 31 Dec. 1927; buried: Erwin; record (1927) # 28466.

PARKER, Willie; age: 5 months; parents: Handy PARKER (North Carolina) and Essie SMITH (North Carolina); death cause: "bronchial pneumonia"; died: 27 Dec. 1927; buried: Martins Creek Cemetery; record (1927) # 28467.

BAILEY, Julia Etta; age: 46 years; born: North Carolina; married; parents: J.H. GARLAND (North Carolina) and Pheba PHILLIPS (North Carolina); death cause: "peritonitis from operation"; informant: John BAILEY; died: 2 Jan. 1928; buried: North Carolina; record (1928) # 2325.

JACKSON, Rlgy (?) Jane; age: 66 years; born: North Carolina; widow; parents: Sam ADAMS (North Carolina) and Caroline MILLER (North Carolina); death cause: "myo-carditis"; informant: Albert JACKSON (Erwin);died: 4 Jan. 1928; buried: Jobe Cemetery; record # 2326.

TAPP, Geter; born: 30 Aug. 1900; married; parents: Bill TAPP and Edna KIRK; death cause: "diabetic coma"; informant: father (Erwin); died: 6 Jan. 1928; buried: Erwin; record (1928) # 2327.

HAYS, Nellie; age: 47 years; born: Ohio; married; parents: father "unknown" and Martha BURKE (Ohio); death cause: "myo-carditis"; informant: Mary HAYS (Erwin); died: 22 Jan. 1928; buried: Martins Creek; record (1928) # 2328.

MILLER, Reba; age: 3 years; parents: Rosco MILLER (North Carolina) and Ruby DUNCAN; death cause: "meningitis"; informant: mother (Erwin); died: 22 Jan. 1928; buried; Martins Creek; record # 2329.

TINKER, James P.; age: 66 years; married; parents: P.P. GUINN and Louise TINKER; death cause: "nephritis"; died: 5 Jan. 1928; buried: Tinker Cemetery; record (1928) # 2330.

LEWIS, Mrs. T.N.; born: 22 Sep. 1887 in North Carolina; married; parents: W.W. BIGGS (North Carolina) and Amanda GRAYBEAL (North Carolina); death cause: "brights disease"; informant: T.J. LEWIS (Erwin); died: 15 Feb. 1928; buried: Martins Creek; record # 4918.

MCLAUGHLIN, W.L.; born: 27 Jul. 1890; married; parents: Emerson MCLAUGHLIN and Mary Ann COLE; death cause: "railroad accident, internal hemorrhage"; informant: wife (Erwin); died: 12 Feb. 1928; buried: Unicoi; record (1928) # 4919.

MCCURRY, Charlotte; age: 5 months and 15 days; parents: J.C. MCCURRY (North Carolina) and Bertha PHILLIPS (North Carolina); death cause: "broncho pneumonia"; informant: father (Erwin);died: 23 Feb. 1928; buried: Jobe Cemetery; record (1928) # 4920.

BOOTH, Lola Dean; age: 58 years; single; parents: Hiram BOOTH and Elizabeth REED; death cause: "influenza and meningitis"; died: 26 Feb. 1928; buried: Erwin; record (1928) # 4921.

HENSLEY, Claude; age: 11 months and 9 days; parents: Lenzy HENSLEY and Hattie MASTERS; death cause: "broncho pneumonia"; died: 20 Feb. 1928; buried; Martins Creek; record (1928) # 4922.

CASH, Margaret Ann; age; 78 years; widow; parents: John SMITH and mother "unknown"; death cause: "bronchial pneumonia"; informant: Roy CASH (Erwin); died: 6 Mar. 1928; buried; Erwin; record # 7513.

SPARKS, Sarah; age: 43 years; born: North Carolina; married; parents: Jim GOUGE (North Carolina) and Jane BUCHANAN (North Carolina); death cause: "apoplexy"; informant: Bob SPARKS (Marion, North Carolina); died: 23 Mar. 1928; buried: Forbes, North Carolina; record (1928) # 7514.

HINE, Lisetta Marie; born: 14 Jan. 183_; age: 78 years, 2 months and 16 days; born: Virginia; single; parents: Thomas L. HINE (Virginia) and Margaret FISER (Virginia); death cause: "carcinoma of breast"; informant: T.H. HINE (Erwin); died: 30 Mar. 1928; buried: Johnson City; record (1928) # 7515.

TITTLE, John; born: 17 Mary 1850; widower; parents: Epthirum TITTLE and Kate PATE; death cause: "old age"; informant: Mrs. Frank BRITT (Erwin); died: 13 Apr. 1928; buried: Erwin; record # 10292.

SIMMONS, J.B.; born: 27 Mar. 1928; parents: N.S. SIMMONS and Annie RENFRO (North Carolina); death cause: illegible; informant: father (Erwin); died: 1 Apr. 1928; buried: Erwin; record # 10293.

BROWN, Ella; born: __ Jan. 1895; age: 33 years; married; parents: Sanders DAY and Sarah WHITE; death cause: "pulmonary embolism, miscarriage"; informant: Fred BROWN (Erwin); died; 4 Apr. 1928; buried: Erwin; record (1928) # 10294.

TITTLE, Howard; born: 1 Apr. 1926; parents: W.H. TITTLE and Ruby CASH; death cause: "infantile paralysis"; informant: father (Erwin); died: 8 Apr. 1928; buried: Erwin; record (1928) # 10295.

MURPHY, Margaret Jane; born: 11 Jun. __; age: 53 years; married; parents: Riley CUPP and Alice BAYLESS; death cause: "brights disease"; informant: Jane EVERETT (Maryville, Tennessee); died: 8 Apr. 1928; buried: Erwin; record (1928) # 10296.

PIERCE, Infant; female; parents: L.W. PIERCE (Virginia) and Pearl Grace RILEY; death cause: "asphyxia neo_ (illegible)"; informant: father (Erwin); died: 9 Apr. 1928; buried; Bristol; record # 10297.

AMBROSE, Ralph William; age: 1 month and 7 days; parents: Charles AMBROSE and Ethel KEESEAKER (West Virginia); death cause: "broncho pneumonia"; informant: father (Erwin); died: 25 Apr. 1928; buried: Fishery Cemetery; record (1928) # 10298.

HARRIS, R.L.; age: 56 years; born: Kentucky; married; parents: "unknown"; death cause: "heart failure"; died: 19 Apr. 1928; buried: Knoxville; record (1928) # 10299.

DOYLE, George; born: 5 Oct. 1913 in West Virginia; parents: Arthur DOYLE (West Virginia) and __ (illegible) MEREDITH (Virginia); death cause: "drowned"; informant: H.H. WILLIAMS (Erwin); died: 29 Apr. 1928; buried; Erwin; record (1928) # 10300.

JOHNSON, R.C.; age: 21 Apr. 1918; parents: R.T. JOHNSON (North Carolina) and Georgia SMITH; death cause: "drowned"; died: 29 Apr. 1928; record (1928) # 10301.

WILLIAMS, Houe; born: 12 Jun. 1911; parents: R.L. WILLIAMS (Virginia) and Myrtle ATKINS (Virginia); death cause: "drowned"; informant: father (Erwin); died: 29 Apr. 1928; buried: Erwin; record (1928) # 10302.

SNIDER, Infant; male; born: 12 Mar. 1928; parents: I.M. SNIDER and Mary ERWIN; death cause: "premature"; died: 14 Mar 1928; buried: Unicoi; record (1928) # 10303.

SNIDER, Bert Harris; born: 13 Mar 1928; parents: I.N. SNIDER and Mary ERWIN; death cause: "premature"; informant: father (Erwin); died: 14 Mar 1928; buried: Erwin; record (1928) # 10304.

BAILEY, Essa; age: 42 years; born: North Carolina; widower; parents: Hiram BAILEY (North Carolina) and Della BIRD (North Carolina); death cause: "typhoid fever"; informant: J.D. BAILEY (Erwin); died: 21 Apr. 1928; buried: Erwin; record (1928) # 10305.

HARRIS, Earne; born: 16 Nov. 1926; parents: B. HARRIS and T.C. HARRIS; death cause: "influenza; informant: father (Erwin); died: 24 Apr. 1928; buried: Erwin; record (1928) # 10306.

CURTIS, Infant; female; born: 10 Apr. 1928; parents: Henry Edwards CURTIS (Washington County) and Bessie RIDDLE; death cause: "unknown, 7 hours old"; died: 11 Apr. 1928; buried: North Carolina; record (1928) # 12900.

DAVIS, Judah; age: 34 years; single; parents: Amos DAVIS and Margaret MORELY; death cause: "heart failure"; informant: James COCHRAN (Unicoi); died: 31 Mar 1928; buried: Gouge Cemetery; record # 12901.

ALLRED, Myrtle M.; born: 11 Apr. 1888 in North Carolina; married; parents: T.C. MAY (North Carolina) and Elizabeth __ (North Carolina); death cause: "brights disease, uremic coma"; informant: T.H. ALLRED (Erwin); died: 2 May 1928; buried: Erwin; record # 12902.

TAYLOR, S.P.; born: __ Aug. 1873; age: 55 years, 8 months and 4 days; born: Virginia; married; blacksmith; parents: W.K. TAYLOR (Virginia) and May COLLINS (Virginia); death cause: "heart disease"; informant:

Mrs. Sam TAYLOR (Erwin); died: 4 May 1928; buried: Erwin; record (1928) # 12903.

DAVIS, W.T.; age: 88 years; married; parents: James C. DAVIS (Virginia) and Sarah LEWIS (Virginia); death cause: "intestinal nephritis"; informant: Bob DAVIS (Erwin); died: 6 May 1928; buried: Erwin; record (1928) # 12904.

BRADFORD, Ethel; age: 30 years; married; parents: George HIGGINS and Julia SPENCE; death cause: "double pneumonia"; informant: father (Erwin); died: 8 May 1928; buried; Erwin; record (1928) # 12905.

EDWARDS, Kathleen; age: 4 years; parents: W.D. EDWARDS and May NELSON; death cause: "burn, nephritis resulted"; informant: father (Erwin); died: 14 May 1928; buried: Erwin; record (1928) # 12906.

ELLIOTT, Hubert Hoover; born: 16 Nov. 1926; parents: R.R. ELLIOTT and Lola SMITH; death cause: "bronchitis, pneumonia"; informant: father (Erwin); died: 14 May 1928; buried: Elizabethton, Tennessee; record (1928) # 12907.

RICE, Nat; born: 1 Jul. 1927; parents: N.B. RICE and Leoth BLANKENSHIP; death cause: "intestinal _ (illegible); informant: father (Erwin); died: 28 May 1928; buried: Flag Pond; record (1928) # 12908.

EDWARDS, Bessie; born: 1 Mar. 1901; married; parents: W.T. WILLIAMS (North Carolina) and Leoth BLANKENSHIP (North Carolina); death cause: "pulmonary tuberculosis"; died: 30 May 1928; buried: Erwin; record (1928) # 12909.

MCINTURFF, Sarah Elizabeth; age: 67 years; married; parents: John CLARK and May BACON; death cause: "double pneumonia"; informant: Jesse MCINTURFF (Erwin); died: 28 Apr. 1928; buried: Erwin; record (1928) # 12910.

JOHNSON, Zeb (?); age: 13 years; parents: Ivery JOHNSON and Georgia SMITH; death cause: "drowned; informant: Tom SMITH (Erwin); died: 29 Apr. 1928; buried: Erwin; record (1928) # 12911.

HENSLEY, Angeline; born: 12 May 1871; married; parents: John NORTON (Madison County, NC.) and Nancy NORTON (Madison County, NC.); death cause: "heart failure"; informant: J.W. HENSLEY (Flag Pond); died: 9 Jun. 1928; buried: Peak Cemetery; record # 15198.

HONEYCUTT, Charley Edward; born: 22 May 1928; parents: C.H. HONEYCUTT (North Carolina) and Ollie PETERSON (North

Carolina); death cause: "broncho pneumonia"; informant: father (Unicoi); died: 6 Jun. 1928; buried: Unicoi; record (1928) # 15199.

SHERRILL, Samuel; parents: Julice Daniel SHERRILL and Talley Jane SHERRILL; death cause: not stated; informant: father (Unicoi); born/died: 4 Jun. 1928; buried: Unicoi; record (1928) # 15200.

HARRIS, Ike; age: 5 months; parents: J.H. HARRIS and Francis SMITH; death cause: "broncho pneumonia"; informant: father (Erwin); died: 8 Jun. 1928; buried: Erwin; record (1928) # 15201.

BAILEY, Mary Elizabeth; born: 14 Apr. 1928; parents: John BAILEY and Mamie BAILEY; death cause: "unknown, found dead in bed"; informant: mother (Erwin); died: 15 Jun. 1928; buried: Erwin; record (1928) # 15202.

HARRIS, William Lester; born: 26 Apr. 1927; parents: R.F. HARRIS and Madge WHITE; death cause: "cholera infantum"; informant: father (Erwin); died: 15 Jun. 1928; buried: Fishery Cemetery; record # 15203.

SHEHAN, Jocie; born: 19 Sep. __; age: 82 years; born: North Carolina; widow; parents: "unknown"; death cause: "heart disease"; died: 28 Jun. 1928; buried: Clear Branch; record (1928) # 15202.

STALLARD, Nathan A.; age: 6 years; parents: Beechem STALLARD (Virginia) and Lizzie COUTHARD (Kentucky); death cause: "colitis"; informant: father (Erwin); died: 29 Jun. 1928; buried: Fishery Cemetery; record (1928) # 15205.

BEAVER, Infant; female; age: 9 months; parents: Red BEAVER (North Carolina) and Grace HAMPTON; death cause: "accidentally burned to death"; informant: J.W. HOWELL (Erwin); died: 30 Jun. 1928; buried: Erwin; record (1928) # 15206.

WHITE, David; born: 15 Jan. 1840; widower; parents: "unknown"; death cause: "carcinoma of bowels"; informant: J.C. WHITE (Erwin); died: 10 Jun. 1928; buried: Fishery Cemetery; record (1928) # 15207.

LOVETT, Guy; born: 22 May 1928; parents: Stewart LOVETT (North Carolina) and Bertha GARLAND (North Carolina); death cause: "bold hives"; informant: father (Erwin); died: 3 Jun. 1928; buried: Bailey Cemetery; record (1928) # 15208.

CUTSHALL, Blanche; born: 26; Jun. 1928; parents: Fowler CUTSHALL (North Carolina) and Kate WALDROP; death cause: "blue baby"; died: 5 Jul. 1928; buried: Cutshall Cemetery; record (1928) # 17941.

WHITSON, Abraham; born: 26 Apr. 1849 in Mitchell County, North Carolina; married; parents: __ (illegible) WHITSON (North Carolina) and Rosie BENNETT (North Carolina); death cause: "diabetes and old age"; died: 17 Jul. 1928; buried: Swingle Cemetery; record # 17942.

ERWIN, Mrs. W.S.; age: 38 years, 3 months and 22 days; married; parents: Ben WOODWARD and Lucinda SAMS; death cause: "goiter"; died: 20 Jul. 1928; buried: Erwin; record (1928) # 17943.

WILLIAMS, Frank; born: 20 Feb. 1887 in South Carolina; married; parents: James WILLIAMS (North Carolina) and Rachel WILLIAMS (North Carolina); death cause: "pellagra"; informant: wife (Erwin); died: 20 Jun. 1928; buried; Martins Creek; record (1928) # 17944.

JONES, Nannie; age: 57 years; married; parents: Dan KIRK and mother "unknown"; death cause: "emphasema"; informant: Henry JONES (Erwin); died: 20 Jun. 1928; buried: Erwin; record (1928) # 17945.

MCVAY, Silas; age: 45 years; born: North Carolina; married; parents: Tom MCVAY (North Carolina) and Sallie STEVINS (North Carolina); death cause: "heart condition and obstruction of liver"; informant: Matt HAMPTON (Erwin); died: 24 Jun. 1928; record (1928) # 17946.

GARLAND, Bertha May; age: 11 years; parents: W.S. GARLAND (North Carolina) and Lottie BROWN; death cause: "typhoid fever"; died: 20 Jul. 1828; buried: Erwin; record (1928) # 17947.

GARLAND, Infant; male; born: 17 Jul. 1928; parents: Hunter GARLAND and Mamie WOODBY; death cause: "unknown"; informant: father (Erwin); died: 24 Jul. 1928; buried: Limestone Cove; record (1928) # 17948.

FORD, Robert; age: 60 years; married; parents: "unknown"; death cause: "cellulitis"; died: 2 Aug. 1928; buried: Erwin; record (1928) # 20394.

INGRAM, Howard; born: 11 Jan. 1923; parents: Brown INGRAM (North Carolina) and Mary BENNETT (North Carolina); death cause: "nephritis"; informant: father (Erwin); died: 6 Aug. 1928; buried: Erwin; record (1928) # 20395.

BELCHER, J.H.; age: 68 years; born: Virginia; married; parents: Wesley BELCHER (Virginia) and Ellse DYE (Virginia); death cause: "brights disease"; informant: wife (Erwin); died: 11 Aug. 1928; buried: Erwin; record (1928) # 20396.

PRICE, Mrs. W.J.; born: 14 Sep. 1873; married; parents: Joe LAWS and Jane LAWS; death cause: "acute brights"; informant: W.J. PRICE (Erwin); died: 13 Aug. 1928; buried: Erwin; record (1928) # 20397.

DAVIS, Mrs. C.D.; born: 29 Mar. 1896 in Canada; married; parents: Soloman HUDGSON (Canada) and Rachel Jane GREY (Canada); death cause: "carcinoma of liver"; informant: C.D. DAVIS (Erwin); died: 17 Aug. 1928; buried: Erwin; record (1928) # 20398.

MCCURRY, Loura; born: 9 Feb. 1892; married; parents: John MCINTURFF and Sarah CLARK; death cause: "tuberculosis"; informant: Mack MCCURRY (Erwin); died: 17 Aug. 1928; buried: Erwin; record (1928) # 20399.

EDWARDS, Tom; age: 47 years; married; parents: Sam R. EDWARDS (North Carolina) and Hannah FOSTER; death cause: "run over by automobile"; informant: wife (Clear Branch); died: 18 Aug. 1928; buried: Clear Branch; record (1928) # 20400.

TOMIE, Curtis H.; born: 17 Sep. 1888 in Virginia; married; parents: W.H. TOMIE (Virginia) and Mattie BUCHANAN (Virginia); death cause: "typhoid"; informant: wife (Erwin); died: 23 Aug. 1928; buried: Saltville, Virginia; record (1928) # 20401.

TONEY, Martha Ellen; age: 1 year and 25 days; parents: H.H. TONEY and Anna Ruth EMERSON; death cause: "gastro enteritis"; informant: father (Erwin); died: 24 Aug. 1928; buried: Erwin; record # 20402.

COLLINS, Alvin; born: 9 Jul. 1927; parents: Shirden COLLINS and Martha Jane HENSLEY; death cause: "cholera infantum"; informant: father (Erwin); died: 28 Aug. 1928; buried: Erwin; record # 20403.

FORD, Thelma J.; born: 10 Feb. 1926; parents: Hiram FORD and Esther BOOTH; death cause: "colitis"; informant: Fred BOOTH (Erwin); died: 28 Aug. 1928; buried; Erwin; record (1928) # 20404.

NELSON, Milley; age: 86 years; married; parents: John MILLER (North Carolina) and mother "unknown"; death cause: "dysentery"; informant: David NELSON (Unicoi); died: 23 Aug. 1928; buried: Erwin; record (1928) # 20405.

NELSON, Sabra; born: 18 Aug. 1861 in North Carolina; married; parents: Harvey PUTMAN (North Carolina) and Jocie EARBY (North Carolina); death cause: "carcinoma of uterus"; informant: Ike NELSON (Erwin); died: 27 Aug. 1928; buried; Erwin; record (1928) # 20406.

FOSTER, Hazel; born: 21 Jul. 1928; parents: Emry FOSTER and Alice JONES; death cause: "unknown"; informant: Emory FOSTER (Erwin); died: 26 Aug. 1928; buried: Erwin; record (1928) # 20407.

HARRIS, __ (illegible) Crettie; born: 28 Apr. 1860 in Kentucky; parents: Wash HENSLEY (North Carolina) and Emeline HENSLEY (North Carolina); death cause: "dysentery"; informant: Jason HENSLEY (Erwin); died: 31 Aug. 1928; buried: Erwin; record (1928) # 20408.

MCLAUGHLIN, Kathleen; born: 2 Jun. 1923; parents: Jess W. MCLAUGHLIN and Stella MCCARTER; death cause: "spinal meningitis"; informant: father (Unicoi); died: 17 Sep. 1928; buried: Jones Cemetery; record (1928) # 22735.

HORTON, Infant; female; parents: Milton HORTON (Bakersfield, North Carolina) and Bulah HAWKINS (Marion, North Carolina); death cause: "premature birth"; informant: Betty NORTON (Unicoi); born/died: 14 Aug. 1928; buried: Horton Cemetery; record (1928) # 22736.

FOSTER, Porter Jr.; age: 2 months; parents: Porter FOSTER and Cordie JOHNSON (North Carolina); death cause: "unknown"; informant: Cordie JOHNSON (Erwin); died: 8 Sep. 1928; record # 22737.

LAWS, Amis; born: 6 Sep. 1846; widower; parents: Bill LAWS and mother "unknown" death cause: "intestinal nephritis"; informant: W.T. LAWS (Elizabethton); died: 12 Sep. 1928; buried: Gouge Cemetery; record (1928) # 22738.

FOSTER, Porter Jr.; age: 2 months; parents: Porter FOSTER and Cordie JOHNSON (North Carolina); death cause: "unknown"; informant: Cordie JOHNSON (Erwin); died: 8 Sep. 1928; buried; Erwin; record (1928) # 22737.

LAWS, Amos; born: 6 Sep. 1846; widower; parents: Bill LAWS and mother "unknown"; death cause: "intestinal nephritis"; informant: W.T. LAWS (Elizabethton); died: 12 Sep. 1928; buried: Gouge Cemetery; record (1928) # 22738.

SLOUDER, Fred; age: 48 years; married; parents: "unknown"; death cause: "dropsy"; informant: wife (Johnson City); died: 17 Sep. 1928; buried: Washington County; record (1928) # 22739.

MCLAUGHLIN, Sindy; born: 16 Sep. 1860; married; parents: Preston NORRIS (North Carolina) and Vennie WHITSON (North Carolina);

death cause: "dysentery"; informant: Miss Drew KEENER (Erwin); died: 16 Sep. 1928; buried: Jobe Cemetery; record (1928) # 22740.

BENNETT, Maude; born: 3 Feb. 1927; parents: Gaither BENNETT and Anne WOODBY; death cause: "cholera infantum"; died: 10 Oct. 1928; buried: Garland Cemetery; record (1928) # 25007.

HOPSON, Angelina; born: 5 Aug. 1927; parents: J.A. HOPSON (North Carolina) and Hassie PETERSON (North Carolina); death cause: "flu and bronchial pneumonia"; informant: father (Unicoi); died: 30 Oct. 1928; buried: Swingle Cemetery; record (1928) # 25008.

HARVEY, Amuil Clety; born: 3 Aug. 1905; married: parents: Thomas V. HARVEY and Mira HENSON; death cause: "tuberculosis of throat and larynx"; informant: James HARVEY (Johnson City); died: 23 Sep. 1928; buried: Erwin; record (1928) # 25009.

JONES, Charley; age: 36 years; married; parents: John JONES and Jane TITTLE; death cause: "dysentery"; informant: Mrs. Charles JONES (Erwin); died: 8 Sep. 1928; buried: Fishery Cemetery; record # 25010.

GUINN, Virginia Lee; age: 2 years, 1 month and 7 days; parents: M.P. GUINN and Florence GILLIS; death cause: "diphtheria"; informant: father (Erwin); died: 27 Oct. 1928; buried: Erwin; record # 25011.

WILLIS, Frankie; born: 25 Oct. 1928; parents: Dave WILLIS and Myrtle JONES; death cause: not stated; informant: father (Clear Branch); died: 28 Oct. 1928; buried: Willis Cemetery; record (1928) # 25012.

EDWARDS, John W.; born: 6 Jul. 1881 in North Carolina; married; parents: Silas EDWARDS (North Carolina) and Mary WOODBY; death cause: "myocarditis"; informant: wife (Erwin); died: 13 Nov. 1928; buried: North Carolina; record (1928) # 27406.

BARNETT, Nannie; age: 46 years; born: North Carolina; married; parents: Jasper LEDFORD (North Carolina) and Elvira BLALOCK (North Carolina); death cause: "paralysis"; informant: Geter BARNETT (Erwin); died: 16 Nov. 1928; buried: Rock Creek; record # 27407.

HASTINGS, Annie Lee; born: 9 Aug. 1928; parents: Ezra HASTINGS and Sallie NORMAN (North Carolina); death cause: "epilepsy"; informant: father (Erwin); died: 19 Nov. 1928; record (1928) # 27408.

WILLIAMS, Glen; age: 17 years; single; parents: W.T. WILLIAMS (North Carolina) and Rana MCCURRY (North Carolina); death cause:

"tuberculosis of hip"; informant: father (Erwin); died: 16 Nov. 1928; buried: Martins Creek; record (1928) # 27409.

BAILEY, Alberta; born: 15 Jan. 1926; parents: Sam BAILEY (North Carolina) and Clara FANNING; death cause: "dysentery"; informant: W.H. FANNING (Erwin); died: 22 Nov. 1928; buried: Martins Creek; record (1928) # 27410.

TIPTON, William; born: 4 Mar. 1907; single; parents: J.H. TIPTON and Nancy BARNETT (North Carolina); death cause: "fell from train severing both legs, hemorrhage"; informant: father (Unicoi); died: 23 Sep. 1928; buried: Unicoi; record (1928) # 30770.

HARVEY, Essie Parker; born: 30 Apr. 1909; widow; parents: W.S. PARKER (North Carolina) and Sindy FRAISOR (North Carolina); death cause: "killed in automobile wreck"; informant: father (Erwin); died: 2 Jun. 1928; buried: Erwin; record (1928) # 30771.

PEAKE, Edith Ruth; born: 5 Jan. 1908; single; parents: J.W. PEAKE and __ HENSLEY; death cause: illegible; informant: Doris PEAKE (Erwin); died: 6 Dec. 1928; buried: Erwin; record (1928) # 30772.

GARLAND, Edd; born: 2 Aug. 1889; married; parents: Thomas GARLAND (North Carolina) and Mary TIPTON (North Carolina); death cause: "homicide, revolver wound in head"; informant: wife (Erwin); died: 11 Dec. 1928; buried: Erwin; record (1928) # 30773.

ROGERS, Elmer; born: 14 Nov. 1928; parents: Joe ROGERS and Stella FRANCIS; death cause: "broncho pneumonia"; informant: father (Embreeville); died: 12 Dec. 1928; buried: Embreeville; record # 30774.

JONES, Catherine; born: 6 May 1856; widow; parents: Jackson EDWARDS and Cressie CLOUSE; death cause: "paralysis"; died in the 5th District, 25 Dec. 1928; buried: Erwin; record (1928) # 30775.

PETERSON, John; born: 2 Feb. 1837 in North Carolina; widower; parents: Hiram PETERSON (North Carolina) and Nancy MASHBURN (North Carolina); death cause: "septic infection"; informant: Bob RENFRO (Erwin); died: 12 Dec. 1928; buried: Relief, North Carolina; record (1928) # 30776.

KEERL, W.T.; born: 3 Dec. 1842 in West Virginia; single; baker; parents: "unknown"; death cause: "nephritis"; informant: Floyd BLANKENSHIP (Erwin); died: 24 Dec. 1928; record (1928) # 30777.

FOSTER, Noma; born: 25 Dec. 1837 in North Carolina; widow; parents: Lark CHANDLER (North Carolina) and Sallie METCALF (North Carolina); death cause: not stated; informant: Frannie SIMMONS (Clear Branch); died: 3 Dec. 1928; buried: Foster Cemetery; record # 30778.

TIPTON, Mary C.; born: 21 Jul. 1857; married; parents: John GILLIS and Ruth TILSON; death cause: not stated; informant: C.C. TIPTON (Clear Branch); died: 10 Dec. 1928; buried: Gillis Cemetery; record 1828 # 30779.

SALTS, Annie; born: 9 Sep. 1886; married; parents: W.P. HOWINGTON (North Carolina) and Martha ETSMON (North Carolina); death cause: "ptomaine poison"; informant: Mack SALTS (Johnson City); died: 21 Jun. 1929; record (1929) # 3758.

TAPP, George; age: 43 years; married; parents: Robert TAPP and Mollie JOHNSON; death cause: "pulmonary tuberculosis"; informant: wife (Erwin); died: 4 Jan. 1929; buried: Fishery Cemetery; record # 3759.

KEENER, Mrs. D.N.; born: 29 Oct. 1840 in South Carolina; parents: Joe ERBY (North Carolina) and Sabra DUNKEN (North Carolina); death cause: "intestinal nephritis"; informant: Drew KEENER (Erwin); died: 8 Jan. 1929; record (1929) # 3760.

RENFRO, Mrs. Cecil; born: 22 Jun. 1912; married; parents: Sam VINSON and Mollie TRUE; death cause: "burn from lighting fire with gasoline"; informant: father (Erwin); died: 8 Jan. 1929; buried: Mayberry, Tennessee; record (1929) # 3761.

HILL, Arthur; age: 28 years; born: Ohio; single; parents: "unknown"; death cause: "fell under train"; died: 13 Jan. 1929; buried: East Liverpool, Ohio; record (1929) # 3762.

LANE, E.B.; age: 67 years; married; parents: John LANE and Elizabeth FOSTER; death cause: "carcinoma of stomach"; informant: Carl LANE (Erwin); died: 13 Jan. 1929; buried: Knoxville; record (1929) # 3863.

GRINDSTAFF, Minnie; age: 39 years; born: North Carolina; married; parents: Flinn THOMAS (North Carolina) and Mary Ann DAVIS (North Carolina); death cause: "influenza and meningitis"; died: 16 Jan. 1929; buried: North Carolina; record (1929) # 3764.

PETERSON, Elmer; age: 11 months; parents: Doss PETERSON (North Carolina) and Darkska BRIANT (North Carolina); death cause:

"pneumonia"; informant: father (Erwin); died: 22 Jan. 1929; buried: Green Mountain, North Carolina; record (1929) # 3765.

COLMAN, Vernie; female; age: 43 years; widow; parents: Dave SMITH and Nan WHALEY; death cause: "intestinal nephritis"; informant: Bob SMITH (Embreeville); died: 20 Jan. 1929; buried: Jones Cemetery; record (1929) # 3766.

NELSON, Rachel; born: 7 Jan. 1843; widow; parents: Henry JONES and Elizabeth FEATHERS; death cause: "influenza"; informant: Will LINVILLE (Unicoi); died: 22 Jan. 1929; buried: Jones Cemetery; record (1929) # 3767.

PATE, S.F.; age: 82 years; born: North Carolina; married; Civil War veteran; parents: "unknown"; death cause: "bronchitis"; died: 22 Jan. 1929; buried: Fishery Cemetery; record (1929) # 3768.

LANE, Mary E.; born: 27 Sep. 1844; married; parents: Daniel ROBERTS (North Carolina) and mother "unknown"; death cause: "influenza"; informant: I.K. LANE (Erwin); died: 17 Jan. 1929; buried: Erwin; record (1929) # 3769.

BENNETT, William R.; born: 22 Jun. 1869 in North Carolina; married; preacher; parents: Amos BENNETT (North Carolina) and Elizabeth LEDFORD (North Carolina); death cause: "catarrh of head"; informant: Oma BENNETT (Clear Branch); died: 7 Jan. 1929; buried: North Carolina; record (1929) # 3770.

GOUGE, Nellie; born: 8 Mar. 1888; divorced; parents: David WHITE and M_ (illegible) GARLAND; death cause: "acute indigestion"; informant: Edith MARSH (Unicoi); died: 9 Feb. 1929; buried: Fishery Cemetery; record (1929) # 6667.

FOSTER, Arthur; age: 40 years; married; parents: father "unknown" and Harriett FOSTER; death cause: "nephritis"; informant: mother (Erwin); died: 7 Feb. 1929; buried: Martins Creek; record (1929) # 6668.

DAVIS, Robert Harry Jr.; born: 29 Dec. 1928; parents: Robert DAVIS and Lula RICE (North Carolina); death cause: "influenza, pneumonia"; informant: father (Erwin); died: 15 Feb. 1929; record (1929) # 6669.

STEWART, W.G.; born: __ Apr. 1872 in North Carolina; married; railroad engineer; parents: James STEWART (North Carolina) and Dellie WISEMAN (North Carolina); death cause: "carcinoma of lower jaw"; informant: wife (Erwin); died: 22 Feb. 1929; record # 6670.

GUINN, Luther Franklin; born: 20 Jul. 1880; single; parents: William GUINN and Mary Jane WOODWARD (North Carolina); death cause: "flu and pneumonia"; informant: M.M. SHELTON (Flag Pond); died: 6 Feb. 1929; buried: Guinn Cemetery; record (1929) # 6671.

TIPTON, Curt; born: 15 Feb. 1850; married; parents: Henderson TIPTON and Elizabeth RANDOLPH; death cause: "flu and pneumonia"; informant: Narcissa HOYLE (Flag Pond); died: 8 Feb. 1929; buried: Blankenship Cemetery; record (1929) # 6672.

SILVERS, Claude; born: 14 Aug. 1926; parents: George SILVERS and Mary E. BLANKENSHIP; death cause: "flu and pneumonia"; informant: father (Flag Pond); died: 28 Feb. 1929; buried: Rice Creek; record (1929) # 6673.

PHILLIPS, Jimmy Lee; born: 19 Jan. 1883; married; parents: J.D. PHILLIPS and Mary L. SAMS; death cause: "flu and pneumonia"; informant: Jimmy HENSLEY (Flag Pond); died: 19 Jan. 1929; buried: Sams Creek; record (1929) # 6674.

WILLIAMS, __ (illegible) Jane; born: 19 Jan. 1929; parents: Arnold WILLIAMS and Jutie TILSON; death cause: "unknown, found dead in bed"; died at Clear Branch on 16 Mar. 1929; buried: Clouse Cemetery; record (1929) # 9575.

GILLIS, Carl; born: 27 Feb. 1888; married; parents: John R. GILLIS and Nancy Jane G_ (illegible); death cause: "syphilis"; informant: Walter GILLIS (Erwin); died: 22 Mar. 1929; record (1929) # 9576.

HATTAN, William Carey; age: 53 years, 3 months and 10 days; born: Beckenridge County, Virginia; married; parents: Mark HATTAN (Virginia) and Jennie SILER (Virginia); death cause: "operation for gangrenous appendix"; died: 25 Mar 1929; informant: wife; buried: Lexington, Virginia; record (1929) # 9577.

FOSTER, Nila; age: 22 days; parents: father not stated and Lena FOSTER; death cause: not stated; informant: J.H. FOSTER; died: 23 Mar. 1929; buried: Foster Cemetery; record (1929) # 9578.

SILVER, Ola; born: 8 Aug. 1921; parents: George SILVERS and Mary E. BLANKENSHIP; death cause: "flu and pneumonia"; informant: father (Flag Pond); died: 1 Mar. 1929; buried: Rice Creek; record # 9579.

COATS, Gabriel; born: 12 Jul. 185_; age: 76 years, 7 months and 26 days; born: Madison County, NC.; married; parents: John COATS (Madison County, NC.) and Emeline RAY (Madison County, NC.); death cause: "dropsy"; informant: John COATS (Flag Pond); died: 8 Mar. 1929; buried: Rice Cemetery; record (1929) # 9580.

BLANKENSHIP, Presley; born: 26 May 1861 in Madison County, NC.; married; parents: David BLANKENSHIP (North Carolina) and mother not stated; death cause: "pneumonia"; informant: Fate BLANKENSHIP (Flag Pond); died: 22 Mar. 1929; buried: Higgins Cemetery; record (1929) # 9581.

HUTCHINS, Julia; born: 13 Mar. 1929; parents: Jesse HUTCHINS (Mitchell County, NC.) and Celia NELSON (Mitchell County, NC.); death cause: "bronchitis"; died: 5 Apr. 1929; buried: Rowe Cemetery; record (1929) # 11917.

ARRWOOD, Sarah Jane; born: _ Oct. 1898 in North Carolina; married; parents: Bill LAUGHRUM (North Carolina) and Ellen JOYCE (North Carolina); death cause: "pellagra"; informant: Burnie ARRWOOD (Erwin); died: 21 Apr. 1929; buried: Huntdale, North Carolina; record (1929) # 11918.

HENSLEY, Jeraldine; born: 18 Mar. 1929; parents: C.B. HENSLEY (North Carolina) and Elen ENGLE; death cause: "unknown"; died: 20 Mar. 1929; record (1929) # 11919.

DICKSON, Nancy Ann; born: 16 Jul. 1858 in Virginia; widow; parents: Duke SMALLING and _ BAKER; death cause: "paralysis"; informant: Matt DICKSON (Erwin); died: 24 Mar. 1929; buried: Milligan College; record (1929) # 11920.

JONES, Elizabeth Ida; born: 20 Jan. 1867; widow; parents: Henry AMBROSE and Martha LYLE; death cause: "pulmonary tuberculosis"; informant: Mrs. John LYLE (Erwin); died: 25 Apr. 1929; buried: Jones Cemetery; record (1929) # 11921.

FOSTER, Silas; born: _ Sep. 1858; married; parents: Thomas FOSTER and A_ (illegible) CHANDLER (North Carolina); death cause: "peritonitis, cystitis"; informant: Jake WOODWARD (Unicoi); died: 29 Jan. 1929; buried: Foster Cemetery; record (1929) # 14219.

TIPTON, Celia; born: 20 May 1851 in Carter County; parents: Elish BENNETT (Mitchell County, NC.) and Pollie JOHNSON (Greene

County, TN.); death cause: "heart disease"; informant: Anderson BENNETT (Erwin); died: 7 May 1929; buried: Swingle Cemetery; record (1929) # 14220.

STEWART, J.M.; born: 29 May 1849 in North Carolina; widower; parents: Robert STEWART (North Carolina) and Rocie GARLAND (North Carolina); death cause: "cerebral hemorrhage"; informant: Robert STEWART (Erwin); died: 8 May 1929; record (1929) # 14221.

BLANKENSHIP, Zeb; born: 19 May 1897; married; parents: Tom BLANKENSHIP and Emma PHILLIPS; death cause: "nephritis, alcoholism"; informant: mother (Erwin); died: 9 May 1929; buried: Flag Pond; record (1929) # 14222.

VANDERGRIFF, E.J.; born: 25 Jun. 1862 in Virginia; married; master carpenter; parents: Thomas VANDERGRIFF (Virginia) and Mary LITTLE (Virginia); death cause: "locked bowels"; informant: Bill VANDERGRIFF (Erwin); died: 11 May 1929; buried: Salem, Virginia; record (1929) # 14223.

HAMPTON, William Woodward; age: 5 years; parents: W.S. HAMPTON and Gertha TIPTON; death cause: "influenza and meningitis"; informant: father (Erwin); died: 14 May 1929; buried: Martins Creek; record (1929) # 14224.

RUNION, Lydia E.; born: 23 Jun. 1849; married; parents: William PARKS and Nancy ERWIN; death cause: "heart disease"; informant: W.K. RUNION (Erwin); died: 10 May 1929; buried: Erwin; record (1929) # 14225.

FURCHES, Durwood; born: 14 Jan. 1928; parents: M.V. FURCHES and Dollie BROYLES; death cause: "meningitis"; died: 25 Jun. 1929; buried: Liberty Cemetery; record (1929) # 16460.

NOELLERT, William; age: 31 years; born: Maryland; single; pottery foreman; parents: John NOELLERT (Maryland) and mother "unknown"; death cause: "automobile accident, neck broken"; died: 30 Jun. 1929; buried: Michigan; record (1929) # 16461.

SAMS, Cora; born: 26 Jul. __; age: 28 years; born: North Carolina; married; parents: Robert SHELTON (North Carolina) and Matt SHELTON (North Carolina); death cause: "pellagra"; informant: Will SAMS (Erwin); died: 19 Jun. 1929; buried: Higgins Creek; record (1929) # 16462.

STALLARD, Ella Marie; age: 1 year, 8 months and 3 days; parents: father not stated and Nannie STALLARD (Kentucky); death cause: "unknown"; informant: mother (Erwin); died: 3 Jul. 1929; buried: Fishery Cemetery; record (1929) # 18968.

MCINTURFF, Dave; born: __ Aug. 1898; single; parents: Bob MCINTURFF and Sadie BAKER; death cause: "homicide, gunshot wound in abdomen"; informant: Nat MCINTURFF (Unicoi); died: 8 Jul. 1929; buried: Unicoi; record (1929) # 18969.

CASEY, Hannah; age: 72 years; widow; parents: James NELSON and Annie HUSKINS; death cause: "nephritis"; informant: Walter CASEY (Embreeville); died: 21 Jul. 1929; buried: Embreeville; record # 18970.

GARLAND, Mary S.; born: __ Aug. 1849 in North Carolina; widow; parents: John TIPTON (North Carolina) and Rauna ROBERTS (North Carolina); death cause: "anemia"; informant: Mrs. Ed GARLAND (Erwin); died: 5 Jul. 1929; buried: Tipton Hill, North Carolina; record (1929) # 16971.

SMITH, Dea O'Dell; born: 1 Sep. 1907; single; parents: John SMITH and Jude DAY; death cause: "pellagra"; informant: mother (Erwin); died: 8 Aug. 1929; buried: Erwin; record (1929) # 21301.

EDWARDS, Lowers; female; born: 19 Aug. 1928; parents: J.F. EDWARDS and Pheba JONES; death cause: illegible; informant: father (Erwin); died: 10 Aug. 1929; buried: Erwin; record (1929) # 21302.

RENFRO, Thelma; born: 10 Jun. 1923; parents: T.B. RENFRO (North Carolina) and Nettie HAMPTON (North Carolina); death cause: "__ (illegible) of right tibia"; informant: father (Erwin); died: 12 Aug. 1929; buried: Martins Creek; record (1929) # 21303.

RULE, Mrs. J.C.; born: 8 Nov. 1873 in Virginia; married; parents: J.M. LINDSEY (Virginia) and Mary __ (illegible) (Virginia); death cause: "nephritis"; informant: Clifford RULE (Erwin); died: 21 Aug. 1929; buried: Roanoke, Virginia; record (1929) # 21304.

VINSON, Mallie Ella; age: 36 years and 10 months; born: Virginia; married; parents: Buck TRUE (Virginia) and Ella KENNEDY (Virginia); death cause: "pulmonary tuberculosis"; informant: Sam VINSON (Erwin); died: 23 Aug. 1929; buried: Virginia; record (1929) # 21305.

MASHBURN, Jacob; born: 19 Apr. 1871; married; parents: Calloway MASHBURN and Rilla PATE; death cause: "typhoid"; informant: Alvin MASHBURN (Erwin); died: 28 Jul. 1929; buried: Jobe Cemetery; record (1929) # 21306.

SHELL, Helen; age: 1 year and 2 months; parents: Alvin SHELL and L_ (illegible) POOR; death cause: "dysentery"; informant: father (Erwin); died: 25 Aug. 1929; buried: Garland Cemetery; record (1929) # 21307.

SHELTON, Visia; born: 15 Sep. 1860 in Yancey County, NC.; widow; parents: John BAILEY and Betsy PHILLIPS; death cause: "carcinoma of face"; informant: Fate SHELTON (Erwin); died: 5 Aug. 1929; buried: Flag Pond; record (1929) # 21308.

BANNER, Dora; born: 19 Jan. 1875; married; parents: Will LOVE and Mary Ann TAPP; death cause: "brights disease"; informant: Henry BANNER (Erwin); died: 17 Aug. 1929; buried: Fishery Cemetery; record (1929) # 21309.

HIGGINS, Infant; born: 10 Aug. 1929; parents: Frank HIGGINS (North Carolina) and Helen DOSER (North Carolina); death cause: "premature birth"; informant: father (Erwin); died: 10 Aug. 1929; buried: Martins Creek; record (1929) # 21310.

JONES, Elbert; age: 78 years; married; parents: William JONES and mother "unknown"; death cause: not stated; died: 4 Aug. 1929; buried: Higgins Cemetery; record (1929) # 21311.

STREET, Pearl; born: 27 Jun. 1910; single; parents: Landon STREET (North Carolina) and Mary COCHRAN; death cause: "pneumonitis both lungs"; informant: Ed STREET (Unicoi); died: 15 Sep. 1929; buried: McInturff Cemetery; record (1929) # 23539.

MCINTURFF, C.B.; born: 22 Oct. 1877; married; parents: Jack MCINTURFF and Marie CROW (North Carolina); death cause: "dysentery"; informant: wife (Erwin); died: 8 Sep. 1929; buried: Fishery Cemetery; record (1929) # 23540.

CONLEY, George; age: 31 years; born: North Carolina; married; parents: James CONELY (North Carolina) and Mallie SLAGLE (North Carolina); death cause: "suicide, drank carbolic acid"; informant: M.F. SPARKS (Tolcane, North Carolina); died: 10 Sep. 1929; buried: Tolcane, North Carolina; record (1929) # 23541.

MATHES, Ruth; born: 8 Sep. 1928; parents: Ben MATHES and Tressie MCCARVER (Missouri); death cause: "diarrhea"; informant: father (Erwin); died: 16 Sep. 1929; buried: Martins Creek; record # 23542.

MOORE, Glennie; born: 28 Jan. __; age: 32 years; married; parents: Russell MOORE and Mary Jane FILLERS; death cause: "intestinal obstruction"; died: 16 Sep. 1929; buried: Liberty Cemetery, Washington County; record (1929) # 23543.

RICE, John Calvin; born: 19 Nov. 1860; widower; parents: Jackson RICE and Matilda BRIGGS; death cause: "nephritis"; informant: Newberry RICE (Erwin); died: 17 Sep. 1929; buried: Rice Cemetery; record (1929) # 23544.

HENSLEY, Cornerly; age: 61 years; born: North Carolina; married; parents: father not stated and Lucindy HENSLEY (North Carolina); death cause: "homicide, gunshot wound"; informant: George W. HENSLEY (Flag Pond); died: 19 Sep. 1929; buried: Jobe Cemetery; record (1929) # 23545.

HENSON, Myrtle Irene; age: 30 years, 2 months and 27 days; married; parents: Thomas BLANKENSHIP and Emma PHILLIPS; death cause: "tuberculosis"; informant: Earl HENSON (Erwin); died: 21 Sep. 1929; buried: Sams Cemetery; record (1929) # 23546.

BAILEY, Johnnie Austin; born: 27 Sep. 1927; parents: Charles P. BAILEY (North Carolina) and Ethel NORRIS; death cause: "broncho pneumonia"; informant: father (Erwin); died: 23 Sep. 1929; buried: Martins Creek; record (1929) # 23547.

BAILEY, M.L.; born: 11 Feb. 1887 in North Carolina; married; parents: Daniel (?) BAILEY (North Carolina) and Mary Jane __ (illegible); death cause: "automobile accident, broken neck"; informant: wife (Erwin); died: 4 Oct. 1929; buried: Jobe Cemetery; record # 25867.

GARLAND, Tom; age: 31 years; born: North Carolina; married; parents: D_ (illegible) GARLAND (North Carolina) and Sarah TIPTON (North Carolina); death cause: "homicide, knife stab"; informant: Rotha GARLAND (Clear Branch); died: 13 Oct. 1929; buried: Martins Creek; record (1929) # 25868.

ANDERSON, Mrs. J.H.; age: 65 years; born: North Carolina; widow; parents: George WILSON (North Carolina) and B_ (illegible) ANDERSON (North Carolina); death cause: "nephritis"; informant:

John ANDERSON (Flag Pond); died: 2 Sep. 1929; buried: Paint Gap, North Carolina; record (1929) # 25869.

BLEVINS, Elmer; born: 8 Oct. 1929; parents: James BLEVINS and Ella CARVER (North Carolina); death cause: "acute indigestion"; informant: father (Unicoi); died: 15 Oct. 1929; buried: Unicoi; record # 28200.

MCKINNEY, Sarah; born: 1 Nov. 1846; widow; parents: Sam MCKINNEY (Carter County) and Litie ATKINS (Carter County); death cause: "aortic insufficiency"; informant: Austin HERRELL (Unicoi); died: 11 Nov. 1929; buried: Herrell Cemetery; record # 28201.

BELL, Hattie; born: 31 Dec. 1859; widow; parents: Jacob B. MILLER and Julie LEONARD; death cause: "carcinoma of liver"; informant: J.B. BELL (Unicoi); died: 14 Nov. 1929; buried: Limestone Cove; record (1929) # 28202.

ROBBINS, James Calvin; born: 27 Feb. 1865 in Virginia; widower; parents: Jackson ROBBINS (Virginia) and Martha Ann ROBBINS (Virginia); death cause: "cerebral hemorrhage"; informant: Guy ROBBINS (Erwin); died: 7 Nov. 1929; buried: Jobe Cemetery; record (1929) # 28203.

DEVAULT, J.W.; age: 55 years; married; parents: William E. DEVAULT and Edna HULL; death cause: "apoplexy"; informant: wife (Erwin); died: 16 Nov. 1929; buried: Johnson City; record # 28204.

HUSKINS, Marie; born: 22 Jun. 1928; parents: Joe HUSKINS and Alice NELSON; death cause: "diphtheria"; informant: father (Erwin); died: 23 Nov. 1929; buried: Garland Cemetery; record (1929) # 28205.

COFFEE, J.W.; age: 58 years; married; parents: Pery COFFEE (North Carolina) and Sarah BERRY (North Carolina); death cause: "thought heart failure"; informant: Byrnie COFFEE (Erwin); died: 30 Nov. 1929; buried: Jones Cemetery; record (1929) # 28206.

JONES, Catherine; born: 3 Oct. 1843; widow; parents: "unknown"; death cause: "nephritis"; informant: T.S. JONES (Erwin); died: 30 Nov. 1929; buried: Fishery Cemetery; record (1929) # 28207.

GUINN, Lennie; age: 74 years; widow; parents: Marion HARRIS and R_ (illegible) HENSLEY; death cause: "cerebral hemorrhage"; informant: M.P. GUINN (Erwin); died: 11 Nov. 1929; buried: Martins Creek; record (1929) # 28208.

PRICE, Mollie; age: 66 years; born: North Carolina; married; parents: Jim PRICE (North Carolina) and __ THOMAS (North Carolina); death cause: "carcinoma of stomach"; informant: T.E. PRICE (Clear Branch); died: 2 Nov. 1929; buried: Ledford Cemetery; record (1929) # 28209.

GENTRY, Lewis G.; born: 22 Feb. 1860 near Mars Hill, North Carolina; married; parents: father not stated and Elizabeth GENTRY (North Carolina); death cause: "acute indigestion"; informant: wife (Flag Pond); died: 12 Dec. 1929; buried: Allison Cemetery; record # 31148.

TIPTON, Margaret Ann; born: 10 Sep __; age: 71 years; widow; parents: Tom FOSTER and Sallie FOSTER; death cause: "heart disease"; informant: Walter TIPTON (Erwin); died: 2 Dec. 1929; buried: Martins Creek; record (1929) # 31149.

WATSON, Jannette Marie; born: 3 Dec. 1929; parents: Dennei WATSON (North Carolina) and Florence HOWELL (North Carolina); death cause: "unknown"; informant: Z.N. HOWELL (Erwin); died: 6 Dec. 1929; buried: Garland Cemetery; record (1929) # 31150.

BOGART, Edd; born: 25 Aug. 1857; married; parents: Sam BOGART and mother "unknown"; death cause: "pellagra"; informant: Bill BOGART (Erwin); died: 26 Dec. 1929; buried: Garland Cemetery; record (1929) # 31151.

FAGAN, Rosa Lee; born: __ May 1884; married; parents: William PAYNE and Hassie PATTON; death cause: "heart condition"; informant: Ethel FAGAN (Erwin); died: 28 Dec. 1929; buried: Milligan College, Tennessee; record (1929) # 31154.

MCLAUGHLIN, N.; born: 27 Oct. __; age: 81 years; widower; parents: W.K. MCLAUGHLIN (North Carolina) and Vennei WHITSON (North Carolina); death cause: "pellagra"; death cause: Drew KEENER (Erwin); died: 29 Dec. 1929; record (1929) # 31153.

WILSON, Samuel; born: 24 Nov. 1929; parents: Isaac WILSON (North Carolina) and Etta BARNETT (North Carolina); death cause: "unknown"; informant: father (Erwin); died: 25 Nov. 1929; buried: Martins Creek; record (1929) # 31154.

WILSON, Onesel; age: 4 years, 7 months and 13 days; parents: Thomas WILSON (North Carolina) and Etta WILSON (North Carolina); death cause: "unknown"; informant: W.F. HENSLEY (Clear Branch); died: 15 Dec. 1929; buried: Hensley Cemetery; record (1929) # 31155.

JILLES, James Brown; born: 7 Oct. 1922; parents: Naddie JILLES and Vivian BARNES; death cause: "nephritis"; died at Clear Branch, 25 Jan. 1930; record (1930) # 2179.

MCINTYRE, Mrs. J.K.; born: 6 Jul. 1872 in Virginia; parents: M. Hugh HERRELL (North Carolina) and Cora MCINTYRE (North Carolina); death cause: "heart disease"; informant: J.K. MCINTYRE (Erwin); died: 1 Jan. 1930; buried: Jobe Cemetery; record (1930) # 2180.

MCINTURFF, Lona D.; born: 4 Oct. 1890; married; parents: John MILLER and Jennie TAPP; death cause: "unknown, sick long time"; informant: D.A. MCINTURFF (Erwin); died: 1 Jan. 1930; buried: Tittle Cemetery; record (1930) # 2181

MCLAUGHLIN, Mrs. J.H.; born: 16 Jan. 1889; married; parents: Elbert RHEA and __ BRIGGS (North Carolina); death cause: "flu and pneumonia"; informant: J.H. MCLAUGHLIN (Erwin); died: 11 Jan. 1930; buried: Jobe Cemetery; record (1930) # 2182.

HINES, Elizabeth; born: 2 Dec. 1839 in North Carolina; widow; parents: Thomas LOUELL (North Carolina) and Eliza WOLFE (North Carolina); death cause: "carcinoma of uterus"; informant: Matte HINES (Erwin); died: 14 Jan. 1930; buried: Monte Vista Cemetery; record (1930) # 2183.

ADKINS, Cass; age: 27 years; born: North Carolina; married; parents: Sam L. ADKINS (North Carolina) and Margaret FINDER (North Carolina); death cause: "homicide, gunshot wound through head"; informant: father (Erwin); died: 18 Jan. 1930; buried: Miller Cemetery; record (1930) # 2184.

RENFRO, Jack; born: 18 Jan. 1930; parents: Rube M. RENFRO (North Carolina) and Francis HONEYCUTT; death cause: "respiratory failure"; informant: R.M. RENFRO (Erwin); died: 28 Jan. 1930; buried: McInturff Cemetery; record (1930) # 2185.

GILLIS, James Brown; born: 17 Oct. 1923; parents: Lattie GILLIS and Vivian BARNS; death cause: "nephritis"; informant: father (Flag Pond); died: 25 Jan. 1930; buried: Rocky Fork; record (1930) # 2185.

MCINTURFF, Genevieve; born: 4 Nov. 1929; parents: Noah MCINTURFF and Myrtle MESON (?); death cause: "acute indigestion, found dead in bed"; informant: father (Erwin); died: 27 Jan. 1930; record (1930) # 2187.

BROWN, Mrs. George; age: 71 years; married; parents: David MCNABB and __ (illegible) COOPER (North Carolina); death cause: "heart disease"; died: 11 Jan. 1930; buried: Fishery Cemetery; record (1930) # 2188.

LYLE, Gracie May; born: 4 Jun. 1909; single; parents: Robert R. LYLE and Rebecca JONES; death cause: "pulmonary tuberculosis"; informant: father (Erwin); died: 30 Jan. 1930; buried: Fishery Cemetery; record (1930) # 2189.

HENSLEY, Wilburn; born: 1 Aug. 1928; parents: W.A. HENSLEY (North Carolina) and Bell TIPTON (North Carolina); death cause: "meningitis"; informant: father (Erwin); died: 5 Jan. 1930; buried: Evergreen Cemetery; record (1930) # 2190.

NELSON, Zeb; age: 59 years; born: North Carolina; married; parents: Ned NELSON (North Carolina) and __ DEATON (North Carolina); death cause: "nephritis"; informant: W.D. NELSON (Erwin); died: 13 Jan. 1930; buried: Yancey County, NC.; record (1930) # 2191.

CHASE, Lillie B.; born: 27 Jan. 1864 in Washington County, Virginia; widow; parents: Harvey ALLEN (Virginia) and mother "unknown"; death cause: "gangrene of foot"; informant: Hubert CHASE (Augusta, Georgia); died: 2 Feb. 1930; buried: Fairview Cemetery, Washington County; record (1930) # 4636.

CROW, Mande; born: 3 Apr. 1895; widow; parents: Robert DAVIS and Lula KEENER (North Carolina); death cause: "pellagra"; informant: Mrs. Bob McInturff (Erwin); died: 7 Feb. 1930; buried: Jobe Cemetery; record (1930) # 4637.

WASHBURN, Myra; born: 6 Sep. 1861; married; parents: Benjamin BIRDWELL and Lydia DUNCAN, death cause: "paralysis"; died: 9 Feb. 1930; buried: Martins Creek; record (1930) # 4638.

BARNETT, T.C.; age: 82 years; born: North Carolina; married; parents: Dave BARNETT (North Carolina) and Hannah STANLEY (North Carolina); death cause: "pneumonia"; informant: wife (Erwin); died: 22 Feb. 1930; buried: Martins Creek; record (1930) # 4639.

HAMPTON, William Parley; born: 5 Mar 1921; parents: W.S. HAMPTON and Girthe TIPTON; death cause: "meningitis"; died: 22 Feb. 1930; buried: Martins Creek; record (1930) # 4640.

FORBS, Jessie; born: 6 Nov. 1891 in North Carolina; single; parents: E.H. FORBS (North Carolina) and Setha STUART (North Carolina); death cause: "nephritis"; informant: R.C. FORBS (Erwin); died: 27 Feb. 1930; buried: Bailey Cemetery; record (1930) # 4641.

CUTSHALL, James; born: 9 Jan. 1862; age: 68 years, 1 month and 25 days; born: North Carolina; married; parents: father "unknown" and Bessie CUTSHALL; death cause: "heart disease"; died: 3 Mar. 1930; buried: Devils Fork; record (1930) # 7315.

HENSLEY, John; born: 7 Mar. 1852; widower; parents: Armp HENSLEY and Barbara HIGGINS; death cause: "dropsy"; died: 6 Mar. 1930; buried: Hensley Cemetery; record (1930) # 7316.

SANGER, Virginia Lydia; born: 19 Feb. 1930; parents: G. Earl SANGER and Ella ASHLEY; death cause: "hemorrhage of umbilical"; informant: father (Unicoi); died: 26 Feb. 1930; buried: Swingle Cemetery; record (1930) # 7317.

MCINTOSH, James; age: 34 years; born: North Carolina; married; parents: Leroy MCINTOSH (North Carolina) and Laura HARRIS (North Carolina); death cause: "homicide, gunshot wound chest"; informant: Oscar BRADFORD (Butch, North Carolina) died: 3 Mar. 1930; buried: Butch, North Carolina; record (1930) # 7318.

HAMPTON, Mattie; age: 68 years; widow; parents: Roy CLICK and Sadie WHITE; death cause: "lobar pneumonia"; informant: W.S. HAMPTON (Erwin); died: 23 Mar. 1930; buried: Martins Creek; record (1930) # 7319.

YOUNG, Missouri Janet Greene; born: 10 Jul. 1874 in North Carolina; married; parents: Landon GREENE (North Carolina) and Louise BURLESON (North Carolina); death cause: "cerebral hemorrhage"; informant: Hobart YOUNG (Erwin); died: 29 Mar. 1930; buried: family cemetery in North Carolina; record (1930) # 7320.

LAWING, Jack; born: 5 Mar. 1928; parents: W.M. LAWING and Bessie THOMAS; death cause: "influenza and operation for __ (illegible)"; informant: father (Erwin); died: 27 Mar. 1930; buried: Martins Creek; record (1930) # 7321.

TITTLE, A.G.; born: 28 May 1853; married; parents: "unknown"; death cause: "heart disease"; informant: Dave SMITH (Erwin); died: 2 Mar. 1930; buried: Jobe Cemetery; record (1930) # 7322.

JONES, Elbert; age: 57 years; widower; parents: John JONES and __ WHALEY; death cause: "lobar pneumonia"; informant: Robert JONES (Saint Paul, Virginia); died: 22 Mar. 1930; buried: Fishery Cemetery; record (1930) # 7323.

HENSLEY, Dorothy; age: 1 year, 11 months and 18 days; parents: Doc HENSLEY and Essie INGRAM; death cause: "double pneumonia"; informant: Walter SHELL (Erwin); died: 7 Mar. 1930; buried: Martins Creek; record (1930) # 7324.

FOWLER, Walter H.; born: 26 Nov. 1858 in North Carolina; single; parents: William J. FOWLER (North Carolina) and Nancy Jane BURGESS (North Carolina); death cause: "nephritis"; informant: A.J. FOWLER (Erwin); died: 14 Mar. 1930; buried: Chapel Hill, North Carolina; record (1930) # 7325.

BOWMAN, Alfred C.; age: 23 years and 11 days; born: Virginia; single; parents: John S. BOWMAN (North Carolina) and Nettie BIRCHFIELD (North Carolina); death cause: "influenza and pulmonary tuberculosis"; died: 21 Apr. 1930; buried: Horton Cemetery; record (1930) # 9936.

REYNOLDS, Emma Jane; born: 16 Feb. 1861 in Pennsylvania; married; parents: __ PORTER (Pennsylvania) and mother "unknown"; death cause: "cerebral hemorrhage"; informant: C.D. MOSS (Erwin); died: 3 Apr. 1930; buried: Roanoke, Virginia; record (1930) # 9937.

JACKSON, Mable; age: 16 years; parents: Edd JACKSON and Bertha DOVE (?); death cause: "lobar pneumonia"; informant: Ruby JACKSON (Erwin); died: 4 Apr. 1930; buried: Jobe Cemetery; record (1930) # 9938.

DOBBINS, Christine; born: 5 Nov. 1928; parents: William DOBBINS and Victoria SIMMONS; death cause: "lobar pneumonia"; informant: W.M. SIMMONS (Erwin); died: 9 Apr. 1930; buried: Jobe Cemetery; record (1930) # 9939.

WHEELER, Infant; male; parents: Fred WHEELER and Mary Emma HENDRIX (Watauga, Tennessee); death cause: "premature"; informant: Mrs. W.O. WHEELER (Erwin); born/died: 14 Apr. 1930; buried: Watauga, Tennessee; record (1930) # 9940.

WILSON, Polly; age: 87 years; born: North Carolina; widow of John WILSON; parents: Tom WILSON (North Carolina) and Hannah LEDFORD (North Carolina); death cause: "carcinoma of breast";

informant: Mrs. W.M. COOPER (Erwin); died: 24 Apr. 1930; buried: Jobe Cemetery; record (1930) # 9941.

CASEY, Hattie; born: 8 Apr. 1881; single; parents: Landon CASEY and Hannah __ (illegible); death cause: "pulmonary tuberculosis"; informant: Walter CASEY (Embreeville); died: 19 Apr. 1930; record # 9942.

CORBIN, Anna; born: 21 Mar. 1905 in Yancey County, NC.; married; parents: L.H. GRIFFITH (Yancey County, NC.) and L_ (illegible) COOPER (Yancey County, NC.); death cause: "pulmonary tuberculosis"; informant: father (Erwin); died: 6 Apr. 1930; buried: Erwin; record (1930) # 9944.

HENSLEY, Amos; age: 83 years; born: North Carolina; husband of Naoma ESTEPP; parents: Wallace HENSLEY (North Carolina) and __ WHITSON (North Carolina); death cause: "myocarditis"; informant: Walter HENSLEY (Erwin); died: 15 Apr. 1930; buried: North Carolina; record (1930) # 9945.

BENNETT, Infant; male; parents: Clayton BENNETT (North Carolina) and Liza THOMAS (North Carolina); death cause: "unknown"; informant: father (Erwin); born/died: 29 Apr. 1930; buried: Martins Creek; record (1930) # 9946.

FOSTER, William Bart; born: __ Apr. 1874; single; parents: Frank FOSTER and Leona HENSLEY; death cause: "tuberculosis"; informant: D.B. FOSTER (Clear Branch); died: 16 Apr. 1930; buried: Foster Cemetery; record (1930) # 9947.

FOSTER, Lonnie Junior; born: 7 Apr. 1930; parents: Roy FOSTER and Leura FOSTER; death cause: not stated; informant: J.H. FOSTER (Clear Branch); died: 25 Apr. 1930; buried: Foster Cemetery; record (1930 # 9948.

TREADWAY, Ethel; born: 7 Apr. 1930; parents: Leonard TREADWAY and Birdie TIPTON; death cause: "flu and pneumonia"; informant: Cordelia TIPTON (Flag Pond); died: 7 Apr. 1930; buried: Sams Creek; record (1930) # 9949.

CANTRELL, J.P.; born: 25 Aug. 1927; parents: James CANTRELL (North Carolina) and Media METCALF; death cause: "pneumonia"; informant: mother (Flag Pond); died: 9 Apr. 1930; buried: Sams Creek; record (1930) # 9950.

TREADWAY, Bethel; born: 7 Apr. 1930; parents: Leonard TREADWAY and Birdie TIPTON; death cause: "flu and pneumonia"; informant: Cordelia TIPTON (Flag Pond); died: 7 Apr. 1930; buried: Sams Creek; record (1930) # 9951.

METCALF, Johnnie; born: 5 Feb. 1930; parents: Dempsy METCALF and Ruby PHILLIPS; death cause: "pneumonia"; died: 27 Apr. 1930; buried: Sams Creek; record (1930) # 9952.

CRAIN, Elua; born: 27 Mar. 1930; parents: Lattie CRAIN and Martha EDWARDS; death cause: "flu and pneumonia"; informant: father (Flag Pond); died: 27 Mar. 1930; buried: Higgins Creek; record # 9953.

RANDOLPH, A.M.; born: 8 Oct. 1876 in North Carolina; married; parents: William RANDOLPH (North Carolina) and Polly HARRIS (North Carolina); death cause: "heart disease"; informant: wife (Erwin); died: 12 May 1930; buried: Martins Creek; record (1930) # 12384.

WRIGHT, John William; born: 4 Sep. 1851; widower; parents: Thomas WRIGHT (Illinois) and Susan SMITHMAN; death cause: "endo carditis"; informant: W.H. WRIGHT (Erwin); died: 8 May 1930; buried: Bell Cemetery; record (1930) # 12385.

GARRISON, James W.; age: "about 48 years"; born: Carter County; married; parents: "unknown"; death cause: "probably apoplexy"; informant: T.E. DOSS (Erwin); died: 30 May 1930; buried: Canton, Georgia; record (1930) # 12386.

CALLAHAN, Alice; born: __ Feb. 1929 in North Carolina; parents: Fred CALLAHAN and Lula RAY (North Carolina); death cause: "lobar pneumonia"; informant: Mrs. Bert CALLAHAN (Erwin); died: 28 May 1930; record (1930) # 12387.

AMBROSE, Hattie McInturff; age: 64 years; wife of James H. AMBROSE; parents: Jackie MCINTURFF and Marlie TIPTON; death cause: "dropsy"; informant: Wade R. AMBROSE (Erwin); died: 21 May 1930; buried: Fishery Cemetery; record (1930) # 12388.

LONG, Harley D.; born: 19 Aug. 1929 in Newell, West Virginia; parents: Dana LONG and Etta SHELTON (North Carolina); death cause: "acute indigestion"; informant: mother (Erwin); died: 8 May 1930; buried: Martins Creek; record (1930) # 12389.

EMMERT, Peter Wesley; born: 4 Oct. 1854 in Carter County; widower; magistrate; parents: William C. EMMERT and Mary RENSHAW;

death cause: "diabetes"; informant: Ben H. EMMERT (Erwin); died: 9 May 1930; buried: Jobe Cemetery; record (1930) # 12390.

TAPP, Infant; male; born: 17 May 1930; parents: Blaine TAPP and Polly FENDER (North Carolina); death cause: "acute indigestion"; informant: father (Erwin); died: 18 May 1930; buried: Martins Creek; record (1930) # 12391.

METCALF, Margaret; age: 74 years and 9 months; born: Madison County, NC.; divorced; parents: William METCALF (Madison County, NC.) and Martha HENSLEY (Madison County, NC.); death cause: "heart leason, pellagra"; informant: Willie METCALF (Erwin); died: 20 May 1930; buried: Metcalf Cemetery; record (1930) # 12392.

TILSON, Elsie Salts; born: 24 May 1908 in Washington County; married; parents: Felix MILLER and Mary Ellen SALTS; death cause: "pellagra"; died: 20 May 1930; buried: Martins Creek; record # 12393.

STOCKTON, Infant; male; parents: Carl STOCKTON and Nola May HENSLEY; death cause: not stated; born/died: 5 May 1930; buried: Mount Pleasant Cemetery; record (1930) # 12394.

TOMPKINS, Rufina Jane; born: 25 Jan. 1870 in North Carolina; married; parents: James Monroe TAYLOR (North Carolina) and Nancy Jane SCROGGINS (North Carolina); death cause: "dropsy and paralysis"; informant: Zippie GUINN (Clear Branch); died: 14 May 1930; buried: Clear Branch Cemetery; record (1930) # 12395.

GARLAND, Sarah A.; born: 15 May 1856 in Carter County; widow; parents: David W. BELL (Belfast, Ireland) and Sarah Alice MCKILDEN (Baltimore, Maryland); death cause: not stated; informant: P.N. GARLAND (Unicoi); died: 16 Jun. 1930; buried: Bell Cemetery; record (1930) # 14931.

PATTON, William S.; born: 10 Jul. 1864 in Carter County; married to Ida HODGE; parents: Joshua PATTON (Ireland) and Julia PHILLIPS (Carter County); death cause: "tuberculosis and pellagra"; informant: Mrs. Ida PATTON (Unicoi); died: 23 Jun. 1930; buried: Simmons Cemetery; record (1930) # 14932.

NORTON, Sallie; born: 3 Oct. 1857 in Virginia; wife of Edward H. NORTON; parents: __ COOK and mother "unknown"; death cause: "colitis"; informant: husband (Unicoi); died: 10 Jun. 1930; buried: Roan Mountain, Tennessee; record (1930) # 14933.

EDWARDS, Gertrude; age: 35 years; born: North Carolina; married; parents: B.H. HUGHES (North Carolina) and Lovie TAYLOR (North Carolina); death cause: "heart lesion"; informant: Arche EDWARDS; died: 9 Jun. 1930; buried: Poplar, North Carolina; record # 14934.

MCCURRY, Velida; age: 5 months and 12 days; parents: Britton MCCURRY and Ruby INGLE; death cause: "found dead in bed wrapped in rubber sheet"; informant: William MCCURRY (Unicoi); died: 18 Jun. 1930; buried: family cemetery; record (1930) # 14935.

RUNION, Thomas C.; age: 70 years, 11 months and 28 days; born: North Carolina; married Sue Emma __; blacksmith; parents: Thomas RUNION (North Carolina) and Betty HARRIS (North Carolina); death cause: "nephritis"; informant: W.C. RUNION (Erwin); died: 25 Jun. 1930; buried; Martins Creek; record (1930) # 14936.

CHARLES, John Valley; born: 24 Mar. 1928 in Kentucky; parents: R.A. CHARLES (Virginia) and Bennie VALLEY (Virginia); death cause: "whooping cough, pneumonia"; informant: C.E. CHARLES (Erwin); died: 25 Jun. 1930; buried: Elkhon City, Kentucky; record # 14937.

PRICE, Ollie Bell; born: 24 Sep. 1928; parents: Furman F. PRICE and Susie ROARKS (Kentucky); death cause: "lobar pneumonia"; informant: father (Erwin); died: 5 Jun. 1930; buried: Martins Creek; record (1930) # 14938.

ANDERS, Rachel Mahala; born: 8 May 1850; widow; parents: William HAMPTON and Malinda LISENBIE; death cause: "pellagra"; died: 16 Jun. 1930; buried: Erwin; record (1930) # 14939.

PETERSON, Joshua; born: 13 Jun. 1865 in Mitchell County, NC.; married to Addie PETERSON; parents: John PETERSON (North Carolina) and Anne RADFORD (North Carolina); death cause: "unknown"; informant: Jesse PETERSON (Erwin); died: 24 Jun. 1930; buried: Erwin; record (1930) # 14940.

JOHNSON, Dartha; age: 4 years and 9 months; parents: Sherman JOHNSON (North Carolina) and Alice BRITT; death cause: "double pneumonia"; informant: mother (Erwin); died: 28 Jun. 1930; buried: Martins Creek; record (1930) # 14941.

FURCHES, Lillian Louise; born: 12 May 1925; parents: Marvin FURCHES and Dolly BROYLES; death cause: "diphtheria"; informant:

father (Erwin); died: 17 Jul. 1930; buried: Liberty Cemetery, Washington County; record (1930) # 17579.

PADGETT, Irene; age: 5 years; parents: Algia PADGETT and Blanche HENSLEY; death cause: "diphtheria"; informant: father (Erwin); died: 20 Jul. 1930; buried: Embreeville; record (1930) # 17580.

HOBBS, Mamie Urekins; born: 16 Feb. 1863 in South Carolina; wife of S.L. HOBBS; parents: J.A.R. UREKINS (Spartainburg, SC.) and Telitha WEBSTER (Union County, SC.); death cause: "typhoid fever"; informant: Mary E. HOBBS (Erwin); died: 20 Jul. 1930; buried: Erwin; record (1930) # 17581.

CLOUSE, Mrs. M.L.; age: 73 years; wife of Robert CLOUSE; parents: William PARKS and Nancy ERWIN; death cause: "heart block"; informant: W.P. CLOUSE (Erwin); died: 22 Jul. 1930; buried: Tinker Cemetery; record (1930) # 17582.

EDWARDS, Aiden Leonard; age: 5 months and 16 days; parents: Arthur EDWARDS and Gertie HUGHES (North Carolina); death cause: "colitis"; informant: father (Chestra, Tennessee); died: 13 Jul. 1930; buried: Chestra; record (1930) # 17583.

HENSLEY, Jessie May; born: 6 Aug. 1928; parents: J.B. HENSLEY and Nellie MILLER (North Carolina); death cause: not stated; informant: mother (Clear Branch); died: 27 Jul. 1930; buried: Foster Cemetery; record (1930) # 17584.

RIDDLE, Lola Wilson; age: 45 years; born: North Carolina; wife of George W. RIDDLE; parents: M.W. WILSON (North Carolina) and Mary RANDOLPH (North Carolina); death cause: "heart lesion"; informant: husband (Erwin); died: 19 May 1930; buried: family cemetery; record (1930) # 17585.

JONES, R.S.; age: 61 years, 3 months and 9 days; born: Virginia; married; parents: Thomas JONES (Virginia) and Annie JOHNSON (Virginia); death cause: "apoplexy"; informant: wife (Erwin); died: 1 Aug. 1930; buried: Evergreen Cemetery; record (1930) # 19894.

HIGGINS, Julia Alberta; age: 65 years; born: Washington County; wife of George HIGGINS; parents: Jim SPEAR and Isabel CARMICHAEL; death cause: "heart disease"; informant: husband (Erwin); died: 9 Aug. 1930; buried: Martins Creek; record (1930) # 19895.

HONEYCUTT, Arthur; age: 55 years; born: North Carolina; husband of Ruth HONEYCUTT; parents: Tom HONEYCUTT (North Carolina) and Melissa WHITSON; death cause: "automobile accident, hemorrhage"; informant: wife (Erwin); died: 3 Aug. 1930; buried: Honeycutt Cemetery; record (1930) # 19876.

BAILEY, Mary Jane; age: 73 years; born: North Carolina; wife of Alfred BAILEY; parents: Albert SLAGLE (North Carolina) and Susie RIDDLE (North Carolina); death cause: "heat"; informant: James BAILEY (Erwin); died: 4 Aug. 1930; buried: Martins Creek; record (1930) # 19897.

COOPER, Thedore; age: 1 year, 10 months and 11 days; parents: M_ (illegible) COOPER and Nellie ALLIS (North Carolina); death cause: "colitis"; informant: father (Erwin); died: 15 Aug. 1930; buried: Martins Creek; record (1930) # 19898.

WILLIS, Lizzie; born: 18 Mar. 1852; married; parents: George TILSON and Nattie BALIS (North Carolina); death cause: not stated; informant: Roda WILLIS (Clear Branch); died: 23 Aug. 1930; buried: Willis Cemetery; record (1930) # 19899.

WHITE, Edward; parents: Hobart WHITE and Pearl BOWMAN; death cause: "premature birth"; informant: Samuel BENNETT (Unicoi); born/died: 7 Sep. 1930; buried: McInturff Cemetery; record # 22935.

WHITE, George; parents: Hobart WHITE and Pearl BOWMAN; death cause: "premature birth"; informant: Samuel BENNETT (Unicoi); born/died: 7 Sep. 1930; buried: McInturff Cemetery; record # 22936.

BOWMAN, Lillian; born: 16 Jun. 1915; parents: Tine BOWMAN and Dora GARLAND (North Carolina); death cause: "pellagra"; informant: father (Unicoi); died: 13 Aug. 1930; buried: Barnett Cemetery; record (1930) # 22937.

GARLAND, Margaret; born: 17 Aug. 1930; parents: Mark MCNABB and Celie GARLAND; death cause: "acute indigestion"; informant: J.W. GARLAND (Erwin); died: 8 Sep. 1930; buried: Jobe Cemetery; record (1930) # 22938.

HUGHES, Margaretta; born: __ Mar. 1864; widow; parents: Robert LOVE (North Carolina) and Jennie TAPP; death cause: "Brights disease and heart lesion"; informant: Mrs. Ervin HENSLEY (Erwin); died: 1 Sep. 1930; buried: Martins Creek; record (1930) # 22939.

METCALF, J.W.; age: 56 years; born: North Carolina; single; parents: Waitsel METCALF (North Carolina) and Margaret METCALF (North Carolina); death cause: "stomach trouble, probably pellagra"; informant: Mandy METCALF (Erwin); died: 4 Sep 1930; buried: Flag Pond; record (1930) # 22940.

MCLEMORE, Julia; born: 18 Oct. 1876; married; parents: Nachin MOSLEY (North Carolina) and Eliza NELSON (North Carolina); death cause: "pellagra"; informant: Henry MCLEMORE (Unicoi); died: 26 Sep. 1930; buried: Mosely Cemetery; record (1930) # 24295.

BIRCHFIELD, Paul Eugene; age: 14 days; parents: Robert BIRCHFIELD and Mande THOMPSON; death cause: "double pneumonia"; died: 26 Oct. 1930; buried: Jobe Cemetery; record # 24296.

SHEHAN, Clifton; born: 31 Aug. 1927; parents: Marcus SHEHAN and Rhetta EDWARDS; death cause: "heart disease"; informant: father (Erwin); died: 27 Oct. 1930; buried: Erwin; record (1930) # 24297.

RENFRO, Zeb; age: 65 years; born: North Carolina; widower; parents: William RENFRO (North Carolina) and Betsy GARLAND (North Carolina); death cause: "pellagra"; informant: Mrs. Bert PETERSON (Erwin); died: 10 Sep. 1930; buried: Green Mountain, North Carolina; record (1930) # 24298.

BLANKENSHIP, Herman; born: 1 May 1902; single; parents: Lewis T. BLANKENSHIP and Laura LAWING; death cause: "pulmonary tuberculosis"; informant: father (Erwin) died: 20 Jul. 1930; buried: Martins Creek; record (1930) # 24299.

SALTS, Margaret; born: 20 May 1930; parents: W.M. SALTS and Jennie KELSEY; death cause: "unknown"; died: 27 Sep. 1930; buried: Anderson Chapel; record (1930) # 26621.

TIPTON, Eliza; age: 81 years, 11 months and 24 days; born: North Carolina; wife of David TIPTON; parents: David TIPTON (North Carolina) and Pattie BRYANT (North Carolina); death cause: "cardio renal"; informant: husband (Unicoi); died: 6 Nov. 1930; buried: Peterson Cemetery; record (1930) # 26622.

WILSON, Bertha Lenore; age: 32 years, 2 months and 3 days; born: North Carolina; wife of John B. WILSON; parents: David BIRCHFIELD (North Carolina) and Ellen BUCHANAN (North

Carolina); death cause: "myocarditis"; informant: husband (Unicoi); died: 9 Nov. 1930; buried; Peterson Cemetery; record (1930) # 26623.

HERRELL, Mrs. Millie A.; born: 30 May 1872 in Georgia; wife of D.C. HERRELL; parents: Presley STANLEY (Georgia) and Elma STONE (Georgia); death cause: "carcinoma in pelvis"; informant: George HERRELL (Unicoi); died: 31 Oct. 1930; record (1930) # 26624.

BROWN, Robert Williams; born: 27 Jul. 1865 in Dublin, Virginia; husband of Roaslie B. BROWN; parents: Alferd P. BROWN (Virginia) and Barbara C. BARNETT (Virginia); death cause: "heart disease"; informant: wife (Erwin); died: 8 Nov. 1930; buried: Alabama (?); record (1930) # 26625.

WHITSON, Tomanda Honeycutt; age: 74 years; born: Yancey County, NC.; widow of I.M. WHITSON; parents: Samuel HONEYCUTT (North Carolina) and Bridget HAMPTON (North Carolina); death cause: "Brights disease"; informant: S.B. HONEYCUTT (Erwin); died: 14 Nov. 1930; buried: Joppa, Tennessee; record (1930) # 26626.

LOVE, Walter W.; age: 56 years; traveling salesman; husband of Bettie LOVE; parents: "unknown"; death cause: "automobile accident, chest crushed"; informant: James R. BUSH (Asheville, NC.); died: 21 Nov. 1930; buried: Wilmington, North Carolina; record (1930) # 26627.

BOOTH, Hiram; age: 90 years, 5 months and 19 days; born: Virginia; husband of Elizabeth REED; parents: John BOOTH and Elizabeth PARKS; death cause: "Brights disease"; informant: W.R. BOOTH (Johnson City); died: 8 Nov. 1930; record (1930) # 26628.

FOSTER, Kyle; born: 19 Jul. 1927; parents: Harrison FOSTER and Della LOWING; death cause: "diphtheria"; informant: father (Erwin); died: 6 Nov. 1930; record (1930) # 26629.

CHANDLER, Richard S.; born: 15 Jul. 1916; parents: Fred A. CHANDLER and Bessie GILBERT; death cause: "flu and pneumonia"; informant: father (Erwin); died: 19 Nov. 1930; buried: Clear Branch; record (1930) # 26630.

CUTSHALL, Infant (s); male; parents: __ (illegible) CUTSHALL and Gertha BISHOP; death cause: not stated, died at birth; died: 20 Dec. 1930; record (1930) # 29594.

BANKS, Ruth; born: 30 Aug. 1913; parents: John F. BANKS and Nannie GRINDSTAFF; death cause: "epileptic fits"; informant: Sam JONES (Unicoi); died: 14 Mar 1930; record (1930) # 29595.

GRINDSTAFF, Sarah Ann; born: 10 Aug. 1853; widow; parents: Seth SNEED (England) and Martha WOODBY; death cause: "apoplexy"; informant: Sherman GRINDSTAFF (Unicoi); died: 26 Sep. 1930; buried: Peterson cemetery; record (1930) # 29596.

WOODBY, Lois; born: 6 Oct. 1929; parents: Barnet WOODBY (North Carolina) and Bessie GADDY (North Carolina); death cause: "lobar pneumonia"; informant: father (Unicoi); died: 7 Dec. 1930; buried: Anderson Chapel; record (1930) # 29597.

WHITE, Opal Carter; male; born: 23 Mar. 1905; U.S. Navy crew member of U.S.S. Arkansas; single; parents: Labe WHITE and Mary E. SMITH; death cause: "homicide, gunshot wound"; informant: father (Unicoi); died: 13 Dec. 1930; buried: Jones Cemetery; record # 29598.

CONLEY, Louisa; age: 66 years, born: Mitchell County, North Carolina; married; parents: Mac GARLAND (Mitchell County) and __ MCKINNEY; death cause: "broncho pneumonia"; informant: Charles W. CONLEY (Unicoi); died: 12 Nov. 1930; buried: Paterson Cemetery; record (1930) # 29599.

PETERSON, Dorothy; age: 3 days; parents: Lum SMITH (North Carolina) and Dorothy PETERSON (North Carolina); death cause: "unknown"; informant: Dave EDWARDS (Erwin); died: 21 Dec. 1930; buried: Erwin; record (1930) # 29510.

INGLE, Fred; born: 20 Nov. 1930; parents: Mark INGLE (Burnsville, NC.) and Mande WILSON (North Carolina); death cause: "acute indigestion"; informant: father (Erwin); died: 26 Dec. 1930; buried: Martins Creek; record (1930) # 29511.

WILSON, Marcus T.; age: 71 years: born: North Carolina; husband of Mary RANDOLPH; preacher; parents: Samuel WILSON (North Carolina) and mother "unknown"; death cause: "aortic stenosis"; informant: E. WILSON (Erwin); died: 27 Dec. 1930; buried: Martins Creek; record (1930) # 29512.

RAMSEY, Mrs. Zeb; age: 50 years; born: North Carolina; wife of Zeb RAMSEY; parents: __ AYERS (North Carolina) and mother "unknown"; death cause: "pulmonary tuberculosis"; informant: Fred D. BOOTHE (Erwin); died: 25 Sep 1930; buried: Erwin; record # 29513.

ERWIN, George R.; born: 26 Apr. 1868; husband of Janie DUNCAN; parents: Samuel ERWIN and mother "unknown"; death cause: "heart disease"; informant: Arthur ERWIN; died: 16 Dec. 1930; buried: Erwin Cemetery; record (1930) # 29514.

CORBY, Kathleen; born: 22 Feb. 1930; parents: Duey CORBY (North Carolina) and Anna May GRIFFITH; death cause: "lobar pneumonia"; informant: Lem GRIFFITH (Erwin); died: 29 Oct. 1930; buried: home cemetery; record (1930) # 29515.

HARRIS, Nathaniel; born: __ Oct. 1929; parents: Luther HARRIS (North Carolina) and Lydia RANDOLPH (North Carolina); death cause: "suspect colic"; informant: Mrs. W.F. BRACKINS (Erwin); died: 28 Jul. 1930; buried: Tinker Cemetery; record (1930) # 29516.

TAPP, Mrs. Ollie; age: 25 years; born: North Carolina; wife of Blaine TAPP; parents: Andy FENDER (North Carolina) and __ LEWIS (North Carolina); death cause: "heart lesion"; informant: Fred D. BOOTHE (Erwin); died: 9 Dec. 1930; buried: Erwin; record (1930) # 29517.

LAUGHREN, William Durent; age: 76 years, 3 months and 23 days; born: North Carolina; husband of Ellen JOYCE; parents: Sam LAUGHREN (England) and __ WEBB (England); death cause: "heart disease"; died: 10 Nov. 1930; buried: Huntdale, North Carolina; record (1930) # 29518.

EDWARDS, Celia M.; born: 28 Aug. 1878; married; parents: Elbert JONES and Margaret EDWARDS; death cause: "heart disease"; informant: Margaret JONES (Clear Branch); died: 13 Dec. 1930; buried: Sams Cemetery; record (1930) # 29519.

HENSLEY, Hester; born: 20 Mar. 1881; single; parents: C.E. HENSLEY and Rebecca J. HENSLEY; death cause: "tuberculosis of bowels"; informant: father (Clear Branch); died: 20 Oct. 1930; buried: Hensley Cemetery; record (1930) # 29520.

BARNETT, Isaac; born: 14 Aug. 1846 in North Carolina; married; parents: Sci BARNETT (North Carolina) and Suanna PERKINS; death cause: "heart leakage"; informant: Smith BARNETT (Unicoi); died: 19 Jan. 1931; buried: Buchanan Cemetery; record (1931) # 2187.

JONES, Jack Roberts; born: 8 Dec. 1930; parents: Paul JONES and Mae BLEVINS; death cause: "croup"; informant: H.C. CARRELL (Unicoi); died: 2 Jan. 1931; buried: Carroll Cemetery; record (1931) # 2188.

WILSON, Thomas; age: 80 years and 7 months; born: North Carolina; widower; widow's name: Nancy Emmaline; parents: Billie WILSON (North Carolina) and Nancy RADFORD (North Carolina); death cause: "pellagra"; informant: W.M. WILSON (Spartainburg, NC.); died: 8 Jan. 1931; buried: Burnsville, North Carolina; record (1931) # 2189.

DUGGER, Infant; female; lived 1 day; parents: M.M. DUGGER and Mary Lou MILLER; death cause: "under nourished infant"; died: 15 Jan. 1931; buried: Erwin; record (1931) # 2190.

BENNETT, Sherman; born: 1860 in North Carolina; marred; parents: Emery BENNETT (North Carolina) and Bashana YOUNG (North Carolina); death cause: "heart lesion"; informant: wife (Erwin); died: 26 Jan. 1931; buried: Fishery Cemetery; record (1931) # 2191.

TAPP, Fannie; born: 7 Nov. 1877; single; parents: Jake TAPP and Axie BALDWIN; death cause: "influenza and pneumonia"; informant: A.M. SMITH; died: 26 Jan. 1931; buried: Erwin; record (1931) # 2192.

COX, Robert; age: 43 years, 2 months and 7 days; born: North Carolina; husband of Lillian May COX; parents: Milburn COX (North Carolina) and Elizabeth FRYE (North Carolina); death cause: "angina pectoris"; informant: wife (Erwin); died: 30 Jan. 1931; buried: Erwin; record (1931) # 2193.

THOMAS, Betty Jane; born: 12 Dec. 1930; parents: Grady F. THOMAS (North Carolina) and Mary __ (illegible) (North Carolina); death cause: illegible; died: 5 Jan. 1931; buried: Martins Creek; record # 2194.

MCCURRY, Monroe; born: 14 Jul. 1876 in North Carolina; widower; parents: D.W. MCCURRY (North Carolina) and Harriett TIPTON (North Carolina); death cause: "vaxination"; informant: Mack MCCURRY; died: 1 Feb. 1931; buried: Swingle Cemetery; record (1931) # 4526.

MCVEY, Anderson; age: 65 years; born: Mitchell County, NC.; husband of Cindy MCVEY; parents: Jordon MCVEY (North Carolina) and Sabra MILLER; death cause: not stated; informant: wife (Unicoi); died: 2 Feb. 1931; buried: Peterson Cemetery; record (1931) # 4527.

RIDDLE, J.M.; age: 78 years, 2 months and 20 days; born: North Carolina; married; parents: John RIDDLE (North Carolina) and Margaret DEATON (North Carolina); death cause: "influenza and pneumonia"; informant: George RIDDLE (Clear Branch); died: 4 Feb. 1931; buried: Unicoi County; record (1931) # 4528.

ADAMS, Charles H.; age: 78 years; born: Boston, Massachusetts; single; merchant; parents: "unknown"; death cause: "cerebral hemorrhage"; informant: J.W. KEGLEY (Erwin); died: 8 Feb. 1931; buried: Martins Creek; record (1931) # 4529.

HARVEY, Nelia Booth; born: 29 May 1887; wife of S.S. HARVEY; parents: Hiram BOOTH and Elizabeth READ (Washington County); death cause: "influenza and pneumonia"; informant: Mrs. Ollie MCCLAIN (Erwin); died: 26 Feb. 1931; buried: Booth Cemetery; record (1931) # 4530.

SHELTON, Infant; female; born: 5 Nov. 1930; parents: Fate SHELTON and Gertha CUTSHALL; death cause: "flu and pneumonia"; died: 6 Feb. 1931; buried: Sweetwater Cemetery; record (1931) # 4531.

HOWELL, Jasper; age: "about 45 years"; married; parents: "unknown"; death cause: "homicide, gunshot wound in head"; informant: Fred D. BOOTHE (Erwin); died: 14 Feb. 1931; buried: home cemetery; record (1931) # 4532.

KIRK, Wolsey; age: 25 years, 9 months and 23 days; married; parents: Bill MCNABB and Nannie KIRK; death cause: "rheumatic __ (illegible)"; informant: wife (Erwin); died: 9 Feb. 1931; buried: family cemetery; record (1931) # 4533.

PARSLEY, Charlotte; born: 30 Mar. 1861 in Kentucky; wife of Mose PARSLEY; parents: Abner JAMES (North Carolina) and Mellie YOUNG; death cause: "dropsy"; informant: George PARSLEY (Erwin); died: 11 Feb. 1931; buried: Martins Creek; record (1931) # 4534.

TIPTON, Nile V.; born: 9 Sep __; age: 5 years and 15 days; parents: Joe H. TIPTON and Polly HIGGINS (North Carolina); death cause: "influenza"; informant: father (Clear Branch); died: 24 Feb. 1931; buried: Taylor Cemetery; record (1931) # 4535.

POPE, William Englise; age: 55 years; husband of Effie TIPTON; parents: Pat POPE (North Carolina) and mother "unknown"; death cause: "post operative emboli"; informant: Ms. Bernie LAWS (Erwin); died: 26 Mar. 1931; buried: Martins Creek; record (1931) # 7114.

BOWMAN, Ed; age: "about 41 years"; husband of Rosa Jones BOWMAN; parents: W. Scott BOWMAN and Alice NICHOLS (Greene County); death cause: "dropsy"; informant: Tine BOWMAN (Unicoi); died: 21 Mar. 1931; buried: Barnett Cemetery; record # 7115.

TINKER, Thelma; born: 5 Feb. 1931; parents: George TINKER (Kentucky) and Leana MULLINS (Kentucky); death cause: "lobar pneumonia"; informant: father; died: 26 Mar. 1931; buried: Dry Creek; record (1931) # 7116.

TUCKER, Columbus; age: 76 years; married; parents: Wilburn TUCKER and Martha LEONARD; death cause: "heart leakage"; informant: George TUCKER (Erwin); died: 28 Feb. 1931; buried: Embreeville; record (1931) # 7117.

BOWMAN, Edward; age: 41 years; married; parents: Scott BOWMAN (Carter County) and Alice NICHOLS (Greene County); death cause: "heart disease"; died: 21 Mar. 1931; buried: Barnett Cemetery; record (1931) # 7118.

MCLAUGHLIN, Susie; born: 18 Jun. 1833; married; parents: David KEENER and Synthia __ (illegible); death cause: "traumatism, fractured leg and hip"; died: 18 Mar. 1931; record (1931) # 7119.

GOUGE, Emery; born: 14 Mar. 1931; parents: Hoy GOUGE (North Carolina) and Delina OVERHULSER; death cause: "bronchitis"; informant: father (Unicoi); died: 25 Mar. 1931; buried: Gouge Cemetery; record (1931) # 7120.

HOWELL, Jasper; born: 18 Apr. 1877 in North Carolina; divorced; parents: Will HOWELL (North Carolina) and Eliza JUSTICE (North Carolina); death cause: "homicide, shot in head"; informant: Ramon HOWELL (Clear Branch); died: 14 Jun. 1931; buried: Howell Cemetery; record (1931) # 7121.

BAILEY, Gladys; born: 18 Jan. 1931; parents: E.D. BAILEY (North Carolina) and Polly DAVIS; death cause: "not stated, found dead in bed"; informant: father (Unicoi); died: 6 Feb. 1931; buried: Woodby Cemetery; record (1931) # 9583.

MCLAUGHLIN, Ed; born: 3 Apr. 1901; husband of Hattie CARVER MCLAUGHLIN; parents: W.B. MCLAUGHLIN and Hiley MILLER

(Carter County); death cause: "tuberculosis"; informant: father (Unicoi); died: 12 Apr. 1931; buried; Peterson Cemetery; record (1931) # 9584.

HAUN, Julia; born: __ May 1860 in Washington County; widow of Peter HAUN; parents: William REED (Virginia) and Marjorie MILLER (Kentucky); death cause: "influenza and pneumonia"; informant: Marjorie AYERS (Erwin); died: 3 Apr. 1931; buried: Haun Cemetery; record (1931) # 9585.

HODGE, Rose Etta; age: 29 years; single; parents: J.M. HODGE and Maggie BENNETT; death cause: "spinal meningitis"; informant: Bob WIDNER (Erwin); died: 3 Apr. 1931; buried: Martins Creek; record (1931) # 9586.

CLARK, Billie; born: 4 Jan. 1930; parents: Dewey CLARK and Sarah RICE; death cause: "double pneumonia"; died: 6 Apr. 1931; record (1931) # 9587.

CAROTHERS, Infant; male; parents: James CAROTHERS and Myrtle HONEYCUTT; death cause: "premature birth"; informant: father (Erwin); born/died: 13 Apr. 1931; buried: Evergreen Cemetery; record (1931) # 9588.

WEBB, Ulysses Jr.; born: 1 Mar. 1927 in Russell County, Virginia; parents: Ulysses WEBB (Mitchell County, NC.) and Louise BYRD (Mitchell County, NC); death cause: "broncho pneumonia"; informant: father (Erwin); died: 13 Apr. 1931; buried: Forbes, North Carolina; record (1931) # 9589.

YOUNG, Margaret Lee; born: 14 Jan. 1916 in North Carolina; parents: W.E. YOUNG (North Carolina) and Bertha HILL (North Carolina); death cause: "flu and pneumonia"; informant: father (Erwin); died: 16 Apr. 1931; buried: Evergreen Cemetery; record (1931) # 9590.

WEBB, Audrey Hilmer; age: 55 years, 10 months and 26 days; born: Virginia; wife of J.R. WEBB; parents: George K. KILMER (Virginia) and Josephine BERTAIN (?) (Virginia); death cause: "carcinoma of uterus"; informant: Mrs. George DISHMAN (Erwin); died : 20 Apr. 1931; buried: Jobe Cemetery; record (1931) # 9591.

CASEY, Zella; born: 30 Apr. 1919; parents: Jim CASEY and Dora BLEVINS; death cause: "pneumonia and meningitis"; died: 2 Apr. 1931; buried: Bumpas Cove Cemetery; record (1931) # 9592.

HUGHES, Infant; male; parents: Dalphus HUGHES (North Carolina) and B_ TAYLOR (North Carolina); death cause: "premature birth"; born/died: 8 Apr. 1931; record (1931) # 9593.

HOLCOMB, Harold Thomas; born: 14 Mar. 1931; parents: Roy HOLCOMB and Amanda FOSTER; death cause: "diphtheria"; informant: J.B. HENSLEY (Clear Branch); died: 24 Apr. 1931; buried: Holcomb Cemetery; record (1931) # 9594.

BUCHANAN, Joseph B.; born: 7 Aug. 1848 in Mitchell County, North Carolina; married; parents: Billie BUCHANAN (Mitchell County) and Polly __; death cause: "gastric hemorrhage"; died: 30 May 1931; buried: Guinn Cemetery; record (1931) # 11886.

MILLER, Jennie; age: 78 years and 25 days; widow of John MILLER Sr.; parents: John TAPP and Polly CLOUSE; death cause: "heart failure"; informant: J.M. BANNER (Erwin); died: 7 May 1931; record (1931) # 11887.

WILSON, Mary Hylmon; born: 26 May 1891 in Yancey County, North Carolina; wife of J.H. WILSON; parents: Thomas HYLMON (Mitchell County, NC.) and Vina BRIGGS (Mitchell County, NC.); death cause: "pregnancy, fibroid, hemorrhage"; informant: husband (Erwin); died: 20 May 1931; buried: McInturff Cemetery; record (1931) # 11888.

CLAUSE, John A.; age: 45 years; single; parents: Robert CLAUSE and Margaret L. PARKS; death cause: "pulmonary tuberculosis"; informant: William CLAUSE; died: 1 May 1931; buried: Tinker Cemetery; record (1931) # 11889.

EDWARDS, Dave; born: 25 Sep 1900; married; parents: John EDWARDS (Virginia) and Hester POOR; death cause: "killed on roadside by automobile"; died: 16 May 1931; buried: Haun Cemetery; record (1931) # 11890.

LOVE, Cena; age: not recorded; born: Missouri; widow of W.C. LOVE; parents: W.C. EMMERT and __ RENSHAW; death cause: "carcinoma of uterus"; informant: R.H. BRADSHAW Jr.; died: 1 May 1931; buried: Martins Creek; record (1931) # 11891.

CROSSWHITE, Nancy; age: 71 years, 8 months and 18 days; wife of I.J. CROSSWHITE; parents: Sam LOVE (North Carolina) and Syndia GREEN; death cause: "Brights disease"; died: 1 May 1931; buried: Martins Creek; record (1931) #11892.

GUINN, David Taylor; born: 17 Apr. 1850; married; parents: Isaac GUINN and Elizabeth LAWING; death cause: "nephritis"; informant: Sarah K. GENTRY (Flag Pond); died: 15 Jun. 1931; buried: Guinn Cemetery; record (1931) # 14099.

RICE, Joe; age: 83 years; born: North Carolina; married; parents: Jess RICE (Madison County, NC.) and Rossie CODY (Madison County, NC.); death cause: "carcinoma of prostate"; informant: R.W. RICE (Faust, North Carolina); died: 22 Jun. 1931; buried: Rice Cemetery, North Carolina; record (1931) # 14100.

BLEVINS, David; age: 81 years, 7 months and 23 days; born: Carter County; husband of Sarah BLEVINS; parents: Charles BLEVINS (Carter County) and Carolina SMITH (Carter County); death cause: "aortic insufficiency"; informant: wife; died: 9 Jun. 1931; buried: Peterson Cemetery; record (1931) # 14101.

BAKER, Edna; born: 9 Jan. 1847; widow of W.H. BAKER; parents: Bert LYLE and mother "unknown"; death cause: "unknown, died suddenly"; informant: Henry LAWS (Unicoi); died: 26 Jan. 1931; buried: Swingle Cemetery; record (1931) # 14102.

WHITSON, John Calvin; age: "about 60 years"; born: Mitchell County, NC.; husband of Julia WHITSON; parents: William WHITSON (North Carolina) and Mary GARTNEY (North Carolina); death cause: "cerebral hemorrhage"; informant: Fayett WHITSON (Erwin); died: 13 Jun. 1931; buried: Relief, North Carolina; record (1931) # 14103.

ELLIOTT, William Herman; born: 8 Jun. 1931; parents: Turner ELLIOTT and Josie RIDDLE (North Carolina); death cause: "acute indigestion"; informant: father (Erwin); died : 15 Jun. 1931; buried: McInturff Cemetery; record (1931) # 14104.

CASEY, Zella; born: 22 Aug. 1914; parents: James CASEY (Washington County) and Dora FOWLER; death cause: "pneumonia and meningitis"; informant: father (Embreeville); died: 2 Apr. 1931; buried: Embreeville; record (1931) # 14105.

HIGGINS, Frank; born: 5 Jan. 1908; husband of Lucy __; parents: Shelby HIGGINS (North Carolina) and __ MCCURRY (North Carolina); death cause: "pulmonary tuberculosis"; informant: Sam LUTTRELL (Erwin); died: 18 Mar 1931; buried: Martins Creek; record (1931) # 14106.

HIGGINS, Samuel; born: 4 Jun. 1931; parents: Ed HIGGINS (North Carolina) and Pearl BAILEY; death cause: "premature birth"; informant: father (Erwin); died: 6 Jun. 1931; record (1931) # 14107.

HARVEY, Maxine; age: 25 years, 3 months and 12 days; single; parents: Tom HARVEY and Maria SLAGLE; death cause: "pulmonary tuberculosis"; informant: Raymond HARVEY (Erwin); died: 6 Jun. 1931; buried: Martins Creek; record (1931) # 14108.

SHELL, Daniel Walter; born: 18 Apr. 1893; husband of Cassie HENSLEY; parents: William SHELL and Angeline JACKSON; death cause: "angina pectoris"; informant: father (Erwin); died: 22 Jun. 1931; buried: Martins Creek; record (1931) # 14109.

BAKER, Martha Charlotte; age: 87 years; widow; parents: Ezekel GRINDSTAFF and Anna DAVIS; death cause: "diabetes, goiter"; informant: Lizzie MCINTURFF (Unicoi); died: 1 Jul. 1931; buried: Cole Cemetery; record (1931) # 16514.

INGRAM, J.C.; born: 21 May 1931; parents: George INGRAM (Mitchell County, NC.) and Flora BANKS (Yancey County, NC.); death cause: illegible; died: 12 Jul. 1931; buried: Swingle Cemetery; record # 16515.

GEER, George; age: "about 75 years"; married; retired soldier; husband of Eletha GEER; parents: Sam GEER and mother "unknown"; death cause: "cerebral hemorrhage"; died: 1 Jul. 1931; record (1931) # 16516.

BENNETT, Roy; born: 17 Jul. 1909; single; parents: W.B. MCNABB and Martha BENNETT; death cause: "cerebral concussion"; died: 1 Jul. 1931; buried: McInturff Cemetery; record (1931) # 16517.

TIBBS, Annie Elizabeth; age: 74 years, 4 months and 15 days; married; parents: father not stated and Mrs. BRACKUS (Campbell County); death cause: "cardio renal"; died: 9 Jul. 1931; buried: Clinton, Tennessee; record (1931) # 16518.

MILLER, Emma; age: 42 years, 6 months and 3 days; born: North Carolina; wife of Bob MILLER; parents: J.W.O. BRYANT (North Carolina) and Omie TIPTON (North Carolina); death cause: "sarcoma"; informant: John MILLER (Unicoi); died: 18 Jul. 1931; buried: Swingle Cemetery; record (1931) # 18862.

HENSLEY, Thomas Carter; born: 16 May 1873; husband of Mary HENSLEY; parents: S.S. HENSLEY (North Carolina) and Cordelia SMITH; death cause: "cardio renal disorder"; informant: Mrs. Mary

HENSLEY (Erwin); died: 4 Aug. 1931; buried: Evergreen Cemetery; record (1931) # 18863.
DAVIS, Raliegh Columbus; age: 11 years, 1 month and 28 days; born: Madison County, North Carolina; parents: H.M. DAVIS (Madison County) and Vertie METCALF; death cause: "typhoid fever"; informant: father (Erwin); died: 6 Aug. 1931; buried: Evergreen Cemetery; record (1931) # 18864.
GEER, George; age: 75 years; married; retired soldier; parents: Sam GEER and mother "unknown"; death cause: "cerebral hemorrhage"; died: 1 Jul. 1931; buried: Johnson City; record (1931) # 18865.
LUTTRELL, Mollie Tittle; age: 56 years; widow of I.W. LUTTRELL; parents: Samuel TITTLE and Annie AMBROSE; death cause: "suicide, hanged herself"; informant: William LUTTRELL (Erwin); died: 29 Jul. 1931; buried: Jobe Cemetery; record (1931) # 18866.
BENNETT, R.E.; age: 3 months and 10 days; parents: Charles BENNETT and Ada BENNETT (North Carolina); death cause: "unknown"; informant: mother (Erwin); died: 15 Aug. 1931; buried: Garland Cemetery; record (1931) # 18867.
ENGLE, Alford; age: 82 years; born: North Carolina; married; parents: Isaac ENGLE (North Carolina) and Polly __ (illegible) (North Carolina); death cause: "carcinoma of signoid"; informant: Blaine ENGLE (Erwin); died: 1 Aug. 1931; buried: Green Cemetery; record (1931) # 18868.
WOODBY, Clyde; born: __ Jan. 1905; married; parents: Charlie WOODBY and Linie SNEED; death cause: "homicide, shot dead"; informant: Dave HYDER (Unicoi); died: 16 Sep. 1931; buried: Hyder Cemetery; record (1931) # 21046.
HASKINS, Martha C.; born: 18 Jul. 1850 in Woodstock, Virginia; parents: father not stated and Martha C. BOWMAN (Woodstock, VA.); death cause: "myocarditis"; died: 9 Sep. 1931; buried: Charleston, TN.; record (1931) # 21047.
HENSLEY, James; born: 1 Sep. 1859 in North Carolina; married; parents: father not stated and Jane SHELTON (North Carolina); death cause: not stated; informant: wife (Flag Pond); died: 18 Sep. 1931; buried: Sweetwater; record (1931) # 23207.

GARLAND, Dorothy; age: 9 years; parents: Bill GARLAND (North Carolina and Dinah MCINTURFF; death cause: illegible; informant: Dewey MCINTURFF (Unicoi); died: 18 Oct. 1931; buried: McInturff Cemetery; record (1931) # 23208.

GOUGE, Frank L.; age: 29 years; born: North Carolina; single; parents: Hoy GOUGE (North Carolina) and Nannie MCKINNEY (North Carolina); death cause: "cardiac __ (illegible)"; informant: father (Unicoi); died: 22 Oct. 1931; buried: Swingle Cem.; record # 23209.

RATLUF, Martia; born: 2 May 1929; parents: William RATLUF and Savanah BENNETT (Mitchell County, NC.); death cause: "gastro enteritis"; died: 28 Oct. 1931; buried: Horton Cem.; record # 23210.

WHITSON, Polly; age: 65 years; born: North Carolina; wife of J.W. WHITSON; parents: Lawson PETERSON (North Carolina) and Camila TIPTON (North Carolina); death cause: illegible; informant: husband (Erwin); died: 6 Sep. 1931; buried: Peterson Cem.; record # 23211.

TINKER, Maggie May; age: 29 years, 6 months and 19 days; single; parents: J.W. TINKER and Annie MCINTURFF; death cause: "badly burned with boiling water, pneumonia"; informant: Cecil TINKER (Erwin); died: 21 Oct. 1931; buried: Jones Cem.; record # 23212.

AYERS, Callie; age: 72 years; widow; parents: Bert BRIGGS and Cindy RAY; death cause: "dysentery"; died: 9 Oct. 1931; record # 23213.

RENFRO, Aliff; born; 25 May 1931; parents: R.M. AYERS (North Carolina) and Francis HONEYCUTT; death cause: "influenza"; informant: Rosco HONEYCUTT (Erwin); died: 25 Oct. 1931; buried; McInturff Cemetery; record (1931) # 23214.

LOWING, Joseph; age: 69 years, 2 months and 16 days; married; parents: Billy LOWING and Lucinda HARRIS; death cause: illegible; died: 10 Oct. 1931; buried: Tullahoma, Tennessee; record (1931) # 23215.

DEFORD, James Brownlow; born: 15 Aug. 1916 in Knoxville; parents: John Loyd DEFORD (Loudon, TN.) and Bessie GILLILAND (Butler, TN.); death cause: "unknown, found dead in bed"; informant: mother; died: 1 Oct. 1931; buried: Knoxville; record (1931) # 23216.

BAILEY, J.C.; age: 2 years, 8 months and 13 days; parents: J.C. BAILEY (North Carolina) and Leona HUGHES (North Carolina); death cause: "diphtheria"; informant: father (Erwin); died: 6 Oct. 1931; buried; Erwin; record (1931) # 23217.

CALLOWAY, Jack; born: 14 Jul. 1927; parents: Gamel CALLOWAY (Greeneville, SC.) and Lizzie SMITH (Yancey County, NC.); death cause: "diphtheria"; informant: father (Erwin); died: 11 Oct. 1931; buried: Jobe Cemetery; record (1931) # 23218.

WHALEY, Virginia Lee; born: 10 Aug. 1931; parents: Charley WHALEY and Rebecca MASHBURN; death cause: not stated; informant: father (Erwin); died: 24 Sep. 1931; buried: Martins Creek; record # 23219.

TIPTON, Alvin; age: 9 months and 25 days; parents: Lattie TIPTON and Henrietta ANDERSON (Virginia); death cause: "rickets and pneumonia"; informant: John D. TIPTON (Erwin); died: 27 Sep. 1931; buried: Jobe Cemetery; record (1931) # 23220.

HATCHER, Catherine C.; born: 2 May 1851 in Sullivan County; wife of J.A. HATCHER; parents: Henry BULLOCK and __ SHIPLEY; death cause: "tuberculosis and myocarditis"; informant: George HATCHER (Erwin); died: 2 Nov. 1931; buried; Martins Creek; record # 25491.

EDNEY, J.B.; age: 4 years, 8 months and 24 days; parents: A.R. EDNEY (North Carolina) and mother "unknown"; death cause: "diphtheria"; informant: J.E. BAILEY (Erwin); died: 3 Nov. 1931; record # 25492.

ROYAL, J.W.; age: 4 months; parents: father not stated and Belle ROYAL; death cause: "bold hives"; informant: Mack DEADERICK (Unaka Springs); died: 30 Oct. 1931; buried; Unaka Springs; record (1931) # 25493.

NELSON, David; age: 80 years; widow; parents: John TIPTON and Millie MILLER; death cause: "old age"; informant: John ANDERSON (Erwin); died: 30 Oct. 1931; buried: Miller Cemetery; record # 25494.

THOMPSON, A.L.; age: 62 years, 7 months and 26 days; born: Ohio; pottery worker; husband of Minnie THOMPSON; parents: W.E. THOMPSON (Pennsylvania) and Kizie REYNOLDS (Washington, D.C.); death cause: "influenza and myocarditis"; informant: W.E. THOMPSON (Erwin); died; 29 Nov. 1931; buried: Martins Creek; record (1931) # 25495.

CLOUSE, Robert; born: 25 Apr. 1856; widower; parents: John CLOUSE and Elizabeth TINKER; death cause: "pellagra"; informant: W.P. CLOUSE (Clear Branch); died: 5 Nov. 1931; buried: Tinker Cemetery; record (1931) # 25496.

GOUGE, Robert C.; age: 73 years; born: North Carolina; married; parents: George W. GOUGE (North Carolina) and Rachel GOUGE (North Carolina); death cause: "dropsy"; informant: Dalton GOUGE (Unicoi); died: 28 Dec. 1931; buried: Gouge Cemetery; record # 28148.

BRUMMETT, Ethel; born: 14 Jan. 1895; married; parents: George WHITE and Ethel WHITE; death cause: "pellagra"; informant: Sam BRUMMETT; died: 5 Nov. 1931; buried: Brummett Cemetery; record (1931) # 28149.

BRUMMETT, Thomas; born: 9 Dec. 1889; married; parents: Tom BRUMMETT and Annie BUCK; death cause: "obstruction of bowels"; informant: wife; died: 6 Oct. 1931; buried: Brummett Cemetery; record (1931) # 28150.

DAVIS, Lydia; born: 22 Nov. 1862 in Mitchell County, NC.; married; parents: John GOUGE and Rachel FORBES (Yancey County, NC.); death cause: illegible; informant: Henry DAVIS (Unicoi); died: 12 Oct. 1931; buried: Bell Cemetery; record (1931) # 28151.

FRYE, Hazel Webb; age: 35 years, 9 months and 2 days; born: West Virginia; wife of Manden (?) FRYE; parents: J.R. WEBB (Virginia) and Audrey KILMER (Virginia); death cause: "carcinoma of bowels"; informant: Mrs. George DISHMAN (Erwin); died: 11 Dec. 1931; buried: Jobe Cemetery; record (1931) # 28152.

TAPP, Nancy; age: "about 69 years"; widow of John AMBROSE and Jake TAPP; parents: __ MILLER and mother "unknown"; death cause: "diarrhea"; informant: Mrs. Andy BUCK; died: 24 Dec. 1931; buried: Jobe Cemetery; record (1931) # 28153.

BANNER, Lillie; age: 50 years; wife of H.B. BANNER; parents: Newt COLLETT and mother "unknown"; death cause: "nephritis"; informant: husband (Erwin); died: 27 Nov. 1931; buried; McInturff Cemetery; record (1931) # 28154.

WHALEY, James; age: 58 years; married; parents: Jake WHALEY (North Carolina) and Della TIPTON (North Carolina); death cause: "cerebral hemorrhage"; informant: wife (Erwin); died: 30 Aug. 1931; buried: Martins Creek; record (1931) # 28155.

LOVE, Ike; age: 84 years; widower; parents: William LOVE (North Carolina) and Nancy HARTSELL; death cause: "hemipliga"; informant:

Robert LOVE (Erwin); died: 30 Oct. 1931; buried: Martins Creek; record (1931) # 28156.

MASHBURN, Mary Louise; born: 15 Jan. 1855 in Madison County, NC.; wife of John MASHBURN; parents: Louise CRANE and mother "unknown"; death cause: "apoplexy"; informant: husband (Erwin); died: 2 Dec. 1931; buried: Flag Pond; record (1931) # 28157.

BANNER, Billie; born: 18 Jan. 1930; parents: Bob BANNER and Julia BAILEY (North Carolina); death cause: "broncho pneumonia"; informant: father (Erwin); died: 5 Dec. 1931; buried: family cemetery; record # 28158.

BAILEY, Mack; age: 59 years; born: Mitchell County, NC.; husband of Nora BAILEY; parents: James BAILEY (North Carolina) and Elizabeth ROBINSON (North Carolina); death cause: "aortic insufficiency"; informant: C.W. BAILEY (Erwin); died: 28 Nov. 1931; buried: Green Mountain, North Carolina; record (1931) # 28159.

ALLEN, Wilma Etta; born: 30 Sep. 1931; parents: Isaac ALLEN and Cassie WHALEY; death cause: "unknown"; informant: father (Erwin); died: 21 Oct. 1931; buried: Martins Creek; record (1931) # 28160.

PRICE, Grady; born: 30 Oct. 1931; parents: Buster PRICE and Amanda JONES; death cause: "jaundice"; informant: father (Clear Branch); died: 5 Dec. 1931; buried: Edwards Cemetery; record (1931) # 28161.

HIGGINS, Pollie; born: 15 Jul. 1904 in North Carolina; married; parents: J.H. HIGGINS (North Carolina) and Manarcha MARR (North Carolina); death cause: "pellagra"; informant: Joe TIPTON (Clear Branch); died: 16 Oct. 1931; buried: Higgins Cemetery; record # 28162.

RIDDLE, James Harmon; born: 13 Feb. 1927; parents: Dewey H. RIDDLE and Lizzie TILSON; death cause: "log rolled on him causing strangulation"; informant: father (Erwin); died: 4 Dec. 1931; buried: Riddle Cemetery; record (1931) # 28163.

CARVER, Monroe; born: 25 Nov. 1852 in Madison County, NC.; married; parents: John CARVER (Madison County, NC.) and Nancy CARVER (Madison County, NC.); death cause: "dropsy"; informant: R.M. SAMS (Flag Pond); died: 17 Dec. 1931; buried: Madison County, North Carolina; record (1931) # 28164.

METCALF, Sarah; born: 13 Sep. 1850; single; parents: Anderson CROWDER (South Carolina) and Peggy BURNS (South Carolina);

death cause: "old age"; informant: Samuel METCALF (Flag Pond); died: 18 Dec. 1931; buried: Sams Creek; record (1931) # 28165.

DOWNS, Harvey D.; age: 33 years; born: Georgia; married; parents: J.M. DOWNS (Georgia) and mother "unknown"; death cause: "run over by automobile driven by unknown party"; informant: father (Gainesville, GA.); died: 14 Nov. 1931; buried: Georgia; record (1931) # 28705.

GOUGE, Robert Castle; born: 16 Oct. 1859 in North Carolina; husband of Ollie GOUGE; parents: John L. GOUGE (North Carolina) and Rachel FORBES (North Carolina); death cause: "myocarditis"; informant: Lloyd GOUGE (Unicoi); died: 28 Dec. 1931; buried: Gouge Cemetery; record (1931) # 28706.

HONEYCUTT, Kizar; age: 77 years; born: North Carolina; wife of Robert V. HONEYCUTT; parents: Wiley TIPTON (North Carolina) and Libbie WHITSON (North Carolina); death cause: "lobar pneumonia"; informant: A.N. HONEYCUTT (Erwin); died: 2 Jan. 1932; buried: Tipton Cemetery; record (1932) # 1784.

WILCOX, Mary Elizabeth Ester; born: 6 Mar. 1857; wife of C.W. WILCOX; parents: Ezekiel Soloman MATHIS and Mary B_ (illegible); death cause: "urethritis, cystitis"; informant: C.N. WILCOX (Unicoi); died: 10 Jan. 1932; buried: Washington College; record (1932) # 1785.

BRUMMETT, Linburg Curtis; age: 7 months and 6 days; parents: Henry A. BRUMMETT (Connecticut) and Martha PHILLIPS (West Virginia); death cause: "whooping cough, pneumonia"; informant: father (Unicoi); died: 13 Jan. 1932; buried: Peoples Cemetery; record (1932) # 1786.

BAILEY, Sam; age: 63 years; born: North Carolina; married; parents: Ancil BAILEY (North Carolina) and Mary BAILEY (North Carolina); death cause: "nephritis, high blood pressure"; informant: Charlie HARRIS (Erwin); died: 5 Jan. 1932; buried: Martins Creek; record (1932) # 1787.

PATE, Ernie Lee; born: 23 Mar. 1928 in Cecil County, Maryland; parents: Neal PATE (Yancey County, NC.) and Martha MILLER; death cause: "pulmonary tuberculosis"; informant: father (Erwin); died: 9 Jan. 1932; buried: Miller Cemetery; record (1932) # 1788.

ALLEN, Jasper; born: 12 Aug. 1869; husband of Edna ALLEN; parents: R.H. ALLEN and Sarah MCINTURFF; death cause: "cardio renal disease"; informant: Isaac ALLEN (Erwin); died: 13 Jan. 1932; buried: Martins Creek; record (1932) # 1789.

HONEYCUTT, Irene Fay; born: 5 May 1928 in Madison County, NC.; parents: George HONEYCUTT and Thelma RAMSEY (Madison County, NC.); death cause: "whooping cough, pneumonia"; died: 10 Feb. 1932; buried: Lone Branch Cemetery; record (1932) # 3851.

WHITSON, Blanch; born: 8 Nov. __; age: 22 years, 2 months and 25 days; single; parents: J.B. WHITSON (North Carolina) and Molly WHITSON (North Carolina); death cause: "influenza and pneumonia"; informant: father (Unicoi); died: 1 Feb. 1932; buried: Swingle Cemetery; record (1932) # 3852.

LENTZ, Rebecca; born: 3 Feb. 1848 in McDowell County, North Carolina; widow; parents: Amos MCCURRY (North Carolina) and mother "unknown"; death cause: "diarrhea"; informant: S.M. HAWKINS (Unicoi); died: 17 Feb. 1932; buried: Latta Cemetery, North Carolina; record (1932) # 3856.

SPARKS, Edna Louise; born: 18 Feb. 1932; parents: G.B. SPARKS (North Carolina) and Belle WEST; death cause: "yellow jaundice"; died: 22 Feb. 1932; buried: Swingle Cemetery; record (1932) # 3857.

TITTLE, Rose Annie; age: 56 years; born: Washington County; widow of George Frank TITTLE; parents: Tom SALTS and Sarah WILLIAMS; death cause: "pulmonary tuberculosis, pneumonia"; informant: John TITTLE (Erwin); died: 8 Feb. 1932; buried: Martins Creek; record (1932) # 3858.

ROBERTS, James C.; age: 84 years; widow; parents: Daniel ROBERTS and mother "unknown"; death cause: "heart disease and influenza"; died: 10 Feb. 1932; buried: Evergreen Cemetery; record (1932) # 3859.

RUNIONS, Mrs. Frank Toney; age: 37 years; pottery employee; wife of Frank Toney RUNION; parents: Henry SPARKS and Layretta HARRIS; death cause: "influenza and pneumonia"; informant: W.C. RUNION (Erwin); died: 26 Feb. 1932; buried: Martins Creek; record (1932) # 3860.

PRICE, Samuel Lee; age: 52 years; husband of Blanch PROFFIT; parents: James L. PRICE and Anne E. FEATHERS; death cause: "acute indigestion"; informant: J.W PRICE; died: 27 Jan. 1932; buried: Evergreen Cemetery; record (1932) # 3861.

PETERSON, Helen Lee; born: 8 Feb. 1932; parents: Geter PETERSON (North Carolina) and Pearl BAILEY (North Carolina); death cause: "unknown"; informant: Doss PETERSON (Erwin); died: 12 Feb. 1932; buried: Washington County; record (1932) # 3862.

EDNEY, Matilda (?); age: 79 years; born: Mitchell County, North Carolina; husband of Bonnie EDNEY; parents: "unknown"; death cause: "cancer"; informant: Lon PRICE (Erwin); died: 29 Feb. 1932; buried: Erwin; record (1932) # 3863.

HASTINGS, Hazel Helen; born: 26 Mar. 1925; parents: E.F. HASTINGS and Sally NORMAN; death cause: "pneumonia"; informant: father (Erwin); died: 17 Feb. 1932; buried: Fishery Cemetery; record (1932) # 3864.

FOSTER H.B.; age: 73 years; married; parents: C_ (illegible) FOSTER and mother "unknown"; death cause: "carcinoma of face"; informant: Mrs. Dora HUGHES (Erwin); died: 3 Feb. 1932; buried: Martins Creek; record (1932) # 3865.

EDWARDS, Wilson; age: 63 years; born: North Carolina; husband of Phinettie HARRIS; parents: Wilson EDWARDS (North Carolina) and mother "unknown"; death cause: "dropsy"; informant: Jason EDWARDS (Erwin); died: 11 Feb. 1932; buried: Martins Creek; record (1932) # 3866.

RAY, Charles Blake; born: 10 Dec. 1930 in Buncombe County, North Carolina; parents: Nelson WRAY and Ida FRANKLIN (North Carolina); death cause: "whooping cough"; informant: Waco WRAY (Flag Pond); died: 7 Feb. 1932; buried: Ray Cemetery; record # 6462.

CARVER, Polly; age: 67 years; widow of Iserell CARVER; parents: Joe SNEED and Susie CAMPBELL; death cause: "heart failure"; informant: J.W. WILLIAMS (Unicoi); died: 22 Mar. 1932; buried: Sneed Cemetery; record (1932) # 6463.

KELLY, Ellen Bruner; age: 81 years, 9 months and 30 days; born: Virginia; widow; parents: John BYERS (Virginia) and Emeline JONES (Virginia); death cause: "influenza and uremia"; informant: J.W. INGRAM (Unicoi); died: 13 Mar. 1932; buried: Kelley Cemetery; record (1932) # 6464.

MORGAN, J.H.; age: 77 years, 2 months and 12 days; widower; parents: Lewis MORGAN (Kentucky) and Laura PATTON; death cause:

"myocarditis"; informant: Frank YOUNG (Erwin); died: 23 Mar. 1932; buried: Garland Cemetery; record (1932) # 6465.

WHITSON, Emma; age: 70 years; divorced; parents: Nathan MOSELY (North Carolina) and Eliza WILSON (North Carolina); death cause: "angina pectoris"; informant: Mrs. Orville HARVEY; died: 24 Mar. 1932; buried: Marbleton; record (1932) # 6466.

BARNETT, Bessie May; age: 19 years; married; parents: Andy MCINTURFF and Malorie MILLER; death cause: "pneumonia"; informant: father (Erwin); died: 2 Mar.. 1932; buried: Erwin; record (1932) # 6467.

O'BRIEN, John; age: 76 years; married; parents: Joe O'BRIEN and Anne BIRCHFIELD; death cause: "cerebral hemorrhage"; informant: Albert O'BRIEN (Erwin); died: 4 Mar. 1932; buried: Martins Creek; record (1932) # 6468.

WHITE, Cora Lee; born: 12 Aug. 1930 in Letcher County, Kentucky; parents: Landon WHITE and Josie HUGHES; death cause: "pneumonia"; died: 9 Mar. 1932; buried: Erwin; record (1932) # 6469.

ERWIN, W.S.; age: 78 years; widower; County Court Clerk; parents: Jesse B. ERWIN and: Elizabeth MCMAHAN (North Carolina); death cause: "influenza and heart disease"; informant: Herman ERWIN (Erwin); died: 25 Mar. 1932; buried: Evergreen Cemetery; record (1932) # 6470.

KEEVER, Rosa Lee; born: 28 Aug. 1915 in Mitchell County, North Carolina; wife of Nelson KEEVER; parents: Don GRIFFITH (North Carolina) and Etta TIPTON (North Carolina); death cause: "suicide, drank carbolic acid"; informant: husband (Erwin); died: 25 Feb. 1932; buried: Martins Creek; record (1932) # 6471.

PRICE, Evelyn; born: 29 Dec. 1931; parents: Furman F. PRICE and Susie ROARKS (Letcher County, Kentucky); death cause: "lobar pneumonia"; died: 9 Mar. 1932; buried: Martins Creek; record (1932) # 6472.

MCINTURFF, W.A.; age: 67 years; widower; parents: J.S. MCINTURFF and Emeline TINKER; death cause: "flu and pneumonia"; informant: Clarence MCINTURFF (Erwin); died: 29 Mar. 1932; buried: Fishery Cemetery; record (1932) # 6473.

SMITH, Nancy; age: 58 years; wife of Henry SMITH; parents: Harrison HUSKINS and Cresa TAPP; death cause: "pernicious anemia"; informant: D.B. BLEVINS (Unicoi); died: 31 Mar 1932; buried: Fishery Cemetery; record (1932) # 6474.

ERWIN, Eugene; age: 10 months; parents: Arthur ERWIN and Bertha MASTERS; death cause: "pneumonia"; informant: father (Erwin); died: 8 Mar. 1932; buried: Erwin Cemetery; record (1932) # 6475.

WELLS, Nancy Matilda; born: __ Oct. 1867 in Yancey County, North Carolina; widow of Billie WELLS; parents: Thomas JENKINS (North Carolina) and __ LUNSFORD (North Carolina); death cause: "flu an pneumonia"; informant: Mrs. B.L. RUNION (Erwin); died: 30 Mar. 1932; buried: Tinker Cemetery; record (1932) # 6476.

TREADWAY, Glenn; born: 12 Sep. 1_31; parents: Leonard TREADWAY and Birdie TIPTON; death cause: "unknown"; informant: Lewis TREADWAY (Flag Pond); died: 28 Mar. 1932; buried: Rice Creek; record (1932) # 6477.

YARBER, John; age: 58 years; married; landscape artist; parents: __ (illegible) YARBER (Washington County) and Nana DANIELS (Greene County); death cause: "cerebritis"; informant: Rachel N. YARBER; died: 10 Apr. 1932; buried: McInturff Cemetery; record (1932) # 8933.

TIPTON, Samuel Y.; age: 76 years; husband of Becky GILLIS; parents: Valentine TIPTON (North Carolina) and mother "unknown"; death cause: "influenza and pneumonia"; informant: Alford LEDFORD; died: 5 Apr. 1932; buried: Washington College, Tennessee; record # 8934.

BOONE, Sullins; age: 77 years; born: North Carolina; husband of Nancy WILLIAMS; parents: Jerry BOONE (North Carolina) and Sallie MCMAHAN (North Carolina); death cause: "cancer of face"; informant: H.K. BOONE (Erwin); died: 24 Apr. 1932; buried: Burnsville, North Carolina; record (1932) # 8935.

CLAYTON, Mary; age: 80 years; born: Hickory, North Carolina; married; parents: Manual AUSTIN (Hickory, NC.) and Marion WILSON (North Carolina); death cause: "carcinoma of stomach"; informant: Mrs. O.P. CLAYTON (Erwin); died: 12 Apr. 1932; buried: Martins Creek; record (1932) # 8936.

LOVE, Marion; age: 8 years and 13 days; parents: Earl LOVE (North Carolina) and Harriett WILSON (North Carolina); death cause: "influenza and meningitis"; informant: father (Erwin); died: 14 Apr. 1932; buried: Evergreen Cemetery; record (1932) # 8937.

TILSON, Hazel Lee; born: 19 Mar. 1931; parents: Ernest TILSON and Gracie GUINN; death cause: "whooping cough"; died: 2 Apr. 1932; buried: Guinn Cemetery; record (1932) # 8938.

BARNETT, D.W.; age: 25 years; born: North Carolina; husband of Mery MOORE; parents: Smith BARNETT (North Carolina) and Mary CARVER (North Carolina); death cause: "syphilis, arsenic poison (being used as treatment)"; informant: father (Unicoi); died: 27 May 1932; buried: Peterson Cemetery; record (1932) # 11306.

ADAMS, Callie Prater; age: 40 years, 6 months and 28 days; wife of C.W. ADAMS; parents: J.R. PRATER and mother not stated; death cause: "pulmonary tuberculosis"; informant: husband; died: 4 May 1932; buried: Jobe Cemetery; record (1932) # 11307.

CORNETT, Mollie Eugenia; age: 48 years, 9 months and 10 days; born: Virginia; wife of T.C. CORNETT; parents: Ellis L. LEMDY (?) (Virginia) and Alice HALE (Virginia); death cause: "carcinoma of breast"; informant: husband (Erwin); died: 7 May 1932; buried: Virginia; record (1932) # 11308.

MCLAUGHLIN, Robbie; age: 17 years, 9 months and 25 days; parents: Alf MCLAUGHLIN and Alice SMITH; death cause: "pulmonary tuberculosis"; informant: Dave SMITH (Unicoi); died: 25 Apr. 1932; buried: Jones Cemetery; record (1932) # 11309.

ROGERS, Roy V.; born: 26 Sep. 1928; parents: Ed ROGERS and Millie BIRCHFIELD; death cause: "colitis"; informant: father (Unicoi); died: 23 Jun. 1932; buried: Birchfield Cemetery; record (1932) # 13470.

MILLER, Mildred Pauline; age: 10 months and 6 days; parents: Fred MILLER and Etta JONES; death cause: "colitis"; informant: father (Unicoi); died: 2 Jun. 1932; buried: Swingle Cemetery; record # 13471.

PARKER, Madge; age: 16 years, 5 months and 13 days; parents: Handy PARKER (North Carolina) and Hessie SMITH; death cause: "myocarditis"; informant: Wesley PARKER (Erwin); died: 11 Jun. 1932; buried: Martins Creek; record (1932) # 13472.

HUGHES, Andrew; age: 10 years, 6 months and 16 days; parents: Nelson HUGHES and Dora FOSTER; death cause: "fell under moving train, legs amputated, loss of blood and shock"; informant: mother (Erwin); died: 20 Jun. 1932; buried: Martins Creek; record (1932) # 13473.

CODY, Noah; age: 70 years, 3 months and 22 days; husband of Hale HARRIS; parents: "unknown"; death cause: "diabetes"; informant: George CODY (West Virginia); died: 16 Jun. 1932; record # 13474.

RUNION, W.S.; age: 75 years, 2 months and 18 days; married; parents: S.V. RUNION and Pollie TINKER; death cause: "Brights disease"; informant: Phil MASTERS (Flag Pond); died: 23 May 1932; buried: Shallow Ford Cemetery; record (1932) # 13475.

EDWARDS, Martha Ann; born: 17 Apr. 1846 in Carter County; widow of Wilson EDWARDS; parents: Tom GOUGE and __ BLEVINS; death cause: "nephritis and uremia"; informant: D.S. EDWARDS (Erwin); died: 5 Jun. 1932; record (1932) # 13476.

BAILEY, Mamie; age: 23 years, 11 months and 8 days; single; parents: John BAILEY and mother "unknown"; death cause: "pulmonary tuberculosis"; informant: Bessie WILLIAMS (Erwin); died: 11 Jun. 1932; buried: Martins Creek; record (1932) # 13427.

TIPTON, Joe Ben; born: 1 May 1876 in North Carolina; married; parents: Charles TIPTON (North Carolina) and Axie COOPER (North Carolina); death cause: "cancer of stomach"; died: 22 Jun. 1932; buried: Mount Pleasant Cemetery; record (1932) # 13478.

DAVIS, Clay; born: 22 Jun. 1932; parents: Will DAVIS and Nola CLARK; death cause: "bold hives"; died: 12 Jul. 1932; buried: Berry Cemetery; record (1932) # 15911.

BYRD, Blake; born: 20 Jul. 1853 in North Carolina; husband of Caroline BYRD; parents: "unknown"; death cause: "abscess of liver, possibly cancerous"; informant: D.J. GARLAND (Unicoi); died: 12 May 1932; record (1932) # 15912.

HORNE, Drew Franklin; age: 46 years; single; parents: Frank HORNE (South Carolina) and mother "unknown"; death cause: "alcoholism"; informant: Lee HORNE (Greeneville); died: 11 Jul. 1932; buried: Martins Creek; record (1932) # 15913.

HIGGINS, Susan; age: 73 years; born: Ball Mountain, North Carolina; married; parents: Andy CRAIN and Polly WITSON (North Carolina);

death cause: "Brights disease"; informant: M.B. HIGGINS (Erwin); died: 15 Jul. 1932; buried: Martins Creek; record (1932) # 15914.

HUGHES, Charles; born: __ Feb. 1848 in North Carolina; husband of Amie HUGHES; parents: "unknown"; death cause: "kidney disease"; informant: L.B. BAXTER (Erwin); died: 13 Jul. 1932; buried: Fishery Cemetery; record (1932) # 15915.

MCINTOSH, Dewey; age: 28 years; born: Yancey County, NC.; divorced; parents: Willie MCINTOSH (North Carolina) and mother "unknown"; death cause: "killed outright in automobile wreck"; died: 19 Jun. 1932; buried: Burnsville, North Carolina; record (1932) # 15916.

MCINTOSH, Claude; age: 23 years; born: North Carolina; husband of Emma MCINTOSH; parents: "unknown"; death cause: "killed instantly in automobile wreck"; buried: Burnsville, NC.; record (1932) # 15917.

ROWLAND, Ivan; age: 29 years; single; parents: McClellan ROWLAND (North Carolina) and mother not stated; death cause: "killed instantly in automobile wreck"; died: 19 Jun. 1932; buried; Burnsville, North Carolina; record (1932) # 15918.

SELLERS, Hollie; born: 6 Nov. 1861; widow parents: Mart BRITT and Lucinda MCINTURFF; death cause: "bronchial pneumonia"; informant: Mrs. W.H. ROWE (Unicoi); died: 1 Aug. 1932; buried: Anderson Chapel; record (1932) # 18092.

COLEMAN, Monte; born: 18 Feb. 1918; parents: J.C. COLEMAN (Carter County) and Betty TOLLEY (Carter County); death cause: "tuberculosis and pneumonia"; informant: father; died: 30 Aug. 1932; buried: Tolley Cemetery; record (1932) # 18093.

PUGH, Betty Lou; age: 22 months; parents: C.R. PUGH and Verna VEST; death cause: "homicide, gunshot wound through heart"; informant: C.G. DAVIS (Erwin); died: 16 Aug. 1932; buried: Evergreen Cemetery; record (1932) # 18094.

PUGH, Verna Louise; age: 32 years; wife of C.R. PUGH; parents: J.W. VEST and Katie WILSON; death cause: "suicide, gunshot wound through heart"; informant: C.G. DAVIS (Erwin); died: 16 Aug. 1932; buried: Evergreen Cemetery; record (1932) # 18094.

RENFRO, Julia; age: 61 years; born: North Carolina; single; parents: Jim MCKINNEY (North Carolina) and Nancy MCKINNEY (North Carolina); death cause: "killed instantly in automobile wreck";

informant: Paul HARVEY (Erwin); died: 17 Jul. 1932; buried: McInturff Cemetery; record (1932) # 18096.

COOPER, Sarah; age: 2 years and 3 months; parents: Nelce COOPER (North Carolina) and Belle COOPER (North Carolina); death cause: "flux"; died: 1 Aug. 1932; buried: Unaka Springs; record # 18097.

HARVEY, Howard; age: 6 years, 7 months and 21 days; parents: Alfred HARVEY and Essie PARKER; death cause: "myocarditis"; informant: Wes PARKER (Erwin); died: 19 Aug. 1932; buried: Martins Creek; record (1932) # 18098.

BRYANT, Thomas Wesley; age: 18 years and 19 days; born: Yancey County, NC.; single; parents: C.W. BRYANT (Yancey County, NC.) and Cordelia MCCURRY (Yancey County, NC.); death cause: "cleaning gun, gunshot wound in chest"; informant: father (Erwin); died: 26 May 1932; buried: Martins Creek; record (1932) # 18099.

SLAGLE, Kelsie; born: 18 Feb. 1911 in Madison County, NC.; married; parents: David SLAGLE (North Carolina) and Harriett SHOOK (North Carolina); death cause: "accidental by circular saw mill"; died: 22 Aug. 1932; record (1932) # 18100.

FERGUSON, Elmer; age: 29 years; husband of Coxie (?) CASEY; parents: Jake FERGUSON and Fannie MOORE; death cause: illegible; died: 5 Sep. 1932; buried: Grays Station; record (1932) # 20008.

CATON, Robert Napoleon; born: 9 Dec. 1870 in Cocke County, Tennessee; husband of Ethel West CATON; parents: Stephen CATON and Matilda HARRISON (South Carolina); death cause: "heart failure"; informant: W.G. CATON (Kingsport); died: 11 Sep. 1932; buried: Evergreen Cemetery; record (1932) # 20009.

MASON, Jeanette; age: 45 years; born: Maryland; wife of Homer L. MASON; parents: William D. LANE (Maryland) and Anna E. PAYNE (Maryland); death cause: "basal cell __ (illegible) of face"; informant: husband (Erwin); died: 22 Aug. 1932; buried: Evergreen Cemetery; record (1932) # 20010.

LEDFORD, Amos Franklin; age: 28 years; husband of Edith LEDFORD; parents: Jason Woodward LEDFORD (Yancey County, NC.) and Mary LOVETTE; death cause: "drowned swimming"; informant: J.W. LEDFORD (Clear Branch); died: 4 Sep. 1932; buried; Edwards Cemetery; record (1932) # 20011.

251

GOUGE, Gene Ray; born: 17 Oct. 1931; parents: Charles H. GOUGE (Mitchell County, NC.) and Hassie PHILLIPS (Mitchell County, NC.); death cause: "meningitis"; informant: father (Erwin); died: 27 Aug. 1932; buried: Erwin; record (1932) # 20012.

BEAN, Myrtle; age: 22 years; born: North Carolina; parents: John BEAN and Hattie RENFRO (North Carolina); death cause: "pulmonary tuberculosis"; informant: Bill BEAN (Erwin); died: 5 Sep. 1932; buried: Martins Creek; record (1932) # 20013.

TITTLE, Leitha; age: 16 years; parents: Ike TITTLE and Blanch LLOYD; death cause: "pernicious anemia"; informant: father (Erwin); died: 8 Aug. 1932; buried: Martins Creek; record (1932) # 20014.

LONG, Pansy May; born: 16 Jun. 1932; parents: father not stated and Myrtle LONG; death cause: "unknown"; informant: John LONG (Erwin); died: 7 Jul. 1932; buried: Martins Creek; record # 20015.

LEWIS, J.W.; born: 14 Aug. 1930; parents: Willard LEWIS (Yancey County, NC.) and Lee TIPTON (Mitchell County, NC.); death cause: "croup and diphtheria"; informant: Samuel LEWIS (Clear Branch); died: 3 Sep. 1932; buried: Lewis Cemetery; record (1932) # 20016.

COATS, John; born: 18 May 1893; single; parents: J.C. COATS (Madison County, NC.) and Eliza ALEN (Yancey County, NC.); death cause: "tuberculosis"; informant: James COATS (Flag Pond); died: 25 Aug. 1932; buried: Flag Pond; record (1932) # 20017.

STREET, Billie Gene; born: 30 Sep. 1932; parents: W.G. STREET and Destie BENNETT (North Carolina); death cause: "marasmus"; died: 11 Oct. 1932; buried: Unicoi; record (1932) # 22200.

INGRAM, Pollie; born: 19 Oct. 1932; parents: Harley INGRAM and Virgie MCINTURFF; death cause: "unknown, premature"; died: 21 Oct. 1932; buried: Swingle Cemetery; record (1932) # 22201.

WILLIAMS, Infant; female; parents: Robert L. WILLIAMS (Giles County, Virginia) and Ann Myrtle ATKINS (Giles County, Virginia); death cause: "weak heart"; informant: father (Erwin); born/died: 10 Oct. 1932; buried: Jobe Cemetery; record (1932) # 22202.

DAVIS, Robert B.; born: 16 Jun. 1876 in Greene County; single; parents: William D. DAVIS and Sophia SEATON; death cause: "possible liver malignancy"; informant: Fred DAVIS (Erwin); died: 17 Oct. 1932; buried: Evergreen Cemetery; record (1932) # 22203.

DAVIS, Martha; age: 62 years; born: Kentucky; widow; parents: B.A. RICE and Tebatha MILLER; death cause: "carcinoma of pelvic bones"; informant: Mrs. R.H. RENFRO (Erwin); died: 4 Oct. 1932; buried: Barboursville, Kentucky; record (1932) # 22204.

HARRIS, William Chester; age: 27 years; husband of Elen HUGHES; parents: Harrison HARRIS and Maggie NELSON; death cause: "fell under train amputating leg, blood loss"; informant: Sam HARRIS; died: 25 Oct. 1932; buried: Fishery Cemetery; record (1932) # 22205.

GILLIS, Ann Marie; age: 2 years and 8 months; parents: Frank GILLIS and Lula SPARKS; death cause: "diphtheria"; informant: father (Erwin); died: 28 Oct. 1932; buried: Martins Creek; record # 22206.

MATHIS, Estelle; born: 22 Sep. 1931; parents: Ben MATHIS (Washington County) and Teressa MCCANN; death cause: "pneumonia"; informant: father (Erwin); died: 4 Oct. 1932; buried: Martins Creek; record (1932) # 22207.

TINKER, Wayne Franklin; born: 8 Aug. 1932; parents: George TINKER and Leona M_ (Illegible); death cause: "broncho pneumonia"; died: 31 Oct. 1932; buried; Jones Cemetery; record (1932) # 22208.

LOVETTE, Bertha; age: 24 years; born: North Carolina; wife of Stuart LOVETTE; parents: Dave GARLAND (North Carolina) and Sarah TIPTON (North Carolina); death cause: "pneumonia"; informant: John LOVETTE (Erwin); died: 14 Oct. 1932; buried: Erwin Cemetery; record (1932) # 22209.

BURK, John; age: 83 years; born: England; widower; parents: "unknown"; death cause: not stated; informant: Smith B. ARNETT; died: 15 Nov. 1932; buried: Peterson Cemetery; record (1932) # 24545.

BRITT, Landon; born: 2 Jan. 1905; married; parents: David BRITT and Rebecca PRICE (Carter County); death cause: "homicide, gunshot wound through chest"; informant: J.M. PETERSON (Unicoi); died: 17 Jan. 1932; record (1932) # 24546.

HORTON, Benjamin Taylor; born: 14 Mar. 1849 in North Carolina; married; parents: Zeph HORTON (North Carolina) and Charlotte MAST (North Carolina); death cause: "gastritis, nephritis"; informant: J.W. HORTON (Hampton, Tennessee); died: 28 Nov. 1932; buried: Horton Hill; record (1932) # 24547.

253

GARLAND, Donald Lynn Jr.; born: __ Aug. 1932; parents: Donald Lynn GARLAND (North Carolina) and Clara DEATON (North Carolina); death cause: "influenza and pneumonia"; died: 3 Nov. 1932; record (1932) # 24548.

MILLER, Alice Jane; born: 17 Jun. 1872 in Mitchell County, NC.; wife of William E. MILLER; parents: Joe B. YOUNG and Susan J. PATTON; death cause: "cerebral hemorrhage"; informant: W.E. MILLER (Erwin); died: 11 Nov. 1932; buried: Unicoi; record # 24549.

POORE, Homer; born: 29 Jun. 1930; parents: Joe POORE and Bessie HUGHES (North Carolina); death cause: "pneumonia"; informant: father (Erwin); died: 15 Nov. 1932; buried; Martins Creek; record (1932) # 24550.

EDWARDS, Joseph; born: 4 May 1854 in Madison County, NC.; married; parents: Floyd J. EDWARDS (North Carolina) and Nancy LEDFORD; death cause: "dropsy"; informant: John EDWARDS (Flag Pond); died: 10 Nov. 1932; buried: North Carolina; record # 24551.

PETERSON, Jerry; born: 26 Dec. 1932; parents: Robert PETERSON (North Carolina) and Goldie HOLBROOK (Coeburn, Virginia); death cause: not stated; informant: mother (Unicoi); buried: Cole Cemetery; record (1932) # 27948.

PETERSON, Mary; born: 26 Dec. 1932; parents: Robert PETERSON (North Carolina) and Goldie HOLBROOK (Coeburn, Virginia); death cause: not stated; informant: mother (Unicoi); buried: Cole Cemetery; record (1932) # 27949.

HOPSON, Joshah; age: 68 years; born: North Carolina; widower; parents: John HOPSON (North Carolina) and Lila STANLEY (North Carolina); death cause: "Brights disease"; informant: Jason HOPSON; died: 17 Aug. 1932; buried: Peterson Cemetery; record (1932) # 17950.

JOHNSON, Harold Vivian; age: 24 years and 11 months; husband of Virginia BICK; parents: W.J. JOHNSON and Cora FRANCIS; death cause: "nephritis"; died: 14 Dec. 1932; buried: Evergreen Cemetery; record (1932) # 27951.

WHITE, Paul; born: 1 May 1932; parents: Landon WHITE and Josie HUGHES; death cause: "pneumonia"; informant: father (Erwin); died: 16 Dec. 1932; buried: McInturff Cemetery; record (1932) # 27952.

GENTRY, Laura A.; born: __ Oct. 1877; wife of J.N. GENTRY; parents: David GUINN and Melinda RUNION; death cause: "cerebral hemorrhage"; informant: Fred GENTRY (Erwin); died: 17 Dec. 1932; buried: Rocky Fork Cemetery; record (1932) # 27953.

LEWIS, Joseph W.; born: __ May 1886 in Saint Louis, Missouri; husband of Arlie Jane LEWIS; parents: "unknown"; death cause: "embolism and gangrene"; informant: wife; died: 27 Dec. 1932; buried: family cemetery; record (1932) # 27954.

SIMMONS, Samuel Moses; born: 15 Sep. 1865 in Franklin County, Virginia; husband of Emma Melvina SIMMONS; parents: George SIMMONS (Virginia) and mother's name illegible; death cause: "myocardial failure"; informant: wife (Erwin); died: 29 Dec. 1932; buried: Roanoke, Virginia; record (1932) # 27955.

BARNETT, Jeter; age: 42 years; born: Mitchell County, NC.; divorced from Vina HYDER; parents: William BARNETT (North Carolina) and Elizabeth GREENE (North Carolina); death cause: "homicide, gunshot skull"; informant: father (Unicoi); died: 30 Nov. 1932; buried: Buchanan Cemetery; record (1932) # 27956.

HONEYCUTT, Peter; age: 92 years, 5 months and 24 days; born: Yancey County, NC.; widower of Annie TIPTON; parents: Zeke HONEYCUTT (Yancey County) and Marie BAILEY (Yancey County); death cause: "flu"; died: 21 Nov. 1932; buried: McInturff Cemetery; record # 27957.

HATCHER, Fred D.; born: 15 Dec. 1932; parents: Henry HATCHER and Sarah __ (illegible); death cause: "pneumonia"; informant: father (Erwin); died: 28 Dec. 1932; buried: Martins Creek; record # 27958.

MCKINNEY, Infant; male; parents: Rex MCKINNEY and Jane LOWING; death cause: "premature"; informant: mother (Erwin); born/died: 5 Dec. 1932; buried: Erwin; record (1932) # 27959.

HENSLEY, Margaret; age: 51; born: North Carolina; divorced from __ (illegible) PHILLIPS; parents: __ (illegible) SHELTON (North Carolina) and __ (illegible) HENSLEY; death cause: "pneumonia"; died: 9 Dec. 1932; record (1932) # 27960.

PRICE, David Junior; age: 17 months and 15 days; parents: Lee PRICE and mother's name illegible; death cause: "convulsions"; died: 13 Dec. 1932; buried: Martins Creek; record (1932) # 27961.

BRADSHAW, Rebecca Garland; age: 69 years and 2 months; born: North Carolina; wife of R.H. BRADSHAW; parents: William GARLAND (North Carolina) and Elizabeth BUCHANAN (North Carolina); death cause: "flu and pneumonia"; informant: husband; died: 21 Dec. 1932; buried: Evergreen Cemetery; record (1932) # 27962.

OLLIS, Franklin D.; born: 24 Oct. 1932; parents: Clarence OLLIS (North Carolina) and Cora HIGGINS; death cause: "pneumonia"; informant: father (Erwin); died: 24 Dec. 1932; record (1932) # 27963.

BAILEY, Curtis Theodore; age: 1 month; parents: Bernie BAILEY (North Carolina) and Pearl TIPTON (North Carolina); death cause: "influenza and pneumonia"; informant: father (Erwin); died: 21 Nov. 1932; buried: Martins Creek; record (1932) # 27964.

BANKS, Infant; female; born: 22 Apr. 1932; parents: Cecil BANKS (North Carolina) and Elsie CALLAHAN; death cause: "unknown"; informant: father (Erwin); died: 11 May 1932; buried: Erwin; record (1932) # 27965.

TILSON, Ethel Bailey; born: 12 Jun. 1880; widow of Robert T. TILSON; postmistress; parents: William W. BAILEY and Lucy SAMS; death cause: "pellagra"; informant: Roy TILSON (Flag Pond); died: 3 Dec. 1932; record (1932) # 27966.

HARKINS, Infant; male; parents: Bill HARKINS (North Carolina) and Sue ANDERSON (North Carolina); death cause: "unknown"; informant: Jim TREADWAY (Flag Pond); born/died: 25 Dec. 1932; buried: Sams Creek; record (1932) # 27967.

WOODBY, Cass; born: ___ Apr. 1914; parents: Joe Bill WOODBY (North Carolina) and Jane HEAD; death cause: "pulmonary tuberculosis"; informant: Barnett WOODBY; died: 6 Jan. 1933; buried: Peterson Cemetery; record (1933) # 2221.

BENNETT, William Lester; born: 19 Apr. 1930; parents: Gather BENNETT and Ann WOODBY (North Carolina); death cause: "pneumonia"; informant: father (Unicoi); died: 21 Jan. 1933; buried: Garland Cemetery; record (1933) # 2222.

LUNDY, Clyde Vance; born: 19 Sep. 1886 in Wytheville, Virginia; husband of Elizabeth Leola LUNDY; parents: Wiley M. LUNDY (Independence, Virginia.) and Rachel E. LEMON (Rockingham County, North Carolina); death cause: "fell, fractured skull"; informant: T.H.

LUNDY (Unicoi); died: 5 Jan. 1933; buried: Evergreen Cemetery; record (1933) # 2223.

ARROWOOD, Infant; male; parents: John W. ARROWOOD (Yancey County, NC.) and Pearl COLE; death cause: "premature"; informant: father (Erwin); born/died: 11 Jan. 1933; buried: Washington County; record (1933) # 2224.

HARRIS, Herman; age: 19 months; parents: C_ (illegible) HARRIS (deceased) and Lula THOMAS (North Carolina); death cause: illegible; informant: Charles HARRIS (Erwin); died: 6 Jan. 1933; buried: Erwin Cemetery; record (1933) # 2225.

GUINN, Loura Ellen; born: 12 Mar. 1853 in Virginia; widow; parents: Jackson EDWARDS and Matilda LETERAL; death cause: "paralysis"; died: 13 Jan. 1933; buried: Clear Branch; record (1933) # 2226.

HARRIS, Jason Carson; born: 15 May 1857; married; parents: Jason HARRIS and Nancy HENSLEY; death cause: "paralysis"; died: 14 Jan. 1933; buried: Guinn Cemetery; record (1933) # 2227.

BRITT, Axie; age: 56 years; born: North Carolina; wife of E.C. BRITT; parents: __ (illegible) MCCURRY (North Carolina) and mother "unknown"; death cause: "bronchial pneumonia"; died: 7 Feb. 1933; buried: Cole Cemetery; record (1933) # 4422.

STREET, William M.; parents: W.M. STREET and Gertie MCINTURFF; death cause: "premature"; born/died: 25 Feb. 1933; buried: Swingle Cemetery; record (1933) # 4423.

BIRDWELL, William; born: 11 Sep. 1903; husband of Virginia Fry BIRDWELL; parents: Jim BIRDWELL and Hester HIGGINS; death cause: "acute alcoholism"; informant: wife (Erwin); died: 5 Feb. 1933; record (1933) # 4424.

STONE, William A.; born: 5 Jun. 1924 in Indiana; parents: George STONE (Macon County, TN.) and Sallie __ (illegible) (Hickory Valley, TN.); death cause: "meningitis"; informant: father (Erwin); died: 11 Feb. 1933; buried: Gallatin, Tennessee; record (1933) # 4425.

SMITH, Karl Augustus; born: 15 Nov. 1850 in Virginia; husband of Nannie B. SMITH; parents: John SMITH (Virginia) and mother "unknown"; death cause: "myocarditis and uremia"; informant: Mrs. O.C. HALE (Erwin); died: 16 Feb. 1933; buried: Evergreen Cemetery; record (1933) # 4426.

CALLAHAN, Margaret; born: 5 Sep. 1842 in Madison County, NC.; widow of Levi CALLAHAN; parents: Braxton KEITH (Virginia) and Katherine ROBERTS (Madison County, NC.); death cause: "pneumonia"; died: 25 Feb. 1933; buried: Bethesda; record # 4427.

TOSTER, Dolly; born: 1 Feb. 1933; parents: Lonnie SMITH (Georgia) and Stella TOSTER; death cause: "pneumonia"; informant: J.H. TOSTER (Erwin); died: 9 Feb. 1933; buried: Fishery Cemetery; record (1933) # 4428.

TITTLE, John Henry; age: 65 years; husband of Jude Smith TITTLE; parents: "unknown"; death cause: "myocarditis"; informant: Charles E. TITTLE (Erwin); died: 16 Jan. 1933; buried: Jobe Cemetery; record (1933) # 4429.

MCINTURFF, William H.; born: 4 Jul. 1868; widower of Lizzie Nelson MCINTURFF; parents: Samuel MCINTURFF and Sarah JONES; death cause: "Brights disease"; informant: William CONSTABLE (Unicoi); died: 6 Feb. 1933; buried: Jones Cemetery; record # 4430.

HARRIS, J.D.; born: 29 Feb. 1932; parents: Dave HARRIS and Isabell HUGHES (North Carolina); death cause: "pneumonia"; died: 17 Feb. 1933; buried: Fishery Cemetery; record (1933) # 4431.

HASTINGS, Henry Franklin; age: 87 years, 7 months and 3 days; born: North Carolina; widower; parents: Clint HASTINGS and Elizabeth HORN; death cause: "heart failure"; died: 20 Feb. 1933; buried: Stockton Cemetery; record (1933) # 4432.

WILLIAMS, Louisa; age: 82 years; born: North Carolina; wife of H.C. WILLIAMS; parents: Sam ESTEP (North Carolina) and mother "unknown"; death cause: "influenza"; informant: Pitman WILLIAMS (Erwin); died: 27 Feb. 1933; buried: Martins Creek; record # 4433.

DAVIS, Margaret L.; born: __ May 1905; wife of Floyd DAVIS; parents: __ (illegible) RUNION and Martha __ (illegible); death cause: "homicide, neck broken, blow to head"; informant: William RUNION (Clear Branch); died: 4 Feb. 1933; record (1933) # 4434.

BLANKENSHIP, Martha M.; born: 19 Nov. 1869 in North Carolina; widow; parents: John T. BLANKENSHIP (North Carolina) and Emerline CULBERTSON (North Carolina); death cause: "heart disease"; informant: J.C. FOSTER (Clear Branch; died: 13 Jan. 1933; buried: Higgins Cemetery; record (1933) # 4435.

PATE, Lizza; age: 60 years; married; parents: Dr. Daniel SHULTS and Pollie SULTIN; death cause: "pellagra"; informant: Frank DAVIS; died: 5 Mar. 1933; buried: Cove Cemetery; record (1933) # 6831.

PETERSON, Noah; age: 53 years; born: Mitchell County, NC.; married; parents: Peters PETERSON (North Carolina) and Sarah Ann TIPTON (North Carolina); death cause: "alcoholism"; informant: Jim PETERSON (Unicoi); died: 29 Mar. 1933; buried: Peterson Cemetery; record (1933) # 6832.

RIDDLE, Thelma; born: __ Dec. 1929 in North Carolina; parents: Charlie RIDDLE (North Carolina) and Mary RAY (North Carolina); death cause: "croup"; informant: J.B. KING; died: 30 Mar 1933; record (1933) # 6833.

CLOUSE, Phyllis Loeta; born: 3 Oct. 1921; parents: Ernest CLOUSE and Johanna ADKINS (Yancey County, NC.); death cause: "ruptured appendix, meningitis"; informant: E.E. CLOUSE (Erwin); died: 2 Mar. 1933; buried: Evergreen Cemetery; record (1933) # 6834.

TINKER, Vadie; age: 27 years; born: Washington County; wife of F.B. TINKER; parents: David BRACKINS and Dora FOSTER; death cause: "unknown"; informant: husband (Erwin); died: 2 Mar. 1933; buried: Mount Wesley Cemetery; record (1933) # 6835.

PHILLIPS, Ruby; age: 4 months; parents: G.S. PHILLIPS (North Carolina) and Carrie GARLAND; death cause: "pneumonia"; informant: father (Erwin); died: 6 Mar. 1933; buried: Tinker Cemetery; record (1933) # 6836.

MCNEELY, Rebecca; age: 43 years; wife of H.T. MCNEELY; parents: James BULLIONS and Sally SMITH; death cause: "blood poison"; informant: husband (Erwin); died: 16 Mar. 1933; buried: Martins Creek; record (1933) # 6837.

HENSLEY, Harm Cornelious; born: 4 Jul. 1862; married; parents: Barnett HENSLEY and Lucinda HENSLEY; death cause: "atrophy of liver"; informant: S.V. HENSLEY (Clear Branch); died: 12 Mar. 1933; buried: Hensley Cemetery; record (1933) # 6838.

PEEK, Hadley Smith; born: __ Apr. 1883 in North Carolina; husband of Sarah PEEK; parents: Dr. W.A. PEEK (North Carolina) and Margaret CONLEY; death cause: "tuberculosis"; informant: wife (Clear Branch); died: 17 Mar. 1933; buried: Tumblin Hill; record (1933) # 6839.

SNEED, Orbie; born: 11 Dec. 1930; parents: A.T. SNEED and Bettie PATE; death cause: "congenital __ (illegible); died: 20 Apr. 1933; buried: Sneed Cemetery; record (1933) # 8858.

FOSTER, Ernest; born: 1 Mar. 1910 in Greene County; single; parents: Marion FOSTER and Nora ADAMS; death cause: "concussion of brain"; informant: father (Limestone); died: 2 Apr. 1933; buried: Limestone; record (1933) # 8859.

GILLIS, Rulbe May; age: 10 years; parents: Frank GILLIS and Lula SPARKS; death cause: "tonsillitis and tooth infection"; informant: father (Erwin); died: 5 Feb. 1933; buried: Erwin; record (1933) # 8860.

MATHIS; Harben Edward; born: 29 Jul. 1932; parents: Edward MATHIS (Washington County) and Alice GREEN; death cause: "pneumonia"; informant: mother (Erwin); died: 17 Apr. 1933; buried: Jobe Cemetery; record (1933) # 8861.

DAY, Pauline; age: 17 years; wife of Woodward DAY; parents: Andy MCINTURFF and Lovie MILLER; death cause: "tuberculosis"; informant: Cloyd AMBROSE (Erwin); died: 12 Apr. 1933; buried: Rock Creek; record (1933) # 8862.

STARNES, Millie; age: 71 years; born: Washington County; widow of Ben STARNES; parents: Billie HENSLEY (Washington County) and Katie SALTS (Washington County) death cause: "myocarditis"; informant: Loff STARNES (Embreeville); died: 10 Mar. 1933; buried: Embreeville; record (1933) # 8863.

BANNER, Will; born: 12 Mar. 1861; husband of Lucretia BANNER; parents: John BANNER and Ruth __; death cause: "unknown, probably malignancy"; informant: J. William BANNER (Erwin); died: 24 Apr. 1933; buried: Martins Creek; record (1933) # 8864.

HUGHES, Bayler; born: 11 Jun. 1869 in North Carolina; widower; parents: __ (illegible) HUGHES (North Carolina) and Betsy WILSON (North Carolina); death cause: "tuberculosis"; informant: Dolphus HUGHES (Erwin); died: 25 Apr. 1933; buried: Ramseytown, North Carolina; record (1933) # 8865.

AMBROSE, Bernie Sherwood; born: 2 Jun. 1931; parents: James AMBROSE and Bessie COFFEE; death cause: "bronchial pneumonia"; informant: Wade AMBROSE (Erwin); died: 24 May 1933; buried: Fishery Cemetery; record (1933) # 10913.

FOSTER, Bud; age: 18 years; parents: Will FOSTER and Maggie GOFORTH; death cause: "dropsy"; informant: W.S. HAMPTON (Erwin); died: 8 May 1933; buried: Unaka Springs; record # 10914.

SHEEHAN, Loretta; born: 12 May 1900; wife of M.S. SHEEHAN; parents: Allen EDWARDS and Sarah WATTS; death cause: "carcinoma of cervix"; informant: husband (Erwin); died: 23 May 1933; buried: Bailey Cemetery; record (1933) # 10915.

BAILEY, Tobie Lee; born: 23 Aug. 1932; parents: O.L. BAILEY and Ethel NORRIS; death cause: "dysentery"; informant: father (Erwin); died: 23 May 1933; buried: Martins Creek; record (1933) # 10916.

LEWIS, Maney; age: 86 years; widower; county home inmate; parents: "unknown"; death cause: "nephritis"; died: 23 Jun. 1933; record (1933) # 13164.

HUSKINS, Charles; age: 66 years; widower; county home inmate; parents: "unknown"; death cause: "carcinoma of stomach"; died: 23 Jun. 1933; buried: Fishery Cemetery; record (1933) # 13165.

HARRELL, Georgia Ray; born: 23 Aug. 1932; parents: D.A. HARRELL and Evaline RIDDLE; death cause: "colitis and pneumonia"; informant: father (Unicoi); died: 22 Jun. 1933; buried: Harrell Cemetery; record (1933) # 13166.

EARLY, Richard Carroll; born: 24 Jun. 1933; parents: Guy EARLY (Marion County, NC.) and Mary Elizabeth ALFORD (Eatonton, Georgia); death cause: "premature"; informant: father (Erwin); died: 25 Jun. 1933; buried: Evergreen Cemetery; record (1933) # 13167.

EARLY, Robert Eugene; born: 24 Jun. 1933; parents: Guy EARLY (Marion County, NC.) and Mary Elizabeth ALFORD (Eatonton, Georgia); death cause: "premature"; informant: father (Erwin); died: 25 Jun. 1933; buried: Evergreen Cemetery; record (1933) # 13168.

NELSON, William Howard; born: 22 Feb. 1925; parents: Martin NELSON and Nettie LUTTRELL; death cause: illegible; informant: father (Erwin); died: 10 Jun. 1933; buried: Jones Cemetery; record (1933) # 13169.

LEWIS, Davie; age: 28 years; born: North Carolina; single; parents: David LEWIS (North Carolina) and Deborah JUSTICE; death cause: "epileptic fits"; informant: Willard LEWIS (Clear Branch); died: 23 Jun. 1933; buried: Lewis Cemetery; record (1933) # 13170.

MCLAUGHLIN, Hattie; age: illegible; born: North Carolina; widow of Ed MCLAUGHLIN; parents: William CARVER (North Carolina) and __ BUTLER; death cause: "pregnancy, streptococoma"; died: 8 Jul. 1933; informant: Sam BRUMMETT (Unicoi); record (1933) # 15518.

RENFRO, Nan Philly; age: 56 years; born: North Carolina; widow; parents: William PHILLIPS and Margaret MCCRACKEN; death cause: "heart failure"; died: 8 Jul. 1933; buried: Jobe Cemetery; record (1933) # 15519.

EVANS, George C.; born: 12 Dec. 1858 in Ohio; marital status: illegible; tailor; parents: "unknown"; death cause: "Brights disease"; informant: Louis BLANKENSHIP (Erwin); died: 26 Jul. 1933; buried: Sams Cemetery; record (1933) # 15520.

CAMPBELL, Elaine; parents: Emmett CAMPBELL and Julia RENFRO (North Carolina); death cause: "premature birth"; born/died: 2 Jun. 1933; buried: Martins Creek; record (1933) # 15521.

SHELL, Clint; age: 3 years; parents: Walter SHELL and Cassie HENSLEY; death cause: "pneumonia"; informant: Martin BANNER (Erwin); died: 1 Jul. 1933; buried: Martins Creek; record # 15522.

HASKETT, Amanda; born: 9 Dec. 1853 in Macon County, NC.; widow; parents: "unknown"; death cause: "breast cancer"; informant: N.C. DUNCAN (Erwin); died: 8 Jul. 1933; buried: Walnut Cemetery, North Carolina; record (1933) # 15523.

SHOOK, John Abraham; born: 22 Aug. 1874 in Madison County, NC.; husband of Cora SHOOK; parents: Augustus SHOOK (Berk County, NC.) and Oma RICE (Madison County, NC.); death cause: "heart lesion"; died: 30 Jul. 1933; buried: Martins Creek; record # 15524.

TILSON, Infant; male; born: 25 Jun. 1933; parents: E.E. TILSON and Gracie TILSON; death cause: not stated; died: 26 Jun. 1933; buried: Guinn Cemetery; record (1933) # 15525.

TOLLEY, Lou Wilcox; age: 77 years, 5 months and 8 days; born: Virginia; parents: John H. WILCOX (Virginia) and Mary MCMILLEN (Virginia); death cause: "senility"; died: 4 Aug. 1933; buried: Monte Vista Cemetery; record (1933) # 17704.

PADGETT, Glenna; born: 6 Oct. 1926; parents: Mack PADGETT and Francis BELL; death cause: "myocarditis"; informant: father (Erwin); died: 24 Aug. 1933; buried: Liberty Cemetery; record (1933) # 17705.

MILLER, John Clifton; born: 30 Sep. 1863 in Rogersville, Tennessee; husband of Maude Holder MILLER; parents: Clifton MILLER and Maude HOLDER; death cause: "pylites"; informant: Fred MILLER (Erwin); died: 29 Aug. 1933; buried: Evergreen Cemetery; record (1933) # 17706.

MOORE, James P.; born: 18 Oct. 1868 in North Carolina; husband of Mary MOORE; parents: Simon MOORE (North Carolina) and Manima MILTON (North Carolina); death cause: "apoplexy"; died: 4 Sep. 1933; record (1933) # 19862.

HOPSON, Ike; age: 32 years; born: North Carolina; single; parents: Joe HOPSON (North Carolina) and Sadie STREET (North Carolina); death cause: "pulmonary tuberculosis"; informant: Smith BARNETT; died: 10 Sep. 1933; buried: Stanley Cemetery; record (1933) # 19863.

MCLAIN, Janette Franklin; born: 23 Dec. 1898 in Altamont, North Carolina; widow of Wade H. MCLAIN; parents: A.D. FRANKLIN (Altamont, NC.) and Emma WELD (Fulox, Maryland); death cause: "phlebitis"; informant: Everett FRANKLIN (Erwin); died: 28 Sep 1933; buried: Jobe Cemetery; record (1933) # 19864.

VANCE, Infant; male; born: 1 Aug. 1933; parents: William VANCE and Evelyn MASTERS; death cause: "premature"; informant: father (Erwin); died: 2 Aug. 1933; buried: Erwin; record (1933) # 19965.

ANDERS, Isaac Grady; age: 18 years and 6 months; parents: Haben ANDERS and Lenia FLETCHER; death cause: "pneumonia"; informant: father (Erwin); died: 21 Aug. 1933; buried: Martins Creek; record (1933) # 19866.

MOORE, Charley; born: 31 Mar. 1927 in Carter County; parents: Lomy HOWELL (Carter County) and Martha MOORE (Carter County); death cause: "infected throat"; died: 2 Oct. 1933; buried: Peterson Cemetery; record (1933) # 22252.

CLARK, Luther; age: 40 years; born: Carter County; married; parents: John CLARK (North Carolina) and Marra MILLER (North Carolina); death cause: not stated; informant: John WOODBY (Unicoi); died: 13 Oct. 1933; buried: Woodby Cemetery; record (1933) # 22253.

GARDNER, Donna; born: 6 Mar. 1913; single; parents: D. GARDNER (North Carolina) and Sallie FORBES (Mitchell County, NC.); died: 12 Oct. 1933; record (1933) # 22254.

TIPTON, Bobbie Lee; parents: Bascom TIPTON (Yancey County, NC.) and Lila PIERSON; death cause: "premature"; informant: father (Erwin); born/died: 21 Oct. 1933; buried: Martins Creek; record (1933) # 22255.

BRUCE, Martha Francis; born: 2 Dec. 1856; widow; parents: Barnett SMITH and Mary E. WITT; death cause: "nephritis"; informant: Golda SAMS (Flag Pond); died: 20 Jul. 1933; buried: Witt Cemetery; record (1933) # 22256.

LLOYD, Joe; age: 41 years, 7 months and 22 days; parents: David LLOYD (North Carolina) and Willie EFFLER; death cause: "injury"; informant: John H. TINKER (Erwin); died: 9 Nov. 1933; buried: Lloyd Cemetery; record (1933) # 24698.

MCBRIDE, Frank M.; age: 55 years; born: County Mays, Ireland; parents: "unknown"; death cause: "cerebral hemorrhage"; died: 16 Nov. 1933; buried: Garland Cemetery; record (1933) # 24699.

BIRCHFIELD, Millie Buchanan; born: 2 May 1896 in Mitchell County, NC.; widow of David Wallace BIRCHFIELD; parents: W.W. BUCHANAN (Mitchell County, NC.) and Sarah WILSON (Mitchell County, NC.); death cause: "breast cancer"; informant: father (Unicoi); died: 17 Nov. 1933; buried: Buchanan Cemetery; record # 24700.

HEAD, William Allen; born: 20 Nov. 1933; parents: J.S. HEAD and Maryann SNEED; death cause: "heart congestion"; died: 23 Nov. 1933; record (1933) # 24701.

HAMMITT, Margaret; born: 14 Mar. 1843; widow of John HAMMITT; parents: Jimmie ROBINSON and Fannie __; death cause: "pneumonia"; died: 13 Nov. 1933; buried: Anderson Cemetery; record (1933) # 24702.

HOPSON, Bessie; born: __ Mar. 1902; married; parents: W.B. MCLAUGHLIN and Pollie MILER; death cause: "myocarditis"; informant: Jason HOPSON; died: 5 Nov. 1933; buried: Peterson Cemetery; record (1933) # 24703.

BUCHANAN, Hazel Gertrude; age: 24 years, 3 months and 26 days; divorced from Carl ROBBINS; parents: Robert BUCHANAN (North Carolina) and Luly BUCHANAN (North Carolina); death cause: "pulmonary tuberculosis"; informant: father (Unicoi); died: 28 Nov. 1933; buried: Swingle Cemetery; record (1933) # 24704.

BUCKLES, C.E.; age: 60 years; husband of Lula BUCKLES; parents: John BUCKLES and Martha VANCE; death cause: "prostate cancer"; informant: Harold BUCKLES (Erwin); died: 26 Nov. 1933; buried: Holston Valley; record (1933) # 24705.

PETERSON, Moses Cling; age: 72 years, 5 months and 19 days; born: North Carolina; husband of Hattie PETERSON; parents: Reuben PETERSON (North Carolina) and Polly HAMPTON (North Carolina); death cause: "carcinoma of liver"; informant: Mrs. W.S. RENFRO; died: 23 Nov. 1933; buried: Martins Creek; record (1933) # 24706.

LEDFORD, Amos; age: 87 years; born: Yancey County, NC.; husband of Sarah Jane LEDFORD; parents: Alfred LEDFORD (North Carolina) and Artie Christine SAMS; death cause: "nephritis"; informant: Alfred LEDFORD (Erwin); died: 9 Nov. 1933; buried: family cemetery; record (1933) # 24707.

TUCKER, Wesley S.; born: 8 Jan. 1854 in Yancey County, North Carolina; husband of Polly Ann TUCKER; former County Court Clerk; parents: Joseph Sevier TUCKER (North Carolina) and Allie MCGINSEY (North Carolina); death cause: "nephritis"; informant: wife (Erwin); died: 3 Dec. 1933; record (1933) # 27503.

LAWS, Billie; born: __ Sep. 1869 in Greene County; widower; parents: Tom MCINTURFF and Elizabeth LAWS (Greene County); death cause: "carcinoma of face"; informant: Mrs. W.R. CAPPS (Erwin); died: 4 Dec. 1933; buried: Jobe Cemetery; record (1933) # 27504.

PARDUE, Urel Warren; born: 17 Dec. 1903 in Washington County; husband of Beatrice Johnson PARDUE; parents: Soloman B. PARDUE (Elkin, North Carolina) and Flora HILBERT (Washington County); death cause: "strept infection"; informant: Clyde PARDUE (Erwin); died: 6 Dec. 1933; buried: Boone Cemetery; record (1933) # 27505.

MURRY, Stalla Pearl; born: 29 Mar. 1879; widow of Jesse B. MURRY; parents: W.S. ERWIN and Julia RAY; death cause: "influenza and pneumonia; died: 13 Dec. 1933; buried: Jobe Cemetery; record # 27506.

HENSLEY, Edna; born: 11 Jul. 1913; single; parents: J.H. HENSLEY (North Carolina) and Lizzie BUTNER (North Carolina); death cause: "burned"; informant: mother (Erwin); died: 13 Dec. 1933; buried: Jobe Cemetery; record (1933) # 27507.

SHELTON, Hobart; age: 10 years; parents: Andrew SHELTON and Sarah RAY; death cause: "run over, killed by automobile"; informant: R.E. MOORE (Erwin); died: 22 Dec. 1933; buried: Erwin; record (1933) # 27508.

AMBROSE, Alto; born: 25 May 1907; wife of Cloyd AMBROSE; parents: Andy MCINTURFF and Lena MILLER; death cause: "pneumonia"; informant: Wade AMBROSE (Erwin); died: 24 Dec. 1933; buried: Fishery Cemetery; record (1933) # 27509.

ROBERTS, Kate; age: "about 72 years"; born: Buncombe County, North Carolina; wife of J.H. ROBERTS; parents: Ramsey BUCHBOARD and mother "unknown"; death cause: "myocarditis"; informant: husband (Erwin); died: 30 Dec. 1933; buried: Higgins Creek; record # 27510.

TIPTON, Zeek; born: 1 Jan. 1908 in North Carolina; husband of Hazel Hughes TIPTON; parents: Charles TIPTON (North Carolina) and __ (illegible) HONEYCUTT (North Carolina); death cause: "tuberculosis"; died: 31 Dec. 1933; record (1933) # 27511.

FANNING, Bill; born: 21 Jul. 1867; married; parents: unknown (adopted); death cause: "aortic stenosis"; died: 28 Oct. 1933; buried: Pleasant Hill; record (1933) # 27512.

COLLINS, Dora; age: 26 years; born: North Carolina; single; parents: "unknown"; death cause: "suicide, drank Lysol"; died: 5 Nov. 1933; record (1933) # 27513.

JEWELL, Infant; female; born: 13 Apr. 1933; parents: father not stated and Mae JEWELL; death cause: "unknown"; informant: Mrs. Lola JEWELL (Erwin); died: 15 Apr. 1933; buried: Martins Creek Cemetery; record (1933) # 27514.

HAYNES, Mary Ida; born: 23 May 1930; parents: Arthur HAYNES (North Carolina) and Janie CHANDLER; death cause: "croup"; died: 14 Dec. 1933; buried: Mount Pleasant; record (1933) # 27515.

HARRIS, Rachel; born: 27 Oct. 1838; widow; parents: Jacob CLOUSE and Sally TILSON; death cause: "paralysis"; informant: J.T. HARRIS (Flag Pond); died: 17 Dec. 1933; buried: Higgins Chapel; record (1933) # 27516.

SHOOK, Jim; born: 17 Dec. 1918; parents: Noel SHOOK (North Carolina) and Sis BLANKENSHIP; death cause: "homicide, gunshot wound by Clemon SANOS; died: 17 Dec. 1933; buried: Blankenship Cemetery; record (1933) # 27517.

GRINDSTAFF, Sallie; born: 11 May 1885 in Carter County; married; parents: Jake MORTON (Carter County) and Delia MCKINNEY (Carter County); death cause: "pellagra"; informant: Alfred GRINDSTAFF (Unicoi); died; 28 Jan. 1934; buried: Lyons Cemetery; record (1934) # 1945.

HOLLAND, Gene; born: 9 Apr. 1929 in Virginia; parents: Thomas HOLLAND (North Carolina) and Lesta COX (Georgia); death cause: "shot in eye with air rifle, eye removed, infection, meningitis"; died: 12 Jan. 1934; buried: Evergreen Cemetery; record (1934) # 1946.

RIDDLE, Mrs. M.J.; age: 75 years; widow; parents: __ CRAWFORD and mother "unknown"; death cause: "influenza, pneumonia"; informant: Sam ROGERS (Erwin); died: 31 Jan. 1934; buried: Embreeville; record (1934) # 1947.

BRITT, Elbert; age: 74 years; widower; parents: Jim BRITT and Nancy UNDERWOOD; death cause: "carcinoma of __ (illegible); informant: W.H. BRITT (Unicoi); died: 5 Jan. 1934; buried: Siota; record # 1369.

GREENE, Glenn; age: 7 years; born: Kentucky; parents: Oliver GREENE (North Carolina) and Janie MULLINS (Kentucky); death cause: "pneumonia"; informant: mother (Erwin); died: 2 Feb. 1934; buried: Jobe Cemetery; record (1934) # 4370.

HAROLD, Marie; age: 3 years; parents: McKinley HAROLD (North Carolina) and Rebecca MILLER (North Carolina); death cause: "pneumonia"; informant: father (Erwin); died: 2 Feb. 1934; buried: Garland Cemetery; record (1934) # 4371.

TAPP, Harvey Clinton Jr.; born: 12 Dec. 1933; parents: Harvey TAPP and Lela HOBBS; death cause: "whooping cough"; died: 17 Feb. 1934; buried: Evergreen Cemetery; record (1934) # 4372.

RUNION, Mary Hensley; born: 7 Jun. 1893; married; parents: James M. HENSLEY (North Carolina) and Sarah HIGGINS; death cause: "breast cancer"; informant: Troy BOONE (Flag Pond); died: 7 Feb. 1934; buried: Higgins Cemetery; record (1934) # 4373.

BONDURANT, S.W.; age: 64 years; born: Virginia; husband of C.V. PORTER; parents: Merrinetine BONDERANT (Virginia) and mother "unknown"; death cause: "influenza"; informant: B.D. BONDURANT (Erwin); died: 4 Mar. 1934; buried: Evergreen Cemetery; record # 7178.

PRITCHARD, Laurence Payne; age: 29 years; born: Knoxville; divorced from Mildred BANNISTER; parents: L.N. PRITCHARD and mother not stated; death cause: "syphilis"; informant: Mrs. Charles PEAKE (Ramseytown, NC.); died: 6 Mar. 1934; buried: Evergreen Cemetery; record (1934) # 7179.

STALLARD, Marcus Dalton Jr.; born: 23 Dec. 1931 in Spruce Pine, North Carolina; parents: Dalton STALLARD (Corburn, NC.) and Janice STUBBLEFIELD (Jefferson City, TN.); death cause: "pneumonia"; informant: father (Erwin); died: 8 Mar. 1934; buried: Evergreen Cemetery; record (1934) # 7180.

NELSON, Ella Belle; born: 22 Mar. 1880; wife of William F. NELSON; parents: Hiram BOOTHE (Washington County) and Elizabeth REED (Washington County); death cause: "struck on public highway by __ (illegible), fractured skull"; informant: Earl NELSON (Erwin); died: 13 Mar. 1934; buried: family cemetery; record (1934) # 7181.

BOGART, Florence Crouch; born: 4 Oct. 1854 in Washington County; wife of Jeremiah BOGART; parents: James CROUCH and Mary Caroline HUNTER; death cause: "heart lesion"; informant: J.E. BOGART (Erwin); died: 16 Mar. 1934; buried: Evergreen Cemetery; record (1934) # 7182.

RIDDLE, Indiana; age: 19 years; born: Cane River, North Carolina; parents: C.C. RIDDLE (North Carolina) and Ella RIDDLE (North Carolina); death cause: "automobile accident"; informant: Glen ANGEL (North Carolina); died: 21 Mar. 1934; buried: North Carolina; record (1934) # 7183.

COX, Milburn; born: __ Apr. 1909 in North Carolina; husband of Emma Gillis COX; parents: Jason COX (Mitchell County, NC.) and Elizabeth GILLIS; death cause: "automobile accident, crushed left thigh"; informant: Bob WILLIS (Erwin); died: 22 Mar. 1934; buried: Clouse Cemetery; record (1934) # 7184.

SIBERT, Maude; born: 21 Aug. 1887 in Ohio; wife of H. SIBERT; parents: "unknown"; death cause: "cancer"; informant: husband (Erwin); died: 22 Feb. 1934; buried: Evergreen Cemetery; record (1934) # 7185.

DUNCAN, W.A.; born: 29 Dec. 1859; husband of Nancy DUNCAN; parents: Frank DUNCAN and Katherine DUGGER; death cause: "Brights"; informant: William DUNCAN (Erwin); died: 22 Jan. 1934; buried: Erwin; record (1934) # 7186.

LOVE, Dillard; born: 3 Sep. 1877; husband of Gertrude LOVE; parents: Bob LOVE and mother "unknown"; death cause: "coronary occlusion"; informant: Joe LOVE (Erwin); died: 5 Mar. 1934; buried: Martins Creek; record (1934) # 7187.

MILLER, Paul Thomas; born: 14 Jan. 1931; parents: Oscar Haun MILLER and Maude DAY; death cause: "influenza, meningitis, pneumonia"; informant: father (Erwin); died: 11 Mar. 1934; buried: McInturff Cemetery; record (1934) # 7188.

HAMPTON, A.S.; born: 3 Mar. 1867; husband of Sarah HAMPTON; parents: Daniel HAMPTON and Katherine __ (illegible); death cause: "influenza, pneumonia"; informant: John HAMPTON (Erwin); died: 29 Mar. 1934; buried: Martins Creek; record (1934) # 7189.

ROGERS, Velma; lived 3 days; parents: George ROGERS and Helen DOOR (Virginia); death cause: "undernourished"; informant: father (Erwin); died: 31 Mar. 1934; buried: Embreeville; record # 7190.

PETERSON, Addie; age: 56 years; born: North Carolina; widow; parents: Andy JONES (Virginia) and Sarah WHITSON (North Carolina); death cause: "heart problem"; informant: Jess PETERSON (Erwin); died: 20 Mar. 1934; buried: Martins Creek; record # 7191.

CLOUSE, Dortha; born: 5 Mar. 1934; parents: Charles FARMER (North Carolina) and Della CLOUSE (North Carolina); death cause: "mother had measles"; informant: Addie TILSON (Flag Pond); died: 6 Mar. 1934; buried: Farmer Cemetery; record (1934) # 7192.

BRIGGS, Elisha Elbert; born: 8 Feb. 1933; parents: Homer BRIGGS and Flora PROFFITT; death cause: "measles"; informant: Tom BRIGGS (Flag Pond); died: 8 Mar. 1934; buried: Blankenship Cemetery; record (1934) # 7193.

TAYLOR, Mary Catherine; born: 18 Apr. 1854; widow; parents: Silas STEPP (Virginia) and __ BENNETT; death cause: "myocarditis"; informant: J.H. TAYLOR (Johnson City); died: 25 Apr. 1934; buried: Anderson Chapel; record (1934) # 9640.

MCLEMORE, Walter L.; born: 19 Aug. 1904 in North Carolina; single; parents: C.L. MCLEMORE (North Carolina) and Mollie ANDERSON; death cause: "killed by truck"; informant: father (Johnson City); died: 5 Apr. 1934; buried: Simmons Cemetery; record (1934) # 9641.

MATHES, William; age: 74 years; born: North Carolina; widower; parents: "unknown"; death cause: "hemiplegia"; informant: George MATHES (Erwin); died: 2 Apr. 1934; buried: Liberty Cemetery; record (1934) # 9642.

ERWIN, Horace; black; age: 15 years; parents: not stated; death cause: "run over by train"; died: 5 Apr. 1934; record (1934) # 9643.

VANDERGRIFF, Sarah Alice; age: 72 years, 2 months and 9 days; born: Bousach, Virginia; widow of E.J. VANDERGRIFF; parents: William Joseph SAWERS (Virginia) and Elizabeth CLARK (Virginia); death cause: "apoplexy"; informant: Maude VANDERGRIFF (Erwin); died: 16 Apr. 1934; buried: Salem, Virginia; record (1934) # 9644.

TIPTON, Lela; age: 3 years; parents: Zeke TIPTON (Mitchell County, NC.) and Hassie HUGHES (Mitchell County, NC.); death cause: "pneumonia"; informant: Britt TIPTON (Erwin); died: 25 Apr. 1934; buried: Martins Creek; record (1934) # 9645.

BRIGGS, Douglas; born: 20 Feb. 1934; parents: Seth BRIGGS and Virgie MCINTOSH; death cause: "measles"; informant: Tom BRIGGS (Flag Pond); died: 20 Apr. 1934; buried: Rice Creek; record # 9646.

BRIGGS, Virgie; age: 33 years; wife of Seth BRIGGS; parents: Dolph MCINTOSH and Mordecie RICE; death cause: "measles, pneumonia"; informant: Winfred FENDER (Flag Pond); died: 14 Apr. 1934; buried: Rice Creek; record (1934) # 9647.

SAMS, Norma Jean; born: 26 Apr. 1934; parents: Raymond WIGARD (Virginia) and Rebecca SAMS; death cause: "premature"; informant: Martha HOWELL (Erwin); died: 26 Apr. 1934; buried: Higgins Creek; record (1934) # 12022.

JONES, Woodward Swain; born: 14 Nov. 1926; parents: Earl Franklin JONES and Lula Annie HIGGINS; death cause: "meningitis"; informant: father (Erwin); died: 10 May 1934; buried: Fishery Cemetery; record (1934) # 12023.

SIZEMORE, Danny; born: 17 Mar. 1934; parents: Jay N. SIZEMORE and C_ (illegible) HARRISON; death cause: "spina bifida"; informant:

father (Erwin); died: 11 May 1934; buried: Martins Creek Cemetery; record (1934) # 12024.
HOWELL, Lorena Mae; born: 1 Jun. 1893; wife of Frank HOWELL; parents: William H. MCINTURFF and Lizzie NELSON; death cause: "pulmonary __ (illegible); died: 28 May 1934; buried: Swingle Cemetery; record (1934) # 12025.
MORELLE, Maggie; age: 66 years; widow of John MORELLE; parents: "unknown"; death cause: "cardiac exhaustion"; informant: J.S. HEADRICK (Erwin); died: 18 Jun. 1934; buried; St. Clair, Tennessee: record (1934) # 14427.
MCLAUGHLIN, C.E.; born: 2 Jul. 1866; married; parents: Nelson MCLAUGHLIN and mother "unknown"; death cause: "coronary occlusion"; informant: Howard KATTOX (Erwin); died: 28 May 1934; buried: Jobe Cemetery; record (1934) # 14428.
WIGGAND, Mrs. Paul P.; born: 12 Aug. 1880 in Virginia; widow; parents: John MARTIN (Virginia) and Ella DANIEL (Virginia); death cause: "kerosene explosion, severe burns, pneumonia"; informant: Dick WIGGAND (Erwin); died: 24 Apr. 1934; buried: Evergreen Cemetery; record (1934) # 14429.
ROBERTS, John Hicks; born: 3 Mar. 1873 in Madison County, NC.; widow; parents: Jack D. ROBERTS (Big Laurel, NC.) and Harriett J. HUNTER (Alexandra, NC.); death cause: "homicide, fractured skull"; informant: A.F. ROBERTS (Alexandra, NC.); died: 16 Jun. 1934; buried: Higgins Cemetery; record (1934) # 14430.
PRINCE, Mrs. Vonnie; born: 27 Jun. 1911 in North Carolina; married; parents: Lee HALE (North Carolina) and Florence HYATT (North Carolina); death cause: "myo carditis"; informant: father (Erwin); died: 21 May 1934; buried: North Carolina; record (1934) # 14431.
BRIGGS, Lee Moore; born: 27 Oct. 1888; husband of Mary BRIGGS; parents: Adolphus BRIGGS and Matilda MOORE; death cause: "tuberculosis of kidney"; informant: .W.W. SMITH (Flag Pond); died: 13 Jun. 1934; buried: Rice Creek; record (1934) # 14432.
BROWN, William Henry; born: 1 Aug. 1861 in Knox County; husband of Annie L. BROWN; bookbinder; parents: William L. BROWN (Knox County) and Nancy Colvin BROWN (Blount County); death cause:

"accidental fall, fractured skull"; informant: wife (Erwin); died: 24 Jul. 1934; buried; Evergreen Cemetery; record (1934) # 17166.

TOMPKINS, George W.; age: 83 years, 9 months and 15 days; husband of Harriett TOMPKINS; parents: John H. TOMPKINS (North Carolina) and Martha TILSON; death cause: "blood poison"; died: 20 Jul. 1934; buried; Clear Branch; record (1934) # 17117.

HAYNES, Nathaniel Taylor; born: 14 Aug. 1860 in Washington County; married; parents: Jonathan MCNABB (Washington County) and Emma HAYNES (Washington County); death cause: "heart failure"; died: 23 Jul. 1934; buried: Clear Branch; record (1934) # 17118.

GARLAND, Sarah; age: 57 years; born: North Carolina; widow; parents: Joe TIPTON (North Carolina) and mother not stated; death cause: not stated; died: 22 Jun. 1934; buried: Martins Creek; record # 17119.

CLOUSE, Thomas; born: 21 Mar. 1841 at Flag Pond; widower; parents: Jacob CLOUSE and mother "unknown"; death cause: "old age"; died: 18 Jul. 1934; buried: Sams Cemetery; record (1934) # 17120.

TIPTON, Rebecca Gillis; age: 77 years, 7 months and 7 days; widow of S.Y. TIPTON; parents: John GILLIS and Ruth TILSON; death cause: "heart failure"; informant: M.E. TIPTON (Erwin); died: 16 Aug. 1934; buried: Washington County; record (1934) # 19429.

PETERSON, Jonas Daniel; born: 30 Nov. 1867 in Mitchell County, NC.; widower of Mary PETERSON; parents: John N. PETERSON (North Carolina) and Emmaline PETERSON (North Carolina); death cause: "portal obstruction"; informant: W.N. PETERSON (Erwin); died: 17 Aug. 1934; buried: Poplar, North Carolina; record (1934) # 19430.

SILVERS, John; age: 78 years, 3 months and 15 days; born: Higgins, North Carolina; husband of Narcissus SILVERS; parents: Marion SILVERS (Higgins, NC.) and Mary HENSLEY (Higgins, NC.); death cause: "paralysis"; informant: Walter SILVERS (Flag Pond); died: 31 Jul. 1934; buried: family cemetery; record (1934) # 19431.

GUINN, William Edwin; born: 19 Jan. 1930; parents: Glen GUINN and Wilsie CAPPS; death cause: "meningitis"; informant: Lattie GUINN (Erwin); died: 23 Sep. 1934; buried: Evergreen; record (1934) # 21712.

FOX, Haskel; born: 22 Jun. 1891 in North Carolina; single; parents: Robert FOX (North Carolina) and Lellith ROBERTS (North Carolina);

death cause: "consumption of stomach"; informant: Marion FOX (Erwin); died: 28 Sep. 1934; buried; Evergreen; record (1934) # 21713.

MCNABB, Madge Eloise; born: 2 Jan. 1917; single; parents: Robert Henry MCNABB and Bessie Lee KEEVER; death cause: "mitral insufficiency"; informant: Elizabeth SMITH (Erwin); died: 3 Sep. 1934; buried: Jobe Cemetery; record (1934) # 21714.

LONG, John Richard; born: 11 May 1931; parents: William LONG (North Carolina) and Cora Mae HIGGINS; death cause: "scarlet fever"; informant: father (Erwin); died: 22 Sep. 1934; buried: Martins Creek; record (1934) # 21715.

WILSON, Loyle Gene; born: 8 Aug. 1934; parents: __ (illegible) WILSON (North Carolina) and Annie __ (illegible) (North Carolina); death cause: "bronchial pneumonia"; died: 23 Sep. 1934; buried: Martins Creek; record (1934) # 21716.

LONG, Mozella; born: 18 May 1933; parents: William Martin LONG (Yancey County, NC.) and Cora Mae HIGGINS; death cause: "scarlet fever"; informant: father (Erwin); died: 25 Sep. 1934; buried: Martins Creek; record (1934) # 21717.

HIGGINS, Paul William; born: 24 Mar. 1934; parents: Floyd HIGGINS and Rosetta HUGHES; death cause: "bronchial pneumonia"; informant: Joe POORE (Erwin); died: 30 Sep. 1934; buried: Martins Creek; record (1934) # 21718.

BRACKINS, Dennis; born: 4 Aug. 1932; parents: Ike BRACKINS (North Carolina) and Jane WILSON (North Carolina); death cause: "colitis"; informant: father (Erwin); buried: Bald Mountain; died: 30 Jun. 1934; record (1934) # 21719.

EFFLER, Pauline; born: 24 Apr. 1921; parents: George EFFLER and Emma MARR; death cause: "bronchial pneumonia"; informant: father (Clear Branch); died: 25 Oct. 1934; buried: Effler Cemetery; record (1934) # 24182.

GARLAND, Dina; age: 45 years; wife of W.M. GARLAND; parents: Dave MCINTURFF and Mary TONEY; death cause: "pneumonia"; died: 14 May 1934; buried: Martins Creek; record (1934) # 24183.

JOHNSTON, John Thomas; birth date not recorded; born: West Virginia; husband of Ethel JOHNSTON; parents: __ (illegible) JOHNSTON (West Virginia) and Catherine __ (illegible) (Pennsylvania); death cause:

"influenza and pneumonia"; informant: wife; died: 3 Oct. 1934; buried: Evergreen Cemetery; record (1934) # 24184.

HUGHES, Amy C.; born: 9 Aug. 1856; widow of Charles HUGHES; parents: David BROOKS and __ GARRETT; death cause: "bronchial pneumonia"; informant: Dave HUGHES (Erwin); died: 8 Oct. 1934; buried: Fishery Cemetery; record (1934) # 24185.

CHAPMAN, David; age: 98 years; born: Glasgon Scotland; husband of Elizabeth TODD; parents: James CHAPMAN (Scotland) and mother "unknown"; death cause: "senile dementia"; informant: J.H. CHAPMAN (Erwin); died: 8 Oct. 1934; buried: Evergreen; record (1934) # 24186.

STALLARD, Mary Elizabeth; born: 2 May 1880 in Locust, Virginia; wife of Samuel Covey STALLARD; parents: Clayton MEADE (Virginia) and Cosby RICHARDSON (Virginia); death cause: "cerebral hemorrhage"; informant: S.C. STALLARD (Erwin); died: 10 Oct. 1934; buried: Evergreen Cemetery; record (1934) # 24187.

TIPTON, Clyde; age: 7 years; born: North Carolina; parents: Lawson TIPTON (North Carolina) and Rettie BEAM (North Carolina); death cause: "pneumonia"; informant: father (Erwin); died: 18 Oct. 1934; buried: Huntdale, North Carolina; record (1934) # 24188.

PHIPPS, Ellen; born: 4 Oct. 1860 in Virginia; widow; parents: __ (illegible) HASH (Virginia) and Alice HALSEY (Virginia); death cause: "carcinoma of stomach"; died: 22 Sep 1934; buried: Jobe Cemetery; record (1934) # 24189.

FALK, James; born: 13 Nov. 1929 in Ohio; parents: Wilbur FALK (Ohio) and Thelma NICHOLS (Ohio); death cause: "run over by automobile, fractured skull"; informant: father (Erwin); died: 8 Jul. 1934; buried: Evergreen Cemetery; record (1934) # 24190.

ARROWOOD, Earl; born: 15 Sep. 1934; parents: Earl ARROWOOD (North Carolina) and Pearl ARROWOOD (Virginia); death cause: "pneumonia"; informant: father (Erwin); died: 7 Oct. 1934; buried: Cherokee Cemetery; record (1934) # 24191.

PHILLIPS, Melvin; born: 17 Dec. 1928; parents: Grant PHILLIPS (Yancey County, NC.) and Carrie GARLAND; death cause: "scarlet fever"; informant: father (Erwin); died: 16 Oct. 1934; record # 24192.

METCALF, George; born: 22 Feb. 1878; widower; parents: John METCALF and Lizzie __ (illegible) (North Carolina); death cause: "indigestion"; died: 17 Oct. 1934; record (1934) # 24193.

HOWELL, Sidney; age: 61 years; born: North Carolina; husband of Minnie HOWELL; parents: James HOWELL (North Carolina) and __ (illegible) ATKINS (North Carolina); death cause: "kidney disease"; informant: John TOLLEY (Erwin); died: 24 Nov. 1934; buried: Swingle Cemetery; record (1934) # 26497.

DANIEL, Charles David; born: 21 Oct. 1934; parents: Harold Thomas DANIEL (Roanoke, Virginia) and Iris JONES (Michigan); death cause: "broncho pneumonia"; informant: father (Erwin); died: 24 Nov. 1934; buried: Jobe Cemetery; record (1934) # 26498.

TONEY, Infant; male; born: 30 Oct. 1934; parents: Hazen House TONEY and Anna Ruth EMMERSON (Greene County); death cause: "blue baby"; informant: father (Erwin); died: 31 Oct. 1934; buried: Jobe Cemetery; record (1934) # 26499.

PETERSON, Walter Noah; born: 16 Oct. 1934; parents: Harry PETERSON and Lula GILLIS; death cause: "lobar pneumonia"; informant: W.T. WOODWARD (Erwin); died: 27 Oct. 1934; buried: Unicoi; record (1934) # 26500.

MILLER, Tempa Ann; born: 8 Jan. 1876 in Mitchell County, NC.; wife of William MILLER; parents: William BENNETT (North Carolina) and Myra BAILEY; death cause: "carcinoma of gall bladder"; informant: Hyder MILLER (Erwin); died: 10 Nov. 1934; buried: Martins Creek; record (1934) # 26501.

PETERSON, Grover; age: 55 years, 4 months and 21 days; born: North Carolina; husband of Treaty PETERSON; parents: Joshua PETERSON (North Carolina) and Martha WARRICK (Virginia); death cause: "heart failure"; informant: Pansy PETERSON (Erwin); died: 1 Aug. 1934; buried: Martins Creek; record (1934) # 26502.

LOVETTE, John; born: 10 May 1910; single; parents: David LOVETTE and Minnie FOSTER; death cause: "tuberculosis"; informant: Stewart LOVETTE (Erwin); died: 4 Nov. 1934; buried: Unaka Springs; record (1934) # 26503.

HIGGINS, William Ellis; age: 74 years; married; parents: Samuel HIGGINS and Lizzie TILSON; death cause: "paralysis"; informant:

Troy BOONE (Flag Pond); died: 6 Nov. 1934; buried: Higgins Chapel; record (1934) # 26504.

BRIGGS, J.H.; born: 6 Nov. 1934; parents: H_ (illegible) SHELTON (North Carolina) and Janie BRIGGS (Higgins, NC.); death cause: "croup and pneumonia"; informant: Shelt RAY (Flag Pond); died: 17 Nov. 1934; buried: Metcalf Cemetery; record (1934) # 26505.

TOLLY, E.K.; born: 1859 in the 3rd District, Carter County; widower; parents: Billy TOLLY (North Carolina) and Nancie WILLIS (North Carolina); death cause: "old age"; informant: D.W. MORRELL; died at Limestone Cove on 3 Sep. 1934; buried: Carter County; record # 39604.

GRINDSTAFF, Susan; age: 72 years, 8 months and 20 days; widow of Russell GRINDSTAFF; parents: Billie DAVIS and Susan DAVIS; death cause: "myo carditis"; died: 22 Jun. 1934; buried: Bell Cemetery; record (1934) # 29605.

WHITE, G.I.; born: 24 Sep. 1870; married; parents: John WHITE and Delia SIMMONS (North Carolina); death cause: not stated; informant: A.I. WHITE (Unicoi); died: 7 Dec. 1934; buried: Brummitt Cemetery; record (1934) # 29606.

MOYERS, Jacob Columbus; born: 9 Oct. __ in Washington County; age: "about 60 years"; parents: Daniel MOYERS (Rockingham County, VA.) and Katherine D__ (illegible) (Rockingham County, VA.); death cause: "pulmonary tuberculosis"; died: 25 Oct. 1934; buried: Jonesboro, Tennessee; record (1934) # 29607.

HOWELL, Frank; age: 41 years; born: North Carolina; widower of Mae HOWELL; parents: Pete HOWELL (North Carolina) and Mary HEADRICK (North Carolina); death cause: "pneumonia"; informant: Edgar HOWELL (Unicoi); died: 13 Jul. 1934; buried: Swingle Cemetery; record (1934) # 29608.

MCLAUGHLIN, R.C. Jr.; born: 8 May 1934; parents: R.C. MCLAUGHLIN and Lottie HORTON (Mitchell County, NC.); death cause: "congenital heart problem"; informant: George MCLAUGHLIN; died: 27 Jun. 1934; buried: family cemetery; record (1934) # 29609.

QUESENBERRY, Tobias Jackson; born: 19 Sep. 1882 in Carroll County, VA.; husband of Tempa Bailey QUESENBERRY; railroad engineer; parents: Enos QUESENBERRY and Rebecca HEWITT; death cause: "dropsy and nephritis"; informant: wife (Erwin); died: 13 Dec. 1934; buried: Jobe Cemetery; record (1934) # 29610.

PETERSON, Albert Lee; born: __ Oct. 1934; age: 1 year and 13 days; parents: James PETERSON (North Carolina) and Mary BRITT; death cause: "found dead in bed, probably suffocation"; informant: father (Erwin); died: 26 Dec. 1934; buried: Peterson Cemetery; record (1934) # 26611.

JONES, James Douglas; age: 2 months; parents: Ernest JONES and Elizabeth BARNETT (North Carolina); death cause: "bronchial __ (illegible); informant: Bud JONES (Erwin); died: 28 Oct. 1934; buried: Martins Creek; record (1934) # 29612.

HENSLEY, J.H. Jr.; age: 9 years; parents: J.H. HENSLEY (North Carolina) and Lizzie B_ (illegible) (North Carolina); death cause: "rheumatic heart"; informant: father (Erwin); died: 5 Aug. 1934; buried: Jobe Cemetery; record (1934) # 29613.

HENSLEY, Howard D.; born: 24 Feb. 1934; parents: Charles B. HENSLEY (North Carolina) and Rosa Ellen ENGLE; death cause: "meningitis"; died: 11 Aug. 1934; buried: Jobe Cemetery; record (1934) # 29614.

HARRIS, Sarah; age: 56 years; born: North Carolina; wife of Dempsy HARRIS; parents: John WOODY (North Carolina) and mother "unknown"; death cause: "cancer of cervix"; informant: Frank HARRIS (Erwin); died: 3 Oct. 1934; buried: Flag Pond; record (1934) # 29615.

MORROW, Ada Marie; born: 16 Feb. 1918; parents: Will MORROW (North Carolina) and Byrdie COFFEE; death cause: "pneumonia"; informant: mother (Erwin); died: 9 Dec. 1934; buried: Fishery Cemetery; record (1934) # 29616.

HOWELL, James; age: 90 years, 10 months and 30 days; born: North Carolina; widower; parents: William HOWELL (North Carolina) and __ HONEYCUTT (North Carolina); death cause: "cerebral hemorrhage"; died: 14 Dec. 1934; buried: Erwin; record # 29617.

MCINTOSH, Helen Ruth; born: 5 Oct. 1933; parents: Fermon MCINTOSH and Orpha Mae CALLOWAY; death cause: "laryngitis"; informant: father (Erwin); died: 31 Dec. 1934; buried: Martins Creek; record (1934) # 29618.

WALDROP, W.B.; born: 14 Nov. 1862 in North Carolina; married; parents: Joe WALDROP (North Carolina) and Minnie BANKS (North Carolina); death cause: "carcinoma of face"; informant: wife (Erwin); died: 12 Oct. 1934; buried: Martins Creek; record (1934) # 29619.

POORE, James; age: 76 years; married; parents: "unknown"; death cause: "pneumonia"; informant: Charles PETERSON (Erwin); died: 29 Oct. 1934; buried: Martins Creek; record (1934) # 29620.

SHELL, Erline; born: 17 May 1934; parents: Willard ALLEN (Illinois) and Cassie SHELL; death cause: "under nourished"; died: 18 May 1934; buried; Martins Creek; record (1934) # 29621.

SHELL, William; born: 17 May 1934; parents: Willard ALLEN (Illinois) and Cassie SHELL; death cause: "under nourished"; died: 18 May 1934; buried: Martins Creek; record (1934) # 29622.

SHELL, Willie Dean; born: 17 May 1934; parents: Willard ALLEN (Illinois) and Cassie SHELL; death cause: "under nourished"; died: 18 May 1934; buried; Martins Creek; record (1934) # 29623.

WILLIAMS, Rige; born: 12 Dec. 1934; parents: Vernon WILLIAMS (North Carolina) and Polly GARLAND (North Carolina); death cause: "hives"; informant: Stewart LOVETTE (Erwin); died: 14 Dec. 1934; buried: family cemetery; record (1934) # 29624.

BRIGGS, John Logan; born: 15 Mar. 1849; born: Tennessee; husband of Ethel BRIGGS; parents: John BRIGGS (Tennessee) and Annie GARLAND (North Carolina); death cause: "paralysis"; informant: Laura CARTER (Flag Pond); died: 21 Nov. 1934; buried: Rice Creek; record (1934) # 30183.

CUTSHAW, S_ (illegible); female; age: "approximately 67 years"; widow of James CUTSHAW; parents: "unknown"; death cause: "unknown"; informant: Gertha CUTSHAW (Flag Pond); died: 31 Dec. 1934; buried: Shelton Cemetery; record (1934) # 30184.

MCNABB, Infant; female; parents: Frank MCNABB and Luria HEAD; death cause: "stillborn"; informant: T.H. HEAD (Unicoi); born/died: 19 Oct. 1934; buried: McInturff Cemetery; record (1934) # 30185.

MCKINNEY, Rex; age: 30 years; born: North Carolina; husband of June MCKINNEY; parents: R.F. MCKINNEY (North Carolina) and Blanche BYRD (North Carolina); death cause: "pulmonary tuberculosis";

informant: mother (Erwin); died: 28 Sep. 1934; buried: Indian Creek Cemetery; record (1934) # 30186.

HENSLEY, Martha; born: 18 Jul. 1934; parents: father not stated and Mildred HENSLEY; death cause: not stated; informant: J.C. FOSTER (Clear Branch); died: 30 Nov. 1934; buried: Patty Cemetery; record (1934) # 30326.

HENSLEY, Mildred; born: 27 Nov. 1910; single; parents: Abe RIDDLE and Martha J. HENSLEY; death cause: "under nourished"; informant: Blake JONES (Clear Branch); died: 18 Dec. 1934; buried: Patty Cemetery; record (1934) # 30327.

MCINTOSH, William Jackson; born: 8 Jan. 1850 in Yancey County, North Carolina; widower of Rossey MOORE; parents: "unknown"; death cause: "old age"; informant: J.W. HOWELL (Erwin); died: 1 Sep. 1934; buried: Erwin; record (1934) # 30572.

ROBINSON, Jessie; born: 11 Jan. 1935; parents: Luke ROBINSON (Madison County, NC.) and Elizabeth HENSLEY (Madison County, NC.); death cause: not stated; informant: mother (Flag Pond); died: 12 Jan. 1935; buried: Loyd Cemetery; record (1935) # 2149.

WATTS, Mary Elizabeth; age: 17 months; born: Greene County; parents: Fred WATTS and Ethel BAINES; death cause: "meningitis"; informant: father (Clear Branch); died: 19 Jan. 1935; buried: Rocky Fork Cemetery; record (1935) # 2150.

LEDFORD, Joe; age: 75 years; husband of Vicie WOODBY; parents: Sam STREET and Mary LEDFORD (North Carolina); death cause: "influenza"; informant: Brown LEDFORD (Erwin); died: 22 Jan. 1935; buried: Bell Cemetery; record (1935) # 2151.

BROWN, Andrew Johnson; born: 4 May 1858 in Washington County; husband of Mary Jane BROWN; parents: Benjamin F. BROWN (Washington County) and Lucretia DAVIS (Washington County); death cause: "uremic poisoning"; informant: Mrs. Elizabeth PALMER (Erwin); died: 14 Jan. 1935; buried: Evergreen; record (1935) # 2152.

DENNIS, Lillian; age: 69 years, 4 months and 5 days; born: Peterstown, West Virginia; wife of Charles William DENNIS; parents: M.M. WARREN (West Virginia) and mother "unknown"; death cause: "cerebral hemorrhage"; informant: Wade DENNIS; died: 30 Jan. 1935; buried: Petersburg, Virginia; record (1935) # 2153.

POORE, Clifton; age: 5 months; born: Cherokee, Washington County; parents: James POORE and Valeria BAILEY (Burnsville, North Carolina); death cause: "pneumonia"; informant: father (Erwin); died: 28 Jan. 1935; buried: Erwin; record (1935) # 2154.

HUGHES, Burnie; born: 11 Jan. 1935; parents: Dolphus HUGHES (Yancey County, NC.) and Bertie TAYLOR (Yancey County, NC.); death cause: "under nourished"; informant: father (Erwin); died: 28 Jan. 1935; buried: family cemetery; record (1935) # 2155.

SMITH, R.C.; born: 8 Jan. 1935; parents: Fred SMITH and Omie MCCLELLAN (Carter County); death cause: "premature"; informant: Frankie MCINTURFF (Unicoi); died: 8 Jan. 1935; buried: Jones Cemetery; record (1935) # 2156.

SMITH, M.B.; 8 Jan. 1935; parents: Fred SMITH and Omie MCCLELLAN (Carter County); death cause: "premature"; informant: Frankie MCINTURFF (Unicoi); died: 8 Jan. 1935; buried: Jones Cemetery; record (1935) # 2157.

TAPP, Matison Love; born: 28 Jan. 1857; husband of Emma TAPP; parents: William TAPP and mother "unknown"; death cause: "Brights disease"; informant: Isaac TAPP (Erwin); died: 24 Jan. 1935; buried: Fishery Cemetery; record (1935) # 2158.

WILSON, Bertie; born: 3 Aug. 1856 in North Carolina; widow; parents: "unknown"; death cause: "cerebral hemorrhage"; informant: D.W. WILSON (Erwin); died: 12 Jan. 1935; buried: Evergreen Cemetery; record (1935) # 2159.

BIRCHFIELD, William; age: 74 years and 7 months; husband of Eliza BOWERS; parents: Ezekiel BIRCHFIELD; and __ GOUGE; death cause: "bronchial asthma"; informant: Deyton MORRELL (Unicoi); died: 18 Jan. 1935; buried: Bell Cemetery; record (1935) # 4667.

FOWLER, Stella Mary; born: 9 Nov. 1888 in Wellsville, Virginia; wife of Harry FOWLER; parents: Dyton PIERCE (New York) and Magdalen CRINE; death cause: "uremia"; informant: husband (Erwin); died: 1 Feb. 1935; buried: Evergreen Cemetery; record (1935) # 4668.

TUCKER, Amanda Cornelia; age: 74 years; born: North Carolina; widow; parents: "unknown"; death cause: "uremia and nephritis"; informant: W.F. TUCKER (Erwin); died: 12 Feb. 1935; buried: Erwin; record (1935) # 4669.

HOLCOMB, Elcie; born: 19 Mar. 1919; parents: William HOLCOMB and Belle GILLIS; death cause: "automobile accident, skull crushed"; informant: mother (Erwin); died: 16 Feb. 1935; buried: Holcomb Cemetery; record (1935) # 4670.

MCINTURFF, Lou; age: 49 years; single; parents: N.K. MCINTURFF and Anne COBBLE; death cause: "anemia"; informant: Skip MCINTURFF (Unicoi); died: 30 Jan. 1935; buried: Jones Cemetery; record (1935) # 4671.

MORRIS, Nan; age: "about 95 years"; parents: Isam MORRIS and Eliza __; death cause: "influenza and pneumonia"; informant: Morgan BAILEY (Erwin); died: 7 Feb. 1935; buried: Martins Creek; record (1935) # 4672.

MILLER, Infant; male; born: 14 Feb. 1935; parents: Hobart MILLER and Amanda WATTS (Yancey County, NC.); death cause: "premature"; informant: father (Erwin); died: 16 Feb. 1935; buried: Martins Creek; record (1935) # 4673.

CRAINE, Andy J.; born: 18 Mar. 1850; husband of Sarah J. CRAINE; parents: Lewis GRAINE (Madison County, NC.) and Lydia TILSON (Flag Pond); death cause: "angina pectoris"; informant: Anderson EDWARDS (Flag Pond); died: 10 Feb. 1935; buried; Higgins Chapel; record (1935) # 4674.

PROFFITT, Elbert S.; born: 22 Jun. 1856 at Bald Creek, North Carolina; husband of Julia PROFFITT; parents: Ben A. PROFFITT (Bald Creek, NC.) and mother not stated; death cause: "pneumonia"; informant: E.A. METCALF (Flag Pond); died: 12 Feb. 1935; buried: Blankenship Cemetery; record (1935) # 4675.

ORREN, Jacob Lundy; age: 75 years and 14 days; widower; parents: Jacob Washington ORREN (North Carolina) and Nancy LUNDY; death cause: "heart __ (illegible)"; informant: C.A. ORREN (Erwin); died: 6 Mar. 1935; record (1935) # 7331.

BLANKENSHIP, John William; age: 44 years, 8 months and 3 days; husband of Cora TREADWAY; parents: John BLANKENSHIP (Yancey County, NC.) and Sarah MATHIS (Yancey County, NC.); death cause: "killed in altercation, fractured skull"; informant: John BLANKENSHIP (Flag Pond); died: 31 Mar. 1935; buried: Blankenship Cemetery; record (1935) # 7332.

MCNICOL, Earl; born: 14 Feb. 1935; parents: Roy MCNICOL (Washington County) and Nina BROYLES (Washington County); death cause: "premature"; informant: father (Erwin); died: 1 Mar. 1935; buried: Liberty Cemetery; record (1935) # 7333.

FRYE, Caroline Sue; born: 13 Dec. 1934; parents: Dewey FRYE (North Carolina) and Ethel HENSLEY; death cause: "meningitis"; died: 21 Mar. 1935; buried: Clear Branch; record (1935) # 7334.

HOWELL, Eliza; age: 76 years; born: Buncombe County, North Carolina; widow of William H. HOWELL; parents: Jake JUSTICE (North Carolina) and __ ROBERTS; death cause: "hit by train on bridge"; informant: Neal HOWELL (Erwin); died: 29 Mar. 1935; buried: Unaka Springs Cemetery; record (1935) # 7335.

PETERSON, Paul Roscoe; born: 1 May 1900 in Knoxville; husband of Ethel Howell PETERSON; parents: Grover PETERSON (Relief, North Carolina) and Trotie JONES (North Carolina); death cause: "lobar pneumonia"; informant: wife (Erwin); died: 24 Feb. 1935; buried: Martins Creek; record (1935) # 7336.

BAILEY, Teddy Ross; born: 13 Aug. 1934; parents: Calvin Burnie BAILEY (Yancey County, NC.) and Pearl TIPTON (North Carolina); death cause: "meningitis"; informant: father (Erwin); died: 18 Mar. 1935; buried: Martins Creek; record (1935) # 7337.

GARLAND, Evelyn; born: 9 Mar. 1922; parents: E.L. GARLAND (Bakersville, North Carolina) and Cora MCINTOSH (Greene County); death cause: "ruptured appendix"; informant: father (Erwin); died: 24 Mar. 1935; buried: Martins Creek; record (1935) # 7338.

TIPTON, Hassel Lee; born: 21 Feb. 1909 in North Carolina; wife of Zeke TIPTON; parents: Bacus HUGHES (North Carolina) and Louie TAYLOR (North Carolina); death cause: "pulmonary tuberculosis"; informant: Whitt HUGHES (Erwin); died: 25 Mar. 1935; buried: Martins Creek; record (1935) # 7339.

TIPTON, Carl; age: 2 years; parents: Frank TIPTON and Lydia GADDY; death cause: "bronchial __ (illegible)"; informant: father (Unicoi); died: 10 Mar. 1935; buried: McInturff Cemetery; record (1935) # 7340.

HOWELL, Jeff; age: 38 years; born: North Carolina; husband of Mary BENNETT; parents: Pete HOWELL (North Carolina) and Mary

HEADRICK (North Carolina); death cause: "pulmonary tuberculosis"; informant: Robert HOWELL (Unicoi); died: 13 Feb. 1935; buried; Swingle Cemetery; record (1935) # 7341.

WHITE, John Christopher; born: 28 Mar. 1848; widower of Delia SIMMONS; Civil War Veteran; parents: Abe WHITE and Emeline MCINTURFF; death cause: "myocardial failure"; informant: J.C. WHITE Jr. (Unicoi); died: 27 Apr. 1935; buried: Jones Cemetery; record (1935) # 9630.

EDENS, Charles David; born: 28 Feb. 1900 in Elizabethton, Tennessee; divorced from Bonnie EDENS; parents: Edwin Lockwood EDENS (Elizabethton) and Margaret SHELL (Elizabethton); death cause: "automobile accident, ruptured spleen, etc."; informant: E.L. EDENS (Elizabethton); died: 14 Apr. 1935; buried: Elizabethton; record # 9631.

MILLER, Ann Lois; born: 8 Jul. 1934; parents: C.M. MILLER and Dessie ARROWOOD; death cause: "meningitis"; informant: father (Unicoi); died: 25 Mar. 1935; buried: Unicoi; record (1935) # 9632.

TUCKER, Joseph L.; age: 58 years, 9 months and 17 days; husband of Mamie TONEY; parents: Wesley TUCKER (North Carolina) and Polly Ann BAILEY; death cause: "heart failure"; informant: Ernest TUCKER (Birmingham, Alabama); died: 12 Apr. 1935; buried: Jobe Cemetery; record (1935) # 9633.

ERWIN, Lydia Harriett Ann; age: 78 years; single; parents: Jesse B. ERWIN and Elizabeth MCMAHAN; death cause: "influenza and pneumonia"; informant: H. ERWIN (Erwin); died: 13 Apr. 1935; buried: Jobe Cemetery; record (1935) # 9634.

ERWIN, Lela Pearl; born: __ Jun. 1888; wife of Charles R. ERWIN; parents: J.W. CALLAHAN (North Carolina) and Rosa JARVIS; death cause: "cerebral hemorrhage"; informant: husband (Erwin); died: 27 Apr. 1935; buried: Martins Creek; record (1935) # 9635.

BIRCHFIELD, William E.; age: 53 years, 8 months and 6 days; husband of Gertrude REEVES; parents: Robert BIRCHFIELD and Mary GARLAND; death cause: "homicide, gunshot wound"; informant: Mrs. Carl NELSON (Erwin); died: 23 Apr. 1935; buried: Jobe Cemetery; record (1935) # 9636.

MCINTURFF, Nathaniel R.; age: 98 years, 3 months and 1 day; widower of Anne COBBLE; parents: "unknown"; death cause: "just dropped dead"; informant: Shep MCINTURFF (Unicoi); died: 30 Apr. 1935; buried: McInturff Cemetery; record (1935) # 9637.

ATKINS, Russell; born: 3 Mar. 1933; parents: J.B. ATKINS (Yancey County, NC.) and Martha Jane FENDER (Yancey County, NC.); death cause: "meningitis"; informant: father (Erwin); died: 29 Apr. 1935; buried: Bee Log, North Carolina; record (1935) # 9638.

RANDOLPH, Sharlean; born: 29 Jan. 1935; parents: Elisha RANDOLPH (North Carolina) and Gerthie HONEYCUTT (North Carolina); death cause: "diphtheria"; informant: father (Clear Branch); died: 16 Apr. 1935; buried: Foster Cemetery; record (1935) # 9639.

MATHES, Belle; born: 8 Aug. 1927; parents: Walter MATHES and Florence METCALF; death cause: "heart problem"; died: 28 Apr. 1935; buried: Metcalf Cemetery; record (1935) # 9640.

BLANKENSHIP, John Jr.; age: 45 years; husband of Carry Treadway BLANKENSHIP; parents: John BLANKENSHIP Sr. (Georgia) and Sarah BLANKENSHIP (Yancey County, NC.); death cause: "altercation, struck on head, fractured skull"; informant: Rebecca HARRIS (Flag Pond); died: 31 Mar. 1935; buried: Blankenship Cemetery; record (1935) # 9644.

BRADLEY, Roy Melborne; age: 42 years, 3 months and 2 days; born: Virginia; husband of Emma ROBINETTE; parents: W.H. BRADLEY (Virginia) and Sarah STALLARD (Virginia); death cause: "pulmonary tuberculosis"; informant: Arthur PATE (Unicoi); died: 10 May 1935; buried: Swingle Cemetery; record (1935) # 11999.

MILLER, Carmen; born: 24 Jun. 1913 in North Carolina; husband of Maude HONEYCUTT; parents: Robert MILLER (Yancey County, NC.) and Emma BRYANT (North Carolina); death cause: "pulmonary tuberculosis"; informant: father (Unicoi); died: 21 May 1935; buried: Swingle Cemetery; record (1935) # 12000.

OVERHOLSER, Thomas B.; age: 69 years; widower; parents: William J. OVERHOLSER and Martha COOPER; death cause: "angina pectoris"; informant: Andy HUMPHREYS (Watauga, TN.); died: 21 Jan. 1935; buried: Carter County; record (1935) # 12001.

BENNETT, Ruth; born: 30 Oct. 1931; parents: William BENNETT (North Carolina) and Mabel INGRAM (Avery County, NC.); death cause: "accidental gunshot wound"; informant: mother (Erwin); died: 9 May 1935; buried: Martins Creek; record (1935) # 12002.

HUGHES, Ernest Casey; born: 4 Oct. 1934; parents: Robert H. HUGHES and Gladys WHISNANT (Morganton, NC.); death cause: "diphtheria"; informant: father (Erwin); died: 7 May 1935; buried: Martins Creek; record (1935) # 12003.

CAMPBELL, James; age: 71 years; widower of Alice Stout CAMPBELL; parents: Billie CAMPBELL and Mary FRY; death cause: "cancer of prostate, nephritis"; informant: Daniel CAMPBELL (Unicoi); died: 20 May 1935; buried: Campbell Cemetery; record (1935) # 12004.

MCNABB, Marie; age: 10 days; parents: Clarence MCNABB and Pansy BARNES; death cause: "cranial hemorrhage"; died: 30 May 1935; buried: Swingle Cemetery; record (1935) # 12005.

PETERSON, Infant; female; parents: W.N. PETERSON (North Carolina) and Edith CASH; death cause: "premature"; informant: father (Erwin); died: 27 May 1935; buried: Martins Creek; record # 12006.

HENSLEY, Robert Lee; born: 7 Jun. 1935; parents: Jim Frank HENSLEY and Callie HARRIS; death cause: "premature birth"; died: 8 Jun. 1935; buried: Gentry Cemetery; record (1935) # 14284.

INGRAM, Helen Christine; age: 1 month and 24 days; parents: Harley INGRAM and Virgie MCINTURFF; death cause: illegible; informant: Shep MCINTURFF (Unicoi); died: 4 Jun. 1935; buried: Swingle Cemetery; record (1935) # 14285.

MCINTURFF, Jennie Earline; born: 14 Mar. 1935; parents: Willard MCINTURFF and Pansy MILLER; death cause: "jaundice"; informant: father (Unicoi); died: 31 Mar. 1935; buried: Unicoi; record # 14286.

HILL, William Clayton; age: 43 years; born: Rutherfordton, North Carolina; husband of Hilda HILL; parents: William HILL (North Carolina) and Emma ALLEN (North Carolina); death cause: "wounds on head and neck, source unknown"; (body found in abandoned railroad car); informant: Hicks HILL (Rutherfordton, NC.); died: "about 2 Jun. 1935; buried: North Carolina; record (1935) # 14287.

BECKELHIMER, William Daniel; age: 73 years, 3 months and 27 days; born: Virginia; widower of Heney Ellen VANCE; parents: William Daniel BECKELHIMER (Virginia) and mother "unknown"; death cause: "coronary __ (illegible); informant: Ray BECKELHIMER (Erwin); died: 16 Jun. 1935; buried: Johnson City; record # 14288.

O'BRIEN, Janice Sue; born: 12 Apr. 1935; parents: George Clifton O'BRIEN and Nancy PETERSON (Yancey County, NC.); death cause: "premature"; informant: father (Erwin); died: 17 Jun. 1935; buried: Jobe Cemetery; record (1935) # 14289.

TONEY, William Clifton; age: 53 years; husband of Christine SCOTT; parents: J.F. TONEY Sr. (North Carolina) and Fannie Bell MILER; death cause: "suicide, gunshot"; informant: Hubert TONEY (Erwin); died: 21 Jun. 1935; buried: Evergreen Cemetery; record # 14290.

SPARKS, Robert Newton; born: 9 Jun. 1873 in Yancey County, North Carolina; husband of Sarah SPARKS; parents: Jack SPARKS (North Carolina) and Carolina WOODY (North Carolina); death cause: "cerebral hemorrhage"; informant: George SPARKS (Marion, North Carolina); died: 21 Jun. 1935; buried: Evergreen Cemetery; record (1935) # 14291.

ELLIOTT, Adeline Braswell; born: 14 May 1873 in Johnson County, Tennessee; wife of Richard ELLIOTT; parents: Wiley A. BRASWELL (North Carolina) and Clarissa ROARK; death cause: "cancer of liver"; informant: Richard ELLIOTT (Erwin); died: 24 Jun. 1935; buried: McInturff Cemetery; record (1935) # 14292.

TIPTON, Hobert; age: 25 years; husband of Sidia TIPTON; parents: William M. TIPTON (North Carolina) and Alice HAMPTON (North Carolina); death cause: "influenza and pneumonia"; informant: George TIPTON (Embreeville); died: 18 Apr. 1935; buried: Embreeville; record (1935) # 14293.

PEAKE, Richard; age: 9 months and 16 days; parents: Oscar PEAKE (North Carolina); and Ida TINKER; death cause: illegible; informant: father (Erwin); died: 24 Jun. 1935; buried: Erwin; record # 14294.

CRAINE, George W.; age: 74 years; born: Yancey County, North Carolina; husband of Lillie CRAINE; parents: "unknown"; death cause: "paralysis"; informant: Andy CRAINE (Flag Pond); died: 12 Jun. 1935; record (1935) # 14295.

TIPTON, Alda; born: 22 Jun. 1933; parents: Leroy TIPTON and Estelle SHELTON; death cause: "flux"; informant: Jake HENSLEY (Flag Pond); died: 22 Jun. 1935; buried: Blankenship; record (1935) # 14296.

RICE, Janell; born: 20 Dec. 1914 in Madison County, North Carolina; wife of Arlin RICE; parents: Wiley METCALF (Madison County, NC.) and Loura CLICK (Greene County); death cause: "flux"; informant: Walter MATHES (Flag Pond); died: 26 Jun. 1935; buried: Madison County, NC.; record (1935) # 14297.

PATE, Arthur R.; age: 51 years; husband of Hannah WHITE; parents: Nathan PATE and Vina GARLAND; death cause: "suicide"; informant: P.N. GARLAND (Unicoi); died: 26 Jul. 1935; buried: Swingle Cemetery; record (1935) # 16686.

MOSLEY, Rebecca; age: 75 years; widow of John MOSLEY; parents: John GREER (Carter County) and Rebecca GREER; death cause: "heart failure"; informant: David MOSLEY (Unicoi); died: 4 Mar. 1935; buried: Harrell Cemetery; record (1935) # 16687.

LILLEY, James Matthew; born: 29 May 1875 in Augusta County, Virginia; husband of Matilda B. LILLEY; parents: Col. John D. LILLEY (Virginia) and Anna SMITH (Virginia); death cause: "coronary __ (illegible)"; informant: wife (Erwin); died: 13 Jul. 1935; buried: Augusta County, Virginia; record (1935) # 16688.

BROYLES, Noah; born: 21 Mar. 1877 in Washington County; husband of Maggie PADGETT; parents: Melvin BROYLES and Louise HOLT; death cause: "heart lesion"; died: 15 Jul. 1935; buried: Liberty Cemetery; record (1935) # 16689.

HUTCHINS, Walter Frederick; born: 14 May 1934; parents: Grady HUTCHINS (North Carolina) and Nellie HERNS (West Virginia); death cause: "polio"; informant: father (Erwin); died: 26 Jul. 1935; buried: Jobe Cemetery; record (1935) # 16690.

BAILEY, Elbert Lenoir; born: 4 Apr. 1848 in Mitchell County, North Carolina; husband of Vista Belle BAILEY; parents: Jessie BAILEY (North Carolina) and Mollie CURTIS (North Carolina); death cause: "heart lesion"; informant: Ralph BAILEY (Erwin); died: 26 Jul. 1935; buried: Erwin; record (1935) # 16691.

HAUN, Jimmy Hobart; born: 5 Apr. 1934; parents: Herman HAUN and Sarah MILLER; death cause: "dysentery"; informant: father (Erwin); died: 11 Jul. 1935; buried: Haun Cemetery; record (1935) # 16692.

POORE, Frank; born: 26 Jun. 1878 in Washington County; husband of Melvina POORE; parents: Robert POORE and Sue STARNES; death cause: "pulmonary tuberculosis"; informant: Joe POORE (Erwin); died: 15 Jul. 1935; buried: Garland Cemetery; record (1935) # 16693.

CAMPBELL, June Carolyn; born: 17 Jun. 1935; parents: Clarence Albert CAMPBELL and Velma Mae THOMPSON (West Virginia); death cause: "spina bifida, meningitis"; informant: W.E. THOMPSON (Erwin); died: 21 Jul. 1935; buried: Erwin; record (1935) # 16694.

BLANKENSHIP, Bobby Lee; born: 3 Jul. 1935; parents: Bob BLANKENSHIP and Zora HIGGINS; death cause: "premature"; informant: Merrett HENSLEY (Flag Pond); died: 3 Jul. 1935; buried: Rice Creek; record (1935) # 16695.

RICE, Catherine; born: 22 Nov. 1934; parents: Alva RICE and Gladys HESTER (Georgia); death cause: "flux"; died: 5 Jul. 1935; buried: Rice Creek; record (1935) # 16696.

STOCKTON, Frank Jimmy; born: 27 Jun. 1935; parents: Roscoe STOCKTON and Leakie THOMAS (Johnson City); death cause: "found dead in bed, croup"; died: 19 Jul. 1935; buried: Stockton Cemetery; record (1935) # 16697.

HENSLEY, Marie; born: 28 Dec. 1934; parents: James HENSLEY and Burly RAY; death cause: "fever"; informant: Shelt RAY (Flag Pond); died: 20 Jul. 1935; buried: Metcalf Cemetery; record (1935) # 16698.

MCINTOSH, Marcina; age: "about 77 years"; born: Yancey County, North Carolina; widow of Newton MCINTOSH; parents: James c. ANGLE (Yancey County) and Ruth RADFORD (Yancey County); death cause: "paralysis"; informant: Sam MCINTOSH (Flag Pond); died: 20 Jul. 1935; buried: Rice Creek; record (1935) # 16699.

JONES, Lora Dean; born: 6 Sep. 1910; single; parents: John JONES (Sullivan County) and Nancy Jane TITTLE; death cause: "eclampsia"; informant: Hiram JONES (Erwin); died: 13 Aug. 1935; buried: Fishery Cemetery; record (1935) # 19040.

LONG, Johnny; born: 29 May 1935; parents: Dana LONG and Etta SHELTON (North Carolina); death cause: "unknown"; informant: mother (Erwin); died: 30 May 1935; buried: Erwin; record # 19041.

FRANK, Garrett Murray; born: 20 May 1849 in Jackson County, North Carolina; husband of Harriett FRANK; parents: Garrett FRANK (North Carolina) and Dicie CALLAHAN (North Carolina); death cause: "heart lesion"; informant: Lydia BEAN (Erwin); died: 4 Aug. 1935; buried: Bailey Cemetery; record (1935) # 19042.

SMITH, Henry; born: 6 Jan. 1860; widower; parents: Alex SMITH and Jane SMITH; death cause: "heart lesion"; died: 15 Aug. 1935; buried: Fishery Cemetery; record (1935) # 19043.

RIDDLE, Homer; born: 26 Dec. 1912; husband of Helen Willis RIDDLE; parents: T.N. RIDDLE and Belle JONES; death cause: "automobile accident, skull crushed"; informant: father (Erwin); died: 29 Aug. 1935; buried: Riddle Cemetery; record (1935) # 19044.

COFFEE, James; age: 66 years, 4 months and 17 days; husband of Margaret ROBERTS; parents: Perry COFFEE (North Carolina) and Sarah Ann BERRY; death cause: "heart disease"; informant: J.Z. ROBERTS (Erwin); died: 7 Aug. 1935; buried: Evergreen Cemetery; record (1935) # 19045.

FOSTER, Viola Erwin; born: 28 Dec. 1914 in Washington County; wife of Guy FOSTER; parents: J.K. ERWIN and Lula JARVIS (Washington County); death cause: "run over by truck, skull crushed"; informant: J.R. ERWIN (Erwin); died: 20 Aug. 1935; buried: Chucky Cemetery; record (1935) # 19046.

WHITSON, Walter; born: 7 Apr. 1935; parents: Robert WHITSON (North Carolina) and Violet GILLIS; death cause: "premature birth"; informant: J.D. WHITSON; died: 25 Aug. 1935; record # 19047.

TREADWAY, Biddie; age: 68 years; widow; parents: William BALES and Sarah __ (unknown); death cause: "paralysis"; informant: Roxie TREADWAY (Erwin); died: 11 Jan. 1935; buried: Garland Cemetery; record (1935) # 19048.

BLANKENSHIP, Betty Jean; born: 28 Feb. 1933; parents: Frank BLANKENSHIP and Sue CRAIN (Madison County, NC.) death cause: "automobile accident"; informant: father (Erwin); died: 19 Aug. 1935; buried: Higgins Cemetery; record (1935) # 21239.

DICKSON, Matthew Columbus; born: 26 Apr. 1890 in Kingsport; husband of Martha Jane DICKSON; parents: Henry DICKSON (Johnson City) and Anne SMALLING (Johnson City); death cause: "pulmonary tuberculosis"; informant: wife (Erwin); died: 3 Sep. 1935; buried: Jobe Cemetery; record (1935) # 21240.

FOX, Orville Henry; born: 20 May 1877 in Illinois; locomotive engineer; husband of Julia SCHUARZ; parents: Orville Edgar FOX (North Carolina) and Lyda MEYERS (Indiana); death cause: "coronary thrombosis"; informant: O.J. FOX (Erwin); died: 10 Sep. 1935; buried: Evergreen Cemetery; record (1935) # 21244.

HENSLEY, Himack; age: 18 years; parents: J.C. HENSLEY and Mary Louise S_ (illegible); death cause: "influenza and cardio _ (illegible)"; informant: father (Erwin); died: 15 Sep. 1935; buried: Bailey Cemetery; record (1935) # 21242.

SCRUGGS, Louis D.; age: 65 years and 2 days; born: North Carolina; husband of Ada __ (illegible); parents: T.V. SCRUGGS (North Carolina) and mother's name illegible; death cause: "cancer of stomach"; informant: wife (Erwin); died: 18 Sep. 1935; buried: Evergreen; record (1935) # 23243.

MATHES, Belle Garland; born: 25 Sep. 1905 in Mitchell County, North Carolina; wife of Laurence MATHES; parents: John L. GARLAND (Mitchell County) and Crety HONEYCUTT (Mitchell County); death cause: "septicemia of face"; informant: John L. GARLAND (Erwin); died: 26 Sep. 1935; buried: Martins Creek; record (1935) # 21244.

HOLLIFIELD, Shirley Joyce; born: 4 Aug. 1935; parents: Ray HOLLIFIELD (North Carolina) and Ruby HOPKINS; death cause: "premature"; informant: C.D. HOLLIFIELD (Erwin); died: 5 Aug. 1935; buried: Jobe Cemetery; record (1935) # 21245.

BOGART, Charles C.; born: 3 Jun. 1869; husband of Daisy BOGART; parents: William BOGART and Sue TREADWAY; death cause: "nephritis"; informant: W.A. BOGART (Erwin); died: 7 Aug. 1935; record (1935) # 21246.

GREEN, Elizabeth; born: 28 Apr. 1933; parents: Tommy GREEN and Trula WILSON (North Carolina); death cause: "pneumonia"; informant: mother (Erwin); died: 4 May 1935; buried: Jobe Cemetery; record (1935) # 21247.

BARNETT, Demps; age: "about 51 years"; born: North Carolina; husband of Addie Williams BARNETT; parents: Waits BARNETT (North Carolina) and Martha WILCOX (North Carolina); death cause: "heart lesion"; informant: wife (Erwin); died: 31 Mar. 1935; buried: Martins Creek; record (1935) # 21248.

BARNETT, Richard Lee; born: 5 Feb. 1935; parents: Demps BARNETT (North Carolina) and Addie WILLIAMS; death cause: not stated; informant: mother (Erwin); died: 5 Feb. 1935; buried: Martins Creek; record (1935) # 21249.

RENFRO, Howard; born: 18 Nov. 1920; parents: McKinley RENFRO (North Carolina) and Glee HAUN; death cause: "typhoid"; informant: father (Clear Branch); died: 19 Sep. 1935; buried: McInturff Cemetery; record (1935) # 21250.

RICE, Tommy Jr.; born: 23 Sep. 1935; parents: Tommy RICE and Thelma HARRIS; death cause: "unknown"; informant: Charley COATS (Flag Pond); died: 23 Sep. 1935; buried: Rice Creek; record # 21251.

HARRIS, Robert Luther; born: 23 Sep. 1935; parents: Luther HARRIS Sr. and Lydia Margaret RANDOLPH; death cause: not stated; informant: Walter HARRIS (Flag Pond); died: 23 Sep. 1935; buried: Higgins Chapel; record (1935) # 21252.

SHELTON, Arson; born: 22 Jun. 1890 in White Rock, North Carolina; husband of Mary SHELTON; parents: Frank SHELTON (White Rock) and Vi HENSLEY (White Rock); death cause: "heart failure or brain hemorrhage"; informant: E.N. SHELTON (Flag Pond); died: 24 Sep. 1935; buried: White Rock, NC.; record (1935) # 21253.

BENNETT, Harrison; born: 7 Nov. 1862 in North Carolina; husband of Callie BENNETT; parents: Arch BENNETT and Jane HENSLEY; death cause: "cancer of prostate"; informant: C.F. BENNETT (Saltville, VA.); died: 18 Oct. 1935; buried: Fishery Cemetery; record # 23546.

GILLILAND, George Arthur; born: 31 Jul. 1895 in Carter County; husband of Bessie GILLILAND; parents: J.B. GILLILAND (Carter County) and Alice GREENWELL (Johnson County); death cause: "automobile accident, compound fractures of legs and thrombosis"; informant: wife (Erwin); died: 2 Oct. 1935; record (1935) # 23547.

HOLLIFIELD, Francis; age: 4 years and 24 days; parents: Max HOLLIFIELD (North Carolina) and Mattie ROGERS; death cause: "diphtheria"; informant: father (Erwin); died: 9 Oct. 1935; buried: Fishery Cemetery; record (1935) # 23548.

TAYLOR, John W.; born: 16 Mar. 1872 in North Carolina; husband of Leucretia ANGLE; parents: Lewis TAYLOR (North Carolina) and

Rebecca HIGGINS; death cause: "dropsy"; informant: J.L. TAYLOR (Erwin); died: 11 Oct. 1935; buried: Jobe Cemetery; record # 23549.

TITTLE, Infant; male; born: 22 Oct. 1935; parents: Brady TITTLE and Ethel TIPTON (Virginia); death cause: "premature"; informant: father (Erwin); died: 23 Oct. 1935; buried: Martins Creek; record # 23550.

HOWELL, Jeff N.; born: 17 Mar. 1878 in Yancey County, North Carolina; husband of Fannie Emma HOWELL; parents: Robert HOWELL and mother unknown; death cause: "pulmonary tuberculosis"; informant: Albert HOWELL (Erwin); died: 25 Oct. 1935; buried: Evergreen Cemetery; record (1935) # 23551.

BANNER, Mathison Lewis; age: 82 years; widower; parents: Lewis BANNER and Viona WHITSON (North Carolina); death cause: "dropsy"; informant: Ralph BANNER (Erwin); died: 15 Oct. 1935; buried: Martins Creek; record (1935) # 23552.

SHELTON, Guy Lee; born: 27 Jun. 1930; parents: Claude SHELTON and Viola FONDREN; death cause: "died in house fire"; informant: Ramon HARVEY (Erwin); died: 7 Oct. 1935; buried: Shelton Cemetery; record (1935) # 23553.

SHOOK, Burlin; female; born: 29 Jul. 1920; parents: Noel SHOOK (Foust, North Carolina) and Sis BLANKENSHIP; death cause: "died in the Claude SHELTON house fire"; informant: Ramon HARVEY (Erwin); died: 7 Oct. 1935; buried: Rice Creek; record (1935) # 23554.

LOWE, Mary; born: 28 Mar. 1872; widow of E.L. LOWE; parents: James BRITT and Nancy UNDERWOOD; death cause: "cerebral hemorrhage"; informant: C.E. LOWE (Greeneville); died: 14 Nov. 1935; buried: Tolly Cemetery; record (1935) # 26991.

DUNCAN, Samuel Thomas; born: 4 Sep. 1876 in McDowell County, North Carolina; husband of Lulu MARTIN; parents: John DUNCAN (McDowell County) and Myra HANKINS (McDowell County); death cause: "coronary thrombosis"; informant: Ada ADAMS (Marion, North Carolina); died: 1 Nov. 1935; buried: Evergreen; record (1935) # 26992.

NOREN, Sarah Lillian Hensley; age: 63 years; born: Mitchell County, North Carolina; wife of K.E. NOREN; parents: S.R. HENSLEY (North Carolina) and Harriett BURLESON (North Carolina); death cause: "heart failure"; informant: Virginia HENSLEY (Erwin); died: 11 Nov. 1935; buried: Bandanna, North Carolina; record (1935) # 26993.

STALLARD, Betty Joyce; born: 16 Nov. 1935; parents: Dalton STALLARD (Virginia) and Janice STUBBLEFIELD (Jefferson City, TN.); death cause: "premature"; informant: father (Erwin); died: 17 Nov. 1935; buried: Evergreen Cemetery; record (1935) # 26994.

WOODBY, Charlie Thomas; born: 2 Jun. 1918; parents: B.W. WOODBY (North Carolina) and Bessie GADDY (North Carolina); death cause: "accidental gunshot in face"; informant: A.J. GADDY (Johnson City); died: 16 Dec. 1935; buried: Anderson Chapel; record (1935) # 29170.

HILMON, Thomas; age: 45 years; born: North Carolina; husband of Birtie ESTEP; parents: Fred HILMON (North Carolina) and Carrie LEWIS (North Carolina); death cause: "gunshot wound, probably by own hands"; informant: wife (9th District); died: 25 Dec. 1935; buried: Honeycutt Cemetery; record (1935) # 29171.

RAY, Thomas Lafayette; born: 1 Mar. 1885; born: Alabama; husband of May B_ (illegible); parents: "unknown": death cause: "heart failure"; informant: wife (Erwin); died: 29 Dec. 1935; buried: Evergreen Cemetery; record (1935) # 29172.

HATCHER, Infant; male; parents: Henry HATCHER (Virginia) and Sarah BARTEE (Texas); death cause: "unknown"; informant: father (Erwin); died: 27 Nov. 1935; buried: Martins Creek; record # 29173.

KEESECKER, Etta May; born: 2 Jul. 1868 at Big Pool, Maryland; wife of A.G. KEESECKER; parents: William E. ALBRIGHT (West Virginia) and Elizabeth MEYERS (Maryland); death cause: "dropsy"; informant: husband (Erwin); died: 6 Dec. 1935; buried: Evergreen Cemetery; record (1935) # 29174.

DAVIS, Horace Mock; born: 5 Sep. 1883 in North Carolina; husband of Vertie DAVIS; parents: A. Jack DAVIS (North Carolina) and Celie RADFORD; death cause: "pulmonary tuberculosis"; informant: G.R. DAVIS (Erwin); died: 17 Dec. 1935; buried: Evergreen Cemetery; record (1935) # 29175.

WHITE, Bessie; born: 17 Dec. 1905 in Michigan; wife of John WHITE; parents: Joe WHITE and Mary MCINTURFF; death cause: "pulmonary tuberculosis"; informant: husband (Unicoi); died: 18 Dec. 1935; buried: Unicoi; record (1935) # 29176.

HOYLE, Fred; age: 27 years; single; parents: Jerry HOYLE (Greene County) and Susie ROBERTS (Virginia); death cause: "lobar pneumonia"; informant: father (Erwin); died: 21 Dec. 1935; buried: Martins Creek; record (1935) # 29177.

HAMPTON, Dan; born: 22 Sep. 1865; married; parents: William HAMPTON and Mellina TOMPKINS; death cause: "__ (illegible) rupture"; informant: Bill HAMPTON (Clear Branch); died: 28 Dec. 1935; buried: Martins Creek; record (1935) # 29178.

BOWMAN, J.C.; born: 23 Nov. 1935 in Mitchell County, North Carolina; parents: J.C. BOWMAN (Mitchell County) and Birdie SHEPPARD (Mitchell County); death cause: "hives"; informant: Wesley STREET; died: 13 Jan. 1936; buried: Street Cemetery; 1936 # 2418.

HUTCHINS, James M.; born: 26 Jun. 1871 in Mitchell County, North Carolina; husband of Francis HUTCHINS; parents: Wright HUTCHINS (North Carolina) and Polly STANLEY (North Carolina); death cause: "inflammatory rheumatism"; informant: wife (Erwin); died: 6 Jan. 1936; buried: Evergreen Cemetery; record (1936) # 2419.

PATE, Eliza; born: 9 Apr. 1859 in North Carolina; widow of Flem PATE; parents: "unknown"; death cause: "lobar pneumonia"; informant: James AMBROSE (Erwin); died: 13 Jan. 1936; buried: Fishery Cemetery; record (1936) # 2420.

COPELAND, George Alvin; born: 17 May 1857 in Thomaston, Maine; single; parents: Oliver COPELAND (Maine) and Rebecca PALMER (Maine); death cause: "nervous system disease"; informant: Mrs. W.J. WILLIAMSON (Erwin); died: 19 Jan. 1936; buried: Tinker Cemetery; record (1936) # 2421.

EDWARDS, Bobby Gene; born: 6 Jan. 1936; parents: Sol EDWARDS (North Carolina) and Mae PETERSON (North Carolina); death cause: "unknown, found dead in bed"; informant: S.K. DAVIS (Erwin); died: 10 Jan. 1936; buried: Martins Creek; record (1936) # 2422.

HENSLEY, Infant; male; born: 27 Jan. 1936; parents: John HENSLEY and Lila TIPTON; death cause: "something like croup"; informant: Henry HENSLEY (Flag Pond); died: 28 Jan. 1936; buried: Higgins Chapel; record (1936) # 2423.

ALLEN, Goldie; born: 22 Dec. 1913; wife of Oscar ALLEN; parents: E.L. GRINDSTAFF and Lottie CARVER; death cause: "pulmonary tuberculosis"; died: 2nd District, 15 Jan. 1936; record (1936) # 5296.

PERRY, Dallas Earl; born: 8 Apr. 1917; parents: Henry PERRY and Pearl WINTERS; death cause: "heart attack"; informant: mother (Shell Creek, Tennessee); died: 5 Feb. 1936; buried: Shell Creek, TN.; record (1936) # 5297.

AYERS, Ernest Allen; age: 3 weeks; parents: Columbus AYERS (North Carolina) and Lissie BENNETT (North Carolina); death cause: "not stated, found dead in bed"; informant: father (Unicoi); died: 12 Feb. 1936; buried: Phillips Cemetery; record (1936) # 5298.

TIPTON, William L.; age: 41 years; born: Mitchell County, North Carolina; husband of Vertie TIPTON; parents: Joseph TIPTON (Kentucky) and Minerva PHILLIPS (Mitchell County); death cause: "homicide, gunshot wound"; informant: Lottie TIPTON (Forbes, North Carolina); died: 8 Feb. 1936; buried: Forbes, NC.; record # 5299.

MCNABB, Ella Belle; born: 16 Dec. 1877; wife of Grover Seldon MCNABB; parents: William S. ERWIN and Hester WOODWARD; death cause: "hysterectomy, pneumonia"; informant: G.S. MCNABB (Erwin); died: 8 Feb. 1936; buried: Jobe Cemetery; record # 5300.

PUTNAM, Mila L.; born: 10 Sep. 1867 in Shelby, North Carolina; husband of Louise __ (illegible); parents: Drewery Alston PUTNAM (Shelby, NC.) and Carolina IRBY (Shelby, NC.); death cause: "pneumonia"; informant: A.D. UPDIKE (Erwin); died: 11 Feb. 1936; buried: Evergreen Cemetery; record (1936) # 5301.

HUGHES, Earl Eugene; born: 26 Dec. 1935; parents: Robert HUGHES and Gladys WHISNANT (Morganton, NC.); death cause: "probably asphyxiation, found dead in bed"; informant: father (Erwin); died: 25 Feb. 1936; buried: Martins Creek; record (1936) # 5302.

MASTERS, Shirley; age: 5 months; parents: C.B. MASTERS and Lea BAILEY (North Carolina); death cause: "pneumonia"; informant: father (Erwin); died: 1 Feb. 1936; buried: Duncan Cemetery; record # 5303.

VANOVER, Georgia; born: 16 Jan. 1933; parents: Robert A. VANOVER and Eula EDNEY (North Carolina); death cause: "whooping cough"; informant: C.E. VANOVER (Erwin); died: 2 Feb. 1936; buried: McInturff Cemetery; record (1936) # 5304.

HENSLEY, Paul Carroll; born: 14 Aug. 1926; parents: Ebb HENSLEY and Florence HARRIS; death cause: "influenza and pneumonia"; informant: father (Erwin); died: 7 Feb. 1936; buried: Evergreen Cemetery; record (1936) # 5305.

ERWIN, Lula Jarvis; born: 12 Jul. 1874 in Washington County; wife of Jessie Kendrick ERWIN; parents: Abner JARVIS (Madison County, NC.) and Sarah SCOTT (Washington County); death cause: "pulmonary tuberculosis"; informant: J.R. ERWIN (Erwin); died: 8 Feb. 1936; buried: Chucky Cemetery; record (1936) # 5306.

HOYLE, Martha; born: __ May 1860 in Rutherfordton County, North Carolina; single; parents: Hiram HOYLE (South Carolina) and Myra PARTON (North Carolina); death cause: "cerebral hemorrhage"; informant: Jerry HOYLE (Erwin); died: 9 Feb. 1936; buried: Martins Creek; record (1936) # 5307.

WILSON, Rose Marie; age: 3 years, 5 months and 10 days; born: Yancey County, North Carolina; parents: U.D. WILSON (Yancey County); and Leona HONEYCUTT (Yancey County); death cause: "pneumonia"; informant: father (Erwin); died: 10 Feb. 1936; buried: Yancey County; record (1936) # 5308.

HICKS, Robert Franklin, II; born: 15 Jan. 1936; parents: George Dewey HICKS (New York) and Anna May VEST; death cause: "pneumonia"; informant: father (Erwin); died: 14 Feb. 1936; buried: Swingle Cemetery; record (1936) # 5309.

KIRK, Billie Jean; born: 11 Jun. 1935; parents: Bill KIRK and Rosa JONES; death cause: "pneumonia"; informant: father (Erwin); died: 16 Feb. 1936; buried: Fishery Cemetery; record (1936) # 5310.

WHITE, Elsie; born: 12 Feb. 1936; parents: Robert Landon WHITE and Ruth HENDERON (Dante, Virginia); death cause: "pneumonia"; informant: father (Erwin); died: 23 Feb. 1936; buried: family cemetery; record (1936) # 5311.

TITTLE, Mary Elizabeth; age: 56 years; widow of C.B. TITTLE; parents: James SIMMONS (North Carolina) and Emmaline MASHBURN (North Carolina); death cause: "pneumonia"; informant: J.F. TITTLE (Erwin); died: 25 Feb. 1936; buried: Evergreen Cemetery; record (1936) # 5312.

MATHIS, Maude Tipton; age: 27 years; born: Burnsville, North Carolina; wife of Sandy MATHIS; parents: J.C. TIPTON (North Carolina) and Minnie PHILLIPS (North Carolina); death cause: "cellulitis in left leg"; informant: Mack TIPTON (Erwin); died: 28 Feb. 1936; buried: Liberty Cemetery; record (1936) # 5313.

RIDDLE, Nancy Jane; born: 25 Aug. 1854; widow of James Marion RIDDLE; parents: John TOMPKINS and Martha TILSON; death cause: "pneumonia"; informant: Dewey RIDDLE (Clear Branch); died: 18 Feb. 1936; buried: family cemetery; record (1936) # 5314.

COATS, Eliza; born: 15 Nov. 1866; born: Madison County, North Carolina; widow of __ (illegible) COATS; parents: Nathan ALLEN and Lucinda WHEELER; death cause: "nephritis, uremia"; informant: James COATS (Flag Pond); died: 10 Feb. 1936; buried: Flag Pond; record (1936) # 5315.

COATS, Gertie; born: 18 Jan. 1895; wife of Charley G. COATS; parents: Robert GENTRY and Lula SAMS; death cause: "pneumonia"; informant: James COATS (Flag Pond); died: 24 Feb. 1936; buried: N.B. RICE Cemetery; record (1936) # 5316.

BRIGGS, Wanda Herrin; born: 18 Feb. 1936; parents: Kick BRIGGS (North Carolina) and Nellie HANEN (North Carolina); death cause: "unknown, found dead in bed"; died: 25 Mar. 1936; buried: Erwin; record (1936) # 8436.

BAILEY, Hiram B.; born: 25 Aug. 1858 in Yancey County, North Carolina; widower; parents: Hiram BAILEY (North Carolina) and Sallie DEYTON (North Carolina); death cause: "general breakdown"; informant: Bernie BAILEY (Erwin); died: 9 Mar. 1936; buried: Martins Creek; record (1936) # 8433.

HUGHES, Infant; male; parents: Dolphus HUGHES (North Carolina) and Bertie TAYLOR (North Carolina); death cause: "premature"; informant: father (Erwin): born/died: 14 Mar. 1936; buried: Bailey Cemetery; record (1936) # 8434.

BANNER, Linda Hensley; born: 8 Jul. 1902; wife of Martin L. BANNER; parents: Zeb HENSLEY and Mary TAYLOR; death cause: "puerperal hemorrhage"; informant: husband (Erwin); died: 16 Mar. 1936; buried: Evergreen Cemetery; record (1936) # 8435.

BRADY, Jennetta A.; born: 2 Aug. 1863 in Indiana; wife of Samuel E. BRADY; parents: father "unknown" and __ VANDEWATER (Indiana); death cause: "pulmonary tuberculosis"; informant: husband (Erwin); died: 21 Mar. 1936; buried: Martins Creek; record (1936) # 8436.

BAILEY, Frank Jarvis; born: 7 Jan. 1936; parents: Hiram BAILEY and Rachel PETERS; death cause: "pneumonia"; informant: J.C. FOSTER (Clear Branch); died: date not recorded; buried: Sams Cemetery; record (1936) # 8337.

MASHBURN, William; born: 1 Jan. 1857; married; parents: Caloway MASHBURN and Marilla PATIE; death cause: "dropsy"; informant: Lizzie TIPTON (Clear Branch); died: 21 Mar. 1936; buried: Tilson Cemetery; record (1936) # 8438.

FARNOR, John Berthafer; born: 24 May 1878 in Greene County; married; parents: Jacob S. FARNOR (Greene County) and Rebecca J. HARDIN (Greene County); death cause: "tuberculosis"; informant: Julia FARNOR (Clear Branch); died: 30 Mar. 1936; record (1936) # 8439.

RUNION, John Roper; born: 26 May 1847 in Dandridge, Jefferson County, Tennessee; husband of Catherine FOSTER; parents: Abram RUNION and mother "unknown"; death cause: "nephritis and uremia"; informant: J.L. HIGGINS (Flag Pond); died: 8 May 1936; buried: Higgins Creek; record (1936) # 8440.

BLANKENSHIP, Jimmie; born: 22 Jun. 1934; parents: father not stated and Texanner BLANKENSHIP; death cause: "bronchial pneumonia"; informant: mother (Flag Pond); died: 16 Mar. 1936; buried: Rice Creek; record (1936) # 8441.

RANDOLPH, Elzora Jane; born: 4 Jun. 1878 in Be Long, North Carolina; wife of T.M. RANDOLPH; parents: Samuel RANDOLPH (North Carolina) and Cordelia HENSLEY (North Carolina); death cause: "paralysis"; informant: Murphy RANDOLPH (Flag Pond); died: 17 Mar. 1936; buried: Rice Creek; record (1936) # 8442.

CRAINE, Wesley O.; born: 2 Feb. 1936; parents: Joe William CRAINE (Madison County, NC.) and Dianah BOICE (West Virginia); death cause: "bronchial pneumonia"; informant: Mrs. Fate BLANKENSHIP (Flag Pond); died: 23 Mar. 1936; buried: Higgins Chapel; record (1936) # 8443.

BUCKNER, Duskie; age: 65 years; born: Cherokee County, Georgia; wife of James A. BUCKNER; parents: __ EDWARDS and mother "unknown"; death cause: "pneumonia"; informant: husband (Flag Pond); died: 26 Mar. 1936; buried: Higgins Chapel; record (1936) # 8444.

CAMPBELL, Bessie Markhan; age: 39 years, 11 months and 29 days; born: Kentucky; wife of James S. CAMPBELL; parents: John MARKHAM and Jane STAPLETON (Virginia); death cause: "child birth, septic infection"; informant: husband (Unicoi); died: 4 Apr. 1936; record (1936) # 11348.

HANKINS, Malinda; born: 28 Mar. 1936; parents: J.F. HANKINS (Cumming, Georgia) and Francis Anne TUCKER; death cause: "premature birth"; informant: father (Erwin); died: 5 Apr. 1936; buried: Jobe Cemetery; record (1936) # 11349.

RIDDLE, Tom; born: 16 Jun. 1869 in North Carolina; husband of Hazel WEBB; parents: David RIDDLE (North Carolina) and Liza RIDDLE (North Carolina); death cause: "hypo static pneumonia and heart failure"; informant: wife (Erwin); died: 18 Apr. 1936; buried: Peterson Cemetery; record (1936) # 11350.

MCKINNEY, William Stokes; age: 55 years, 7 months and 13 days; born: North Carolina; husband of Donna Elizabeth MCKINNEY; parents: J.W. MCKINNEY (North Carolina) and Margaret BURRIS (North Carolina); death cause: "heart failure"; informant: Ellen MCKINNEY (Johnson City); died: 19 Mar. 1936; buried: Erwin; record 91936) # 11351.

WILSON, Mable; born: 25 May 1915; wife of John R. WILSON; parents: Charles CASEY and Bessie DETHRIDGE; death cause: "pleurisy and pneumonia"; informant: father (Embreeville); died: 20 Mar. 1936; buried; Embreeville Cemetery; record (1936) # 11352.

SHEHAN, Virginia; parents: Melvin SHEHAN and Mollie HILL (North Carolina); death cause: "unknown"; born/died: 7 Apr. 1936; buried: family cemetery; record (1936) #11353.

WHALEY, Mary Demona; born: 22 Feb. 1881; widow of James Franklin WHALEY; parents: Will HUSKINS and Mary POORE; death cause: "hypo static pneumonia"; died: 19 Apr. 1936; buried: Martins Creek; record (1936) # 11354.

GARLAND, Hugh Ray; parents: Celbert GARLAND and Susanna WILLIAMS; death cause: "unknown"; born/died: 29 Mar. 1936; buried: Limestone Cove; record (1936) # 11355.

TIPTON, Bettie Joe; born: 20 Jan. 1936; parents: J.M. TIPTON and Juanita FORBES; death cause: "influenza and pneumonia"; informant: father (Unicoi); died: 15 Feb. 1936; buried: McInturff Cemetery; record (1936) # 11356.

INGRAM, Leona; born: __ May 1934; parents: Manassa INGRAM (Mitchell County, NC.) and Rosa BARNETT (Virginia); death cause: "pneumonia"; informant: father (Unicoi); died: 5 Apr. 1936; buried: Peterson Cemetery; record (1936) # 11357.

BOWMAN, Mary Susan; born: 14 Oct. 1872; single; parents: D.E. BOWMAN and Nancy BUCK; death cause: illegible; informant: Andrew BRUMMITT (Unicoi); died: date not recorded; buried: Brummitt Cemetery; record (1936) # 11358.

BRUMMETT, Hattie Carver; born: 17 Oct. 1905; wife of Andrew BRUMMETT; parents: John CARVER and Caroline MOORE; death cause: "pupural septicemia and pneumonia"; informant: husband (Unicoi); died: 29 Feb. 1936; record (1936) # 11359.

TILSON, Eliza J.; born: 29 Sep. 1860; wife of L.S. TILSON; parents: William E. PARKS and June DAVIS; death cause: "cerebral hemorrhage"; informant: Lela BUCKNER (Erwin); died: 4 May 1936; buried: Jobe Cemetery; record (1936) # 13939.

PETERS, Vreeland Franklin; born: 2 Dec. 1901 in Halifax County, Virginia; husband of Alice Caroline PETERS; parents: T.H. PETERS (North Carolina) and Minnie Belle BRENTLEY (Wythe County, VA.); death cause: "sarcoma of liver"; informant: father (Erwin); died: 5 May 1936; buried: Evergreen Cemetery; record (1936) # 13940.

BOONE, Samuel; born: 7 May 1884 in Burnsville, North Carolina; husband of Irene WALTER; parents: J.S. BOONE (North Carolina) and E_ (illegible) RAY (North Carolina); death cause: "heart failure"; informant: wife (Erwin); died: 6 May 1936; buried: Jobe Cemetery; record (1936) # 13941.

COOPER, John D.; born: 14 Mar. 1914; born: Yancey County, North Carolina; single; parents: Samuel COOPER and Oma TIPTON (Yancey County, NC.); death cause: "ruptured ulcer, peritonitis"; informant:

Mose COOPER (Erwin); died: 24 May 1936; buried: Martins Creek; record (1936) # 13942.

MCINTOSH, Alexander; born: 12 Sep. 1932; parents: Sam MCINTOSH (Yancey County, NC.) and Bessie TREADWAY; death cause: "probably diphtheria"; informant: Maud RANDELL (Flag Pond); died: 17 May 1936; buried: Hog Skin Cemetery; record (1936) # 13943.

STOCKTON, Will; age: 75 years; husband of Theen STOCKTON; parents: Samuel STOCKTON and Elizabeth HORNE; death cause: "nephritis and uremia"; informant: T.E. SAMS (Flag Pond); died: date not recorded; buried: Hog Skin Cemetery; record (1936) # 13944.

STOCKTON, Vertie Florence; born: 21 Dec. 1935; parents: Cotner SHELTON and Annie Mae ENGLE; death cause: "whooping cough"; died: date not stated; buried: 19 Jun. 1936; record (1936) # 16397.

EDWARDS, Allie Jane; born: 23 Jun. 1898; wife of John Henry EDWARDS; parents: C.C. WHITE (Georgia) and Mary SIMMONS (North Carolina); death cause: "appendix ruptured, operation"; informant: husband (Erwin); died: 3 Jun. 1936; buried: McInturff Cemetery; record (1936) # 16398.

KEESECKER, Adrian Garrett; born: 8 Aug. 1867 in Tomahawk, West Virginia; husband of Etta May KEESECKER; parents: Jacob KEESECKER and Elizabeth JORDAN; death cause: "heart failure"; informant: W.O. KEESECKER (Erwin); died: 11 May 1936; buried: Evergreen Cemetery; record (1936) # 16399.

DOVER, Infant; male; parents: father not stated and Lucy DOVER (North Carolina); death cause: "premature birth"; born/died: 23 Mar. 1936; buried: Erwin; record (1936) # 16400.

DOVER, Infant; male; parents: father not stated and Lucy DOVER (North Carolina); death cause: "premature birth"; born/died: 23 Mar. 1936; buried: Erwin; record (1936) # 16401.

HUGHES, Ruby; age: 19 years; wife of Gather HUGHES; parents: William LOWING and Bessie THOMAS (North Carolina); death cause: "tuberculosis"; informant: father (Erwin); died: 28 Jun. 1936; buried: Bailey Cemetery; record (1936) # 16402.

BYRD, Myrtle Marie; parents: Laurence BYRD (Yancey County, NC.) and Velva WILLIS (Yancey County, NC.); death cause: not stated;

informant: father (Clear Branch); born/died: 20 Jun. 1936; buried: Willis Cemetery; record (1936) # 16403.

SILVERS, Edward; born: 28 Jun. 1927; parents: Thore SILVERS and Florence HENSLEY; death cause: "accidental gunshot wound by smaller brother"; informant: mother (Flag Pond); died: 12 Jun. 1936; buried: Silvers Cemetery; record (1936) # 16404.

TIPTON, Earl; born: 18 Feb. 1916; single; parents: Leroy TIPTON and Estell SHELTON (Shelton Laurel, NC.); death cause: "heart failure"; informant: father (Flag Pond); died: 14 Jun. 1936; buried: Blankenship Cemetery; record (1936) # 16505.

HURT, Ruth; age: 2 months and 2 days; parents: M.L. HURT (North Carolina) and Phina MCKINNEY (Carter County); death cause: not stated; informant: father (Unicoi); died: 4 Aug. 1936; buried: Bryant Cemetery; record (1936) # 21440.

NORRIS, Lucinda; born: 21 Nov. 1863; single; parents: Chester NORRIS and Rachel MCINTURFF; death cause: not stated; informant: W.S. NORRIS (Johnson City); died: 17 Jul. 1936; buried: Peoples Cemetery; record (1936) # 21441.

CRIGGER, Lucille Virginia; born: 12 Aug. 1936; parents: W. Kyle CRIGGER (Grayson County, VA.) and Eula Mae WEAVER (Riner, VA.); death cause: "premature"; informant: father (Erwin); died: 13 Aug. 1936; record (1936) # 21442.

MATHES, Loda; born: 9 May 1875 in Washington County; husband of Sarah MATHES; parents: Will MATHES (North Carolina) and Hester BAILEY; death cause: "paralysis"; informant: George W. MATHES (Erwin); died: 29 Aug. 1936; buried: Martins Creek; record # 21443.

NELSON, Sadie Loetta; age: 60 years; born: Yancey County, North Carolina; widow of Joseph NELSON; parents: Silas STEVENS (North Carolina) and Jane HUGHES (North Carolina); death cause: "bronchial asthma"; informant: H.R. NELSON (Erwin); died: 27 Aug. 1936; buried: Jobe Cemetery; record (1936) # 21444.

WILLIAMS, Jeff; born: 18 Apr. 1917; single; parents: Hiram R. WILLIAMS (Yancey County, NC.) and Jaunita LOVELACE; death cause: "tubercular spine"; informant: father (Erwin); died: 9 Jun. 1936; buried: Martins Creek; record (1936) # 21445.

TIPTON, Ruth; born: 2 Feb. 1930; parents: Charlie TIPTON and Bertie CALLAHAN; death cause: "broncho pneumonia"; informant: father (Embreeville); died: 16 Apr. 1936; buried: Bethesda Cemetery; record (1936) # 21446.

SHELTON, Pearl Elizabeth; age: 24 years; wife of Andrew SHELTON; parents: Silas STEVENS (North Carolina) and Rosa HOUSTON (North Carolina); death cause: "heart lesion"; informant: Norman EDWARDS (Erwin); died: 10 Jul. 1936; buried: Ray Cemetery; record (1936) # 21447.

EDWARDS, Sarah; born: __ Apr. 1868 in Mitchell County, North Carolina; single; parents: Wilson EDWARDS (North Carolina) and Martha GOUGE; death cause: "malignant uterine growth"; informant: Nat EDWARDS (Erwin); died: 23 Jul. 1936; buried: Martins Creek; record (1936) # 21448.

SMITH, Arlene; born: 22 Feb. 1857 in Sullivan County; wife of James SMITH; parents: "unknown"; died in the 4th District, 19 Aug. 1936; record (1936) # 21449.

DAVIS, Julia Bernice; born: 25 Apr. 1936; parents: William DAVIS and Nola CLARK (Carter County); death cause: "epilepsy"; informant: Monroe CLARK (Erwin); died: 27 Sep. 1936; buried: Berry Cemetery; record (1936) # 26132.

BENNETT, Callie; born: 25 Jul. 1870; widow of Harrison BENNETT; parents: Wilson BRITT and Addie PHILLIPS; death cause: "carcinoma of bladder"; informant: J.J. BENNETT (Unicoi); died: 22 Aug. 1936; buried: Phillips Cemetery; record (1936) # 26133.

INGRAM, Smith Woodward; parents: Manassa INGRAM (Mitchell County, NC.) and Rosa BARNETT (Wise County, VA.); death cause: "premature"; informant: N.A. INGRAM (Unicoi); born/died: 19 Apr. 1936; buried: Peterson Cemetery; record (1936) # 26134.

INGRAM, Mary; parents: Manassa INGRAM (Mitchell County, NC.) and Rosa BARNETT (Wise County, VA.); death cause: "premature"; informant: N.A. INGRAM (Unicoi); born/died: 19 Apr. 1936; buried: Peterson Cemetery; record (1936) # 26135.

INGRAM, William; parents: Manassa INGRAM (Mitchell County, NC.) and Rosa BARNETT (Wise County, VA.); death cause: "premature";

informant: N.A. INGRAM (Unicoi); born/died: 19 Apr. 1936; buried: Peterson Cemetery; record (1936) # 26136.

SMITH, Clara; born: 1 May 1861; wife of Thomas M. SMITH; parents: Robert ALLEN and Sara MCINTURFF; death cause: "cerebral hemorrhage"; informant: husband (Erwin); died: 12 Oct. 1936; buried: Martins Creek; record (1936) # 26137.

JONES, Roy Harrison; born: 30 Sep. 1914 in North Carolina; husband of Dorothy JONES; parents: Manuel JONES (North Carolina) and Mollie LAUGHERN (North Carolina); death cause: "crushed between wagon and tree"; informant: Zeb JONES (Unicoi); died: 12 Oct. 1936; buried: Barnett Cemetery; record (1936) # 28694.

DEVAULT, Francis Julia; born: 12 Sep. 1879 in Zanesville, Ohio; widow of J. Wilbur DEVAULT; parents: Charles CALLISTER (Ohio) and Olive VESTAL (Ohio); death cause: "cerebral hemorrhage"; informant: Eva C. CLICK (Columbus, Ohio); died: 18 Nov. 1936; buried: Oak Hill Cemetery, Johnson City; record (1936) # 28695.

HUGHES, James William; born: 30 Nov. 1914 in Shelby County, Tennessee; single; parents: W.F. HUGHES (Shelby County) and Minnie Sue BLAIN (Fayette County, TN.); death cause: "run down by automobile, head injury"; died: 26 Nov. 1936; buried: Colliersville, Tennessee; record (1936) # 28696.

TAPP, Annie June; age: 4 months and 18 days; parents: Frank TAPP and Rachel JONES; death cause: "whooping cough"; informant: father (Erwin); died: 11 Nov. 1936; record (1936) # 28697.

BANNER, Howard Lawrence; born: 16 Jun. 1936; parents: Walter Ernest BANNER and Retta GARLAND (Mitchell County, NC.); death cause: illegible; informant: father (Erwin); died: 16 Nov. 1936; buried: Martins Creek; record (1936) # 28698.

HENSLEY, Sulvania; age: "about 66 years"; single; parents: father "unknown" and Polly HENSLEY (Madison County, NC.); death cause: not stated; informant: Jim SPARKS (Flag Pond); died: 30 Nov. 1936; buried: Hensley Cemetery; record (1936) # 31669.

HONEYCUTT, Edna Mae; age: 5 years, 2 months and 8 days; parents: George Washington HONEYCUTT (Foster Creek, NC.) and Thelma RAMSEY (Faust, NC.); death cause: "malignant neoplasm of abdomen"; informant: father (Clear Branch); died: 5 Oct. 1936; buried: Shelton Cemetery; record (1936) # 31670.

BROWN, William; born: 3 Sep. 1849 in Troutville, Virginia; husband of Mary Virginia BROWN; parents: "unknown"; death cause: "heart disease"; informant: E.A. BROWN (Erwin); died: 2 Dec. 1936; buried: Evergreen Cemetery; record (1936) # 31671.

WHITE, David J.; parents: J.C. WHITE and Bessie HARRIS (North Carolina); death cause: "premature"; informant: father (Erwin); born and died: 26 Dec. 1936; buried: Jobe Cemetery; record (1936) # 31672.

MILLER, James M.; age: 59 years, 9 months and 14 days; born: Carter County; married; parents: Wesley MILLER (Yancey County, NC.) and Eliza MILLER (Wilkes County, NC.); death cause: "myo carditis"; informant: Thomas MILLER (Erwin); died: 29 Dec. 1936; buried: Johnson City; record (1936) # 31673.

FISHER, Louie Clyde; born: 23 Feb. 1879; husband of Virlie May MOYERS; parents: Henry FISHER (Virginia) and Amanda Jane DUKES; death cause: "heart failure"; informant: wife (Erwin); died: 13 Dec. 1936; buried: Evergreen Cemetery; record (1936) # 31674.

HENSLEY, Robert Edward; born: 19 May 1930; parents: Wallace HENSLEY and Mary ROGERS; death cause: "meningitis and influenza"; informant: father (Erwin); died: 18 Dec. 1936; buried: Martins Creek; record (1936) # 31675.

HIGGINS, John Henry; age: 55 years; born: Yancey County, North Carolina; widower of Minorca HIGGINS; parents: John Henry HIGGINS (North Carolina) and Anna HIGGINS (North Carolina); death cause: "heart failure"; informant: Shelby HIGGINS (Erwin); died: 15 Dec. 1936; buried: Higgins, North Carolina; record (1936) # 31676.

TREADWAY, Albert J.; born: 4 Nov. 1936; parents: Lewis TREADWAY and Kate PHILLIPS; death cause: "pneumonia"; informant: father (Flag Pond); died: 23 Nov. 1936; buried: Sams Creek; record (1936) # 31677.

MCINTURFF, Peggy Jane; born: 22 Jan. 1936; parents: Willard MCINTURFF and Pansia MILLER; death cause: "jaundice"; informant: father (Unicoi); died: 25 Jan. 1936; buried: Sams Cemetery; record (1936) # 32303.

TIPTON, Charles F.; born: 14 Aug. 1889; husband of Birtie TIPTON; parents: Will TIPTON and Alice HAMPTON; death cause: "hepatic cirrhosis and peritonitis"; informant: wife (Embreeville); died: 23 Oct. 1936; buried: Bethesda; record (1936) # 32304.

BARNES, James Berry; born: 5 Aug. 1864 in Asheville, North Carolina; husband of Mary Magdaline BARNES; parents: William BARNES (London, England) and Ellen MAYS (England); death cause: "paralysis"; informant: W.C. BARNES (Clear Branch); died: 9 Mar. 1936; buried: Rocky Fork Cemetery; record (1936) # 32652.

INDEX

ABELL, Thomas B. 68 Thomas F. 68 T.F. 68
ABNER, English 6
ADAMS, Ada 291 Anee Lee 52 Callie Prater 247 Charles H. 231 C.W. 247 Mrs. C.W. 140 James 52 Nora 259 Sam 195
ADKINS, B_ 131 Cass 216 Jim 131 Johanna 258 Lilly 168 Mynter 90 Rickels 126 Sam L. 216
AKERS, J.O. 172
ALBERTSON, Catherine 99 Infant 47 Jack 47
ALBRIGHT, William E. 292
ALDRIDGE, William A. 188
ALEN, Eliza 251
ALEXANDER, F. 39 Mary Catherine 39
ALFORD, Mary Elizabeth 260
ALFRED, Parlee 136
ALLEN, Ada 193 Edna 242 Emma 284 Eva 139 Emma 284 Eva 139 Goldie 294 Harvey 148 217 Isaac 82 241 243 I.G. 57 James Virgil 82 Jasper 242 Jennie 143 Mary A. 38 Nancy 34 Nathan 296 Oscar 294 Rachel 25 Robert 303 R.H. 242 Sarah 57 Willard 277 William 148 Wilma Etta 241
ALLISON, Ellie 47 N.H. 66 Sarah Elizabeth 66
ALLIS, Nellie 225
ALLRED, B.M. 187 Mrs. B.M 187 Joseph 187 Myrtle M. 198 T.H. 198
ALLRES, B.M. 41
ALTMAIER, Peter 157
AMBERUST, Carolina 24
AMBROSE, Alfred M. 168 Alto 265 Annie 74 132 237 Bernie Sherwood 259 Charles 168 197 Cloyd 259 265 Fannie 141 Hattie McInturff 221 Henry 57 159 209 Hester 96 James 259 293 James H. 144 221 John 141 144 240 Ralph William 197 Wade 259 265 Wade R. 221
AMBROS, Annie 171
ANDERSON, B_ 213 Henrietta 239 Isaac 37 I.H. 37 Jake 190 James 7 John 214 239 John F. 147 Josephine 29 Mrs. J.H. 213 J.R. 175 Lillian 110 Lucinda 94 Mary 3 7 Mollie 269 Shep M. 37 Sue 255 Taylor 8 William Loyd 16
ANDERS, Essie May 28 E.G. 38 40 Haben 262 Isaac Grady 262 Lola May 105 Nancy 38 40 Rachel Mahala 223 Wordin 28
ANDREWS, Elsie 137 E.B. 137
ANGEL, David 52 Glen 267
ANGLER, Emma 111
ANGLE, Leucretia 290 Noma 189
ARNETT, Edwin 83 John 83 Smith B. 252
ARROWOOD, Dessie 282 Earl 273 Infant 256 John W. 166 256 Madeline 166 Pearl 273
ARRWOOD, Burnie 209 Sarah 118 Sarah Jane 209

ARWOOD, Leveasy 36 Sinda 66
ASHBIN, Hobert Lee 116
ASHLEY, Ella 218
ATKINS, __ 274 Ann Myrtle 251
  Clingman 84 Jason 131 J.B. 283
  Litie 214 Myrtle 198 Russell 283
  Tillie 73
AUSBIN, Hobert 116
AUSBON, Ida 4
AUSTIN, Manual 246
AYERS, __ 228 Callie 238
  Columbus 294 Ernest Allen 294
  R.M. 238 Tilda 7
B__, Cordelia 173 Eugen 173
BACON, May 199
BAILEY, Alberta 205 Alfred 225
  Ancil 242 A.B. 126 A.L. 66 121
  A.S. 42 Bashie 116 Bernie 255
  296 Calvin Burnie 281 Catherine
  181 Charles P. 213 Cordelia 98
  Cordia 70 Curtis Theodore 255
  C.W. 241 Dalia 136 Daniel 213
  David 162 Delcina 174 Delie 129
  Don 109 Earl 189 Edd 162 Edgle
  118 Elbert Lenoir 286 Ellen 73
  Essa 198 E.D. 189 232 E.L. 53
  Frank Jarvis 297 Gladys 232
  Hester 301 Hiram 174 198 296
  297 Hiram B. 296 Infant 32 35
  162 James 225 241 Jane 26 27
  119 Jeff 100 Jena 149 Jessie 286
  John 70 73 97 162 195 200 212
  248 Johnnie Austin 213 Julia 241
  Julia Etta 195 June 181 J.C. 238
  J.D. 198 J.E. 239 Lea 294 Lonn
  97 Mack 241 Mamie 200 248
  Marie 183 254 Mary 30 106 118
  242 Mary Elizabeth 200 Mary
  Jane 225 Mary Lee 145 Milton
A. 35 Milton O. 22 Minnie L. 19
  Morgan 32 99 145 280 Myra 274
  M.L. 213 M_ 98 Narion 99 Nora
  241 O.L. 260 Pearl 236 244 Polly
  Ann 282 Reece 189 Sally 127
  Sam 181 183 205 242 S.G. 119
  Teddy Ross 281 Tempa 275
  Texie 109 Theodore 22 Tobie
  Lee 260 Vista Belle 286 William
  W. 255 Willis 95
BAILS, Katie 175
BAILY, Ed 101 Effie 139 John
  Lester 73 Rosy 101 W.F. 73
BAINES, Ethel 278
BAKER, __ 209 Anna 89 Cassie
  28 Charles A. 34 C.H. 58 David
  6 D.W. 41 Edna 235 Edna Lyle
  26 Ezekiel 171 Ezkill 171 Fina
  162 Fine 139 Floyd 118 Frank
  W. 183 F.W. 150 Jane 58 Jessie
  120 J.W. 41 Love Lee 66 Maggie
  66 Martha Charlotte 236 Martha
  C. 171 Mildred 118 Minerva 184
  Nat 1 Polly 21 Sadie 211 Vina
  125 Will 41 William 26 Wilson
  137 171 W.H. 235
BALDWIN, Axie 230
BALES, Katy 184 Lizzie 188 Lula
  81 William 288 W.N. 29
BALEY, A.L. 86 John 80 Mary 80
BALIS, Jessie 24 Nattie 225
  Rebecca 67
BALLARD, Lucy 166
BALL, George 179 Lula 179
BANKS, Birt 151 Cecil 255 Flora
  236 Helen Marie 173 Infant 255
  James 17 John 159 John F. 228
  Minnie 277 Moses 159

BANKS (continued) Nancie 159
Robert 173 Ruth 228 Walter 173
BANNER, __ 190 Alvin Lee 139
Billie 241 Bob 241 David S. 164
Dora 212 D.S. 164 Febe 48
Henry 212 Howard Lawrence 303
H.B. 240 John 259 Jude 105 Julia
E. 27 J. William 259 J.M. 234
Lewis 170 291 Lillie 240 Linda
Hensley 296 Louis 49 Lucretia
259 Martin 185 261 Martin Lee
139 Martin L. 296 Mary 158
Mathison Lewis 291 Mollie 123
Monroe 158 Paul 185 Phebe E.
29 Phoeba Ann 74 Ralph 291 S_
98 Walter Ernest 303 Will 259
BANNET, Mollie E. 194
BANNISTER, Mildred 267
BARE, J.E. 123
BARLOW, Chafon 48
BARNES, Geneva 89 James Berry
305 Lizzie 18 Mary Magdaline
305 Parker 12 Vivian 37 104 134
216 William 305 W.C. 305
BARNETT, Addie Williams 289
Aron 126 Barbara C. 289 Barnett
170 Bell 178 Bessie May 245
Bettie 142 Charles S. 49 Dave
217 Demps 289 290 D.W. 247
Elizabeth 118 276 Etta 215 Geter
113 194 204 Henry 111 Infant 87
161 Isaac 111 229 Jack 115
James 112 Jeter 254 J.D. 126
J.M. 99 Mrs. J.W. 156 Marial
Alderson Snead 47 Marie 110
Marion 110 Martha 112 Nancy
49 102 170 172 205 Nannie 204
Nellie 1 Phillip 136 Richard Lee
290 rosa 299 302 R.C. 115 Sarah
160; Sci 229 Sinda 85 Smith 87
229 247 262 S.B. 193 S.E. 110
T.C. 217 Walker 63 William 170
254 Willie Denton 98 W.J. 170
BARNET, Pansy 284
BARNS, Vivian 216
BARRON, Infant 140 Roy L. 140
BARRY, David 95 David M. 91
Everett J. 34 John 41 91 160
John W. 160 Julie 176 L.C. 160
Manetia 95
BARR, Florence Virginia 113
W.M. 113
BARTEE, Sarah 292
BARTLEY, J.W. 69 Martha E. 169
W.E. 169
BARTTIG, John W. 49
BATES, Hoogis 155 James C. 155
Robert 155
BAUMGARDNER, Ruth Ann 138
T.C. 138
BAXTER, Bird D. 57 Green 57
Infant 41 Letticia 57 L.B. 249
L.D. 41 May 178
BAYER, A.L. 69 Francis Louise
69
BAYLESS, Alice 197 Lee 114
Sallie 179
BEALE, John 55
BEALS, John 30 Joseph M. 98
T.A. 98
BEAM, Daniel 147 Mary 147
Rettie 273 Sarah 156
BEAN, Bill 251 John 251 Kate
113 Lydia 288 Myrtle 251
BEAVER, Infant 200 Red 200
BECKELHIMER, Ray 285
William Daniel 284
BECKET, Floyd 155 Infant 155

BECK, Infant 23 Julian J. 23 Mrs. J.J. 23
BEESON, Sarah 180
BELCHER, J.H. 201 Wesley 201
BELLYSE, __ 76
BELL, David W. 222 Francis 261 Harriett 157 Hattie 214 J.B. 214
BENEFIELD, Mary 156
BENETT, Cora 46 James 62 Matt 48 62
BENFIELD, Emely 93
BENNETT, __ 268 Ada 80 237 Amos 22 179 207 Anderson 210 Arch 194 290 A.N. 78 Bayless 179 Bessie 146 148 Binder 89 Callie 290 302 Charles 237 Clayton 220 Cora 74 C.F. 290 C.I. 194 Derkie 78 Destie 251 Destie Lee 179 Elish 209 Elizabeth 157 Emery 230 Essie 36 Frank 22 Gaither 204 Gather 255 Harrison 79 290 302 Mrs. Ike 194 Infant 220 Jonnie 167 Josephine 12 19 J.J. 302 Lee 179 Lissie 294 Mae 140 Maggie 233 Manda 147 Martha 135 236 Mary 201 281 Mat 140 Matthew 157 Maude 204 Mytrle 135 Oma 207 Paddie 45 Rice 89 Rosie 201 Roy 236 Ruth 283 R.E. 237 Sallie 122 Samuel 225 Savanah 238 Sherman 230 T_ 191 Walter Lee 167 William 79 157 274 283 William Glen Street 78 William Lester 255 William R. 207
BENNET, Cordi 48 Nancy 63
BENSON, Wyeth 14
BERRY, Margaret 45 Sarah 214 Sarah Ann 288

BERTAIN, Mrs. George
BETTIS, Darthula J. 41
BICK, Virginia 253
BIDDIX, Arthur 107 Cordie 107
BIETZ, Annie 193
BIGGS, W.W. 196
BIRCHFIELD, Anne 245 Charley 38 Cordelia 176 David 176 226 David Wallace 263 Ezekiel 51 279 H. 21 Infant 5 49 Isaac 153 Julia 5 Lenore 63 Martha 29 Mattie C. 41 Millie 247 Millie Buchanan 263 M.E. 21 93 N. 51 Nathan 38 Nathaniel 51 Nettie 170 219 Paul Eugene 226 Robert 21 226 282 Rosa Leah 153 Sallie 155 Samuel 6 Sarah 5 S.L. 49 Vistie 16 William 16 279 William E. 282 W.C. 112
BIRDWELL, __ 90 Benjamin 217 Fry 256 Jim 256 William 256
BIRD, __ 191 Della 198
BISHOP, Andrew J. 57 Duffey 153 Duffy 153 Gertha 227
BLACKBURN, __ 92 Andrew Jackson 59 Silas 59 Mrs. Silas 59
BLACK, G.B. 175 G.S. 175 Ralph 175
BLAIN, Minnie Sue 303
BLAKELY, May 80
BLAKE, Howard 81 Infant 81
BLALOCK, Elvira 204
BLANKENSAY, Leota 130
BLANKENSHIP, Betty Jean 288 Bob 287 Bobby Lee 287 Carrie Treadway 283 Cling 54 David 209 Debie Jane 33 Dosha 132 Dwight 39 Earl 54 Estell 17 105 Ettter Isabell 55 Fate 120 209

BLANKENSHIP (continued) Mrs.
Fate 297 Floyd 205 Frank 288
Fred 15 George W. 55 Grace 120
Hattie 46 Herman 226 Horace 39
Infant 10 25 Jasper 19 169
Jimmie 297 John 56 188 280
John Jr. 283 John Sr. 283 John
T. 257 John William 280 J.M. 50
68 Mrs. J.O. 42 Lenore Lillian
161 Leota 155 Loeth 199 Lewis
J. 161 Lewis T. 226 Louis 261
Lydia 95 120 L.E. 32 M_ 149
Martha M. 257 Mary E. 208
Mattie 14 Mildred 56 Minnie 54
Oscar 39 Presley 209 Ray 65
Sallie 151 Sarah 283 Sis 265 291
Texanner 297 Thiery 54 Thomas
213 Tom 169 210 Walter 30
William E. 65 W.B. 25 Zeb 210
Zisa 157
BLANTON, John 39
BLASY, Hellen Lola 191 John 191
BLEVINS, _ 248 Alfred Sr. 102
Bertie 125 Biddie 186 Bill 43
Callie 133 Charles 35 235
Charlie 146 David 235 Dora 147
233 D.B. 96 246 Elmer 214 Ethel
142 Fine 43 Frank 51 Infant 51
James 214 Lockie 96 Lura 121
Mae 230 Maggie 103 Martha 43
Oscar Silas 146 Polly 163 Sarah
163 235 Walter 102 170 William
121 William M. 35
BOGART, Bill 215 Charles 26 107
Charles C. 289 C.G. 51 Edd 215
Elizabeth 12 E.G. 60 E.P. 60
Florence Crouch 267 Gerturde 51
Infant 26 51 107 Jeremiah 267

J.E. 267 Kate 126 Sam 215 S.W.
60 William 289 W.A. 289
BOICE, Dianah 297
BOLMAN, Mrs. Everet 194
BONDERANT, Merrinetine 266
B.D. 267 S.W. 266
BONNER, Lizzie 188
BOONE, Charles 117 Charles P.
161 Charley 161 Grace 102 H.K.
246 H.P. 109 Infant 78 104 104
117 148 Jerry 246 Jim 159 J.S.
109 299 Mary 111 Mont 148
Mort 148 Paul 102 Paul 103 Sam
91 104 111 Samuel 299 Sullins
246 Troy 78 266 275 Troy
Sherman 78 Zeb 91 Zeb Vance
109
BOOSHE, Charles 25
BOOTHE, Elizabeth 134 Fred D.
229 231 Hiram 267 John 97 Lora
134 M.F. 97
BOOTH, Augusta P. 124 A.V. 124
Esther 202 Fred 202 Hiram 196
227 231 Ida 1 John 227 Lola
Dean 296 Mary 124 W.R. 227
BORDEON, Virginia 7
BORDERS, Lucenda 23
BORING, Hattie 162
BOWERS, Eliza 279 H.V. 129
Infant 129 V.B. Jr. 129
BOWING, Louis 1
BOWMAND, Tine 225
BOWMAN, Alfred C. 219
Christopher 94 Cleda 104 Daniel
135 D.E. 299 Earnest Taylor 170
Ed 232 Edd 151 Edward 232 Ella
71 Ellia 85 Emeline 16 Gravir 20
Hattie 15 Ida 67 Ida Pearl 81 J.
151 John 170 John S. 219

BOWMAN (continued) Joseph 9 135 Joseph Arlee 18 J.C. 293 Lee 104 Lillian 225 Lillian Virginia 104 Lizzie 103 Loyd 16 Martha C. 237 Mary Susan 299 Pearl 225 Rosa Jones 232 Ruth Geneve 151 Scott 128 232 Tine 232 U.S. 173 Vena 150 W. Scott 232

BOYD, Clyde Eldrige 96 D.A. 141 Hassaltine 101 Infant 141 William 96

BRACKINS, David 258 Dennis 272 Ike 272 Mrs. W.F. 229

BRADFORD, Bessie Marie 190 Callie 23 Ethel 80 93 199 J.E. 190 Oscar 218 Rettie 177

BRADLEY, John 180 Roy Melborne 283 W.H. 283

BRADSHAW, Elizabeth 141 Rebecca Garland 255 R.H. 255 R.H. Jr. 234

BRADY, Jennetta A. 297 Samuel E. 297

BRAKINS, Dora 75

BRAKSUS, __ 236

BRANCH, Sidney 93

BRASWELL, Wiley A. 285

BRENTLEY, Minnie Belle 299

BREWER, Dolly 131

BRIANT, Darkska 206

BRICE, Hezekiah 120 William 120

BRIDGES, Eather 24

BRIGGS, William H. 30

BRIGGS, __ 216 Ada 131 Adolphus 270 Altha 32 Annie 277 Bell 37 51 Bert 238 Bertha 79 Callie 31 Cinda 127 Douglas 269 Elisha Elbert 268 Fairy 124 Flora May 154 Harriett 184 Homer 124 154 173 268 Infant 42 154 James Holt 80 Jane 105 Janie 275 John Logan 277 Julia Finettie 173 J.H. 275 Kirk 296 Lee Moore 270 Lockie 51 Lucindy 169 Lue 23 Margaret M. 167 Mary 31 270 Matilda 213 P. 30 Peter 172 Polly 123 Rebecca 37 Rosco 42 Rosie 30 Seth 269 Therman 172 tom 268 269 Vina 234 Virgie 269 Walter 80 Wanda Herrin 296

BRINKLEY, Belle 28 John 80 M.B. 92 Sallie 80

BRITTON, Cauthus 104

BRITT, Alice 74 128 223 Axie 256 David 74 252 Elbert 266 E.C. 256 Mrs. Frank 197 Infant 146 Isaac 117 Jacob 151 James 14 117 151 171 291 Jim 266 Landon 252 Malinda 62 Mart 249 Martha 85 Mary 276 Melinda 44 156 183 Minnie E. 176 Nancy 171 Rachel E. 149 Roxy 83 Sinda 134 Wilson 302 W.H. 146 266

BROCKINS, Betsy 188 John 188 M.R. 188

BROKUS, D. 35

BROOKINS, Serley 190

BROOKS, __ 130 Ader 13 David 273 Robert 27 Vernie Elizabeth 27

BROWN, Alfred P. 227 Andrew Johnson 278 Annie L. 270 Barbara Elizabeth 136 Benjamin F. 278 Blanch 43 Catherine 170 Charity 89 167 Ella 197 E.A. 193 304 Floyd Ray 43 Fred 197

BROWN (continued) Mrs. George 217 Infant 45 74 Jane 48 79 Jesse 46 114 Joseph A. 46 J.W. 36 Latten 117 Lettie 156 183 Lizzie Lucille 193 Lottie 183 Louise 43 Lucinda Jane McInturff 189 Margaret 79 Margaret Elizabeth 128 Mary 44 Mary E. 179 Mary Jane 278 Mary Virginia 304 M.J. 170 Nancy Colvin 270 Roasile B 227 Robert Williams 227 R.L. 136 Sam 45 74 S.H. 81 William 47 170 304 William Henry 270 William L. 270 W.H. 128 W.S. 8
BROYLES, Dollie 163 210 Dolly 223 Frank E. 49 102 Jacob 49 Jane 52 John Sumerfield 49 Mrs. John 102 Lucinda 49 Melvin 286 Nina 281 Noah 286
BRUCE, Martha Francis 263
BRUMETT, James 44 J. 62 Thomas J. 62 William 44 William P. 62
BRUMITT, Thomas 44
BRUMMETT, Andrew 299 Casey 166 Celia 92 David 156 Dewitt 120 Dorotyh Mae 53 Elizabeth 112 Ethel 105 240 Hattie Carver 299 Henry A. 242 Infant 56 James 53 164 Joe 53 J.R. 120 Linburg Curtis 242 Lissie 53 Nancy Evangeline 122 Roscoe 115 Sam 56 179 183 240 Samuel 105 166 Sarah Ann 192 Sarah Louise 183 Susan 93 Thomas 115 179 240 Tom 240 William 92 134 156 183
BRUMMITT, Andrew 299

BRYANT, __ 182 C.W. 250 Darliskey 143 Eliza 101 Emma 283 Franky Jean 70 J.W.O. 236 Luvina 146 Marrie 162 Meniva 152 Pattie 226 Polly 180 Rosa 151 Sam 14 141 Sisey 168 Thomas 118 Thomas Wesley 250
BUCHANAN, A. 103 Are 103 Ave 151 Billie 234 Carolina 44 Celia 64 Clarence 103 Dora 114 Dot 49 Elizabeth 255 Ellen 226 Elvira A. 100 Hazel Gertrude 263 Infant 151 Jane 196 Joseph B. 234 Luly 263 Mattie 202 Mollie 151 Robert 263 Sallie 44 Vertie Flora 49 W.W. 263
BUCHBOARD, Ramsey 265
BUCKLES, C.E. 264 Harold 264 Iva 180 John 264 Lula 264
BUCKNER, Duskie 298 Elizabeth 185 Eugenie Kate 169 George W. 169 James A. 298 Lela 299
BUCK, Mrs. Andy 240 Anne 115 Annie 179 240 Nancy 299 Rosha 193
BULLIONS, James 258
BULLOCK, Henry 239 Ollie 169
BUNDY, Addie G. 140
BURGEN, Ellen 3
BURGESS, Edward 59 Mrs. Edward 59 E.D. 28 Mitchell 59 Nancy Jane 219 Roy 28
BURGNER, Birdie L. 158 Wilma 158
BURKE, Martha 196
BURK, John 252
BURLESON, Harriett 291 Jane 46 Louise 218 Phebe 45

BURLISON, D.W. 25 Isaac 25
Margaret E. 25
BURNET, Cania 64
BURNS, Jack 161 Mary_ 123
Peggy 241 Susey 112
BURRIS, Margaret 298
BURTON, Mrs. M.J. 157
BUSH, James R. 227
BUSTER, Martha 49 69
BUTCHER, Allie 61
BUTLER, _ 261 Mary Jane 108
Obediah 106 Tilha 87
BUTNER, Lizzie 264 Mary 29
Sam 131 Selma 131
BYERS, John 244 R.L. 185
BYRD, _ 143 Arthur 143 Blake 248 Blanche 277 Bob 80 Caroline 248 Charles 174 Dora 175 189 Ira Kenneth 93 Jacob B. 93 J.B. 93 Laurence 300 Louise 144 233 Molly 158 Myrtle Marie 300 R.V. 20
CALDWELL, Jim 67
CALLAHAN, Albert 21 Alice 221 Mrs. Bert 221 Bertie 302 Dicie 287 Dora 132 Emily 95 Fred 221 Jane 51 J.A. 133 J.W. 132 282 Levi 257 Margaret 257 William 18 William Elbert 152 William Elbert Jr. 152
CALLISTER, Charles 303
CALLOWAY, Dan 68 Daniel 68 Gamel 239 Jack 239 Orpha Mae 276 Saunders 68
CAMPBELL, Addie 128 148 Alice Stout 284 Allice 110 Annie 6 Arthur 137 Brady 163 Bessie Markham 298 Betsy 175 Billie 284 Brownlow 165 C_ 177 Cad

165 Carolina 33 Caroline 56 Cinda 45 163 Clarence Albert 287 Daniel 284 David 71 85 113 175 Dorris 113 Edith 88 Elaine 261 Elenor Kirkwood 73 Elisha 194 Ellen 110 Emeline 106 Emmett 261 Eray 174 Harmon 137 Henry 52 Infant 29 147 Ivens 175 Jack 174 Jackson 88 James 85 110 284 James S. 298 John 71 163 John C. 85 John Wiley 73 June Carolyn 287 J.L. 165 J.W. 73 Lois Reed 24 Mary 86 Mattie 164 Sabra 62 Sarah 174 Susan 131 Susie 244 William 57 71 113 194 William E. 147 W.a. 29 W.E. 113
CANADY. Sarah 23
CANTRELL, James 220 J.P. 220
CAPPS, Edith 155 John 109 M.R. 28 109 Ruth 28 Sana 131 William Manual 109 Wilsie 271 Mrs. W.R. 264
CAPP, Luda L. 187 Willie 187
CARL, Sarah 9
CARMICHAEL, Isabel 224
CAROL, James 104
CAROTHERS, Infant 233 James 233
CARPENTER, Frank 34 John W. 34
CARRELL, Andy 175 D. 170 George 175 H.C. 230
CARROLL, Arter 16 David 191 Delia 68 Edmon 115 Edward 122 George 191 Greenberry 68 Mattison 4 Nancy 120 Norma Edna 192 Opal 175 Rosy 4

CARROLL (continued) Sarah A.
Brummett 179 William 115 192
CARTER, Bill 165 Ethel 16
Francis Marion 165 Frank 165
Hester 128 Infant 130 John
Henry 105 Laura 277 Minta 105
William 105 W.B. 130
CARVER, Charlotte 38 150 Doc
82 109 Ella 214 George 38 Hattie
82 232 Iserell 244 Joe 106 John
241 299 John William 109 Lottie
294 Mary 87 247 Monroe 241
Nancy 241 Polly 106 244 P.P. 59
Stacy 59 William 38 261
CARVIN, James 72
CARY, Anie 40
CASEY, Charles 298 Clifton 101
Clyde Garnett 97 Coxie 250
Ernest 56 George B. 97 G.B. 107
Hannah 211 Hattie 220 James
235 Jim 233 Joe 56 101 Landon
220 Lula B. 107 Walter 211 220
Zella 233 235
CASH, Edith 284 Gertrude 26 107
John 48 164 Margaret Ann 196
Roy 196 Ruby 197
CASTEEL, Amanda 61 126 Bill
163 Infant 61 Jack 61 126 163
Mrs. Jack 163 Jane 139 John 78
140 John David 126 Millard 78
140 Mrs. Millard 78
CASTELL, Amanda 61
CASWELL, Hattie 176
CATON, Ethel West 250 Robert
Napoleon 250 Stephen 250 W.G.
250
CAUDELL, Mattie 95
CAWTHEN, Jim 141
CHALDLER, I.T. 53

CHALLAHAN, Elsie 255
CHANDLER, A_ 209 Annie E. 67
Arthur 93 C_ 179 Clyde 12
Creola 146 Dessie 11 Dora 11
Elmira 27 Elvina 179 Emeline
188 Estell 38 134 Esteller 192
Fannie 174 Fred A. 227 G.B. 61
192 Ida 164 Infant 93 Isaac 179
Jane 25 135 Janie 265 John 169
J.F. 174 J.H. 53 159 166 J.P. 67
J.W. 22 Lark 61 206 Litty 53
Mary 159 Naoma 37 75 Nervie
Jane 151 Oma 187 Richard S.
227 Sarah 153 Silas L. 61 Vestel
8 Wiley 166 Wolford 166
CHANDLEY, Anorman 25 Banner
125 Cullen 125 Howard 125
CHAPEEL, Sarah 62
CHAPMAN, David 273 James 273
J.H. 273 Robert 147
CHARLES, C.E. 223 John Valley
223 R.A. 223
CHASE, Daniel 147 Hubert 217
Mrs. Hubert 147 Lillie B. 217
CHITWOOD, Harvey 27
CHURCH, Katherin 111 Larkin
111
CLAIBORNE, Uisie 193
CLARKSON, Louisa 109 193
CLARK, Autie 131 Billie 233
Dewey 233 Elizabeth 269
Florence 189 John 199 262
Lockey 56 Luther 42 262 Luther
Jr. 42 Monroe 302 Nancy 17
Nola 248 302 Sarah 142 202
CLAUSE, John A. 234 Martha 108
Robert 234 William 234
CLAWSON, Ben 59

CLAYTON, Edna 107 Mary 246
Odis P. 107 Mrs. O.P. 246
CLEVELAND, Infant 145 M.C.
145
CLICK, Eva E. 303 Julia 21 Lora
86 Loura 286 Roy 218
CLINE, Catherine 135
CLOCESE, Grover 96 Infant 96
CLOUD, Daisy Lee 2
CLOUSE, Cressie 205 Della 268
Dortha 268 Ernest 258 E.E. 258
Georgia 65 Groar 111 Infant 111
Jacob 65 265 271 James M. 183
John 183 239 J.M. 62 Mary J. 37
Mrs. M.L. 224 Phyllis Leota 258
Polly 160 234 Rachel 47 Robert
224 239 Thomas 271 W.J. 37
W.P. 224 239
CLOYD, Blanch 162
CL_, Martha J. 67
COATS, Charley 290 Charley G.
296 Eliza 296 Gabriel 209 Gertie
296 James 251 296 John 41 209
251 J.C. 251 R_ 34 Rentha 41
COBBIL, Maggie 63
COBBLE, Ann 282 Anne 280
Barbara Ann 127
COCHRAN, Amanda 70 Delia 127
George 191 Hannah 70 Hattie 38
James 64 198 J.T. 191 Manda 65
Mary 34 212 Robert 64 192
CODA, Cordelia 107
CODY, Charlie 77 George 248
Harrie 77 78 Noah 75 248 Rossie
235 W.C. 77 78
COFFEE, Bessie 259 Byrdie 276
Byrnie 214 James 288 Judy 152
J.W. 152 214 Maggie 119 Perry
288 Pery 214

COGGINS, Charlie 113 Will 113
COIN, Cleo 139 Harvey Lee 81
S.A. 81
COLBAUGH, Lucina 117
COLDWELL, M_ 43 Thomas J. 43
COLEMAN, Bettie 123 Dorchis
Marie 192 James 84 John 42 J.C.
123 192 249 M_ 92 Minnie 42
Monte 249 Roy 112 Will 112
COLE, E.L. 120 Jesse 45 Mary
Ann 35 196 Mildred 120 Pearl
166 256 S.W. 166 256 S.W. 53
Mrs. S.W. 51
COLLETT, Newt 240
COLLIER, L.D. 132
COLLINS, Alvin 202 Dora 265
Georgia Lee 70 G.V. 70 L.C. 149
May 198 Minnie 149 Nellie 177
Shirden 202
COLMAN, Vernie 207
COLVIN, Nancy 270
CONELY, James 212 Martha Ann
172
CONLEY, Charles W. 228 George
212 Lida 109 Louisa 228
Margaret 258
CONSTABLE, William 257 W.J.
64
COOK, __ 222 Alice 49 Betsy 180
Ester 119
COOPER, __ 217 Andy 46 April
69 Axie 248 Belle 250 Emma 21
46 Ethel 160 Guy 35 Hubert 81
Infant 35 James 36 James Taylor
46 James T. 21 Joel 141 John D.
299 L_ 220 Landon Nathaniel 21
M_ 110 225 Martha 283 Milburn
36 Mose 300 Nelce 250 Neuona
107 Orville 36 160 Rebecca 59

COOPER (continued) Sam 107 110 Samuel 299 Sarah 250 Theodore 225 William 287 Mrs. W.M. 220
COPELAND, George Alvin 293 Oliver 293
COPESTICK, Daniel Bellyse 76 Mrs. D.B. 76 William 76
CORBIN, Anna 220
CORBY, Duey 229 Kathleen 229
CORM, Cleo 33
CORNETT, Mollie Eugenia 247 T.C. 247
COR_, John 81
COROTHEN, Jim 141 Pauline 141
CORRELL, Nancy 139 Sid 140
COTHRAN, James Whitlock 64
COUSINS, Isaac S. 76 Mrs. Isaac 76 W.M. 76
COUTHARD, Lizzie 200
COWELL, Belle 65
COX, Emma Gillis 267 Jason 267 Lesta 266 Lilliam May 230 Milburn 230 267 Robert 230 Ruth 155 Sarah 132
CRAINE, Andy 285 Andy J. 280 George W. 285 Joe William 297 Lewis 280 Lillie 285 Sarah J. 280 Wesley O. 297
CRAIN, Andy 248 Annie 93 96 Arthur 192 Berry 34 Billie 54 Braddie 41 Bradie 34 Carl 50 Cordie 124 Eula 221 Hezekiah 46 Infant 41 121 149 J. 93 Jennie 120 Joe 50 146 149 Junior 146 Lair 25 Lattie 121 221 Lewis E. 54 Mack 32 Mamie 11 Martha 121 R_ 32 Radie 39 Ralph Elroy 46 Retha 19 Sam 146 Sue 288

Vaughn 10 Vira Eulalia 192 Louise 241
CRAWFORD, __ 266
CREECH, Parrott 23
CRIGGER, Lucille Virginia 301 Mary 136 W. Kyle 301
CRINDSTAFF, Elbert 38
CRINE, Magdalen 279
CROSSWHITE, George 143 I.J. 234 Maggie E. 143 Nancy 234
CROUCH, James 267
CROUSE, Cinthia 31
CROWDER, Anderson 241 Jane 63
CROWELL, Jasper 100
CROW, A.C. 75 Charlie Lee 112 Ed 93 Edward Marshall 93 Elizabeth 48 Joe 186 Mande 217 Marie 212 Marshall 112 William 186 William Edward 75
CRUMLEY, Stacy 119
CULBERTSON, Emerline 257
CULBERT, Hannah 91
CUPP, Riley 197
CURTIS, Henry Edward 198 Infant 198 Ralph 286
CUTSHALL, Bessie 218 Blanche 200 Fowler 200 Gertha 231 Girtha 26 Infant 227 James 218 Virgie 59
CUTSHAW, Gertha 277 James 277 S_ 277
DALTON, Lewis 180 L.C. 180
DANIELS. Jane 176 Nana 246 Nora 27 Riley B. 65
DANIEL, Charles David 274 Ella 270 Harold Thomas 274 Infant 26 W. 26
DARTER, Mary A. 88

DAUGHERTY, Infant 62 James 42 174 Joseph 174 Minnie 187 Thomas 42 62 174
DAVIDSON, Horace 87 James 87
DAVIS, Acey 20 Allice 175 Amos 65 198 Anne 236 Annie 178 A. Jack 292 Billie 275 Bob 199 Charley 33 153 Chevis 88 Clay 248 C.D. 202 Mrs. C.D. 202 C.G. 249 Elizabeth 112 175 Ernest 171 Floyd 257 Frank 258 Frank L. 27 33 Fred 251 Gladys 164 G.R. 292 Hazel Elton 29 Henry 240 Horace Mock 292 H.M. 237 Infant 145 Jackson 4 James 87 James C. 42 199 Jane 46 John 20 88 171 176 John M. 164 Judah 198 Julia Bernice 302 June 299 Mrs. J.C. 42 Litha 85 Lucretia 278 Lydia 27 100 240 Margaret 6 112 Margaret L. 257 Martha 252 Mary 80 Mary Ann 206 Mollie 97 Netron 145 Nora 124 Ollie 5 Pollie 101 Polly 189 232 Rachel 44 Raleigh Columbus 237 Rebecca 164 Robert 207 217 Robert B. 251 Robert Harry Jr. 207 Ruthie 159 R.H. 29 Susan 112 275 Thomas 87 Thomas D. 42 Thurla 171 Vertie 292 Walter 124 Will 248 William 124 153 302 William D. 251 W.D. 8 W.T. 199
DAY, Alexander 93 C.W. 93 Jude 211 Martishy J. 131 Maude 268 Molly 125 Pauline 259 Sanders 197 Walter 194 Mrs. Walter 194 William 53 William Done 93

William Leonard 53 Woodward 259
DEADERICK, Mack 239 Mary A. 193 Paul 193
DEADRICK, Elizabeth 36
DEAN, Hewy 103
DEATHRIDGE, Bessie 298
DEATON, __ 217 Betsy 72 C_ 94 Clara 253 F.H. 94 F.R. 195 Infant 94 Joe 182 J.W. 195 Margaret 231 Nathan 144 Sarah 117 Zora 166
DEAVER, R.K. 130
DEFORD, James Brownlow 238 John Loyd 238
DEHAVEN, Mary R. 7
DENNIS, Charles William 278 Lillian 278 Wade 278
DENTON, Bessie 33 H.M. 98 Jane 175
DEVAULT, Francis Julia 303 Gerogia Sprinkle 69 Infant 78 James T. 78 J. Wilbur 303 J.J. 78 J.W. 214 William E. 214
DEVERT, Tom 70
DEWITT, Berzillia 48
DEYTON, Dolly 182 May 76 Sallie 296
DICKERSON, H. 170 Mrs. O.E. 36
DICKSON, Henry 288 James 65 95 Martha Jane 288 Matt 209 Matthew Columbus 288 Monica Brown 95 M.C. 95 Nancy Ann 209 Nola 65
DILLINGER, Liza 84
DISHMAN, Mrs. George 240
DIXON, R_ 109 William Henry 109

DOBBINS, Christine 219 William 219
DOBSON, Bod 123
DOOR, Helen 268
DOSER, Helen 212
DOSS, T.E. 221
DOUGALL, Anna May 153
DOUGLAS, Archie 2 Polly 97
DOVER, Infant 300 Lucy 300
DOVE, Bertha 219 Catherine 54
DOWNS, Harvey D. 242 J.M. 242
DOYLE, Arthur 197 A.P. 75 Mrs. A.P 75 George 197 George P. 75
DRAPER, Minnie 40
DRYMAN, C.F. 118 Olga 118
DUFFY, Hattie 90
DUGGER, Catherine 36 Infant 230 Jacob 44 Datherine 268 Margaret 92 M.M. 230 Rosa 167
DUKES, Amanda Jane 304
DUNBAR, Annie 167 Joseph 184 Loade 139 Loade Jr. 139 L.A. 162
DUNCAN, Abner 36 David 25 76 Dora 150 Dovie 76 Frank 84 268 Franklin Madison 36 Ida 20 Infant 143 150 Isaac 77 Janie 229 John 77 176 291 John Columbus 154 John Samuel 20 Mrs. John 77 J.L. 36 69 J.N. 143 Lillian 183 Lydia 217 Malisa 154 Mary Catherine 44 Nancy 268 N.C. 261 Pauline 84 Pearl 3 Rosa 165 Ruby 196 S. 114 Samuel 154 Samuel Thomas 291 Samuel T. 20 William 268 W.A. 268 W.F. 44 69 W.G. 150
DUNKEN, Anzo 14 Fred 14 Sabra 206 Walter 14

DUNKLEBURGER, A.C. 99 Mabel Leone 99
DURBAN, Charles Thomas 60
DURBIN, Infant 60
DYE, Ellse 201
EALEM, Polly 111
EARBY, Jocie 202
EARLY, Guy 260 Richard Carroll 250 Robert Eugene 260 Virginia 171
EATON, Frank L. 163 Mrs. F.L. 163 William F. 163
EDENS, Bonnie 282 Charles David 182 Edwin Lockwood 282 Ernest 127 Etta T. 162 E.L. 182 H.K. 162 Infant 127 Manda 182 M.F. 182
EDNEY, A.R. 239 Bonnie 244 Eula 294 J.B. 239 Matilda 244
EDWARDS, __ 167 180 298 A. 39 Aiden Leonard 224 Allen 260 Allie Jane 300 Amanda 90 Anderson 280 Andrew 156 Andy 90 Archie 223 Arthur 224 Bertha 68 Bessie 199 Bobby Gene 293 Bonnie 181 Catherine 154 Celia M. 229 Clifton 146 166 167 Clyed 14 D. 68 Dave 228 234 Delia 159 Dessie 105 Dolly 95 D.S. 248 Edd 68 95 Eliza 9 Elizabeth 107 Ell 81 Ellen 45 Emaline 100 Ester 102 Floyd J. 253 Frank 107 Fred 100 G. 30 Garrett 176 George 63 105 122 Gertie 20 Gerturde 223 G.W. 83 Harve 12 Hester 83 Howell 102 Infant 59 68 95 146 148 163 165 166 167 Ira 123 Jackson 205 256 Jane 128 Jason 148 244

EDWARDS (continued) John 123 165 234 253 John Henry 300 John W. 204 Joseph 253 Joseph B. 102 J.F. 59 211 J.S. 163 Kathleen 199 L_ 141 Lizzie 82 Lowers 211 Lula 102 143 Lydia 39 Margaret 50 229 Martha 221 Martha Ann 248 Mary 181 Mile 195 Millie 151 Mollie 103 Morton 83 M.G. 176 Nancy 28 Nat 302 Norman 302 O.B. 68 Rhetta 226 R.A. 151 R.G. 11 R.R. 199 Sallie 190 Sam R. 202 Sarah 150 302 Silas 204 Sol 293 Stella M. 181 Theidry 30
EDWARDS, Tom 202 Vinna 122 Willard 20 William 102 143 William A. 183 Wilson 28 68 248 302 W.B. 68 W.E. 24 W.M. 119 W.T. 177
EDWARD, Bertha Lee 9
EFFLER, Clerie Bell 15 Dathia Evelyn 48 Everette 48 George 98 272 Infant 98 Jane 48 Magie 50 Pauline 272 Willie 263
ELDRIDGE, Jacob 102
ELLIOTT, Adeline Braswell 285 C.B. 116 Hubert Hoover 199 James O. 116 Jess 85 Jessie 85 Razor 85 Richard 285 R.T. 199 Turner 235 Walter Logue 116 William Herman 235
ELLIS, Alice 26 Charles D. 47 Dan M. 72 Infant 151 Jack Keith 72 Landon 47 Rebecca 85 R.J. 151
EMERSON, Anna Ruth 202
EMMERSON, Anna Ruth 274

EMMERT, Ben H. 222 Peter Wesley 221 William C. 221 W.C. 234
ENGLAND, Mamie 28 Nancy 161
ENGLE, Alford 237 Annie Mae 300 Blaine 237 Elen 209 Garth 104 Isaac 237 Nancy 187
ENGLISH, Anderson 120 Duie 120 W.G. 120
EPPERSON, Ernest 187 J.B. 187
ERBY, Joe 206
ERWIN, Annie Thelma 45 Arthur 229 246 Bell 31 Belle 95 Bertie 30 Charles R. 282 C.H. 182 D.J.N. 182 Eliza 136 Ella B. 115 128 Eugene 246 George R. 229 G.C. 45 H. 282 Herman 245 Horace 269 Jack Stuart 41 Jesse B. 52 245 282 Jessie 100 J.K. 288 Mrs. J.L. 30 J.R. 288 295 Lela Pearl 282 Lula Jarvis 295 Lydia Harriett Ann 282 Mary 18 198 Nancy 210 224 Pearl 21 Phillip 21 39 184 R.H. 41 Sam 184 Samuel 113 229 William M. 76 William Ryburn 76 William S. 294 Mrs. William 169 W.M. 184 W.S. 161 183 245 264 Mrs. W.S. 201
ESKEW, Nonie 136
ESTEPP, Naoma 220
ESTEP, Bessie 57 87 Birtie 292 Infant 87 Sam 257
ETSMON, Martha 206
EVANS, George C. 261 G.C. 69 Mabel 78 Sadie Jane 69
EVERETT, Jane 197
EXXLER, George 162 Infant 162 Verna 153

F_, Alvin 164
FAGAN, Bessie M. 71 Eliza 117
Ethel 215 James M. 26 Robert T.
26 Mrs. Robert 48 Rosa Lee 215
FALK, James 273 Wilbur 273
FANNING, Bill 265 Clara 181 183
205 Frank 89 Ruby 89 W.H. 205
FARMER, Charles 268 Francis
164 Martha E. 172
FARNOR, Jacob S. 297 John
Barthafer 297 Julia 297
FEATHERS, Anne E. 243
Elizabeth 61 92 207
FELTY, H.R. 175
FENDER, Andy 229 Marier 90
Martha Jane 283 Polly 222
Winfred 269
FERGUSON, Elmer 250 Jake 250
Sis 60
FILLERS, Mary Jane 213
FINCHER, Bessie 152
FINDER, Bonnie 188 Caroline 176
Margaret 216
FISER, Margaret 197
FISHER, Elizabeth 143 Henry 304
Louie Clyde 304
FLACK, Mary 74
FLETCHER __ 71 Alta 159 Lenia
262
FOISTER, Tildy 187
FONDREN, Viola 291
FORBES, Juanita 299 Masey 66
Melinda 160 Milburn 65 Minnie
Lucille 65 Rachel 158 240 Sallie
262 Sarah 45 Wiley 167
FORBS, E.H. 218 Jessie 218 R.C.
218
FORD, Ethel 47 George 103
Hiram 202 Josh 80 Mart 80
Robert 201 Robert Joseph 103
R.E.L. 112 Sara Rosa 112
Thelma J. 202
FOREMAN, Addie B. 99
FORNER, J.S. 56 Jacob 56
FORTUNE, Hubert 148 Infant 74
148 J.E. 74
FOSTER, Adline 181 Amanda 234
Andy 53 157 Arthor 146 Arthur
207 Axie 152 Bud 260 C_ 244
Catherine 297 Cecil 9 Charles
172 Charlie 13 C.B. 46 Dan 130
David 25 143 Dora 248 258
Dortha E. 190 D.B. 220 D.C. 88
Eda 187 Elbert 130 Eliza 38 146
Elizabeth 206 Elmer 84 Emma
97 Emory 39 203 Emry 203
Ernest 259 Ethel 8 Frank 220
Fred 157 Gladys 39 Guy 288
G.W. 288 Hannah 202 Harriett
207 Harrison 227 Hazel 203
Hobart 146 H.B. 244 Infant: 41
53 69 97 152 James Luther 162
Jean 38 John 130 Johnathan 143
Jonathan 157 J.C. 162 257 278
297 J.H. 41 75 89 190 208 220
Kyle 227 Lena 208 Leona 152
Leora 190 Leura 220 Lonnie
Junior 220 Lora 156 172 Lula 46
Marion 259 Mary 105 Mary Jane
55 Maud 18 89 110 Minnie 274
M.C. 124 162 Nila 208 Noma
206 Porter 203 Porter Jr. 203 Roy
220 Sallie 98 159 215 Sarah 124
Sarah Beck 155 Sarah B. 69
Silas 69 209 Thomas 18 37 75
159 209 Tilda 89 Tom 187 215
Viola Erwin 288 Will 260

FOSTER (continued) William Arthur 84 William Bart 220 William David 25 W.B. 88
FOWLER __ 60 A.J. 219 Dora 235 George D. 36 60 Harry 279 John 9 60 Stella Mary 279 Walter H. 219 William J. 219
FOX, Charles Burnie 88 Charlie B. 88 C.B. 88 153 Gladys 139 Guindolyn 153 H_ 164 Haskel 271 Henry Grady Jr. 156 Hershel 164 H.G. 156 John 145 Marion 272 M.S. 139 Orville Edgar 289 Orville Henry 289 O.J. 289 Robert 271 Ula 145
FRAISOR, Sindy 205
FRANCIS, Bell 159 Cora 253 Dr. Joseph 6 Stella 205
FRANKLIN, A.D. 262 Emma 165 Everett 262 Fred 178 Harry 176 Hester 178 Ida 61 Infant 176
FRANK, Garrett 287 Garrett Maurray 287 Harriett 287
FRAZIER, Andy 66 Bessie 65 66 Eriasey 107
FREEMAN, Ann Eliza 156 Bash 168 Bashie 124 G.A. 156 Ola 59
FREOY, Forest 190 I.G. 190
FRITTS, Lula Pearl 69 Rally 13 Willie 13
FRITZ, Andy H. 22 Infant 22 Lula Duncan 22
FRYE, Caroline Sue 281 Della 168 Dewey 281 Elizabeth 230 Hazel Webb 240 H.M. 157 168 Manden 240
FRY, Clayton 79 Dewey 124 Henry 161 Lucy 4 Mary 57 194 284 Matilda 4 Michel 112

FULLER, Frank 139
FULTON, B.F. 195
FULWILDER, Abraham 172
FURCHESS, Earl 163 Will 191
FURCHES, Durwood 210 Elsie May 60 Lillian Louise 223 Marvin 163 223 M.V. 210 M.Z. 60 61 Nancy 104 Nancy 104 Nancy Ruth 187 Rena Jane 83 Sheridan 177 Virgie 61 W.F. 104 W.J. 83 W.T. 187
G_, Elizabeth 113 Nancy Jane 208
GADDY, Bessie 228 Eva 1 J.J. 292 Lydia 281 Sara A. Bowman 128
GALLOWAY, Edna Leah 109 Joseph H. 109 Mary 91 Maude 109
GAMBOL, Anna 75
GANT, Elcany 150 L. James 150
GARDNER, D. 262 Dock 45 Donna 262 Infant 45
GARLAND, __ 66 Ander 171 Andie 171 A.G. 66 116 Bertha 165 200 Bertha May 201 Betsy 226 Biddie 137 171 Biddy 171 Bill 168 238 Bonnie 84 Callie 84 Carcil M. 168 Carrie 258 273 Celbert 299 Celia 28 Celie 225 Charles 69 Christianbury 46 Citta 61 D_ 213 Dave 252 David 90 104 Delia 6 Dina 272 Donald Lynn 253 Donald Lynn Jr. 253 Dora 225 Dorothy 238 Dutrey 79 D.J. 248 Earl 172 Mrs, Ed 178 211 Edd 205 Elisha 46 Evelyn 281 E.L. 281 Guss 134 Gutch 137 Harley 69 Hobart 144 Howard Allen 83 Hugh Ray 299 Hunter 201 Infant 90 104 201

GARLAND (continued) Isabell 137 Jane 40 John 58 83 84 John L. 289 Julias 66 J.H. 195 J.W. 225 Lacy 79 Lila 51 M_ 207 Mac 228 Margaret 225 Martha 95 Mary 282 Mary S. 211 Minnie 40 Mynete 116 Nancy 122 144 Ollie 93 Paulin 117 Polly 277 P.N. 222 286 P.T. 46 Retta 303 Rhota 213 Rocie 210 Sarah 271 Sarah A. 222 Stakes 117 Sudie 191 Susan 69 Thomas 205 Tom 144 213 Valdine 172 Verna 41 Verna Erwin 134 Vina 86 286 Will 69 William 255 W.A. 84 W.M. 272 W.S. 201
GARRETT, __ 273 Infant 105 James 105
GARRISON, James 91 James W. 221 Mrs. J.W. 123 W.T. 91
GARTNEY, Mary 235
GEER, Eletha 236 George 236 237 Ransom 140 Sam 236 237
GEISLER, L.H. 71 Mavine 71
GENTRY, A.R. 128 C.P. 41 Elizabeth 15 215 Fred 254 Guy 8 John 128 179 John B. 128 J.N. 254 Kabe 179 Laura A. 254 Lewis G. 215 Mary Louise 59 Newton 59 Robert 296 Sarah 89 Sarah K. 235 W.R. 86 95
GHANDLER, Vestel 8
GIBBS, Bell 36 Ella 69 Grace 103 Thomas 102
GIBSON, Laky 168
GILBERT, Bessie 227 Carl R. 108 Darsie 184 Edward Floyd 108 Elvira 56 Fannie E. 85 Guy F. 184 Henry 48 Margaret 74 Mary 41 48 Mary E. 39 184 Melvira 90 R.W.H. 170 Sarah E. 170 Steve 82 S.C. 48
GILBER, H.W. 132
GILLE, Belle 280
GILLILAND, Bessie 238 290 George Arthur 290
GILLIS, Alfred 85 Ann Marie 252 Becky 246 Belle 22 Bessie 187 Carl 208 Celia 147 David Lewis 134 D.C.S. 46 D.S. 107 Eliza J. 64 Elizabeth 267 Emiline 11 E.J. 184 Florence 204 Frank 252 259 Infant 46 James Brown 216 John 161 206 271 John R. 208 Lattie 37 134 216 Leonard Ezekiel 37 Lula 274 Mary Ellen 128 Minnie Belle 188 Nancy 19 Orville 104 Rulbe May 259 Violet 288 Walter 156 208 William J. 85 William L. 104 W. Lattie 134
GLENARD, Infant 9
GLOVER, Oma 176 177
GOFORTH, Maggie 260
GOODWIN, Celia 194
GOOD, A.C. 67 Margaret Louise 67
GOUGE, __ 279 Adda 147 A.M. 144 Bonnie 6 Bulow 45 B.L. 23 Charles H. 251 D. 35 Dalton 163 240 David 44 Dora 174 Emery 232 Ezekiah 35 Frank L. 238 Fuda 171 Gene Ray 251 George W. 240 Georgia 100 Hettie 163 Howard 13 Hoy 100 232 238 Infant 23 James 158 163 James Denman 142 Jim 196 John 17 240 John L. 242 J.w. 158 Leonard 45 Lloyd 242 L.T. 142

GOUGE (continued) Martha 28 119 302 Nat 29 Nellie 207 Ollie 242 Phebe 45 144 Rachel 240 Robert 35 Ruben 134 Sarah 120 Thomas 163 Tina 66 Tom 248 Walter 23 William 29
GOUGH, Cheerfully 6
GRAYBEAL, Amanda 196
GRAY, A.M. 95 Infant 95 R.M. 185
GREENE, Elizabeth 254 Glenn 266 Hattie 49 Landon 218 Oliver 266 Roscoe 186 R.L. 186 W.M. 186
GREENFIELD, __ 111 Kate 111
GREENWAY, Laura Jane 123
GREENWELL, Alice 290 Ed 75 Infant 75
GREEN, __ 127 Alice 259 Anna 135 Elizabeth 289 Ida 146 Kathrn 149 Lena 149 Missouri 53 Percy 149 Syndia 234 Thomas Duncan 147 Tommy 289 William 147
GREER, Ed 40 Helen 40 John 286 Rebecca 286 Harrison 92 138 Hester Beale 55 John 92 John M. 138 Julius D. 92 J.H. 138 Nettie 142 Orville 142
GREY, Rachel Jane 202
GRIDSTAFF, Etta 189
GRIFFIN, Pat 173
GRIFFITH, Adina M. 134 Adine 116 Anna May 229 Bertha 176 Charles 101 Don 245 Eliza 174 Ethel 75 G. 167 Infant 167 J.T. 75 Lem 229 L.H. 118 220 W.M. 176

GRINDSTAFF, __ 5 Alf 194 Alfred 266 Anna May 5 A.J. 86 Earl 150 Elbert 150 Eliza 171 Ella 145 Ezekiel 236 E.L. 294 Isaac 77 Jackson 194 Jane 77 187 Jessie 38 Jim 194 Josie 130 Julia 77 Julie 77 Louise 158 194 Novada 125 Mary 5 52 Minnie 206 Mollie 77 Nannie 228 O.H. 37 Russell 178 275 Mrs. Russell 178 Sallie 266 Sarafina 42 Sarah Ann 228 Sarah A. 86 Sherman 125 228 Susan 275 Zack 178
GUINN, Annie 98 A.b. 50 58 Clide 50 C.F. 60 David 254 David Taylor 235 D.T. 152 Emeline 85 Frank 108 Glen 271 Gracie 247 G.F. 34 50 58 82 Infant 11 110 Isaac 54 235 Jalinee 117 Julina 102 Lattie 271 Laura 59 Lennie 214 Lilly B. 59 Loura Ellen 256 Luther Franklin 208 Malinda 19 Mary Ann 20 M.P. 204 214 Nettie Geneva 58 Orville 110 Pearl 77 P.P. 196 Sue E. 34 Virginia Lee 204 William 208 William Edwin 271 William Franklin 54 Zippie 222
GUIN, Vale 16
GUTHRIE, Polly 54
HAIRE, George 46 Georgia Pearl 46
HAIR, Cale 38
HALE, Alice 247 Lee 270 Mary C. 52 O.C. 125 134 Mrs. O.C. 256
HALL, Hannah 30 Harrison 46
HALSEY, Alice 273
HAMBRICK, Samuel 80 Samuel W. 80

HAMILTON, Rebecca 70
HAMMER, Daniel W. 20 Mary
 Ella 20
HAMMETT, John 35 Newton 35
HAMMET, Maggie 85
HAMMIET, John 85
HAMMITT, John 170 263
 Margaret 263
HAMMIT, Infant 192 J.S. 192
HAMPTON, __ 116 Alice 285 305
 A.S. 22 268 Bessie 29 Bill 293
 Bridget 227 Dan 203 Daniel 99
 143 268 Ellen 70 97 Fred 151
 George 24 127 151 Grace 200
 Grant 194 Hannah 143 Infant 24
 John 268 Katherine 116 Laurie
 108 Lizzie 127 194 M. 127
 Malina 83 Mary 43 Matt 194 201
 Mattie 218 Millie 72 Myrtle 53
 Nettie 211 Phebia E. 169 Phoebe
 117 Polly 264 Robert A. 99
 Sarah 73 83 149 194 268
 Sherman 73 William 83 223 293
 William Parley 217 William
 Woodward 73 210 W.S. 96 99
 108 210 217 218 260
HANEN, Nellie 296
HANKINS, J.F. 298 Malinda 298
 Myra 291
HARDING, Ford 181 Sam 181
HARDIN, Carl 166 Dessie 166
 Jane 165 J.A. 101 122 Rebecca
 56 Rebecca J. 297 W.H. 166
HAREN, Elizzie Pearl 77
HARES, Nancy 91
HARE, Grave 16
HARISON, James 91 William 91
HARKINS, Bill 255 Infant 255

HARMON, Arthur L. 47 Harold
 Francis 47
HAROLD, Marie 266 McKinley
 266
HARRELL, A. 33 D.A. 260
 Georgia Ray 260 Nancy 52 Wiley
 B. 88
HARRINGTON, Fred 80 W.B. 80
HARRISON, C_ 269 Carry B. 164
 C.L. 108 James 91 Matilda 250
 Robert Taylor 19 William 91
 W.B. 75
HARRIS, __ 203 A. 61 Ada 32
 145 Adeline 138 Allice 106
 Archlene 112 Armstrong 158
 Bessie 304 Betty 223 B. 198 C_
 256 Carl 176 177 Charles 176
 256 Charlie 138 242 Clay Daniel
 122 Dave 257 Dempsy 276 Dora
 3 Dwight 33 Earne 198 Estel 158
 Estell 137 Fletch 33 39 Florence
 295 Frank 60 276 Gather 31 Hale
 248 Harrison 105 190 252 Henry
 188 Herman 256 Horace 31
 Hugh 105 Ike 200 Infant 19 124
 Jake 112 James 191 Jane 106
 Jason 105 110 158 256 Jason
 Carson 256 Jocinth 61 John 105
 Joseph 61 Jossie 170 Jude 60
 Judy 188 J.D. 257 J.F. 33 118
 J.H. 200 J.L. 101 J.M. 33 J.T.
 265 K. Callie 284 Kissie 118
 Laura 218 Layretta 243 Lindy
 170 Lucinda 67 238 Lula 68 Lula
 May 147 Luther 177 229 290
 Lydia 39 Marion 214 Maud 111
 Minnie 4 Nancy 61 Nancy Ann
 56 Nathaniel 229 Patty 110 191
 Phinettie 244 Pinkston 158

HARRIS (continued) Polly 221
Quillin 124 Rachel 265 Rebecca
283 Rheuhana 90 Richard 106
Richard Pinkston 105 Robert
Luther 290 Ruthanna 62 R.F.
200 R.L. 197 Sam 187 252 Sarah
276 Siddie Pearl 101 Thelma 290
Tom 33 T.C. 198 Walter 39 290
Will 31Willard Brady 187
William 170 176 William
Chester 252 William Harrison
118 William Lester 200
HARR, Clara 159
HARTMAN, Sofia 66
HARTSELL, Nancy 240
HARTSEL, Nancy C. 170
HARTSOCK, Winnie Elizabeth 140
HARVEL, Maggie 46
HARVEY, Alfred 173 250
Amanda 99 Amuil Clety 204 Bob
110 Dewey 174 Essie Parker 205
Howard 250 James 204 Jim 167
Mariah 173 Mary Francis 110
Maxine 236 Nelia Booth 231
Mrs. Orville 245 Paul 250
Ramon 291 Raymond 236 Sam
173 174 S.S. 231 Thomas 173
Thomas V. 174 204 Tom 236
W.D. 99
HARVICK, Mary 140
HASH, __ 273
HASKETT, Amanda 261
HASKINS, Martha C. 237
HASTINGS, Annie Lee 204 Clint
257 Elizabeth 177 Ezra 204 E.F.
244 Hazel Helen 244 Henry
Franklin 257 J.C. 177 Nancy
Jane 177

HASTON, Vertie 133
HATCHER, Catherine C. 239 Fred
D. 254 George 239 Henry 254
292 Infant 292 J.A. 239 William
124
HATTAN, Mark 209 William
Carey 208
HAUN, Daniel 122 Effie 142 Ethel
6 George 114 Glee 290 G.W. 122
Herman 286 Jimmy Hobart 286
Julia 114 233 Peter 133 Retta
122 Rose 43 R.L. 114
HAWKINS, Bulah 203 S.M. 243
HAYMON, Virginia 54
HAYNES, Anna Lee 87 Arthor
135 Arthur 265 A.W. 87 Buena
Vista 88 Emma 271 Frank 135
Frank 135 George G. 150 John
58 J.K. 88 Lesley 16 Madison P.
150 Mary Ida 265 Matilda 180
Nathaniel Taylor 271 Nathaniel
T. 150 Samuel 58 William 58
HAYS, Mary 196 Bekkue 196
HEADRICK, J.S. 270 Mary 275
282 Millie 35
HEAD, Amanda Cochran 192
Blake 175 189 Carl 175 Elbert
158 Eller 65 Hunter 85 Infant 85
Jane 21 255 Jessie 189 John 65
Julia 85 J.S. 263 Lucy 158 Luria
277 Mary 65 S.J. 189 Thurman
34 T.H. 277 William 34 William
Allen 263 W.J. 175
HEATON, Dashia 71
HEDNRICK, E.D. 36
HEDRICK, Lina 94 M.A. 94
HELTON, Dasha 85 Infant 135
Oscar 135
HENDERSON, Ruth 295

HENDRIX, Mary Emma 219
HENLEY, Charlie 104 Rose 104
HENLINE, Mary 66
HENSLEY, __ 205 254 Albert 153
Amos 220 Ana May 120 Andrew
90 Angeline 125 199 Anis 55
Annie 90 April 5 Armp 218
Armstrong 104 Banner 114
Barbery 16 Barnet 104 Berry 34
Billie 259 Blanche 224 B.L. 52
Carlotta 36 Cassie 236 261
Charles 150 Charles B. 276
Claude 196 Calyton 8 Clingman
121 Cordelia 297 Cornerly 213
Critty 158 C.B. 209 C.E. 32 41
229 C.J. 167 Della 98 Doe 219
Dora 29 Dorothy 219 Dortherly
188 Ebb 295 Edna 264 Effie 80
Eliza 59 Elizabeth 96 105 278
Elizer 110 Ella 146 Elsie 31
Elvira 12 Elzie 82 Emeline 203
Mrs. Ervin 225 Ethel 281 Evert
14 Florence 301 Francis 180
Frank 114 George W. 213 Gladys
127 Golman 8 G.B. 112 Harm
Corenlius 258 Harrie 37 Harrison
98 Harry 115 Henry 29 Hester
229 Himack 289 Hobart 140 141
Howard 195 Howard D. 276 H.C.
52 Infant 29 43 44 45 110 140
293 Irene 86 Jake 285 James 42
188 237 287 James M. 266 James
Thomas 2 Jane 102 194 290
Jason 203 Jeraldine 209 Jessie
121 Jessie May 224 Jim Frank
284 Jimmy 208 Joe 44 45 Joel
179 John 90 98 136 184 218 293
Joseph 17 Joseph H. 141
Josephine 99 Julia Ann 27 J.A.
10 J.B. 43 145 224 234 J.C. 89
91 289 J.E. 43 J.H. 264 276 J.H.
Jr. 276 J.N. 152 J.W. 152
Larance 55 Lenzy 196 Leon 42
Leona 220 Lewsindy 5 Linda 139
Lindy 185 Lizzie 137 Lofton 41
Louisa 152 Lucinda 258 Lucindy
213 Lula 54 73 L.E. 88 Maggie
88 133 148 Margaret 96 134 254
Marie 287 Marion 96 Martha 43
222 278 Martha Jane 202 Martha
J. 278 Mary 37 54 86 90 102 114
126 136 236 271 Matly 121 May
93 158 McKinley 145 Merrett
287 Mildred 278 Mollie 111
M.E. 172 Nancy 110 138 158
256 Noah 54 89 Nola May 222
Oscar 99 Paul Carroll 295 Polly
303 R_ 214 Rebecca J. 41 229
Rena 78 Reuben 114 Robert
Edward 304 Robert Lee 284
Robert W. 12 Rome 153 Rosco
37 R.b. 184 R.C. 104 R.J. 82
Sallie 161 Sally 145 Sarah 164
181 Starling S. 34 Sulvania 303
S.R. 291 S.S. 236 S.V. 258 Texie
99 Thomas Carter 236 Tomes 15
T.C. 34 Dr. T.C. 31 Vance 137
Vernon 12 Vi 290 Vira 112
Virginia 291 Wallace 304 Walter
86 110 158 220 Wash 203
Wilburn 217 Willard L. 150
William 52 62 133 William K.
27 Wylie 115 W.A. 184 217
W.F. 215 W.H. 24 195 W.K. 44
45 W.R. 179 Zeb 296 Zeb D.
Vance 136
HENSON, Bell 122 Earl 213
Hubert 122 Mattie 107 Mollie 81

HENSON (continued) Myrtle
  Irene 213 Rebecca 44 Vira 204
HEREN, Z.G. 77
HERNS, Nellie 286
HERRELL, Austin 214 D.C. 227
  George 227 72 Julia 163 Millie
  A. 227 M. Hugh 216 Samuel 28
  Spencer 72 William 28
HERRILL, Celia 28
HESTER, George 106 137 Gladys
  287
HESTER, Roy 106
HEWITT, Rebecca 275
HICKS, Carry 72 Catherine 114
  Elbert 173 Ella 116 George
  Dewey 295 H.H. 52 Jane 140
  John 139 Robert Franklin II 295
  Sarah 52
HIGGINBOTHOM, Lora Tilson
  129
HIGGINS, Amanda E. 84 139
  Anna 304 Arthur 68 180 Barbara
  218 Bethel 190 Bonnie 179 Celia
  37 Cinda 184 Cora 255 Cora
  Mae 272 Dora 50 149 D.C. 86
  Ed 236 Edgar 64 Elizabeth 20
  181 Ellis 84 134 Enidien 186
  Ernest 148 Floyd 272 Frank 212
  235 George 157 199 224 G.W.
  36 Hanah 97 Hester 256 Infant
  19 180 212 Jane 32 91 131 143
  John 66 John Henry 304 John H.
  36 Julia Alberta 224 J.D. 148
  J.H. 11 241 J.H. Sr. 12 J.L. 93
  297 J.T. 160 Leroy 96 130 Lizzie
  106 Lula Annie 269 Lydia May
  127 L.D. 127 L.J. 97 Mamie 141
  Mary 93 Mildred 159 Minorca
  304 M.B. 159 249 Nevoy 81 Otis
  189 Pansey 86 Pansy 68 Paul
  William 272 Pollie 241 Paul
  William 272 Pollie 241 Polly 231
  Ralph Gay 133 Rebecca 291 Sam
  134 Samuel 106 181 236 274
  Sarah 235 266 Shelby 304
  Stewart 130 Stuart 182 Susan
  248 Texie 32 Thugie 37 Vance
  14 William 64 William Ellie 274
  William L. 64 William T. 84
  Woodward 133 W.E. 64 86 181
  Zora 287
HIGGIN, Sarah M. 50
HILBERT, Flora 264 Mae 114
HILL, Arthur 206 Bert 70 Bertha
  233 Bertie 109 Bertie L. 82 Hicks
  284 Hilda 284 Howard 62 70
  H.H. 24 Mollie 298 William 284
  William Clayton 284
HILMAN, Mattie 52
HILMON, Fred 292 Thomas 292
HINES, Elizabeth 216 Matttte 216
HINE, Lisetta Marie 197 Thomas
  L. 197 T.H. 197
HINSON, Rebecca 144
HOBBS, Lela 266 Mamie Urekins
  224 Mary E. 224 S.L. 224
HOBGOOD, Blanche 193
HODGE, Ida 222 John 55 J.M. 233
  Rose Etta 233
HOGAN, Bessie 194
HOLBROOK, Goldie 253
HOLCOMB, Abner 22 Earl 22
  Elcie 280 Elizabeth 11 Enid 32
  Harold Thomas 234 Roy 234
  Sarah 139 U.S. 32 William 280
  William M. 22 W.P. 22
HOLDER, Maude 262

HOLLAND, Bessie 165 Gene 266 Thomas 266
HOLLIFIELD, C.D. 289 Francis 290 Max 290 Ray 289 Shirley Joyce 289
HOLLOWAY, Nellie 176
HOLT, Louise 286
HONEYCUTT, __ 265 276 Arthur 225 Arvill Lee 168 A.N. 242 Charley Edward 199 Connie 195 Credy 83 Crety 289 C.C. 168 C.H. 178 199 Dave 144 Dawson 136 Dicey 29 Dillard 36 Dina 158 Edna Mae 303 Elisha 142 Elizabeth 114 Ezekiel 106 Francis 216 238 F.B. 118 George 243 George Washington 303 Gerthie 283 Hanah 98 Hick 25 Infant 57 62 Irene Fay 243 Jack 36 John 152 Julia 164 Kizar 242 Lemuel 142 Leona 295 Litha 152 Loretta 176 Lucy 178 Martha C. 118 Mary M. 27 Matt 62 Maude 283 Minnie 60 Myrtle 141 233 M.R. 160 Peter 254 Polly 25 Robert V. 242 Rosco 238 Ruth 225 Sadie 57 58 Sam 160 Samuel 227 Sarah 144 175 Sidney 144 S.B. 227 Tom 225 William 25 William M. 25 W.R. 136 Zeke 254
HOPKINS, Martha Jane 123 Ruby 289
HOPSON, Angelina 204 Bert 20 Bessie 263 Bob 178 Delia 79 Delila 133 Etta 3 George 131 133 Ike 263 Jake 131 Jason 253 263 Joe 262 John 253 Joshah 253 J.A. 20 178 204 M. 103 Neoma 178 Nick 131 Paul 103 Phoeba 80 W.C. 133
HORD, Fisher 138
HORNE, Drew Franklin 248 Elizabeth 300 Frank 248 Lee 248
HORN, Elizabeth 257 Frank 31 Idy 15 Lee 31
HORTON, Annie 123 Benjamin Taylor 252 David M. 150 Elvira 51 Infant 203 Isaac 112 J.W. 252 Lewis 7 Lottie 275 Milton 203 Taylor 123 Zeph 252 Zephine 150
HORVILLE, John 42 William 42
HOUSTON, Rosa 302
HOWARD, Pollie 62
HOWELL, Albert 291 Christine 74 Dave 152 Dudley J. 44 E. 42 Edgar 275 Effie 23 Eliza 281 Emegene 2 Emma 291 Florence 215 Frank 22 270 275 Geter 74 Harmon 3 Infant 22 44 James 274 276 James Ray 123 Jasper 231 232 Jeff 281 Jeff N. 291 J.W. 64 70 83 90 92 105 181 200 278 Lillie 94 Lomy 262 Lorena Mae 270 Luke 159 Luvada 126 Mae 275 Martha 269 Mattie 144 Minnie 159 274 Neal 281 Pete 275 281 Polly 52 Ramon 232 Robert 282 291 Rufus 9 Ruth 152 Sid 159 Sidney 274 Teter 180 Tinetta 92 Will 169 232 William 276 William H. 281 W.T. 123 Zeb 152 Z.N. 215
HOWE, Jim 179
HOWINGTON, W.P. 206
HOYLE, Andrew 157 Diana 64 65 147 Fred 293 Hiram 157 295

HOYLE (continued) Jerry 293 295
Martha 295 Narcissa 208 Sara
Cordelia 64 Thomas 34
HOYL, Dora 27 H.S. 10 J.M. 27 L.
Zira 10
HUDGSON, Soloman 202
HUFFINE, Franklin Taylor 114
John 114 J. Adison 123
HUFF, __ 137
HUGHES, Amie 249 Amy C. 273
Andrew 248 Bacus 281 Bayler
259 Bessie 253 Burnie 279 B.H.
223 Caroline 144 Celia 80
Charles 249 273 Dalphus 234
Dave 273 David 101 153 David
A. 133 Dolphus 259 279 296
Dora 115 244 Earl Eugene 294
Elen 252 Elizabeth 41 Ernest
Casey 284 Garth 182 Gather 300
Gertie 224 Hassie 269 Holden
182 Infant 38 234 296 Isabell
257 James William 303 Jane 301
Joe 106 John 59 Josie 182 245
253 Julia 122 J.E. 80 Leona 162
238 Maggie 42 Margaretta 225
Mary 165 Nelson 248 Oma 89 P_
144 Paul 153 Rachel 125
Rebecca 101 Robert 294 Robert
H. 284 Rosetta 272 Ruby 300
Toma 115 Walter 38 White 281
Will 125 Willie 115 W.F. 303
HUGHS, Cliford L. 14
HULING, Sarah 46
HULL, Edna 214
HUMPHREYS, Andy 283 Nannie
43 Rebecca 75
HUMPHREY, Henry 116 Mary 83
Nanie 116 Nannie 83

HUNTER, Caroline 267 Harriett J.
270 Huldy 65
HURDT, James 172
HURD, Flossie 125 Luther C. 125
Virginia Caroline 125
HURT, M.L. 301 Ruth 301
HUSKINS, __ 92 Anna Lee 41
Annie 211 Charles 260 E_ 97
Elbert 58 Ellie 118 Geneva 157
Harrison 246 H.E. 126 Idie 91
Jane 41 61 Joe 214 John 21 187
Josie 38 136 J. 118 J.E. 27 38 54
59 J.H. 187 J.W. 37 Lizzie 21
Louzretia 37 Marie 214 Mary
192 Mary Ann 44 Nancy 54
Nancy D. 98 Rena 191 Robert 21
Samuel 41 Vina 83 W_ 187 Will
298 William 58
HUTCHENS, Dora 147 Jess 147
Francis 293 Grady 129 286
James M. 293 Jess 135 Jesse 209
Julia 209 Rosa 135 Walter
Frederick 286 Wright 293
HUTTON, Arthur D. 81 Ralph 81
HYATT, Florence 270
HYDER, Dave 237 Emaline 85
100 Golf 71 Robert 111 Vina 254
HYLMAN. David 76
HYLMON, Thomas 234
INGLE, A. 24 __ Clamon 42
Clifford 51 Elizabeth J. 147
Ellen 150 Estel 24 Fred 228
Isaac 51 Mark 228 Menerva 156
Polly 188 Ruby 223 Savannah 77
T.C. 150 Willie Viola 42 W.G.
147
INGRAM, Brown 201 Essie 219
F.H. 138 George 236 Harley 251
284 Hattie 126

INGRAM (continued) Helen Christine 284 Howard 201 J.C. 236 J.W. 244 Leona 299 Mabel 283 Manassa 299 302 Mary 302 Mary 302 Nathaniel 135 N.A. 302 303 Pollie 251 Sallie 170 Sam 125 Smith Woodward 302 William 135 138 302 W.H. 135
IRBY, Carolina 294
ISAACS, Lois 129
JACKSON, Albert 195 Angeline 236 Austin 51 Bertha 135 Calvin 135 C.B. 19 Edd 219 Edward 135 Everett 159 G.C. 130 Infant 159 Jarrett 130 Mable 219 Martha 137 Rlgy 195 Ruby 219 W.C. 51 Mrs. W.C. 51
JACOBS, Carrow 169
JAMES, Abner 231 Margaret 188
JARRETT, George 35 Infant 35
JARVIS, Abner 295 Lula 288 Rosa 282
JENKINS, Julia 73 175 Thomas 246
JENNINGS, Charles E. 61 Leta 32
JERVIS, Margaret 132
JESSE, Ruth 72
JEWELL, Charley 105 Eliza 26 27 George 27 64 George Raymond 26 Infant 265 John 64 Lola 265 Mae 265 Robert 105
JEWEL, Catherine 61 Ellen 181 Infant 181 Lola 181
JILLES, James Brown 216 Naddie 216
JIMISON, Mary 186
JINKER, John 89
JOHNAS, Dela 112

JOHNSON, Adie 84 Annie 224 Clarcia Emmie 142 Corda 146 84 203 Dartha 223 D.A. 189 Emma 27 Enylu 110 Eva May 66 E. 94 E.L. 94 G.B. 46 G.W. 143 Harold Vivian 253 Hester 58 111 Ivery 199 Jake 110 James 12 189 J.A. 191 Mrs. J.A. 191 Leuria 46 Lizzie 161 Marshall 162 Mollie 91 206 Moses 25 Patrick H. 189 Pollie 209 Rachel R. 143 R.C. 198 R.T. 198 Sarafina 94 Sherman 223 Simpson 66 William 75 W.J. 253 Zeb 199
JOHNSTON, __ 272 Ethel 272 John Thomas 272
JONES, __ 31 Albert 79 Alice 39 203 Amanda 241 Andy 268 A.S. 57 Barbara Ellen 66 Belle 288 Birdie 16 Blake 278 Bud 146 276 Catherine 157 205 214 Celia 83 105 Cenia 34 Charles 91 Mrs. Charles 60 Charley 204 Mrs. Charley 204 Chester 129 Chester 139 159 Cora Belle 119 C.B. 60 Daicy 87 Danal 49 Dartha 146 Davis Silas 81 Delia 48 Dorothy 303 Earl Franklin 269 Elbert 50 212 219 229 Elizabeth Ida 209 Emeline 244 Ernest 276 Ethel 91 Etta 247 E.L. 119 Gaither B. 126 George C. Jr. 129 Gilbert 161 H_ 33 Henry 61 92 128 195 201 207 Hiram 287 Hoy 116 Infant 139 Iris 274 Jack Roberts 230 James Douglas 276 James E. 81 Jennie 182 Joe A. 87 John 87 92 107 204 219 287 Julia A. 9 Julia B. 91 J.E. 80 161 183 J.M. 22 92

JONES (continued) Katherine 154 Leonard 39 Leonard Hester 159 Dr. Lewis 26 27 Lizzie 12 Lora 60 Lora Dean 287 Louis David 195 Margaret 229 Martha 49 145 Martha Ann 116 Myrtle 204 M.J. 1833 Nancy 186 Nannie 201 Naomi 47 Oran Hutsel 83 Orra Clive 89 Paul 27 230 Pauline 26 Perl 49 Pheba 211 Pheoba 16 Rachel 303 Ransom 47 Rebecca 217 Rhoda 145 Robert 154 157 219 Roda 157 Rosa 295 Roy Harrison 303 Rufus 83 R.D. 118 R.P. 37 R.S. 224 Sallie 98 Sam 159 228 Sarah 257 Thomas 224 Thomas J. 128 Trotie 281 T.S. 214 Urah Haskell 91 Van 37 Virgie 80 Walter 79 William 51 William 212 William H. 75 Woodward Swain 269 W.H. 26 56 89 126 128 143 Zeb 303
JORDAN, Elizabeth 300
JOYCE, Ellen 209 229
JOY, Henry 86
JULIAN, G.L. 28 Polly Eveline 28
JUSTICE, Deborah 260 Eliza 232
KAGLEY, Harold Westley 193 J.H. 193
KATTOX, Howard 270
KEEBLER, Frank 39
KEENER, Claud 135 Cordie 140 C.C. 133 David 71 232 Drew 204 206 215 Mrs. D.N. 206 Florence Cordie 141 Lula 217 Maude 112 Stella 133 Susan 64 Will 133
KEENE, Enoch 125 G.F. 125 William Mathis 125
KEERL, W.T. 205

KEESEAKER, Ethel 197 Adrian Garrett 300 A.G. 292 Etta May 292 300 Jacob 300 Wilbur 185 W.A. 185 W.O. 185 300
KEEVER, Bessie Lee 272 Drew 151 D.N. 151 Jacob 151 Nelson 245 Rosa Lee 245
KEGLEY, J.W. 231
KEITH, __ 34 Braxton 257
KELEY, J.M. 98 May 98 R.M. 98 Ellen Bruner 244 Flossie 138
KELSEY, Jennie 226
KEMPFIELD, Georgia 154
KENEDY, C.A. 105 Linnie 105
KENLY, Mabel 171
KENNEDY, Ella 211
KEPLINGER, Josie 155 Paul K. 104 Vestie 3
KERNS, Annie 124 J.D. 124 Myrtle Jane 191 William 124
KILBY, James Albert 53 J.H. 53
KILMER, Audrey 240 George K. 233
KINARD, John Andrew 66 Mrs. J.A. 66 Martin Luther 66
KING, Andy 191 Harry H. 31 Ida 150 J.B. 258 Peggy 52 W.L. 31
KINNING, Paul S. 102
KIPPLING, W.F. 87
KIPPLIN, W.F. 58
KIRK, Becky 116 Bill 295 Billie Jean 295 Dan 201 Daniel 70 Edny 195 Jim 70 Nannie 231 Robert 70 Wolsey 231
KISSICKER, Ethel 168
KITE, Hazel C. 88 Luther 88 L.D. 102 Rosetta 102
KRIDER, Mary 76
KUNER, Margaret 41

KUSECKER, Infant 18
LACY, Sammie 32
LAMBERT, Helen May 80 W.G. 80
LAMON, Ira 96 Irene 96
LANDERS, Maggie Hensley 188
LAND, E.B. 206 F.E. 158 Infant 158
LANE, Betty A. 111 Carl 206 I.K. 207 John 206 J.A. 107 Marie 107 Mary E. 207 William D. 250
LAUGHREN, Arcinus 148 Dosser M. 148 Hannah 79 Mollie 303 William Durent 229
LAUGHRUM, Bill 209
LAWING, Clara Bell 145 Daniel 26 D.T. 191 Mrs. D.T. 191 Elbert 60 67 111 Elizabeth 54 235 Flossie 106 124 Infant 136 Jack 218 John 2 Julina 152 J.B. 37 102 117 152 Laura 226 Laura E. 161 Leonard 26 Maud 112 Pearl 60 Stanley 102 William 67 145 W.A. 136 W.M. 67 180 218
LAWSON, Deffina D. 49 James Wesley 156 R.W. 138 156 183 Thomas 49 69 Walter Hubert 183
LAWS, Amis 203 Amos 203 Annie May 28 Becky 160 Ms. Bernie 232 Bill 203 Billie 254 Bob 161 D.M. 132 Elizabeth 164 Henry 235 Infant 126 132 Jane 202 Joe 202 John 126 J.W. 125 Lizzie 145 Netta 125 Rettie 36 Robert 160 R.L. 115 Sarah 115 161 W.T. 203
LEACH, E.W. 125 Will H. 125
LEDERWOOD, Cynthia 180

LEDFORD, __ 190 Alford 58 246 Alfred 131 264 Amos 264 Amos Franklin 250 Blanch 9 Brown 278 E. 190 Edith 250 Elizabeth 207 Fred 146 Hannah 219 Infant 183 Jane 88 Jason Woodward 250 Jasper 204 Joe 278 J.W. 20 40 250 Kitty L. 11 Louttie 20 M_ 68 Mary 40 63 278 Nancy 253 O.M. 68 183 Polly 92 Rachel 55 Sarah Jane 264 Susan 14 Texie 90 Troy E. 58 W.C. 90
LEMDY, Ellis L. 247
LEMON, Rachel E. 255
LENTZ, Rebecca 243
LEONARD, John 116 Ki;oe 214 Martha 232 Ralph 116
LETERAL, Matilda 256
LETTERMAN, B.L. 169 Dessie 169 Ed 144 Hannah 44 161 Mary J. 24 Milton 44 Noah 44 Sarah Jane 144
LEWIS, __ 73 93 229 Altha 82 Arlie Jane 254 Atha 22 Audie 114 Betsy 166 Bill 33 Carrie 292 Charles Edgar 93 Cora L. 29 Mrs. C.E. 93 David 33 50 260 Davie 260 Deborah 33 Dora 141 Elizabeth 128 Evert 167 Fred F. 149 Haret 50 Henry 14 Ida 169 Jessie L. 149 John M. 131 Joseph W. 254 J.W. 251 Leroy 25 Lida 8 Lilly 25 Lula 174 Luther 25 L.J. 131 Mallie 114 Maney 260 Mary 15 Mary Jane 173 M. Daniel 25 N.S. 31 Ora 31 Rody 159 Samuel 251 Sarah 50 199 T.J. 196 Mrs. T.N. 196 Willard 251 260 Willard Ray 48 W.S. 29 48 167

LILBURNE, Nancy 150
LILLBURN, Marien 135
LILLEY, James Matthew 286 John D. 286 Matilda B. 286
LINDSAY, Mary A. 94
LINDSEY, Caroline 169 Frank 169 J.M. 211
LINKINS, Fannie 163
LINVILLE, Dana Landon 43 Emily 71 Howard Ray 32 James 43 116 John 83 Loyd 83 Minnie Ray 116 Perna 2 Will 207 William A. 32 W.A. 71 91
LIPE, Abraham 117 William 117 Mrs. W.F. 117
LISENBIE, Malinda 223
LITTERFORD, Sara 113
LITTLE, Elizabeth 126 Gracy Pearl 1 Mary 210
LLOYD, Blanch 251 David 263 Gleason 85 Joe 263 Lattie 85
LOCKNER, Fred 192 Ida 192
LOGAN, George 31 Larkin 24 Manaley Erwin 24 Mollie 31
LOID, Dary 15
LONG, Dana 190 221 287 Dana Jr. 190 Harley D. 221 John 190 251 John Richard 272 Johnny 287 Martha 30 Mozella 272 Myrtle 251 Pancy May 251 William 272 William Martin 272
LOOPER, Vinie 178
LOUDY, Dave 155
LOUELL, Thomas 216
LOUGHREN, Sam 229
LOURY, Marie 166
LOVELACE, Heta 164 Jaunita 301 Nita 100

LOVETTE, Bertha 252 David 274 John 252 274 Mary 250 Stewart 274 277 Stuart 252
LOVETT, Guy 200 Infant 165 Stewart 200 Stuart 165
LOVE, Bettie 227 Bob 268 Cena 234 D. 49 Dillard 67 68 124 268 Earl 247 Gertrude 268 Gladie 124 Grant 68 Ike 240 I.R. 149 Joe 268 John R. 7 Lola 86 Marion 247 Martha C. 49 Paul 67 Phoeba 134 Robert 225 241 Roy 67 Sam 234 Sarah Ann 194 Virginia A. 94 Walter 144 Walter W. 227 Will 212 William 94 170 240 W.C. 170 234 W.P. 151
LOWE, C.E. 291 E.L. 291 Mary 291 Sinda Tipton 111
LOWING, Billy 238 Della 227 Jane 254 Joseph 238 William 300
LOWRY, Charles M. 100
LOYD, Ben 75 119 138 Blanch 137 Edward 119 Eller 148 Flow Ellen 55 Fred 178 Infant 138 I.A. 55 Laddie 178 Velma 75
LOY, Artie Louise 180 S.W. 180
LUCAS, Infant 168 Julia Katherine Creech 23 J.W. 23 Troy 168 Uncella 178
LUNCEFORD, Brownlow 167 M.P. 167
LUNDY, Clyde Vance 255 Elizabeth Leola 255 Nancy 280 Terry Jr. 54 T.H. 54 256 Wiley M. 255
LUNSFORD, __ 246
LUTS, Jane 101

LUTTRELL, Albert 127 Dora 135
Infant 127 184 Isaac Washington
129 I.W. 237 Linda 129 Mollie
Tittle 237 Nattie 260 Sam 235
William 184 237
LYLE, Bert 235 Edna 26 Floyd
Alvey 47 Frank 47 Gracie May
217 John 57 Mrs. John 147 209
Martha 209 Martha J. 57 Robert
R. 217
LYONS, Mary 55
MACDOUGALL, Anna 165
MACKINTOSH, Cora Lee 173
MAHAFFEY, Mary 192
MAHATHEY, Mary 64
MAMAHAN, Estelle 148
MARKHAM, John 298
MARKIN, Garfield 63 Infant 63
MARKLAND, Blain 43 D.W. 186
Emory Alfred 43 Nelson 186
MARLOW, Nancy Isabel 141
MARRIS, Mary 18
MARR, Emma 272 Manarcha 241
MARSH, Edith 207 George 155
Gracy Louise 155
MARTIN, Bak 153 Clifton 156
Helen Lea 130 J. 125 John 125
Lula B. 20 Lulu 291 L.G. 156
172 Marvin 172 Samuel 130 154
Sherman 114 Warren G. 154
MASHBURN, Alvin 212 Andy
Clifford 38 Bessie 15 Bob 56
Calloway 212 297 Carl 55 Cora
56 71 140 Dora 65 87 174 Elizie
186 Emmaline 45 295 Helen 189
Infant 134 Jacob 212 Jake 189
James 124 John 106 241 Liza 64
124 Malinda 106 Martha May 17
Mary Louise 241 Melvin 38

Nancy 205 Rebecca 57 239 T.M.
38 134 T.N. 32 William 297
W.M. 57 62
MASON, Homer L. 250 Jeanette
250
MASSEY, Mandy 113
MASTERS, Alexander 79 Annie
51 Bertha 246 C.B. 294 Dicie 29
Dicy 138 Evelyn 262 Hattie 196
Ida May 18 Jacob 80 J.W. 51
Kate 143 Katie 99 L_ 68 Lidia
154 Maggie E. 111 Nancy A. 111
Phil 248 Rhoda 127 Senia E. 73
Shirley 294 Worley 29 Worly
138
MAST, Charlotte 252
MATHES, Altha 54 Amanda 187
Belle 283 Belle Garland 289 Ben
213 Emeline 52 George 269
George W. 301 Joseph 52
Laurence 289 Lenrie 48 Lizzie
46 Loda 46 301 Lucy 74 101
Ninah 48 Ruth 213 Sanis 48
Sarah 301 Velma 54 Walter 283
286 Will 301 Willard 166
William 269
MATHIS, Ben 155 166 252
Clarence David 155 Edward 259
Estelle 252 Ezekiel Soloman 242
Harben Edward 259 John 38
Lena 162 Maude Tipton 296
Phenchca 19 Sandy 296 Sarah
280 Uma 145 Walter 131
MATHUS, Brigett 107
MATON, Elizabeth 44
MAUK, Abe 189 Mary 71 T.M.
189
MAYNARD, James 112 Victoria
113

MAYS, Ellen 305
MAY, T.C. 198
MCADOUGALL, Anna 173
MCALF, Sallie 61
MCANICH, Mary 86
MCBEE, Mabel 107
MCBRIDE, Frank M. 263
MCCALL, Julia 179 Louvina 62 Martha 148
MCCAMEY, Nancy 139
MCCANDLESS, Clarence A. 130 Della 130
MCCANN, Teressa 252 Tressie 166
MCCAN, Trissie 155
MCCARTER, Stella 203 Tressie 213
MCCLAIN, Mrs. Ollie 231
MCCLELLAN, Omie 279
MCCORKLE, A.E. 47 Sam 117
MCCOUGALL, Anna 179
MCCRACKEN, Margaret 261
MCCURRY, __ 22 118 235 256 Amos 243 Britton 223 Charlotte 196 Cleophus 135 Cora 193 Cordelia 250 D.W. 230 Elvira 118 Ernest 157 Essie 97 Ethel 156 157 Harrison 178 Ike 193 Infant 47 145 Jane 79 Jay M. 39 J.C. 145 196 J.H. 135 Lillie Howell 169 Loura 202 Luther 31 L.M. 94 Mack 202 230 Malcolm 72 Maxine 178 May 185 Monroe 230 Myrtle 34 M.C. 31 Oliver 72 185 Pauline 192 Pink 192 Rana 204 Rena 185 186 Retha 94 Rosie 150 Ruby 157 Sid 94 Sidney 169 Velida 223 V.S. 96

Wash 16 William 47 223 W.M. 39 Mrs. W.M. 34
MCCURY, Germa 97 Loyd 3 Sarah 94
MCDOUGALL, Anna 155
MCEWEN, Calvin 43 Leroy 12 Will 43
MCFARLINGTON, Infant 10
MCGEE, Betsy 68
MCGINSEY, Allie 264
MCGLAUGHLIN, Malinda 2
MCINTOSH, Alexander 300 Betsy 17 Claude 249 Clifford 90 Cora 281 Cullus 65 Dewey 249 Dolph 269 Earl 190 Ellen 59 Elmira 102 Elsie 90 Emma 249 Fermon 276 Helen Ruth 276 Infant 175 Isaac 19 I.N. 15 James 218 Leroy 218 Lincoln 175 Marcina 287 Mark 145 Mary 63 Newton 287 Rausa 123 Ray 145 Robert 111 Sam 287 300 S.J. 102 Virgie 269 William Jackson 278 Willie 249 W.J. 123
MCINTRUFF, A_ 50 Andy 245 259 265 Annie 238 Basel 77 Bob 211 Mrs. Bob 217 Bruce K. 144 Charles 137 Clarence 245 C.B. 212 Dave 211 272 David 8 70 Dewey 238 Dinah 238 Dlith 81 D.A. 216 D.J. 23 77 110 Earnest Ray 21 Edna Lee 1 Elizabeth 37 Elizabeth J. 66 Emeline 282 Enos 117 E.M. 13 Frankie 279 Gabriel 57 Genevieve 216 Gertie 256 Infant 85 Infant 85 107 117 153 Jack 212 Jackie 221 James 81 107 Jennie Earline 284 Jesse 142 199 Jessie 21 John 82 142

MCINTURFF (continued) John 202 John C. 189 Julia Neal 26 J.A. 165 J.S. 245 Laura 31 Lizzie 61 236 Lizzie Nelson 257 Lena D. 216 Lou 280 Lucinda 146 249 Mae 22 Mande 109 Margaret 156 Mary 165 292 Mattie 142 Nat 211 Nathaniel R. 282 Noah 153 216 N.J. 144 N.K. 23 127 280 Peggy Jane 304 Rachel 136 301 R.N. 109 Samuel 12 257 Sara 303 Sarah 74 242 Sarah Elizabeth 199 Sarah Ellen 162 Scott Howard 71 Shep 283 284 Sindy 106 Skip 280 Tom 264 Ula Louise 188 Virgie 251 284 Walter 71 85 110 Wesley 70 Willard 284 304 William H. 257 270 William R. 23 Willy 16 W.A. 50 106 245 W.H. 66 162

MCINTYRE, Cora 216 J.K. 216 Mrs. J.K. 216

MCINURFF, William 155

MCKAY, James 108 Josie 108

MCKILDEN, Saran Alice 222

MCKINNEY, __ 228 B_ 145 Delia 266 Donna Elizabeth 298 Ellen 298 Henry 177 Infant 254 Jim 249 John W. 123 June 277 J.W. 298 Mae 173 Mary 167 Nancy 249 Nannie 238 Ollie 120 Peggy 91 Phina 301 Poly 140 Reuben 184 Rex 184 254 277 Robert T. 184 R.F. 277 Sam 214 Sarah 214 Tabitha 43 T.W. 96 177 Mrs. T.W. 177 William Stokes 298

MCLAIN, C.L. 94 Janette Franklin 262 O.L. 72 Wade H. 94 262

MCLAUGHLIN, Alf 247 Alvin 3 Amanda 99 C.E. 270 Doxine 185 Ed 232 261 Emerson 196 E.B. 35 Hattie 261 Hattie Carver 232 Jess W. 203 J.H. 99 216 Mrs. J.H. 184 216 Kathleen 203 Kendrick 64 Lola 82 Mary Ann 45 M. Ephram 35 N. 215 Nelson 270 Oscar 185 Robbie 247 Robert 82 R.C. 275 R.C. Jr. 275 Sindy 203 Susie 232 Wic 4 Wilder 101 Willetta Manson 173 William 101 William K. 173 W.B. 232 263 W.K. 215 W.L. 196

MCLEMORE, C.L. 269 Henry 49 226 Julia 226 Nathan 60 Rouben 52 Velma 60 Venie 49 Walter L. 269

MCMAHAN, Elizabeth 52 100 245 282 Sallie 246

MCMILLEN, Estella 24 Mary 261

MCMURRY, Ernest 157

MCNABB, Annie Elizabeth 115 A.W. 178 Bill 231 Charles 178 Clarence 284 Clinton 193 David 217 Davie 178 Eliza 1 Ella Belle 294 Emma 48 Frank 277 Gertrude 144 Grover 128 Grover Seldon 294 Grover S. 115 G.S. 31 95 294 hannah 39 Infant 95 277 Isaac 9 Jessie 193 Joe 121 John Wilson 1 Jonathan 271 Madge Eloise 272 Madine 121 Margaret 36 Margaret K. 21 Marie 284 Mark 225 Myrtle Marie 44 Ralph 31 Robert 82 Robert Henry 272 R.G. 39 Sarah Ellen 175 Taylor 44 144 William Clifton 128 W.B. 236

MCNEELY, H.T. 258Rebecca 258
MCNICOL, Earl 281 Roy 281
MCVAY, Lula 117 Mary 153 Silas 201 Tom 201
MCVEY, Anderson 230 Cindy 230 Jordon 230 Sarah Jane 112 Silas 112
MCWEEN, Mrs. Calvin 43
MEADE, Clayton 273
MEADOWS, Joseph 21
MEAD, John 140
MEEK, Elizabeth Jane 109
MELTON, M_ 160
MERCEY, Ruby 99 William S. 99
MEREDITH, __ 197 Anna Virginia 182 J.F. 182 Thurman B. 69 W.R. 91
MESON, Mytrle 216
METCALF, __ 133 Ada 177 Anettie 42 Dempsy 221 Elizabeth 185 Estell 86 E.A. 280 Florence 283 George 82 96 274 Ham 126 Hobart 53 Hobert 121 Jennie 126 John 126 274 Johnnie 221 J.W. 226 Laura 121 Lovada 96 Mandy 226 Margaret 222 226 Media 220 Richard 149 Sallie 206 Sam 54 Samuel 242 Sarah 241 Velma 143 Vertie 237 Victor 121 Waitsel 226 Wesley 177 Wiley 286 William 222 Willie 86 222 Woodrow Edward 82 W.E. 121
METTOL, Agnes 73
MEYERS, Elizabeth 292 Lyda 289
MILER, Pollie 263
MILLER, __ 240 Alice Jane 253 Allie 83 168 Andy 23 Ann Lois 282 Arther 103 Bob 236 Carmen 283 Caroline 195 Cecil M. 96

Clifton 262 C.M. 282 C.N. 175 C.O. 178 Daniel 85 Edna 24 Elbert C. 149 Eliza 304 Elkanan 63 Ellen 110 Emma 236 Ernest 179 Ester 136 Ethel 24 Fannie Bell 285 Felix 222 Francis 170 Frank 183 Fred 247 Fuller 24 George 96 Goldie 152 Hattie 62 Helen 179 Henry 48 Hiley 232 Hobart 280 Hyder 96 274 Infant 111 126 168 183 280 Jacob B. 214 James M. 304 Jennie 234 Joda 72 John 126 141 216 234 236 John Clifton 262 John K. 146 John Preston 40 72 Johny S. 126 Julia 64 J.B. 5 J.F. 141 J.O. 120 Lena 265 Lillie 144 Lovie 259 Malorie 245 Margaret 129 Marjorie 233 Marra 262 Martha 134 242 Mary 93 Mary Lou 230 Maude Holder 262 Mildred Pauline 247 Millie 88 239 Minnie 48 113 Mollie 153 Nan 144 Nancy 141 Nancy Isabel 141 Nat 111 Neal 4 Nellie 224 N.T. 27 Ollie 12 Ora Ellen 175 Oscar 73 Oscar Haun 268 Pansia 304 Pansy 284 Paul Thomas 268 Ralph 73 Reba 196 Rebecca 266 Robert 283 Rosco 196 Rosetta 112 Sabra 230 Salda 81 Sam 103 Sam Ray 63 Samuel K. 72 Samuel Washington 122 Sarah 286 Shepperd 40 Smith 85 Soloman 23 Susan Carolina 40 Susie 153 T. 122 Tebatha 252 Tempa Ann 274 Thomas 304 Wayne 178 Wesley 304 Willard 27 William 64 79 149 274

MILLER (continued) William
  Elbert 120 William E. 253 W.E.
  73 253 W.M. 191
MILLIE, Ollie 18
MILTON, Manima 262
MINTON, Mrs. L.L. 26
MITCHELL, Caroline 63
  Elizabeth Lee 25 John 187 J.H.
  25 187 Rosa 25 Rosa Florence
  187
MONK, Edward L. 58 J.C. 58
MONTGOMERY, Clarence 182
  Hugh 182 Jones 182
MOORE, Andy 123 Caroline 185
  299 Charity 87 95 Charley 262
  Etter 130 Fannie 250 Frank 121
  Glennie 213 Infant 122 132
  Jackson 180 James P. 262 Jennie
  59 Julius 180 Mrs. Julius 180
  J.L. 132 Martha 262 Mary 262
  Matilda 270 Mery 247 Ralph 30
  Rebecca Jane 185 Rossey 278
  Russel 213 R.E. 265 R.L. 122
  Samuel 10 87 89 167 Simon 262
  S.J. 160 Thomas Henry 30
  William N. 30 41 121
MOOSHA, Essie McCurry 96
  Infant 97 William E. 96
MORELAND, Orville 7
MORELLE, John 270 Maggie 270
MORELY, Margaret 198
MORE, Eliza 65 Mamey 20 Miller
  65
MORGAN, Ashley 108 C. 114
  Clarence 173 Elan Woods 114
  John C. 114 J.H. 244 Laura C.
  173 Lewis 244
MORLEY, Esther 55

MORRELL, __ 137 Callie 93
  Deyton 279 D.W. 275 H.F. 137
MORRISON, Jennie 116
MORRIS, __ 181 Clara 26 Dudly
  H. 162 Isam 280 Mary Lois 162
  Nan 280 William 166 W.H. 166
  Mrs. W.H. 166
MORROW, Ada Marie 276 Annie
  162 Emma 98 Kittie 178 Kitty 85
  Will 276
MORTON, Jake 266
MOSELY, David 286
MOSELY, John 286 Nathan 245
  Rebecca 286
MOSER, Mary Ann 104
MOSLEY, Edward 44 Harriett 65
  Julia 49 Martha 72 Nachin 226
  William 44
MOSS, C.D. 219 Margaret 67
MOYERS, Daniel 275 Jacob
  Columbus 275 Virlie May 304
MOYER, Elizabeth 72
MULLINS, Janie 266 Leana 232
  Leona 185
MURAY, Jessie 161
MUREY, Yety 15
MURPHY, Margaret Jane 197
MURRAY, Joseph 138 Pearl 64
  Thomas 17
MURRY, Geter 140 Jesse B. 264
  Joe 188 Miney 140 Sarah 78
  Stalla Pearl 264
MYERS, Margaret 166
MYNATT, H.C. 189 Sawyers 189
  William C. 189
NAVE, Elizabeth 20
NEAL, Marion Albert 32 R.A. 32
NEAS, George 31 George M. 32

NELSON, Alice 214 Barbara Ellen 61 Blanie 51 Mrs. Carl 282 Celia 209 Charles 66 David 202 239 David Samuel 88 Earl 267 Effie 184 Eliza 226 Elizabeth 30 Ella Belle 267 Harold M. 93 H.r. 301 Ike 92 202 Infant 97 Isaac 7 James 211 Jasper 91 Joe 80 97 147 John 54 91 92 147 Joseph 301 Lizzie 162 270 Mae 143 Maggie 252 Martha 7 77 Martha 260 Martin 260 Mary E. 80 May 199 Milley 202 Myrtle 144 153 Nancy 91 Nancy Elizabeth 32 Ned 217 Newton 54 Mrs. N. 32 Phillip 88 Rachel 207 Ralph 80 Ralph M. 93 Sabra 202 Sadie Leotta 301 Silvin 7 Tom 125 Willl 51 William F. 267 William Howard 260 W.D. 217 Zeb 217
NEWEL, Edwin Tollison 182 Sam H. 182
NEWMAN, John 180
NICHOLS, Alice 232 Lizzie 120 Thelma 273
NICKLAS, Mary 108
NOELLERT, John 210 Willaim 210
NOLAND, Valda 13
NOREN, K.E. 291 Sarah Lillian Hensley 291
NORMAN, Sallie 204 Sally 244
NORRIS, Alex 158 A.C. 136 Ben 127 Charles 84 Chester 301 C.C. 136 C.T. 194 D.B. 9 Ethel 213 260 H.F. 146 Infant 149 Jim 154 Josephine 155 Lucinda 301 Mary Elizabeth 146 Nannie A. 106 Mrs. Otto 154 Pres 125 Preston 165 203 Rena 127 Richard 158 Richard Herman 84 Richard M. 146 R.N. 18 Shelor 155 William P. 136 Willie 89 W. Otto 154 W.S. 301
NORTH, Gertrude 148
NORTON, Alfred 128 Betty 203 Edward H. 222 John 199 Liza 77 78 Nancy 199 Sallie 222 Singleton 160 Stella Iris 128
O'BRIAN, Clifton 163 Infant 163
O'BRIEN, Albert 245 Benjamin Fletcher 86 Carry 130 Charles 101 Clifton 183 Emma 101 George Clifton 285 Jack 183 Janice Sue 285 Joe 245 John 245 Joseph 130 Sarah 29 William D. 86
ODEN, Anne 135
ODOM, Nancy 146
OLIVER, John 139 William 139
OLLIS, Arther 115 Clarence 255 Franklin D. 255 Infant 129 James 128 129 Margaret 128 Mary 174 Sallie 42 Tilman 115
ORREN, C.A. 280 George Washington 280 Jacob Lundy 280
ORTON, Julia 119
OSBORNE, John 130 Mrs. John 130 Joseph 130 Sarah E. 125
OVERBEY, Haley 63
OVERHOLSER, Thomas B. 283 William J. 283
OVERHULSER, Delina 232
OWENS, Hugh 170
OXENDINE, Luther 102 Rosa Eveline 102
P_, Sarah, 28

PACE, Benjamin Franklin 72
Infant 72
PACK, M.O. 173
PADGETT, Algia 224 Algire 93
Daisy 127 Ed 129 Emily 127 Fay
93 Glenna 261 H.J. 129 Infant 89
Irene 224 Mack 89 261 Maggie
286 S. 129 Sadie 89
PAGETT, Claude 159 Mack 159
PAGGET, Charlie 113 Dasie 113
PAINTER, George Ernest 57
George K. 127 Infant 127 James
57
PAISLEY, G.W. 154 Margaret
Marion 154
PALMER, Elizabeth 278 Rebecca
293
PARDUE, Beatrice Johnson 264
Clyde 264 Soloman B. 264 Mrs.
S.B. 158 Urel Warren 264
PARISH, Nannie 26
PARKER, Dollie 10 Elisah 87
Essie 250 Handy 72 247 Madge
247 Manerva 69 Manuel Love 72
Martha 134 Miley 87 Richard 67
Vagan 10 Wes 250 Wesley 247
W.S. 72 205
PARKLEY, Mose 188
PARKS, Eliza J. 129 Elizabeth 227
Margaret L. 234 Mary 97 113
Polly 184 William 210 224
William E. 299
PARR, George Washington 50
R.C. 50
PARSLEY, Charlotte 231 Edna 43
George 231 Mose 231 Thomas J.
112 113 T.J. 113 Victoria 112
Vivian Pearl 113

PARSONS, Richard C. 138 R.D.
138
PARTLEY, Miss F.P. 69
PARTON, Myra 295
PASE, Infant 55 T.V. 55
PATERSON, David 171 S.G. 171
PATE, Arthur 283 Arthur R. 286
Bettie 179 259 Betty 160 Dewey
85 Eddie Burton 107 Elbert 149
Eliza 293 Ella Tipton 90 Ernie
Lee 242 Eson 98 Fannie 60 111
Flem 293 Infant 64 85 149 John
131 J.E. 14 Kate 197 Linda 66
Lizza 258 Margaret 101 Milton
107 M.S. 131 N. 69 Nathan 98
286 Neal 242 Reuben 74 Rilla
212 Sallie 77 S.F. 207 Tom 64
Zeb 149
PATIE, Marilla 297
PATRICK, George 46 George
William 46
PATTERSON, Jack 117 J.C. 117
M.C.
PATTON, Hassie 215 Ida 222
John 173 Joshua 222 Laura 244
Lurla 104 Susan J. 253 William
S. 222
PAUL, A.E. 139 Infant 139
PAYNE, Alex J. 81 Anna E. 250
A.J. 67 Blanch 138 Blanche 75
119 Daniel 65 Jennie 55 Reba
Maudann 81 Selmon Jesse 81
Vivian Margaret 67 William 215
PEAKE, Mrs. Charles 267 Doris
205 Edith Ruth 205 Julia 24 J.W.
24 205 Oscar 285 Richard 285
PEAK, Helen Boone 111 Rachel
176 Rube 111 H.S. 124 Infant
124

PEEK, Hadley Smith 258 Susan 105 Dr. W.A. 258
PELINGS, Susan 105
PENERAL, Rebecca 123
PENLAND, Louise Poteet 42 Milton 51 Milton F. 51 R.L. 43
PEOPLES, William J. 92 W.J. 92
PERKINS, Suanna 229
PERRY, Dallas Earl 294 Henry 294 Margaret 122
PETERSON, __ 140 Ada 78 Addie 223 268 Albert Lee 276 Allie 178 Ben 171 Mrs. Bert 226 Bindett 79 Birdie 176 Boyd 171 Caroline 152 Cemillie 193 Charles 79 277 Charles C. 176 Chester 143 C_ 107 Cora 192 Dave 80 David 171 Dorothy 228 Doss 143 182 206 244 Elmer 206 Emmaline 271 Esther 71 Ethel Howell 281 Geter 244 Glenna 97 Grover 274 281 Hannah 27 Harry 274 Hassie 20 204 Hattie 264 Ina 39 47 Infant 71 80 136 182 284 James 168 276 Jerry 253 Jess 268 Jesse 223 Jim 258 John 160 168 205 223 John N. 271 Jonas Daniel 271 Joshua 223 274 J.D. 1 J.M. 252 Lawson 94 193 238 Lee 166 Lizzie 77 Loyd 171 Mae 293 Mary 253 271 Mary L. 22 35 Massy 140 May 163 Millie 182 Moses Cling 264 N. 94 Nancy 23 163 183 285 Naoh 193 258 Ollie 199 Pansy 142 274 Paul Roscoe 281 Peter 50 94 Mrs. Peter 50 Peters 258 Polly 191 Reuben 264 Robert 71 79 136 253 Samuel 168 Sarah A. 160 Thomas 104

Tice 166 Treaty 274 Uisie 193 Walter Noah 274 W.N. 271 284
PETERS, Alice Caroline 299 Francis Love 92 G.W. 30 Hugh 28 119 J.F. 119 J.S. 30 Nealey Belle 84 Rachel 297 T.H. 28 92 299 Vreeland Franklin 299
PETTET, Daniel 166
PEW, Dora 100
PHIBBS, William Davis 54 W.W. 54
PHILIPS, Carson 104 Jack 104 Matilda 104 Visa 177
PHILLIPS, __ 254 Addie 302 Allas 161 Bertha 39 145 196 Bessie 7 Betsy 212 Callie 268 Clara 165 C.W. 120 Diana 33 Dorthy Ryden 138 Dwight 151 Emma 210 213 Fidel 151 Fidell 120 George 191 Grant 273 G.S. 258 Hassie 251 Henderson P. 149 Homer 138 Jennie 147 Jimmy Lee 208 John 147 Julia 222 J.D. 208 Kate 87 304 Lizzie 53 Martha 242 Melvin 273 Minerva 294 Minnie 296 Muncy 102 Myra Jane 130 Pheba 195 Rebecca 92 Robin 120 Ruby 221 258 Thomas Warren 149 Veney 120 William 261 W.C. 120 W.L. 149 189 W.M. 39 W.W. 120 Zeb 151
PHILLIP, Bertha May 105 W.W. 105
PHILPOT, J.T. 142
PHIPPS, Ellen 273 Jackson 123 Larkin 123
PICKERING, Infant 111 Robert 111

PIERCE, Dyton 279 Infant 197
James H. 3 L.W. 197
PIERCY, Hattie 100 Hubert 100
  Vostie 150
PIERSON, Lila 263
PITMAN, A.M. 148
PLOTT, Catherine 21
POLAND, Jamima 41
POORE, Aroura 183 Burnie 62
  124 Clifton 279 Estell 124 Frank
  286 Homer 253 Isaac 102 James
  277 279 Jim 159 Joe 253 272 287
  Mary 104 298 Melvina 286
  Robert 286 William 62
POOR, Hester 234 L_ 212
POPE, Henry C. 142 John Richard
  142 Pat 231 William 231
PORTER, _ 219 C.V. 266
POTEAT, Susie 119
POTEET, A.E. 190
POTTER, Clyde 91 Oscar 91
  Wesley J. 91
PRATER, J.R. 247 Salina Geer
  140
PRESNELL, Alha 164 Charley
  153 David A. 88 Elizabeth 154
  Ernest 13 Gilbert 63 Harrison 88
  Joseph 153 Nancy 73 Peter 88
  Pheba 153 Soloman 63 Wesley
  63
PRICE, Annie 58 Beca 107 128
  Buster 241 David Junior 254
  Evelyn 245 Furman F. 223 245
  Grady 241 Infant 22 36 180
  James L. 243 Jane 95 Jim 107
  215 J.W. 243 Laura 179 Lee 254
  Lon 244 Minnie 53 Mirra 173
  Mollie 215 Nolie Mae 53 Nora
  23 Ollie Bell 223 Paris 180
  Rachel 70 177 Rebecca 252
  Samuel Lee 243 Sarah 185 T.E.
  215 Will 36 W.J. 202 Mrs. W.J.
  202 W.P. 23
PRICHARD, Charles 55 N.D. 55
PRINCE, Mrs. Vonnie 270
PRITCHARD, Laurence Payne 267
  Lena J. 172 L.N. 172 267
  Malinda 86
PROFFITT, Blanch 243 Elbert S.
  280 Flora 124 268 Flora May
  173 Julia 280 Lokie 79 May 129
  Wesley 79
PROFFIT, Ben A. 280
PROPST, Kate 67
PUGH, Betty Lou 249 C.R. 249
  Verna Louise 249
PUTMAN, Harvey 202 Drewery
  Alston 294 Mila L. 294
QUESENBERRY, Enos 275
  Tempa Bailey 275 Tobias
  Jackson 275
R_, Edith 96
RADFORD, Anne 223 Celie 292
  Nancy 230 Ruth 287
RAIDER, Ella 69
RAILY, Mary 51
RAINBOLT, Hannah 69
RALDOLPH, Vissie 191
RAMSEY, Elizabeth 101 Glenn
  Fowler 59 Hester 95 Infant 26
  107 128 James 101 John 59
  Johny 15 J.W. 17 Liney 6 Linnie
  10 M.B. 26 Rachel 65 Rebecca
  141 Thalma 243 Thelma 303
  Will 107 128 Zeb 228 Mrs. Zeb
  228
RANDELL, Maud 300

RANDOLPH, Annie 159 A.M. 221
Birtha 57 Elisha 283 Elizabeth
11 208 Elzora Jane 297 Haden
71 Lizzie 57 Lydia 229 Lydia
Margaret 290 Martha 11 Mary
224 228 Murphy 297 M.Z. 177
Samuel 297 Sharlean 283 T.M.
297 V.L. 11 Walcie 11 William
177 221 W.M. 71
RANGE, George 186 George E.
186 John 186 Ruth 186
RATCLIFF, Hattie 23
RATLUF, Martia 238 William 238
RAYBURN, Margaret Sarah 188
RAY, __ 9 79 Aga 55 Albert 61
Angie 121 Arch 55 69 121 Burly
287 Caldona 21 Charles Blake
244 Cindy 238 Claude 101 E_
299 Edd 35 61 62 Elbert 184
Emeline 209 Emely 109 Gathen
C. 184 Infant 10 17 55 95 James
Harrison 50 Jane 69 Julia 19 264
Lula 221 M_ 62 Mary 179 258
Mary Ellen 69 Nelson 61 244
R.W. 121 Riley 50 Sarah 181
265 Shelt 55 275 287 Sirelda 95
101 Stephen 108 Thomas 108
Thomas Lafayette 292 Vista 24
Waco 244
READ, Elizabeth 231
REAVES, Kittie 175 R.B. 175
REECE, Mary 70
REEDY, Rebecca 155
REED, A.M. 24 Elizabeth 196 227
267 John 66 William 134 233
REESE, Nancy 108
REEVES, Edna 177 Gertrude 282
RENFRO, Aliff 238 Annie 176
197 Bob 205 Mrs. Cecil 206

Eistella 72 Hattie 251 Howard
209 Jack 216 John 182 Mrs. John
174 Julia 249 261 Nan Philly 261
Pansy 75 Rube M. 216 Mrs. R.H.
252 R.M. 216 Thelma 211
Thomas 72 T.B. 211 William
226 Mrs. W.S. 264 Zeb 226
RENSHAW, __ 234 Mary 221
REYNOLDS, Emma Jane 219
Kizie 239
RHEA, Elbert 216
RICE, Alice 26 Alva 287 Arlin
286 Betsie 97 Billie 122 B.A.
252 Catherine 287 Cora 10 Dana
129 Denlie 32 Elizith 90 E.J. 23
79 Flossie 77 Floyd 15 George 77
78 Henry 122 Infant 23 79 155
I.M. 26 Jackson 213 James C.
132 Janell 286 Jess 235 Jessie 73
Joe 235 John Calvin 74 213
Joshua Taylor 17 J.C. 74 J.W. 23
Lewis 1 Lizzie 15 Lola 29 Lu
Case 107 Lula 207 Malinda 174
Malinda Jane 132 Marion 107
122 Mary 15 129 Matilda 73 78
Mordecie 269 Nancy 23 78 84
Nat 199 Newberry 155 213 N.B.
130 155 199 296 Oma 261
Quillan 78 R.W. 235 Sarah 233
Tilda Mae 42 Tommy 290
Tommy Jr. 290 T.G. 32 V. 130
William Jackson 74 W.A. 73
W.S. 78
RICHARDSON, Alern 192 Cosby
273 Irene 192 John S. 43 J.S. 43
Lovada 162 William 43
RICH, Frank 193
RIDDLE, Abe 278 Bessie 198
Carrie 166 Carrie Martha 167

RIDDLE (continued) Charlie 258
Cornelius 159 C.C. 267 Dewey
296 Dewey H. 241 Ella 267 Ella
267 Evaline 260 Florence 32
George 50 231 George W. 224
Helen Willis 288 Homer 288
H.L. 63 Indiana 267 Infant 159
James harmon 241 James Marion
296 John 50 231 Josie 235 J.M.
231 Leroy 9 Liza 298 Lola
Wilson 224 Lucy 168 Mamie 179
Molly 134 Mrs. M.J. 266 M.L.
34 58 Nancy Jane 296 Pearl 177
Richard 152 Sarah 183 Susie 225
Thelma 258 Thomas 70 Tom 177
298 T.N. 288 Viola 152 W.L.
134
RIGGS, Ellis J. 92 Emma 92 E.J.
41 Gladys 13 16 Jessie 92
RILEY, Ermer 103 Pearl Grace
197
RILE, May 1
ROARKS, Susie 233 245
ROARK, Clarissa 285
ROBARDS, Ida 56
ROBBINS, A.D. 76 Carl 263 Guy
214 Jackson 214 James Calvin
214 Laura 76 Martha Ann 214
Nora 72 Thomas Arson 76
ROBERSON, Maggie 85 Margaret
133 W.E. 133
ROBERTS, __ 281 Annie 190
Benni 154 Bob 170 190 Chester
23 Cora 138 Daniel 207 243
George 64 Jack D. 270 James C.
243 Jim 138 John 114 John
Hicks 270 J.C. 126 J.E. 64 J.H.
265 J.Z. 288 Kate 265 Katherine
257 Lellith 271 Margaret 288

Mary 22 Mary Jane 50 Rauna
211 S. 27 Susie 293 Mrs. Tom
138 T.B. 154 T.Z. 23 Velma 283
ROBINETTE, Emma 283
ROBINSON, Elizabeth 241 Ethel
Mae 117 E.B. 117 Jack Owen
188 James A. 188 Jessie 278
Jimmie 263 Luke 278 Maggie
170 M.M. 104 Sallie 122
Thomas 104
ROBISON, Mary 40 Corbet 28
David 191 Ed 247 Elihue 61
Elmer 205 George 268 Infant
162 Joe 139 205 Mary 304
Mattie 290 Millie 56 Mollie 101
Reana 154 Roy V. 247 Sam 266
Velma 268 Vergie 60 Will 28
139 W.M. 162
ROGINS, Myrtle 124
ROSEMAN, Martha 19
ROSS, Matta 158
ROWE, Bessie 84 Cirfina 137 Dill
84 Guy 4 W. Harrions 84 Mrs.
W.H. 249
ROWLAND, Ivan 249 McClellan
249
ROWMAN, Martha Carroll 115
ROYAL, Belle 239 J.W. 239
RULE, Clifford 211 Mrs. J.C. 211
Mary L. 94
RUNIONS, Brask 93 Carie L. 51
Dolphus 93 Mrs. Frank Toney
243 Rhue Nanie 127
RUNION, __ 257 Abram 297 Mrs.
B.L. 246 Cornelius 47 David 47
106 Frank Toney 243 Infant 133
James 133 James S. 143 John
Roper 297 Lindy 152 Linda E.
210 Maggie 113 Margaret 119

RUNION (continued) Mary Hensley 266 Melinda 254 Polly 169 Rebecca 121 Ruth G. 106 S.V. 248 Thomas 223 Thomas C. 223 William 257 Wilma 143 W.C. 223 243 W.F. 119 W.K. 133 210 W.S. 248 W.T. 119
RUNNIAN, Vestal Ray 63 W.J. 63
RUNNION, David 113 Infant 34 Louise 113 Thomas C. 34
RUNYON, Julia 45 Minnie Lee 172
RYBURN, Allie 76 Antom 2 Rowina 169 S.W. 119 Walter 76 Walter Jr. 76
RYDEN, __ 138
RYNON, B. 185
S_, Elizabeth 92 Virginia B. 97
SALTS, Annie 206 Katie 259 Kittie 185 Mack 206 Margaret 226 Mary Ellen 222 Tom 243 W.M. 226
SALTZ, William 133
SAMMONS, Cinthy 54 Leander 190
SAMPSON, __ 138
SAMS, Amelda 41 Annis 46 Artie Christine 264 Carl 54 55 Catherine 181 Clinton 156 Conway 155 156 Cora 210 Darkey 76 89 Elizabeth 45 Ezekel G. 86 E.B. 24 89 162 Galden 171 Jack Gleason 53 James 161 John 86 127 John B. 121 John Dan 154 155 Joshah 17 Katherine 136 171 Leonard 40 Leroy S. 194 Lucinda 201 Lucy 255 Lula 296 L.S. 154 155 Margaret Lee 184 Mary 189 Mary L. 151 208 M.S. 40 Norma Jean 269 Rebecca 269 Robert 1 171 Rufus 53 R.M. 120 241 Sarah 161 T.C. 155 T.E. 300 Will 181 210 W.A. 20 35 43 44 46
SANGER, G. Earl 218 Thomas E. 63 Virginia Lydia 218
SANOS, Clemon 266
SAWERS, Joseph 269
SAYLOR, J.S. 194 Sarah 120
SCARBOUGH, Ollie 143
SCHURAZ, Julia 289
SCOTT, Addie V. 115 Christine 146 285 Emma 67 Gladys 67 L.D. 18 Rachel 189 Sarah 295
SCROGGINS, Nancy Jane 222
SCRUGGS, Louie Davis, Jr. 67 Louis D. 289 L.D. 67 100 T.V. 289
SEATON, Elizabeth 175 Sophia 251
SELF, William 105
SELLERS, Hollie 249 Infant 10
SHANAN, Nancy 24
SHEEHAN, Loretta 260 M.S. 260
SHEHAN, Aaron 145 164 Albert 114 Bessie E. 114 Celia 154 Clifton 226 E_ 136 Elizabeth 145 Ethel 114 George 136 Harry 167 Jack 8 Jocie 200 John 164 Marcus 226 Martha 136 Melvin 298 Ned 145 Shely 154 Viola 167 Virginia 298
SHELL, Alvin 212 Cassie 277 Clint 261 Daniel Webster 236 Erline 277 Helen 212 Kate 151 Margaret 282 Samuel 6

SHELL (continued) Walter 219
  261 William 236 277 Willie
  Dean 277
SHELTON, __ 80 156 254 Allis
  149 Amanda 21 Andrew 265 302
  Arson 290 Arvile 1 Billie 31
  Celia M. 92 Champ 26 Claude
  291 Coatney 168 Cora 181
  Cotner 300 Creed 62 C.L. 77
  David 15 137 Eli 132 Eliphus 15
  Eliza 114 Elvira 81 106 Esau 35
  Estell 301 Estella 158 285 Etta
  190 221 287 E.N. 290 Fate 26
  212 231 Faye 101 Frank 290 Guy
  Lee 291 G.W. 137 H_ 275
  Hobart 265 Ike 114 115 Infant 33
  36 115 168 231 Jane 237 Jasper
  132 Jesse 18 John 133 174 John
  B. 31 Julia Ann 50 Levi 21
  Malinda 74 Marion W. 17 Mary
  18 44 45 290 Matt 210 Melvin
  77 Millard 133 Milton 36 Minny
  130 M.M. 208 Nancy 137
  Nathan Garfield 21 Neley 1 Nella
  77 Nicy 137 Norman 13 Pearl
  Elizabeth 302 Purel 6 Robert 210
  Rod 33 Stella 110 Sylvia 62
  Visia 212 William 149
SHEPARD, Frank 142 Rhoda 142
SHEPPARD, Birdie 293 Sallie 35
SHEPPEARD, Arthur 123 Fred
  123
SHERILL, Charles 176
SHERRILL, Julice Daniel 200
  Samuel 200 Talley Jane 200
SHEVLEY, M. 8
SHIPLEY, __ 239 Fred 133
  Geneve 37 Mrs. J.A. 148 May 37
  Roy 37 133 148 Vivian 148
SHIPLEY, Vivian 148
SHOOK, Augustus 261 Burlin 291
  Cora 261 Harriett 250 Jim 265
  John Abraham 261 Noel 265 291
SHOUN, Infant 89 Roy 89
SHULLAND, Hobert 105 Melvin
  105
SHULL, Francis Ellen 103 G.F.
  103
SHULTS, Daniel 258
SHULTZ, __ 142 A.W. 142 Daniel
  89 Jack 89 Mary Lee 168
SHUTLER, Dan N. 103 Infant 103
SIBERT, H. 267 Maude 267
SILER, Jennie 208
SILVERS, Claude 208 Edward 301
  George 208 John 271 Marion
  271 Narcissus 271 Nellie 150 Ola
  208 Rose 195 Thore 301 Tom
  150 Walter 271
SIMERLY, Sarah 81
SIMMONS, Annie 190 Birdie 184
  delia 275 282 Emma Melvina
  254 Evelin 176 Frannie 206 Fred
  67 George 254 George W. 67 190
  G. William 67 Henry 125 James
  45 295 J.B. 197 Leander 88 186
  Mary 300 Noah 176 N.S. 197
  Samuel Moses 254 Sana 125
  Victoria 219 Will 45 108
  William Harry 108 W.M. 219
SIMONS, Sarah E. 34
SIZEMORE, Danny 269 Jay 164
  Jay N. 269 Joseph M. 164 Magra
  126
SLAGEL, W.J. 108
SLAGLE, Alzie 20 Bill 163 Carie
  47 Claude Elizabeth 163

SLAGLE (continued) David 52
250 Joanna 90 Kelsie 250 Mallie
212 Maria 236 Susan 66
SLIGER, Elizabeth 172
SLOUDER, Fred 203
SMALLING, Anne 288 Duke 209
SMITHMAN, Susan 221
SMITH, Alec 194 Alex 288
Alexander 192 Alice 247
Amanda 99 Amanda E. 64 Anna
139 286 Anna Bell 159 Anna
Belle 129 Arlene 302 A.L. 192
A.M. 230 Barnett 263 Besssie 88
Bob 207 Boyd 48 Carolina 235
Clara 303 Clay 126 Cordelia 236
Dave 152 207 218 247 David 119
192 Davis 84 Dea O'Dell 211
Deckey 167 Elizabeth 68 272
Ella 3 Essie 72 195 Francis 101
200 Fred 192 279 Georgia 198
199 Glenna 132 Harrison 54
Henry 54 91 246 288 Hessie 247
Hilda 99 Infant 129 148 James
302 Jane 288 John 126 196 211
256 Karl Augustus 256 Kelly
Lena 74 Lilly 82 Lizzie 96 239
Lola 199 Lonnie 257 Lum 228
Mary E. 135 153 228 M.B. 279
Nancy 54 246 Nannie B. 256
Pauline 171 Pearl 101 Press 129
Rachel 60 Rever 148 R.C. 279
Sallie 87 258 Sam 74 132 148
171 Thomas 139 Thomas M. 303
Tom 199 W.W. 270
SMYER, Earl 115 L.T. 115
SNEAD, H.C. 170 Mary Jane 47
Ralph 47

SNEED, Alford 160 A.T. 259
Jessie L. 160 Joe 244 Linie 237
Maryann 263 Orbie 259 Seth 228
SNEYD, Alven 6 A.T. 179 Blain
100 Daisey Lee 179 Dasha
Sousana 121 Emma 137 Isaac 5
Infant 30 128 James 128 148
Jewel 5 Joseph 121 Joseph 131
Lizzie 111 Maryan 85 Samantha
100 Sara 100 Seth 131 Walter
148 Will 30
SNEY, Seth 121
SNIDER, Bert Harris 198 Infant
198 I.N. 198
SOUGER, Christian 171 Thomas
Early 171 Mrs. T.E. 172
SOUTHERLAND, Dope 156
SPAIRS, Ellen 139
SPARIES, Green 78
SPARKS, Bob 196 D.C. 83 Edna
Louise 243 George 285 Green
181 G.B. 181 243 Henry 243
Infant 76 152 165 Jack 285 Jim
303 Joseph William 83 J.B. 76
79 Lewis 165 Lula 252 259
Marie 178 M.F. 212 Nelly 71
Ralph 181 Robert Newton 285
Sarah 196 285 Sidney 83 Sindy
84 Tom 178 V.R. 152 Will 23
SPEAR, Jim 224
SPENCE, Julia 199
SPRINKLES, Cordelia 95
STACK, C.E. 180 Elizabeth 180
STAFFORD, B.H. 103 Henry Jank
103
STALLARD, Beechem 200 Betty
Joyce 292 Dalton 267 292 Ella
Marie 211 Marcus Dalton Jr. 267
Mary Elizabeth 273 Nannie 211

STALLARD (continued) Nathan A. 200 Samuel Covey 273 Sarah 283 S.C. 273
STALLINGS, G.E. 143 Maggie E. 143
STALLING, Emma 115
STANELY, Hannah 217
STANIFORTH, Edward P. 97 Infant 97
STANLEY, Claricy 25 Delia 131 Grace 82 Lila 253 Polly 84 2293 Presley 227
STANTON, Billie 52 Clint 52 Edwin 127
STAPLETON, Jane 298
STARNES, Ben 259 Loff 259 Millie 259 Oscar 70 Oscar Caney 70 Sue 286 William 133
STEPHENS, Isaac 13 Ora 13
STEPP, Silas 268
STEVENS, Ed 100 Eva Gertrude 84 42 Silas 301 302
STEVINS, Sallie 201
STEWARD, Gertrude 67 68 124 James 397 J.M. 210 Robert 210 Ruth 152 W.G. 207
STILLMAN, Lede Elizabeth 8
STOCKTON, Alta Madge 174 Betsy Jane 65 Caldonie 160 Carl 222 Edd 87 Eliza 165 Frank Jimmy 187 Gladys Hazel 143 Infant 147 222 Luthe 147 Luther 87 L.H. 174 Nellie 87 Roscoe 287 R.W. 143 Samuel 177 300 Theen 300 Vertie Florence 300 Will 300
STOCTON, Infant 11 91 James H. 37 J.W. 37 Minty 10 Olla May 17 T.J. 37 Wesley 91

STONE, Elma 227 George 256 William A. 256
STORY, Anna 98 Ed 159 Hattie 159
STOUT, _ 134 Alice 284 Dicey 50 James 110 Zela 121
STRAFFINSTEAD, Elizabeth 123
STREET, A.W. 2 Billie Gene 251 Charles 137 Clingman 40 David 40 Doak 63 Don 42 Dosser 63 Ed 212 Fonzo 66 Glenn 78 179 Hassie Mae Garland 137 Helen Maria 179 Infant 30 34 James 40 James C. 131 John 135 147 John A. 164 Mrs. Joseph 51 Landon 34 212 Martha 73 Mary 81 Milton 63 Monroe 30 Pearl 212 Sadie 262 Sam 278 Stephen G. 131 Ulyses C. 131 Vista 53 Wesley 293 William M. 256 W.G. 251 W.M. 256
STROND, Oma 172
STRONG, George 118 John 118 Ollie 118
STUART, Setha 218
STUBBLEFIELD, Janice 267 292
SULLINS, Maggie 118
SULTIN, Pollie 258
SUMMONDS, Julia 47
SUTPHIN, Alice 14 Glenna May 173 Maud 173 Maude 146
SUTS, Kattie 133
SWAFORD, Edna 96
SWANNER, Rachel 38 174
SWANN, Harriett E. 174
SWATHARD, Betsy 147
SWATZEL, Mary A. 47
SWEENEY, Susan 72
SWINEY, John 129

SWINIE, Adam 153 Vicy 153
TABB, Annabeth 176
TALLEY, E.K. 24 William Albert 24
TAPP,__ 37 Annie Jane 303 Bill 195 Blaine 222 229 Cresa 246 Emma 279 Fannie 230 Frank 303 George 206 Geter 195 Harvey 266 Harvey Clinton Jr. 266 Ida Ray 185 Infant 222 Isaac 279 Jake 160 230 240 Mrs. Jake 160 Jenie 225 Jennie 216 John 160 234 Julia 195 Lottie 143 Martha 47 Mary Ann 212 Matison Love 279 Matt 44 Matt L. 142 Nancy 240 Ollie 229 Rebecca 55 149 Robert 206 Robert L. 91 Sada 34 Sarah 2 T.M. 55 William 44 279 William Henry 142
TATEMAN, John 95
TAYLOR, Annie 75 Annie L. 40 B_ 234 Bertie 279 296 Bob 69 Bula Grace 122 Carry 110 C.A. 120 Elizabeth 46 Frank 45 48 Gracy 2 Infant 45 Jacob 98 James Monroe 222 Jeff 98 122 John W. 290 J.H. 268 J.L. 291 Leala Kate 2 Lewis 290 Louie 281 Louttia 48 Lovie 223 Mary 82 296 Mary Catherine 268 Mike 98 Neater May 1 Nora 134 Prescilla 177 R. 125 Rebecca 36 R.L. 168 Sam 186 Mrs. Sam 199 S.P. 198 Wesley 168 W.J. 168 W.K. 198
TEAGUE, Bell 35 John 117 189 Julia 117 Nola 35 Sad Allen 189
THACKES, George W. 75

THOMAS, __ 215 Bessie 145 218 300 Betty Jane 230 Billie 119 Dempsy 119 Flinn 206 Goldie 60 Grady 174 Grady F. 230 Infant 145 150 John R. 30 Leakie 287 Liza 220 Lula 256 L.D. 31 Maggie 119 Pat 145 Paul 30 Pearl 60 Ruby 174 William 60 W.C. 150
THOMPSON, A.L. 239 Mande 226 Minnie 239 Velma Mae 287 W.E. 239 287
THURMAN, Robert 167
TIBBS, Annie Elizabeth 236
TILSON, Addie 268 Andy 98 Axie 175 A.B. 64 184 Barbara 134 Brownlow 12 Catherine 8 Dellar Mae 141 Elen 25 Eliza J. 299 Elizabeth 30 130 Elsie Salts 222 Elzie 89 Ernest 247 Essie Mae 56 Ethel Bailey 255 E_ 29 Eva May 108 E.D. 172 E.E. 261 G> 184 Gennet 47 George 30 175 225 George W. 64 Gracie 261 G. Tilman 45 G.F. 64 Hazel Lee 247 Henry 45 H.G. 83 Infant 29 161 John 20 98 175 John A. 67 John S. 79 Jutie 208 Leroy S. 171 Lizzie 241 274 Lydia 280 L.S. 34 36 52 95 98 129 136 147 155 169 299 Dr. L.S. 29 Margaret 47 67 Martha 271 296 Nora 29 P_ 34 Rebecca 24 Rhoda 57 Robert T. 255 Rody 159 Roy 255 Ruth 84 161 206 271 Sallie 65 Sally 265 Sam 96 Sarah 172 Thomas 47 Tildy 184 Walter 56 William 108 William E. 34 136 171 William Harrison 20

TILSON (continued) William H. 184 W.A. 47 65 W.E. 171 Zora 50 58
TIMBERLAKE, Ida L. 109
TIMMERSON, Mary R. 88
TIMPKINS, John 296 Rufina Jane 222
TINKER, Cecil 238 Charlie 99 Edward 153 Elizabeth 183 239 Ellen 190 Emeline 245 F.B. 258 George 232 252 185 Hazeline 141 Ida 285 Ina 141 Infant 99 140 153 James P. 196 John 76 89 135 John H. 263 J.C. 71 J.F. 141 J.W. 193 238 Kathleen 185 Lizzie 56 Louise 196 Maggie 238 Maree R. 55 Margaret 180 Melda 108 Nelson 51 Palmer 77 Phillip Edmon 56 Pollie 248 Rachel 122 Robert 193 Robert C. 180 Rosie 99 Sada 89 Sam 76 Samuel 50 S.W. 140 55 56 Thelma 232 Vadie 258 Virginia 21 132 Wayne Franklin 252 Wesley 71 Willard Oliver 77 W.S. 56
TIPTON, __ 93 193 Aaron Burl 164 Alda 285 Alvin 165 239 Amanda 99 Annie 254 A.B. 58 111 Bascom 263 Beckie 98 Bell 217 Bettie Joe 299 Biddie 141 Birdie 220 221 246 Birtha 49 Birtie 305 Bobby Lee 263 Britt 269 Camelia 94 Camile 238 Carl 281 Carrie 149 Celia 209 Charles 33 139 248 265 Charles F. 305 Charles Sherman 102 Charlie 302 Clyde 273 Cora 193 Cordelia 220 221 Curt 208 C.C. 206 Daniel 122 David 70 226 Della 240 Dianna 32 Dock 153 Earl 301 Effie 231 Eliza 70 226 Elizabeth 96 Eller 64 Emma 45 Ethel 291 Etta 245 Eula 74 Frank 170 181 Mrs. Frank 172 Fred 134 G_ 96 George 285 Gertha 210 Gertie 108 Girthe 217 Harriett 230 Harrison 113 Hassel Lee 281 Hazel Hughes 265 Henderson 208 Hobart 156 285 H.G. 63 Infant 33 61 146 178 Isaac 58 Iva An 86 James Oscar 113 Jane 192 Joe 195 241 271 Joe Ben 248 Joe H. 231 Joel 241 John 107 211 239 John D. 32 90 113 152 239 Joseph 49 128 164 170 172 294 Julia Ann 51 J.C. 296 Mrs. J.D. 90 J.H. 102 186 205 J.M. 299 Kathern 139 Lattie 239 Lawson 273 Lee 251 Lela 269 Leroy 285 301 Lila 293 Lizzie 297 Lottie 294 Mack 1 61 296 Margaret Ann 215 Marlie 221 Martha 19 Mary 8 63 205 Mary C. 206 Mary Jane 58 May 151 Melissa 96 Mollie 143 Mose 152 Moses 64 M.C. 111 113 M.E. 271 M.J. 11 Neoma 170 172 Nile V. 231 Oma 199 Omie 236 Ora 134 Pearl 255 281 Rebecca Gillis 271 Richard 186 Rosa Belle 141 rousa 99 Ruba Mae 22 Rucker 64 Ruth 302 Sam 127 156 178 Samuel Y. 246 Sarah 22 213 252 Sarah Ann 258 Sarah Elizabeth 38 Sidia 285 Steve 141 151 Strom 96 Su Ema 81 S.C. 99 S.Y. 271 Tom 127 Valentine 246 Vertie 294

TIPTON (continued) Walter 146 215 Wiley 242 Will 305 William 205 William L. 294 William Monroe 13 William M. 285 Zeek 265 Zeke 269 281
TITTLE, Addie 101 Alex 92 Anna 159 A.G. 218 Back 73 Brady 291 Charles E. 257 Charlie 116 Charlie Bean 149 Cora 174 Cora Lee 141 C.B. 295 Elizabeth 130 Elmer 186 Epthirum 197 Frank 186 George Frank 243 Hazel 74 Howard 197 Ike 137 162 251 Infant 92 154 162 291 James 154 James F. 149 Jane 204 John 55 116 197 243 John Henry 257 John R. 55 Jude Smith 257 Julia 139 J.F. 295 Leitha 251 Loretta 189 Mary C. 10 Mary Elizabeth 295 Millie 42 Nancy 116 Nancy Jane 287 Rosa 186 Rose Annie 243 Russell 149 Sam 116 Samuel 237 Sarah Alice 187 Walter 74 101 187 Wayne 137 W.H. 197
TODD, Elizabeth 273
TOLLEY, Betty 249 Clarenc 81 Clarence 152 Clerica 192 Darkey 42 Edna May 81 E.K. 57 Francis 42 H.A. 126 Ida Susand 57 John 274 J.A. 123 J.R. 90 Lace 57 Lou Wilcox 261 Mary L. 152 Nancy Jane 57 Rex 90
TOLLISON, Evelyn 182
TOLLY, Avery 78 Billy 275 E.K. 275 Nancy An 87 Nancy Ann 79
TOMIE, Curtis H. 202 W.H. 202
TOMPKINS, Emmie 81 George W. 271 G.W. 47 Harriett 271 Martha 47 Mellina 293

TOMPKIN, Martha 39
TONEY, Cindy 165 E.K. 78 Fanny B. 58 Harry 146 Hazen House 274 Hubert 285 H.H. 202 Infant 274 J.F. Sr. 285 J.G. 74 Lucinda 4 Mamey 101 Mamie 75 282 Martha Ellen 202 Mary 110 272 Ruby 7 William Clifton 285 W.C. 3 146
TOPP, Infant 24 Jim 24 M.L. 27 Vinson 24
TOSTER, Dolly 257 J.H. 257 Stella 257
TOWNSEND, Mary Lou 183 Waits 35 W.J. 183
TRAYLOR, Bill 169 Hazel Katherine 169
TREADWAY, Albert J. 304 Bessie 300 Bethel 221 Biddie 288 Bill 194 Carrie 283 Carver 121 Cora 280 Ethel 220 Glenn 246 Infant 121 Jane 121 Jim 255 Leonard 220 221 246 Lewis 246 304 Roxie 288 Sarah 164 Sue 289
TREDWAY, Berthe 14 Carver 69 Infant 69
TRICKETT, Rachel 191
TROUTMAN, Bunia 120 Eveline 40 Hobart 57
TRUE, Buck 211 Millie 206
TUCKER, Amanda Cornelia 279 Columbus 232 Ernest 282 Francis Anne 298 George 232 Joe L. 75 Joe L. Jr. 75 Joseph L. 282 Joseph Sevier 264 J.L. 75 101 Lyda 117 Lydia 161 Paul Lewis 101 Polly Ann 264 Wesley 282 Wesley S. 264 Wilburn 232 W.F. 279

TUGGLE, Amanda 116
TURBYFIELD, George 158
Homer 158
TURNER, __ 187 Abraham 61
Milus Edward 61 Richard 188
TUTTLE, Lula M. 41
UNDERWOOD, Nancy 117 151 266 291
UPDIKE, A.D. 294
UREKINS, J.A.R. 224
URST, William 52
VALLEY, Bennie 223
VANCE, Beckie 128 Helen Ellen 284 Infant 262 Mark 3 Martha 264 Mary 29 55 140 Polly 57 Sam 42 57 William 262
VANDEGRIFF, Thomas 126
VANDERGRIFF, Bill 210 E.J. 210 269 John W. 126 Maude 269 Sarah Alice 269 Thomas 210
VANDEWATER, __ 297
VANOVER, C.E. 294 Gerogia 294 Robert A. 294
VAUGHN, Lona E. 43
VESTAL, Olive 303
VEST, Anna May 295 J.W. 249 Verna 249
VINES, D.A. 165 Lafayett 165 William 165
VINSON, Mallie Ella 211 Sam 206 211
WAKEFIELD, Elizabeth 46 114
WALDROP, Carrie 121 Infant 121 Joe 277 Jordan Fields 18 Kate 200 Milla 18 Tilda 140 W.B. 277 Zeb 84 121
WALDRUP, Joe 23 Martha 23
WALKER, B.S. 65 Carrie 14 Fayette 158 Frank 53 Infant 36 158 James H. 193 J.H. 109 53 Wash 36 W.A. 53 Luther 40 Mary 40 S.W. 40
WALLIN, Bessie 62
WALL, Carrie 129 Ellen 103
WALTERS, Cynthia 71 Irene 91 104
WALTER, Irene 299
WARD, William Reese 82 William Reese Jr. 82
WARLICK, Alfred 143
WARLISK, Jane 160
WARREN, Infant 30 J.M. 30 M.M. 278
WARRICK, Fredlen 119 Martha 274 Mary Imogene 119
WASHBURN, Myra 217
WATKINS, R.A. 52
WATSON, Annie 193 Dannel 215 Edith C. 57 Jennette Marie 215 William 57
WATTIS, Bert 22 Infant 22
WATTS, Amanda 280 Anderson 73 112 Arthur 9 82 Bert 73 82 Bessie 186 Betsie 97 Clay 73 Dempsy 181 Ellis 97 Fred 278 John 13 J.M. 73 Lizie 89 Lizzie 106 Mary Elizabeth 12 278 Monroe 86 Nelson 11 N.J. 181 Rosa Belle 86 Sam 188 Sarah 133 260 Silas 112 Texie P. 73 Usby 31 Ushy 54 Usley 73 William 73 181 186
WAUGH, John 49 Julia Ann 49
WEAVER, A.C. 40 Eula Mae 301 William S. 40
WEBB, __ 229 Audrey Hilmer 233 Cinda 140 Fannie 70 Hazel 298 J.R. 233 240 Mary 132 Texie 131

WEBB (continued) Ulys 131
Ulysses 233 Ulysses Jr. 233 Will
131
WEBSTER, Telitha 224
WEEKS, Cleo 172 Oscar 12
WELCH, Sallie 182
WELD, Emma 262 Lewis 165
WELLS, Billie 246 Nancy Matilda
246
WESLEY, Eliza 52
WESTALL, Herman 29 T.B. 29
WEST, Bell 76 Belle 181 243
Burna 118 James 118 John 73
Martha 164 Thomas J. 73
William 118
WHALEY, __ 219 C_ 127 Cassie
82 241 Charley 239 Elizabeth
107 Frank 183 Jake 240 James
127 240 James Franklin 298
Jennie 60 Lizzie 87 Lizzy 63
Mary Demona 298 Nan 152 207
Nancy 84 Virginia Lee 239
WHEELER, Fred 219 Infant 219
Lucinda 296 Mrs. W.O. 219
WHISNANT, Gladys 284 294
WHITBURN, Elizabeth 100
WHITEHEAD, Anna Thakes 75
A.L. 169 Betsy 108 Cloyd 75
Hannah 138 John 69 Julia 175
Kincaid 169 Susan 20 78 123
Susand 58
WHITEHORN, Lottie 19
WHITE,__ 119 Abe 282 Alis 123
Allie 165 A.I. 275 Bessie 292
Carrie Adlin 117 Catherine 36
169 Charles 38 Charles Jr. 38
Christopher 56 Cora Lee 245
Cordie 4 Criss 74 C.C. 56 108
142 300 Daniel 108 David 200

207 David J. 304 Dora 81 D.J. 95
Edith Louise 83 Edna May 188
Edward 225 Elizabeth 108 142
Elsie 295 Emma 71 Emma Erwin
100 Ethel 56 105 166 240 Evert
127 E.T. 11 Fannie 156 Fay
Banner 21 Flecher 119 Fred 119
F.B. 188 George 225 240 G.I.
275 Hannah 286 Harrel 132
Hester 115 Hobart 225 Ida J. 67
Irene 182 James W. 117 169 Jane
95 Jesse 83 114 Joe 292 John 275
292 John Christopher 282 J.C. 21
132 200 304 J.C. Jr. 282 J.D. 34
Labe 228 Landon 182 245 253
Lee 114 Lenis 51 Madge 200
Margaret 34 Margaret Adelia
186 Mary 56 Mary E. 127 Mary
Lucinda 88 Masy 170 Mrs. M.C.
194 Opal Carter 228 Paul 253
Quillen 43 Robert Landon 295
Sadie 218 Salie 218 Sarah A. 71
Tommy 18 Will 95 Will W. 108
William 74
WHITLOCK, Vada 192
WHITRUN, Birtha 1
WHITSON, __ 146 Abraham 201
Alzina 52 Ancrinua 65 Arnold
Lee 13 Blanch 243 E_ 131
Emma 115 122 245 Fayett 235
I.M. 227 Jennie 35 Jessie Ida 76
John 3 20 John Calvin 235 John
F. 65 Julia 235 J.b. 243 J.D. 288
J.w. 191 238 Libbie 242
Margaret 155 Mary Adams 26 27
Melissa 225 Mollie 191 Molly
243 Nancy 54 Polly 238 248
Robert 288 Ruth 13 Sarah 268
Tomanda Honeycutt 227

WHITSON (continued) Vennie
203 215 Viana 49 170 Viona 291
Walter 288 William 235 William
Matt 65
WHITTAMORE, Amanda 38
Deck 40 Florence 68 Maggie 110
Mrs. Matt 71 Samuel 40 Tom 40
WIDNER, Bob 233
WIGGAND, Dick 270 P.P. 187
Mrs. Paul P. 270 Raymond 142
Virginia 142
WILCOX, Celia 135 C.N. 27 45
242 C.W. 242 Francie E. 173
John H. 261 Martha 289 Mary
Elizabeth Ester 242
WILLIAMSON, Dora Bell
Callahan 132 George 132 Infant
132 Ozy 175 Mrs. W.J. 293
WILLIAMS, __ 208 Addie 290
Anna 97 Arnold 208 Bessie 87
248 Betie 122 Bradie 82 Celia
151 153 Celie 24 Child 164 C.R.
59 82 David 135 Dora 127 Dr.
180 Edith May 186 El_ 38 Ernest
100 Ethel 188 Frank 38 40 201
Glen 204 Harley 59 H. 24 Hiram
59 164 Hiram R. 301 Houe 198
H.C. 257 H.H. 197 Infant 90 169
177 251 James 138 201 Jeff 301
Jessie 29 Joe 138 Joe A. 131 J.H.
182 J.W. 244 Kid Turley 135
Leona 40 Louisa 257 Mable 116
Millard 116 Minnie 144 Nancy
246 Nellie Clo 118 N.E. 31 P_
130 Pinkney 43 Pitman 97 257
Rachel 86 138 201 Retman 188
Rex Frank 116 Rigg 277 Robert
L. 251 Ruth 180 R.L. 90 198
Sam 97 Sanders 185 Sarah 243
Silas 130 Steve 169 Susan 111
Susanna 299 Vannis 29 Vernon
277 William 177 W.T. 118 185
186 199 204
WILLIS, Dr. A.J. 57 Bert 79 Bob
79 267 Dave 204 D.F. 25 Frankie
204 Hester 50 Juda 42 J.C. 50
Lela 129 Lizzie 225 Mary 132
Mary Ann 122 May 10 Nancie
275 Orpha 96 111 Pery 172
Robert 24 32 87 Robert C. 33
Roda 225 Rossie Elen 87 Sarah
76 T.F. 154 Velva 300 Walter
188 W.J. 33
WILLS, Ardella 172
WILOUGHBY, Flossie 147
WILSON, __ 272 Bertha Lenore
226 Bertie 279 Betsy 259 Billie
230 Delia 167 D.M. 62 D.W. 279
E. 228 Eliza 245 Emily 165 Etta
215 Garfield 102 George 213
Harriett 247 Harry 139 Infant 63
122 Isaac 215 Jane 272 John 94
163 219 John B. 63 226 John M.
62 John R. 298 J.H. 234 Katie
249 Lela 8 Lilian E. Dalton 180
Loyle Gene 272 Lukinzie 186
Mable 298 Mande 228 Marcus T.
228 Marion 246 Mart 102 Mary
53 Mary A. 94 Mary Hylmon 234
Mattie 76 Mattie Molloy 76
Milly 102 M.W. 28 224 Nancy
25 Nancy Emmaline 230 Onesel
215 Polly 219 Rose Marie 295
R.C. 139 Samuel 215 228 Sara
146 Sarah 263 Thomas 215 230
Tom 219 Trula 289 U.D. 295
Vinetta 115 Walts 122 W.A. 62
W.M. 230 W.T. 166 Zeb 146

WINDELL, Jane 147
WINNIGER, Katherine 58
WINTERS, Pearl 294
WINTZER, Antonette 76
WISEMAN, Dellie 207 Sarah 177
WISE, Rosa 162
WITCHER, Infant 129 Ruben 129
WITSON, Polly 248
WITT, Mary E. 263
WOHLFORD, Charlott 7 C.R. 119 Stacy Rogetta 119
WOLDRUP, Joe 178
WOLFE, Eliza 216 Mary 114
WOLF, Henry 82 Phill 82
WOMACK, Elizabeth 32 E.L. 32 61 Lela 32 Stella 103
WOODBY, Alford 56 90 Alfred 85 Ann 255 Anne 204 Barnet 228 255 Bertie 100 B.W. 292 Cass Charley 161 Charlie 237 Charlie Thomas 292 Clyde 237 Cordelia 62 Docis 6 D.F. 34 58 Ephases 56 Eppy 97 E.P. 33 90 George 33 Gladys Sally 33 Henry 32 Hezekiah 97 Infant 5 32 34 176 James 97 Jim 176 Joe Bill 255 Joe B. 21 John 91 100 262 Junior 161 J.L. 20 Lockie 42 Lois 228 Mamie 201 Marry 33 Martha 228 Mary 74 153 204 Mary Elizabeth 74 Maud Ailene 58 R.L. 32 Samuel 21 Susan 38 Vicie 278 William 85 William P. 74 Willie 2
WOODFIN, David Oscar 174 John 174
WOODLEY, Charles 134 Elizabeth 134 Teddy 4

WOODLY, Cany L. 27 F.W. 30 John 27 Ollie 30 Sarah 17
WOODS, Bessie 114
WOODWARD, Ben 201 Hester 294 Infant 103 Jake 209 J.B. 103 Lockie 161 Lucinda 161 Mary Jane 103 208 W.T. 274
WOODY, Carolina 285 John 276 Ollie 35
WORSHAM, Anna 132 James 22 Rebecca 21 Thelma 90 W.J. 90
WRAY, Nelson 244 Waco 244
WRIGHT, Elizabeth 39 Infant 33 John William 221 Ollie 33 Thomas 221 Thomas J. 4 W.H. 221
WYATT, Lela Yarnell 157 Penley 6
WYNNE, Lamar Andrew 150 Lamar Anderw Jr. 150
YARBER, John 246 Rachel N. 246
YARNELL, James S. 157 Martin 157
YATES, G.M. 133
YELTON, Carroll Reese 125 Effie Isabell Bailey 53 H.L. 125
YODER, J.S. 144
YOUNG, Anderson 124 168 Bashana 230 Bob 176 Della 157 Frank 245 F.W. 53 Hellen 124 Hobart 218 Ileen 167 Infant 99 Joe B. 253 Margaret Lee 233 Martha 49 Mellie 231 Missouri Janet Greene 218 Ralph 99 Sam H. 167 Susan C. 182 S.H. 167 Wilma 53 W.E. 233
ZACHARY, Alizy 189

www.ingramcontent.com/pod-product-compliance
Lightning Source LLC
Chambersburg PA
CBHW071953220426
43662CB00009B/1112